Toward a Theology of the Septuagint

Septuagint and Cognate Studies

Wolfgang Kraus, General Editor

Editorial Board:
Robert Hiebert
Arie van der Kooij
Siegfried Kreuzer
Philippe Le Moigne

Number 74

Toward a Theology of the Septuagint

Stellenbosch Congress on the Septuagint, 2018

Edited by
Johann Cook and Martin Rösel

Atlanta

Copyright © 2020 by SBL Press

All rights reserved. No part of this work may be reproduced or transmitted in any form or by any means, electronic or mechanical, including photocopying and recording, or by means of any information storage or retrieval system, except as may be expressly permitted by the 1976 Copyright Act or in writing from the publisher. Requests for permission should be addressed in writing to the Rights and Permissions Office, SBL Press, 825 Houston Mill Road, Atlanta, GA 30329 USA.

Library of Congress Cataloging-in-Publication Data

Names: International Organization for Septuagint and Cognate Studies. Congress (2018 : Stellenbosch, South Africa) | Cook, Johann, editor. | Rösel, Martin, editor.
Title: Toward a theology of the Septuagint : Stellenbosch Congress on the Septuagint, 2018 / edited by Johann Cook and Martin Rösel.
Description: Atlanta : SBL Press, 2020. | Series: Septuagint and cognate studies; 74 | Includes bibliographical references and index.
Identifiers: LCCN 2019059617 (print) | LCCN 2019059618 (ebook) | ISBN 9781628372700 (paperback) | ISBN 9780884144298 (hardback) | ISBN 9780884144304 (ebook)
Subjects: LCSH: Bible. Old Testament. Greek—Versions—Septuagint—Theology—Congresses. | Bible. Old Testament. Greek—Versions—Septuagint—Congresses.
Classification: LCC BS744 .I58 2020 (print) | LCC BS744 (ebook) | DDC 221.4/8—dc23
LC record available at https://lccn.loc.gov/2019059617
LC ebook record available at https://lccn.loc.gov/2019059618

In memory of Klaus Koch (1926–2019), a great theologian who long before others recognized the theological significance of LXX studies.

Im Andenken an Klaus Koch (1926–2019), einen großen Theologen, der lange vor anderen die eigenstständige Bedeutung der LXX erkannt hat.

Contents

Preface..xi
Abbreviations.. xiii

Part 1. Introduction and Questions of Methodology

Projektvorstellung: Theologie der Septuaginta – Methodische
Grundlegung und Fallstudien
    Martin Rösel 3

The Interaction between Theological and Text-Critical Approaches
    Emanuel Tov 23

Theology and Septuagint Corpora: A Proposal and Some Questions
    Gideon R. Kotzé 47

Product Received: Influence of "the Old in the New" on the
Formulation of Theologies of "the" Septuagint
    Kyle Young..71

Part 2. Septuagint and Plato: Methodological Considerations and Models of Interpretation

Platons *Politeia* und die Theologie der LXX
    Evangelia G. Dafni 95

Part 3. Theological Aspects of the Greek Bible 1: Translations

Interpretive Intent and the Legal Material of the Septuagint
Pentateuch
    Dirk Büchner 115

„Aber nicht wie die Ägypter formierte er seine Kunstwerke aus Backstein und Granit…" Bild-Gottheiten in der Septuaginta
   Stefanie Peintner 141

"You Saw No Form When YHWH Spoke to You at Horeb" (Deut 4:15): Antianthropomorphisms in the Greek Deuteronomy
   Hans Ausloos 163

Holiness and the Levites in MT and LXX Chronicles: An Avenue for Exploring the Theology of LXX Chronicles?
   Louis C. Jonker 179

Theology and Translation Technique in the Old Greek Version of Job 28
   Jessie Rogers 201

The Septuagint of Proverbs as a Jewish Document
   Johann Cook 225

"To Shine" or "To Show"? A Conceptual and Theological Exploration of Light in the LXX
   Joel D. Ruark 245

   Part 3. Theological Aspects of the Greek Bible 2: Greek Literature

Sophia as Second Principle in Wisdom of Solomon
   Johan C. Thom 263

The Joseph Narratives in the LXX, Philo, and Josephus
   Philip R. Bosman 277

Toward Defining the Fourth Quest in 2 Maccabees Theological Research
   Pierre J. Jordaan 295

Contributing toward Theologies of the LXX: The Use of the Terms θεός and κύριος in 1 and 2 Maccabees
   Peter Nagel 317

Israel und die Völker in Texten der Septuaginta
    Wolfgang Kraus 335

Septuagint Influence on the Formation of Early Christian Theology:
ἐπαγγελία in the Book of Hebrews and Its Substantiation from the
LXX Pentateuch
    Gert J. Steyn 371

„Binde die Gebote auf Deine Seele". Zum Einfluss anthropologischer
Begrifflichkeiten der Septuaginta auf die patristische Ethik
    Ulrich Volp..397

Contributors..421
Ancient Sources Index..423
Modern Authors Index...435

Preface

Scholars have been engaged in innovative Septuagint research for some decades now. Whereas in previous centuries text-critical analysis was the focus of this research, recently hermeneutical research has predominated. Various research projects developed, with one in particular gaining in urgency: the formulation of a theology of the Septuagint. It was decided to formally register a research project in this regard. Martin Rösel and Johann Cook have independently published some suggestions as to what is necessary to construe such a theology. The former obtained research funds from the "Kultusministerium des Landes Mecklenburg-Vorpommern" in Germany in order to pursue this research project. He was granted a sabbatical by the University of Rostock and had sufficient funds to invite a number of specialists to participate in a conference in collaboration with Johann Cook from Stellenbosch University. Cook in turn obtained additional funds from the South African National Research Foundation (SANRF) and Stellenbosch University. They invited eight international specialists and nine scholars from South Africa. With an eye to the future, two students—Joel Ruark and Kyle Young—were also invited to present papers.

The congress took place 17–19 August 2018 in the Department of Ancient Studies of Stellenbosch University, and the proceedings are hereby published. Shortly after the congress, Martin Rösel was one of the reviewers of the dissertation by Stefanie Peintner (born Plangger), a former student of Eberhard Bons at the University of Strasbourg. Since her work fits very well with the theme of the conference, she was asked to contribute an essay to the proceedings. So, a total of nineteen papers are published.

This project turned into a *Riesenarbeit*, and so many specific individuals and instances need to be thanked. First, Stellenbosch University allowed us to make use of their excellent research facilities. The chairperson of the Department of Ancient Studies, Professor Annemaré Kotzé, received us with open arms and made us feel at home. The Vice-Rector: Research of the university, Professor Eugene Cloete, made funds available to make the congress possible. We also express our gratitude for the generous scholarship and additional funding provided by the "Theoria-Kurt von Fritz Science Program" in Mecklenburg-Vorpommern, Germany. Without this financial assistance, the congress would not have been possible. The preparation for and running of the conference itself as well as the postcongress activities were ably orchestrated by various individuals: Mrs. Louise Damons, current Administrative Officer of the Department of Ancient Studies, and two student assistants of this Department: Jacques Cilliers and Marcus Joubert. Many thanks also to Luise Gerber and Gertrud Frenzel (both Rostock, Germany) for the preparation of the German essays for publication. A special word of appreciation is in order to Gideon Kotzé from Potchefstroom, who took responsibility for the final preparations of the collection for publication. Finally, we thank the participants for their willingness to collaborate to make the congress not only possible but such a success.

Johann Cook
Martin Rösel

Abbreviations

AASF	Annales Academiae scientiarum fennicae
AB	Anchor Yale Bible
AGJU	Arbeiten zur Geschichte des antiken Judentum und Urchristentums
AnBib	Analecta biblica
ANRhAW	Abhandlungen der Nordrhein-Westfälischen Akademie der Wissenschaften
ANRW	*Aufstieg und Niedergang der römischen Welt. Geschichte und Kultur Roms im Spiegel der neueren Forschung*
ArBib	The Aramaic Bible
ASV	American Standard Version
ATA	Alttestamentliche Abhandlungen
ATD	Das Alte Testament Deutsch
AThANT	Abhandlungen zur Theologie des Alten und Neuen Testaments
BBB	Bonner biblische Beiträge
BdA	La Bible d'Alexandrie
BDAG	Bauer, Walter, Frederick William Danker, William F. Arndt and F. Wilbur Gingrich, *A Greek-English Lexicon of the New Testament and Other Early Christian Literature*. 3rd ed. Chicago: University of Chicago, 2000.
BDB	Brown, Francis, Samuel R. Driver and Charles A. Briggs, *A Hebrew and English Lexicon of the Old Testament*. Oxford: Clarendon Press, 1906.
BETL	Bibliotheca ephemeridum theologicarum lovaniensium
BGrL	Bibliothek der griechischen Literatur
BHQ	*Biblia Hebraica Quinta*
BHS	*Biblia Hebraica Stuttgartensia*. Edited by Karl Elliger and Wilhelm Rudolph. Stuttgart: Deutsche Bibelgesellschaft, 1997.

BibLeb	*Bibel und Leben*
BIOSCS	Bulletin of the International Organization for Septuagint and Cognate Studies
BIS	Biblical Interpretation series
BJS	Brown Judaic Studies
BKAT	Biblischer Kommentar, Altes Testament
BKV	Bibliothek der Kirchenväter
BN	*Biblische Notizen*
BO	*Bibliotheca orientalis*
BR	*Biblical Research*
BThS	Biblisch-theologische Studien
BTS	Biblical tools and studies
BU	Biblische Untersuchungen
BWANT	Beiträge zur Wissenschaft vom Alten und Neuen Testament
BZ	*Biblische Zeitschrift*
BzA	Beiträge zur Altertumskunde
BZABR	Beihefte zur Zeitschrift für Altorientalische und Biblische Rechtsgeschichte
BZAW	Beihefte zur Zeitschrift für die alttestamentliche Wissenschaft
BZNW	Beihefte zur Zeitschrift für die neutestamentliche Wissenschaft
CATSS	Computer Assisted Tools for Septuagint/Scriptural Studies
CBET	Contributions to Biblical Exegesis and Theology
CBQ	*Catholic Biblical Quarterly*
CBQMS	Catholic Biblical Quarterly Monograph Series
CCSL	Corpus Christianorum: Series latina
CEJL	Commentaries on Early Jewish Literature
CHANE	Culture and History of the Ancient Near East
ClQ	*The Classical Quarterly*
ConBOT	Coniectanea biblica: Old Testament Series
CPG	*Clavis patrum graecorum.* Edited by Maurice Geerard. 5 vols. Turnhout: Brepols, 1974–1987.
CSEL	Corpus scriptorum ecclesiasticorum latinorum
DCH	*The Dictionary of Classical Hebrew.* 9 vols. Edited by David J. A. Clines. Sheffield: Sheffield Academic Press, 1993–2016.
DCLS	Deuterocanonical and Cognate Literature Studies

DJD	Discoveries in the Judaean Desert
EDNT	*Exegetical Dictionary of the New Testament*. Edited by Horst Balz and Gerhard Schneider. 3 vols. Grand Rapids: Eerdmans, 1990–1993.
EJL	Early Judaism and Its Literature
ESV	English Standard Version
EvT	*Evangelische Theologie*
FAT	Forschungen zum Alten Testament
FC	Fathers of the Church
FKDG	Forschungen zur Kirchen- und Dogmengeschichte
FRLANT	Forschungen zur Religion und Literatur des Alten und Neuen Testaments
GAT	Grundrisse zum Alten Testament
GCS	Die griechische christliche Schriftsteller der ersten [drei] Jahrhunderte
GELS	Muraoka, Takamitsu, *A Greek-English Lexicon of the Septuagint*. Leuven: Peeters, 2009.
Ges[18]	Gesenius, Wilhelm, *Hebräisches und Aramäisches Handwörterbuch über das Alte Testament*. 18. Aufl. Bearbeitet und herausgegeben von Herbert Donner. Heidelberg: Springer, 2013.
GKC	Gesenius, Wilhelm, *Gesenius's Hebrew Grammar*. Edited by Emil Kautzsch. 2nd English ed. by Arthur E. Cowley. Oxford: Clarendon Press, 1910.
HALAT	Koehler, Ludwig, Walter Baumgartner, und Johann Jakob Stamm, *Hebräisches und Aramäisches Lexikon zum Alten Testament*. 2 vols. Leiden: Brill, 2004.
HALOT	Koehler, Ludwig, Walter Baumgartner and Johann Jakob Stamm, *The Hebrew and Aramaic Lexicon of the Old Testament*. Translated and edited under the supervision of M. E. J. Richardson. 2 vols. Leiden: Brill, 2001.
HBM	Hebrew Bible Monographs
HBS	Herders biblische Studien
HeBAI	*Hebrew Bible and Ancient Israel*
HR	Hatch, Edwin, and Henry A. Redpath. *Concordance to the Septuagint and Other Greek Versions of the Old Testament*. 2 vols. Oxford: Clarendon Press, 1897. Supplement, 1906.
HS	*Hebrew Studies*
HThKAT	Herders Theologischer Kommentar zum Alten Testament

HTR	*Harvard Theological Review*
HUCA	*Hebrew Union College Annual*
IBHS	Waltke, Bruce K., and Michael O'Connor. *An Introduction to Biblical Hebrew Syntax*. Winona Lake, IN: Eisenbrauns, 1990.
ICC	International Critical Commentary
JAJ	*Journal of Ancient Judaism*
JBL	*Journal of Biblical Literature*
JBLMS	Journal of Biblical Literature Monograph Series
JBTh	*Jahrbuch für Biblische Theologie*
JECH	*Journal of Early Christian History*
JEOL	*Jaarbericht van het Vooraziatisch-Egyptisch Gezelschap (Genootschap) Ex oriente lux*
JM	Joüon, Paul and Takamitsu Muraoka, *A Grammar of Biblical Hebrew*. Rome: Editrice Pontificio Istituto Biblico, 2006.
JPS	Jewish Publication Society Tanakh
JSem	*Journal for Semitics*
JSCS	*Journal of Septuagint and Cognate Studies*
JSHRZ	Jüdische Schriften aus hellenistisch-römischer Zeit
JSJ	*Journal for the Study of Judaism*
JSJSup	Supplements to the Journal for the Study of Judaism
JSNTSup	Journal for the Study of the New Testament: Supplement Series
JSOTSup	Journal for the Study of the Old Testament: Supplement Series
JTS	*Journal of Theological Studies*
JudChr	Judaica et Christiana
JudUm	Judentum und Umwelt
KAT	Kommentar zum Alten Testament
KEK	Kritisch-exegetischer Kommentar über das Neue Testament
L&N	*Greek-English Lexicon of the New Testament: Based on Semantic Domains*. Edited by Johannes P. Louw and Eugene A. Nida. New York: United Bible Societies, 1996.
LCL	Loeb Classical Library
LEH	*A Greek-English Lexicon of the Septuagint*. Edited by Johan Lust, Erik Eynikel and Katrin Hauspie. 3rd ed. Stuttgart: Deutsche Bibelgesellschaft, 2015.

LHBOTS	The Library of Hebrew Bible/Old Testament Studies
LSJ	Liddell, Henry George, Robert Scott, Henry Stuart Jones, *A Greek-English Lexicon*. 9th ed. with revised supplement. Oxford: Oxford University Press, 1996.
LXX	Septuagint
LXX.D	Septuaginta Deutsch
LXX.H	Handbuch zur Septuaginta
MGWJ	*Monatschrift für Geschichte und Wissenschaft des Judentums*
MSU	Mitteilungen des Septuaginta-Unternehmens
MT	Masoretic text
MVEOL	Mededelingen en Verhandelingen van het Vooraziatisch-Egytisch Genootschap „Ex Oriente Lux"
NA[28]	*Novum Testamentum Graece*, Nestle-Aland, 28th ed.
NCB	New Century Bible
NETS	New English Translation of the Septuagint
NICNT	New International Commentary on the New Testament
NIGTC	New International Greek Testament Commentary
NIV	New International Version
NJahrb	*Neue Jahrbücher für das klassiche Altertum*
NJPS	New Jewish Publication Society of America Tanakh
NovTSup	Novum Testamentum Supplements
NRSV	New Revised Standard Version
NSKAT	Neuer Stuttgarter Kommentar Altes Testament
NTD	Das Neue Testament Deutsch
OBO	Orbis Biblicus et Orientalis
OG	Old Greek
OTE	*Old Testament Essays*
ÖTK	Ökumenischer Taschenbuch-Kommentar
OTL	Old Testament Library
OTS	*Old Testament Studies*
PFES	Publications of the Finnish Exegetical Society
PG	Patrologia graeca. Edited by Jacques-Paul Migne. 162 vols. Paris: Imprimerie Catholique, 1857–1886.
PNT	De Prediking van het Nieuwe Testament
PTS	Patristische Texte und Studien
QD	Quaestiones disputatae
ResQ	*Restoration Quarterly*

*RGG*³	*Religion in Geschichte und Gegenwart.* Edited by Kurt Galling. 7 vols. 3rd ed. Tübingen: Mohr Siebeck, 1957–1965.
*RGG*⁴	*Religion in Geschichte und Gegenwart.* 4th ed. Edited by Hans D. Betz et al. Tübingen: Mohr Siebeck, 2000.
RTP	*Revue de théologie et de philosophie*
RVV	Religionsgeschichtliche Versuche und Vorarbeiten
S	Peshitta
SAPERE	Scripta Antiquitatis Posterioris ad Ethicam Religionemque pertinentia
SBB	Stuttgarter biblische Beiträge
SBLRBS	Society of Biblical Literature Resources for Biblical Study
SBS	Stuttgarter Bibelstudien
SC	Sources chrétiennes
SCS	Septuagint and Cognate Studies
SNT	Studien zum Neuen Testament
SP	Samaritan Pentateuch
ST	Studienbücher Theologie
StS	Studia Samaritana
TCSt	Text-Critical Studies
T^{NF}	Targum Neofiti
T^{O}	Targum Onkelos
T^{Ps-J}	Targum Pseudo-Jonathan
TEH NF	Theologische Existenz heute, Neue Folge
TDOT	*Theological Dictionary of the Old Testament.* Edited by G. Johannes Botterweck, Helmer Ringgren and Heinz-Josef Fabry. 15 vols. Grand Rapids: Eerdmans, 1975–2015.
TDNT	*Theological Dictionary of the New Testament.* Edited by Gerhard Kittel and Gerhard Friedrich. Translated by Geoffrey W. Bromiley. 10 vols. Grand Rapids: Eerdmans, 1964–1976.
THAT	*Theologisches Handwörterbuch zum Alten Testament.* Edited by Ernst Jenni and Claus Westermann. 2 vols. Gütersloh: Chr. Kaiser / Gütersloher Verlagshaus, 2004.
ThB	Theologische Bücherei
ThQ	*Theologische Quartalschrift*
ThViat	*Theologia viatorum*
TSAJ	Texte und Studien zum antiken Judentum

TWAT	*Theologisches Wörterbuch zum Alten Testament.* Edited by G. Johannes Botterweck, Helmer Ringgren and Heinz-Josef Fabry. 9 vols. Stuttgart: Kohlhammer, 1970–2000.
TWNT	*Theologisches Wörterbuch zum Neuen Testament.* Edited by Gerhard Kittel and Gerhard Friedrich. 10 vols. Stuttgart: Kohlhammer, 1932–1979.
TZ	*Theologische Zeitschrift*
VC	*Vigiliae Christianae*
VCSup	Supplements to Vigiliae Christianae
VetE	*Verbum et Ecclesia*
VT	*Vetus Testamentum*
VTSup	Supplements to Vetus Testamentum
VWGTh	Veröffentlichungen der Wissenschaftlichen Gesellschaft für Theologie
WBC	Word Biblical Commentary
WMANT	Wissenschaftliche Monographien zum Alten und Neuen Testament
WO	*Die Welt des Orients*
WUNT	Wissenschaftliche Untersuchungen zum Neuen Testament
ZAW	*Zeitschrift für die alttestamentliche Wissenschaft*
ZBK	Zürcher Bibelkommentare
ZThK	*Zeitschrift für Theologie und Kirche*

Part 1
Introduction and Questions of Methodology

Projektvorstellung:
Theologie der Septuaginta – Methodische Grundlegung und Fallstudien

Martin Rösel

ABSTRACT: The essay is meant as a short introduction to the project of a "Theology of the Septuagint." In a first step, the most important results from the history of research and the discussion of methodological issues are presented. They are based on elaborated chapters of the book, which were sent to the participants of the symposium in advance. These texts are the first part of an intended book of about 150 pages, which shall serve as a "methodological foundation" of a theology of the Septuagint. In its second part several "case studies" on selected topics will demonstrate the outcome of the proposed compilation of theologically motivated deviations between Hebrew and Greek Bible. Several methodological considerations are made. First, a "twofold comparative approach" is proposed: the comparison of the Hebrew and Greek texts as a first step, and the comparison of the Greek translations with each other as a second, so that accordances and differences between the individual translations and their theological profiles become visible. Another important issue is the question for the concept of "theology," which consists of elements of reflection and systematization: Ongoing reflection on the Hebrew text and its meaning lead to more systematic categorizations through the use of distinct and at times more uniform vocabulary. Finally, the growth of the Septuagint as a collection of scriptures and its manifold character has to be taken into account. Therefore, the material will be presented in a diachronic approach in three stages and in systematic order according to the most important topics that were identified during the history of research.

Das Rostock-Stellenbosch-Symposion zur Theologie der Septuaginta hatte eine Struktur, die etwas von der Organisation anderer Tagungen abwich: Hintergrund war ein Forschungsstipendium, das mir vom

Kultusministerium des Landes Mecklenburg-Vorpommern bewilligt wurde, um meine Überlegungen zur Theologie der griechischen Bibel weiterführen zu können. Im Rahmen dieses Projekts konnte auch das Symposion zu großen Teilen finanziert werden. Während der Laufzeit des Stipendiums konnen zwei umfangreiche Abschnitte des geplanten Buches mit dem Titel „Theologie der Septuaginta – Methodische Grundlegung und Fallstudien" erarbeitet werden: die Forschungsgeschichte und die Methodik. Diese Ausarbeitungen wurden den Teilnehmerinnen und Teilnehmern des Symposions vorab zugesandt, verbunden mit der Bitte, in ihren Beiträgen darauf Bezug zu nehmen und konstruktive Kritik zu üben. Zu Beginn der Tagung habe ich als Einführung in die Thematik meine Schlussfolgerungen aus Forschungsgeschichte und Methodik kurz vorgestellt. Dieser Beitrag soll im Folgenden dokumentiert werden. Er führt frühere Überlegungen weiter, weshalb Überschneidungen in einzelnen Fällen nicht zu vermeiden sind.[1] Die beiden ausführlichen Kapitel werden Teil der endgültigen Publikation sein, sie sind vorab auf academia.edu zugänglich.

1. Das Projekt

In den letzten beiden Jahrzehnten hat die Beschäftigung mit der LXX einen gänzlich unerwarteten Aufschwung erlebt. Das hat nach meiner Beobachtung zu zwei gegenläufigen Tendenzen geführt. Zum einen ist über die neu angefertigten Übersetzungen der LXX – allen voran NETS, LXX.D und in Teilen auch BdA – der Zugang zur griechischen Bibel auch für Nicht-Spezialisten einfacher als je zuvor. Unterschiedlich ausführliche Einführungen, sowohl in den jeweiligen Übersetzungen als auch separat publiziert,[2] ermöglichen zudem einen Eindruck von Charakteristik und Problematik der jeweiligen Übersetzungen. Allerdings sind diese Einführungen von sehr unterschiedlicher Qualität und setzen zudem oft nicht die gleichen Schwerpunkte bei der Auswahl der zu behandelnden Gegenstände.[3]

---

1. Die gemeinten Aufsätze sind jetzt leicht zugänglich in Rösel 2018, 253–72, 273–90.

2. Zu nennen sind hier vor allem: Aitken 2015; Karrer und Kraus 2011; Kreuzer 2016; dazu noch die Abschnitte zur LXX in Lange und Tov 2017.

3. Um nur ein Beispiele für die zweite Behauptung zu geben: Im Fall der Exodus-Übersetzung für LXX.D war der Übersetzer Jürgen Roloff verstorben. Die Kommen-

Daneben hat sich als zweite Entwicklungslinie eine sehr hoch spezialisierte Detailforschung etabliert. Ihre Ergebnisse werden in Dissertationen und Tagungsbänden veröffentlicht, die über den engeren Kreis der Spezialisten hinaus kaum wahrgenommen werden. Das soll nicht kritisiert werden, da solche Forschung an den Grundlagen der Disziplin absolut nötig ist und zudem wichtige Ergebnisse und neue Orientierungen bringt. Was aber nach meinem Eindruck fehlt, ist eine zusammenfassende Darstellung dieser Forschungsergebnisse, die es z.B. den Nachbardisziplinen ermöglicht, sich einen Überblick über den theologisch relevanten Ertrag der LXX-Forschung zu verschaffen und für die eigenen Forschungen zu nutzen.[4] Ein Indiz dafür ist etwa die Tatsache, dass in der alttestamentlichen Wissenschaft nur in Ausnahmefällen im Rahmen einer Theologie des AT auf die LXX kaum je eingegangen wird[5] oder dass in wissenschaftlichen Kommentaren die LXX über den Bereich der Textkritik hinaus genutzt wird, um ihr wirkungsgeschichtliches Potential zu dokumentieren.[6] Allerdings ist für den Bereich des Neuen Testaments zu konstatieren, dass die Bedeutung der Septuaginta immer stärker in Rechnung gestellt wird.[7]

Ich selbst habe mich schon länger mit der Frage beschäftigt, ob und wie es möglich ist, eine Zusammenfassung der theologischen Besonderheiten der griechischen Bibel als „Theologie der Septuaginta" zu verfassen.

---

tare im Begleitband wurden daher von Joachim Schaper erstellt, der natürlich nicht die Übersetzungen Roloffs begründen konnte, sondern inhaltliche Kommentare nach eigenen Kriterien gab. Bei allen genannten Werken ist festzustellen, dass manche Artikel von Autoren/innen verfasst wurden, die sich noch nicht intensiv mit der LXX und ihren spezifischen Fragestellungen befasst hatten, weshalb sich notwendig ein unterschiedliches Niveau ergab. Auf die Nennung von Beispielen verzichte ich.

4. Damit soll nicht der Wert von Einleitungen oder Einführungen wie denjenigen von Jennifer Dines, Michael Tilly, Natalio Fernández Marcos, Karen Jobes/Moises Silva oder Folker Siegert geschmälert werden. Sie stellen die Breite der mit der LXX zusammenhängenden Fragestellungen in unterschiedlicher Ausführlichkeit dar, sind aber nicht auf theologisch relevante Fragestellungen fokussiert.

5. Vgl. aber Feldmeier und Spieckermann 2011, die fast durchgängig auch die Akzente im Blick haben, die die LXX bei der Übersetzung von Gottesprädikaten etc. verändert; vgl. etwa S. 30, Anm. 34 zu Ex 3,14 oder S. 162–75 zur Vorstellung des Allmächtigen/*pantokrator*.

6. Das gilt etwa für die Psalmenkommentare von Frank-Lothar Hossfeld/Erich Zenger (HThK) oder Friedhelm Hartenstein/Bernd Janowski (BKAT, neue Bearbeitung).

7. Vgl. neben den vielfältigen Beiträgen von Wolfgang Kraus und Martin Karrer v.a. Müller 2018.

Es scheint mir sinnvoll zu sein, eine solche Arbeit so zu positionieren, dass sie nicht nur die Spezialisten des Faches anspricht, sondern auch für die Nachbardisziplinen gut nutzbar ist. Andererseits ist aber gerade die Kernfrage, ob man überhaupt so etwas wie eine Theologie verfassen kann, höchst strittig.[8] Das Verfahren bedarf einer differenzierten Begründung, soll es Aussicht auf Akzeptanz haben. Daher habe ich mich dazu entschlossen, das Projekt in zwei Schritten anzugehen.

Im ersten Schritt soll eine „Grundlegung einer Theologie der Septuaginta" entstehen. Sie setzt sich aus zwei wesentlichen Elementen zusammen: Der erste Teil besteht aus einer methodischen Grundlegung, die ihrerseits aus den Ergebnissen der Forschungsgeschichte erwächst. Er soll die bisherige Diskussion bündeln und als Voraussetzung für die weitere Beschäftigung dienen. Der zweite Teil ist mit „Fallstudien" überschrieben. Hier wird nicht eine umfassende Theologie geboten, sondern anhand einiger ausgewählter Themenfelder soll deutlich werden, wie ich mir vor dem Hintergrund der methodischen Probleme die Darstellung einer solchen Theologie denke. Auswahl und Anordnung der Themen werden am Ende dieser Einführung vorgestellt werden. Die so beschriebene, vorläufige Formulierung des Projekts soll dem Umstand Rechnung tragen, dass die Forschung zu diesen Fragen derzeit in vollem Gange ist. Johann Cook hat daher die methodische Forderung erhoben, dass eine Theologie der LXX erst dann geschrieben werden könne, wenn Kommentare zu allen Büchern der LXX vorliegen.[9] Ich will natürlich nicht ausschließen, dass sich durch die Arbeit an den Kommentaren das Bild noch verändert und präzisiert. Doch ich habe den Eindruck, dass bereits jetzt so viele Informationen gesammelt wurden, dass erste Versuche lohnend und weiterführend sind. Das Projekt ist also ein Zwischenschritt zwischen den einzelnen thematischen Untersuchungen, wie ich sie bisher erarbeitet habe, und einer ausführlichen Theologie.[10] Es soll vor allem der Erprobung und der Kritik dienen, auch in Hinblick auf die Nachbardisziplinen.

2. Ergebnisse der Forschungsgeschichte

Blickt man auf die Forschungsgeschichte zur Frage nach der eigenständigen Theologie der LXX, so können einige der im Laufe der Zeit

---

8. Vgl. dazu als jüngste Stellungnahme Ausloos 2017.
9. Cook 2017a; vgl. bereits Cook 2010 und Cook 2017b.
10. Vgl. die vorläufige Skizzierung eines solchen Buches in Rösel 2018, 264–65.

verhandelten Fragen als geklärt angesehen werden, andere sind weiterhin aktuell und verdienen Aufmerksamkeit.

Zu den Problemkreisen, bei denen nach meinem Eindruck kein großer Diskussionsbedarf mehr besteht, gehört die Frage nach der Stellung der Septuaginta innerhalb der religionsgeschichtlichen Entwicklung des Judentums. Die ersten Arbeiten von Zacharias Frankel und Abraham Geiger hatten sich ja darum bemüht, die griechische Bibel in der Kontinuität der geistesgeschichtlichen Entwicklung des Judentums zu sehen.[11] Dies geschah einerseits durch die Beobachtung, dass sich in der LXX der Gebrauch exegetischer Techniken zeigen lässt, die im späteren rabbinischen Judentum ebenfalls angewendet wurden. Zum anderen wurden Parallelen bei inhaltlichen Themen aufgezeigt, etwa bei halachischen Fragestellungen, der Ausweitung monotheistischer Aussagen oder auch bei der Frage nach messianischen Vorstellungen.

Über die Forschungen des Philosophen August Ferdinand Dähne kam schon im 19. Jahrhundert eine weitere Dimension in die Diskussion.[12] Dähne hatte erkannt, dass an einigen Stellen der Einfluss hellenistischer Elemente auf die Übersetzung festzustellen ist. Dies konnte zunächst positiv als Zeichen für die Aufgeschlossenheit des hellenistischen Judentums für die Fragestellungen seiner Umwelt gewertet werden. Die LXX wurde dann als ältestes Zeugnis für spezifische theologische Entwicklungen gesehen, die fragmentarisch bei Autoren wie etwa Aristobul greifbar waren und dann bei Philo von Alexandrien zu voller Ausprägung gelangten. Dieses Verständnis der LXX lässt sich als evolutionär bezeichnen. Das frühe hellenistische Judentum, dem sie ihre Entstehung verdankt, wird als in sich folgerichtige Entwicklung von bestimmten theologischen und religiösen Prozessen verstanden, etwa der spät-nachexilischen Diasporaliteratur oder dem stärker universalistischen Denken Deutero- und Tritojesajas. Durch die historische Entwicklung, die zum Untergang des alexandrinisch-hellenistischen und der Vormachtstellung des rabbinischen Judentums geführt hat, ist auch dieser theologische Prozess beendet worden; seine Wirkungsgeschichte ist vor allem im frühen alexandrinischen Christentum greifbar.

Demgegenüber haben Adolf Deissmann, Joseph Ziegler und vor allem Georg Bertram die Position formuliert, dass die LXX Zeichen für eine

---

11. Frankel 1841, 1851; Geiger 1928.
12. Dähne 1834.

kategorial verschiedene Religionsform ist.¹³ Während die hebräische Bibel als nationalistisches und gesetzliches Dokument gesehen wird, sei die LXX Zeichen für eine vom Universalismus und der Gnadengabe Gottes geprägte Religion. Als Beleg sei nur Deissmanns berühmtes Diktum zitiert: „Die Bibel, deren Gott Jahveh heißt, ist die Bibel eines Volkes; die Bibel, deren Gott κύριος heißt, ist die Weltbibel".¹⁴ Diese Position lässt sich heute nicht mehr halten, unter anderem deshalb, weil wir nach den Funden von Qumran ein sehr viel besseres Bild von der Vielschichtigkeit des hellenistischen und protorabbinischen Judentums haben. Besonders die Arbeiten Bertrams sind zusätzlich belastet durch sein Engagement bei den „Deutschen Christen" und seine Arbeit als wissenschaftlicher Leiter des „Instituts zur Erforschung und Beseitigung des jüdischen Einflusses auf das deutsche kirchliche Leben", dessen Existenz er auch nach 1945 weiterführen wollte¹⁵. Ebenso problematisch ist die Abwertung der LXX durch Robert Hanhart, der sie als Zeichen des Nieder- und Übergangs bewertete.¹⁶ Für den heutigen Umgang mit der LXX stellt sich daher für christliche Forscher die Aufgabe, ohne antijudaistische Verhältnisbestimmungen auszukommen und die LXX im Sinne Isac Leo Seeligmanns vornehmlich als Dokument jüdischer Theologie zu verstehen.¹⁷ Zugleich besteht die Aufgabe, das Verhältnis zwischen einer Theologie der LXX und einer Theologie der hebräischen Bibel zu bestimmen.¹⁸

Als weitere Einsichten aus der Forschungsgeschichte sind einige methodische Prinzipien zu nennen. Grundlegend ist seit Zacharias Frankel, dass die LXX nicht vorschnell als Einheit zu verstehen ist, sondern dass die einzelnen Bücher zunächst separat zu bearbeiten sind, um ihr je charakteristisches Übersetzungsprofil zu erkennen.¹⁹ Um dieses größere Bild zu erhalten, ist es aber nötig, dass parallele Stellen mit gleichen oder

---

13. Deissmann 1903; Ziegler 1937, 1962; Bertram 1954–1959, 1957.

14. Deissmann 1903, 175.

15. Vgl. dazu Heschel 2008, 67–105. Siehe auch die umfassende Darstellung von Schuster 2017, 253–55 zur Zeit nach 1945.

16. Hanhart 1967, ibs. 42–52.

17. Seeligmann 1948, ibs. 220–32.

18. Siehe dazu den Versuch von Glenny 2016.

19. Vgl. sein Vorgehen im Buch von 1851: Die Behandlung der Bücher erfolgt weitgehend parallel; für jedes Buch wird zunächst eine allgemeine Einführung gegeben, darauf folgt eine Fülle von Belegen für Charakteristika der jeweiligen Übersetzungsweise, dann Hinweise zur philosophischen und religiösen Exegese und schließlich Diskussionen über Textstellen, die später in den Text eingedrungen seien.

gleichartigen Phänomenen zusammengeordnet werden, dies seit dem methodischen Vorgehen von Martin Flashar zum Septuaginta-Psalter.[20] Staffan Olofsson hat dies später noch um die Überlegung erweitert, dass auch parallele Entwicklungen in unterschiedlichen Büchern betrachtet werden müssen, um das Ausmaß theologischer Exegese festzustellen, das in ihnen stattgefunden hat.[21]

Ein offenes Problem in der Forschungsgeschichte bleibt aber die Frage, was eigentlich als theologische Exegese gelten kann, die charakteristisch für die theologische oder religiöse Überzeugung des jeweiligen Übersetzers ist. Das soll an einem besonders instruktiven Beispiel erläutert werden: Von Dtn 32,4 an wurde צוּר „Fels" als metaphorische Aussage über Gott nicht wörtlich übersetzt, sondern mit θεός „Gott" oder, so besonders in den Psalmen, mit βοηθός „Helfer" übersetzt (vgl. Ps 18 [17],3). Während mir dieses Phänomen als eine buchübergreifende theologische Modifikation erscheint, die in einer Theologie der LXX zu würdigen wäre, gilt für Anneli Aejmelaeus die Rede von Gott als „Fels" als in der hellenistischen Zeit erstarrte, tote Metapher. Die nicht-wörtliche Übersetzung mit „Gott" ist daher nicht als theologisch motiviert zu verstehen, sondern als einfache Übersetzungsleistung.[22] Noch weiter geht Melvin Peters, der nachzuweisen versucht, dass für die Vorlage des Deuteronomium-Übersetzers nicht צוּר „Fels", sondern אֱלֹהִים „Gott" anzunehmen ist, die getreu wiedergegeben wurde.[23] Demnach ist auch für ihn nicht mit theologisch motivierter Übersetzung zu rechnen.

Methodisch lässt sich hier nur weiterkommen, wenn man vom Einzelphänomen absieht und *patterns* erkennt, denen zufolge bei vergleichbaren Problemstellungen des Ausgangstextes ähnliche Übersetzungslösungen angewendet wurden. Im konkreten Fall צוּר–θεός wäre dies die Beobachtung, dass ἀντιλήμπτωρ „Beschützer, Unterstützer" in vergleichbaren Fällen verwendet wurde, wenn von Gott als מָגֵן „Schild" (Ps 3,4); מִשְׂגָּב „Burg" (2.Kgt 22,3; Ps 18 [17],3) oder סֶלַע „Fels" (Ps 42 [41],10) die Rede ist.[24]

---

20. Flashar 1912.
21. Olofsson 2001, 296: "It is easier to detect a theological tendency in one book in relation to other books of the LXX than to focus only on the Book of Psalms".
22. Aejmelaeus 2006, 35.
23. Peters 2012.
24. Eine ausführlichere Diskussion dieses Problems findet sich bei Rösel 2019.

Eine weitere offene Frage besteht darin, ob es überhaupt möglich ist, eine umfassende Theologie der LXX zu formulieren. In der Regel wird nicht bestritten, dass es einzelne Fälle von theologisch motivierter Exegese gibt, dies vor allem bei freier übersetzten Büchern wie Genesis, Jesaja, Hiob oder den Proverbien (so etwa Emanuel Tov 1987 oder Jan Joosten 2000). Dabei handele es sich aber vor allem um *ad hoc*-Übersetzungslösungen, die auf ein konkretes Textproblem reagieren. Daneben wird oft auch die Existenz einiger buchübergreifender Phänomene akzeptiert, etwa der Umgang mit Aussagen über die Möglichkeit Gott zu sehen im Pentateuch[25] oder die Verwendung der Übersetzung παντοκράτωρ für צְבָאוֹת (2.Kgt 5,10; 7,8; durchgehend im Dodekapropheton) oder שַׁדַּי (Hiob 11,7; 22,17) in jüngeren Schriften. Allerdings lasse sich aus diesen Einzelphänomenen keine einheitliche Theologie zusammenstellen.[26] Prominent wird etwa von Johann Cook formuliert und in einigen Aufsätzen vorgeführt, dass nur die Theologie von Einzelschriften, also etwa der Bücher Proverbien oder Hiob formuliert werden könne.[27]

Diese Zurückhaltung wird etwa von Jan Joosten mit der These begründet, dass die Übersetzer gar keine eigene Theologie formulieren wollten. Ihr hermeneutischer Ansatz sei demgegenüber gewesen, dass sie im Bewusstsein, eine heilige Schrift bzw. Gottes Wort zu übersetzen, den Sinn des hebräischen Textes so genau wie möglich übersetzen wollten, dies allerdings in der Weise, wie sie ihn verstanden haben.[28] Auf diese Weise sei es dann zu Abweichungen vom mutmaßlichen Ursprungssinn des Textes gekommen, unter anderem auch zu theologischen Aktualisierungen.[29]

Dieser Position kann ich durchaus zustimmen. Allerdings gehe ich insofern darüber hinaus, dass in der Summe aus den so beschriebenen Änderungen eben doch eine Schriftensammlung mit einer veränderten Aussage entstanden ist. Bisher ist noch keine umfassende Zusammenstellung von solchen theologisch motivierten Einzelübersetzungen oder *patterns* vorgelegt worden.[30] Eine „Theologie der LXX" auf kleinstem

---

25. Lust 1997.
26. So Tov 1987, 244-45.
27. Cook 2010, 636-37.
28. Joosten 2000, 41-42.
29. Vgl. auch De Sousa 2018.
30. Allerdings ist gerade in der Reihe „Handbuch zur Septuaginta" (LXX.H) ein Band zur Theologie erschienen (2020), herausgegeben von Hans Ausloos und Bénédicte Lemmelijn, in dem verschiedene theologisch relevante Themen bearbeitet werden.

gemeinsamem Nenner könnte also darin bestehen, dass nachgezeichnet wird, an welchen Stellen in der LXX sich religiöse oder theologische Überzeugungen zeigen, die vom hebräischen Text abweichen.

Zur Orientierung oder zur Strukturierung können dabei die Themen gelten, die bereits im Verlauf der bisherigen Forschungsgeschichte benannt worden sind. Bei ihnen gibt es eine Reihe von Übereinstimmungen bei verschiedenen Forschern, so dass mit einer hohen Akzeptanz gerechnet werden kann. Folgende Themenfelder sind dabei genannt worden; sie werden auch in meiner Skizze berücksichtigt werden:

- Zacharias Frankel und Abraham Geiger: Gottesbild, mit den besonderen Aspekten des Wohnens Gottes und der Anthropomorphismen.
- Armand Kaminka: Die Erhabenheit des göttlichen Wesens, die Heiligkeit Israels, Jenseitsvorstellungen, Apologie des Judentums.[31]
- Isac Leo Seeligmann: Gott (mit Abgrenzung zu anderen Göttern), Israel und sein Messias, die Tora und ihre Bedeutung.[32]
- Leo Prijs: Torazentrik und Eschatologie.[33]
- Georg Bertram: Septuaginta-Frömmigkeit, Anthropologie, dabei besonders der Erziehungsgedanke, das Sündenverständnis, Gottesvorstellungen, Eschatologie und Messianismus.[34]

3. Überlegungen zur Methodik

In den eben geäußerten Überlegungen zur Forschungsgeschichte sind bereits wichtige methodische Fragen angesprochen worden. Meine eigene Position möchte ich im Anschluss daran knapp zusammenfassen, erneut werden die in Anm. 1 genannten Arbeiten vorausgesetzt.

3.1. Doppelter Vergleich

Es ist eindeutig, dass die spezifischen theologischen Aussagen der griechischen Übersetzung vor allem an den Differenzen zwischen dem hebräischen und dem griechischen Text zu erheben sind. Dieses Vergleichen hat zunächst auf der Ebene des einzelnen Buches zu geschehen,

---

31. Kaminka 1928, 272–73.
32. Seeligmann 1948, 96: "an outline of certain religious conceptions".
33. Prijs 1948, 62–75.
34. Bertram 1954–1959, vgl. auch zusammenfassend: Bertram 1961.

wobei die je spezifische Übersetzungsweise des Buches zu berücksichtigen ist. Die zweite Ebene des Vergleichs ist dann die der griechischen Bücher untereinander. Ich gehe also davon aus, dass die in der Forschungsgeschichte als nötig erkannte methodische Beschränkung auf nur ein Buch zwar als erster Schritt der Untersuchung wichtig ist. Sie reicht aber nicht aus, um angemessen zu beschreiben, welche theologischen Veränderungen sich in der LXX vollzogen haben.[35] Zur Verdeutlichung greife ich ein Beispiel wieder auf, das ich bereits genannt hatte:

Instruktiv ist der Umgang mit den Gottesbezeichnungen צְבָאוֹת und אֵל שַׁדַּי nämlich insofern, als frühe Übersetzungen noch keine spezifischen Übersetzungslösungen kannten. In der Genesis wird אֵל שַׁדַּי mit „mein Gott" (Gen 17,1) oder „dein Gott" (Gen 35,11) wiedergegeben; צְבָאוֹת wird in 1.Kgt 1,3 transkribiert und in Ps 24 (23),10 mit δύναμις übersetzt. In späteren Übersetzungen zeigt sich dann eine andere inhaltliche Füllung und theologische Konkretion, wenn צְבָאוֹת oder אֵל שַׁדַּי mit παντοκράτωρ „Allherrscher" (Am 3,13; Hi 22,17) oder אֵל שַׁדַּי als ὁ ἱκανός „der alleinreichende"; „sufficient One" (so NETS; Rut 1,20). Erst durch den Vergleich der Bücher untereinander erschließt sich diese theo-logische Weiterentwicklung.[36] Damit ist zugleich deutlich, dass dieser doppelt vergleichende Zugang notwendig eine diachrone Dimension hat. Das verhindert die in der Forschungsgeschichte als problematisch erkannte Wahrnehmung der LXX als Einheit.

3.2. Standard-Äquivalente und Semantik

Der doppelt vergleichende Zugang setzt voraus, dass sich die theologischen Besonderheiten vor allem an den Differenzen zwischen Ausgangstext und Übersetzungsergebnis fassen lassen. Das ist unmittelbar einleuchtend, allerdings erscheinen hier weitere Problemfelder am Horizont. Das erste liegt in der Frage nach der Bestimmung der Semantik der gewählten Übersetzungsäquivalente. So stellt die Wahl von κύριος für den Gottesnamen oder von νόμος für תּוֹרָה zwar das jeweilige Standard-Äquivalent dar,

---

35. Vgl. die oben Anm. 21 wiedergegebene Position von Oloffson 2001, 296, wonach theologische Tendenzen durch den Vergleich verschiedener Bücher leichter zu erkennen sind.

36. Ein weiteres gutes Beispiel ist die Verwendung von εἴδωλον zur Wiedergabe verscheidener hebräischer Lexeme, vgl. dazu den Beitrag von Stefanie Peintner in diesem Band.

doch unterscheidet sich der Sinngehalt der griechischen Wörter deutlich von dem der hebräischen.[37] Das zeigt sich auch in den Fällen, in denen die Übersetzer gerade nicht das Standard-Äquivalent verwendet haben, sondern ein anderes Lexem zur Wiedergabe wählten; etwa bei צְדָקָה nicht δικαιοσύνη, sondern z.B. ἐλεημοσύνην (Ps 24 [23],5) wählten; die semantischen Differenzierungen waren ihnen also bewusst.[38] Es ist noch ein offenes Problem, wie mit dieser Fragestellung umzugehen ist und wie diese Differenzen auszuwerten sind.

3.3. Das Problem der Differenzen zwischen hebräischem und griechischem Text

Ein weiteres Problemfeld liegt darin, was eigentlich als Differenz zu gelten hat.[39] Hier ist zunächst der weite Bereich abweichender Vorlagen zu nennen; in vielen Fällen ist nicht sicher zu sagen, ob eine Differenz daher rührt, dass der Übersetzer einen abweichenden Text vor sich hatte. Ein zweiter Bereich ist der der sprachlichen Decodierungen; der Übersetzer hat seinen Text sprachlich anders verstanden, als er offenkundig gemeint war. Ein Paradebeispiel dafür ist der Umgang mit den Verneinungen in Ps 7 und 90 (89):

Ps 7,12: וְאֵל זֹעֵם בְּכָל־יוֹם wurde zu μὴ ὀργὴν ἐπάγων καθ' ἑκάστην ἡμέραν.
Aus: „ein Gott, der täglich zürnt" (Zürcher) wurde: „der nicht jeden Tag (seinen) Zorn aufkommen lässt" (LXX.D).

Ps 90 (89),2-3: אַל[3] תָּשֵׁב אֱנוֹשׁ עַד־דַּכָּא: wurde zu μὴ ἀποστρέψῃς ἄνθρωπον εἰς ταπείνωσιν.

---

37. Auf dieses Problem hatte bereits Dodd 1954, 3-95 aufmerksam gemacht. Vgl. jüngst Zurawski 2016.
38. Hinweis von Jean Maurais, Montreal. Als Hinweis auf die Problematik vgl. auch Lee 2010; und als eindrückliches Beispiel für die Komplexität der semantischen Bestimmung Joosten 2012, der darauf hinweist, dass ἔλεος offensichtlich seine hellenistische Prägung behalten hat.
39. Dieses grundlegende Problem wird in nahezu allen Publikationen zum Thema angesprochen. Vgl. beispielsweise Olofsson 2009, hier ibs. 14-27; oder Aejmelaeus 2006, 26-37.

Aus: „Gott. Du lässt den Menschen zum Staub zurückkehren" (Zürcher) wurde: „Führe den Menschen nicht fort in die Erniedrigung." (LXX.D).

Es ist eindeutig, dass sich in diesen Fällen die theologische Aussage der griechischen Version von der des hebräischen Textes erheblich unterscheidet. Sie kann daher für die Bestimmung der Theologie der griechischen Psalmen herangezogen werden. In methodologischer Hinsicht plädiere ich daher für die Reduzierung der Konzentration auf den Übersetzer als alleine verantwortliche Person oder Instanz. Zudem konnten auch Abschreiber eines hebräischen Textes theologisch denken und Änderung vornehmen, wie sich an einer Vielzahl textkritischer Varianten zeigt.[40] Hinzu kommt, dass immer dann, wenn sich ein *pattern* erkennen lässt, wenn sich also ein Phänomen mehrfach feststellen lässt, die Wahrscheinlichkeit groß ist, dass es sich bei der Änderung nicht um einen Zufall der Textüberlieferung handelt. Eine Einzelstelle muss dann nicht die Beweislast alleine tragen; die Existenz des theologischen Interpretationsmusters (*pattern*) wirkt unterstützend.[41]

3.4. Der Begriff „Theologie": Reflexion und Systematisierung vorgegebener biblischer Aussagen

Aus der Fülle der Veränderungen, seien es nun einzelne Phänomene oder übergreifende *patterns*, lässt sich kein umfassendes theologisches System rekonstruieren, das die Übersetzer gehabt hätten.[42] Damit stellt sich die Frage, wie der Begriff „Theologie" in meinem Projekt zu verstehen ist. Hier habe ich vorgeschlagen, dass es um ein Nachzeichnen und Zusammenstellen der Reflexionsleistungen und Systematisierungen geht, die sich in der LXX erkennen lassen.[43] Dies nimmt die oben genannten, in

---

40. Vgl. aber die entgegengesetzte Argumentation von Screnock 2017, der davon ausgeht, dass die LXX nicht theologisch oder ideologisch auszuwerten sei, weil man in der Regel nicht unterscheiden könne, ob Differenzen zwischen hebräischem und griechischem Text auf einen Abschreiber oder den Übersetzer zurückgehen. Vgl. auch Perkins 2013, 18, der es ebenfalls für nachrangig erachtet, ob eine Variante auf der Ebene der hebräischen oder der griechischen Textüberlieferung entstanden ist.

41. So auch Aejmelaeus 2006, 21.

42. Vgl. dazu als instruktives Beispiel in diesem Band Wolfgang Kraus' Untersuchung zur Problematik des Landes in der LXX.

43. Vgl. die vergleichbare Definition von McLay 2010, 610: "Theology is a reflec-

der Forschungsgeschichte bereits identifizierten Themen auf, bei denen theologisch bedeutsame Veränderungen stattgefunden haben. Als instruktive Beispiele wären etwa die Übersetzung der Altar-Terminologie und die Differenzierung zwischen θυσιαστήριον und βωμός für israelitische und fremde Altäre zu nennen, aber auch die Frage nach der Sichtbarkeit Gottes[44] oder der Abgrenzung zu den εἴδωλα „Götzen". Bei diesen Themen lässt sich überzeugend deutlich machen, dass ein theologischer Gestaltungswille hinter der Übersetzung steht.

3.5. Das Problem der LXX als Schriftensammlung und die diachrone Anlage einer „Theologie"

Schließlich ist auf das Problem der Darstellung einer Theologie der LXX angesichts der Vielfalt der Schriften und angesichts des sukzessiven Wachstums dieser Schriftensammlung einzugehen. Es wird dadurch erschwert, dass die hermeneutischen Grundüberzeugungen der Übersetzer nicht einheitlich waren, wie sich am gewählten Übersetzungsstil zeigt. Hinzu kommen übergreifende Entwicklungen, wie die seit dem 2. Jh. feststellbare Tendenz zur Stabilisierung der hebräischen Textüberlieferung, die im zweiten Schritt zur Revision von früheren, weniger wörtlichen Übersetzungen führte.

Hier schlage ich anders als der Theologie-Band in der Reihe „Handbuch zur LXX" (s. oben Anm. 30) vor, schon in der Anlage des Buches das diachrone Wachstum der LXX nachzuvollziehen und das Material in drei Stufen oder Epochen zu präsentieren, wobei die jeweils wichtigsten Themen der Schriften besonders betont werden. Einen ersten Entwurf für einen möglichen Aufbau des zweiten Teils des Buches habe ich skizziert (siehe unten), der hiermit zur Diskussion gestellt sei. Dabei sind bereits jetzt zwei Problemkreise erkennbar. Der eine besteht darin, dass die Datierung der Übersetzungen und damit die Zuordnung zu Epochen mit mancherlei Unsicherheiten behaftet ist. Der zweite besteht in der angestrebten Kürze der Darstellung, die zu einem Verzicht auf ausführliche Exegesen und zu einer hohen Verdichtung nötigt.

---

tive activity in which the content of religious expressions is to some extent abstracted, contemplated, subjected to reflection and discussion, and deliberately reformulated".
44. Vgl. dazu die Aufsätze in Dafni 2017 und van der Meer 2019.

3.6. „Fallstudien"

Abschließend sei kurz skizziert, wie der zweite Hauptteil der Studie nach Forschungsgeschichte und Methodik konzipiert sein kann. Geplant sind kurze Kapitel, die für Nicht-Spezialisten verständlich sind und einen Überblick über das Material und die entscheidenden theologischen Veränderungen geben sollen.[45] Dabei wird keine vollständige Darstellung angestrebt, sondern es soll demonstriert werden, bei welchen Themenkomplexen es theologisch bedeutsame Unterschiede zwischen den Versionen gibt. Zugleich soll die theologische Weiterentwicklung innerhalb der Schriftensammlung „Septuaginta" erkennbar werden.

Die einzelnen Abschnitte sollen folgendem Muster folgen: Jeder Hauptteil wird eröffnet mit einer kurzen Charakterisierung der Epoche. Darin werden angesprochen: Historische Ereignisse; übersetzte Bücher; Besonderheiten im Umfeld, die die „hermeneutische Großwetterlage" beeinflusst haben. Die einzelnen Übersetzungen werden kurz charakterisiert, es werden Hinweise bzw. der Diskussionsstand zur relativen und absoluten Datierung und zur Lokalisierung gegeben.

Die Kapitel/Fallstudien orientieren sich an den vorgegebenen Themen. Die Ergebnisse der einzelnen Bücher werden getrennt dargestellt und am Ende zusammengefasst. Besonderheiten einzelner Bücher, die nicht in anderen begegnen, können im Rahmen der Zusammenfassung mitgeteilt werden. Im Mittelpunkt der Kapitel sollen die jeweiligen Texte stehen, auf die sich die Beobachtung oder These stützt. Hebräische und griechische Texte werden übersetzt. Literaturangaben werden nur sparsam gegeben, so dass interessierte Leser die Ergebnisse oder nötige Diskussionen nachvollziehen können. Am Ende jedes Hauptteils wird eine Zusammenfassung gegeben.

Die Themen im Einzelnen:

1. Pentateuch: Die LXX des 3. Jahrhunderts; dargestellte Themen sind:
   Theo-Logie: Das Bild Gottes
   Schöpfung: Plato und die Bibel
   Das Gesetz: Auf dem Weg zu einer neuen Soteriologie

---

45. Vgl. auch die entsprechende Darstellung bei Müller 2020.

Anthropologie: Der hebräische Mensch im griechischen Gewand
Gottesdienst: Gemeinde ohne Tempel
Die Zukunft: Messianische Erwartungen

2. Propheten und Psalmen: Die LXX in der Mitte des 2. Jahrhunderts
Die Darstellung der Geschichte Israels
Die Propheten und das Gesetz
Aktualisierung der Prophezeiungen: Messianismus und Eschatologie
Gott wird *Pantokrator*
Anbetung und Klage: Gotteslob in griechischen Worten

3. Weisheit, Apokalyptik und Auseinandersetzung: Die LXX im 1. Jahrhundert
Wort Gottes – Wörtliches Übersetzen (erste Revisionen)
Weisheit und Philosophie – Die Rolle des Menschen in der Welt
Gott und die Götter – Gott und die Könige
Gottesreich und Auferstehung: Die Zukunft des Menschen

Auswahl und Anordnung der Themen wurden im Rahmen des Symposions diskutiert. Auf breite Zustimmung stieß der Vorschlag, in Abschnitt II und III die Themen zu unterteilen oder auf konkrete Bücher zu konzentrieren, etwa die Gruppe Dodekapropheton, Jeremia und Ezechiel, oder Hiob und Proverbien, dies wegen der vergleichbaren Charakteristik der Übersetzungen. Ein weiterer Vorschlag war, Abschnitte zur Semantik zentraler Lexeme oder Wortfelder aufzunehmen, etwa δικαιοσύνη, ἐλεημοσύνη, παιδεία oder διαθήκη. Beide Fragestellungen werden bei der konkreten Ausarbeitung berücksichtigt werden.

In der Diskussion über das Projekt fand zum einen die Forderung Zustimmung, dass die Befunde der einzelnen Bücher separat zu erheben und darzustellen seien, zum anderen der prinzipielle methodische Zugang des „doppelten Vergleichs". Keine Einigung gab es bei der auch im allgemeinen Diskurs strittigen Frage, welche Phänomene des griechischen Textes als „Theologie" gewertet werden können. Hier hat besonders Emanuel Tov darauf hingewiesen, dass ein subjektives Element nicht ausgeschlossen werden kann; er benennt dies mit dem Terminus „*intuition*", womit die Intuition der heutigen Forschenden gemeint ist.

Diskutiert wurde außerdem die Notwendigkeit eines reflektierten Umgangs mit Phänomenen der Rezeptionsgeschichte der griechischen Bibel. Es ist zu vermeiden, spätere Interpretationen in die Übersetzungstexte hineinzulesen. Allerdings wurde durch den Beitrag von Ulrich Volp exemplarisch deutlich, dass der Umgang der Kirchenväter mit Texten aus der LXX einen hohen heuristischen Wert haben kann. Durch die spätere Rezeption wurde im konkreten Fall eine theologische Akzentuierung in mehreren Büchern deutlich, die bei der Bearbeitung der Einzelschriften nicht aufgefallen wäre.

Die Diskussion des hier umrisshaft beschriebenen Konzepts im Rahmen des Symposions hat ergeben, dass ein Projekt dieser Art grundsätzlich zu begrüßen ist. Es zeigt, dass die griechische Bibel als Teil eines theologischen Diskurses des hellenistischen Judentums zu verstehen ist, in dem auf offene Fragen oder Problemstellungen des hebräischen Bibeltextes reagiert wird. Die LXX will damit die hebräische Bibel und ihre Theologie nicht ersetzen, sondern explizieren, präzisieren oder fallweise auch aktualisieren. Eine Darstellung der veränderten theologischen Aussagen der griechischen Bibel ist damit als wesentlicher Teil sowohl einer gesamtbiblischen Theologie als auch einer Religionsgeschichte Israels zu verstehen.

Literatur

Aejmelaeus, Anneli. 2006. „Von Sprache zur Theologie. Methodologische Überlegungen zur Theologie der Septuaginta." Seiten 21–48 in *The Septuagint and Messianism*. Hrsg. von Michael A. Knibb. BETL 195. Leuven: Peeters.

Aitken, James K. ed. 2015. *The T&T Clark Companion to the Septuagint*. London: Bloomsbury.

Ausloos, Hans. 2017. „Sept défis posés à une théologie de la Septante." Seiten 228–50 in *Congress Volume: Stellenbosch, 2016*. Hrsg. von Louis C. Jonker, Gideon R. Kotzé, und Christl M. Maier. VTSup 177. Leiden: Brill.

Bertram, Georg. 1954–1959. „Vom Wesen der Septuaginta-Frömmigkeit." *WO* 2:274–83.

———. 1957. „Praeparatio Evangelica in der Septuaginta." *VT* 7:225–49.

———. 1961. „Septuaginta-Frömmigkeit." *RGG3* 5:1707–9.

Cook, Johann. 2010. „Towards the Formulation of a Theology of the Septuagint." Seiten 621–40 in *Congress Volume: Ljubljana, 2007*. Hrsg. von André Lemaire. VTSup 133. Leiden: Brill.

———. 2017a. „Interpreting the Septuagint." Seiten 1–22 in *Congress Volume: Stellenbosch, 2016*. Hrsg. von Louis C. Jonker, Gideon R. Kotzé, und Christl M. Maier. VTSup 177. Leiden: Brill.

———. 2017b. „A Theology of the Septuagint." *OTE* 30: 265–82.

Dähne, August F. 1834. *Geschichtliche Darstellung der jüdisch-alexandrinischen Religions-Philosophie: Zweite Abtheilung*. Halle: Buchhandlung des Waisenhauses.

Dafni, Evangelia G. Hg. 2017. *Gottesschau – Gotteserkenntnis*. Studien zur Theologie der Septuaginta 1. WUNT 387. Tübingen: Mohr Siebeck.

Deissmann, Adolf. 1903. „Die Hellenisierung des semitischen Monotheismus." *NJahrb* 11:162–77.

De Sousa, Rodrigo. 2018. „The Righteous King in LXX Isa 32:1-4: Hope and Ideology in Translation." *JSCS* 51:140–55.

Dodd, Charles H. 1954. *The Bible and the Greeks*. London: Hodder & Stoughton.

Feldmeier, Reinhard, und Hermann Spieckermann. 2011. *Der Gott der Lebendigen: Eine biblische Gotteslehre*. Topoi biblischer Theologie 1. Tübingen: Mohr Siebeck.

Flashar, Martin. 1912. „Exegetische Studien zum Septuagintapsalter." *ZAW* 32:81–116, 161–89, 241–68.

Frankel, Zacharias. 1841. *Vorstudien zu der Septuaginta*. Leipzig: Vogel.

———. 1851. *Ueber den Einfluss der palästinischen Exegese auf die alexandrinische Hermeneutik*. Leipzig: Barth.

Geiger, Abraham. 1928. *Urschrift und Übersetzung der Bibel in ihrer Abhängigkeit von der innern Entwickelung des Judentums*. Zweite Auflage mit einer Einführung von Paul Kahle. Frankfurt am Main: Madda.

Glenny, W. Edward. 2016. „The Septuagint and Biblical Theology." *Themelios* 41:263–78.

Hanhart, Robert. 1967. „Die Bedeutung der Septuaginta-Forschung für die Theologie." Seiten 38–64 in *Drei Studien zum Judentum*. Hrsg. von Robert Hanhart. TEH NF 140. München: Kaiser.

Heschel, Susannah. 2008. *The Aryan Jesus, Christian Theologians and the Bible in Nazi Germany*. Princeton: Princeton University Press.

Joosten, Jan. 2000. „Une théologie de la Septante? Réflecions méthologiques sur l'interprétation de la version greque." *RTP* 132:31–46.

———. 2012. „חסד, 'Benevolence', and ἔλεος, 'Pity': Reflections on Their Lexical Equivalence in the Septuagint." Seiten 97-111 in *Collected Studies on the Septuagint: From Language to Interpretation and Beyond*. Hrsg. von Jan Joosten. FAT 83. Tübingen: Mohr Siebeck.
Kaminka, Armand. 1928. „Studien zur Septuaginta an der Hand der zwölf kleinen Prophetenbücher." *MGWJ* 72:49-60, 242-73.
Karrer, Martin, und Wolfgang Kraus. 2011. *Septuaginta Deutsch: Erläuterungen und Kommentare zum griechischen Alten Testament*. Stuttgart: Deutsche Bibelgesellschaft.
Kreuzer, Siegfried. 2016. *Einleitung in die Septuaginta*. LXX.H 1. Gütersloh: Gütersloher Verlagshaus.
Lange, Armin, und Emanuel Tov, Hrsg. 2017. *Textual History of the Bible: The Hebrew Bible*. Vol. 1. Leiden: Brill.
Lee, James A. 2010. „Review of T. Muraoka, *A Greek-English Lexicon of the Septuagint*." *BIOSCS* 43:115-25.
Lust, Johan. 1997. „Septuagint and Messianism, with a Special Emphasis on the Pentateuch." Seiten 26-45 in *Theologische Probleme der Septuaginta und der hellenistischen Hermeneutik*. Hrsg. von Henning Graf Reventlow. VWGTh 11. Gütersloh: Gütersloher Verlagshaus.
McLay, R. Timothy. 2010. „Why Not a Theology of the Septuagint?" Seiten 607-20 in *Die Septuaginta - Texte, Theologien, Einflüsse*. Hrsg. von Wolfgang Kraus, Martin Karrer, und Martin Meiser. WUNT 252. Tübingen: Mohr Siebeck.
Meer, Michaël N. van der. 2019. „*Visio Dei* in the Septuagint." Seiten 171-205 in *XVI Congress of the International Organization for Septuagint and Cognate Studies: Stellenbosch, 2016*. Hrsg. von Gideon R. Kotzé, Wolfgang Kraus, und Michaël N. van der Meer. SCS 71. Atlanta: SBL Press.
Müller, Mogens. 2018. „Die Bedeutung der Septuaginta für die Entfaltung neutestamentlicher Theologie." Seiten 730-56 in *Die Septuaginta - Geschichte, Wirkung, Relevanz*. Hrsg. von Martin Meiser, Michaela Geiger, Siegfried Kreuzer, und Marcus Sigismund. WUNT 405. Tübingen: Mohr Siebeck.
———. 2020. „Theology in the LXX?" In *The Oxford Handbook of the Septuagint*. Hrsg. von T. Michael Law and Alison Salvesen (im Druck).
Olofsson, Staffan. 2001. „Law and Lawbreaking in the LXX Psalms - A Case of Theological Exegesis." Seiten 291-330 in *Der Septuaginta-Psalter: Sprachliche und theologische Aspekte*. Hrsg. von Erich Zenger. HBS 32. Freiburg im Breisgau: Herder.

———. 2009. *Translation Technique and Theological Exegesis: Collected Essays on the Septuagint Version*. ConBOT 57. Winona Lake, IN: Eisenbrauns.

Perkins, Larry. 2013. „The Greek Translator of Exodus, Interpres (*translator*) and Expositor (*interpretor*): His Treatment of Theophanies." *JSJ* 44:16–56.

Peters, Melvin K. H. 2012. „Revisiting the Rock: Tsur as a Translation of Elohim in Deuteronomy and Beyond." Seiten 37–51 in *Text-Critical and Hermeneutical Studies in the Septuagint*. Hrsg. von Johann Cook und Hermann-Josef Stipp. VTSup 157. Leiden: Brill.

Prijs, Leo. 1948. *Jüdische Tradition in der Septuaginta*. Leiden: Brill.

Rösel, Martin. 2018. *Tradition and Innovation: English and German Studies on the Septuagint*. SCS 70. Atlanta: SBL Press.

———. 2019. „Vorlage oder Interpretation? Zur Übersetzung von Gottesaussagen in der Septuaginta des Deuteronomiums." Seiten 250–62 in *Ein Freund des Wortes*. Festschrift Udo Rüterswörden. Hrsg. von Sebastian Grätz, Axel Graupner, und Jörg Lanckau. Göttingen: Vandenhoeck & Ruprecht.

Schuster, Dirk. 2017. *Die Lehre vom »arischen« Christentum: Das wissenschaftliche Selbstverständnis im Eisenacher »Entjudungsinstitut«*. Kirche – Konfession – Religion 70. Göttingen: Vandenhoeck & Ruprecht.

Screnock, John. 2017. *Traductor Scriptor: The Old Greek Translation of Exodus 1-14 as Scribal Activity*. VTSup 174. Leiden: Brill.

Seeligmann, Isac L. 1948. *The Septuagint Version of Isaiah: A Discussion of Its Problems*. MVEOL 9. Leiden: Brill.

Tov, Emanuel. 1987. „Die Septuaginta in ihrem theologischen und traditionsgeschichtlichen Verhältnis zur hebräischen Bibel." Seiten 237–65 in *Mitte der Schrift? Ein jüdisch-christliches Gespräch*. Hrsg. von Martin A. Klopfenstein. JudChr 11. Bern: Lang.

Ziegler, Joseph. 1937. *Dulcedo dei: Ein Beitrag zur Theologie der griechischen und lateinischen Bibel*. Alttestamentliche Abhandlungen 13/2. Münster: Aschendorf.

———. 1962. *Die Septuaginta: Erbe und Auftrag*. Würzburger Universitätsreden 33. Würzburg: Julius-Maximilians-Universität. Wieder abgedruckt in Ziegler, 1971. *Sylloge: Gesammelte Aufsätze zur Septuaginta*. MSU 10. Göttingen: Vandenhoeck & Ruprecht, 590–614.

Zurawski, Jason M. 2016. „From *Musar* to *Paideia*, from *Torah* to *Nomos*: How the Translation of the Septuagint Impacted the Paideutic Ideal in Hellenistic Judaism." Seiten 531–54 in *XV Congress of the International Organization for Septuagint and Cognate Studies: Munich, 2013.* Hrsg. von Wolfgang Kraus, Michaël N. van der Meer, und Martin Meiser. SCS 64. Atlanta: SBL Press.

The Interaction between Theological and Text-Critical Approaches

Emanuel Tov

ABSTRACT: This chapter focuses on the interaction between theological and other approaches to the LXX, especially text-critical approaches. In my view, the recognition of theology in a translation is not a solid fact, nor does it reflect an objective statement about what we identify in the translation, but a subjective recognition of a way of understanding elements in the translation. The description of theology in a translation can hardly ever be descriptive, since there is always an element of interpretation involved: deviations from MT that look to us like theological could have been caused by other factors as well. The theological and textual approaches represent two different disciplines that are usually mutually exclusive. If a deviation of the LXX from MT reflects a Hebrew variant, it cannot reflect theological exegesis at the same time, because a deviating Hebrew reading does not reflect the translator's intentions. By the same token, if that deviation was caused by the translator's techniques in transferring the message of the Hebrew into Greek, that detail does not reflect theology either. After a methodological introduction, I exemplify how certain differences between MT and the LXX can be approached by either a text-critical or a theological approach. I discuss approaches, not necessarily textual evidence of a certain type. In many cases, no decision can be made, and we often also change our mind. No one approach is preferable to another, since much depends on our intuition. Both Rösel and I use both approaches at different times, but with different frequencies; Rösel turns more to the theological approach and I more to the text-critical approach.

1. Background

This study focuses on the interaction between theological and other approaches to the LXX, especially the text-critical approach. In my view, the recognition of theology in a translation is not a solid fact, neither does it reflect a statement about what we identify in the translation, but it is a subjective recognition of a way of understanding elements in the translation.[1] The description of theology in a translation can hardly ever be descriptive, since there is always an element of interpretation involved: deviations from MT that appear to us to be theological also could have been caused by other factors.

On the other hand, other approaches to the translation such as the studies of translation technique and linguistic analysis can be descriptive. For example, one can conduct a study of the presentation of the Hebrew verbal tenses in the LXX of 2 Kings within the framework of a study of its translation technique. Regardless of the nature of the data, there will always be something factual to report. By the same token, a study on the use of Hebraistic phrases in LXX 2 Kings is always meaningful, although this investigation is more complicated, because one first needs to prove that a certain phrase is indeed Hebraistic. This topic provides a good comparison with the study of theology, since the very recognition of a Hebraism is subjective. Therefore, if someone claims that a certain rendering reflects acceptable Greek diction, and not a Hebraism, there is nothing to report at the level of Hebraisms. By the same token, any study of possible theological elements does not necessarily yield positive results, since the recognition of such elements may pertain only to the views of those scholars who recognize them. A presumed theological interpretation derived possibly from translation technique, from a different *Vorlage*, or from a different type of exegesis, etc.

What is theology of a translation? Theological exegesis of the LXX may be defined as any theological element added to the source text by the translator. In rare cases, the noninclusion in the translation of elements appearing in the source text may reflect theological censorship.[2] A similar definition also applies to other forms of exegesis. Most exegetical elements are reflected in the lexical choices themselves, which were influenced by the immediate context or the conceptual world of the translators. Theological exegesis relates to the description of God and his acts, the Messiah,

---

1. See my earlier publications: Tov 1987, 1999b.

2. The short form of the Greek translation of 1 Sam 16–18 is often presented as a case of theological shortening. See the views of Dominique Barthélemy and David Gooding in Barthélemy et al. 1986.

the exile, as well as the whole spectrum of religious experiences.³ Martin Rösel treated this question extensively in his position paper.⁴

In my view, the theology of the LXX should deal with the theological intentions of the translators, or the intentions that presumably were in the minds of the translators. However, not all scholars adhere to this view. Some include the theological implications of the LXX canon beyond the intentions of the translators. Hans Ausloos made a useful distinction between a "théologie de la Septante" and an "interprétation théologique de la Septante."⁵ I have only the former in mind and I believe that we should aim at the translators; otherwise we will reconstruct imaginary theological meanings that were not intended by the translators. Translators were sometimes influenced by other units in the LXX canon, but the default position should be that they were not, since each book was rendered by a separate translator, while many of them were influenced by the translation of the Torah. There is no proof of cooperation between the translators although sometimes clusters of books display shared equivalents. We need not think in terms of projects, neither regarding the Torah nor the post-Pentateuchal books.

This situation complicates the writing of a theology of the canon of the LXX. The same problem plays a role in the writing of a theology of Hebrew Scripture. Hebrew Scripture also became a unit only after it was canonized. However, it is more difficult to write a theology of the LXX because not every theological element in the LXX is relevant for the translator, while every element in the Hebrew Bible may be relevant for Hebrew Scripture. The main benefit of consulting a theology of the LXX and the Hebrew Bible is for those who take these literatures as completed units, which in the case of the LXX are the church fathers and the believing communities.⁶

The fact that the LXX is a translation should guide every detail of our analysis of the theological elements found in it. We therefore should not include elements common to the Hebrew and Greek texts in the analysis, for these provide no indication of the intellectual and religious world of the translators. It is a common misconception in analyses of this kind to

---

3. A somewhat narrower definition was suggested by Seeligman 1990, 224: "God, Israel, comprising the Messianic idea as a national redemptive force, and the Torah" (original version: Seeligman 1940).
4. See Rösel's chapter in this volume.
5. Ausloos 2017.
6. On the theological aspects of textual criticism in general, see Kreuzer 2018.

include elements that are shared with the Hebrew,[7] as was already pointed out eloquently by Isac Seeligmann in 1940.[8] We thus are not interested in elements in the LXX that reflect Hebrew theological variants. Such variants have a bearing on the manuscripts from which the translation derived, not on the translators.

The theological and textual approaches represent two different philosophies that usually are mutually exclusive. If a deviation in the LXX from MT reflects a Hebrew variant, it cannot reflect theological exegesis because the variant does not reflect the translator's intentions. I therefore allow myself to disagree with Martin Rösel's analysis of the theological importance of Exod 15:3 κύριος συντρίβων πολέμους ("The Lord, who shatters wars") for MT יְהוָה אִישׁ מִלְחָמָה:

Exod 15:3	MT	יְהוָה אִישׁ מִלְחָמָה
	SP	יהוה גיבור במלחמה
	LXX	κύριος συντρίβων πολέμους
	= ?	יהוה שבר מלחמה

The Greek version does form a theological statement in Jdt 9:7, where it is quoted from Exodus.[9] However, does the Greek text of Exod 15:3 carry the same powerful message? Larry Perkins and Martin Rösel[10] reply in the

---

7. See the argumentation in Tov 1999b. For example, several scholars scrutinized the LXX of the Torah in order to sketch a picture of Moses or other biblical figures even when the data in the LXX were compatible with those of the Hebrew Bible. Thus, Horbury 2006 deals extensively with "a ruling prophet like Moses" and with "the profile of Moses" in an otherwise valuable discussion about the Greek shape of these traditions, although usually the text is shared by the MT and LXX. Such an analysis would be more significant for the study of the reception of the LXX. The same problem pertains to similar analyses of other Septuagintal traditions. The discussion of "biblical women" in Dines 2013 provides philological details comparing the MT and LXX, but in most cases the two texts agree. Both studies, as well as many other ones, deal with theological issues.

8. Seeligmann 1990, 223: "Moreover, many of the high-standard discourses about the theology of the LXX have not entirely escaped the danger of finding in the translation more than the translators intended. Most of these studies were written by New Testament scholars, their main interest being the question of to what degree the LXX paved the way for early Christian thought."

9. See Perkins 2007; Schmitz 2014.

10. Perkins 2007; Rösel 2018, 34.

affirmative, but Alex Douglas does not believe so.[11] Douglas thinks that the LXX may be based on a different Hebrew *Vorlage*; Rösel disagrees with him and speaks of the uncertainty of reconstructing that Hebrew *Vorlage*, or any *Vorlage*, quoting as support the fact that the reconstruction is not supported by any evidence. Further, Douglas refers to Scripture parallels that could support the reading of יהוה שבר מלחמה.[12] This is not manuscript evidence, but suffices to support the assumption of a variant. Even more so, the fact that the SP reflects a variant יהוה ג(י)בור במלחמה, which differs in only one letter (ש/ג) from the presumed יהוה שבר מלחמה, further strengthens the assumption of a variant.

In my view, the burden of proof should not be on those who assume a Hebrew variant, as claimed by Rösel, but on those who see here the reflection of theology in the LXX: as long as we have no certainty that κύριος συντρίβων πολέμους was produced by the translator's creative thinking, we cannot use this instance as a productive case for analyzing theology.

By the same token, neither would a deviation caused by the translator's techniques in transferring the message of the Hebrew into Greek reflect theology.

Before analyzing the different approaches, let me briefly describe some points of my credo regarding theological elements in the LXX.

1. The freer a translation unit is, the better the chances that a specific equivalent or series of equivalents reflect a theological interpretation. In literal translation units, there is much less opportunity for that kind of interpretation. This kind of reasoning is not objective, but neither is the evaluation of theology objective. We therefore expect little or no theological interpretation in the *kaige*-Th sections but more in the other sections, especially in the midrashic translation of 1 Kings (3 Kingdoms); less in Ecclesiastes, Ruth, and Th-Daniel and more in Esther; less in Jeremiah and more in Proverbs and Isaiah; less in Leviticus and more in the other four books of the Torah. This is merely a general thought, not an absolute truth, but I would not go as far as Rösel, who trusts the faithfulness of the translators and expects theological renderings in literal translation units as well.[13]

---

11. Douglas 2012.

12. For example, Hos 2:20 וּמִלְחָמָה אֶשְׁבּוֹר מִן־הָאָרֶץ and Ps 76:4, where God is described as שָׁמָּה שִׁבַּר רִשְׁפֵי־קָשֶׁת מָגֵן וְחֶרֶב וּמִלְחָמָה.

13. Rösel 2018, 35. Rösel quotes studies on Ruth and Qoheleth that are among the most literal in the LXX canon and therefore not representative for that corpus.

2. There is no theological system of the LXX as a whole or even of blocks of texts.[14] The inclusion of theological elements in the translation of individual books was based on the insights of each individual translator, and since the books of the LXX were translated by many individuals, many expressions of theology may be visible in the various units. In practice, we can probably isolate only the theological systems of the translators of Isaiah, Proverbs, Job, Esther, and Daniel.[15] This was claimed, among others, by Johan Lust in a study about Isaiah.[16] While various optimistic voices have raised the possibility of writing an overall theology of the LXX,[17] Rösel's most recent contribution is more realistic. He now hopes to combine an analysis of the character of small units with a description of the overall character of larger groups of translations.[18] The future will show how utopian this plan is, as we know neither the sequence of the translation units nor details regarding their clustering.

3. Although there are clear indications of *messianic* interpretation in the LXX,[19] many of the examples analyzed in the professional literature are problematic. I agree with the caution expressed by Johan Lust in his analyses of this topic.[20] Thus the messianic exegesis detected by Joachim Schaper (1995) in the LXX of Psalms has been criticized much by Pietersma, Lust, and Joosten in their reviews of that monograph,[21] all of whom claim that these messianic ideas may also have been extant in the Hebrew sources of the LXX.

---

14. For the problems involved, see Seeligmann 1990; Tov 1999b; Joosten 2000, 2005; Douglas 2012. On the other hand, for Abraham Geiger blocks of books in the LXX formed a unit. See n. 40 below.

15. On Isaiah, see Seeligmann 1948, 95–121; Lust 1979. On the other hand, Troxel 2008, 73–132, taught us to consider the translation as basically faithful to the message of the Hebrew and to consider *theologoumena* as exceptions rather than the rule. On Proverbs, see Cook 1997, 2010. On Daniel, see Amara 2005.

16. See Lust 1979.

17. See Rösel as quoted in n. 4; see further Rösel 2006; Dafni 2002.

18. Rösel's essay in this volume.

19. For example, Gen 49:10; Num 24:7, 17. See the material analysed by Lust 1985, 1995, 1997, 2004.

20. See the general conclusion of Lust 2004, 151: "The Septuagint version of the Pentateuch does not seem to emphasize individual messianism. This general statement is to be nuanced in the respective cases."

21. Pietersma 1997; Lust 2003; Joosten 2005, 104–5.

4. The study of the *antianthropomorphisms* in the LXX is closely connected with the name of Fritsch, who detected several such features in the Pentateuch, especially in Exodus, and further in Numbers and Deuteronomy, but almost none in Genesis and Leviticus.[22] The importance of this study is greatly exaggerated, and it suffers from many imprecisions.[23]

5. The description of major biblical figures could have been colored theologically, but as far as I know this has not happened, as shown in detail in my study of Moses.[24]

6. If a theological tendency has been identified in the renderings of one translator, for example, that of צבאות יהוה by παντοκράτωρ, the same theological awareness did not persist with the next translators who accepted this equivalent. They may have used this equivalent without thinking about its implications. I assume that the awareness of this rendering developed in the translation unit in which this phrase occurred frequently, namely in the Minor Prophets and Jeremiah. However, we do not know the exact sequence of the translators, and therefore this equivalent also could have been created in another translation unit in which it occurred: 2 Sam 5:10; 7:8, 27; 1 Kgs 19:10, 14; 1 Chr 11:9; 17:7, 24.

---

22. Fritsch 1943, 62.

23. Today this monograph would not have been accepted as a dissertation in most universities because the individual renderings are not subjected to a detailed analysis, and alternative views have not been taken into consideration. In my view, only a few examples are convincing, and most of them should be assigned to the realm of translation technique and a few to different Hebrew readings. Good examples are included in chapter 7 and some in chapter 1. The number of the valid examples is much smaller than suggested by Fritsch, as shown by Orlinsky and his students in a series of monographs: Orlinsky 1956; Soffer 1957; Orlinsky 1959; Orlinksy 1961; Wittstruck 1976; Zlotowitz 1981. Unfortunately, Fritsch did not take into consideration negative evidence, that of the literal translation of the same words in other verses. After all, as a rule the translators did not shrink away from the plastic depictions of God.

24. Tov 2018a. When examining various postbiblical compositions in which Moses is mentioned, the expectations of finding relevant material in the LXX are high, as many traditions not found in the MT of the Torah found their way into these sources. However, despite these great expectations, the scriptural source of Philo, Ezekiel the Tragedian, and Josephus, namely, the LXX itself, has little interest in exegetical traditions regarding Moses. The Greek books of the Torah reflect unmistakable contextual, theological, and legal exegesis, while on the other hand the figure of Moses did not receive such interest. This is the case also for the other biblical figures so far as I have been able to see.

Against this background, the writing of a full-fledged theology of the LXX needs to be determined by its natural limitations, and Martin Rösel is aware of them.[25] In the analysis of theology we are directed by both knowledge and intuition, but we ought to be honest in admitting that what guides us most often is intuition, and that that premonition cannot be bound by rules. Thus, our approach to each translation unit is determined by intuition, and scholars have different intuitions. For example, with regard to the text-critical value of the Greek Genesis scholars have different feelings. Martin Rösel suggested that "the text-critical value of the Septuagint version of Genesis should be regarded less highly than its value for the history of interpretation and reception."[26] Here we disagree. If we espouse that view, we imply that the Greek Genesis contains many exegetical readings, including several theological interpretations. But I do not believe this to be so, and indeed two scholars have recorded their disagreement with Rösel.[27] I believe that LXX Genesis is a valuable textual witness; for example, it reflects many Hebrew harmonizing readings as well as a different redaction of the genealogies in chapters 5 and 11.[28] The practical result of this disagreement is that both Rösel and I use relevant arguments, and we ought to admit that our inclinations are based much on intuition, although we both turn to evidence.

2. Theological or Textual Approach?

In the previous paragraph, I expressed my view that the recognition of theology is not based on absolute facts, but reflects an approach. The theological explanation competes with other approaches to deviations from MT in the translation. After all, the translation could also reflect: (1) a Hebrew theological variant; (2) another type of exegesis, such as linguistic or contextual, or one of the categories of translation technique; (3) inner-Greek developments, such as errors. These three areas reflect different approaches, applied in different circumstances. In this study, we focus on the textual approach, as it is the most serious competitor to the

---

25. See Martin Rösel's systematic and judicious position paper prepared for the conference: "Theologie der Septuaginta-Theology of the Septuagint Teil II. Methodische Grundlegung" (https://tinyurl.com/SBLPress0474a).
26. Rösel 1998, 69.
27. Hendel 1999; Brown 1999.
28. For my most recent statement, see Tov 2018b.

assumption of theological exegesis. In the next pages, I will exemplify how certain differences between MT and the LXX can be approached by either a text-critical or a theological approach. In many cases, no decision can be made. From the outset, there is no preferable approach, and the choice of one depends much on our intuition. Rösel and I use both approaches at different times, but in different frequencies; Rösel is more inclined toward the theological approach and I more to the text-critical approach.

3. A Theological Approach Is Preferable

The existence of theological exegesis in the LXX is well established. The best examples relate to equivalents that do not allow for the possibility of Hebrew variants. In these cases, there is no need to turn to an alternative approach.

(1) For example,

Prov 1:10	MT	אִם־יְפַתּוּךָ חַטָּאִים
	NJPS	if sinners entice you …
	LXX	μή σε πλανήσωσιν ἄνδρες ἀσεβεῖς
	NETS	let not impious men lead you astray

Here, as often elsewhere in this translation, a general term for sinners (חַטָּאִים) has been rendered by a religious term (ἀσεβεῖς – "impious"), implying that the text speaks about sins committed against religion. Also elsewhere, the Greek translation of Proverbs colors religiously the world of the Hebrew Proverbs.[29]

(2) In the case of the garments of God, שׁוּלָיו was avoided in the LXX and Targum of Isa 6:1, being replaced with "glory."

Isa 6:1	MT	ושוליו (מלאים את ההיכל)
	NJPS	and *the skirts of His robe* (filled the Temple.)
	T^J	ומזיו יקריה (אתמלי היכלא)
		(and the temple was filled with) *the brightness of his glory*.
	Cf. LXX	τῆς δόξης αὐτοῦ … *of his glory*

---

29. See Cook 1997.

For this translator, δόξα ("glory") serves as one of the central characteristics of God.[30] This equivalent is intentional, as it is unlikely that the translator did not know this word.[31]

(3) The Greek translator(s) of the Latter Prophets (except for Isaiah) who rendered the phrase יהוה צבאות (literally: "the Lord of armies") consistently with κύριος παντοκράτωρ ("the Lord omnipotent") must have had a certain view of the nature of the Hebrew phrase. For him (them), צבאות signified not just a body of "angels" or "armies" but encompassed everything in the universe. Thus, when choosing this rendering, the translator(s) rendered the Hebrew word exegetically when opting for a term that is also known from the world of the Greek gods, some of whom were described as παντοκράτωρ.[32]

(4) Also when a textual solution is in sight, sometimes a theological solution may be preferable.

1 Sam 2:2	MT	וְאֵין צוּר כֵּאלֹהֵינוּ
	NJPS	There is no rock like our God.
	LXX	καὶ οὐκ ἔστιν δίκαιος ὡς ὁ θεὸς ἡμῶν
	NETS	and there is none righteous like our God.

The first question when analyzing this translation relates to the equivalent of the quoted Hebrew half-stich.[33] The LXX clearly presents a different sequence. If the three stichs of MT are presented as *abc*, the LXX presents a sequence *acb* with small differences in details:

a	אֵין־קָדוֹשׁ כַּיהוָה	a	ὅτι οὐκ ἔστιν ἅγιος ὡς κύριος,
b	כִּי אֵין בִּלְתֶּךָ	c	οὐκ ἔστιν <u>ἅγιος</u> πλὴν σοῦ
c	וְאֵין צוּר כֵּאלֹהֵינוּ	b	καὶ οὐκ ἔστιν <u>δίκαιος</u> ὡς ὁ θεὸς ἡμῶν

The added element in stich c of the LXX (= stich b of MT), ἅγιος, is probably to be reconstructed as קדוש, but the really interesting issue is the equivalent צור – δίκαιος in stich c of MT (= stich b of the LXX).

---

30. See Brockington 1951, 23–32.

31. The word is rendered correctly, though in different ways, in the tabernacle chapters in Exodus (5x) and elsewhere (Jer 13:22, 26; Nah 3:5; Lam 1:9).

32. See Tov 1999b, 263.

33. כִּי אֵין בִּלְתֶּךָ וְאֵין צוּר כֵּאלֹהֵינוּ אֵין־קָדוֹשׁ כַּיהוָה – ὅτι οὐκ ἔστιν ἅγιος ὡς κύριος, καὶ οὐκ ἔστιν δίκαιος ὡς ὁ θεὸς ἡμῶν· οὐκ ἔστιν ἅγιος πλὴν σοῦ.

At first sight, it seems as if this equivalent points to a *Vorlage* that differs from MT צור, but the Greek rendering should be seen rather in the light of the diverse renderings of צור elsewhere in the LXX. The various Greek equivalents of this word reflect an avoidance of a literal rendering of צור as a designation of God. The LXX consistently avoided a literal translation of צור ("rock") as an appellation of God, probably because a literal rendering would have created the impression of paganism.[34] Such a theological tendency may also be assumed in this verse. It is thus unsound to reconstruct צדיק here based on the graphic similarity between the two Hebrew words.[35]

(5) The Greek Esther reflects a free reworking of the Hebrew text. Probably the most characteristic feature of that version is the addition of a religious background to the earlier Hebrew version that lacks the mentioning of God's name. Such details are added not only in the large expansions but also in small pluses such as Esth 2:20; 4:8; 6:13, and in changes in 6:1 and 4:13–14.[36] However, there is a thin dividing line between changes made by the translator and those found in his midrashic *Vorlage*; the additions of God's name probably were made by the translator. Likewise, God's involvement is mentioned everywhere in the midrash and targum.[37]

4. A Textual Approach Is Preferable

I now turn to the textual approach to deviations in the LXX. Several Greek renderings reflect theological exegesis but, unlike in Section 3, other theological renderings need to be approached textually. These renderings do

---

34. The translator of Deuteronomy, who was the first to face this issue, consistently rendered this word with θεός ("God") in poetic contexts in Deut 32:4, 15, 18 (parallels: אל and אלוה [θεός]), 30 (parallel: יהוה [κύριος]), 31, 37. The most frequent equivalents elsewhere in the LXX are: θεός ("God"), βοηθός ("helper"), φύλαξ ("guardian"), and ἀντιλήμπτωρ ("protector"). See Wiegand 1890; Passioni dell' Acqua 1977; Oloffson 1990, 35–45; Meiser 2008, 328–29.

35. The reconstruction צדיק in CATSS is incorrect.

36. Cf. De Troyer 2003, 9–28.

37. Thus Esther's concern for dietary laws in C 27–28 should be compared with b. Meg. 13a, Targum Rishon, and Targum Sheni 2:20. See Grossfeld 1991. For LXX Esth 2:7, "he trained her for himself as a wife (MT "Mordecai adopted her <Esther> as his own daughter"), cf. b. Meg. 13a: "A Tanna taught in the name of R. Meir: Read not 'for a daughter' [*le-bat*], but 'for a house' [*le-bayit*] <that is, a wife>." For a different view on the relation between the LXX and the Midrash, see Zipor 2006.

not reflect the translators' exegesis, but a variety of Hebrew nontheological variants or pseudo-variants.

4.1. Nontheological Variants

Amos 7:1   MT   וְהִנֵּה־לֶקֶשׁ אַחַר גִּזֵּי הַמֶּלֶךְ
the late-sown crops after *the king's reaping*.[38]

LXX   καὶ ἰδοὺ βροῦχος εἷς Γωγ ὁ βασιλεύς
and behold, one locust <was> *Gog the king*.[39]

Representing a theological approach, Frederick Bruce found links between the various Greek translations of the prophetic books since for him "to the Septuagint translators the prophetical books formed one sacred canon."[40] The text of Amos has an agricultural background, although it also mentions a locust (גבי), and Bruce claims that the translator connected this verse to the locust of Joel 2:25 and the description of Gog in Ezek 39:4–29. The king (mentioned in Ezekiel) and the locust in Joel are then combined into one picture in the LXX of Amos, viz., that of Gog, the king of the locusts. In the same study, Bruce provides several similar examples of theological interpretations in which a textual argumentation is preferable.

A textual approach requires us to ask what "Gog the king" is doing in this verse in MT that deals with the destruction of the late crops by locusts. The Hebrew context is not easy, as it involves a *hapax legomenon* לֶקֶשׁ ("late-sown crops") and a rare word גז ("shearing, mowing"), occurring three times in Scripture. Both words have been rendered by different Greek words probably representing ילק ("locust")[41] and גוג ("Gog").[42] The Hebrew and Greek contexts are completely different, involving a third

---

38. The JPS translation is accompanied by a footnote: "Meaning of Hebrew uncertain. The king's reaping of fodder apparently occurred near the end of the rainy season, and whatever the locust destroyed after that could not be replaced for another year."

39. My own translation. Βροῦχος is either a "locust" or a "locust larva," according to LSJ. The latter meaning is reflected in the translation of NETS: "one locust larva, Gog the king." This rendering does little to improve the rather absurd LXX translation.

40. Bruce 1979, 19. By the same token, for Abraham Geiger (1928) blocks of books in the LXX formed a unit.

41. This word is not badly chosen, as it has two letters in common with the presumed *Vorlage* לקש and belongs to the vocabulary of the context. The word must have been difficult for the translator, as its first occurrence in the verse was left untranslated.

42. This word has one letter in common with the presumed *Vorlage* גז, involving

interchange of letters in the LXX. In the new context of the LXX, אחר made no sense, requiring the translator to read this word with a *dalet/resh* interchange as אחד. As a result, according to MT, God created (יוֹצֵר) the plague of locusts when the late crops (לקש) were beginning to sprout after the king's reaping (גז). However, according to the LXX, there was a plague of locusts, and "one locust <was> Gog the king." While MT is certainly not easy, it does make sense,[43] while this cannot be said of the LXX.

4.2. Nontheological Pseudo-variants

In another subgroup of variants, which I named pseudo-variants,[44] we likewise see the tension between the two different approaches. The difference between this group and the others is that these variants presumably never existed. Pseudo-variants look like variants, but they are not. Some scholars described some of them as theological changes made by the translators, while others took a text-critical approach to them.

Gen 3:17	MT	ארורה האדמה בעבורך
	NJPS	Cursed be the ground because of you.
	LXX	ἐπικατάρατος ἡ γῆ <u>ἐν τοῖς ἔργοις σου</u>
	NETS	Cursed is the earth *in your labors*.
Gen 8:21	MT	לא אסף לקלל עוד את האדמה בעבור האדם
	NJPS	Never again will I doom the earth *because of man*.

---

an interchange of *gimmel* and *zayin* and producing a rendering that is very remote from the context.

43. Paul 1991, 227: "It is probably a reference to a prerogative of reaping (for example, fodder for horses) that took place toward the end of the late-rain season."

44. The methodological background of the recognition of this special type of variants has been explained in Tov 2015b, 178–87. On pp. 98–99 I point out that few retroversions are certain and that, even if a retroversion should be considered reliable, the retroverted variant may have existed only in the mind of a translator. With regard to errors, it can never be known whether the error was made by the translator or was already present in his *Vorlage*. Nevertheless, also such retroversions must be called "variants" because of the lack of suitable controls. One must accept the fact that some reliable retroversions never existed in writing. In the discussion of pseudo-variants we go one step further, since in these cases according to at least some scholars these variants did not exist in writing.

> LXX   οὐ προσθήσω ἔτι τοῦ καταράσασθαι τὴν γῆν <u>διὰ τὰ ἔργα τῶν ἀνθρώπων</u>
> I will not proceed hereafter to curse the earth *because of the deeds of men.*

A theological approach has been suggested by Georg Bertram, who detected a theological slant in these renderings, claiming that "thus the negative attitude of Hellen[istic] Judaism to work decisively affects the text."[45] This theological interpretation is based on the LXX, in complete disregard of alternative possibilities.[46] Marguerite Harl reflects a different type of theological approach, as she sees a theological slant in the LXX of Gen 8:21: "God does not take the nature of human beings into consideration, but the actions of everyone."[47]

The textual approach starts with the suggestion that the translator may have misinterpreted the prepositional phrase בעבור ("because of …"). This word occurs here for the first time in Scripture, and in other cases also the translator of Genesis, presumably being the first translator, struggled with the meanings of words met for the first time.[48] On the other hand, when the word occurs later in the book, its correct meaning is sometimes recognized.[49] In Gen 3:17, 8:21, the translator presumably did not understand the prepositional phrase בעבור, and it was but a small step for him to interpret the graphic sign ר/ד not as a *resh*, but a *dalet*. In both verses, the idea of tilling the ground in the LXX is suggested by the context. However, there is more involved than just the *dalet/resh* interchange, since the translator manipulated the letters of בעבוד/ר, adapting them to the context, having in mind something like בעבודתיך, without having such a word in front of him.[50]

> Jer 31:8   MT   וקבצתים מירכתי ארץ בָּם עִוֵּר וּפִסֵּחַ הָרָה וְיֹלֶדֶת יַחְדּוֹ קָהָל גָּדוֹל יָשׁוּבוּ הֵנָּה
> and I shall gather them from the farthest parts of

---

45. Bertram 1964, 643–44.
46. The anti-Jewish attitude of Bertram has been described extensively by Rösel in his chapter in this volume.
47. Harl 1986, 139.
48. See Tov 2015a; van der Louw 2018.
49. Gen 12:13, 16; 18:26, 29, 31; 26:24, etc. the word is rendered as ἕνεκεν and διά.
50. A similar process, with the same words, took place in Jer 14:4 בעבור האדמה – καὶ τὰ ἔργα τῆς γῆς.

		the earth, among them the blind and the lame, the pregnant woman, and the one in labor, together, a great multitude shall return hither.
Jer 38:8	LXX	καὶ συνάξω αὐτοὺς ἀπ' ἐσχάτου τῆς γῆς ἐν ἑορτῇ φασεκ καὶ τεκνοποιήσῃ ὄχλον πολὺν καὶ ἀποστρέψουσιν ὧδε
		and I will gather them from the farthest part of the earth at the feast of phasek (Pesach), and you will give birth to a great multitude, and they shall return hither (implying: בְּמוֹעֵד פֶּסַח).

Reflecting a theological approach, Seeligmann sees in this rendering the translator's tendency to ascribe the time of the "future redemption of the Jewish people" to the time of Passover.[51] A similar idea is reflected in the targum to Song 1:1 (not referenced by Seeligmann): "At the time when they go out from their exile, the children of Israel will utter the tenth song, which is thus written and explained by Isaiah: This song will be for your joy as on the night that is sanctified for the festival of Passover, and (as) a joyful heart is in the people who go to appear before the Lord three times per year with all kinds of music and the sound of the drum while ascending the mountain of the Lord to worship before the Mighty One of Israel." This text alludes to the song sung at night in Isa 30:29 although that text does not refer to Passover.[52]

Taking a textual approach to the text, we note that the Greek translator had a content in mind that differed completely from MT, and was based on a text that differed very little from MT in letters and vowels (see above).[53] Once the words "among them the blind and the lame" (MT) had been read as "at the feast of Pesach," the context was changed completely, and the translator was impelled, as it were, to conceive of additional details in a different way from MT. In particular, the words "the pregnant woman and the one in labor, together" (הרה וְיֹלֶדֶת יחדו) did not suit the new context. This caused the translator to introduce a second verb, parallel to the first

---

51. Seeligmann 1990, 230.
52. "For you, there shall be singing as on a night when a festival is hallowed; there shall be rejoicing as when they march with flute, with timbrels, and with lyres to the Rock of Israel on the Mount of the Lord."
53. MT has the appearance of originality: עִוֵּר and פִּסֵּחַ occur together in Lev 21:18; Deut 15:21; 2 Sam 5:6, 8; Mal 1:8; Job 29:15.

one, by vocalizing וְיָלַדְתְּ instead of וְיָלְדָה. Furthermore, he left out both הרה and יחדו. The upshot of this maneuvering was a rendering καὶ τεκνοποιήσῃ ὄχλον πολύν ("and you will give birth to a great multitude"). Seemingly, the translator's *Vorlage* was וקבצתים מירכתי ארץ בְּמוֹעֵד פֶּסַח וְיָלַדְתְּ, but the existence of that reading and vocalization must be strongly doubted.

4.3. Deviations due to Translation Technique

Some presumed theological deviations were created by translation choices that reflect the translators' techniques. In these cases, too, the textual approach is preferable to the theological approach.

Exod 33:7	MT SP	ומשה יקח את האהל וְנָטָה־לוֹ מִחוּץ לַמַּחֲנֶה = T^{O, F} V
	NRSV	Now Moses would take the tent and pitch it outside the camp.
	LXX	Καὶ λαβὼν Μωυσῆς τὴν σκηνὴν <u>αὐτοῦ</u> ἔπηξεν ἔξω τῆς παρεμβολῆς
	NETS	And Moyses took *his* tent and pitched it outside the camp.

The addition of the pronoun "his" is shared with S (ܡܫܟܢܗ) and T^{Ps-J} "his tent for teaching the Torah" (במשכן אולפן אורייתא דיליה), and not continued in v. 8. The suggestion that the LXX had theological intentions when naming Moses' tent (the tent of meeting) "his tent" is attractive. Indeed, this complicated verse may present a view of the tent[54] of meeting that differs from that in other chapters. Some scholars connect this small detail in the Greek translation of verse 7 to theories about the Documentary Hypothesis or to theological concepts about the nature of the tent of meeting.[55]

However, most likely there is no special theological thought behind the addition of the pronoun in verse 7, which should be viewed as a translation technical change.[56] Probably לוֹ, without direct equivalent in the

---

54. Moses's tent was referred to earlier, in Exod 18:7. For an analysis of the problems involved in this verse and the verses in the context, see Sommer 2000, 53.

55. See Lustig 2018; Sommer 2000, 53.

56. The Hebrew article in הָאֹהֶל, which represents a form of determination, is often represented in Greek by the pronominal suffix, representing another form of determination (e.g., Josh 2:9). The same phenomenon also occurs vice versa, e.g., Exod 19:10 שִׂמְלֹתָם – τὰ ἱμάτια.

context (וְנָטָה־לֹו), is represented by αὐτοῦ.⁵⁷ The pronoun creates a distinction between the tent of Moses and the tents of "all the people" mentioned in verse 10 ("all the people would rise and bow low, each at the entrance of *his tent*"). The Greek translator may have felt the need to explain which tent is being referred to in verse 7. This small change at the translational level was deemed necessary by the Greek translator and likewise, probably independently, by S (ܡܫܟܢܗ) and T^(Ps-J).

5. Vacillations between the Textual and Theological Approach

We often vacillate between the two approaches.

(1) The first examples are taken from Exodus.

Exod 19:3	MT	ומשה עלה אל האלהים
	NJPS	And Moses went up to God.
	LXX	καὶ Μωυσῆς ἀνέβη εἰς <u>τὸ ὄρος</u> τοῦ θεοῦ· ≈ T^(Ps-J)
	NETS	And Moses went onto *the mountain of* God.

The Greek translation of verse 3 (≈ T^(Ps-J)) created a distance between Moses and God, possibly reflecting a theological tendency, even though this was not done in v. 4: ואבא אתכם אלי – καὶ προσηγαγόμην ὑμᾶς πρὸς ἐμαυτόν. However, there is a remote possibility that the LXX is based on a variant הר האלהים, for which see, for example, Exod 3:1; 4:27; 18:5; 24:13.

At the same time, in the light of a similar theological change in LXX Exodus, it is more likely that the translator nevertheless inserted a theological change in 19:3:

Exod 24:10	MT	ויראו את אלהי ישראל = SP
	NJPS	And they saw the God of Israel.
	LXX	καὶ εἶδον <u>τὸν τόπον, οὗ εἱστήκει ἐκεῖ</u> ὁ θεὸς τοῦ Ισραηλ·
	NETS	And they saw *the place where* the God of Israel *stood*.

In order to reduce the possibility that the people would see God, the translator added "the place where (the God of Israel) stood." In a similar

---

57. Thus Lustig 2018, 175.

fashion, the targumim avoided the direct viewing of God by inserting the concept of glory, as in T^{Ps-J}: וחמון ית איקר אלקא דישראל ("and they saw the glory of the God of Israel"), and T^O, T^{NF} ("Then they saw the glory of the Shekhinah of the Lord").

(2) LXX Joshua contains several nomistic changes (changes in accord with the Torah), but it is hard to know whether they were inserted by the translator or his *Vorlage*.

According to Num 10:8–9, only priests could sound the trumpets when Israel would go to war. However, Joshua, who was told to follow the laws of the Torah day and night (Josh 1:8), gave orders that nonpriests should be involved in sounding the trumpet during the encircling of Jericho (MT Josh 6:9, 13). Remarkably, these texts were changed in the LXX on three occasions:

Josh 6:9b	MT	לִפְנֵי הַכֹּהֲנִים תָּקְעוּ [תֹּקְעֵי] הַשּׁוֹפָרוֹת וְהַמְאַסֵּף הֹלֵךְ אַחֲרֵי הָאָרוֹן הָלוֹךְ וְתָקוֹעַ בַּשּׁוֹפָרוֹת
	NJPS	in front of the priests who were blowing the horns, and the rear guard marched behind the ark, with the horns sounding all the time.
	LXX	καὶ <u>οἱ ἱερεῖς</u> οἱ οὐραγοῦντες ὀπίσω τῆς κιβωτοῦ τῆς διαθήκης κυρίου πορευόμενοι καὶ σαλπίζοντες.
	NETS	and the priests who bring up the rear, behind the ark of the covenant of the Lord, as they walk and trumpet.
Josh 6:13	MT	וְהַמְאַסֵּף הֹלֵךְ אַחֲרֵי אֲרוֹן יְהוָה הוֹלֵךְ [הָלוֹךְ] וְתָקוֹעַ בַּשּׁוֹפָרוֹת
	NJPS	and the rear guard marched behind the Ark of the Lord, with the horns sounding all the time.
	LXX	καὶ ὁ λοιπὸς ὄχλος ὄπισθε τῆς κιβωτοῦ τῆς διαθήκης κυρίου· <u>καὶ οἱ ἱερεῖς</u> ἐσάλπισαν ταῖς σάλπιγξι
	NETS	and the rest of the crowd behind the ark of the covenant of the Lord, and the priests sounded with the trumpets.
Josh 6:20	MT	יָרַע הָעָם וַיִּתְקְעוּ בַּשֹּׁפָרוֹת
	NJPS	So the people shouted when the horns were sounded.

LXX	καὶ ἐσάλπισαν ταῖς σάλπιγξιν <u>οἱ ἱερεῖς</u>·
NETS	And the priests sounded with the trumpets.

The text of the LXX is far from clear, but it is evident that the priests have been added to the base text.[58] In MT, the priests sound the trumpets in v. 9a, but not in vv. 9b, 13, and 20, while they do in the LXX (and in the targum in vv. 9b and 13). Furthermore, the horns of v. 8 have been transformed to sacred horns, so that only priests can sound them:

Josh 6:8	MT	וְשִׁבְעָה הַכֹּהֲנִים נֹשְׂאִים שִׁבְעָה שׁוֹפְרוֹת הַיּוֹבְלִים
	NJPS	the seven priests carrying seven rams' horns
	LXX	καὶ ἑπτὰ ἱερεῖς ἔχοντες ἑπτὰ σάλπιγγας <u>ἱεράς</u>
	NETS	and seven priests holding seven sacred trumpets

In the LXX, the "trumpets made of rams' horns" have been transformed to "sacred trumpets." If there was a Hebrew equivalent, it would have been שופרות הקודש (for MT שופרות היובלים) which is unattested in Hebrew Scripture. The textual relation between the LXX and MT is unclear since the LXX also leaves out several elements in this passage, possibly because they were considered "verbose" (vv. 6:3b, 4, 6b, 9a).

In a detailed analysis, Leah Mazor (1995) ascribes these nomistic changes to the *Vorlage* of the LXX, basing herself on internal analysis and on the external parallel of the targum and Josephus. However, Josephus may depend on the LXX. On the other hand, the nomistic changes, also partially reflected in the targum, may reflect a theological midrash-like tradition of the LXX, similar to other instances in Joshua.[59] I find it difficult to reach a decision.

In sum, this study focuses on the interaction between theological and other approaches to the LXX, especially the text-critical approach. In my view, the recognition of theology in a translation is not a solid fact, neither does it reflect a statement about what we identify in the translation; rather it is a subjective recognition of a way of understanding elements in the translation. Over the years, I have learned much from the judicious stud-

---

58. The rear guard is rendered with different terms in vv. 9 and 13. Οὐραγέω does not occur elsewhere in the LXX, while οὐραγία occurs in Deut 25:18 and Josh 10:19 for the verb זנב.

59. See Tov 1999a.

ies of Martin Rösel and even more so now from his very learned position paper. I agree with some of his basic assumptions and disagree with others; we also agree and disagree with regard to specific instances. It is important to realize that the decision to ascribe a deviation to a theological or textual factor depends on a scholar's personal inclination. In this chapter, I gave some examples of elements that I ascribe to theological factors and other examples that I ascribed to textual factors. In yet other cases, I remain undecided. More than anything else I emphasize the role of intuition in the decision process.

Bibliography

Amara, Dalia. 2005. "Theological Corrections in the Various Versions of the Book of Daniel." Pages 61–76 in *On the Border Line: Textual Meets Literary Criticism*. Edited by Zipora Talshir and Dalia Amara. Beer-Sheva 18. Beer Sheva: Ben-Gurion University of the Negev Press. [Hebrew]

Ausloos, Hans. 2017. "Sept défis posés à une théologie de la Septante." Pages 228–50 in *Congress Volume: Stellenbosch, 2016*. Edited by Louis C. Jonker, Gideon R. Kotzé, and Christl M. Maier. VTSup 177. Leiden: Brill.

Barthélemy, Dominique, et al. 1986. *The Story of David and Goliath, Textual and Literary Criticism: Papers of a Joint Venture*. OBO 73. Fribourg: Éditions universitaires; Göttingen: Vandenhoeck & Ruprecht.

Bertram, Georg. 1964. "ἔργον, ἐργάζομαι." *TDNT* 2:635–55.

Brockington, Leonard Herbert. 1951. "The Greek Translator of Isaiah and His Interest in δόξα." *VT* 1:23–32.

Brown, William P. 1999. "Reassessing the Text-Critical Value of LXX-Genesis 1: A Response to Rösel." *BIOSCS* 32:35–39.

Bruce, Frederick F. 1979. "Prophetic Interpretation in the Septuagint." *BIOSCS* 12:17–26.

Cook, Johann. 1997. *The Septuagint of Proverbs, Jewish and/or Hellenistic Colouring of LXX Proverbs*. VTSup 69. Leiden: Brill.

———. 2010. "Towards the Formulation of a Theology of the Septuagint." Pages 621–40 in *Congress Volume: Ljubljana, 2007*. Edited by André Lemaire. VTSup 133. Leiden: Brill.

Dafni, Evangelia. 2002. "Theologie der Sprache der Septuaginta." *TZ* 58:315–28.

De Troyer, Kristin. 2003. *Rewriting the Sacred Text: What the Old Greek Texts Tell Us about the Literary Growth of the Bible.* TCSt 4. Atlanta: Society of Biblical Literature.

Dines, Jennifer M. 2013. "What If the Reader Is a She? Biblical Women and Their Translators." Pages 56–82 in *The Reception of the Hebrew Bible in the Septuagint and the New Testament: Essays in Memory of Aileen Guilding.* Edited by David J. A. Clines and J. Cheryl Exum. HBM 55. Sheffield: Sheffield Phoenix.

Douglas, Alex. 2012. "Limitations to Writing a Theology of the Septuagint." *JSCS* 45:104–17.

Fritsch, Charles T. 1943. *The Anti-anthropomorphisms of the Greek Pentateuch.* Princeton: Princeton University Press.

Geiger, Abraham. 1928. *Urschrift und Übersetzungen der Bibel in ihrer Abhängigkeit von der innern Entwickelung des Judentums.* 2nd ed. Frankfurt am Main: Madda, 1928.

Grossfeld, Bernard. 1991. *The Two Targums of Esther, Translated with Apparatus and Notes.* ArBib 18. Collegeville, MN: Liturgical Press.

Harl, Marguerite. 1986. *La Genèse.* BdA 1. Cerf: Paris.

Hendel, Ronald S. 1999. "On the Text-Critical Value of LXX-Genesis: A Reply to Rösel." *BIOSCS* 32:31–34.

Horbury, William. 2006. "Monarchy and Messianism in the Greek Pentateuch." Pages 79–128 in *The Septuagint and Messianism.* Edited by Michael A. Knibb. BETL 195. Leuven: Peeters.

Joosten, Jan. 2000. "Une théologie de la Septante? Réflexions méthodologiques sur l'interprétation de la version grecque." *RTP* 132:31–46.

———. 2005. "Considering the Septuagint's Theological System" [Hebrew]. Pages 99–112 in *On the Border Line: Textual Meets Literary Criticism.* Edited by Zipora Talshir and Dalia Amara. Beer-Sheva 18. Beer Sheva: Ben-Gurion University of the Negev Press. [Hebrew]

Kreuzer, Siegfried. 2018. "Textgeschichte und Theologie." Pages 1–24 in *Textgeschichte und Theologie: Septuaginta und Masoretischer Text als Äußerungen theologischer Reflexion.* Edited by Frank Ueberschaer, Thomas Wagner, and Jonathan Miles Robker. WUNT 407. Tübingen: Mohr Siebeck.

Louw, Theo van der. 2018. "The Evolution of the LXX Genesis Translator." Pages 146–57 in *Die Septuaginta – Geschichte, Wirkung, Relevanz.* Edited by Martin Meiser, Michaela Geiger, Siegfried Kreuzer, and Marcus Sigismund. WUNT 405. Tübingen: Mohr Siebeck.

Lust, Johan. 1979. "The Demonic Character of Jahweh and the Septuagint of Isaiah." *Bijdragen* 40:2–14.

———. 1985. "Messianism and Septuagint." Pages 174–91 in *Congress Volume: Salamanca, 1983*. Edited by John A. Emerton. VTSup 36. Leiden: Brill.

———. 1995. "The Greek Version of Balaam's Third and Fourth Oracles. The ἄνθρωπος in Num 24:7 and 17. Messianism and Lexicography." Pages 233–57 in *VIII Congress of the IOSCS: Paris, 1992*. Edited by Leonard Greenspoon and Olivier Munnich. SCS 41. Atlanta: Scholars Press.

———. 1997. "Septuagint and Messianism, with a Special Emphasis on the Pentateuch." Pages 26–45 in *Theologische Probleme der Septuaginta und der hellenistischen Hermeneutik*. VWGTh 11. Edited by Hennig Graf Reventlow. Gütersloh: Gütersloher Verlagshaus.

———. 2003. "Messianism in Ezekiel, in Hebrew and in Greek, Ezek 21:15 (10) and 20 (15)." Pages 619–31 in *Emanuel: Studies in Hebrew Bible, Septuagint, and Dead Sea Scrolls in Honor of Emanuel Tov*. Edited by Shalom M. Paul, Robert A. Kraft, Lawrence H. Schiffman, and Weston W. Fields. VTSup 94. Leiden: Brill.

———. 2004. *Messianism and the Septuagint*. BETL 178. Leuven: Leuven University Press.

Lustig, Christian. 2018. "Moses eigenes Zelt: Zur Unterscheidung zweier Zeltkonzeptionen im griechischen Exodusbuch." Pages 168–80 in in *Die Septuaginta – Geschichte, Wirkung, Relevanz*. Edited by Martin Meiser, Michaela Geiger, Siegfried Kreuzer, and Marcus Sigismund. WUNT 405. Tübingen: Mohr Siebeck.

Mazor, Leah. 1995. "A Nomistic Re-working of the Jericho Conquest Narrative Reflected in LXX to Joshua 6:1–20." *Textus* 18:47–62.

Meiser, Martin. 2008. "Samuelseptuaginta und Targum Jonathan als Zeugen frühjüdischer Geistigkeit." Pages 323–35 in *Die Septuaginta – Texte, Kontexte, Lebenswelten*. Edited by Martin Karrer, Wolfgang Kraus, and Martin Meiser. WUNT 219. Tübingen: Mohr Siebeck.

Oloffson, Staffan. 1990. *God Is My Rock: A Study of Translation Technique and Theological Exegesis in the Septuagint*. ConBOT 31. Lund: Almqvist & Wiksell.

Orlinsky, Harry M. 1956. "The Treatment of Anthropomorphisms and Anthropopathisms in the LXX of Isaiah." *HUCA* 27:193–200.

———. 1959. "Studies in the Septuagint of the Book of Job III." *HUCA* 30:153–67.

———. 1961. "Studies in the Septuagint of the Book of Job III (Continued)." *HUCA* 32:239–68.
Passioni dell' Acqua, Anna. 1977. "La metafora biblica di Dio Roccia e la sua soppressione nelle antiche versioni," *Ephemerides Liturgicae* 91:417–53.
Paul, Shalom M. 1991. *Amos*. Hermeneia. Minneapolis: Fortress.
Perkins, Larry. 2007. "'The Lord is a Warrior' – 'The Lord Who Shatters Wars': Exod 15:3 and Jdt 9:7; 16:2." *BIOSCS* 40:121–38.
Pietersma, Albert. 1997. "Review of J. Schaper, *Eschatology in the Greek Psalter*." *BO* 54:185–90.
Rösel, Martin. 1998. "The Text-Critical Value of Septuagint-Genesis." *BIOSCS* 31:62–70.
———. 2006. "Towards a 'Theology of the Septuagint.'" Pages 239–52 in *Septuagint Research: Issues and Challenges in the Study of the Greek Jewish Scriptures*. Edited by Wolfgang Kraus and R. Glenn Wooden. SCS 53. Atlanta: Society of Biblical Literature.
———. 2018. "Eine Theologie der Septuaginta? Präzisierungen und Pointierungen." Pages 25–43 in *Textgeschichte und Theologie: Septuaginta und Masoretischer Text als Äußerungen theologischer Reflexion*. Edited by Frank Ueberschaer, Thomas Wagner, and Jonathan Miles Robker. WUNT 407. Tübingen: Mohr Siebeck.
Schaper, Joachim. 1995. *Eschatology in the Greek Psalms*. WUNT 2/76. Tübingen: Mohr Siebeck.
Schmitz, Barbara. 2014. "κύριος συντρίβων πολέμους 'The Lord Who Crushes Wars' (Exod 15:3^{LXX}): The Formative Importance of the Song of the Sea (Exod 15:1–18^{LXX}) for the Book of Judith." *JSCS* 47:5–16.
Seeligmann, Isac L. 1940. "Problemen en perspectieven in het modern Septuaginta onderzoek." *JEOL* 7:339–90.
———. 1948. *The Septuagint Version of Isaiah: A Discussion of Its Problems*. MVEOL 9. Leiden: Brill.
———. 1990. "Problems and Perspectives in Modern Septuagint Research." *Textus* 15:169–232.
Soffer, Arthur. 1957. "The Treatment of Anthropomorphisms and Anthropopathisms in the Septuagint of Psalms." *HUCA* 28:85–107.
Sommer, Benjamin D. 2000. "Translation as Commentary: The Case of the Septuagint to Exodus 32–33." *Textus* 20:43–60.
Tov, Emanuel. 1987. "Die Septuaginta in ihrem theologischen und traditionsgeschichtlichen Verhältnis zur hebräischen Bibel." Pages 237–68 in *Mitte der Schrift? Ein jüdisch-christliches Gespräch. Texte der Berner*

Symposions 1985. Edited by Martin Klopfenstein et al. JudChr 11. Bern: Lang.

———. 1999a. "Midrash-Type Exegesis in the LXX of Joshua." Pages 153–63 in *The Greek and Hebrew Bible: Collected Essays on the Septuagint*. Edited by Emanuel Tov. VTSup 72. Leiden: Brill.

———. 1999b. "Theologically Motivated Exegesis Embedded in the Septuagint." Pages 257–69 in *The Greek and Hebrew Bible: Collected Essays on the Septuagint*. Edited by Emanuel Tov. VTSup 72. Leiden: Brill.

———. 2015a. "The Septuagint Translation of Genesis as the First Scripture Translation." Pages 504–20 in vol. 3 of *Textual Criticism of the Hebrew Bible, Qumran, Septuagint: Collected Essays*. Edited by Emanuel Tov. VTSup 167. Leiden: Brill.

———. 2015b. *The Text-Critical Use of the Septuagint in Biblical Research*. 3rd ed. Winona Lake, IN: Eisenbrauns.

———. 2018a. "Moses in the Septuagint." Pages 3–20 in *Figures Who Shape Scriptures, Scriptures That Shape Figures: Essays in Honour of Benjamin Wright III*. Edited by Géza G. Xeravits and Greg Schmidt Goering. DCLS 40. Berlin: De Gruyter.

———. 2018b. "Textual Harmonization in the Five Books of the Torah: A Summary." Pages 31–56 in *The Bible, Qumran, and the Samaritans*. Edited by Magnar Kartveit and Gary N. Knoppers. StS 10. Berlin: De Gruyter.

Troxel Ronald L. 2008. *LXX-Isaiah as Translation and Interpretation: The Strategies of the Translator of the Septuagint of Isaiah*. JSJSup 124. Leiden: Brill.

Wiegand, A. 1890. "Der Gottesname צור und seine Deutung in dem Sinne Bildner und Schöpfer in den alten jüdischen Literatur," *ZAW* 10:85–96.

Wittstruck, Thorne. 1976. "The So-Called Anti-anthropomorphisms in the Greek Text of Deuteronomy." *CBQ* 38:29–34.

Zipor, Moshe. 2006. "When Midrash Met Septuagint: The Case of Esther 2, 7." *ZAW* 118:82–92.

Zlotowitz, Bernard M. 1981. *The Septuagint Translation of the Hebrew Terms in Relation to God in the Book of Jeremiah*. New York: Ktav.

Theology and Septuagint Corpora: A Proposal and Some Questions[1]

Gideon R. Kotzé

ABSTRACT: Research on the theology represented by the literary writings included in Septuagint corpora is not the only field of study that has the religious ideas and convictions underlying the subject matter of a limited corpus of ancient literature as object. For example, some of the same challenges that confront the study of Old Testament theology also face research on the theology reflected by Septuagint corpora. These challenges involve, but are not limited to, (1) the diversity of the corpora, their texts, and subject matter, (2) differing definitions of "theology," (3) the theological pluralism evidenced by the collections, (4) the correspondences in divine imagery and ideas to theologies outside of the corpora, (5) the relationship with the New Testament and Rabbinic Judaism, and (6) the question of the intended target audiences who might benefit from presentations of the "theology" witnessed by the ancient literary writings included in pre-determined corpora. This chapter proposes that research on the theology represented by Septuagint corpora should be recognized as an interdisciplinary endeavor. This means that the object and the objectives of such research should not be conceptualized in isolation from other disciplines that use the same resources, process the same data, and produce information that is relevant to more than one of these fields of study. In this regard, the chapter identifies a number of questions that may, in future discussions of theology and Septuagint corpora, play a positive role in the conceptualization of research on the topic.

---

1. In conducting the research for this chapter, I greatly benefited from discussions with Dr. Manitza Kotzé over matters regarding doctrinal theology. The views expressed here, however, are my own.

1. Introduction

Research on the theology represented by the literary works included in Septuagint corpora has the potential to play a positive part in the interpretation of these ancient cultural artefacts.[2] Such research is still in its infancy, and its enthusiasts are still finding their feet as regards its theoretical and practical challenges.[3] Seeing as this research is not the only field of study that deals with the religious ideas and convictions reflected by the subject matter of a limited corpus of ancient literature, it may learn from scholars' attempts to examine and expound the theology implied by the writings in other collections. Old Testament theology immediately comes to mind as a possible partner for fruitful dialogue concerning matters of method and theory. Indeed, some of the same challenges that confront this discipline also face research on the theology represented by Septuagint corpora. These challenges involve, but are not limited to, (1) the diversity of the corpora, their texts, and subject matter, (2) differing definitions of "theology," (3) the theological pluralism evidenced by the collections, (4) the correspondences in imagery and ideas of the divine to theologies outside of the corpora, (5) the relationship with the New Testament and Rabbinic Judaism, and (6) the question of the intended target audiences who might benefit from presentations of the "theology" witnessed by the ancient literary works included in pre-determined corpora. I briefly elaborate on each of these challenges in turn.

(1) Like "the" Septuagint, there is no single Old Testament corpus, and the subject matter of the compositions in the various Old Testament and Septuagint collections are not fixed in one language or transmitted in a uniform textual form. The evidence, especially from the Qumran scrolls, suggests that, in the period of early Judaism (when the literary works included in the Septuagint corpora were first produced and transmitted), there was no generally accepted list of authoritative scriptures, and that the texts of important and influential writings circulated in dif-

---

2. By Septuagint corpora, I have collections of Jewish literary works in Greek, such as those of early codices, in mind. Swete (1914, 201–2) provides lists of the books in Codex Vaticanus, Codex Sinaiticus, Codex Alexandrinus, and Codex Basiliano-Venetus. See also Hengel 2002, 57–60; McDonald 2007, 442; and Schmid 2019, 118–22.

3. Cf., e.g., Rösel 2006, 2018.

ferent versions.⁴ The nature of the differences between manuscripts imply that, during this period, scribes continued to tinker with the details of the wordings and subject matter of literary writings when they made new copies of them. This pertains not only to the Hebrew or Aramaic versions of early Jewish writings, but to the Greek versions as well. The diversity of corpora, languages, and versions of writings' subject matter have significant implications for the study of Old Testament theology, especially if it is approached as a historical endeavor. First, the extent of the corpus chosen for study in the discipline has to be defined and justified. Second, the data concerning various scribal practices in producing and transmitting literary compositions indicate that there is little justification, from the perspectives of textual history and subject matter, to use only one particular version of an Old Testament writing as a resource in examining theology. These two implications are also relevant to research on the theology represented by Septuagint corpora, seeing as most of the discussions on this topic appear to have a restricted focus on the Greek translations of Hebrew Bible writings, and more specifically, on the so-called Old Greek versions of these translations.⁵

(2) There is no consensus regarding the task of Old Testament theology, which speaks to disagreements over what is meant by "theology," the object of study.⁶ In one of the classic Old Testament Theologies of the twentieth century, Walther Eichrodt argues that this field of study has the task "die alttestamentliche Glaubenswelt in ihrer strukturellen Einheit zu

---

4. Cf., e.g., VanderKam 2002; Karrer and Kraus 2008, 12–25; Lim 2010; Tov 2012, 183–87; Brooke 2013, 213–20; 2019, 123; Kraus 2014, 6–7, 9–10; Ulrich 2015; Fabry 2016, 40–59; Lange 2016, 132–48; Pajunen 2019, 369–70.

5. Cf., e.g., Cook 2010, 2017a, 2017b. While Cook and others insist that the theology of the Septuagint deals with the ideas, beliefs, or convictions of the original translators, Rösel (2018, 34–35) argues that the focus in research on this topic should be less on the translators and more on the communities who circulated the texts and whose ideas and convictions are mediated through the texts: "Ich würde also dafür plädieren, die Konzentration auf den Übersetzer als schöpferische Persönlichkeit zu reduzieren. Eher sollte die Theologie der LXX als gemeinsamer Prozess der Reflexion und Systematisierung in hellenistischen Gemeinden betrachtet werden, deren so formierte religiöse Überzeugung in die Überlieferung der Texte einfließt und daher an diesen Texten abgelesen werden kann. Ob diese Interpretationsleistungen auf der Ebene der hebräischen Textüberlieferung oder beim Wechsel in die griechische Sprache stattfanden, halte ich daher für weniger relevant; entscheidend ist, dass sie in der griechischen Bibel greifbar ist."

6. Cf. Schmid 2019, 13–44.

begreifen und unter Berücksichtigung ihrer religiösen Umwelt einerseits, ihres Wesenszusammenhanges mit dem Neuen Testament andererseits in ihrem tiefsten Sinngehalt zu deuten."[7] He disagrees with another influential exponent of the discipline, Gerhard von Rad, who takes a different position: "Der Gegenstand, um den sich der Theologe bemüht, ist ja nicht die geistig-religiöse Welt Israels und seine seelische Verfassung im allgemeinen, auch nicht seine Glaubenswelt, welches alles nur auf dem Weg von Rückschlüssen aus seinen Dokumenten erhoben werden kann, – sondern nur das, was Israel selbst von Jahwe direkt ausgesagt hat."[8] Given such differences in opinion over the task of Old Testament theology, it is not surprising that there is little agreement on how to accomplish its task. Rainer Albertz has identified the lack of consensus over the task of Old Testament theology, as well as its structure and method, as one of the discipline's major drawbacks.[9] This weakness is compounded by the fact that there is almost no dialogue between the designs of the various Theologies, which means that new attempts at compiling such a work hardly ever engage with the shortcomings of previous designs in an effort to arrive at a demonstrably better solution.[10] Without such constructive critical dialogue between its practitioners, no real advancement is achieved in the discipline. Regarding the Septuagint, much discussion has been devoted to the methodological challenges involved in isolating those differences between Greek translations and their presumed Semitic source texts, or the Masoretic text, which can be attributed to the "original" translators.[11] The theology of the Septuagint is often sought only in these differences between Greek and Hebrew versions of passages in early Jewish writings.[12] There is, however, almost no constructive critical dialogue about whether

---

7. Eichrodt 1968, 4.
8. Von Rad 1969, 117–18. Cf. also Westermann 1985, 5.
9. Albertz 1995, 6–7.
10. Albertz 1995, 6.
11. Cf., e.g., Ausloos 2017, 240–43.
12. Cf., e.g., Joosten 2000, 33; Dafni 2002, 324, 327; Aejmelaeus 2006, 23; Cook 2010, 622; 2017a, 13; 2017b, 277; Douglas 2012, 106. Rösel (2018, 30, 35–36, 37) suggests a double comparative approach to the theology of the Septuagint (see also his chapter in this volume). It should include a comparison between the Greek and Hebrew texts and then a comparison of the theological expressions of the Greek books with one another. A theology of the Septuagint that follows such an approach will necessarily have a diachronic structure and therefore will not be restricted to the original translations but include later revisions as well.

this focus on the translators' interpretations of passages is a proper understanding of the theology of Septuagint corpora. An important exception is the stimulating contribution of Timothy McLay.[13] Based on the presupposition that "theology of/in the Septuagint is not limited to or controlled by the intentions of the translator,"[14] he discusses three points that merit close attention in future discussions on the topic: (a) theology of/in the Septuagint, is not limited to the Old Greek text;[15] (b) theology of/in the Septuagint is not limited to differences between the Greek texts and the presumed Semitic source texts; and (c) theology of/in the Septuagint may be examined and described with the same legitimacy and using the same basic principles as a theology of the Old Testament/Hebrew Bible or New Testament.[16] Proponents of a different view ignore these points, and McLay's arguments, only to the detriment of their own designs.

(3) Whether "theology" is taken to refer to the religious ideas and convictions that may be inferred from the texts (their implicit world of thought and belief), or their assertions about the divine (the texts' religious statements), the Old Testament witnesses to theological pluralism.[17] According to Rolf Knierim, this pluralism is the central problem of the Old Testament, and Old Testament theology has the task of examining the correspondence and relationship between the coexisting theologies.[18] Attempts to establish the coherence of the theology of the Old Testament, especially those that seek to identify a center of the Old Testament,[19] are

---

13. McLay 2010.
14. McLay 2010, 608.
15. Cf. also Dafni 2009, 446.
16. McLay 2010, 608.
17. Cf. Gerstenberger 2001, 9.
18. Knierim 1995, 1–2, 7. By contrast, Gerstenberger (2001, 9) does not see the theological plurality and syncretism evidenced by the Old Testament writings as a problem: "Die Mannigfaltigkeit der Theologien öffnet uns den Blick für andere Völker, Zeiten und Gottesvorstellungen, sie enthebt uns dem Zwang, ängstlich im Auf und Ab der Geschichte und der Theologien nach *der einen*, geschichtslosen, unwandelbaren, absolut verpflichtenden Vorstellung und Richtlinie zu suchen. Sie befreit uns zu der aufrichtigen, gelassenen Würdigung der theologischen Leistungen unserer geistlichen Vorväter und Vormütter, die sie verdienen, und sie macht uns fähig, im Dialog mit ihnen und mit den Religionen der Welt den ‚richtigen', d.h. heute und jetzt zu verantwortenden Gottesglauben für unser Wende- (und End?)zeitalter zu finden und zu formulieren."
19. Cf. Hayes and Prussner 1985, 257–60.

frustrated by the fact that, by any definition of the corpus, the Old Testament is not a book,[20] but a library of different kinds of literature, whose diverse imagery and ideas of the divine developed, circulated, and co-occurred over an uncertain length of time into the period of early Judaism and beyond. Septuagint corpora are also libraries of assorted literature. The Greek translations, as well as the writings and passages originally composed in Greek, were produced and transmitted in different locations over the span of many years. During this time, the existing diversity of imagery and ideas of the divine continued to circulate, and coexisted alongside novel developments. Martin Rösel is therefore justified in his criticism of early attempts to determine a theology of the Septuagint, which viewed it as a unity "without considering that the individual books have been translated by different people at different times not only in Alexandria but also elsewhere."[21] He concludes from this that "a 'Theology of the Septuagint' cannot be based on the leveling of differences among the individual books or the specific profiles of the translators for the sake of a common edifice of ideas."[22] This, however, does not mean that there is no room for some form of synthesis in the description of the theology represented by Septuagint corpora.[23] As is the case with Old Testament theology, there are more than one organizational principle that may give structure to the exposition of this theology. The principle may be historical, systematic, and/or thematic.

(4) The study of archaeological finds, iconography, and ancient Near Eastern literature has indicated that the religions of Israel and Judah were "typical northwest Semitic religions of the first millennium."[24] Similarly, data from material and textual sources suggest that all of early Judaism (Semitic- and Greek-speaking communities, as well as multilingual ones, in Judea and the Diaspora) was influenced in complex and variegated ways by Hellenism.[25] Furthermore, the images and ideas of the divine witnessed

---

20. Cf. Keel 2001, 91.
21. Rösel 2006, 240.
22. Rösel 2006, 240.
23. Rösel 2006, 241–42.
24. Niehr 1995, 50; 2010. Cf. also the comments of Uehlinger 2015, 12–14; and Schmid 2019, 84–85.
25. Nickelsburg and Kraft 1986, 11–12. They note that a close investigation of the available information has called for the correction of the oversimplified distinction in earlier scholarship between "Palestinian" and "Hellenistic" Judaism: "It is now clear that even as an independent Maccabean/Hasmonean kingdom, Jewish Palestine is best viewed as part of the larger 'hellenized' world, whether its representatives were

by the early Jewish texts included in the Old Testament and Septuagint corpora are comparable to counterparts in visual and textual sources from various periods and places of the eastern Mediterranean region. Indeed, the religious ideas and convictions inferable from the texts did not exist in isolation, and they did not develop *ex nihilo*; rather, they belonged to large, encyclopedic networks of knowledge. From this perspective, research on Old Testament and Septuagint theology can ill afford to ignore the connections with the theologies evidenced by the cultural products that shared an intellectual environment with the compositions in these collections.

(5) It has been contended that Old Testament theology is an essentially Christian discipline, a part of Christian theology,[26] and that it is concerned with how writings the church inherited from its Jewish parent function as Christian scripture.[27] In this regard, some Old Testament theologians see the Old Testament's relationship with the New Testament as of paramount importance.[28] Hartmut Gese even claims that the application of the Old Testament in the Christian church can only be grounded within the context of such a relationship.[29] It is, therefore, not surprising that, although a few Old Testament theologians have argued that the discipline should reflect theologically solely on the Old Testament texts,[30] others have seen

---

speaking and writing in Greek or in a Semitic dialect (Aramaic or Hebrew). That there were different Jewish responses to that world is also clear, but they are not defined primarily along linguistic or geographical lines. To state the issue more generally, the relations of Jews and Judaism to the Hellenistic environment was similar to that of other identifiable 'subcultures' (e.g., in Egypt or Syria) and is treated most satisfactorily by accepting Hellenism as the norm against which to judge similarities and differences, rather than by positing some 'pure' form of (Palestinian) Judaism as the norm." Cf. also Hengel 1973, 191–95.

26. Childs 1985, 7.
27. See Childs 1979, 660–71; 1985, 7–10.
28. See Barr 1999, 172; Schmid 2019, 89–90.
29. Gese 1970, 417.
30. Childs 1985, 9: "I would argue that the Old Testament functions within the Christian scripture as a witness to Jesus Christ precisely in its pre-Christian form. The task of Old Testament theology is, therefore, not to Christianize the Old Testament by identifying it with the New Testament witness, but to hear its own theological testimony to the God of Israel whom the church confesses also to worship. Although Christians confess that God who revealed himself to Israel is the God and Father of Jesus Christ, it is still necessary to hear Israel's witness in order to understand who the Father of Jesus Christ is. The coming of Jesus does not remove the function of the divine disclosure in the old covenant."

the establishment of connections with the New Testament as an essential purpose of the discipline.[31] The connections between the Old and New Testaments do not include only agreements but disagreements as well. In order to shed light on these agreements and disagreements, it would be necessary for an Old Testament theology to incorporate early Jewish literature, especially the texts from Qumran, and the research on the Septuagint in the discussion of the relationship between the two testaments.[32] Indeed, Old Testament theologians cannot simply ignore the early Jewish literature outside the Hebrew Bible and Old Testament corpora, given that they, as contemporaries of the Old Testament and New Testament writings, are invaluable resources of information about the intellectual and cultural environment in which the Old Testament and New Testament writings came into being and were transmitted. A case can also be made for the relevance of later Jewish writings, such as rabbinic literature.[33] Old Testament theology is thereby challenged to include the diversity of Jewish literature outside of the narrow confines of the Hebrew Bible or Old Testament corpora in its examination of theology. With regard to Septuagint corpora, there can be little doubt that early Jewish texts in Greek influenced the vocabulary, formulations of subject matter, and theology of the New Testament writings.[34] In fact, it is justified to presuppose that "the Jewish Scriptures in Greek provided the principal cultural, liturgical, theological, and literary context for the NT writers as they reflected on the way in which Jesus had fulfilled the expectations of God's covenant people according to the Scriptures."[35] In the same way as the New Testament writings, the early Jewish texts in Greek were not created and developed in a vacuum, but in environments where translations into other languages, such as Aramaic, were made, the wordings and subject matter of existing literature were adapted when they were copied, and new compositions of

---

31. Cf., e.g., Eichrodt 1968, xi–xii; von Rad 1968, 413–14; Westermann 1985, 192–203.

32. Jeremias 2015, 479.

33. According to Harrington (2002, 206), one of the reasons why early and later Jewish writings should be taken seriously today, even if they are not part of communities' canons, is that "renewed attention to the Old Testament apocrypha, as well as to the works of Josephus and Philo, the Dead Sea scrolls, the Old Testament pseudepigrapha, and the rabbinic writings, can help all Christians (and Jews) better to understand the Jewishness of Jesus and of the earliest Christian movement."

34. McLay 2003, 144–70.

35. McLay 2003, 138.

different genres were put into writing. Research on the theology of Septuagint corpora will do well not to proceed as though the prodigious literary activity during the period of early Judaism and the diversity of contemporary writings have no or only limited relevance for an understanding of the composition and ideas of the literary works in the collections.

(6) The recent Old Testament theology of Jörg Jeremias opens with the following striking statement: "Eine ‚Theologie des Alten Testaments (AT)' zielt darauf ab, die Ergebnisse der wissenschaftlichen Bemühungen um das Verständnis der alttestamentlichen Texte sowohl für die Theologie als auch für die Kirche zu bündeln und insbesondere die zentralen Gottesaussagen des Alten Testaments zu erheben."[36] On this view, the compilation of an Old Testament theology makes the results of scientific efforts to understand the Old Testament texts available to its two main beneficiaries, (Christian) theology and the church. Yet, Old Testament theology has in the past faced strong opposition from scholars who are of the opinion that it is not the business of biblical criticism to cater to theology, as well as theologians who point out that the religious statements of Old Testament texts are not theology in the proper sense of the word.[37] This raises the important question who the target audience(s) of research on divine images and ideas witnessed by Old Testament texts should be. This is an important question, because its answer determines the goal of compiling such research, as the quote from Jeremias implies. Rösel recognizes that a theology of the Septuagint should also address this question. He claims that there is a very simple answer: "All scholars who are interested in the meaning of the Hebrew Bible/Old Testament in Hellenistic times need such a book and will use it."[38] Does this mean, however, that the compilation of a theology of the Septuagint is not supposed to hold interest for anyone who is not concerned with the narrow focus on how the Hebrew Bible/Old Testament was understood in the Hellenistic period? In other words, is the goal of a Septuagint theology merely to serve the interest of a small group of specialists without regard for wider audiences in contemporary religious communities and other theological disciplines?

This cursory sketch outlines some of the challenges confronting both research on the theology represented by Septuagint corpora and Old

---

36. Jeremias 2015, 1.
37. Barr 1999, 223–25, 231–32, 240–52.
38. Rösel 2006, 243.

Testament theology. These shared challenges are the first of two factors that govern my proposal in this chapter. The second one is the fact that research on the theology represented by Septuagint corpora is based on many of the same resources and processes much of the same data as other disciplines. The data in question are the depictions of the divine in various types of resources, such as written, pictorial, and material cultural artefacts. With these two factors in mind, I propose that research on the theology represented by Septuagint corpora should be approached as an interdisciplinary endeavor. This means that the object and objectives of research on the topic should not be conceptualized within the confines of Septuagint studies alone, or in isolation from other disciplines that use the same resources, process the same data, and produce information that is relevant to more than one of these fields of study. Examples of disciplines that share resources and data with research on the theology represented by Septuagint corpora are biblical theology, history of religion, and doctrinal theology. In order to tease out some of the implications of this proposal for the conceptualization of research on the theology represented by Septuagint corpora, I shall, in what follows, briefly mention connections between Septuagint corpora and the three disciplines, and then raise questions for further reflection.[39] My aim in this chapter is not to provide answers to these questions. My goal is simply to put the questions on the agenda of researchers who examine and expound the theology witnessed by Septuagint corpora in the hope that the proposal will play a positive role in future conceptualizations of this field of study.

2. Septuagint Corpora and Biblical Theology

James Barr's comprehensive discussion of the concept shows that it is difficult to define what "biblical theology" is.[40] Indeed, both words, *biblical* and *theology*, are open to more than one interpretation, and how these terms are understood influences the definition of the concept. The adjec-

---

39. Biblical theology, history of religion, and doctrinal theology are, of course, not unambiguous concepts. The nature, aims, and procedures of these disciplines can be understood in different ways; therefore, it is imperative to be clear what I mean by these concepts. In matters of definition, I have chosen James Barr as a guide, whose extensive work on biblical theology has also treated the subjects of history of religion and doctrinal theology.

40. Barr 1999, 2–17.

tive *biblical* indicates that the theology in question relates to the Bible. *Bible*, however, is a slippery term that means different things to different communities, whether Jewish, Protestant, Roman Catholic, or Orthodox.[41]

> Despite its familiarity to Christians who have grown up reading it in English translations, "Bible" is actually a complex phenomenon. What it is relates not only to the question of *which books* are "scripture" but also *which languages* function as "scripture" for *which community* and *which texts or manuscripts* of those selected books are authoritative and inspired.[42]

For the church, this complexity is compounded by the fact that its "Bible" is comprised of two parts, the Old and New Testaments. In order to avoid confusion in terminology, I shall follow Barr's lead and treat Old Testament theology and New Testament theology as subdivisions of the larger category of "biblical theology."[43] He uses the term "pan-biblical theology" for a theology that encompasses both parts of the Christian Bible.[44] To be clear, in this section, I have the connection between Septuagint corpora and biblical theology, not panbiblical theology, in view.[45]

Although, in scope and texts, Septuagint corpora are not the same as the Hebrew Bible or the Old Testaments of the church,[46] there are overlaps.[47] This means that research on the theology of Septuagint corpora and biblical theology, in the sense of Old Testament or Hebrew Bible theol-

---

41. Wooden 2008, 130–31. The lists of books in the Jewish, Orthodox, Roman Catholic, and Protestant Hebrew Bible/Old Testament canons are conveniently presented side by side in McDonald 2007, 443–44.

42. Stuckenbruck 2011, 177, emphasis original.

43. Barr 1999, 1.

44. Barr 1999, 1. Panbiblical theology has been approached in different ways. See, e.g., Childs 1993, 11–26, 85; Westermann 1985, 203–5; Schmidt 1996, 439–46.

45. Glenny 2016 has recently tackled the issue of the role the Septuagint might play in determining a panbiblical theology. He discusses different views on this role and concludes that the Septuagint has at least four functions in a Christian biblical theology. It functions (1) as a source of such a theology, (2) as a commentary on the biblical text, (3) as a bridge or link between the Old Testament and the New Testament, and (4) as a complement to the Hebrew scriptures.

46. Cf. Jeppesen 2006, 58.

47. Interestingly, Septuagint corpora have also featured in debates on what the Old Testament of the church should be, especially the status of the so-called deuterocanonical books, as well as in discussions over the proper textual base for interpreta-

ogy, share resources. The important question for both fields of study is whether their treatments of the resources should be "descriptive" or "constructive." Biblical theology, says Barr, can either describe theology "as it existed or was thought or believed within the time, languages and cultures of the Bible itself," or it can refer to a theology "which we, or other persons of modern times, create upon the basis of the biblical texts."[48] Barr is of the opinion that the term "biblical theology" only has clarity when it is understood in the former sense; that is, biblical theology has the theology that underlies the biblical texts in view.[49] Its task is to make this implicit theology explicit, because the texts themselves do not state the theology explicitly.[50] The texts, of course, make religious statements and are full of God-talk, but Barr cogently argues that

> religious opinions, expressions and aspirations, however strongly expressed, are not thereby theology. Theology is a reflective activity in which the content of religious expressions is to some extent abstracted, contemplated, subjected to reflection and discussion, and deliberately reformulated. Much of the Bible does not have this character.[51]

Biblical theologians, therefore, are not tasked with bringing together and synthesising the myriad of different and differing assertions about the divine in passages of biblical texts, as they were probably intended to function rhetorically in historical contexts; rather, the biblical theologian studies

> the intellectual and cultural world-image that lies behind the individual texts and their individual meanings. He or she considers the presup-

---

tion and translations into modern languages. See, e.g., Barr 1999, 376–77; Wagner 2008; Wooden 2008, 131; Stuckenbruck 2011, 177; Glenny 2016, 266.

48. Barr 1999, 4. Cf. also the introductory remarks of Childs 1993, 3: "It has long been recognized that the term 'Biblical Theology' is ambiguous. It can either denote a theology contained within the Bible, or a theology which accords with the Bible. The first definition understands the task of Biblical Theology to be a descriptive, historical one which seeks to determine what was the theology of the biblical authors themselves. The second understand the task of Biblical Theology to be a constructive, theological one which attempts to formulate a modern theology compatible in some sense with the Bible."

49. Barr 1999, 4, 74.

50. Barr 1999, 248.

51. Barr 1999, 249. Cf. the discussion of Schmid 2019, 45–49.

positions from which the writers (and later readers) may have started, the connections with other concepts which have been used elsewhere, or with concepts that may have been used but are avoided, the general world-picture that may have been assumed, the network of connections and indications that may have been involved.[52]

In short, according to this understanding, biblical theologians attempt to construct the conceptual world that underlies and informs the religious statements in the biblical texts. It goes without saying that the biblical texts are not the sole evidence for this conceptual world. Other resources, such as realia of the material culture, iconography, inscriptions, and literary texts of other cultures, are equally important for the construction of the conceptual world of which the biblical texts partook. So are the early Jewish texts outside of the "Bible," those that are sometimes called apocryphal or pseudepigraphical, as well as the majority of the Dead Sea Scrolls.[53] Moreover, Barr correctly notes that "if we come down to this time—and after all the canonical Daniel brings us down to it—we can hardly fail also to include the earliest beginnings of the traditions which were later to mature in Rabbinic tradition."[54] The upshot of this is that biblical theology is not built upon the canonical books alone: "It is built upon what was *thought*; its base lies *behind* the canonical books, in the life of ancient Israel."[55] The literary works of Septuagint corpora are, of course, not excluded from the resources of biblical theology, but the question remains whether expounding the theology implied by these corpora should be a descriptive exercise in the same way as Barr argues regarding biblical theology. In other words, should research on the topic focus on and attempt to construct the conceptual world, especially the ideas and images about the divine, which underpins the explicit religious statements in Septuagint corpora? Or should research on the theology of Septuagint corpora be conceptualized in a completely different way from biblical theology, as Barr describes the latter, despite the fact that these disciplines share resources?

---

52. Barr 1999, 248.
53. Barr 1999, 578–80.
54. Barr 1999, 580.
55. Barr 1999, 578.

3. Septuagint Corpora and History of Religion

For the purposes of this chapter, history of religion deals with the changes and developments, as well as the stable aspects of the religious domain of ancient cultures, such as images, ideas, and convictions regarding divine entities and spheres, cultic practices, times, and personnel. The study of history of religion attempts to understand and explain these changes, developments, and stable elements through time, their interrelatedness with other facets of culture, and their comparability with phenomena in religions of neighboring peoples. For information on these matters, historians of religion interpret the data culled from different resources, for example, cultic objects, buildings and places, material images, documentary texts, inscriptions, and literary writings.[56] Regarding early Judaism, the material, pictorial, and textual resources are many and varied. The literary texts, which are relevant to the study of the ideas and convictions about the divine in early Judaism during the period from the downfall of the kingdom of Judah to the Bar Kochba revolt, include a myriad of writings of different genres in Hebrew, Aramaic, and Greek, as well as translations of compositions into these languages. The great number and diversity of these literary texts are exemplified by the sectarian and non-sectarian literature among the Dead Sea Scrolls, other apocalyptic, historiographic, narrative, sapiential, and testamentary literature, hymns, prayers, and other poetic compositions, (popular) philosophical texts,[57] the New Testament writings, and rabbinic literature. The translations and other compositions in Septuagint corpora are only a small number of the resources available to historians of religion during the period of early Judaism. Like the other resources, the textual artefacts in these corpora are cultural products whose religious ideas and convictions were part of a large pool of encyclopaedic knowledge that was fed from different sources and evidently fostered by peoples in the eastern Mediterranean region over a long period of time. Furthermore, changes and stable elements in these ideas and convictions cannot be understood apart from developments in related aspects of the larger cultural environment, such as developments in the political, socio-economic, and geographical domains. This raises

---

56. Cf., e.g., Keel 2001, 99–100; Keel and Uehlinger 2010, 10–12.

57. Popular philosophy refers to philosophical knowledge that was not limited to a particular philosophical tradition and that was accessible to people without formal philosophical training. See Thom 2012; 2014.

the questions whether designs of theologies of Septuagint corpora can do justice to their implied religious ideas and convictions as products of a broad cultural milieu that bear the stamps of temporally and geographically diverse influences, and whether it would not be more appropriate to incorporate them in a history of religion. In this connection, Albertz has argued that, as far as the Old Testament writings are concerned, a history of religion is not plagued by the same, theoretical, methodological, and conceptual problems as Old Testament theology, and that research should be devoted to the former, rather than the latter.[58] Other scholars, however, have seen the relationship of the two disciplines as one of overlap and mutual enrichment.[59] According to Collins, biblical theology is an area of historical theology, and, therefore, "it necessarily overlaps with the history of religion. Within the history of the religion, it focuses on the portrayal of God in one group of texts, the Bible."[60] Similarly, Barr expresses the opinion that the difference between the two disciplines lies in their scope and field:

> The one, Old Testament theology, is related to *certain texts* and to the theology *implied* by them; the other, the history of religion, is related to a large social and intellectual field, for which these texts are part of the evidence, and often indirectly so, through hints they give of the contemporary world rather than through the values that they directly affirm.[61]

Can the relationship between history of religion and the theology represented by Septuagint corpora be conceptualized along similar lines, or not? A positive answer to this question would raise two more questions. First, how narrowly should the borders of the Septuagint be drawn; that is, on the theology implied by which texts should the research focus? Second, what are the historical parameters for the theology; that is,

---

58. Albertz 1992, 37–38; 1995, 14–16.
59. Cf., e.g., Schmidt 1996, 17; Barr 1999, 135; Keel 2001, 107; Schmid 2019, 85: "Die theologische Substanz alttestamentlicher Texte lässt sich nicht allein textintern erschließen … vielmehr muss sie auch in ihren historischen Interaktionen, sei es mit anderen Texten oder mit geschichtlichen Erfahrungen, beschrieben werden. Insofern setzt die Theologie des Alten Testaments die Geschichte und Religionsgeschichte des antiken Israel und Juda voraus und baut darauf auf."
60. Collins 2005, 26.
61. Barr 1999, 133, emphasis original.

should the research be restricted to the Hellenistic period, or include earlier and later times?

4. Septuagint Corpora and Doctrinal Theology

Doctrinal theology is here conveniently restricted to ideas of the Christian religion, and understood as the study of articles of Christian faith, including their foundations in traditions, reason, and experience, their development over time, their relationships with each other, and their applicability to the concerns of contemporary religious communities.[62] Although "the Bible" is sometimes referred to as a source of doctrinal theology,[63] Barr argues that this is not completely accurate:

> The Bible may in a certain sense be the norm, or rather one of the norms, but it cannot, strictly speaking, be the source. The source is a theological tradition which *preceded* the Bible and accompanied it, guiding and influencing its utterances, as well as following it.[64]

Doctrinal theology is, therefore, not primarily about the Bible as such, even though it uses biblical texts,[65] and has exegesis as a dialogue partner.[66] In this regard, I suggest that biblical texts are some of the resources of data that doctrinal theology processes to obtain information that is pertinent to its study of articles of Christian faith. The texts in Septuagint corpora can also be counted among these resources, for, to the best of our knowledge, ideas and convictions about the divine that may be inferred from their wordings circulated before, during, and after the period of early Judaism, and, therefore, form part of the larger traditions that are foundational to articles of Christian faith. If Septuagint corpora, as a whole, or in part, are regarded as "biblical" or "canonical" and, in one way or another, as divinely "inspired," some theologians may even allocate more weight to them, relative to other resources, in the interpretation of articles of faith, especially their continued applicability. Biblicism, that is, "any conception that

---

62. Cf., e.g., McGrath 2007, 101–2.
63. Cf., e.g., McGrath 2007, 105–6.
64. Barr 1999, 75, emphasis original.
65. Barr 1999, 74, 242.
66. See Schmid 2017; 2019, 95.

suggests that the Bible alone is the final decisive authority in theology,"[67] should, however, be avoided. The reason is that, for doctrinal theology, the ideas and convictions about the divine, which may be inferred from the texts, are relevant (not particular versions of texts' wordings, or passages' uses of divine images and ideas for specific rhetorical purposes), and the texts are not the sole transmitters of these ideas and convictions. Given that Septuagint corpora can be a useful pool of data for doctrinal theology, on the one hand, and that the ideas and convictions about the divine inferable from these texts are not accessible only through them, on the other hand, the question for research on the theology represented by Septuagint corpora is how such research may be conducted and presented in a way that may help doctrinal theology steer a course between the Scylla of disregard for these texts, and the Charybdis of biblicism.

To summarize, the preceding discussion of connections between Septuagint corpora and the disciplines of biblical theology, history of religion, and doctrinal theology, raises the following questions: (1) Should research on the theology represented by Septuagint corpora describe the conceptual world that underlies the religious assertions of the literary works in the collections? (2) Can this research adequately expound and present the stable elements and developments in ideas and images of the divine, as well as their temporally and geographically diverse influences that may be inferred from the literary works in the collections? (3) How can it assist doctrinal theology to engage with the ideas and images of the divine that are implied by the early Jewish writings in Greek, without making the formulations of these ideas and images in the texts the decisive arbiter of theological "truth"? These are not the only questions that come to mind when reflecting on research on the theology represented by Septuagint corpora as an interdisciplinary undertaking. Another important issue is how such research should be related to modern readers' exegesis of the literary works in Septuagint corpora, the process of reading and making sense of these ancient texts "in which factors of language, of literary form, of history, of environing culture, or knowledge of geography and other *realia*, intertwine and from which theological conclusions may be drawn."[68] Would the subject matter of this research only be a by-product of exegesis,

---

67. Barr 1999, 70.
68. Barr 1999, 249.

and would the research itself merely be an attempt to synthesize the results of exegetical endeavors? Or can research on the theology represented by Septuagint corpora make a contribution to exegesis? Can the research be conceptualized in such a way that a book or multivolume work on the topic may serve as a tool that exegetes can use to elucidate individual passages of literary works in Septuagint corpora?

5. Closing Remarks

In this chapter, I propose that researchers who are interested in the theology represented by Septuagint corpora would do well to approach the study of this topic as an interdisciplinary endeavor. Their research designs will leave much to be desired if they conceptualize their studies in isolation from other disciplines, such as biblical theology, history of religion, and doctrinal theology, that also count early Jewish literature in Greek among their resources. Martin Rösel's project on a "theology of the Septuagint"[69] will no doubt stimulate much debate and future research. His projected volumes do not aim to be the last word on the subject, and, in this regard, I have identified some questions that will, I hope, be addressed in discussions and conceptualizations of research on the topic that will follow in the wake of Rösel's project. At a minimum, my proposal calls for a reconsideration of the notion that research on the topic of Septuagint corpora and theology can properly be restricted to the narrow foci in Septuagint studies on translation technique and differences between Greek and Hebrew versions of passages that may be ascribed to the supposed intentional interpretations of "original" translators. Moreover, the proposal suggests that the potential usefulness of the theology of Septuagint corpora for exegesis needs to be on the agenda of researchers of the topic. Indeed, these literary works merit much more attention from exegetes, and it remains to be seen how research on the theology represented by Septuagint corpora will contribute to the understanding of these ancient cultural artefacts.

Bibliography

Aejmelaeus, Anneli. 2006. "Von Sprache zur Theologie: Methodologische Überlegungen zur Theologie der Septuaginta." Pages 21–48 in *The*

---

69. See his chapter in this volume.

Septuagint and Messianism. Edited by Michael A. Knibb. BETL 195. Leuven: Peeters.

Albertz, Rainer. 1992. *Religionsgeschichte Israels in alttestamentlicher Zeit*. Vol. 1. GAT 8/1. Göttingen: Vandenhoeck & Ruprecht.

———. 1995. "Religionsgeschichte Israels statt Theologie des Alten Testament! Plädoyer für eine forschungsgeschichtliche Umorientierung." *JBTh* 10:3–24.

Ausloos, Hans. 2017. "Sept défis posés à une théologie de la Septante." Pages 228–50 in *Congress Volume: Stellenbosch, 2016*. Edited by Louis C. Jonker, Gideon R. Kotzé, and Christl M. Maier. VTSup 177. Leiden: Brill.

Barr, James. 1999. *The Concept of Biblical Theology*. Minneapolis: Fortress.

Brooke, George J. 2013. "The Scrolls from Qumran and Old Testament Theology." Pages 211–27 in *Reading the Dead Sea Scrolls: Essays on Method*. EJL 39. Atlanta: Society of Biblical Literature.

———. 2019. "Scrolls and Early Judaism." Pages 119–28 in *T&T Clark Companion to the Dead Sea Scrolls*. Edited by George J. Brooke and Charlotte Hempel. London: Bloomsbury.

Childs, Brevard S. 1979. *Introduction to the Old Testament as Scripture*. Philadelphia: Fortress.

———. 1985. *Old Testament Theology in a Canonical Context*. Philadelphia: Fortress.

———. 1993. *Biblical Theology of the Old and New Testaments: Theological Reflection on the Christian Bible*. Minneapolis: Fortress.

Collins, John J. 2005. *Encounters with Biblical Theology*. Minneapolis: Fortress.

Cook, Johann. 2010. "Towards the Formulation of a Theology of the Septuagint." Pages 621–40 in *Congress Volume: Llubljana, 2007*. Edited by André Lemaire. VTSup 133. Leiden: Brill.

———. 2017a. "Interpreting the Septuagint." Pages 1–22 in *Congress Volume: Stellenbosch, 2016*. Edited by Louis C. Jonker, Gideon R. Kotzé and Christl M. Maier. VTSup 177. Leiden: Brill.

———. 2017b. "A Theology of the Septuagint?" *OTE* 30:265–82.

Dafni, Evangelia G. 2002. "Theologie der Sprache der Septuaginta." *TZ* 58:315–28.

———. 2009. "Theologie der Sprache der Septuaginta im Horizont des altgriechischen Schrifttums und Denkens." *JSem* 18:434–57.

Douglas, Alex. 2012. "Limitations to Writing a Theology of the Septuagint." *JSCS* 45:104–17.

Eichrodt, Walther. 1968. *Theologie des Alten Testaments*. Vol. 1. 8th ed. Stuttgart: Klotz; Göttingen: Vandenhoeck & Ruprecht.

Fabry, Heinz-Josef. 2016. "Der Text und seine Geschichte." Pages 37–66 in *Einleitung in das Alte Testament*. 9th ed. Edited by Erich Zenger et al. ST 1.1. Stuttgart: Kohlhammer.

Gerstenberger, Erhard. 2001. *Theologien im Alten Testament: Pluralität und Synkretismus alttestamentlichen Gottesglaubens*. Stuttgart: Kohlhammer.

Gese, Hartmut. 1970. "Erwägungen zur Einheit der biblischen Theologie." *ZThK* 67:417–36.

Glenny, W. Edward. 2016. "The Septuagint and Biblical Theology." *Themelios* 41:263–78.

Harrington, Daniel J. 2002. "The Old Testament Apocrypha in the Early Church and Today." Pages 196–210 in *The Canon Debate*. Edited by Lee Martin McDonald and James A. Sanders. Peabody, MA: Hendrickson.

Hayes, John H., and Frederick C. Prussner. 1985. *Old Testament Theology: Its History and Development*. Atlanta: John Knox.

Hengel, Martin. 1973. *Judentum und Hellenismus*. 2nd ed. WUNT 10. Tübingen: Mohr Siebeck.

———. 2002. *The Septuagint as Christian Scripture: Its Prehistory and the Problem of Its Canon*. Edinburgh: T&T Clark.

Jeppesen, Knud. 2006. "Insider—Not Outsider: A Plea for the Septuagint." Pages 48–59 in *Kanon: Bibelens tilblivelse og normative status*. Edited by Troels Engberg-Pedersen, Niels Peter Lemche, and Henrik Tronier. Forum for Bibelsk Eksegese 15. Copenhagen: Museum Tusculanums Forlag.

Jeremias, Jörg. 2015. *Theologie des Alten Testament*. GAT 6. Göttingen: Vandenhoeck & Ruprecht.

Joosten, Jan. 2000. "Une théologie de la Septante? Réflexions méthodologiques sur l'interprétation de la version grecque." *RTP* 132:31–46.

Karrer, Martin, and Wolfgang Kraus. 2008. "Umfang und Text der Septuaginta: Erwägungen nach dem Abschluss der deutschen Übersetzung." Pages 8–63 in *Die Septuaginta – Texte, Kontexte, Lebenswelten*. Edited by Martin Karrer, Wolfgang Kraus, and Martin Meiser. WUNT 219. Tübingen: Mohr Siebeck.

Keel, Othmar. 2001. "Religionsgeschichte Israels oder Theologie des Alten Testaments?" Pages 88–109 in *Wieviel Systematik erlaubt die Schrift?*

Auf der Suche nach einer gesamtbiblischen Theologie. Edited by Frank-Lothar Hossfield. QD 185. Freiburg: Herder.

Keel, Othmar, and Christoph Uehlinger. 2010. *Göttinnen, Götter und Gottessymbole: Neue Erkenntnisse zur Religionsgeschichte Kanaans und Israels aufgrund bislang unerschlossener ikonographischer Quellen.* Fribourg: Academic Press.

Knierim, Rolf P. 1995. *The Task of Old Testament Theology: Substance, Method, and Cases.* Grand Rapids: Eerdmans.

Kraus, Wolfgang. 2014. "Die hermeneutische Relevanz der Septuaginta für eine Biblische Theologie." Pages 3–25 in *Die Septuaginta – Text, Wirkung, Rezeption.* Edited by Wolfgang Kraus and Siegfried Kreuzer. WUNT 325. Tübingen: Mohr Siebeck.

Lange, Armin. 2016. "Ancient Hebrew-Aramaic Texts." Pages 82–166 in vol. 1A of *Textual History of the Bible: The Hebrew Bible.* Edited by Armin Lange and Emanuel Tov. Leiden: Brill.

Lim, Timothy H. 2010. "Authoritative Scriptures and the Dead Sea Scrolls." Pages 303–22 in *The Oxford Handbook of the Dead Sea Scrolls.* Edited by Timothy H. Lim and John J. Collins. Oxford: Oxford University Press.

McDonald, Lee Martin. 2007. *The Biblical Canon: Its Origin, Transmission, and Authority.* Peabody, MA: Hendrickson.

McGrath, Alister E. 2007. *Christian Theology: An Introduction.* 4th ed. Oxford: Blackwell.

McLay, R. Timothy. 2003. *The Use of the Septuagint in New Testament Research.* Grand Rapids: Eerdmans, 2003.

———. 2010. "Why Not a Theology of the Septuagint?" Pages 607–20 in *Die Septuaginta – Texte, Theologien, Einflüsse.* Edited by Wolfgang Kraus, Martin Karrer, and Martin Meiser. WUNT 252. Tübingen: Mohr Siebeck.

Nickelsburg, George W. E., and Robert A. Kraft. 1986. "Introduction: The Modern Study of Early Judaism." Pages 1–30 in *Early Judaism and Its Modern Interpreters.* Edited by Robert A. Kraft and George W. E. Nickelsburg. Atlanta: Scholars Press.

Niehr, Herbert. 1995. "The Rise of YHWH in Judahite and Israelite Religion: Methodological and Religio-Historical Aspects." Pages 45–72 in *The Triumph of Elohim: From Yahwisms to Judaisms.* Edited by Diana Vikander Edelman. CBET 13. Kampen: Kok Pharos.

———. 2010. "'Israelite' Religion and 'Canaanite' Religion." Pages 23–36 in *Religious Diversity in Ancient Israel and Judah.* Edited by Francesca Stavrakopoulou and John Barton. London: T&T Clark.

Pajunen, Mika. 2019. "Bible." Pages 367–75 in *T&T Clark Companion to the Dead Sea Scrolls*. Edited by George J. Brooke and Charlotte Hempel. London: Bloomsbury.

Rad, Gerhard von. 1969. *Theologie des Alten Testaments*. Vol. 1. Munich: Kaiser.

———. 1968. *Theologie des Alten Testaments*. Vol. 2. Munich: Kaiser.

Rösel, Martin. 2006. "Towards a 'Theology of the Septuagint.'" Pages 239–52 in *Septuagint Research: Issues and Challenges in the Study of the Greek Jewish Scriptures*. Edited by Wolfgang Kraus and R. Glenn Wooden. SCS 53. Atlanta: Society of Biblical Literature.

———. 2018. "Eine Theologie der Septuaginta? Präsizierungen und Pointierungen." Pages 25–43 in *Textgeschichte und Theologie: Septuaginta und Masoretischer Text als Äußerungen theologischer Reflexion*. Edited by Frank Ueberschaer, Thomas Wagner, and Jonathan Miles Robker. WUNT 407. Tübingen: Mohr Siebeck.

Schmid, Konrad. 2017. "Dogmatik als konsequente Exegese? Überlegungen zur Anschlussfähigkeit der historisch-kritischen Bibelwissenschaft an die Systematische Theologie." *EvT* 77:327–38.

———. 2019. *Theologie des Alten Testaments*. Neue Theologische Grundrisse. Tübingen: Mohr Siebeck.

Schmidt, Werner H. 1996. *Altestamentlicher Glaube*. 8th ed. Neukirchen-Vluyn: Neukirchener Verlag.

Stuckenbruck, Loren T. 2011. "Apocrypha and Septuagint. Exploring the Christian Canon." Pages 177–201 in *Die Septuaginta und das frühe Christentum – The Septuagint and Christian Origins*. Edited by Scott Caulley and Hermann Lichtenberger. WUNT 277. Tübingen: Mohr Siebeck.

Swete, Henry Barclay. 1914. *An Introduction to the Old Testament in Greek*. Cambridge: Cambridge University Press.

Thom, Johan C. 2012. "Popular Philosophy in the Hellenistic-Roman World." *Early Christianity* 3:279–95.

———. 2014. "Populêre Filosofie en die Nuwe Testament," *LitNet Akademies* 11:401–28.

Tov, Emanuel. 2012. *Textual Criticism of the Hebrew Bible*. 3rd ed. Minneapolis: Fortress.

Uehlinger, Christoph. 2015. "Distinctive or Diverse? Conceptualizing Ancient Israelite Religion in Its Southern Levantine Setting." *HeBAI* 1.4:1–24.

Ulrich, Eugene. 2015. *The Dead Sea Scrolls and the Developmental Composition of the Bible*. VTSup 169. Leiden: Brill.

VanderKam, James C. 2002. "Questions of Canon Viewed through the Dead Sea Scrolls." Pages 91–109 in *The Canon Debate*. Edited by Lee Martin McDonald and James A. Sanders. Peabody, MA: Hendrickson.

Wagner, J. Ross. 2008. "The Septuagint and the 'Search for the Christian Bible.'" Pages 17–28 in *Scripture's Doctrine and Theology's Bible*. Edited by Markus Bockmuehl and Alan J. Torrance. Grand Rapids: Baker Academic.

Westermann., Claus. 1985 *Theologie des Alten Testaments in Grundzügen*. 2nd ed. GAT 6. Göttingen: Vandenhoeck & Ruprecht.

Wooden, R. Glenn. 2008. "The Role of 'the Septuagint' in the Formation of the Biblical Canons." Pages 129–46 in *Exploring the Origins of the Bible: Canon Formation in Historical, Literary, and Theological Perspective*. Edited by Craig A. Evans and Emanuel Tov. Grand Rapids: Baker Academic.

Product Received: Influence of "the Old in the New" on the Formulation of Theologies of "the" Septuagint

Kyle Young

ABSTRACT: Septuagint scholars have significantly advanced the discussion over how modern interpreters should articulate the theologies of septuagintal materials. Nevertheless, significant impasses still exist (e.g., whether Old Greek manuscripts alone or non–Old Greek manuscripts as well deserve analysis; determining an instance of a theological "difference" between source and target texts). This paper attempts to demonstrate how New Testament authors quoted a diverse range of material contextually, thereby encouraging LXX scholarship to develop theologies that take all extant evidence into account. By distinguishing between theological *changes* and *choices*, this paper builds on the first argument and shows how indiscreet definitions of "differences" already tend toward analyses that assess the text as *received* rather than *produced*.

Some Septuagint scholars are suggesting that, with due precautions, acting on a methodologically sound way of establishing "a theology of the Septuagint" is desirable. If by "the Septuagint" one means reconstructed Old Greek (OG) texts such as those represented by the Göttingen efforts; and by "a theology" one means not theology but theologies of individual OG texts; and by "theology" one means only ascertainable differences between Semitic sources and Greek derivatives—if all *that* is meant by "a theology of the Septuagint," some agreement exists that the task should be undertaken.

Two scholars in particular, Martin Rösel and Johann Cook, have repeatedly contended for sound means of formulating theologies.[1]

I thank Johann Cook and Martin Rösel for inviting me to present the original form of this paper in Stellenbosch, especially Prof. Cook for taking a chance with a "young" scholar. Cook, Rösel, an anonymous reviewer, Rob Hiebert, and my wife all made valuable suggestions for revisions. The errors that remain (along with those that do not) are solely my responsibility. Thanks are also due to my recent professors at

Both agreed initially on the need to (1) address septuagintal[2] material as a diversity, perceived diachronically; (2) regard the texts as translational materials, always analyzed in conjunction with their (extant or reconstructed) Hebrew *Vorlagen*; and (3) focus solely on perceived differences between the theologies of the Greek and Hebrew texts. On two additional issues they have differed: (4) Rösel would articulate the theologies topically, whereas Cook prefers to derive theologies by pericope (e.g., chapter by chapter, book by book, and then compare). Furthermore, (5) Cook thinks scholars should address just the OG, yet Rösel wishes to incorporate revisional and non-OG materials. More recently, Rösel has clarified that by incorporating revisional materials, he intends to articulate theologies of septuagintal materials based not just on their topic but time period, which *de facto* includes whatever manuscripts are extant.[3] In addition, Cook has emphasized a need to use exegetical commentaries on the LXX.[4] Both have refined, clarified, and developed their preferred methodologies, yet neither has retreated on original tenets—at least in their print publications until now. Concerning the disagreement between Cook and Rösel over focusing on OG manuscripts alone versus OG manuscripts and non-OG manuscripts and as well as the issue of what constitutes a "difference," I would like to consider how insights from studying the "Old in the New" should influence how we formulate theologies of septuagintal materials.[5]

Westminster Theological Seminary, Philadelphia, for teaching me to think critically but reverently. All feedback is welcome at kyle.young@pbti.org.

1. Cf. Rösel 2006; Cook 2010.

2. Given the thorny nature of nomenclature surrounding *the Septuagint* and how the term potentially designates the OG Pentateuch, versus OG translations of the Hebrew Bible, versus Greek compositions, versus revisions used in early codices, etc., I prefer to use the adjective *septuagintal* when possible to refer to all or some of these senses. By doing so, I hope to avoid accusations of misunderstanding the difference between *Septuagint* in its original sense and subsequent applications.

3. Rösel 2018, 283–84.

4. Cook 2017a, 22; Cook 2017b, 277–79. Rösel agrees that exegetical commentaries are an important resource and should be utilized where they have been written; see his paper in this volume.

5. A few sources I was unable to consult include Ausloos 2017; Aejmelaeus 2006; and Joosten 2000.

1. The Present Debate

To understand the crux of the conflict, one might question what those interested in formulating theologies of the LXX are trying to achieve. Cook has noted that, for better or worse, scholars are articulating theologies.[6] Thus, he desires to see sound principles established. Moreover, many more resources are available now than in prior years, such that, in fear and trembling, theologizing is the next step.[7] But that still does not address *why* or *for whom* one would develop theologies. Whom would the scholarship serve? Stated otherwise, who is the intended audience? Rösel has contended that such efforts would aid those studying the historical development of religion, or *Religionsgeschichte*, but he also believes scholars from other fields would find valuable resources in the production of theologies.[8] Other reasons for articulating theologies of the LXX have been articulated by McLay: septuagintal theologies have implications for "the Old in the New," and thereby for Christian theology.[9] His interests in these matters are undoubtedly in mind when he argues for theologizing based on texts in their entireties rather than the differences between Greek translations and their Hebrew *Vorlagen*,[10] but that "would be a different project" from what Rösel is designing.[11] When such disagreements exist over the explicit goals and audience, one should not be surprised to find disharmony over methodology.

2. Considerations from a New Testament Perspective

2.1. Septuagint and New Testament Studies

The "Old in the New" has relevant insights that can influence the goals of theologizing septuagintal materials and potentially even the audience for whom theologizing would occur. Septuagint studies and New Testament

---

6. Cook 2017b, 265–67, 279.
7. Cook 2017a, 1–2.
8. Rösel 2018, 284–85; 2006, 251.
9. See McLay 2010, 616–20; 2003. McLay's contentions warrant attention. We argue for similar goals, though we make distinct arguments.
10. McLay 2010, 608, 616–20.
11. Rösel 2018, 283. The most up-to-date version of this project is described in his chapter in this volume.

studies, far from being in competition, are complementary. Scholars have placed increasing weight upon appreciating the relevancy of the New Testament for textual criticism of septuagintal materials, as voiced by De Vries and Karrer, Kreuzer, Jobes, and Wilk.[12] Tov has pointed out that the New Testament helps lexicographers understand the diachronic development of words found in the septuagintal corpus, insofar as some lexemes shift semantically after the Greek translations.[13] On the other hand, many such as Steyn and Cox are warning that New Testament scholars need to exercise more caution against indiscriminately asserting some biblical author quotes *the* LXX,[14] a problem that multiple publications have tried to rectify.[15] Reciprocal profit arises from interdisciplinary study.

How LXX and New Testament studies can benefit each other concerning the topic at hand might seem opaque. Oftentimes discussions on the theology of the Septuagint focus on how septuagintal materials theologically influence the New Testament.[16] Law claims the theology of the LXX and MT are overarchingly dissimilar.[17] Given how prevalently New Testament authors quote or reference septuagintal materials, Law proceeds to say that New Testament theology is different from how it would appear if the New Testament writers had interacted with the MT more directly. Therefore, New Testament scholars need to attend more carefully to septuagintal resources. Ten years before Law, McLay asserted that "it would seem reasonable to assume, based on his use of the Jewish Scriptures in Greek, that Paul (and all the other NT writers) was influenced in his theological thinking because of reading the Scriptures in Greek."[18] McLay also mentioned how septuagintal vocabulary and quotations influenced the New Testament. Stating the matter imperatively, Rösel urges that "Christian biblical theology should no longer be performed without taking the LXX into account."[19] These contentions are appreciable but somewhat perplexing. Septuagint scholars still drastically disagree over how to

---

12. De Vries and Karrer 2013; Kreuzer 2015; Jobes 2006; Wilk 2006.
13. Tov 1999b, 93–94.
14. Cf., e.g., Steyn 2008; Cox 2014.
15. Cf., e.g., Jobes and Silva 2015; Beale 2012; McLay 2003.
16. A note Tov makes in 1999a, 258.
17. Law 2013, 167–71. Law claims Anneli Aejmelaeus and Ross Wagner think the MT and LXX materials are largely the same theologically, whereas Law enlists Martin Rösel among supporters of his position.
18. McLay 2003, 145; see also 2003, 16, 30, 144.
19. Rösel 2018, 284–85.

understand septuagintal theology, let alone how to understand its effect (versus the effect of its *Vorlagen*) on the New Testament. As agreeing upon adequate methodology for formulating theologies of the Septuagint is still a *desideratum*, asking how the Old in the New impacts articulating a theology the Septuagint seems more appropriate.

2.2. Old [Greek] in the New

In response to Rösel's claim about the widespread profitability of a project that focuses on differences alone, resources documenting and outlining only theological *differences* would possess miniscule profit from the perspective of New Testament studies.[20] Incorporating all manuscripts (i.e., OG plus others) from a given era is important, which Rösel proposes and Cook argues against. Nevertheless, for a project to be of more use to New Testament scholarship, the venture would need to investigate (1) all available manuscripts that can be traced prior to or are contemporaneous with the development of the New Testament and (2) theologies of entire texts when the translated texts are viewed independently from their source texts.

2.2.1. Manuscripts in the New Testament

The apostles quoted a wide range of manuscripts.[21] Silva writes that, out of an estimated twenty-four quotations in the Pauline corpus from the Psalter, twenty-two are easily attributable to the OG and another two plausibly so.[22] Sometimes significant disagreements exist between the MT and OG, but most often not. As for Pauline quotations that match the OG greatly but not entirely, examples include a verbal modification from second- to third-person between Ps 62 (61):13 in Rom 2:6 and Ps 8:7 in 1 Cor 15:27. One instance of a stark difference between the OG and Paul is with ἔλαβες in Ps 68 (67):19 and ἔδωκεν in Eph 4:8, which Silva sees as coming from an alternative Christian reading or Aramaic tradition of the text, but not a

---

20. See Rösel's paper in this volume; 2018, 284–85; 2006, 251.

21. By *apostles*, I do not mean to suggest that every New Testament book was written by an apostle, as church history indicates otherwise. *Apostles* is a convenient shorthand that I use here synecdochally, using the designation that applies to some of the New Testament authors for all of them.

22. Silva 2001, 287–88.

text besides the OG.[23] When one examines the Psalter in Paul, even with alternations, nearly everything seems to come from the OG. Concerning Matthew, van der Kooij illustrates another side of apostolic quotations.[24] Van der Kooij would argue that when Matthew quotes from Isaiah, five of the quotations agree with the OG, and three do not.[25] In his examination of one difference, that of Isa 42:1–4 in Matt 12:18–21, van der Kooij asserts that Matthew "worked with two texts, LXX and Theodotion/*kaige*-recension."[26] Finally, Steyn's work on Hebrews deserves consideration.[27] Steyn has remarked many times about the frequent correlation between Hebrews (or *Ad Hebraeos*) and the Dead Sea Scrolls over and against the proto-MT and septuagintal manuscripts. Thus, by surveying Silva, van der Kooij, and Steyn, one sees textual plurality as the resultant picture within New Testament quotations.

2.2.2. Contextual Interpretation

A growing number of scholars contend the apostles had a thorough awareness of the contexts from which they quoted. Arguing along these lines are Jobes, Beale, Carson, Law, and Wilk, to name a few.[28] Law gives one minor example of how the apostles quoted contextually in Rom 15:7–14.[29]

---

23. For what follows, see Silva 2001, 280–84.

24. Van der Kooij 2013.

25. Cf. van der Kooij 2013, 201. Van der Kooij says that Isa 8:23b–9:1 in Matt 4:15–16; Isa 53:4 in Matt 8:17; and Isa 42:1–4 in Matt 12:18–21 do not agree with OG Isaiah, whereas the following do: Isa 7:14 in Matt 1:23; Isa 40:3 in Matt 3:3; Isa 6:9–10 in Matt 13:13–15; Isa 29:13 in Matt 15:8–9; and Isa 56:7 in Matt 21:13.

26. Van der Kooij 2013, 216.

27. Steyn 2016, 2011. Here I might note a personal conversation with Steyn on 18 August 2018 about determining sources in quotations. Steyn encourages "keeping the conversation open" concerning citations that have no obvious *Vorlage* among extant manuscripts: texts could have been modified for rhetorical or whatever other purposes ([+extant, +modified]), or quotes could come from a nonextant *Vorlage* that we do not (otherwise) possess ([-extant, -modified]). I would further distinguish the possibilities to include other conceivable complexity: quotes could represent modifications of translations we do not possess ([-extant, +modified]). When quotes do not match an existing *Vorlage* ([+extant, -modified]), probable cases must be made from these three possibilities.

28. Law 2013, 91–94; Beale 2012; Beale and Carson 2007, xxiii–xxviii; Jobes 2006, 323–33; Wilk 2006, 263.

29. Law 2013, 91–93. Also, by "contextually," I mean minimally that the apostles

Although one might construe Paul's conglomerate quotation of four different passages in these eight verses as quoting from a *testimonia*, the surrounding discourse in Romans suggests otherwise. In particular, though the reference to Ps 117 (116):1 comes in Rom 15:11, Ps 117 (116):2 seems to infiltrate Rom 15:8–9: both allude to ἀληθείας θεοῦ (or ἡ ἀλήθεια τοῦ κυρίου in Ps 117 [116]:2) and ἐλέους (or τό ἔλεος αὐτοῦ in Ps 117 [116]:2), which are verbal parallels outside the direct quotations.

On the flip side, scholars can overstate the extent to which septuagintal materials influenced the apostles. McLay tries to demonstrate how "theological reflection" on OG Jonah heavily influenced Matthew.[30] In ten pages, by looking at OG Jonah in conjunction with Matthew, McLay purportedly finds evidence of the "descent into Hades" and solves the *crux interpretum* of the resurrected saints in Matt 27:51b–53. Consider the following chart:[31]

	BHS	OG	NA[28] (italics original)
Jonah 2:1b // Matt 12:40a	וַיְהִי יוֹנָה בִּמְעֵי הַדָּג שְׁלֹשָׁה יָמִים וּשְׁלֹשָׁה לֵילוֹת:	καὶ ἦν Ιωνας ἐν τῇ κοιλίᾳ τοῦ κήτους τρεῖς ἡμέρας καὶ τρεῖς νύκτας.	ὥσπερ γὰρ ἦν Ἰωνᾶς ἐν τῇ κοιλίᾳ τοῦ κήτους τρεῖς ἡμέρας καὶ τρεῖς νύκτας,
Jonah 2:2	מִמְּעֵי הַדָּגָה	ἐκ τῆς κοιλίας τοῦ κήτους	
Jonah 2:3	מִבֶּטֶן שְׁאוֹל	ἐκ κοιλίας ᾅδου	
Jonah 2:4 Jonah 2:7 // Matt 12:40b	מְצוּלָה בִּלְבַב יַמִּים ... יָרַדְתִּי הָאָרֶץ בְּרִחֶיהָ בַעֲדִי לְעוֹלָם	εἰς βάθη καρδίας θαλάσσης ... κατέβην εἰς γῆν, ἧς οἱ μοχλοὶ αὐτῆς κάτοχοι αἰώνιοι	... ἐν τῇ καρδίᾳ τῆς γῆς τρεῖς ἡμέρας καὶ τρεῖς νύκτας.

A glance at the first row from OG Jonah 2:1b and Matt 12:40a confirms the verbatim quotation. In the final row, that καρδίᾳ τῆς γῆς in Matt 12:40b alludes to words from OG Jonah 2:4 and 7 is certainly conceivable as well (see καρδίας in Jonah 2:4 and γῆν in 2:7). For the middle two rows, the Greek κοιλία replacing both בֶּטֶן, "internal organs" and מֵעֶה, "womb" offers

---

knew and exhibited evidence of knowing the surrounding contexts and discourses of pericopes from which they quoted.

30. McLay 2003, 159–69.
31. The OG is taken from Ziegler 1984.

no significant divergence from the Hebrew, though two nouns indeed collapse into one.³² McLay insists the Greek translations affect Matthew theologically, but without ever establishing any substantial differences (especially "theological") between the MT and OG! Presuming the MT is the *Vorlage*, as McLay does, a near one-to-one parallel exists between the MT and OG in word order and lexical correspondence, notwithstanding the morphosyntactic constraints of the receptor language. McLay offers profitable insights in his discussion. But as he hardly mentions how the Greek and Hebrew texts differ, and his purpose in the example is to trace theological influence from the context of the OG, he does not justify the dazzling dividends. Why could someone not have reached the same conclusions as McLay while reading Matthew and the MT apart from the OG, however unadvisable that might be? Regardless, McLay does establish that Matthew interacted with much of the context from Jonah. As McLay has also said, "the texts *as complete texts* were the scriptural sources that became a source for theological reflection …"³³ Examples from other scholars could be given to show how aware the apostles were of the contexts from which they quoted,³⁴ but these examples, both positive and negative, are sufficient for our purposes.

2.2.3. Diverse Manuscripts Plus Texts as Received

The apostles used multiple manuscripts besides the OG and interacted with whole texts, which are significant facts. To the extent that the apostles quoted a diverse range of septuagintal materials, ranging from the OG to revisions that are and are not extant elsewhere, those wishing to trace the theological influence of septuagintal materials in the New Testament would need to examine all manuscript evidence available. Moreover, to the extent that the apostles were familiar with the contexts of their scriptural sources, articulating theological differences alone will not suffice. The apostles would not have quoted differences *as* differences. They would

---

32. LSJ lists both senses found in the Hebrew words under the entry for κοιλία. More specifically, *HALOT* (609–10) gives the entry euphemistically for מֵעֶה with the use in Jonah as "that part of the **body** through which people come into existence" (emphasis original).

33. McLay 2010, 619. I would change this to say that they became *the* source for theological reflection.

34. Cf. above n. 28.

simply have quoted whatever differences happened to be present in the contexts from which they quoted. If anything, focusing on differences alone will perpetuate unproven biases that septuagintal and Masoretic texts are overarchingly dissimilar theologically. LXX scholars would do well to remember these realities when deciding whether (1) to theologize just the "differences" as attributed to the perspective of translators versus the texts as received and (2) to include just OG versus OG and non-OG manuscripts as the loci of efforts for theologizing.

3. Our Differences

3.1. Perspectives on the Nature of the LXX

At this point, I have mentioned how LXX and New Testament studies are mutually beneficial. I have also discovered what kinds of resources would assist efforts to address how theologies of the LXX have influenced New Testament theology, especially efforts addressing the claim that the New Testament differs from how it would have looked had the apostles quoted from the proto-MT text group directly. But these are not goals shared by scholars more broadly in the LXX community; problems largely independent of New Testament studies still need resolution. Returning now to a discussion of unresolved methodological issues within LXX studies on "best practices" for formulating theologies, the discrepancies between Rösel and Cook need to be placed within their broader contexts. A large part of the issue pertains to how the OG itself is to be understood. Referencing Pietersma's interlinear paradigm with the distinction between the *text as produced* versus *the text as received*, which is parallel to Marguerite Harl's *amont* ("upstream") versus *aval* ("downstream") division, Kraus outlines how NETS heavily emphasizes the *text as produced* or *amont* angle in translation, whereas *La Bible d'Alexandrie* (BdA) emphasizes the *text as received* or *aval* approach in translation.[35] On the other hand, *Septuaginta Deutsch* (LXX.D) approaches "the text in its present outlook," which essentially recognizes that the Greek translators were trying to do more than provide Greek speakers a hued inlet into the Hebrew parent text.[36] Rather, the translators were providing a translation that would

---

35. Kraus 2006, 67–70.
36. Kraus 2006, 70.

"mediate between the tradition and the contemporary situation" as they produced a text that was dependent in its origins but sufficient as a stand-alone document.[37]

With these perspectives on the nature of the OG in mind, the differences between Rösel and Cook are likely not coincidental. Cook, who was a translator for NETS, explicitly adheres to the interlinear paradigm, since in his perspective "it indicates a *linguistic* relationship between two texts."[38] Thus he focuses only on the OG when formulating theologies and approaches the text as it was produced. Comparatively, Rösel, who was involved in the LXX.D project, desires to develop theologies from "a production-oriented perspective."[39] This has significant overlap with what Cook proposes. Rösel is interested in what he terms the *genitivus subjectivus*, meaning "the implicit theology that emerges from the intentional decisions of the translators," rather than the *genitivus objectivus*, which he defines as "the theological systematization resulting from the translated texts."[40] Nevertheless, Rösel goes on to say that *genitivus objectivus* may be found in some septuagintal corpora, such as the Wisdom of Solomon, where theology is presented in "the form of doctrinal exposition or apology."[41] Scholars should distinguish between the two (*genitivus subjectivus* and *objectivus*) but recognize that instances of both may be found in the corpora. Rösel would also like to use reception history to inform how texts as produced are understood, since Greek-speaking recipients might have insights into the language that better reveal the translators' intent.[42] This requires a greater sensitivity to the texts as received. Rösel also wishes to include whatever revisional materials are extant in a given era, which, to borrow from the philosophy of LXX.D, reflects "the texts in their present outlooks." Cook and Rösel attempt to develop theologies of septuagintal materials under the influence of their work in modern-day translation projects. The impasse is linked to ideas that have been operable in both scholars' methodologies for years. Neither have principally changed their positions concerning a need to proceed (or not) beyond the OG. These are

---

37. Kraus 2006, 78; see also 83.
38. Cook 2017a, 9.
39. Rösel 2018, 283.
40. Rösel 2018, 279.
41. Rösel 2018, 279.
42. Personal conversation with Rösel on 18 August 2018. Of course, this hearkens to similarities with BdA.

differences for which compromise is necessary if more cohesive collaboration is to ensue.

On the issue of using just the OG versus all manuscripts in an era, Rösel's suggestion is preferable. The interlinear paradigm, which tethers Cook's agenda to the (hypothetically reconstructed) OG, cannot be construed solely as a heuristic device for detecting "differences."[43] The reason why is because the intended scope of the paradigm is to define definitively what "the Septuagint" was in terms of its original purpose and function, to the exclusion of other accounts. As Cameron Boyd-Taylor explains,

> On the assumption of interlinearity, the Septuagint *qua* translation would have originally lacked the status of an independent text within the target culture. Rather it would have formed the Greek half of a virtual Greek-Hebrew diglot ... *if taken seriously* the assumption of interlinearity would prove *more than just a heuristic* for conceptualizing the role of the Hebrew text in translating the Septuagint.[44]

The interlinear paradigm makes ontological claims about "the Septuagint," for example, that the original purpose of the translations was to be (metaphorically or otherwise) a lens through which to perceive the Hebrew or Aramaic source. In other words, the Septuagint was not meant to be independent from the sources. The way in which the purpose of the interlinear paradigm has routinely confused scholars calls into question whether the theory is too elaborate to be helpful. Regardless, as far as Boyd-Taylor is concerned, the paradigm applies beyond the OG even to the καίγε-group and Aquila texts.[45] What this entails is that insofar as the interlinear paradigm is a valid theory, the paradigm is descriptive of non-OG manuscripts. Therefore, nothing inherent within the theory necessitates avoiding non-OG manuscripts in theologizing septuagintal materials.[46]

In addition to the fact that the interlinear paradigm does not intrinsically preclude examining non-OG manuscripts, the paradigm still should not be the arbiter for understanding theologies of septuagintal materials. Three points support this claim. (1) A primary reason why Pietersma

---

43. Pietersma 2017, 2002. Cf. also Boyd-Taylor 2006. For the most elaborative exposition of the interlinear paradigm, see Boyd-Taylor 2011.
44. Boyd-Taylor 2011, 5–6. Emphasis added.
45. Boyd-Taylor 2011, 175–266; see also 316–17.
46. That is, provided one does not presuppose that, by definition, anything other than the OG is not properly *the* Septuagint.

originally designed the paradigm was to account for why scholars access the source texts to understand the translations: "it is only the interlinear paradigm with its articulated vertical dimension that can legitimize what Septuagint scholars in fact routinely do, namely, have recourse to the parent text in order to account for the translated text."[47] Therefore, the paradigm is not necessary for LXX scholars to have recourse to the source, and scholars already do this "routinely." Pietersma constructed the paradigm to legitimize the practice. But as was the case before the paradigm existed, so afterwards those who reject the paradigm may (and do) access the source text to account for the translations. (2) Insofar as the translators occasionally did not understand Hebrew well, a point Pietersma helpfully makes, the "unusual use of the receptor language" is explained by poor comprehension of Hebrew.[48] The theory, which should simplify thorny issues, is superfluous for justifying "sub-par" Greek when such is present. No one should anticipate a clear translation wherever the translators did not comprehend what they translated. (3) Despite "unusual use of the receptor language" at times, early readers made sense of the texts, as is apparent in how the apostles (and many others) utilized the OG and other revisions. To use Pietersma's tongue-in-cheek caricature, according to the apostles, "the Greek isn't all that bad!"[49] Just because translators translated poorly (by some standards)[50] does not mean that the translators used incomprehensible language, even if someone claims early interpreters misunderstood the translators. To say that the interpreters failed to understand the translations because they did not understand the *translational* intent assumes a priority for the translators' perspective that requires any meaning worth ascertaining to be filtered through the source text. Scholars thereby neglect artificially the meaning that the translation portrays when viewed independently of the source.[51]

---

47. Pietersma 2002, 355.

48. Pietersma 2002, 356–57.

49. Pietersma 2002, 357. Of course, the same would be true of all who used the septuagintal materials, not just the apostles. Aejmelaeus (2007a, 295–97) also makes the point that others understood the Greek translations, and so the Greek cannot be as impoverished as some would like to construe it.

50. Although I do not have the space here to address the issue, scholars need to dedicate much more attention to developing criteria for what qualifies as "bad" language use.

51. Thankfully, Bible translation protocols in the twenty-first century include comprehension checks, whereby native speakers of the language receiving translation

Developers and advocates of the interlinear paradigm have provided valuable conceptions by distinguishing between the text-as-produced and the text-as-received, among other ideas. But the interlinear paradigm itself is not necessary to appreciate the translational nature of the translations, nor should its agenda influence LXX scholars away from interacting with non-OG manuscripts or from theologizing texts by taking into account how early readers received and perceived them. If LXX scholars wish to elicit the theological distinctiveness of the translators or translations by focusing on perceived differences within OG or non-OG manuscripts, they may do so without subscribing to the ontological and theoretical claims about septuagintal materials that the interlinear paradigm promotes.

3.2. Differences about "Differences"

In addition to disagreements about the scope of the texts that scholars should assess while formulating theologies, another controversy concerns what constitutes a difference.[52] Besides McLay, all in favor of writing a theology of the Septuagint conclude that theologizing should focus only on differences between the translations and underlying forms.[53] Even those not necessarily enthralled with writing theologies per se are concerned about the differences.[54] Douglas insists we focus on the differences, without exerting much effort in defining *differences*.[55] But agreement over what constitutes a theological disagreement has not been attained. A primary problem pertains to attributing theologically motivated exegesis to so-called stereotyped equivalents. Tov and Boyd-Taylor claim that

---

are asked about what they understand the meaning of the text to be before publication ever ensues. That way, translators minimize undesired discontinuities between what the translators intend and what the audience interprets.

52. Another controversial matter concerns who has the burden of proof in establishing the *Vorlagen* of translated texts, as there can only be theological differences if there are, well, *differences*. The majority of scholars seem to insist that the onus of responsibility resides with the theologians. Whereas Douglas and Tov would say the theologian must bear burden of proof for establishing the correct *Vorlagen*, Rösel argues contrarily; Douglas 2012, 112–16; Tov's chapter in this volume; Rösel 2018, 281. On the need to establish *Vorlagen*, see also Tov 1999a, 259; and Aejmelaeus 2007a, 296, 310.

53. Cf. Cook 2010, 622, 632; Rösel 2018, 283.

54. Cf. Tov 1999a, 257–69; Douglas 2012, 105–6.

55. Douglas 2012, 105–6.

the precedent of earlier translators (e.g., in the Pentateuch) leaves those following in their footsteps with default or "stereotyped" renderings that would not have been theologically motivated.[56] On the other hand, Rösel says stereotyped equivalents may represent the theological motivation of a translator.[57] Cautioning against Tov and others who implement the stereotyped distinction without utmost attention to "literal" versus "periphrastic translations," Olofsson notes, "the more the translator takes the meaning of the Hebrew and the demands of the target language into account, the more misleading becomes statistics that is built on the rendering of single words."[58] In other words, if a translator was sensitive to multiple senses of Hebrew words when making translational choices, then observations about how often word X is translated as word Y need to be equally sensitive to the contexts wherein X was translated as Y. Aejmelaeus similarly warns against using statistics without checking what sense of polysemous words is intended in both source and target languages.[59] Some say stereotypes are not theologically motivated, others say they may be, while others warn against misleading use of "stereotypes" altogether. The problem of stereotypes is open for further reflection and debate.

One issue that can muddle discussions about stereotyped equivalents in particular and differences in general is the influence of theological presuppositions on differences between source and target texts. For clarity's sake, one must categorically distinguish between (1) theological *presuppositions* that are always operable in choosing adequate phrases and senses of lexemes for translation and (2) theological *changes* between the source and target texts that may or may not result from theological *choices*.[60] If

---

56. Tov 1999a, 260–64; Boyd-Taylor 2006, 29–31. Boyd-Taylor is following Tov's precedent.

57. Rösel 2018, 282 n. 46.

58. Olofsson 2009, 59; see also 50–66. Although at first (and even second) glance Olofsson seems to have a grammatical error here, he appears to be using *statistics* as a singular word for the discipline (e.g., *Linguistics is fun!*).

59. Aejmelaeus 2007b, 213–17.

60. I thank Jessie Rogers for our lengthy discussion on this topic that helped me (and hopefully her) clarify the issue at stake; personal communication, 17 August 2018. My distinction between *choice* and change has resonance with Emanuel Tov when he says, "theological exegesis … may be expressed through theologically motivated choices of translation equivalents, in changes in words and verses (either large or small) or in expansions or omissions of ideas considered offensive" (Tov 2012, 120). I use the distinction between *choice* and *change* more discriminately than he does.

(1) translating the Hebrew Bible (proto-MT or otherwise) ubiquitously requires theological presuppositions to function due to the text's inherent (theological) nature and the theological decisions that translators encounter, and (2) "theological differences" are defined as instances in which translators make translational decisions by applying theological reasoning, then (3) articulating theologies based on "theological differences" becomes futile. Furthermore, without distinguishing between constant interaction of theological presuppositions and theologically motivated *choices* that result in theological *changes*, one might as well articulate theological agreements too because those resulted from theologically motivated choices, even when changes did not occur. By this distinction, every instance of a theological *choice* would necessarily entail a theological *change*, but not every theological *change* would be a theological *choice* (i.e., some choice the translator consciously made to change the text).

To discuss the tension between theological choices versus changes, an example from Ausloos is helpful.[61] Ausloos mentions the translator(s) for OG Genesis could have theoretically misconstrued the meaning of Gen 1:2. Looking at the MT (and presuming the proto-MT is the *Vorlage* of OG Genesis for the sake of the argument), *BHS* states, ורוח אלהים מרחפת על פני המים, or "the Spirit of God was hovering over the face of the water." OG Genesis presents a translation along these lines: καὶ πνεῦμα θεοῦ ἐπεφέρετο ἐπάνω τοῦ ὕδατος.[62] However, as Ausloos notes, *IBHS* §14.5.b lists a use of אלהים deemed the *absolute superlative*, whereby divine names in a construct chain connote a superlative meaning. Ausloos therefore poses the question: what if the Hebrew author meant אלהים as an absolute superlative, such that רוח אלהים had the meaning of "a mighty wind"? In this case, the translator of OG Genesis (and translations taking their cue from the Greek) produced a hugely divergent translation. By all accounts, such a translation would have introduced a theological *change*. The question, then, is whether the translator would have intentionally *chosen* to render the text with a meaning besides what he suspected was intended. For someone to claim a theological choice has occurred, one must assume (1) the original meaning of the text is known to the biblical scholar who is trying to assess theological differences; (2) the translator(s) in question knew alternative

---

61. Hans Ausloos shared this example with me in a conversation during the congress in Stellenbosch (17–19 August 2018). Thereafter he shared the example with all attendees at the final roundtable discussion.

62. Wevers 1974.

senses (e.g., "Spirit of God" versus "a mighty wind"); (3) the translator(s) disfavored what he supposed to be the more likely sense; and (4) the translator felt free (or obligated) to choose the less likely sense because of theological bias. Translators might have foregone a theoretically viable translation because of their theological presuppositions (among other relevant matters like obligatory receptor language grammar and surrounding discourse), but unless the translators attempted to suppress what they supposed to be the intention of their source texts, no foundation exists upon which to posit a theological *choice*. To discover such suppression, factors related to translation technique, source texts, scribal tendencies, and evidence from other extant manuscripts become vital.

Apart from the question of stereotyped equivalents, another outstanding issue concerns the value of writing about theological changes that were unintentional (i.e., that were not theological choices). Theological changes due to semantic shifts might result from (at least) three causes: intentional choices attributable to the translator alone; intentional choices due to communally-held beliefs; or unintentional changes, such as when a translator used a stereotyped translation for a word that did not adequately convey the underlying sense, or a translator misunderstood the Hebrew.[63] If the focus of a project is on theological "differences," theologizing should only encompass theological choices or at least categorically distinguish between theological choices and changes. The question then becomes how intentional theological changes can be sorted from unintentional changes. In Rösel's estimation, the more one sees a pattern repeat, the likelihood increases that some intentional change is involved, though Tov believes intuition is the ultimate factor for ascribing theological motivation after one has assessed the translation technique of the translator in question, *Vorlagen*, precedent among other translators, and so on.[64] Certainly, no one would want to ascribe an intentional theological change unless translation techniques within individual books had already

---

63. Both Tov (1999a, 259) and Rösel (2018, 281–82) stress the need to understand changes due to influence from communities. However legitimate the distinction between individual versus communal choices might be, the distinction between intentional choices and unintentional changes is more important.

64. Martin Rösel, personal communication in an email on 11 November 2018; Tov in this volume. My thanks to Rösel for his suggestion that I clarify how to identify an intentional change and give an example of a theological choice that resulted in change.

been established.⁶⁵ Nevertheless, considering the criteria that are prerequisite before claiming a theological *choice* has occurred,⁶⁶ one would need to establish that a translator was aware of words' multiple meanings and chose to translate unlikely senses anyway. A translator's awareness of multiple meanings could be demonstrated by showing how words, phrases, or clauses had been translated differently by earlier translators. If a single translator translated elements from the source text with various words in the same book, one would also have evidence of awareness. Thus, rigid repetition of a pattern might not denote a theological choice unless one can claim the translator knew the source text could have – and likely should have – been translated another way. Even if alternative criteria can be offered for establishing how to identify theological choices, only intentional choices would reflect distinct theological beliefs that might have been present in the translators and/or their communities. To theologize about theological changes that were not intentional would be a discussion of *reception*, which, again, "would be a different project."

4. Conclusion

Insofar as New Testament authors quoted diverse manuscripts contextually, theologies based on septuagintal texts in their entireties would be necessary for tracing theological influence between septuagintal materials and the New Testament: entire texts of OG plus non-OG manuscripts. Theologies of whole texts would be important for areas of study such as Hellenistic Judaism and the early church as well.⁶⁷ Within LXX scholarship, no reason exists why the interlinear paradigm should inhibit scholars from theologizing based on non-OG manuscripts. Moreover, to the degree that *intentional theological changes* are not in view, the project

---

65. By *translation technique*, I have something in mind along the lines of Anneli Ajemaelus: though suited to the task, "'translation technique' should not be thought of as a system acquired or developed or resorted to by the translators." Indeed, we should keep in mind that all and "every kind of Septuagintal studies" is influenced by the reality of "(1) the text of the translation, (2) the text of the *Vorlage*, and (3) translation technique" (Aejmelaeus 2007b, 206).

66. See the discussion above concerning Gen 1:2.

67. See contributions in this volume on Philo and Josephus by Phlip Bosman and on the early church by Ulrich Volp for examples of projects that would profit from a resource that articulated theologies of septuagintal materials in their contexts—agreements and disagreements alike.

to theologize would already be moving in the direction of understanding the text as received, as it would not reflect theological changes in the beliefs of translators but only their misunderstandings of source texts. Contrary to its aspirations, the proposed project[68] would serve a small portion of scholarship, mainly those interested in the history of religions as perceived in the theological perspectives of translators and their communities. Either as an addendum to the current project, if such is possible, or as a separate enterprise, articulating whole theologies of septuagintal corpora would be a profitable project, even if different.

Bibliography

Aejmelaeus, Anneli. 2006. "Von Sprache zur Theologie: Methodologische Überlegungen zur Theologie der Septuaginta." Pages 21–48 in *The Septuagint and Messianism*. Edited by Michael A. Knibb. BETL 195. Leuven: Peeters.

———. 2007a. "Levels of Interpretation: Tracing the Trail of the Septuagint Translators." Pages 295–312 in *On the Trail of the Septuagint Translators: Collected Essays*. Edited by Anneli Aejmelaeus. CBET 50. Leuven: Peeters.

———. 2007b. "What We Talk about When We Talk about Translation Technique." Pages 205–22 in *On the Trail of the Septuagint Translators: Collected Essays*. Edited by Anneli Aejmelaeus. CBET 50. Leuven: Peeters.

Ausloos, Hans. 2017. "Sept défis posés à une théologie de la Septante." Pages 228–50 in *Congress Volume: Stellenbosch, 2016*. Edited by Louis C. Jonker, Gideon R. Kotzé, and Christl M. Maier. VTSup 177. Leiden: Brill.

Beale, Greg K. 2012. *Handbook on the New Testament Use of the Old Testament: Exegesis and Interpretation*. Grand Rapids: Baker Academic.

Beale, Greg K., and D. A. Carson, eds. 2007. *Commentary on the New Testament Use of the Old Testament*. Grand Rapids: Baker Academic.

Boyd-Taylor, Cameron. 2006. "In a Mirror, Dimly—Reading the Septuagint as a Document of Its Times." Pages 15–32 in *Septuagint Research: Issues and Challenges in the Study of the Greek Jewish Scriptures*. Edited

---

68. Cf. Rösel in this volume.

by Wolfgang Kraus and R. Glenn Wooden. SCS 53. Atlanta: Society of Biblical Literature.

———. 2011. *Reading between the Lines: The Interlinear Paradigm for Septuagint Studies.* BTS 8. Leuven: Peeters.

Cook, Johann. 2010. "Towards the Formulation of a Theology of the Septuagint." Pages 621–40 in *Congress Volume: Ljubljana, 2007.* Edited by André Lemaire. VTSup 133. Leiden: Brill.

———. 2017a. "Interpreting the Septuagint." Pages 1–22 in *Congress Volume: Stellenbosch, 2016.* Edited by Louis C. Jonker, Gideon R. Kotzé, and Christl M. Maier. VTSup 177. Leiden: Brill.

———. 2017b. "A Theology of the Septuagint?" *OTE* 30:265–82.

Cox, Claude E. 2014. "Some Things Biblical Scholars Should Know about the Septuagint." *ResQ* 56.2:85–98.

De Vries, Johannes, and Martin Karrer. 2013. "Early Christian Quotations and the Textual History of the Septuagint: A Summary of the Wuppertal Research Project and Introduction to the Volume." Pages 3–20 in *Textual History and the Reception of Scripture in Early Christianity.* Edited by Johannes de Vries and Martin Karrer. SCS 60. Atlanta: Society of Biblical Literature.

Douglas, Alex. 2012. "Limitations to Writing a Theology of the Septuagint." *JSCS* 45:104–17.

Jobes, Karen H. 2006. "Septuagint Textual Tradition in 1 Peter." Pages 311–44 in *Septuagint Research: Issues and Challenges in the Study of the Greek Jewish Scriptures.* Edited by Wolfgang Kraus and R. Glenn Wooden. SCS 53. Atlanta: Society of Biblical Literature.

Jobes, Karen H., and Moisés Silva. 2015. *Invitation to the Septuagint.* 2nd ed. Grand Rapids: Baker Academic.

Joosten, Jan. 2000. "Une théologie de la Septante? Réflecions méthologiques sur l'interprétation de la version greque." *RTP* 132:31–46.

Kooij, Arie van der. 2013. "The Septuagint, the Recension of Theodotion, and Beyond: Comments on the Quotation from Isaiah 42 in Matthew 12." Pages 201–18 in *Textual History and the Reception of Scripture in Early Christianity.* Edited by Johannes de Vries and Martin Karrer. SCS 60. Atlanta: Society of Biblical Literature.

Kraus, Wolfgang. 2006. "Contemporary Translations of the Septuagint: Problems and Perspectives." Pages 63–83 in *Septuagint Research: Issues and Challenges in the Study of the Greek Jewish Scriptures.* Edited by Wolfgang Kraus and R. Glenn Wooden. SCS 53. Atlanta: Society of Biblical Literature.

Kreuzer, Siegfried. 2015. "The Place and Text-Critical Value of the New Testament Quotations from Dodekapropheton in the Textual History of the Septuagint." Pages 233–52 in *The Bible in Greek: Translation, Transmission, and Theology of the Septuagint*. Edited by Siegfried Kreuzer. SCS 63. Atlanta: SBL Press.

Law, Timothy M. 2013. *When God Spoke Greek: The Septuagint and the Making of the Christian Bible*. New York: Oxford University Press.

McLay, R. Timothy. 2003. *The Use of the Septuagint in New Testament Research*. Grand Rapids: Eerdmans.

———. 2010. "Why Not a Theology of the Septuagint?" Pages 607–20 in *Die Septuaginta – Texte, Theologien, Einflüsse*. Edited by Wolfgang Kraus, Martin Karrer, and Martin Meiser. WUNT 252. Tübingen: Mohr Siebeck.

Olofsson, Staffan. 2009. *Translation Technique and Theological Exegesis: Collected Essays on the Septuagint Version*. ConBOT 57. Winona Lake, IN: Eisenbrauns.

Pietersma, Albert. 2002. "A New Paradigm for Addressing Old Questions: The Relevance of the Interlinear Model for the Study of the Septuagint." Pages 337–64 in *Bible and Computer: The Stellenbosch AIBI-6 Conference; Proceedings of the Association Internationale Bible et Informatique "From Alpha to Byte," University of Stellenbosch 17–21 July, 2000*. Edited by Johann Cook. Leiden: Brill.

———. 2017. "The Society of Biblical Literature Commentary on the Septuagint: Basic Principles." Pages 1–16 in *The SBL Commentary on the Septuagint: An Introduction*. Edited by Dirk Büchner. SCS 67. Atlanta: SBL Press.

Rösel, Martin. 2006. "Towards a 'Theology of the Septuagint.'" Pages 239–52 in *Septuagint Research: Issues and Challenges in the Study of the Greek Jewish Scriptures*. Edited by Wolfgang Kraus and R. Glenn Wooden. SCS 53. Atlanta: Society of Biblical Literature.

———. 2018. "A Theology of the Septuagint? Clarifications and Definitions." Pages 273–90 in *Tradition and Innovation: English and German Studies on the Septuagint*. Edited by Martin Rösel. SCS 70. Atlanta: SBL Press.

Silva, Moisés. 2001. "The Greek Psalter in Paul's Letters: A Textual Study." Pages 277–88 in *The Old Greek Psalter: Studies in Honour of Albert Pietersma*. Edited by Robert J. V. Hiebert, Claude E. Cox, and Peter J. Gentry. JSOTSup 332. Sheffield: Sheffield Academic.

Steyn, Gert J. 2008. "Which 'LXX' Are We Talking about in NT Scholarship? Two Examples from Hebrews." Pages 697–707 in *Die Septuaginta – Texte, Kontexte, Lebenswelten*. Edited by Martin Karrer, Wolfgang Kraus, and Martin Meiser. WUNT 219. Tübingen: Mohr Siebeck.

———. 2011. *A Quest for the Assumed LXX Vorlage of the Explicit Quotations in Hebrews*. FRLANT 235. Göttingen: Vandenhoeck & Ruprecht.

———. 2016. "The Importance of the Dead Sea Scrolls for the Study of the Explicit Quotations in Ad Hebraeos." *HTS Teologiese Studies/Theological Studies* 72.4:1–9.

Tov, Emanuel. 1999a. "Theologically Motivated Exegesis Embedded in the Septuagint." Pages 257–69 in *The Greek and Hebrew Bible: Collected Essays on the Septuagint*. Edited by Emanuel Tov. VTSup 72. Leiden: Brill.

———. 1999b. "Three Dimensions of Words in the Septuagint." Pages 85–94 in *The Greek and Hebrew Bible: Collected Essays on the Septuagint*. Edited by Emanuel Tov. VTSup 72. Leiden: Brill.

———. 2012. *Textual Criticism of the Hebrew Bible*. 3rd ed. Minneapolis: Fortress.

Wevers, John W. 1974. *Genesis*. Septuaginta Vetus Testamentum Graecum Auctoritate Academiae Scientiarum Gottingensis editum 1. Gottingen: Vandenhoeck & Ruprecht.

Wilk, Florian. 2006. "The Letters of Paul as Witnesses to and for the Septuagint Text." Pages 253–72 in *Septuagint Research: Issues and Challenges in the Study of the Greek Jewish Scriptures*. Edited by Wolfgang Kraus and R. Glenn Wooden. SCS 53. Atlanta: Society of Biblical Literature.

Part 2
Septuagint and Plato: Methodological Considerations and Models of Interpretation

Platons *Politeia* und die Theologie der LXX

Evangelia G. Dafni

ABSTRACT: The paper will discuss some basic problems and methodological steps concerning the encounter between Hebrews and Greeks in the classical period and its impact on the Hellenistic era. The relationship between the Old Testament Greek and ancient Greek literature and theology will be examined on the basis of the Pentateuch and Plato's *Politeia*. The following considerations and models of interpretation can arise from the analysis of Plato's *Politeia* compared to M- and LXX-Pentateuch: (1) Ancient Greek writers were familiar with Old Testament oral or written traditions through improvised translations. They prepared the way for the LXX and, in their compositions, were in dispute with them although they do not make specific references to the Hebrews and their literature. (2) Hebrew authors knew the works of ancient Greek authors and used Greek philosophical terminology, which they creatively adapted to Semitic models. (3) Both models are possible.

Platon ist, soweit uns bekannt ist, der erste, der das Wort „Theologie" verwendet.[1] Im mittelplatonischen Dialog *Politeia* (379a) wird nach den Arten angemessenen Redens der Dichter über Gott in einem idealen Rechtsstaat gefragt und drei Typen der Theologie festgelegt (τύποι περὶ θεολογίας): der epische, der lyrische und der tragische Typus. Aber auch die platonische Philosophie selbst „auf ihrer höchsten Stufe" hielt Werner Jaeger für „Theologie",[2] da sie „in gewisser Weise das eigentliche Ziel und Zentrum seines Denkens" ist.[3] Damit wird also dem Reden der Dichter von Gott das Reden der Philosophen beigefügt und von ihm deutlich abgehoben. Denn die Dichter erfinden mithilfe der Phantasie im Grunde Unwahrheiten vom Göttlichen, während die Philosophen nach der Wahrheit suchen.

---

1. Weischedel 1998, 49.
2. Jaeger 1953, 13. Vgl. Weischedel 1998, 48–49.
3. Jaeger 1953, 221.

Den Begriff „Theologie" bei Platon und im Alten Testament zu vergleichen heißt, wie man mit Johannes Hessen sagen könnte, „auf der Menschheit Höhen wandeln", „zu ragenden Gipfeln im Lande des Geistes aufsteigen, die vom Hauch der Ewigkeit umweht sind".[4] Dabei sprach Hessen von einer vergleichenden Darstellung zweier unterschiedlicher Geisteswelten, die gemeinsam die abendländische Geistesgeschichte zutiefst beeinflusst haben, wie die Höhepunkte der mittelalterlichen (Augustin, Thomas von Aquin), der neuzeitlichen (Reformation, deutscher Idealismus), sowie der zeitgenössischen Philosophie und Theologie im 20. Jh. (Phänomenologie, Existenzphilosophie, Dialektische Theologie) deutlich zum Ausdruck bringen.[5] Damit zeichnete Johannes Hessen als systematischer Theologe und Philosoph einen Weg, den die Biblische Theologie seit Gabler zu vermeiden suchte, indem sie sich zur historischen Wissenschaft erklärte. Während im 20. Jh. der Gedanke besonders hervorgehoben wurde, dass für die Fundierung und die Systematisierung des Offenbarungsgehaltes die Theologie auf die Hilfe der Philosophie angewiesen ist, versuchen alttestamentliche Theologen vergebens, Theologien des Alten Testaments aufgrund des alttestamentlichen Sprachinstrumentariums zu verfassen, ohne von philosophisch geprägten bzw. scholastisch belasteten Begriffen Gebrauch zu machen. Der Vorbehalt und die Voreingenommenheit, mit der heutige LXX-Forscher dem Vergleich Platons mit dem Alten Testament begegnen, beruht darauf, dass man von der Rezeptions- und Wirkungsgeschichte nicht Platons sondern des Platonismus ausgeht und einseitig nach Einflüssen des platonischen Denkens auf die LXX suchte, wobei die scheints Beeinflusste unterschätzt und u.U. abgewertet wurde. Mir geht es aber hierbei nicht um die Frage nach einseitigen Einflüssen, sondern um den *kreativen, kulturellen Austausch* beider Geisteswelten, Platons und der LXX, in der Klassik und im hellenistischen Zeitalter.[6]

Im vorliegenden Beitrag möchte ich der Frage der Theologie anhand von ausgewählten Texten aus Platons *Politeia* und der LXX näherkommen, um sprachliche und gedankliche Formen und Inhalte Platons und der LXX vergleichend auf Denkmotive und Denkstrukturen zurückführen. Damit würde es auch leichter gelingen, das Bleibende im Wandel der historisch verwurzelten Traditionen, das Spezifische, das Typische und

---

4. Hessen 1955, 9.
5. Hessen 1955, 10–11.
6. Dazu Dafni 2010.

das Allgemeingültige ins Auge zu fassen, sowie die Art und Weise eines kulturellen und theologischen Austausches in der Klassik und im Hellenismus plausibel zu machen.

1. Platons *Politeia*[7]

Der aus 10 Büchern bestehende platonische Dialog *Politeia* lässt sich als eine große Abhandlung zur Kernfrage der Gerechtigkeit und ihrer Verwirklichung in einem idealen Staat lesen. Als zentrale Texte zur Definition und zum Wesen der Gerechtigkeit, sowie zu den Konsequenzen ihrer Anwendung auf das Leben des Einzelnen und der Gesellschaft heben sich die abwechselnden Redegänge von Glaukon, Adeimantos und Sokrates (368c–433e) von der Mitte des zweiten bis zur Mitte des vierten Buches heraus. Für die Gesamtdeutung des Dialogs entscheidend ist das von Glaukon eingeführte, weit verbreitete Zugeständnis, dass es eigentlich gut sei, Unrecht zu tun, wenn man davon Vorteile hat, während Unrecht zu leiden schlecht sei, wenn man nicht dazu in der Lage ist, Vergeltung zu üben (357a–362c). Adeimantos fügt die ebenso verbreitete Meinung hinzu, dass der Wert der Gerechtigkeit sich aus ihren Folgen ergibt, ob man also Ansehen bei den Menschen und Gunst bei den Göttern genießt (362d–367e).[8] Sokrates führt die Diskussion zum hypothetischen Staat, den er und seine Gesprächspartner „in Gedanken und vor ihren Augen entstehen lassen" (369a) mit dem Ziel, am Beispiel des Staates zu untersuchen, was das Wesen und die Ausdrucksformen der Gerechtigkeit sind. Sokrates meint, dass „die Entstehung des Staates darauf zurückzuführen ist, dass der Einzelne sich nicht selbst ist, sondern vieler Helfer bedarf" (369c). Der ideale Staat wird aufgrund der menschlichen Bedürfnisse gegründet. Sokrates meint: „jeder von den Staatsbürgern müsste seine Leistung allen übrigen mit zugutekommen lassen" (369e). Angesichts der Tatsache, dass „von Natur keiner dem anderen völlig gleich ist, sondern jeder verschiedene Anlagen hat, der eine für dieses, der andere für jenes Geschäft" (370b), und dass es nicht besser ist, „wenn man als Einzelner viele Künste betreibt", sondern „wenn man nur eine betreibt", kommt man zur Strukturierung des idealen Staates aufgrund ihrer Lebensbedürfnisse in drei Kategorien von Bürgern: (a) die Handwerker bzw. Bauern, Freiberufler und allgemeinen Händler der materiellen Elemente, die die

---

7. Ich bediene mich im Folgenden der Übersetzung von Apelt 1920.
8. Horn, Müller, und Söder 2009, 50.

Mehrheit bilden und die allernotwendigsten Grundbedürfnisse des Überlebens sichern, (b) die *Epikouroi*, bzw. die Wehrpflichtigen, die den Staat vor äußeren und von inneren Feinden beschützen und das Wohlergehen des Staates gewährleisten und (c) die Wächter, die wenigen, die in ihren Händen die Verwaltung geistiger Zustände haben und einer speziellen Erziehung zum Aufbau einer sanften und zugleich beherzten Sinnesart bedürfen, was musische Bildung für die Seele und Gymnastik für den Leib mit einschließt (375c). Sokrates glaubt, dass derjenige zum Wächterdienst tauglich sein sollte, der „neben Beherztheit auch noch eine philosophische Naturanlage besitzt" (375e). Daraus ergeben sich die Fragen (376c–d): (a) Wie sollen die Wächter erzogen und ausgebildet werden? (b) Kann die Beantwortung dieser Frage uns zu der Erkenntnis führen, wie Gerechtigkeit und Ungerechtigkeit im Staate entstehen?

Hinsichtlich der Erziehungsart, die den Wächtern dargeboten wird, soll – so Sokrates – als Beste die aus uralter Zeit überlieferte bevorzugt werden (376e). „Da der Anfang bei jedem Geschäft das Wichtigste ist" (377a, Ἀρχὴ παντὸς ἔργου μέγιστον), meint der platonische Sokrates, dass man bei den Kindern erst mit der musischen Erziehung anfangen soll, die man durch Worte mitteilt, um dann zur Gymnastik überzugehen. Die Worte können wahr oder unwahr sein. „Beides", sagt der platonische Sokrates, „gehört zur Erziehung, zunächst aber das Unwahre" (377a). Damit weist er auf den Mythos[9] bzw. auf mythische Erzählungen hin, die er im Groben zwar als unwahr betrachtet, in denen man aber auch etwas Wahres finden könne. Damit setzt er sich in sehr ernster Weise mit dem von Anthropomorphismen und Anthropopathismen geprägten Reden von Gott und dem überlieferten Götterglauben im Altgriechentum auseinander. Im idealen Staat solle man nicht zulassen, dass die Kinder Mythen anhören und Ansichten aufnehmen, die im Widerspruch mit denen stehen, die sie in reiferen Jahren haben sollten (377c). Daher solle man die Werke der Dichter beaufsichtigen und zensieren (377d–383c), um die misslungenen Erzeugnisse der Dichterphantasie abweisen zu können und die Dichter zu unterweisen, wie sie von Gott angemessen reden müssen (380c). Um diese pädagogische Auffassung zu begründen und in die Erziehungspraxis umsetzen zu können, müsse man sich zuerst im Klaren darüber sein, „wie etwa der Gott ist" (379a). Auch hier verwendet der platonische Sokrates

---

9. In den deutschen Übersetzungen wird μῦθος durch „Märchen" oder „Fabel" wiedergegeben.

das ursprüngliche Prinzip, beim Größeren anzufangen, um das Kleinere beleuchten und erklären zu können (vgl. 368e). So benennt er die zwei größten Dichter Griechenlands, Homer und Hesiod, und übt Kritik an ihre Vorstellungen vom Göttlichen. Daraus sind wichtige Schlüsse auch für unsere Fragestellung bezüglich der Theologie der Septuaginta zu ziehen. Aus der Kritik am Gottesbegriff der Dichter ergibt sich der Gegenstand der Theologie der Philosophen bzw. ihrer Reflexion über das Sosein der Rede vom Gott in einem idealen Rechtsstaat, was für eine Einführung in die Theologie der Septuaginta von Nutzen sein könnte.

Die Dichter ersinnen unwahre Göttererzählungen, die von Generation zu Generation weitererzählt werden (377e). Selbst wenn sie wahr wären, dürften sie vor unverständigen und jungen Leuten nicht erzählt werden, am besten wäre es, wenn sie ganz verschwiegen würden (378a). Der Grund dafür ist Folgender: „Der jugendliche Hörer ist nicht imstande zu unterscheiden, was Allegorie ist und was nicht, sondern das, was er in solchem Alter in seinen Vorstellungskreis aufgenommen hat, das bleibt in der Regel auch haften, unauslöschbar und unwandelbar" (378e). Darum ist es wichtig, dass die jungen Leute Erzählungen „von durchaus sittlicher Art hören, um tugendhaftes Leben zu erstreben": κάλλιστα μεμυθολογημένα πρὸς ἀρετήν (378e). Welche mythischen Erzählungen der Dichter sind nach Sokrates' Meinung abzuweisen? Genannt werden Erzählungen, „die die Unwahrheit noch mit der Hässlichkeit verbinden" (377e).

Die Dekonstruktion der antiken griechischen Mythologie fängt mit den Vorstellungen von Rache und Vergeltung für verübte Freveltaten der Götter bzw. mit den Erzählungen von schonungsloser Züchtigung des Vaters für begangenes Unrecht an und setzt sich fort mit den Erzählungen vom Streit und den mannigfachen Feindschaften unter den Göttern und Heroen, sowie von den Götter- und Gigantenkämpfen. Die gedachten Gründer einer Stadt müssen nicht als Dichter denken und handeln. Ihnen „liegt es ob, das Gepräge zu kennen, das für die Darstellungen der Dichter maßgebend sein muss (...) selbst aber brauchen sie keine Erzählungen zu dichten" (379a). Zu bemerken ist hier, dass der platonische Sokrates weder vom Göttlichen, wie in deutschen Übersetzungen, noch von Göttern sondern von einem einzigen Gott redet. Apollo und das Orakel in Delphi nehmen in seiner Argumentation einen besonderen Platz ein. Diesem Gott haben die Gründer des idealen Staates zu folgen und sich „vom keinem anderen beraten zu lassen als von dem, der ihren Vätern heilig war" (427c), „der über alle diese Dinge allen Menschen als angestammter Berater, im Mittelpunkt der Erde auf dem Nabel thronend,

Auskunft erteilt". Dabei sind folgende Elemente der Gesetzgebung des delphischen Apollon gemeint: „die Gründung von Heiligtümern, die Opfer, der sonstige Kult von Göttern, Daimonen und Heroen, die Bestattung der Verstorbenen und die Leistungen an die im Jenseits Weilenden zur Erlangung ihrer Gunst" (427b).

Das Interesse des platonischen Sokrates gilt vor allem den Mustern oder Normen des richtigen Redens von Gott, die die ideellen Gründer des Staates zu bestimmen haben. Aufgrund dieser normativen Muster müssten dann die Dichter ihre Göttermythen erdichten und von denen dürften ihre Gedichte nicht abweichen. Er betont, dass ein Gott immer dargestellt werden soll, „wie er in Wirklichkeit ist" (379a). Welche sind es aber die Maßstäbe der Gottesvorstellungen, die Sokrates der epischen, lyrischen und tragischen Dichtung setzen würde? Die recht verstandenen Gottesvorstellungen sollen von zweierlei Prämissen ausgehen: die Vollkommenheit und die Unwandelbarkeit Gottes:

(a) „Gott ist in Wahrheit gut und kann nicht die Ursache von allem sein, sondern nur vom Guten". „Er kann nicht die Ursache des Schädlichen sein und ein Übel oder Böses verüben" (379b). „Für das Übel oder Böse muss man andere Ursachen suchen" (379c).

(b) „Gott ist wandellos und unveränderlich in seiner eigenen Gestalt und ist in jeder Beziehung vollkommen". „Er ist kein Zauberer oder Gaukler, der mit wohlberechneter List jetzt in dieser und dann wieder in anderer Gestalt erscheint, bald wirklich persönlich allerlei Gestalten annehmend und seine eigene dagegen vertauschend, bald bloß uns täuschend und in Scheinbild von sich uns vorspiegelnd. Er ist ein durchaus einfaches Wesen, das nun und nimmermehr aus seiner eigenen Gestalt heraustritt" (380e). Denn wenn man eine andere Gestalt annimmt, dann bedeutet das notwendig, dass die Veränderung von ihm selbst oder von etwas anderem bewirkt wird, das sich in bestem leiblichen oder geistigen Zustand befindet. Veränderung würde also bedeuten, dass ihm etwas zur vollen Schönheit und Tugend fehlte. Sokrates geht aber davon aus, dass Gott unübertrefflich gut und schön ist.

Zum Verhältnis Gottes zur Lüge nimmt der platonische Sokrates folgendermaßen Stellung: „Es gibt für Gott keinen Grund zu lügen" (382e) und die Menschen durch Lügen irreführen in Wort oder in Tat (383a). Nicht nur Gott sondern auch alles Gottentstammte und Göttliche ist völlig bar der Lüge (382e). „Die wahre Lüge wird (...) von allen Göttern und Menschen gehasst" (382a). „Die Lüge in Worten ist nur eine Nachahmung des Vorganges in der Seele, später entstanden, ein Nachbild, nicht völlig unvermischte Unwahrheit" (382b–c).

In der Form eines Credos stellt Sokrates fest, dass Gott „durchaus einfach und wahr in Tat und Wort ist und sich weder ändert noch andere täuscht, weder durch Erscheinungen noch durch Worte noch durch Sendung von Zeichen, sei es an Wachende oder an Träumende" (382e). Somit wird aber Kritik an die Theophanien und die Anthropomorphismen Homers und Hesiods geübt. Sokrates kommt zu dem Schluss, dass im idealen Rechtsstaat die musische Bildung der Wächter von solchen Mythen gebrauchen sollte, die die Wächter gottesfürchtig und göttlich machen, soweit dies den Menschen möglich ist (383c, vgl. Gen 1,26). Dieser Vorschrift solle Gesetzeskraft verliehen werden.

2. Zur Theologie der Septuaginta

Nun stellt sich die Frage: Kennt denn die Septuaginta die Frage nach der Unwandelbarkeit und Vollkommenheit Gottes, und wie geht sie damit um? Um die Voraussetzungen für eine richtige Schau und fruchtbare Untersuchung der treibenden Motive und ihre Auseinandersetzung im platonischen Denk- und Sprachsystem und in der Septuaginta zu schaffen, wende ich mich hier drei Beispielen aus Maleachi und Hiob zu, die sich mit dem Gebrauch der Übersetzungsäquivalente ἀλλοιόομαι, πτερνίζω und κρύπτω verbunden sind und auf Genesis 3 zurückverweisen.

2.1. ἀλλοιόομαι

Genesis 3 bildet in vielerlei Hinsicht die theologische Grundlage, auf die sich die LXX-Übersetzung des Maleachibuches stützt. Die Abweichungen der LXX des Maleachibuches scheinen im Übersetzer-Verständnis von Genesis 3 verankert zu sein. Die Tendenz, dass die Gottesvorstellung von LXX Maleachi auf Genesis 3 bezogen ist und entsprechend ausgelegt werden sollte, macht sich besonders in der Wahl der Äquivalente ἀλλοιόομαι (Mal 3,6 und Gen 3,5) und πτερνίζω (Mal 3,8f. und Gen 3,15) bemerkbar.

Das Verb ἀλλοιόομαι (Passiv) ist in unterschiedlichen Verwendungen in Umlauf. Dass sich darin die Problematik von Genesis 3 und die in den Worten der Schlange implizierte Frage verbirgt, ob Gut und Böse

Gott zuzuschreiben wären (Gen 3,5 ἔσεσθε ὡς θεοὶ γινώσκοντες καλὸν καὶ πονηρόν), ergibt sich aus Mal 3,6f., wo göttliches und menschliches Denken, Wollen und Handeln gegenübergestellt werden:

Διότι ἐγὼ κύριος ὁ θεὸς ὑμῶν,   כי אני יהוה
καὶ οὐκ ἠλλοίωμαι·   לא שניתי

LXX.D   Lutherbibel (2017)
Denn: Ich, der Herr, bin euer Gott   Ich, der HERR,
Und habe mich nicht verändert   wandle mich nicht;

Die deutschen Übersetzungen lesen in MT und LXX Mal 3,6 eine Aussage der Unveränderlichkeit und Unwandelbarkeit Gottes. Die LXX aber verwendet hier das griechische Verb ἀλλοιόομαι, dessen Sinngehalt mit dem eher neutralen deutschen Verb „wandeln" zu schwach zum Ausdruck kommt. Denn das Verb ἀλλοιόομαι ist vor allem mit Assoziationen des Verfaulens von Früchten und Nahrungsmitteln oder der Zersetzung von Tier- oder Menschenkörpern nach dem physischen Tod verbunden. Metaphorisch gebraucht, bringt es einprägsam die ethisch-moralische Verdorbenheit des Menschen zum Ausdruck. Sein Gebrauch in Mal 3,6 besagt, dass der Herr weder verdorben, wie die Ungerechten, noch der Anstifter des Bösen und des Todes wie jene alte Schlange von Genesis 3 ist. Dieser Gedanke ergibt sich zwar hier indirekt aus dem Verb ἀλλοιόομαι; er wird aber explizit in Weish 1,13f. und 2,23f. formuliert. Die Israeliten haben eigenwillig Ungerechtigkeit getrieben und die Gebote Gottes nicht bewahrt (LXX Mal 3,7 ἐξεκλίνατε νόμιμά μου καὶ οὐκ ἐφυλάξασθε). Ihr böses Handeln ist mit dem Handeln der ersten Menschen im Paradies vergleichbar, die das Gebot übertraten und von der verbotenen Frucht aßen, um wie Götter zu werden, wissend was gut und was böse ist. Die Wortbedeutung „verfaulen/verderben" für ἀλλοιόομαι und die damit verbundenen Assoziationen werden in LXX Mal 3,11 bestätigt. Dort werden die Umkehr des ungehorsamen Volkes und der göttliche Segen mit den Früchten und dem Weinstock versinnbildlicht, die Gott nicht verderben lassen wird (οὐ μὴ διαφθείρω). Erinnert wird damit auch an LXX Ps 15,10 und an die Hoffnung des Frommen, der sagt (LXX.D): „Denn du wirst meine Seele nicht der Unterwelt preisgeben noch zulassen, dass dein Frommer das Verderben/die Vernichtung sieht".

2.2. πτερνίζω

Die Problematik von Genesis 3 ist auch in Mal 3,8f. erkennbar, wo die Rede von der Versuchung Gottes durch Menschen ist, die laut Sapientia Salomonis zum Anteil Satans gehören.

⁸ εἰ πτερνιεῖ ἄνθρωπος θεόν;   היקבע אדם אלהים
διότι ὑμεῖς πτερνίζετέ με.   כי אתם קבעים אתי
καὶ ἐρεῖτε   ואמרתם
Ἐν τίνι ἐπτερνίκαμέν σε;   במה קבענוך
ὅτι τὰ ἐπιδέκατα   המעשר
καὶ αἱ ἀπαρχαὶ μεθ᾽ ὑμῶν εἰσιν·   והתרומה:
⁹ καὶ ἀποβλέποντες ὑμεῖς   ⁹במארה אתם
ἀποβλέπετε,   נארים
καὶ ἐμὲ ὑμεῖς πτερνίζετε·   ואתי אתם קבעים

LXX.D
8 Hintergeht etwa ein Mensch Gott?
Denn: Ihr hintergeht mich.
Und ihr werdet sagen:
„Worin haben wir dich hintergangen?"
Deshalb, weil der Zehnte
und die Erstlingsgaben bei euch bleiben
⁹ Und ihr seht bewusst weg,
Und ihr hintergeht mich:

Lutherbibel (2017)
Ist's recht, dass ein Mensch Gott betrügt?
Doch ihr betrügt mich.
Ihr aber sprecht:
„Womit betrügen wir dich?"
Mit dem Zehnten
und der Abgabe!
⁹ Ihr seid verflucht,
mich betrügt ihr allesamt.

Die Lutherbibel übersetzt das hebräische Verb קבע mit „betrügen". Aber eigentlich handelt es sich in der LXX nicht allein um Betrug. Denn das Verb πτερνίζω wird von πτέρνα abgeleitet, was in LXX Gen 3,15 erstmalig gebraucht wurde, um die verwundbare Stelle des Samens der Frau zu bezeichnen. Der Same der Frau wird den Kopf der Schlange zertreten und die Schlange vernichten, während sie ihm aber nur die Ferse verletzen wird: αὐτός σου τηρήσει κεφαλήν, καὶ σὺ τηρήσεις αὐτοῦ πτέρναν. Damit wird gezeigt, dass der Anstifter des Bösen und des Todes nur eingeschränkt Macht über die Menschen hat. Das Bild der verwundbaren Ferse ruft die Achilles-Ferse ins Gedächtnis. Achilles stirbt zwar den leiblichen Tod; er wird aber dann als unsterblich in die Elysischen Gefilde entrückt (Platon, *Symp.* 180b).

2.3. κρύπτω

In Genesis 3 wird Gott von der Schlange eigentlich der Arglist beschuldigt. Indem sie nur die halbe Wahrheit sagt, führt sie ihre menschlichen Gesprächspartner zu dem Gedanken, Gott verheimliche bewusst seine eigentliche Absicht. Er verbietet den Verzehr vom Baum der Erkenntnis des Guten und des Bösen, damit der Mensch angeblich nicht vergöttert werden kann. Ein zwar vergleichbarer, aber spiegelverkehrter Gedanke drückt sich mithilfe des Verbes κρύπτω an zwei Parallelstellen des Hiobbuches aus, die sich in der LXX und im MT quantitativ sowie qualitativ voneinander unterscheiden. Auch ihre Übersetzungen ins Deutsche weichen voneinander und von ihren Vorlagen deutlich ab. Indem man sich bemüht, allgemeinverständliche, konventionelle Sprache zu verwenden, lässt man bewusst oder unbewusst Bedeutungsnuancen der bildhaften biblischen Worte, die für die Ideologie und die Theologie äußerst wichtig zu sein vermögen, verloren gehen.

In Hi 38,2 wird die von Hiob lange ersehnte Antwort Gottes aus dem Wettersturm mit einer Frage eingeleitet: EÜ „Wer ist es, der den Ratschluss verdunkelt mit Gerede ohne Einsicht?". Die Formulierung ist allgemein gerichtet, aber die Leitwörter עֵצָה, מִלִּין und דַּעַת erinnern an die Begegnung der Schlange mit den Menschen im Paradies, wo sie nicht mit Taten, sondern mit Worten, die das göttliche Gebot verdunkeln, die Menschen verführt. Der Wortlaut der Einheits- und der Lutherbibel weist auf ein Orakel hin, welches den Ratschluss Gottes den Menschen verdunkelt und in unverständlichen Worten gekleidet mitteilt, wie etwa die Orakel von Pythia in Delphi. Die LXX hingegen liest:

Τίς οὗτος ὁ κρύπτων με βουλήν,
συνέχων δὲ ῥήματα ἐν καρδίᾳ,
ἐμὲ δὲ οἴεται κρύπτειν;

מי זה מחשיך עצה
במלין
בלי דעת:

LXX.D
Wer ist dieser,
der vor mir eine Absicht verbirgt
und der Worte im Herzen festhält
und glaubt,
(sie) vor mir zu verbergen?

Lutherbibel (2017)
Wer ist's,
der den Ratschluss verdunkelt
mit Worten ohne Verstand?

Die LXX ersetzt das hebräische Verb חשׂך mit κρύπτω und macht aus במלין den Partizipialsatz συνέχων δὲ ῥήματα ἐν καρδίᾳ („Worte im Herzen festhalten"), wobei die Aussage συνέχων ἐν καρδίᾳ anstelle der hebräischen Präposition ב steht und ihren Sinn erläutert. Anstelle von בלי דעת – wörtlich ohne Erkenntnis bzw. ohne wahre Erkenntnis – setzt die LXX den Satz ἐμὲ δὲ οἴεται κρύπτειν (wörtlich „man denkt, mich verbergen zu können"). Wenn man also ἐμέ als Akkusativobjekt des Verbes κρύπτω versteht, dann lautet der LXX Text etwa: „Wer will von mir seine Absicht verbergen, indem er Worte in seinem Herzen verheimlicht, und denkt damit, mich verbergen zu können?" Damit wird auf ein absichtliches, arglistiges Wortgeschehen hingewiesen. Man verheimlicht Worte bzw. sagt die halbe Wahrheit, um Gott zu verleugnen, und denkt dabei, dass seine Absicht vor Gott verborgen bleibt. LXX.D übersetzt beides, με und ἐμέ, mit der Präpositionalverbindung „vor mir" und macht daraus ein Wort, welches auf den Versuch hinweist, menschliche Worte und Taten im Angesicht des Allwissenden Gottes zu verbergen. Somit geht aber der spezielle Bezug auf Gott und auf die Gottesleugnung verloren und es wird die Unmöglichkeit des Verbergens und Verheimlichens im Angesicht Gottes unterstrichen.

Hi 42,1–6 enthält die zweite Erwiderung Hiobs auf Gottes Worte und signalisiert eine Steigerung gegenüber der ersten (40,3–5), da Hiob umkehrt und sich vor Gott, seinem Schöpfer und Retter unterwirft. Den Rechtsstreit mit Gott erklärt Hiob für beendet bezugnehmend auf die Anfangsworte Gottes: „Wer ist es, der ohne Einsicht den Rat verdunkelt? So habe ich denn im Unverstand geredet über Dinge, die zu wunderbar für mich und unbegreiflich sind" (42,3; EÜ).

τίς γάρ ἐστιν ὁ κρύπτων σε βουλήν;   מי זה מעלים עצה
φειδόμενος δὲ ῥημάτων   בלי דעת
καὶ σὲ οἴεται κρύπτειν

τίς δὲ ἀναγγελεῖ μοι   לכן הגדתי
ἃ οὐκ ᾔδειν,   ולא אבין
μεγάλα καὶ θαυμαστὰ   נפלאות ממני
ἃ οὐκ ἠπιστάμην;   ולא אדע:

LXX.D   Lutherbibel (2017)
Wer ist es denn,   Wer ist der,
der vor dir eine Absicht verbirgt und   der den Ratschluss verhüllt
        Worte zurückhält
und glaubt, sie vor dir zu verbergen?   mit Worten ohne Verstand?

Und wer wird mir verkünden,
Was ich nicht wusste,   Darum habe ich ohne Einsicht geredet,
Großes und Wunderbares,   was mir zu hoch ist
was ich nicht kannte?   und ich nicht verstehe.

Die quantitativen und qualitativen Unterschiede zwischen der LXX und dem MT sind hier noch deutlicher als in Hi 38,2. Die LXX spricht nicht im ich-Stil wie der MT, sondern sie benutzt das unbestimmte Pronomen τίς. Sie macht Hiob zum Objekt des Redens eines anderen und nicht zum Redenden wie im MT; so stellt sie einen unbestimmten anderen als Anstifter des Streits Hiobs mit Gott in den Vordergrund. Damit wird der Leser direkt auf den Prolog des Hiobbuches (Hi 1–2) und auf die Himmelsszene hingewiesen, wo das schwere Leid und die Schicksalsschläge Hiobs zwar mit Gottes Erlaubnis, aber von Satan zugefügt werden. Anstatt des hebräischen בלי דעת („ohne Erkenntnis") wird in der LXX der Partizipialsatz φειδόμενος δὲ ῥημάτων (wörtlich „derjenige, der sich Worte erspart/ sich jeder Äußerung enthält") sowie der Hauptsatz καὶ σὲ οἴεται κρύπτειν (wörtlich „und denkt dabei, dich verbergen zu können") hinzugefügt. Mit dieser Textänderung wird Hi 42,3 an Hi 38,2 sprachlich und gedanklich angeschlossen. Darüber hinaus fügt die LXX den Fragesatz τίς δὲ ἀναγγελεῖ μοι („wer wird mir verkündigen") hinzu, womit sie in den prophetischen Texten das Kommen eines Gottesboten bzw. des Messias verkündigt.[10] Was in der LXX darauf folgt, ist die Schilderung der großen und wunderbaren Taten Gottes in der Weltgeschichte, die Hiob nicht geahnt hatte. Auch hier fügt die LXX das Wort μεγάλα ohne hebräische Entsprechung hinzu, um Gottes überwältigendes Eingreifen in der Weltgeschichte zu signalisieren oder zu veranschaulichen. Die deutschen Übersetzungen des MT hingegen bringen die Selbstvorwürfe und den Selbsttadel Hiobs vor den allwissenden Gott zum Ausdruck. Hiob erkennt an, dass seine Wissensmöglichkeiten begrenzt sind und dass er den Willen Gottes nicht völlig begreifen kann. Die LXX drückt aber die Hoffnung aus, dass die göttlichen Geheimnisse geoffenbart werden.

In Hi 38,2 (Τίς οὗτος ὁ κρύπτων με βουλήν) handelt es sich um eine Frage Gottes. In Hi 42,3 (τίς γάρ ἐστιν ὁ κρύπτων σε βουλήν;) geht es um die Frage eines Menschen. In beiden Fällen ist das Verb κρύπτω mit zwei Akkusativobjekte verbunden. Diese Syntax ist in der LXX nicht üblich. Die in LXX.D dargebotenen Wiedergaben „vor mir" für με und „vor dir" für σε

---

10. Siehe z.B. Am 4,13; Jes 2,3; Jer 4,15. Vgl. Mi 6,8.

scheinen von der Verbindung des Verbums mit einem Präpositionalobjekt und einem Akkusativobjekt auszugehen, wie z.B. in 1Kgt 3,17f. (vgl. 20,2; Tob 12,11), wo uns die Aussage κρύπτω ῥῆμα in der Bedeutung „Worte verheimlichen" zum ersten Mal begegnet. Eli fragt dort Samuel nach dem geoffenbarten Wort Gottes und warnt ihm davor, nichts zu verheimlichen, damit Gott ihn nicht bestraft. Samuel teilt ihm alles mit, und Eli erkennt, dass der Herr gesprochen hat. Eli wird daraufhin tun, was *vor ihm* gut ist.

¹⁷ καὶ εἶπεν Τί τὸ ῥῆμα τὸ λαληθὲν πρὸς σέ; μὴ δὴ κρύψῃς <u>ἀπ' ἐμοῦ</u>· τάδε ποιήσαι σοι ὁ θεὸς καὶ τάδε προσθείη, ἐὰν κρύψῃς <u>ἀπ' ἐμοῦ</u> ῥῆμα ἐκ πάντων τῶν λόγων τῶν λαληθέντων σοι ἐν τοῖς ὠσίν σου.
¹⁸ καὶ ἀπήγγειλεν Σαμουηλ πάντας τοὺς λόγους καὶ οὐκ ἔκρυψεν ἀπ' αὐτοῦ, καὶ εἶπεν Ηλι Κύριος αὐτός· τὸ ἀγαθὸν ἐνώπιον αὐτοῦ ποιήσει.

¹⁷ ויאמר מה הדבר אשר דבר אליך אל נא תכחד ממני כה יעשה לך אלהים וכה יוסיף אם תכחד ממני דבר מכל הדבר אשר דבר אליך:
¹⁸ ויגד לו שמואל את כל הדברים ולא כחד ממנו ויאמר יהוה הוא הטוב בעינו יעשה:

Lutherbibel (2017)

¹⁷ Er sprach: Was war das für ein Wort, das er dir gesagt hat? Verschweige mir nichts. Gott tue dir dies und das, wenn du mir etwas verschweigst von all dem, das er dir gesagt hat.
¹⁸ Da sagte ihm Samuel alles und verschwieg ihm nichts. Er aber sprach: Es ist der HERR; er tue, was ihm wohlgefällt.

Charakteristisch ist hier, dass mit dem Präpositionalobjekt ἀπ' ἐμοῦ auf die Person hingewiesen wird, vor der etwas verheimlicht wird. Das Nicht-Verheimlichen der Wahrheit vor dem König verbunden mit einem Eidspruch auf das eigene Leben (Seele) kommt in 2Kgt 14,18f. zur Sprache. Dass die Verheimlichung der Worte bzw. der Wahrheit den Tod nach sich zieht, begegnet uns an zwei jeremianischen Stellen, in denen es um die Befragung Jeremias durch den König und die Amtsträger geht: In Jer 38 (45),14 fragt der König:

Ερωτήσω σε λόγον, καὶ μὴ δὴ κρύψῃς <u>ἀπ' ἐμοῦ</u> ῥῆμα
Ich will dich etwas fragen; verhehle mir nichts! (Lutherbibel 2017)

In Jer 38 (45),25 fragen die Amtsträger:

'Ανάγγειλον ἡμῖν τί ἐλάλησέν σοι ὁ βασιλεύς· μὴ κρύψῃς <u>ἀφ' ἡμῶν</u>, καὶ οὐ μὴ ἀνέλωμέν σε.

Sag an, was hast du mit dem König geredet; verbirg es uns nicht, so wollen wir dich nicht töten. (Lutherbibel 2017)

Theologisch interessant ist Hi 31,33: אם כסיתי כאדם פשעי לטמון בחבי עוני (Lutherbibel: „Hab ich meine Übertretungen, wie Menschen tun, zugedeckt, um heimlich meine Schuld zu verbergen...?"). Im Unterschied zum MT liest LXX Hi 31,33: εἰ δὲ καὶ ἁμαρτὼν ἀκουσίως ἔκρυψα τὴν ἁμαρτίαν μου (LXX.D: „und wenn ich auch, nachdem ich unfreiwillig gesündigt hatte, meine Sünde verborgen hätte"). Ein Präpositionalobjekt fehlt dabei. Mit der Zufügung des Adverbs ἀκουσίως[11] ohne hebräische Entsprechung führt die LXX den Begriff der unbewussten Verfehlung gegenüber der bewussten Böswilligkeit ein, was an das sokratische „niemand ist bewusst böse" bzw. „niemand ist freiwillig böse" (*Polit.* 589c) erinnert[12] und soteriologische Implikationen hat; vgl. die Opfer- und Sühnevorschriften in Levitikus 4 und Numeri 15. Mit der Zufügung des Adverbs ἀκουσίως wird Hi 31,33 besonders qualifiziert und von anderen abgehoben. Denn im Fall einer versehentlichen, unwissenden, unbeabsichtigten, unfreiwilligen Handlung gegen die Befehle des Herrn, wird, wenn sie bekannt wird, ein Opfer dargebracht und nicht die Todesstrafe verlangt. Levitikus spricht von entsprechenden Handlungen der ganzen Volksversammlung, der Herrscher und des Einzelnen, in Numeri werden noch die Proselyten hinzugefügt. In Bezug auf diejenigen, die Menschen versehentlich erschlagen haben, sind Asyl- oder Fluchtstätte vorgesehen, damit sie am Leben bleiben (vgl. Jos 20,3.9; so auch in Deut 19,4)

In den Psalmen 39 (40) und 118 (119) finden sich an zwei Stellen scheinbar widersprüchliche Aussagen. Einmal wird gesagt, dass der Gerechte die Worte Gottes in seinem Herzen verbirgt[13] und einmal, dass der Gerechte die Gerechtigkeit, die Wahrheit und die Rettung Gottes in seinem Herzen nicht verbirgt.

---

11. Erinnert sei daran, dass das Adverb uns 18mal in der LXX begegnet, 2mal ohne hebräische Entsprechung (Lev 4,13), 1mal als Wiedergabe von בבלי רעת (Dtn 19,4) und 15mal als Wiedergabe von שגגה (Lev 4,2.13.22.27; 5,15; Num 15,24.27.28.29; 35,11.15. Jos 20,3.9; Hi 31,33).

12. Dazu Dafni 2016.

13. Vgl. Hi 23,12; LXX Prov 2,1; 7,1; 25,2.

Ps 40 (39),11
τὴν δικαιοσύνην σου οὐκ ἔκρυψα ἐν τῇ καρδίᾳ μου,
τὴν ἀλήθειάν σου καὶ τὸ σωτήριόν σου εἶπα,
οὐκ ἔκρυψα τὸ ἔλεός σου καὶ τὴν ἀλήθειάν σου ἀπὸ συναγωγῆς πολλῆς

צדקתך לא כסיתי בתוך לבי
אמונתך ותשועתך אמרתי
לא כחדתי חסדך ואמתך
לקהל רב

LXX.D
Deine Gerechtigkeit habe ich nicht in meinem Herzen verborgen,
(von) deiner Wahrheit und deinem Heil habe ich gesprochen,
ich habe dein Erbarmen und deine Wahrheit nicht vor der großen Versammlung verborgen.

Lutherbibel 2017
Deine Gerechtigkeit verberge ich nicht in meinem Herzen;
von deiner Wahrheit und von deinem Heil rede ich.
Ich verhehle deine Güte und Treue nicht
vor der großen Gemeinde.

Ps 119 (118),11
ἐν τῇ καρδίᾳ μου ἔκρυψα τὰ λόγιά σου,
ὅπως ἂν μὴ ἁμάρτω σοι.

בלבי צפנתי אמרתך
למען לא אחטא לך

LXX.D
In meinem Herzen habe ich deine Worte verborgen,
damit ich nicht gegen dich sündige.

Lutherbibel 2017
Ich behalte dein Wort in meinem Herzen,
damit ich nicht wider dich sündige.

Dabei wird den Aussagen κρύπτω τὴν δικαιοσύνη σου und κρύπτω τὰ λόγιά σου die Ortsbestimmung ἐν τῇ καρδίᾳ μου beigefügt. Der Sinn der Aussagen ergibt sich aus dem Kontext. Im ersteren Fall bezieht sich das Verb auf die Verinnerlichung des Gotteswillens und im letzteren auf die Veräußerlichung der Güte und Treue Gottes vor der großen Gottesgemeinde.

Die Aussagen ἐμὲ δὲ οἴεται κρύπτειν (Hi 38,2) und σὲ οἴεται κρύπτειν (Hi 42,3), denen keine Präpositionalobjekte oder Ortsbestimmungen beigefügt sind, haben zwar keine hebräische Entsprechung; sie werden aber in der LXX.D behandelt, als ob sie ein Präpositionalobjekt hätten. Man scheint davon ausgegangen zu sein, dass das Präpositionalobjekt aus stilistischen Gründen getilgt wurde. Dies ist aber m.E. nicht der Fall. Syntaktisch fehlt den Aussagen nichts. Sie bringen kurz und deutlich den bewussten Versuch zur Sprache, die Gegenwart Gottes in der Weltgeschichte und im Menschenleben zu verheimlichen. Dies dürfte als ein weiterer Aspekt des menschlichen Hochmuts angesehen werden, neben dem Aspekt der Versuchung Gottes durch den Menschen, der mit dem Verb πτερνίζω in Mal 3,8 zum Ausdruck kommt.

3. Ausblicke

Mit der Gottesaussage οὐκ ἠλλοίωμαι bringt LXX Maleachi eben das zum Ausdruck, was der platonische Sokrates mit Unwandelbarkeit und Vollkommenheit Gottes meint, nämlich dass Gott mit der Lüge und dem Übel in der Welt und im Leben des Menschen nichts zu tun hat. Der platonische Sokrates spricht nicht vom Verbergen bzw. von der Verheimlichung des göttlichen Wortes vor Menschen, sondern von der Verheimlichung der Worte jener Dichter, die bewusst lügen und das Göttliche noch ins Hässliche ziehen, dies vor den Zöglingen, die später zu Wächtern werden und noch nicht imstande sind, zwischen wahr und falsch zu unterscheiden. Gegenüber dem alttestamentlichem Jahweglauben scheint der platonische Sokrates aber Apollo als den einzigen Gott der Wahrheit zu sehen. Erinnert sei daran, dass diesem einzigen Gott, den Sokrates anerkennt, der delphische Spruch γνῶθι σεαυτόν („erkenne dich selbst") zugeschrieben wird, den Sokrates zum seinem Lebensmotto gemacht hat. Dieser Spruch lässt sich mehrmals im Alten Testament, genauer: im Deuteronomium in der Formulierung πρόσεχε σεαυτῷ wiedererkennen (4,9; 6,12, 12,13 u.ö.); er lenkt die Aufmerksamkeit auf die Gerechtigkeit Gottes. Was der intuitive Reichtum der sokratischen Religionskritik in helles Licht rückte und die LXX vollbrachte, haben die sogenannten deuterokanonischen Schriften vollauf bestätigt und präzisiert, nämlich dass es keine (anderen) Götter gibt.[14] Die Zeit nach Platon und der LXX ist durch ein intensives Studium der Vorstellungen des einen wahren Gottes Israels charakterisiert.

Literatur

Apelt, Otto. 1920. *Platon, Sämtliche Dialoge, 5. Der Staat*. 5. Aufl. Leipzig: Meiner.

Dafni, Evangelia G. 2003. „Οἱ οὐκ ὄντες θεοί in der Septuaginta des Jeremiabuches und in der Epistel Jeremias. Ein Beitrag zur Erforschung des Werdegangs des sogenannten alexandrinischen Kanons." Seiten

---

14. Dafni 2003. Vgl. auch Dafni 2014.

235–45 in *The Biblical Canons*. Hrsg. von Jean-Marie Auwers und H. Jan de Jonge. BETL 163. Leuven: Peeters.

———. 2010. *Genesis, Plato und Euripides. Drei Studien zum Austausch von Griechischem und Hebräischem Sprach- und Gedankengut in der Klassik und im Hellenismus*. BThS 108. Neukirchen-Vluyn: Neukirchener Verlag.

———. 2014. "Ἡ Μονοθεΐα εἰς τὸ Βιβλίον τοῦ Ἰερεμίου καὶ τὴν Ἐπιστολὴν Ἰερεμίου." *Vetus Testamentum et Hellas* 1:66–106.

———. 2016. "Οὐδεὶς ἑκὼν κακός? Euripides' Hippolytus and Genesis." *Vetus Testamentum et Hellas* 3:58–70.

Hessen, Johannes. 1955. *Platonismus und Prophetismus. Die antike und die biblische Geisteswelt in struktur-vergleichender Betrachtung*. 2. Aufl. München: Reinhardt.

Horn, Christoph, Jörn Müller, und Joachim Söder, Hrsg. 2009. *Platon Handbuch. Leben – Werk – Wirkung*. Stuttgart: Metzler.

Jaeger, Werner. 1953. *Die Theologie der frühen griechischen Denker*. Stuttgart: Kohlhammer.

Weischedel, Wilhelm. 1998. *Der Gott der Philosophen. Grundlegung einer philosophischen Theologie im Zeitalter des Nihilismus*. 3. Aufl. Darmstadt: Wissenschaftliche Buchgesellschaft.

Part 3
Theological Perspectives of the Greek Bible 1: Translation

Interpretive Intent and the Legal Material of the Septuagint Pentateuch

Dirk Büchner

ABSTRACT: A language such as Greek, with a much larger vocabulary and syntactical structures than Hebrew, is able to be more precise where the Hebrew is ambiguous. The question is whether, like the Targums, the LXX is closer to Hebrew style and less faithful to Hebrew meaning, to borrow a phrase from David J. Lane. If the former, the task of the one searching for a hermeneutical purpose in the translation is to determine whether there are more than simply isolated attempts at creating new meanings in the Greek. This paper will present a number of passages from LXX Leviticus where interpretation is clearly evident but also, as a control sample, other cases in which the material does not appear to have the kind of meaning associated with a liturgical text. If, in a book containing sacred laws and precepts, there is uneven clarity of purpose, it forces the researcher to think in terms of the expectations that the translation would have had to meet. Such expectations reside in the community rather than in the mind of the translator. Nonetheless, it adds to the picture of what one might call a diaspora "theology."

To find a way to talk about theology or theologies of the Septuagint is a worthy quest, especially if, through methodological care, we can identify ways in which the translators, by reason of their place geographically and historically, would have subconsciously, and perhaps also consciously, rendered Hebrew words in such a way that the resulting words in the target language communicated ideas that fitted with their own world and satisfied the needs and expectations of their community.[1]

---

1. It has been a pleasure to participate in this symposium, and my sincere thanks to the organizers for inviting me. They have stimulated me to undertake the process of writing on the topic of Jewish Exegesis in the Septuagint after a hiatus of nearly two

This chapter hopes to contribute to the question of theological exegesis from the angle of the Pentateuch's legal material. We begin our approach from the question about the relationship that exists between linguistic usage and meaning, with special focus on the nature of the Greek Pentateuch's linguistic evidence. We will then consider two proposals about its usefulness as a source of theological and juridical information. Following that, some evidence will be presented against viewing the Greek Pentateuch as being intentionally theological or legally precise. We will present a test case of a pentateuchal text dealing with the matter of "living by the Torah" and end with some suggestions for further inquiry.

1. The Character of the Septuagint Pentateuch

Having had no comparable project against which to measure their own enterprise, the Septuagint Pentateuch's translators constantly tried out new strategies of rendering their parent text, now literal, now free, now merely representing the shape of the Hebrew, now communicating with style in Greek. The result is that in the Greek Pentateuch we find less systematization and more experimentation compared to some of the later translated works. Its renderings are creative, spontaneous, and resistant of rigidity.

At the same time, it is commonly accepted that the translators shared an intention to create a Greek equivalent to the Hebrew original that corresponded fairly closely to it in the quantity of lexemes and in the order of lexemes, with varying degrees of elasticity from place to place and book to book. Hebrew words and phrases were matched with Greek words and phrases, and, though the Greek syntax was patterned on Hebrew syntax, the resulting product was a comprehendible Greek text. Translators seemed not always to have an expectation of automatic semantic agreement between the items that were paired up. Meaning was not intended to be transferred from Hebrew to Greek in a mechanical way; rather, the Greek text often communicates in its own direction.

Numbers 22:18 may serve as an illustration of the way in which the Hebrew text is transposed item for item into intelligible Greek, with some elasticity of equivalence and meaning transfer.

---

decades in my own scholarship. In this I owe a debt of gratitude to the guidance and stimulus of Johann Cook.

Hebrew	Greek
ויען בלעם ויאמר	καὶ ἀπεκρίθη Βαλααμ καὶ εἶπεν
אל עבדי בלק	τοῖς ἄρχουσιν Βαλακ
אם יתן לי בלק	ἐὰν δῷ μοι Βαλακ
מלא ביתו	πλήρη τὸν οἶκον αὐτοῦ
כסף וזהב	ἀργυρίου καὶ χρυσίου
לא אוכל לעבר	οὐ δυνήσομαι παραβῆναι
את פי יהוה אלהי	τὸ ῥῆμα κυρίου τοῦ θεοῦ
לעשות	ποιῆσαι
–	αὐτό
קטנה או גדולה	μικρὸν ἢ μέγα
–	ἐν τῇ διανοίᾳ μου

The ingredients of the Hebrew sentence are carried over into ingredients of a Greek sentence that preserves the Hebrew word order. Some overt adjustment in meaning is achieved by ἄρχων supplied for עבד and ῥῆμα for פה. Some inadvertent adjustment of meaning results from the infinitive ποιῆσαι that matches the Hebrew infinitive for the sake of syntactical equivalence. While Hebrew infinitives loosely connected to the main verb express circumstance "by doing," Greek infinitives tend to express purpose.[2] Elasticity of quantitative equivalence is found in αὐτό added as object for ποιῆσαι and in the additional words ἐν τῇ διανοίᾳ μου, possibly originating in a harmonized *Vorlage* but, if not, a decision made by the translator himself.[3]

2. The Septuagint Pentateuch and Exegesis

Scholarship on the topic of septuagintal exegesis has a long history, and the two organizers of this symposium have made no small contribution to the field.[4] Of particular interest to the topic of this chapter, the cult, is a recent

---

2. LXX.D: "um es zu tun"; NETS: "to do it." These grammatical features will be explained in greater detail below.
3. See Rösel and Schlund 2001, 483. For full commentary, see Jones 2017.
4. Johann Cook, whose later work concentrated on the book of Proverbs, from very early on in his career had an instinct for Jewish exegesis in the Septuagint Pentateuch. See Cook 1983, in which he draws our attention to the value of Alexandria as center of Hellenistic intellectual activity and the place at which philosophical currents such as Platonism as well as Jewish thought converge to provide influences that shaped

article by Martin Rösel on the cult in which he identifies motivations observable in the translator of Numbers, whose work is shaped both by the constraints of the Hebrew source and by exegetical traditions known to him.[5] Rösel finds that the Numbers translation distinguishes more starkly between true religion and false religion than does the original Hebrew text. If the realm of the cult is the one in which correct versus incorrect practice is the most pressing concern, it appears that the Numbers translator takes care to ensure that there are no contradictions in the stipulations for priestly roles and duties. Rösel is able to conclude that the translator's mode of work is one in which eliminating ambiguities takes priority above providing a faithful rendering of the parent text. From this principle, illustrated by a generous set of examples, it is for Rösel a logical conclusion that the legal parts of the Greek Pentateuch were tailor-made for the internal use of the Alexandrian Jewish community. He finds that the Greek book of Numbers shows for the benefit of the Jewish community a demarcation of the boundaries between true and false religion, illustrated by the paradigmatic wilderness community.[6]

This is an important study because it brings to the fore questions about a theology of law, or a legal theology of the Septuagint, and points to the actual juridical situation of the Alexandrian community. It also raises the potential for reflection on how exactly the initial audience of the LXX in Alexandria might have viewed and used the legal content of their Torah translation. From this potentiality, one might pose a number of questions. For instance, would a translation serve the needs of a Greek-speaking Jewish community who were well-integrated into their surrounding cultural environment? To what extent might the Alexandrian Jewish community have conducted legal decisions by the requirements of the Greek Pentateuch?

---

the Greek translation of Genesis. Of Martin Rösel's many works, a recent synopsis of his approach may be found in Rösel 2006, in which he makes a plea for a theology of the Septuagint as something that (1) could showcase the development from the theology of the Hebrew Bible to the LXX or highlight the differences between them and (2) show how the LXX may be said to be part of the *Religionsgeschichte* of the Hebrew Bible and biblical theology, particularly since it was recognized to be unified Scripture by early Judaism.

5. Rösel 2001.
6. Rösel 2001, 36–39.

3. The Greek Pentateuch as *Nomos*

These matters have occupied recent scholarly inquiry. In particular, Modrzejewski's study *The Septuagint as Nomos* sheds some light on the questions posed above.[7] His arguments are worth summarizing. To begin, he alerts us to some unique characteristics that are shared between the Greek Pentateuch and an Egyptian collection of legal materials known as the Legal Manual of Hermopolis. Both the Torah and the Manual of Hermopolis were translated into Greek during the reign of Ptolemy II, and both became official documents much later, in the second century CE: the LXX became the Bible of the church and the Manual of Hermopolis a recognized part of Egyptian ideology even as late as the time of Antonine Egypt, judging by the existence of a copy whose text is found in P.Oxy. 46.3285. Another important characteristic shared by the two corpora is found in the fact that we know nothing about the translators of the Egyptian Manual, just as we also know no more about the LXX translators than the legendary information provided by the Letter of Aristeas. Furthermore, both documents may have played a role in the administration of Ptolemaic justice. Modrzejewski describes the Egyptian Manual as a legal case book, a collection of styles for the use of indigenous judges and notaries. It was the Egyptian priests who worked on it and who were anxious to preserve it. It is known that, in Ptolemaic jurisprudence, use could be made in disputes of a νόμος τῆς χώρας, that is, a set of native laws agreed upon and practiced by native Egyptians, no doubt by means of the Greek translation that was made of the Manual. The question then arises whether in the administration of justice involving Jews a similar view might have been taken by the Ptolemaic administration of the law of the Jews, the νόμος τῶν Ἰουδαιῶν. Modrzejewski is sure that this was indeed so, citing the well-known dispute in Krokodilopolis between the Jews Dositheos and Herakleia, recorded in P.Petr. 3.29. From it we learn that, among the hierarchy of applicable rules of law, judges could appeal to civic laws (πολιτικοὶ νόμοι), especially when the πρόσταγμα or διαγράμμα of the regent failed to provide the necessary answers.[8]

Of all the foreign peoples in Ptolemaic Egypt, the Jews were the only group who would have brought a law from their place of origin. Modrze-

---

7. Modrzejewski 2001.

8. Modrzejewski 2001, 191. For a full discussion of the terminology found in this papyrus, see Cadell 1995, 217–18.

jewski suggests that Egyptian judges could find, just as they did in the laws of the population of the *Chora*, legal precedent in the law of the Jews translated into Greek. Unfortunately, there is no extant text that gives an indication of exactly how this might have happened, but the possibility exists that parts of the Greek Pentateuch might have lent themselves to the arbitration of civic disputes, particularly regarding marriage. A case is known involving a Greek woman, Helladote, married to a Jew named Jonathas as recorded in CPJud. 1.128. Within her plea to the regent is a sentence containing both the term συγγραφή, the word in common use for Alexandrian marriage contracts, and a clause explaining that her marriage was contracted [κατὰ τόν νόμον πολιτικόν] τῶν Ἰουδαιῶν. This is for Modrzejewski an indication that "the actual role of the Septuagint in the life of the Jewish communities in Egypt" is an established historical fact. In spite of this, he continues, Jewish law perhaps did not always have the last word in disputes. The Pentateuch does not contain regulations for contracting marriage, only for disposing of an unwanted wife, the latter in contradiction to Greek custom. Thus Alexandrian Jews may have used συγγραφαί to contract marriage and the regulations of the Torah to dissolve them. Such a compromise between the two legal systems regarding repudiating a wife is suggested by a text describing a Jewish husband's return of a dowry to his ex-wife's family in accordance with Alexandrian practice. Modrzejewski's conclusion from the papyrological evidence is that Jews did not feel constrained to be bound by the regulations of the Torah but conducted civic legal decisions by what he calls a "fluid *halakhah*," often in tension with the written law.[9]

Given then that the educated members of the Jewish community were well-adapted to their Greek environment and perhaps did not feel overly bound by the Torah translated into Greek, what does this tell us about the translator's intention to make theologically motivated changes to the text? That question is brought into sharper focus by Michael Knibb's observation that Alexandrian interpreters of the Septuagint were removed from matters of concern to Palestinian exegetes. There is, for instance, no evidence that messianic ideas were of great interest to the Alexandrian community.[10] If there were a larger population who lived by Greek custom, then who was the target audience for which the translation of the legal material was

---

9. Modrzejewski 2001, 192–96.
10. Knibb 2006, 15.

made, and with what intention? These are not easy questions to answer, but perhaps a partial answer will emerge in what follows.

In terms of a "theology of law," one could at this point assert that there are a number of things about which there is no doubt and some about which there is uncertainty. There is no doubt that the legal parts of the LXX Pentateuch contain wording that conveys alternate ideas to the Hebrew original.[11] This wording may have been selected with the religious or doctrinal needs of communities in mind. But there exists some uncertainty over the likelihood that the Septuagint's legal materials were designed to be clear and to function as a guide for legal or religious practice.[12] If the Numbers translator was less concerned with faithfulness to his *Vorlage* and more concerned with ironing out contradictions in Scripture, Greek Leviticus might be shown to take the opposite strategy of being concerned more with faithfulness at the word level and less at the level of meaning.[13] Perhaps a parallel to these divergent attitudes exists in the fact that priests preserved the Egyptian Manual. If a similar class was responsible for the translation and promulgation of the Pentateuch, it is likely that their internal disputes and divergent attitudes toward the parent text finds expression in the diversity of interpretive strategies found in the five books.

The work of the Leviticus translator will now be featured more closely, by means of syntactic and lexicographical examples.

4. Greek Leviticus and Legal Meaning

As an opening illustration of his activity, one might consider the way in which Greek pronouns are used in the cultic prescriptions of that book. By their gender or position in a sentence, they often change the meaning of the Hebrew instruction, but not in a way that is evident of intentionality.

1. Lev 3:9 καὶ προσοίσει ἀπὸ τῆς θυσίας τοῦ σωτηρίου κάρπωμα τῷ θεῷ, <u>τὸ στέαρ</u> καὶ τὴν ὀσφὺν ἄμωμον· σὺν ταῖς ψόαις περιελεῖ <u>αὐτό</u>. In

---

11. In the case of Leviticus, see Büchner 2008.
12. See the comments made about the legislation for sacrifice involving inadvertent sins in Lev 5 in Büchner 2013.
13. This phenomenon is most eloquently treated in a work written over a century ago: Huber 1913.

Hebrew, it is the tail that is to be removed; in Greek, it is the fat that is to be removed.

2. Lev 6:3 καὶ ἀφελεῖ τὴν κατακάρπωσιν, ἣν ἂν καταναλώσῃ <u>τὸ πῦρ</u> τὴν ὁλοκαύτωσιν, ἀπὸ τοῦ θυσιαστηρίου καὶ παραθήσει <u>αὐτὸ</u> ἐχόμενον τοῦ θυσιαστηρίου. In Hebrew, the ashes are to be put next to the altar, but the Greek instruction suggests that the fire is to be put next to the altar.

3. Lev 14:32 οὗτος ὁ νόμος, ἐν ᾧ ἐστιν ἡ ἁφὴ τῆς λέπρας. In Hebrew, the relative clause is headless, pointing to the one in whom there is a skin disease. The Greek is simply representing the relative, but the result suggests that it is the law tainted by the disease.[14]

4. Lev 23:41 τοῦ ἐνιαυτοῦ· νόμιμον αἰώνιον εἰς τὰς γενεὰς ὑμῶν· ἐν τῷ μηνὶ τῷ ἑβδόμῳ ἑορτάσετε <u>αὐτήν</u>. In Hebrew, a feast is to be celebrated, but in Greek it is uncertain exactly what is to be celebrated, since there is no referent for the feminine pronoun.[15]

5. Lev 25:22 καὶ σπερεῖτε τὸ ἔτος τὸ ὄγδοον, καὶ φάγεσθε ἀπὸ τῶν γενημάτων παλαιά· ἕως τοῦ ἔτους τοῦ ἐνάτου, ἕως ἂν ἔλθῃ τὰ γενήματα αὐτῆς, φάγεσθε παλαιὰ παλαιῶν. In the Hebrew regulation, it is the year's yield that is referred to; in Greek, the possessive pronoun is in the feminine, meaning that it is not the year's yield but the yield of something unknown.[16]

---

14. See Den Hertog 2001, 78.

15. In the MT, the referent is חג, twice appearing in this particular set of regulations but twice omitted in the translation. In v. 39, the rendering ἑορτάσετε τῷ κυρίῳ omits the internal accusative ἑορτή. The second case of omission (v. 40) is possibly because of homoioteleuton, but there the shorter sentence makes perfect sense, and one wonders if the first omission of the noun had anything to do with it. Without the presence of ἑορτή, the pronoun refers back to "day" some verses prior, but making it do so is out of character for pronouns operating in Greek Leviticus.

16. See Wevers 1997, 413. For Wevers, the feminine referent can only be the land mentioned a few verses previously, and, indeed, LXX.D and BdA add "the land" for clarification. Huber (1913, 36), on the other hand, felt that the translator is here rendering the feminine suffix for the sake of formal precision (SP and OG read the suffix also in v. 21) and that to regard the referent as the land is no more than an emergency

These examples indicate that the translator's chief intention is representing Hebrew pronouns to preserve Hebrew word order rather than to carry across the exact meaning of the original. The resultant changes in meaning are only the result of accident. If he were producing a legal document for a juridical setting, such an intention is somewhat surprising, but if he were producing a faithful translation of a sacred text, it is unsurprising.

On another level of inquiry, one might examine words that are more theologically significant than pronouns and their referents. The matter to weigh is whether or not translators might have selected Greek words for their intrinsic theological value. Two fairly prominent terms, νόμος and δικαίωμα, come to mind. Both words are taken up by later communities in contexts that require the connotation of the Hebrew words with which they were originally matched rather than their connotation in normal Greek usage. In the case of νόμος, that Hebraic connotation is "divine law," and for δικαίωμα, the Hebraic connotation is "precept required by divine law." Two issues need to be settled. The first is to discover why these words were selected by the translators of the Pentateuch. The second is to propose the process by which they underwent semantic development in order to be understood by later communities in meanings that native Greek speakers who did not know Hebrew would not have associated with them.

Let us make a basic assertion about the audience of the LXX Pentateuch. They were highly educated Jews who were trained in classical scholarship. Honigman, in writing about Aristeas's audience, points out that as a writer he was demanding of his readership and expected them to be receptive to contemporary literary allusions.[17] The same would be true for the readers of the Septuagint. When, therefore, words appear in the Septuagint whose meanings are out of kilter with classical usage, its readers must have expressed some surprise in reaction. The only way to make sense of this is that there must have been an ancillary purpose behind their use, in other words, that the translators had a purpose beyond conveying meaning in context. To the word νόμος we now turn our attention. A fitting place to start our discussion is with a comment made by Modrzejewski that it is unfortunate that the Pentateuch later became known as ὁ νόμος, since νόμος and תורה differ conceptually. The decrees that make up the תורה, as is well known, reside in the cultural context of ancient Semitic

---

measure. Wevers (1997, 413), having made the remark about the land, adds that the possessive makes sense legally only if it refers to the eighth year.

17. Honigman 2003, 28.

law codes, that is, sets of laws given on the initiative of a divine figure for a prominent human mediator to promulgate in a specific geographic location. Greek νόμοι, on the other hand, are not given to human leaders by divinities but are a collection of normative propositions originating in the will of the social group organized as a civic body.[18] Thus in Plato, νόμοι are customs observed, but not through force of law.[19] There are other, more suitable terms for laws that are given by a higher authority or might carry the name of a lawgiver. The word θεσμός is the most obvious one and is in fact a term expressing divine law in Greek literature. So, too, are διαγράμμα and πρόσταγμα, words in common use for the kinds of decrees promulgated by a regent for their subjects to obey. Of these three, only πρόσταγμα is found in the Greek Pentateuch.

Of course, νόμος does appear in the Pentateuch in its natural meaning: that which humans agree on as normative. For instance, οὗτος ὁ νόμος followed by a genitive of the thing described often translates words of the חקק family in the sense of "firmly established usage, custom."[20] Likewise, νόμος is found as an appropriate rendering for תורה when it means "regulation or instruction for a ritual" (e.g., the Passover in Exod 12:43 and the sacrifices in Lev 6). Its regular Greek usage therefore does overlap with those of its main Hebrew equivalents. Having said this, however, the theological context in which such customs and usages are found is a set of instructions that originates from the deity who speaks it to the human lawgiver representing him. Because of frequent usage, νόμος paired with תורה at later periods in time came to mean divine law. Although θεσμός would have been the better and more appropriate word to convey the precise meaning of תורה for these later communities, it was by accident of translational convention that it was never employed. In other words, νόμος was chosen in a less theologically overt manner, and its original usage does not demonstrate theological intent but rather that its selection was due to its presence in the broad semantic domain of what is established norm for conduct. Through familiarity, and with frequent use, νόμος became synonymous with divine law. From this one might say that an important theological term of the Hebrew that was intended by the Priestly writers

---

18. Modrzejewski 2001, 184. See also LSJ, s.v. "νόμος," 1180: "that which is in habitual practice."

19. See Plato, Leg. 715d: where magistrates are servants of the law, wholeness and divine blessings follow.

20. BDB, s.v. "חֻקָּה," 350.

to convey divine law was rendered by a word that at first did not exactly convey the sense of the Hebrew, but for later communities it mediated the idea found in the Hebrew. Stated otherwise, the theological value of the word for later communities does not reside in the Septuagint itself but only in the way that those communities took it up.

The same is true for δικαίωμα, a prominent legal term of the Greek Pentateuch occurring in Ptolemaic legal texts and taken up in the New Testament and early Jewish literature. We begin by noting its appearance in Num 36:13: αὗται αἱ ἐντολαὶ καὶ τὰ δικαιώματα καὶ τὰ κρίματα ἃ ἐνετείλατο κύριος ἐν χειρὶ Μωυσῇ ἐπὶ δυσμῶν Μωαβ ἐπὶ τοῦ Ιορδάνου κατὰ Ιεριχω. In this context, as it is in the majority of other occurrences in the Pentateuch, the noun is found in the same semantic range as ἐντολή, or that which is authoritatively commanded, in this case, by the deity. The noun is well-attested during the Hellenistic epoch, especially in relation to Ptolemaic jurisprudence, but not in the meaning just mentioned. Instead, it connotes a "document of justification attached to a dossier in a plea of right" in order for the proceedings to commence or from which one is able to arrive at a judgment.[21] That is to say, it is a piece of evidence that human individuals have in their possession rather than a charge emanating from a regent, human or divine. Cadell removes any doubt about this by citing a dozen legal texts in which individuals supply these justificatory documents from which to make a defense. This, as she observes, is in contrast with the usage of the word when employed in the Greek Pentateuch, where it evokes something that emanates from God to be put into practice by humans.[22] Harl and Dogniez similarly express some reservation over the meaning "règles du droit" proposed by Le Boulluec and Sandevoir.[23] Among the many Ptolemaic papyri containing this word, the one that most clearly illustrates how δικαίωμα is employed as a category distinct from διαγράμμα, decree or regulation, is the one containing the dispute mentioned above (P.Pet. 3.29). While BDAG cites P.Oxy. 8.1119 from the 200s CE in support of the Hebraic meaning,[24] there are some reasons why its applicability to the Septuagint is in doubt. Cadell provides a careful

---

21. LSJ, s.v. "δικαίωμα," 429; Pape 1954, 627, who has "Rechtsanspruch."
22. Cadell 1995, 216.
23. Dogniez and Harl 1992, 53. See Le Boulluec and Sandevoir 1989, 43, who cite the papyrological evidence but in spite of it accept the Hebraic meaning based on context.
24. BDAG is followed by Tov 1990, 92.

explanation of the language of that text, explaining that the δικαιώματα in question were the special privileges granted by Hadrian to the inhabitants of the city of Antinoe. Hadrian exempted them from liturgical duties at their places of residence outside the city. For this reason, she argues that appealing to this papyrus text for support of the meaning in the Pentateuch is unfounded, since its very precise historical and administrative context is too far removed from that of the Greek Pentateuch and does not support the sense that it appears to take there, not least for the fact that the papyrus postdates the Greek Pentateuch by almost six centuries. To return to what we may know, says Cadell, the word, on the one hand, means a collection of justificatory documents required at a trial, pieces that would have been able to support a plaintiff's case; on the other hand, the word as used in the Pentateuch always appears to connote something a deity may claim as emanating from, and belonging to, the deity.[25] How, then, to account for the disjunct between the two? Cadell's solution is that the Septuagint translators had a perception of the whole (justification) standing in for the parts (the kinds of documents that would emanate from officials, such as a local edict or magistrate's letter). However trusting this solution may be of the translator's capabilities, it nevertheless relies upon an expectation that he did not make semantic mismatches. We know this is not the case, since translators often disregarded the conventions of the living language.[26]

Further support for regarding her view as a compositional fallacy may be found in Philo, who trades upon the frequent juxtaposition of δικαίωμα with words for divine commands in the Septuagint. He seems to regard this as unusual and in need of some explanation. In his exposition of Gen 26:5 (QG 4.184), he cites the Septuagint's δικαιώματά μου καὶ τὰ νόμιμά μου and comments as follows:

διαφέρει δικαιώματα νομίμου· τὰ μὲν γάρ πως δύναται συνίστασθαι φύσει, τὰ δὲ νόμιμα θέσει. πρεσβύτερα δὲ τῶν θέσει τὰ φύσει, ὥστε καὶ τὸ δίκαιον νόμου.

δικαιώματα are different from νόμιμά, since rights can somehow exist by nature, while laws (do so) by convention. But those things (existing) by

---

25. Cadell 1995, 220.
26. One thinks of the use of ἐξομολογέω in Gen 29:35.

nature are older than those (existing) by convention, and so, what is right (is older) than custom.[27]

LXX.D, to my mind, is correct with the decision for *Rechtsentscheide* at Lev 25 and *Rechtssätze* at Num 36:13. The best English rendering one can offer for δικαίωμα, to be fair to the data, is "act of right," or "right action," which would suit Rom 5:16 and 18, as well as Rev 15:4 and 19:8. However, when Paul in Rom 1 and 2 or the writer of Heb 9 engage in discourse on the Jewish-legal level, δικαίωμα occurs as it does by allusion to the LXX's language. It has become familiar to Jewish-Christian audiences through frequency of use, but that says nothing about the word's meaning in the Ptolemaic era.

Two further lexical examples will illustrate the supposition that, in the legal material, translators worked on the word level during the process of translation and that what resulted from that activity is not designed to be pedantic on a legal level. In the Septuagint, the word νυμφή is without variation the rendering for כלה. This equivalence is based upon the latter's meaning of "bride," occurring only in the later books of Isaiah, Jeremiah, and Micah (e.g., Mic 7:6). The Greek word's meaning outside of the LXX and the New Testament is limited to "young bride." It is therefore a good match for כלה in the prophetic literature. When the Hebrew word occurs in the Pentateuch and the historical books, it does not mean bride but daughter-in-law, in each case taking a masculine possessive pronoun referring to the father-in-law. It is of some interest that the translator of Genesis decided that the meaning of the Hebrew word found in the prophetic literature is the meaning that he would like to apply to its occurrence in the Pentateuch. The result is that three times in Gen 38 Tamar is Judah's "young bride," which makes no legal sense at all. Neither is there a warrant for the supposition that the meaning daughter-in-law is part of the semantic range of νυμφή. There is a suitable Greek term for daughter-in-law, νυός; being found only in the Homeric corpus, it was possibly unknown to the translator of Genesis. Word matching was more important than meaning transfer.

A final lexical example to consider is the use in the Pentateuch of the verb μιαίνω. Outside of Leviticus, it expresses the natural active meaning of "defile," as when Shechem defiles Dinah or the people by their actions

---

27. The translation is my own, with some dependence on Marcus's translation of the Armenian (Marcus 1953, 467).

defile the land or the sanctuary. In the passive, it may mean "be defiled" or the tolerative "allow oneself to be defiled," as in Num 5:19 (so LXX.D). When, however, one encounters the active of μιαίνω in Lev 13, the verb's subject is the priest and its object an individual consulting the priest in order to be cleansed. The priest defiles the one needing to be cleansed. In Hebrew, this problem does not exist, since טהר *piel* can mean defile as well as declare defiled. Not so the Greek verb. One can only imagine an educated Alexandrian reader sensing that something is amiss in the usage. To assume from the context a declarative meaning for the Greek word, as it exists for the Hebrew usage, is to clutch at straws. The simpler explanation is that the translator was working on the word level and would not deviate from a predetermined matching of טהר *piel* with μιαίνω. Meaning was not his intention.

The words considered here, with the exception of μιαίνω, became adopted by later reading communities in Hebraic meanings, based on the Septuagint's faithfulness in pairing them with a Hebrew word. It was the Hebrew meaning that persisted via the Greek as a kind of conduit of it. To read that "conducted" meaning back onto the Greek of the Septuagint is to my mind without support from the evidence and contrary to established lexicographical method.

Two examples of imprecise legal prescriptions from Greek Leviticus may round off the argument that mechanical matching of language was for the translator the highest good.

In the Hebrew regulations prohibiting incest in Lev 18:14 and 20:20, one is forbidden to marry the wife of one's father's brother (here called דדה). In the Septuagint, she is classed as συγγενής, that is, a blood relative.[28]

In Lev 3:4, 10, and 15, the Hebrew regulations require that fat against the spine in the region of the kidneys be removed together with the kidney fat and the appendage of the liver. The equivalent regulation found in the Septuagint suggests that the kidney fat and the fat on the μηρία, that is, a part of the leg, are to be removed more or less simultaneously (καὶ ἀμφοτέρους τοὺς νεφροὺς καὶ τὸ στέαρ τὸ ἐπ' αὐτῶν τὸ ἐπὶ τῶν μηρίων καὶ τὸν λοβὸν τὸν ἐπὶ τοῦ ἥπατος σὺν τοῖς νεφροῖς περιελών). Again, this is something an educated reader would find illogical.

Altogether, this evidence points to a matter worth airing: there are renderings in the Septuagint Pentateuch that appear to be intentionally

---

28. Milgrom (2000, 1528) is somewhat surprised by this inaccuracy.

lacking in communicative clarity and deliberately framed so as to be unsuitable for the kind of vocabulary designed for rules by which a religious community could live. Some of these terms did, however, become theologically significant for later communities who read the Pentateuch.

In short, one would have to decide what relationship may be identified between sporadic occurrences of septuagintal usage that in the eyes of a well-educated audience diminishes meaning and sporadic instances of changes with obvious intention to produce sense. Let us pay some attention to the noticeable diversity of approach to the legal parts of the Greek Pentateuch. A book that contains more free renderings (e.g., Numbers) certainly creates the impression that there was a theologically motivated purpose for the translation of the Pentateuch. By the same token, a book that is not as prone to interpretation (e.g., Leviticus) provides support for the perspective that there was more of a linguistic purpose behind the Pentateuch's translation than a theological one. Related to this question of divergent attitudes is the degree to which the Pentateuch translators worked independently from one another or followed one another's lead in some kind of identifiable progression.

5. Who Depended on Whom?

There is clearly some interdependence observable in the way the translators of Leviticus and Exodus share legal and cultic vocabulary, but it is equally apparent that Leviticus often prefers his own course even though existing choices were available and known to him. On the order in which the books were translated, there exists some scholarly division. Den Hertog believes in the priority of Deuteronomy and doubts that Exodus would have been translated early on, owing to its polemical subject matter.[29] He argues from a number of examples that the Leviticus translator depended on, or even improved on, the choices of Deuteronomy's translator, though he leaves room for arguments to the contrary. Martin Rösel, on the other hand, believes Deuteronomy to be the last of the pentateuchal books to be translated.[30] The question of dependence and serial order is difficult to settle. There are, for example, some renderings common to Greek Exodus, Leviticus, and Deuteronomy, such as קדש in the meaning "holy thing"

---

29. Den Hertog 2004.
30. Rösel 2001, 28 and n. 14.

by the neuter plural ἅγια and the rendering of ערוה in its various applied meanings ("shame, intercourse") by ἀσχημοσύνη ("embarrassment") rather than a direct translation equivalent such as γύμνωσις. On the other hand, Leviticus deviates from Exodus and Deuteronomy by using a variety of Greek verbs of slaying for זבח, whereas Exodus and Deuteronomy do not vary from θύω. Sometimes the Greek renderings of Leviticus tend toward a greater degree of literalism, such as when it comes to manufacturing items of false worship. Exodus and Deuteronomy employ ποιέω + ἑαυτου for עשה followed by ל. Leviticus does not use the reflexive pronoun but, in more literalistic fashion, the personal pronoun in the dative. It has been shown that Leviticus more frequently makes use of ὅτι *causale* than does Exodus.[31] A quick survey of the ratio between use of γάρ by Leviticus and Deuteronomy versus ὅτι shows that Leviticus uses γάρ and ὅτι in roughly equal proportion, while Deuteronomy's use of ὅτι to γάρ is about 4:1. This would count in favor of Deuteronomy's technique tending toward the literal and therefore being late. My own impression is that, if one goes by the rule of thumb that literal means later, there is room to believe that Exodus with its use of better Greek and Numbers with its freedom to engage in exegetical correction must precede Deuteronomy and Leviticus, which tend to be more literal.

It may be useful to suggest that different segments of translation found in the Greek Pentateuch may reflect nothing more than the kinds of attitudes to the prominence and priority of the source text held by the priestly guardians of legal material. Whether they were concerned to write Scripture for their community to live by is a question whose answer may be inaccessible to us.

6. Searching for a Systematic Exegetical Tradition

Without rehashing what is a well-worn debate, that exegesis in the Septuagint cannot be argued unless one is quite clear that differences between the Hebrew and its translation[32] are not the result of translation technique,

---

31. Aejmelaeus 1993.

32. Pietersma wants to stress that discovering the extent to which exegesis is located in a text requires rules that are "rooted in the textual-linguistic make-up of the translational unit" (2006, 36). As a result, in a translation marked by excessively quantitative equivalence such as the Psalms, it is highly likely that the function of any given word in the target language is merely to represent a word in the source language. If the range of a lexical item so used on the word level is made to extend beyond that

it is worth noting a number of remarks made by Michael Knibb in his introduction to his 2006 BETL edited volume on the Septuagint and messianism, to guide us in approaching the evidence of the LXX Pentateuch's legal material, with special attention to Leviticus.[33]

First, if a matter such as messianism, of great concern to Palestinian communities, was of little or no importance to the Alexandrian community, this would apply to other topics also. Second, although there is no doubt that translators made renderings that were different from the intent of the Hebrew, the question is how consistently this happened and to what extent it was more than sporadic or accidental. Along the way of adjudicating such things in larger studies, some rigorous criteria are to be employed for each case of what may be deemed exegesis. Significant differences must exist between the Hebrew and the Greek words, there must be a contemporary external tradition for comparison, and there needs to be a clear assessment of how isolated instances of change relate to the translator's overall translational ethos and procedure.[34]

Since the theme of this chapter is living by the Torah in Greek, let us now consider Lev 18:4–5, where living by the Torah is indeed the subject. It is a passage that plays a prominent role also in Ezek 18 and 20, where obedience to the Torah is the basis for life. Below, the Hebrew and Greek clauses are grouped together, with their respective English translations (NRSV/NETS), followed by comments on the more weighty terms. By examining the full range of linguistic usage and the possibilities that arise from that, it will be possible to come to some understanding of the relationship between meaning in Hebrew and meaning in Greek and to suggest ways in which the Greek may be taking an interpretive line.

Lev 18:4

את משפטי תעשו
My ordinances you shall observe

τὰ κρίματά μου ποιήσετε
My judgments you shall perform

---

to the phrase level or even to the discourse level, we are, says Pietersma, on uncertain ground.
33. Knibb 2006, 15–17.
34. Knibb 2006, 18–19.

ואת חקתי תשמרו
and my statutes you shall keep

καὶ τὰ προστάγματά μου φυλάξεσθε
and my ordinances you shall keep

ללכת בהם
Walking by them

πορεύεσθαι ἐν αὐτοῖς
to walk by them

Lev 18:5

ושמרתם
You shall keep

καὶ φυλάξεσθε
And you shall keep,

את־חקתי ואת משפטי
my statutes and my ordinances

πάντα τὰ προστάγματά μου καὶ πάντα τὰ κρίματά μου
all my ordinances and all my judgments

———

καὶ ποιήσετε αὐτά
and you shall do them

אשר יעשה אתם האדם
by doing so

ἃ ποιήσας ἄνθρωπος
as for the things a person does
LXX.D: nachdem er sie getan hat
BdA: c'est en les exécutant que

וחי בהם
one shall live

ζήσεται ἐν αὐτοῖς
he shall live by them

18:4. φυλάξεσθε. Milgrom explains that, in Hebrew, guarding in the context of prohibitions means guarding against their violation, but used in the context of performative stipulations, as it is here, guarding means heeding or respecting.³⁵ In similar fashion, the Greek verb may mean to observe, cherish a command.³⁶

πορεύεσθαι. The Hebrew epexegetical infinitive is more loosely connected to the preceding verb and explains or defines more exactly the preceding action.³⁷ Such a function does not reside in the Greek infinitive. Instead, qualification of the main action, in the form of a supplementary predicate, is a function of the participle, not the infinitive, especially when the subject of the main verb and the attendant verb is the same.³⁸ Accordingly, NETS renders here in a way that suggests a purpose, and compare BdA "pour y trouver votre voie" and LXX.D "in ihnen zu wandeln." Goodwin mentions that, in Homer, the simple infinitive expressed consequence: "so as to."³⁹ The Hebrew instructs: obey the Torah (by) conducting your life in accordance with it. The Greek instructs: obey the Torah in order to conduct your life in accordance with it. Or stated differently, in Hebrew, good conduct is a requirement for a way of obedience, but in Greek there is an adjustment: a way of obedience is the requisite for good conduct. Again, this cannot be said to be a deliberate coloring by the translator, since it is merely the consequence of his activity on the word level. But consider the next verse.

18:5. καὶ ποιήσετε αὐτά. This presupposes a double reading of the existing consonants, or a harmonizing addition presupposing ועשיתם אתם that does indeed accompany the command "to keep" four times in MT Leviticus following this passage. If so, then it means that the translator was conscious of the full Hebrew formula and augmented the incomplete formula he noticed here. He may also have been mindful of the proximity of "walking" and "keeping" in the previous verse.

---

35. Milgrom 2000, 1522.
36. LSJ, s.v. "φυλάσσω," 1961.
37. JM §124o; GKC §114o.
38. Smyth 1984, §2054, who provides the example γελῶν εἶπε ("he said, laughingly").
39. Goodwin 1977, §1533.

ἃ ποιήσας ἄνθρωπος. The first half of the clause אשר יעשה אתם האדם expresses potentiality by a special use of אשר with subject and a *yiqtol* verb and equates to the protasis of a conditional sentence (identical cases are found at 4:22 and 5:22). It may be understood to say "when one does them," or as Milgrom translates, "if one does them."[40] The Leviticus translator rendered the previous two similar constructions by ἐάν and subjunctive, but in this instance he resorts to a relative pronoun as proleptic object of a participle immediately following it. By rendering the neuter plural relative pronoun for אשר, he succeeds in accounting for the Hebrew relative without needing to render the object אתם. This allows the verbs doing and living to stand closer together without intruding words. How much weight does one give his choice to use the participle? Vahrenhorst regards the participle as fulfilling two functions: it subordinates the action of performing, thereby emphasizing living and indicating that the commandments are the gift of life; the use of the aorist signifies a temporal progression from doing to living, an idea taken up by later exegetes.[41] This may be true. It is just as plausible to regard the aorist participle's attendant action as coincident with the leading verb ζήσεται.[42] The result is that there is a circumstantial or conditional sense to the entire sentence: it is in doing them, that one will live by the laws. One might observe that, though MT Ezekiel, in chapters 18 and 20, cites the Hebrew formula verbatim a number of times, the Greek translator of Ezekiel does not cite LXX Leviticus precisely but places the first verb in the future: ἃ ποιήσει ἄνθρωπος καὶ ζήσεται ἐν αὐτοῖς. If the later translator was aware of the interpretive value of the former's rendering, he did not capitalize on it. We now come to all-important statement ζήσεται ἐν αὐτοῖς. Milgrom explains that, by including the instrumental "by them," the Hebrew suggests that the fulfillment of the laws gives life, that is, that the laws themselves are life-giving, in contrast with the Deuteronomistic Code, according to which it is God who grants life to the obedient person.[43] The Leviticus translator's rendering, though a close transposition of the original, is nevertheless worth exploring as an expression in its own right. Is it as natural to say in Greek as it is in Hebrew that one lives "by something"? Harlé and Pralon also ask this question: How does one define "to live" in this verse? For them it implies keeping away from the death implicit

---

40. Milgrom 2000, 1522.
41. Vahrenhorst 2011, 388.
42. See Goodwin 1977, §187; Smyth 1984, §1872c2.
43. Milgrom 2000, 1522.

in breaking any of the commandments of Lev 18. That is, it means staying alive in contrast to dying.⁴⁴ The question is whether the translator's usage of ζάω + ἐν + an abstract suggests a different line of interpretation to the Hebrew, in which, as Milgrom explains, "to live" is the opposite of "being cut off."⁴⁵ In the extrabiblical Greek context, it is in Plato that one observes the closest parallel to the LXX's close rendering of the Hebrew in 18:5. In *Phaed.* 68d is found a reference to those who despise the body and "live by" philosophy: τοῖς μάλιστα τοῦ σώματος ὀλιγωροῦσίν τε καὶ ἐν φιλοσοφίᾳ ζῶσιν. In *Leg.* 770e one reads that laws that are able to effect something are the kind of laws one should accept with open arms and by which one should live: ταῦτα ἡμεῖς τε ἔμπροσθεν συνωμολογησάμεθα, καὶ νῦν ὑμεῖς ἡμῶν εἰς ταῦτα ἑκάτερα βλέποντες ἐπαινεῖτε καὶ ψέγετε τοὺς νόμους ὅσοι μὴ ταῦτα δυνατοί, τοὺς δὲ δυνατοὺς ἀσπάζεσθέ τε καὶ φιλοφρόνως δεχόμενοι ζῆτε ἐν αὐτοῖς· ("adopting them wholeheartedly, rule your lives by them").⁴⁶ In other words, here the Greek of the Septuagint accounts for the Hebrew in idiomatic fashion and does not add to its meaning. With all this in view, one can now consider a shift in understanding resulting from the whole stipulation of 18:4–5 in Greek, when compared to the Hebrew. The Greek stipulation appears to make a logical progression from the formulation in 18:4, "keep my ordinances in order to conduct your life by them," to "one lives by whatever one does" in 18:5. By emphasizing the life-giving effect arising from doing, the LXX offers a different interpretation from one that emphasizes the inherent life-giving aspect of the law itself. This may be regarded as being consistent with Deuteronomy and Ezekiel. When the words "doing" and "living" occur together in MT Deuteronomy, the idea is "do so that you may live." The Greek translation follows suit by expressing purpose with ἵνα throughout. Both MT and LXX Ezekiel hold a similar view that doing results in life. The Greek of Ezek 18:22 adds some color to what this means. It is in doing that the living happens: ἐν τῇ δικαιοσύνῃ αὐτοῦ ᾗ ἐποίησεν ζήσεται. It is too early to say that such shifts in meaning follow a consistent trajectory, and, as has been observed thus far, changes such as these are often the accidental result of fairly close pairing of Greek and Hebrew items.

---

44. Harlé and Pralon 1988, 160.
45. Milgrom 2000, 1522.
46. Bury 1926, 454–55.

7. Future Lines of Inquiry

Space does not allow further detailed probes, but possible lines of interpretation in Greek Leviticus to investigate in future studies include the following:

1. The ratio of Hebrew stipulations that become more vague when translated into Greek (as treated above) to those stipulations that become more direct or specific, as in in Lev 18:11, where MT's ambiguity is reduced by the addition of ὁμοπατριά.

2. The ratio of changes that appear to take a polemical stance against Alexandrian religion and culture to other instances where this is clearly of no concern.

3. The ratio of words of disapproval that have a moral connotation (ἀσέβημα) to those that involve a human emotional or sensory negative reaction (μυσερόν, βδέλυγμα).

4. The ratio of changes that seem to hold a more sympathetic view of victims to language that does not appear to do so; an example of the former is the snare, σκάνδαλον, that is placed before the blind (LXX Lev 19:14) rather than the stumbling block of MT.

8. Conclusion

There is no doubt that the Septuagint's legal corpus contains interpretive changes of a theological nature. It is also possible that, on the juridical level, some regulations of the Torah in Greek may have served the needs of the Ptolemaic courts in settling disputes unique to the Jewish community. But it could be argued with equal force that a large proportion of the legal corpus in the Greek Pentateuch contains language that is too vague or meaningless for it to be considered as a conveyor of legal or theological ideas. In arbitrating between these positions, it would be safe to say that the Greek Pentateuch's diversity of interpretive focus reflects, on the one hand, sporadic debates within priestly or intellectual groups and, on the other, variant attitudes toward rendering the words of a sacred text. That the receptor communities derived theological meaning from the Septuagint's language is not always an indicator that the text was framed with a theological purpose in mind. Nevertheless, much work remains to be done in gathering and analyzing interpretive changes that, however fortuitously, contribute to our knowledge about the expectations of the Jewish community of what a translation of the Torah ought to mean for their religious and civic life.

Bibliography

Aejmelaeus, Anneli. 1993. "OTI *causale* in Septuagintal Greek." Pages 17–36 in *On the Trail of the Septuagint Translators: Collected Essays*. Edited by Anneli Aejmelaeus. Kampen: Kok Pharos.

Büchner, Dirk. 2008. "'You Shall not Give of Your Seed to Serve an Archon'. Leviticus 18:21 in the Septuagint." Pages 183–96 in *Translating a Translation: The Septuagint and Its Modern Translations in the Context of Early Judaism*. Edited by Hans Ausloos et al. BETL 213. Leuven: Peeters.

———. 2013. "Writing a Commentary on the Septuagint." Pages 525–38 in *XIV Congress of the International Organization for Septuagint and Cognate Studies: Helsinki, 2010*. Edited by Melvin K. H. Peters. SCS 59. Atlanta: Society of Biblical Literature.

Bury, R. G., ed. and trans. 1926. *Plato IX. Laws*. Vol. 1. LCL. Cambridge: Harvard University Press.

Cadell, Hélène. 1995. "Vocabulaire de la législation ptolemaique: probléme du sens de dikaiôma dans le Pentateuque." Pages 207–21 in Κατά τοὺς ο': *Selon les Septante; Hommage à Marguerite Harl*. Edited by Gilles Dorival and Olivier Munnich. Paris: Cerf.

Cook, Johann. 1983. "Die Belang van die Septuagint vir die Teologie." *Tydskrif vir Geesteswetenskappe* 23:165–77.

Dogniez, Cécile, and Marguerite Harl. 1992. *Le Deutéronome*. BdA 5. Paris: Cerf.

Goodwin, William. 1977. *A Greek Grammar*. 3rd ed. London: MacMillan.

Harlé, Paul, and Didier Pralon. 1988. *Le Levitique*. BdA 3. Paris: Cerf.

Hertog, Cornelis den. 2001. "The Treatment of Relative Clauses in the Greek Leviticus." Pages 65–98 in *Helsinki Perspectives on the Translation Technique of the Septuagint*. Edited by Raija Sollamo and Seppo Sippilä. PFES 82. Göttingen: Vandenhoeck & Ruprecht.

———. 2004. "Erwägungen zur relativen Chronologie der Bücher Leviticus und Deuteronomium." Pages 216–28 in *Studien zur Bedeutung und Entstehung der griechischen Bibel*. Vol. 2 of *Im Brennpunkt: Die Septua-*

ginta. Edited by Siegfried Kreuzer and Jürgen Peter Lesch. BWANT 161. Stuttgart: Kohlhammer.

Honigman, Sylvie. 2003. *The Septuagint and Homeric Scholarship in Alexandria: A Study in the Narrative of the* Letter of Aristeas. London: Routledge.

Huber, Karl. 1913. *Über den Sprachcharakter des griechischen Leviticus*. Giessen: Töpelmann.

Jones, Spencer A. 2017. "Balaam, Pagan Prophet of God: A Commentary on Greek Numbers 22.1-21." Pages 123–68 in *The SBL Commentary on the Septuagint: An Introduction*. Edited by Dirk Büchner. SCS 67. Atlanta: SBL Press.

Knibb, Michael A. 2006. "The Septuagint and Messianism: Problems and Issues." Pages 3–20 in *The Septuagint and Messianism*. Edited by Michael A. Knibb. BETL 195. Leuven: Peeters.

Le Boulluec, Alain, and Pierre Sandevoir. 1989. *L'Exode*. BdA 2. Paris: Cerf.

Marcus, Ralph. 1953. *Philo: Questions on Genesis*. LCL. Cambridge: Harvard University Press.

Milgrom, Jacob. 2000. *Leviticus 17–22*. AB 3A. New York: Doubleday.

Modrzejewski, Joseph Mélèze. 2001. "The Septuagint as Nomos: How the Torah Became a 'Civic Law' for the Jews of Egypt." Pages 183–99 in *Critical Studies in Ancient Law, Comparative Law and Legal History*. Edited by John W. Cairns and Olivia F. Robinson. Oxford: Hart.

Pape, Wilhelm. 1954. *Griechisch-Deutsches Handwörterbuch*. Vol. 1. Graz: Akademische Druck- u. Verlagsanstalt.

Pietersma, Albert. 2006. "Exegesis in the Septuagint: Possibilities and Limitations (The Psalter as a Case in Point)." Pages 33–46 in *Septuagint Research: Issues and Challenges in the Study of the Greek Jewish Scriptures*. Edited by Wolfgang Kraus and R. Glenn Wooden. SCS 53. Atlanta: Society of Biblical Literature.

Rösel, Martin. 2001. "Die Septuaginta und der Kult: Interpretationen und Aktualisierungen im Buch Numeri." Pages 25–40 in *La Double Transmission du Texte Biblique: Études d'Histoire du Texte Offertes en Hommage à Adrian Schenker*. Edited by Yohanan Goldman and Christoff Uehlinger. OBO 179. Göttingen: Vandenhoeck & Ruprecht.

———. 2006. "Towards a 'Theology of the Septuagint.'" Pages 239–52 in *Septuagint Research: Issues and Challenges in the Study of the Greek Jewish Scriptures*. Edited by Wolfgang Kraus and R. Glenn Wooden. SCS 53. Atlanta: Society of Biblical Literature.

Rösel, Martin, and Christine Schlund. 2011. "Arithmoi / Numeri / Das Vierte Buch Mose." Pages 431–522 in *Septuaginta Deutsch: Erlaüterungen und Kommentare zum griechischen Alten Testament*. Vol. 1. Edited by Martin Karrer and Wolfgang Kraus. Stuttgart: Deutsche Bibelgesellschaft.

Smyth, Herbert. 1984. *Greek Grammar*. Revised by Gordon Messing. Cambridge: Harvard University Press.

Tov, Emanuel. 1990. "Greek Words and Hebrew Meanings." Pages 83–125 in *Melbourne Symposium on Septuagint Lexicography*. Edited by Takamitsu Muraoka. SCS 28. Atlanta: Scholars Press.

Vahrenhorst, Martin. 2011. "Leuitikon / Leviticus / Das Dritte Buch Mose." Pages 325–430 in *Septuaginta Deutsch: Erläuterungen und Kommentare zum griechischen Alten Testament*. Vol. 1. Edited by Martin Karrer and Wolfgang Kraus. Stuttgart: Deutsche Bibelgesellschaft.

Wevers, John W. 1997. *Notes on the Greek Text of Leviticus*. SCS 44. Atlanta: Scholars Press.

„Aber nicht wie die Ägypter formierte er seine Kunstwerke aus Backstein und Granit...":
Bild-Gottheiten in der Septuaginta

Stefanie Peintner

ABSTRACT: In the Septuagint the Greek term εἴδωλον is used as terminus technicus to denote foreign deities, with a focus on the visible representation. Specific for this expression is that deity and image are merged; the noun was used by the translators for both foreign deities and their manifestations (cult images) as well. In contrast to the more general term θεός it explicitly designates other deities than Israel's God. The term εἴδωλον could well be part of a Jewish sociolect for foreign deities. This is probably result of a theologically motivated choice by translators, because the notion covers all essential elements associated with foreign gods. Thus a clear distinction is made between the God of Israel and all other gods. The Greek term occurs in central documents of the Old Testament such as the Decalogue (Exod 20) or the the Song of Moses (Deut 32). The common denominator underlying the term εἴδωλον, regardless of context, can be named as "visible manifestation."

Aber nicht wie die Ägypter formierte er seine Kunstwerke aus Backstein und Granit...

Dieser Vers stammt aus einem Gedicht Heinrich Heines, der die fundamentale Unterscheidung zwischen den Völkern und Israel auf poetische Weise zum Ausdruck bringt. Mose selbst wird darin als großer Künstler bezeichnet, der statt Kunstwerken aus Stein und Metall Israel erschaffen habe: „ein großes, ewiges, heiliges Volk, ein Volk Gottes".[1]

Israel grenzt sich also dadurch von allen übrigen Völkern ab, weil es keine Gottesbilder in Form von Statuen und Denkmälern kennt. Das Bild

---

1. Das Zitat befindet sich in „Geständnisse", vgl. Heine 1987.

Gottes ist nach alttestamentlichem Verständnis in der Menschheit selbst zu finden, das von einer Generation zur nächsten vererbt wird (vgl. dazu Gen 5,1–3). Die Frage nach dem Umgang der Septuaginta mit fremden Gottesvorstellungen und -bildern zielt daher auf das Zentrum alttestamentlicher Religiosität und sollte daher auch in einer „Theologie der Septuaginta" berücksichtigt werden.

1. Gründe für die Begriffswahl von εἴδωλον für die Fremdgötter(bilder)

In der Septuaginta dient der griechische Begriff εἴδωλον als *terminus technicus*[2] für die Fremdgottheiten, wobei der Fokus auf der sichtbaren Erscheinungsform liegt. Das Besondere am Ausdruck εἴδωλον ist die Verschmelzung zwischen Gottheit und Bild. Das Substantiv meint nämlich sowohl fremde Gottheiten als auch deren Erscheinungsformen (Kultbilder). Im Unterschied zum Ausdruck θεός sind damit explizit andere Gottheiten gemeint.

Im griechischen Alten Testament wird εἴδωλον zu einem religiösen Terminus, dessen Wesenskern bis heute im modernen Sprachgebrauch erhalten geblieben ist. In der Gegenwart hat sich das *Idol* zwar in die Trivialsphäre des Personenkultes verlagert, enthält aber immer noch Spuren des antiken Wortsinnes, denn während der *Star* Bewunderung genießt, wird das Idol in übertriebenem Maße verehrt.

Der Idolbegriff betont demnach stärker das Moment der Verehrung, darin liegt auch die Krux: die Kombination aus Adoration und Bildhaftigkeit steht nämlich im Widerspruch mit der alttestamentlichen Theologie der bildlosen Alleinverehrung JHWHs.

Die Bezeichnung εἴδωλον ist möglicherweise Teil eines jüdischen Soziolekts für Fremdgottheiten.[3] Dabei handelt es sich wahrscheinlich um eine theologisch-begründete Begriffsauswahl der Übersetzer, weil mit diesem Ausdruck alle wesentlichen Elemente der Fremdgötter abgedeckt sind. Dadurch kommt es zu einer klaren Unterscheidung zwischen dem Gott Israels und allen anderen Göttern.

Der gängige Erklärungsversuch, ein neutraler, allgemeiner Götterbildbegriff wie z.B. das in der griechischen Literatur geläufige ἄγαλμα sei von den Übersetzern der Septuaginta bewusst vermieden worden, lässt sich

---

2. Vgl. Rösel 2015, 62 (unter Berücksichtigung von Seeligmann 2004, 263).
3. Joosten 2016, 251–52.

als Begründung für die Wahl von εἴδωλον nicht halten.⁴ Ein standardisierter Ausdruck für das Götterbild existierte nämlich offenbar gar nicht. Die Begriffsauswahl hing stattdessen stark von der Präferenz des einzelnen Autors ab. Das Fehlen eines allgemeinen Kultbildbegriffes lag möglicherweise am Mangel eines verbindlichen heiligen Buches als Zentrum der Religiosität. Das Lexem ἄγαλμα wird gerne als positiver, allgemeiner Kultbildbegriff angeführt, jedoch lässt er sich nicht wie εἴδωλον grundsätzlich auf eine Art der Bildhaftigkeit zurückführen.⁵

---

4. Jan Joosten sieht dagegen die Quintessenz von εἴδωλον in seiner negativen Konnotation, die seiner Ansicht nach ausschlaggebend für die LXX-Übersetzer war. Siehe Joosten 2016, 254–5; Rösel 2015, 61, assoziiert εἴδωλον im Zusammenhang des Trügerischen. Eindeutig lässt sich diese Verbindung jedoch nur in Tob 14,6 G^II feststellen. In Jer 16,19 und Hab 2,18 ist lediglich ein Vergleich belegt und bei Habakuk bezieht sich die Täuschung sogar vordergründig auf χώνευμα. In der griechischen Literatur begegnet εἴδωλον zwar manchmal als Trugbild, dennoch kann diese kontextuelle Verwendungsweise nicht als Grundbedeutung des Begriffes bezeichnet werden. Gegen Seeligmann 2004, 263. Eine Verengung und Verkürzung des griechischen Terminus wird begünstigt durch eine willkürliche Reihung in einschlägigen Lexika wie in LSJ, die zu inadäquaten Schlüssen in der Rezeption führen können. Bereits Aitken 2014, 193, weist auf diese Problematik hin, wobei er LSJ kritisiert, weil an erster Stelle die Übersetzung „phantom" (vgl. LSJ, s.v. „εἴδωλον," 483) angeführt wird. Dabei scheint die Bedeutung allerdings mit der Referenz verwechselt worden sein. Aitken führt als Beispiel Homer an: „In Homer's Hades we find 'representations' of mortals, indicating that they are ghosts, but that does not mean the 'images' of humans are to be translated as phantoms". Aitken betrachtet auch die Bewertung biblischer Kommentatoren, laut denen der Begriff εἴδωλον „Idole" bezeichne, die bloß Nichtse oder Phantome sind, als fragwürdig [mit dem Verweis auf Meadors 2006, 12; Hayward 2007, 42]. Er plädiert daher für die grundlegende Bedeutung „image", „representation", weil es seltsam wäre, eine „Repräsentation" als solche zu benennen und sie im gleichen Atemzug als nicht real zu bezeichnen.

5. Das in der griechischen Literatur relativ häufige Wort ἄγαλμα bedeutet aber nicht zwangsläufig „Tempelkultbild" oder „Götterbild". Etymologisch lässt es sich von ἀγάλλω („schmücken"), ἀγάλλομαι („prunken, sich über etwas freuen") ableiten. In der Ilias und der Odyssee hat der Begriff die Hauptbedeutung „wertvolles Geschenk". Homer und Hesiod verwendeten das Wort allerdings nicht als „Bild der Gottheit". Seine beiden Hauptbedeutungen „Zierde" und „Statue" sind bei Aristophanes bezeugt (Vesp. 314). Ab dem 5. Jh. zeichnet sich eine Schwerpunktverlagerung ab: ἄγαλμα bezeichnet tendenziell ein „rundplastisches Götterbild", aber nicht ausschließlich. Herodot benennt mit dem griechischen Ausdruck häufig eine Götterstatue, und sogar das spezifische Tempelbild (Scheer 2000, 13–14). Ab dem 5. Jahrhundert und in den darauffolgenden Jahrhunderten muss ἄγαλμα nicht notwendigerweise ein Bild im Tempel oder ein Götterbild meinen. Es handelt sich um einen allgemeinen Begriff,

Die Visualität als Identitätsmarker für andere Völker bzw. Nationen, im Unterschied zur Bildlosigkeit Israels, ginge verloren (siehe unten 1.Makkabäer), wenn man ἄγαλμα gewählt hätte. Als gemeinsamer Nenner von εἴδωλον, unabhängig vom Kontext, kann nämlich die „sichtbare Erscheinungsform" genannt werden, die dem Begriff zugrunde liegt (vgl. εἴδομαι „[er]scheinen, gleichen").[6] Eine Anspielung auf die Kultbildtheologie Ägyptens ist mit dem Ausdruck εἴδωλον ebenfalls gewährleistet. Laut diesem religiösen Konzept kann die Gottheit in dem Bild präsent sein, in dem sie einwohnt. Besonders in den Tempeln der griechisch-römischen Zeit (ab 3. v. Chr.) wird dieser freiwillige Akt der Gottheit bezeugt. Papyrologische Quellen stützen die Verwendung von εἴδωλον als Götter(bild)bezeichnung; dabei werden die Kultstatuen mit Gottheiten identifiziert (P.Strasb. 2.91; P.Worp 7; PSI 8.901).

Die entscheidende Frage bei der Worterklärung/Begriffsbestimmung lautet indes: Handelt es sich bei εἴδωλον um einen pejorativen Ausdruck? Auf der semantischen Ebene lässt sich eine vordergründig negative Konnotation des Substantivs εἴδωλον nicht nachweisen. Für eine ausschließlich negative Bezeichnung wäre indessen βδέλυγμα „Gräuel" prädestiniert.[7]

„der ohne zusätzliche Information der Quellen weder auf ein spezifisches Material oder einen bestimmten Standort, geschweige denn auf den Platz der Statue in einer kultischen Hierarchie schließen läßt" (Scheer 2000, 18). Ausführlicher zu ἄγαλμα siehe Scheer 2000, 8–18.

6. Vgl. Griffith 2002, 99. Vgl. auch Saïd 1987, 310. Nach Vernant 1990, 233, drückt der Ausdruck εἴδωλον drei Arten von Phänomenen aus: „l'apparition surnaturelle, *phasma*, le songe, *oneiros* (*onar*), l'âme-fantôme des défunts, *psuché*".

7. Der Ausdruck βδέλυγμα ist eindeutig pejorativ und kommt häufiger im Kontext der Fremdgötterverehrung vor, deshalb steht er auch in Verbindung mit εἴδωλον. Vgl. βδέλυγμα in Bezug auf fremde Gottheiten und parallel zu εἴδωλον in Dtn 29,17[16]; in 1.Kön/3.Kgt 11,33; 2.Kön/4.Kgt 21,11; Ez 8,10; In Weish 14,11 wird βδέλυγμα eindeutig auf die εἴδωλα bezogen; unabhängig von εἴδωλον, aber auch im Zusammenhang der Fremdgötterverehrung vgl. auch Sir 49,2; Der Begriff ist wahrscheinlich ein Neologismus der LXX Pentateuch-Übersetzer für Dinge (Handlungen oder Speisen), die religiös als abscheulich gelten; daher ist βδέλυγμα als Spezialbegriff für israelitische Kult- und Ernährungsverbote zu betrachten. LEH, 105: „abomination," es handelt sich um einen Neologismus; GELS, 115: „loathsome;" „object of pagan worship"; Foerster 1933, 599. In 1.Kön 11,7/3.Kgt 11,5 ist εἴδωλον zweimal als Äquivalent für שׁקץ belegt, das anderswo wörtlich mit βδέλυγμα übersetzt wird (vgl. 3.Kgt 11,6). Das hebräische Äquivalent שׁקץ ist stark pejorativ und abwertend. Obgleich εἴδωλον auch als Degradierung interpretiert werden kann, lässt sich durch diese Wortwahl der LXX auch eine Verschiebung der Aussageabsicht feststellen, die den Fokus auf die sichtbare

Allerdings hätte dieser Begriff den Nachteil, dass er nicht auf die Fremdgötterthematik eingegrenzt werden kann.

Die pejorative Konnotation von εἴδωλον erschließt sich erst sekundär auf der interpretativen Ebene: Insofern die εἴδωλα Fremdgottheiten mitsamt sichtbaren Darstellungsarten bezeichnen, sind diese als falsch (Gottheiten) und illegitim (Bilder) zu bewerten.

Im Vergleich dazu kann der Ausdruck εἰκών nicht generell als positives Pendant zu εἴδωλον herangezogen werden. Auch wenn dieser Bildbegriff zwar die Gottebenbildlichkeit des Menschen zum Ausdruck bringt (z.B. in Gen 1,26.27; Weish 7,26), fungiert er sowohl innerhalb der LXX als auch außerhalb in der griechischen Literatur teilweise als Synonym für εἴδωλον (vgl. dazu Weish 14,15: kultisch verehrtes Erinnerungsbild; Herdodot, *His.* 1,51; Plutarch, *Is. Os.* 359B; 362C–D).[8] Im Buch Daniel dient εἰκών als Komplementärbegriff zu εἴδωλον. Während εἰκών das Standbild Nebukadnezars bezeichnet, repräsentieren die εἴδωλα die Gottheiten selbst (vgl. Dan 3,12.18 LXX). In der LXX kommt es dadurch zu einer stärkeren Verschmelzung zwischen Gottheit und Bild auf der begrifflichen Ebene.

Die Begriffsweite und Ambivalenz des Terminus εἴδωλον, der sich nicht auf die kultische Sphäre eingrenzen lässt, könnte möglicherweise den seltenen Gebrauch als Götterbild in der griechischen Literatur erklären. Des weiteren lässt sich εἴδωλον (vgl. auch εἰκών) im Unterschied zu anderen Begriffen (vgl. ἄγαλμα, ἀνδριάς, βρέτας oder ξόανον) etymologisch auf „Erscheinung", „Anschein" zurückführen. Daraus erklärt sich auch das breite Spektrum seiner Verwendung. Der Ausdruck kann alle Formen von handwerklich hergestellten Bilddarstellungen bezeichnen, aber auch mentale „Bilder".[9]

Dafür ist der umfassende und allgemeine Charakter ein ideales Äquivalent für die Bezeichnung der Fremdgötter bzw. deren Bilddarstellungen

---

Seite der Fremdgottheiten legt. Hätte bei der Übersetzung ein pejorativer Wortsinn die oberste Priorität gehabt, dann wäre wohl die wörtliche Entsprechung βδέλυγμα ausgewählt worden.

8. Im Bereich der Gräzistik ist Vernant 1990 zu nennen, der auf die Gemeinsamkeiten zwischen εἴδωλον und εἰκών hinweist und sich auch für einen synonymen Gebrauch ausspricht.

9. Siehe Vernant 1990, 228. Zu den anderen Begriffen wie ἄγαλμα, ἀνδριάς, βρέτας oder ξόανον siehe Vernant 1990, 225–28. Vgl. auch Saïd 1987, 310.

innerhalb der LXX. Mit nur einem Begriff werden damit wesentliche Aspekte der „anderen" Götter abgedeckt.[10]

Im Hinblick auf die hebräischen Äquivalente unterscheiden sich εἴδωλον und εἰκών aber deutlich. Ersteres dient nämlich als Äquivalent für eine Vielzahl von zum Teil sehr unterschiedlichen Begriffen. Folgende Wortfelder ergeben sich aus einer Begriffsanalyse: Bildliche Repräsentationen – Götterbezeichnungen – Kultvokabular.[11] Demgegenüber lassen sich die hebräischen Entsprechungen von εἰκών alle den „bildlichen Repräsentationen" zuordnen (Hauptäquivalent: צלם, besonders häufig im Buch Daniel). Anhand der unterschiedlichen und vielseitigen hebräischen Entsprechungen zeigt sich in der LXX eine Tendenz hin zu einer Begriffsbündelung. Während im hebräischen Text die anderen Götter als פסל, עצב oder גלולים in Erscheinung treten oder mit אלהים bzw. אליל, הבל oder בעל benannt werden, fließen die feinen Nuancierungen der hebräischen Götter(bild)terminologie allesamt in den griechischen Begriff εἴδωλον in der LXX zusammen. Die Verflechtung zwischen Gottheit und sichtbarer Erscheinungsform prädestiniert εἴδωλον geradezu als ideale Wortwahl der Übersetzer, um Fremdgottheiten zu benennen.

2. Die Kunstform Mosaik und das Bedeutungsspektrum von εἴδωλον

Das Bedeutungsspektrum des komplexen griechischen Ausdrucks εἴδωλον ähnelt der Zusammensetzung eines Mosaiks. Erst das Zusammenfügen der heterogenen Elemente unterschiedlicher Natur mit je eigenen Farbschattierungen ergibt ein Muster bzw. ein Gesamtbild. Diese Form der Kunstbildherstellung kann auf die Begriffsdeutung von εἴδωλον übertragen werden. Die Analogie erweist sich als hilfreich für die Begriffs(er)klärung und dient dazu, die Komplexität sichtbar zu machen. Die nachfolgende Zusammenschau beinhaltet die wesentlichen Aspekte und Eckpfeiler des Ausdrucks, damit wird ein Gesamtbild von εἴδωλον sichtbar. Allerdings bleiben wie bei einem Mosaik die einzelnen Steine bzw. Elemente für sich bestehen, d.h. die Facetten dieses vielschichtigen Begriffes werden nicht zugunsten einer einheitlichen Begriffsdeutung aufgegeben.

---

10. Vgl. dazu Griffith 2002, 99.
11. Für detaillierte Einzelnachweise zu den Wortfeldern vgl. meine Studie: Plangger 2018, 52–69.

2.1. Fremdartigkeit

Ein wesentliches Kennzeichen von εἴδωλον besteht in seiner hohen Affinität dem „Fremden" gegenüber. Im Hinblick auf Israel stellt ein εἴδωλον stets einen „Fremdkörper" dar und befindet sich beispielsweise in Besitz von Laban, dem Aramäer/Syrer (ארם/Σύρος[12]), in Gen 31,18.34.35. Auch im Buch Numeri werden die εἴδωλα explizit fremden Personen zugeordnet, nämlich den Töchtern Moabs (Num 25,2). In Num 25,1–3 liegt ein zweifaches Fremdgehen vor – auf der zwischenmenschlichen Ebene („Israels Hurerei mit den Moabiterinnen") – und auf der Beziehungsebene zwischen Israel und seinem Gott (Abfall zu Baal-Peor). Im unmittelbaren Kontext (Numeri 22–24) befindet sich die Perikope rund um die Gestalt Bileam aus Aram/Mesopotamien (Num 23,7).

In Num 33,52 beauftragt JHWH Israel sogar mit der Vernichtung der Landesbewohner mitsamt ihren Kultobjekten. In Deuteronomium 29 werden die Ägypter namentlich mit den εἴδωλα in Verbindung gebracht und insgesamt als „Wiege der Bildgottheiten" genannt (Dtn 29,16[15]–17[16]). In Ps 151,6 gehören die εἴδωλα dem Philister (Andersstämmigen) Goliat (vgl. dazu 1.Kgt 31,9 die εἴδωλα der „Philister").

2.2. Fremdgottheiten

In Num 25,2 bezeichnen die εἴδωλα die sichtbaren Erscheinungsformen von Fremdgottheiten; namentlich genannt wird die Gottheit *Baal-Peor* (Num 25,3). Die griechische Übersetzung der hebräischen Gottesbezeichnung אלהים mit den εἴδωλα bewirkt eine Näherbestimmung und Fokusverschiebung, was die anderen Gottheiten betrifft. In unmittelbarer Weise werden dadurch ihre Sichtbarkeit und Bildhaftigkeit ins Zentrum der Aufmerksamkeit gerückt. Auf einer interpretativen Ebene kann die abweichende Wiedergabe auch als Degradierung bewertet werden.

In den Büchern der Königtümer lassen sich wie in Numeri 25 semantische Veränderungen beobachten, weil εἴδωλον ebenfalls als Äquivalent von אלהים dient. Die Verwendungsweise in 3.Kgt 11 spricht sogar für die Austauschbarkeit zwischen εἴδωλον (11,2) und θεός (11,4), weil beide Verse

---

12. Wegen der Identifizierung von (ארם) פדן (Gen 31,18) mit Μεσοποταμία bezeichnet in LXX Genesis Σύρια, wahrscheinlich das seleukidische Syrien, das im 3. Jahrhundert v. Chr. auch das Zweistromland umfasste. In Gen 25,20; 33,18 und 46,15 wird פדן ארם mit Μεσοποταμία Σύρια übersetzt, siehe dazu Rösel 1994, 239.

sich auf die fremden Gottheiten der ausländischen Frauen Salomos beziehen. Besonders im Buch Daniel ist diese Bedeutungsverschiebung sehr ausgeprägt, da εἴδωλον immer als Äquivalent für das aramäische אלהין verwendet wird. Erwähnenswert ist besonders das Vorkommen in Dan 3,12 LXX, an dieser Stelle bezeichnen nämlich die Chaldäer mit εἴδωλον die Gottheiten Nebukadnezars (εἰσὶ δέ τινες ἄνδρες Ιουδαῖοι, οὓς κατέστησας ἐπὶ τῆς χώρας τῆς Βαβυλωνίας, Σεδραχ, Μισαχ, Αβδεναγω, οἱ ἄνθρωποι ἐκεῖνοι οὐκ ἐφοβήθησάν σου τὴν ἐντολὴν οὔτε τῷ εἰδώλῳ [אלה] σου οὐκ ἐλάτρευσαν καὶ τῇ εἰκόνι [צלם] σου τῇ χρυσῇ, ἧ ἔστησας, οὐ προσεκύνησαν).

Auf exegetischer Ebene lässt sich daher keine primär negative Bezeichnung wie z.B. bei βδέλυγμα, das unabhängig vom Kontext ausschließlich negativ konnotiert ist, nachweisen. Natürlich kann man dagegen einwenden, dass fremde Gottheiten im alttestamentlichen Kontext immer negativ bewertet werden, aber die Unterscheidung zwischen exegetischer und interpretativen Ebene dient einer präzisen und sorgfältigen Auslegung, in der feine Nuancierungen und Zwischentöne wie in Daniel 3 wahrgenommen werden können. In diesem Fall lässt sich auf der Textebene 1 (direkte Rede) keine negative Beurteilung ausmachen. Stattdessen bezeugt das Buch Daniel, wie 3.Kgt 11, die synonyme Verwendung von εἴδωλον und θεός. In Dan 3,14 LXX spricht nämlich Nebukadnezar von seinen Göttern (θεός) und bezieht sich auf die in 3,12 LXX genannte „Bild-Gottheit" (εἴδωλον im Singular!).

Im Buch Jesaja werden die fremden Gottheiten (אלהים) in der LXX auch mit εἴδωλον wiedergegeben (vgl. Jes 37,19).

Im Kontext des Mosliedes (Dtn 32) fungieren die εἴδωλα als Näherbestimmung für den *Nichtgott* (οὐ θεός), mit dem Israel JHWH eifersüchtig gemacht hat. Das hebräische Äquivalent הבל steht in Zusammenhang mit der Bedeutung „Atemhauch", „Luft- bzw. Windhauch", beschränkt sich aber im Unterschied zu רוח, auf die sichtbare Seite „Dunst, Dampf, Rauch".[13] Die Bedeutung „Hauch" beinhaltet die Vorstellung des „Vergänglichen", „Flüchtigen". Möglicherweise sollte in der LXX der Fokus der Vergänglichkeit und Flüchtigkeit auf die sichtbaren Erscheinungsformen von Fremdgottheiten gelenkt werden, die der Zerstörung anheimfallen konnten. Bei einer Vernichtung der Bild-Gottheiten kommt ihre Machtlosigkeit, d.h. ihre Vergänglichkeit und Vorläufigkeit zum Vorschein.

---

13. Siehe Seybold 1977, 338. Die Übersetzung „Nichtigkeit" erweist sich jedoch oft als problematisch, weil sie stark wertend und manchmal schwer nachvollziehbar ist.

Vereinzelt dient εἴδωλον als Übersetzung für die Fremdgötterbezeichnung בעלים (vgl. 2.Chr 17,3; 28,2); im Buch Jeremia ist sogar die Rede von einem tradierten Abfall zu den Baalen (vgl. Jer 9,14 [13]). Diese kollektive verallgemeinernde Benennung der anderen Gottheiten korrespondiert mit dem griechischen Ausdruck εἴδωλον, der noch dazu eine Verknüpfung zur Bildhaftigkeit herzustellen vermag.

Die Wiedergabe von Goliats Göttern mit εἴδωλον (1.Kgt 17,43^A; Ps 151,6) anstatt mit der Gottesbezeichnung θεοί (vgl. 1.Kgt 17,43), der wörtlichen Übersetzung von אלהים, kann auf zweierlei Weise gedeutet werden.

Möglicherweise wollten die Übersetzer vermeiden, andere Gottheiten als solche zu bezeichnen, oder εἴδωλον wurde bewusst ausgewählt, weil dadurch eine präzisere und nähere Bestimmung bzw. Charakterisierung der Fremdgötter ermöglicht wird. Diese Wortwahl macht ebenso eine klare Unterscheidung zwischen den Völkern und Israel sichtbar. So kommt es im „Epilog" des Psalters (in Psalm 151 in der Septuaginta-Fassung) zu einer Kontrastierung zwischen Goliats „Göttern" und dem Gott Davids. Die Sichtbarkeit und die Verbindung zur Divination (vgl. die Verfluchungsversuche Goliats unter Zuhilfenahme seiner εἴδωλα „Bild-Gottheiten" in Ps 151,6[14]) steht dem Gebet Davids zu seinem „unsichtbaren" Gott diametral entgegen. Die Anrufung der εἴδωλα durch Goliat spricht auch für die göttliche Verehrung dieser, da er all seine Hoffnung im bevorstehenden Kampf auf sie setzt. Das Vorkommen am Ende des Psalters macht die zentrale Bedeutung des Themas *Fremdgötterverehrung* deutlich und spricht für eine bewusste Wortauswahl, besonders an so einer exponierten Stellung. Der Epilog kann, von hinten gelesen, als „Kampfbuch"[15] gegen die Fremdgötter(bilder) betrachtet werden.

Ein wertvolles Zeugnis von εἴδωλον ist in 2.Makk 12,40 belegt, das einen neuen Aspekt in die Begriffsinterpretation mit einbringt. Archäologischen Funden zufolge handelt es sich an der besagten Textstelle um Götterminiaturen auf Anhängern: ἱερώματα τῶν ἀπὸ Ἰαμνείας εἰδώλων (vermutlich aus Glas).[16] Folgt man dieser Deutung, repräsentieren die εἴδωλα im 2. Buch der Makkabäer eindeutig fremde Gottheiten.

---

14. 151,6: ἐξῆλθον εἰς συνάντησιν τῷ ἀλλοφύλῳ, καὶ ἐπικατηράσατό με ἐν τοῖς εἰδώλοις αὐτοῦ·

15. Vgl. Hossfeld und Zenger 2008, 890.

16. Die Objekte (ἱέρωμα) symbolisieren ganz konkret die Götter von Jamneia, *Herakles* und *Hauran*. Beide Gottheiten werden in zwei Inschriften (ID 2308–2309), entdeckt in Delos, als Gottheiten von Jamneia genannt, und zwischen dem späten

2.3 Divination

Ein wesentliches Charakteristikum von εἴδωλον ist seine kontextuelle Verortung im Bereich der Divination. Bereits im ersten Vorkommen innerhalb des Alten Testaments, in Genesis 31, lässt sich, nicht zuletzt wegen seines hebräischen Äquivalents תרפים (Gen 31,19.34.35), eine Verbindung zur Divination ausmachen.[17] Die תרפים/εἴδωλα bezeichnen in Genesis 31 die „Hausgötter" Labans.

Im Kontext der Kultreform Joschijas stellt die Reinigung von divinatorischen Praktiken einen Schwerpunkt dar. Innerhalb einer Begriffsaufzählung zum Wortfeld „Divination", reiht sich εἴδωλον ein, das auf θεραφιν (vgl. Gen 31) folgt und eine Brückenfunktion innehat. Das Lexem εἴδωλον weist einerseits eine Affinität zur Mantik und zu Orakelhandlungen auf, andererseits werden mit dieser Wortwahl explizit Fremdgottheiten zur Sprache gebracht (vgl. 4.Kgt 23,24). Eine Polemik gegen die gängige Praxis der Orakelbefragung befindet sich im Buch Jesaja wie die rhetorische Frage JHWHs an die εἴδωλα in Jes 41,28 bezeugt: ἀπὸ γὰρ τῶν ἐθνῶν ἰδοὺ οὐδείς, καὶ ἀπὸ τῶν εἰδώλων αὐτῶν οὐκ ἦν ὁ ἀναγγέλλων· καὶ ἐὰν ἐρωτήσω αὐτούς Πόθεν ἐστέ, οὐ μὴ ἀποκριθῶσίν μοι. Der Begriff εἴδωλον hat zwar kein hebräisches Äquivalent, könnte aber aufgrund des Orakelkontextes bewusst ausgewählt worden sein. Diese Textstelle ist ein weiterer Beleg dafür, dass εἴδωλον im Rahmen der Divination seine Verwendung findet. Es besteht ein direkter Zusammenhang zwischen den εἴδωλα und dem Ausdruck ἀναγγέλλων „Verkünder" (Part. von ἀναγγέλλω). Ein divinatorischer Kontext lässt sich auch in Levitikus 19 beobachten (vgl. 19,31: Verbot der Divination) und in Num 25,3 (vgl. die Anspielung auf die Mysterienkulte[18]; Numeri 22–24: Perikope rund um die Gestalt

---

zweiten Jh. v.Chr. bis ins frühe erste Jh. v. Chr. datiert. Siehe Bruneau 1970, 410, 475. Siehe auch Fischer und Jackson-Tal 2003, 35–36, mit dem Verweis auf weiterführende Literatur; Zur Datierung: Spaer et al. 2001, 162.

17. Vgl. dazu Wenham 1994, 273. Rabbinische Texte deuten den Diebstahl Rahels folgendermaßen: Rachel entwendet die Figur (תרפים), damit Laban keine Orakelbefragung über Jakobs Fluchtort durchführen kann. Der Zusammenhang mit dem Phänomen Orakel kann auch unter Einbeziehung des Kontextes erschlossen werden vgl. Gen 30,27: das Verb נחש (Piel) „wahrsagen", „Vorzeichen suchen und geben"; griechisches Äquivalent ist das Verb οἰωνίζομαι "to divine from omens", "to learn by divination"; Siehe *HALAT*, 652. LEH, 432. Fabry 1986, 385.

18. Für Mysterienkulte spricht besonders die griechische Übersetzung des Verbs צמד (Nifal) „das Joch eines Gottes tragen", „ihm dienen", „hängen an" (siehe dazu

Bileam). Außerbiblisch ist εἴδωλον im Kontext einer Nekromantie belegt, die unter einem Apfelbaum (s. unten 2. „Baumkult") stattfand und üblicherweise dazu diente die Zukunft vorauszusagen (vgl. dazu den Beleg in P.Chester Beatty XVI). Der Magier Jambres bezweckt damit, das εἴδωλον – die sichtbare Erscheinungsform seines Bruders – aus dem Hades heraufzubeschwören.[19]

2.4. Dekalog

Die semantische Weite des Begriffes εἴδωλον unterstreicht und betont noch stärker die allgemeine Ausrichtung des zweiten Dekaloggebotes in Ex 20,4[LXX]. Der Ausdruck lässt sich nämlich nicht auf ein bestimmtes Material reduzieren, er kann auch andere Gottheiten bezeichnen, und im Vergleich mit anderen Belegen innerhalb des Pentateuchs zeigt sich, dass ihm etwas Fremdes, nicht zu Israel gehöriges anhaftet (vgl. Gen 31,19.34.35; Num 25,2; 33,52; Dtn 29,17 [16]). Dies könnte ein möglicher Grund dafür sein, dass die Übersetzer von der wortwörtlichen Übersetzung des Kultbildbegriffes פסל „etwas Behauenes (aus Stein) oder Geschnitztes (aus Holz)" abwichen, weil durch εἴδωλον das Bedeutungsspektrum noch ausgeweitet wird. Eine stärkere Verbindung zwischen Fremdgötter- und Bilderverbot kommt damit zum Ausdruck. Das Fremdgötter- und Bilderverbot kann in der Septuaginta sogar als Einheit betrachtet werden, da mit εἴδωλον eine Verschmelzung zwischen Gottheit und Bild geschieht. In Ex 20,4[LXX] handelt es sich aller Wahrscheinlichkeit nach um eine bewusste aus theologischen Gründen gewählte Abweichung.[20]

Ges[18], 1122; Seebass 2003, 41: „to go in a yoke, to harness oneself") mit dem Ausdruck τελέω, der an dieser Stelle „zu Mysterien einweihen" bedeutet. Die Übersetzung kann als Aktualisierung für die griechischen Leser interpretiert werden, weil dieses Verb auf die Einführung in die Mysterien der griechischen Religion verweist. Die Religion Moabs wird damit auf den griechischen Kontext übertragen. Siehe Dorival 1994, 174.
    19. Siehe dazu Pietersma 1994, 220–1.
    20. Im Unterschied dazu wird der hebräische Terminus פסל im zweiten Dekaloggebot in Dtn 5,8 LXX, nach der Lesart von Papyrus 963, mit dem ihm entsprechenden griechischen Begriff γλυπτόν wiedergegeben. Vgl. dazu Wevers 1978, 133. Im Buch Deuteronomium bevorzugt der Übersetzer – im Vergleich zum Buch Exodus (Ex 20,4) – eine stärker dem Wortsinn entsprechende Übersetzung (vgl. auch die einheitliche Übersetzung von פסל mit γλυπτόν in Dtn 4.16.23.25, ebenfalls im Kontext des Bilderverbots). Die innere Kohärenz im Buch Deuteronomium zogen die LXX-Übersetzer einer identischen Wiedergabe der beiden Dekalogfassungen offensichtlich vor.

Im Buch Levitikus befindet sich eine depotenzierende Aktualisierung des Fremdgötterverbotes (Lev 19,4). Die griechische Übersetzung des hebräischen Ausdrucks אליל mit εἴδωλον stellt eine direkte Verbindung zum Dekalog her und damit wird die Verknüpfung zwischen Fremdgötter- und Kultbilderverbot bestätigt.[21] Das Defizitäre tritt in der Sichtbarkeit und Gegenständlichkeit eines εἴδωλον in Erscheinung.

Die Wendung θεοὶ χωνευτοί bezeugt möglicherweise eine Integration der Goldenen-Kalb-Erfahrung in das Fremdgötter- und Kultbilderverbot.[22] Die Parallelisierung der εἴδωλα mit den θεοὶ χωνευτοί bestätigt das Ineinanderfließen von Fremdgötter- und Kultbilderverbot, weil beide Begriffe sowohl Gottheiten als auch deren Bilddarstellungen zum Ausdruck bringen.

2.5. Kult

Ein weiteres Spezifikum des Ausdrucks ist seine bevorzugte Verwendung in kultischen Kontexten, besonders wenn εἴδωλον als Äquivalent für גלולים fungiert. Das Buch Ezechiel stärkt insgesamt das Verständnis von εἴδωλον als Kultbegriff. In unterschiedlichen Kultkontexten ist es nämlich die favorisierte Wiedergabe für גלולים.[23] In Ez 6,5 (vgl. die Parallelstelle in Lev 26,30; Ez 6,13; Ez 8,10; 16,16; Ez 37,23; Ez 44,12) ist εἴδωλον ein wesentlicher Bestand eines Höhenheiligtums. Gemeint sind eindeutig

---

Die interne Texttreue bezeugt und fokussiert die Eigenständigkeit des Horebdekalogs. Siehe ausführlicher, Plangger 2018, 77–79, 86–89.

21. Lev 19,4: οὐκ ἐπακολουθήσετε εἰδώλοις (אלילים) καὶ θεοὺς χωνευτοὺς (אלהי מסכה) οὐ ποιήσετε ὑμῖν ἐγὼ κύριος ὁ θεὸς ὑμῶν. Hieke (2014, 714) deutet die Verwendung des Begriffes אלילים sogar als Weiterentwicklung gegenüber dem Dekalog.

22. Lev 19,4 ist als Reaktion auf die gemeinschaftlich erfahrene Verfehlung durch die Herstellung des Urgötterbildes, als die „größte anzunehmende Sünde" zu betrachten. Siehe Hieke 2014, 714. Die Identifikation der „gegossenen/edelmetallenen Götter" mit dem *Goldenen Kalb* lässt sich auch durch die Nähe zum Privilegrecht aus Ex 34,17 (אלהי מסכה / θεοὶ χωνευτοί, vgl. Ex 32,4.8) begründen. Unmittelbar davor befindet sich die Schilderung der Perikope rund um das *Goldene Kalb*.

23. Der Übersetzer setzte offenbar ein weites Bedeutungsspektrum des Ausdrucks גלולים voraus, das sich von „bösen Gedanken", „schlechten Gewohnheiten" bis hin zu „verwerflichen Kultobjekten bzw. Praktiken erstreckt, siehe Lust 2008, 324. Die anderen griechischen Äquivalente betreffen alle das Innenleben des Menschen wie z.B. ἐπιτηδεύματα „Lebensweisen", ἐνθυμήματα „(eigene) Gedanken" oder διανοήματα „Gedanken". In Ez 6,9 steht גלולים in einem allgemeineren nicht explizit kultischen Zusammenhang, da sich der Begriff auf die innere Haltung des Menschen bezieht.

materielle, konkrete Objekte, deren Zerstörung JHWH neben Kultinventar wie Altären, heiligen Bezirken androht. In Ezechiel 36 kommt es durch die Begriffswahl εἴδωλον zu einer Neuakzentuierung, d.h. die Verunreinigung Israels kommt in der LXX konkret durch die Fremdgötterverehrung zur Sprache. Im Gegensatz dazu fokussiert der hebräische Text auf das Fehlverhalten Israels (Äquivalent: עלילות vgl. Ez 36,17).

Im Buch Numeri ist die Rede von Opferhandlungen für die εἴδωλα (Num 25,2). Eine explizite Verbindung zu Kultopfern ist zwar nicht häufig belegt, bezeugt aber den dramatischen Abfall von JHWH, der sich in der Verehrung, Anbetung bis hin zu Opferriten für andere Gottheiten offenbart. Die Opfer an die εἴδωλα als Höchstform des Glaubensabfalles liegt in 1.Makk 1,43 explizit vor, in unmittelbarer Weise steht der Ausdruck in Verbindung zum Opferkult. Parallel dazu befindet sich die Entweihung des Sabbats, der ein Handeln gegen die Schöpfungsordnung als auch gegen die Tora beinhaltet (vgl. Ex 20,8-10; Dtn 5,12-14). Der Sabbat ist ein identitätsstiftendes Unterscheidungsmerkmal Israels, in dieser Weise verhält es sich auch mit dem Bund zwischen JHWH und Israel und der damit verbundenen Kultbildlosigkeit. Hervorzuheben ist die drastische Opferkritik in Ez 23,39, an dieser Stelle ist die Rede von der Opferung der eigenen Kinder für die εἴδωλα.

2.6. Baumkult

Eine Besonderheit ist der Zusammenhang zwischen den εἴδωλα und den „heiligen Bäumen", die sich an Kultorten, oft an sogenannten Kulthöhen befanden. "Unter einem schattigen Baum" fanden Kulthandlungen (Orakelbefragungen, Opferhandlungen) für Fremdgottheiten statt (Hos 4,13 // Ez 6,13).

Im Buch Jesaja fungiert εἴδωλον sogar als griechische Wiedergabe für „Terebinthe" (אילים: Jes 1,29; Jes 57,5),[24] damit wird ein lebendiger Baum-

---

24. אילים „Terebinthen," איל II „mächtiger Baum," HALAT, 39; אלה I „mächtiger Baum" – die Baumarten Eiche und Terebinthe sind damit gemeint, HALAT, 50; Die Übersetzung der LXX wird mit 1QJes^a in Verbindung gebracht, wo אלים steht, was im Sinne von „Götter" gedeutet werden kann, vgl. Ulrich und Flint 2010, 4. Als Rechtfertigung für die griechische Übersetzung wird neben dem Qumranbeleg (siehe oben) auch die Parallelstelle Jes 57,5 angeführt, wo εἴδωλον das Äquivalent von אלים „Götter" ist. Allerdings kann diese Wortform, die in 1QJes^a wie auch im MT von Jes 57,5 belegt ist, auch als Defektiv-Schreibung von אילים angesehen werden. In Jes 1,29

kult zu Ehren von Fremdgottheiten bezeichnet. Die Begriffsauswahl in der LXX kann als theologisch und kulturell bedingte Übertragung betrachtet werden. Es lassen sich einige Gemeinsamkeiten zwischen den Terebinthen und den Bild-Gottheiten (εἴδωλα) feststellen: (1) Auch Bäume sind Orte der Gegenwart des Göttlichen. In Hos 14,9 kommt es sogar zu einer positiven Umkehrung der kritisierten Baumkulte, weil der Gott Israels metaphorisch mit einem Wacholder verglichen wird. Der Baum als Lebenssymbol und Sinnbild für vitale Kraft prädestiniert ihn für einen Vergleich mit dem Göttlichen. (2) Die sichtbaren Kultobjekte – im Falle der Bäume handelt es sich um lebendige Verehrungsobjekte – können wie die εἴδωλα (fremde) Gottheiten repräsentieren (vgl. die Aschere als Kultsymbol der Göttin Aschera). „Heilige Bäume" stehen wie die εἴδωλα in Zusammenhang mit Orakelpraktiken. Die Verwendung von εἴδωλον führt in der LXX zu einer Verallgemeinerung, weil die kritisierten Kulte sich nicht mehr auf bestimmte unter Bäumen vollzogene Praktiken eingrenzen lässt.

Daher ist εἴδωλον als theologische Aktualisierung zu deuten; ähnlich wie in Deuteronomium 32, wo die LXX „Fels" im Sinne einer Metapher für JHWH mit θέος wiedergibt.[25]

2.7. Schrift – Bild

Das erste Buch der Makkabäer belegt eine fundamentale Scheidung zwischen Israel und den Völkern. Verdichtet kommen zwei diametral entgegengesetzte Theologien zur Sprache: Auf der einen Seite steht die SCHRIFT – die Tora Israels –, und auf der anderen Seite das BILD – die Bild-Gottheiten der Völker: καὶ ἐξεπέτασαν τὸ βιβλίον τοῦ νόμου περὶ ὧν ἐξηρεύνων τὰ ἔθνη τὰ ὁμοιώματα τῶν εἰδώλων αὐτῶν (1.Makk 3,48).

---

spricht jedenfalls der Parallelismus mit גנה/κῆπος „Gärten" eindeutig für die „heiligen Bäume" (אילים). Seeligmann interpretiert das hebräische Lexem mit den „Heiligen Bäumen", betrachtet die Übersetzung mit εἴδωλον aber als Missverständnis, siehe Seeligmann 2004, 152: „Here אילים as a parallel of גנות is surely the plural of אלה = sacred tree (terebinthe?)".

25. Einerseits scheint die Felsmetapher in einem alexandrinischen Kontext obsolet geworden zu sein, andererseits könnte dieses Gottesbild auch in Verbindung zu Fremdgottheiten stehen und würde das Alleinstellungsmerkmal JHWHs dadurch gefährden. Peters (2012) wendet sich gegen die Auffassung, der Übersetzer habe die wörtliche Wiedergabe der Metapher Fels bewusst vermieden. Siehe dazu die Kritik bei Rösel 2019. Zur Metapher Fels als Gottesbezeichnung, siehe auch Olofsson 1990, 43.

Während für Israel die Tora als Richtschnur gilt, haben die Völker ihre Bilderkulte, die oft divinatorische Handlungen mit sich bringen. In 1.Makk 3,48 (Kontext: Kampfhandlung) ist die öffentliche Toralesung das Symbol der Gegenwart Gottes. Im Gegensatz dazu befragen die Nationen die „Abbilder" (ὁμοιώματα) ihrer εἴδωλα. An dieser Stelle werden mit den εἴδωλα eindeutig die Gottheiten selbst bezeichnet, und der Bildcharakter wird dadurch noch verstärkt bzw. hervorgehoben. In einer verallgemeinernden Art und Weise ähnelt diese Schlachtvorbereitung (1.Makk 3,48) dem Kampf Davids gegen Goliat, wo das Gebet Davids mit der Kommunikation zwischen Goliat und seinen Bild-Gottheiten kontrastiert (vgl. Ps 151).

2.8. Tod und Verderben

Die εἴδωλα symbolisieren Unheil und Tod für Israel, weil die Hinwendung zu den leblosen Bild-Gottheiten gleichzeitig eine Abwendung vom lebendigen Gott Israels nach sich zieht. Ihre Zerstörung ist ein Sinnbild für die Leblosigkeit der durch sie repräsentierten Fremdgottheiten und ihrer Verehrer (vgl. dazu Lev 26,30; Ez 6,4.13). In Weish 14,29 werden die Bildgottheiten sogar explizit als unbelebt (ἄψυχος) genannt. Das antonyme Wortpaar „Tod und Leben" prägt die Götter(bild)thematik besonders im Buch der Weisheit. Das Vertrauen auf die εἴδωλα führt zum Fall für seine Verehrer (vgl. Ps 151,7: Goliats Tod; die Schmach der Fremdgötterverehrer in Ps 97 [96],7).

Die εἴδωλα sind σκάνδαλα „Stolpersteine", „Fallen"[26] für Israel (Hos 4,17), d.h. Ursache des Verderbens und Gegenstand von größter Sünde. Die Falle besteht in der Sichtbarkeit der Götter(bilder), damit sind die Fremdgötter im Gegensatz zum Gott Israels visuell erfahrbar. Dies wird ihren Verehrern zum Verhängnis und führt Israel zu Fall. Im übertragenen Sinne und auf einer interpretativen Ebene täuschen sie eine göttliche Gegenwart vor. Dieser Bundesbruch führt Israel aber ins Verderben, weil die Beziehung zu seinem Gott essentiell für die Identität Israels ist. Die lebensbedrohliche Komponente der Hinwendung zu Fremdgottheiten wird im Buch der Weisheit noch stärker entfaltet, weil die εἴδωλα als σκάνδαλα für die „Seele/das Leben" beschrieben werden (Weish 14,11).

---

26. Stählin 1964, 340.

In Hos 4 lässt sich eine Dynamik des Untergangs beobachten, der sich von Orakelpraktiken (4,12) zu Opferkulten auf Höhen mit „Heiligen Bäumen" (4,13) und Wallfahrten zu entehrten Kultstätten (4,15) erstreckt. Der dramatische Höhepunkt besteht in der Hinwendung zu den εἴδωλα, wodurch der Bruch mit JHWH besiegelt wird. Dabei handelt es sich nicht mehr nur um eine Kritik an falscher Kultpraxis, sondern eindeutig um die Verehrung fremder Gottheiten.

Die Verehrung der εἴδωλα wird im Buch der Weisheit sogar als umfassend böse bewertet (Weish 14,27), weil der Abfall zu Fremdgottheiten verwerfliche Kulthandlungen beinhaltet, die beide Dekalogtafeln betreffen (vgl. Weish 14,23–26).[27]

2.9. Schöpfung

Das Kultbilderverbot innerhalb des Dekalogs (Ex 20,4/Dtn 5,8) dient auch zur Deutung von Texten, die gegen die Herstellung und Verehrung von Bilddarstellungen primär schöpfungstheologisch argumentieren.[28] Das Dekaloggebot kann als ein den Kosmos umspannendes Verbot betrachtet werden, das nicht nur ein Handeln gegen den Bundesgott (vgl. die Dekalogeinleitung: Ex 20,2; Dtn 5,6), sondern auch gegen den Schöpfergott thematisiert.[29] Diese Verbindung wird durch die drei Sphären der Schöpfung, der Gesamtheit der geschaffenen Welt durch Himmel, Erde und Wasser ausgedrückt (Ex 20,4/Dtn 5,8: ὅσα ἐν τῷ οὐρανῷ ἄνω καὶ ὅσα ἐν τῇ γῇ κάτω καὶ ὅσα ἐν τοῖς ὕδασιν ὑποκάτω τῆς γῆς). Die Aufzählung versinnbildlicht eine Abwärtsbewegung, je weiter ein potentielles Abbild vom Himmel als göttlichen Bereich entfernt ist, desto größer scheint die Abartigkeit der Nachbildung.[30]

Die zweifache Ausrichtung verdeutlicht, dass im Kontext des zweiten Dekaloggebotes die Idolatrie auch als Handeln gegen die Schöpfungsordnung und gegen Gott als Schöpfer zum Ausdruck kommt. Grundsätzlich ist es widersinnig vom Menschen nach einer Gestaltung zu suchen, die

---

27. Vgl. dazu Engel 1998, 230.
28. Die Ablehnung von Götterbildern auf Basis des Schöpfungsglaubens ist besonders in Deuterojesaja belegt, siehe z.B. Jes 40,12–14.18).
29. Bereits von Rad (1935, 379) betont den Zusammenhang zwischen Bilderverbot und Schöpfungsglauben.
30. Siehe dazu auch Jacob 1997, 556–57. Besonders ausführlich in Dtn 4,16–18 entfaltet, siehe dazu Plangger 2018, 79–86.

JHWH entsprechen könnte, da seine Gestalt für die Menschen nicht sichtbar ist.[31]

Die Abbildung eines Geschöpfes wäre außerdem bloß ein künstlich von Menschenhand hergestelltes Bild, eine Nachbildung entspricht auch nicht der Aufgabe des Menschen.

Besonders ausgeprägt ist die Kultbildherstellung und Verehrung als Zuwiderhandeln gegen den Schöpfergott in Hosea 13. Dabei handelt es sich um eine verkehrte *Imitatio Dei*. In Hos 13,2 kommt es zu einer Verschmelzung zwischen der bundestheologischen und schöpfungstheologischen Argumentation gegen fremde Gottheiten.

So erinnert die Herstellung eines Gussbildes an den konkreten Sündenfall, das *corpus delicti*, das „Goldene Kalb", das eine Übertretung des Kultbilderverbotes des Dekalogs symbolisiert. Jeder nachfolgende Bruch führt die Bundesbrecher real zurück nach Ägypten.[32] Die Thematik Bundesbruch spielt generell im Buch Hosea eine große Rolle (kritische Auseinandersetzung mit dem Baalskult, Hos 13,1). Die Anspielung auf den Schöpfungsakt Gottes wird in der LXX (Gen 1,26–27), durch die Wendung κατ' εἰκόνα ausgedrückt, die als verkehrte *Imitatio Dei* bewertet werden kann: καὶ ἐποίησαν (עשו) ἑαυτοῖς χώνευμα ἐκ τοῦ ἀργυρίου αὐτῶν κατ' εἰκόνα (כתבונם) εἰδώλων (עצבים). Die Anfertigung eines Gussbildes nach dem Vorbild der εἴδωλα spricht wiederum für den allgemeinen Charakter des Ausdrucks. Sie stehen sozusagen als Prototyp, Modell für konkrete „Gussbilder" (χώνευμα) oder „Schnitzbilder" (γλυπτά).

Die Quintessenz von Gottes Kreation ist die Lebendigkeit – dagegen vermag der Mensch nur Leblosos handwerklich herzustellen. Die eigene Sterblichkeit macht es unmöglich, etwas Lebendiges hervorzubringen, daher ist die Errichtung eines Götterbildes bloß eine schlechte Imitation des Schöpfergottes. Immer wieder kommt es zu einer Reduzierung der Bild-Gottheiten als Menschenwerk, der Mensch ist somit Erschaffer, Kreator der εἴδωλα.

---

31. Vgl. dazu die Begründung und Erklärung des Kultbilderverbots in Dtn 4,12.

32. Der Begriff χώνευμα steht auch in den Parallelstellen im Kontext des (Bundes-)Bruches und ruft die Erfahrungen am Sinai in Erinnerung (explizit: Dtn 9,12; 4.Kgt 17,16; implizit: Jer 10,3; Hab 2,18). Die Aussage in Hos 8,13 enthält auch eine metaphorische Bedeutung: ... αὐτοὶ εἰς Αἴγυπτον ἀπέστρεψαν bei jeder Abkehr Israels von JHWH hin zu fremden Kulten und Göttern, kehrt es zurück nach Ägypten. Ausführlicher dazu in Plangger 2018, 174–96.

Der Mensch überschreitet seine Kompetenz, weil er nicht die ihm von Gott aufgetragene Aufgabe erfüllt, an seiner Stelle Sorge für die übrigen Geschöpfe zu tragen (siehe Gen 1,26b).

Die Verschmelzung zwischen Bundesbruch und Zuwiderhandeln gegen JHWH als Schöpfer wird durch den LXX Zusatz in Hos 13,4 gestärkt, wo der Gott Israels als umsichtiger Organisator und Architekt den stümperhaften Handwerkern gegenübergestellt wird.

Die εἴδωλα sind ein Gräuel in der Schöpfung Gottes (Weish 14,11), da sie nicht von Gott erschaffen worden sind. So wie der Tod kamen sie erst später durch das Fehlverhalten der Menschen in die Welt und erweisen sich als unbeständig und zeitlich begrenzt (vgl. Weish 14,13).

Ein außergewöhnliches hebräisches Äquivalent ist in Num 33,52 belegt, das eine direkte Verbindung zur Schöpfungsthematik herstellt. Der hebräische Ausdruck צלם umfasst eine große Bandbreite an Bedeutungen in oft sehr unterschiedlichen Zusammenhängen und wird sogar als Bezeichnung für die Gottebenbildlichkeit des Menschen verwendet (vgl. Gen 1,26-27; 5,3; 9,6; Ps 39,7 und 73,20; Ez 23,14).

Primär repräsentiert der religiöse Begriff צלם das Dargestellte machtvoll, das Moment des Abbildens steht dagegen weniger stark im Fokus. Das Wort hat eine zweifache Ausrichtung: positiv wird damit der Mensch als „Repräsentant"/"Bild Gottes" genannt (Gen 1,26; griechisches Äquivalent εἰκών), negativ bezeichnet צלם Repräsentationen von Fremdgottheiten.[33]

Bei εἴδωλον steht auch die Repräsentation einer Gottheit bzw. mehrerer Gottheiten im Vordergrund und nicht primär eine bestimmte Art der Bilddarstellung. Bei εἰκών ist stärker das Bild selbst im Fokus (vgl. die Verwendung von εἴδωλον und εἰκών im Buch Daniel). Auch wenn in Gen 1,26-27 εἰκών verwendet wird, das auch ganz allgemein eine Bilddarstellung zum Ausdruck bringen kann, gibt es Überschneidungen mit εἴδωλον. Möglicherweise wollte der Übersetzer eindeutig eine Verbindung zu den Fremdgottheiten, den Götter(bildern) mit seiner Begriffswahl bezwecken. Auch wenn sich eine direkte Verbindung zur Erschaffung des Menschen in der Genesis nur durch צלם nachweisen lässt, könnte die seltene Übersetzung mit εἴδωλον als negative Umkehrung erklärt werden, da in eindeutiger Weise handwerklich hergestellte, künstliche Repräsentationen von Gottheiten gemeint sind. Das Bild Gottes ist nicht in Stein gemeißelt

---

33. Ausführlicher zur Begriffsklärung bzw. -bedeutung, siehe Stendebach 1989; Schroer 1987, 322-24; Berlejung 1998, 62-63; Garr 2003, 137.

(wie in Num 33,52 die Götter[bilder]), sondern zeichnet sich im Menschen selbst ab, das beständig und lebendig von Generation zu Generation weitergegeben wird (Gen 5,3).[34]

3. Ertrag

Die Studie hat gezeigt, wie differenziert die einzelnen Übersetzer mit dem Problem der Benennung fremder Gottesvorstellungen und -bilder umgegangen sind. Es ist deutlich geworden, dass der hebräische Text zu je neuen Interpretationsleistungen nötigte, die vom Übersetzer zu erbringen waren. Dabei ging es um die Markierung der Grenzlinie zwischen eigenem und fremden Glauben, um Abwägungen darüber, was im Rahmen der Religion Israels sagbar war und was nicht. Insofern war die theologische Urteilsbildung der Übersetzer gefordert, eine Reflexion darüber, wie der hebräische Sinn angemessen in die neue sprachliche und kulturelle Verstehenssituation transferiert werden konnte. Damit erfüllt das Thema der *eidola* eines der Hauptkriterien dafür, was als Thema einer „Theologie der Septuaginta" zu bearbeiten ist.[35]

Literatur

Aitken, James K. 2014. „Outlook." Seiten 183–94 in *The Reception of Septuagint Words in Jewish-Hellenistic and Christian Literature*. Hrsg. von Eberhard Bons, Ralph Brucker, und Jan Joosten. WUNT 2/367. Tübingen: Mohr Siebeck.

Berlejung, Angelika. 1998. *Die Theologie der Bilder. Herstellung und Einweihung von Kultbildern in Mesopotamien und die alttestamentliche Bilderpolemik*. OBO 162. Freiburg: Universitätsverlag; Göttingen: Vandenhoeck & Ruprecht.

Bruneau, Philippe. 1970. *Recherches sur les cultes de Délos à l'époque hellénistique et à l'époque impériale*. Bibliothèque des Écoles Françaises d'Athènes et de Rome 217. Paris: de Boccard.

Dorival, Gilles. 1994. *Les Nombres*. BdA 4. Paris: Cerf.

---

34. Weitere Kategorien, die für das Bedeutungsverständnis von εἴδωλον erhellend sind: *Größe und Beschaffenheit*; *Materialzugehörigkeit*; *Herstellungsprozess*; *Namen*; *Ohnmacht / Machtlosigkeit / Nutzlosigkeit*; Siehe dazu ausführlicher in: Plangger 2018, 268–80.

35. Siehe Rösel 2018.

Engel, Helmut. 1998. *Das Buch der Weisheit.* NSKAT 16. Stuttgart: Katholisches Bibelwerk.

Fabry, Heinz-Josef. 1986. „נחש." *TWAT* 5:384–97.

Fischer, Moshe, und Ruth E. Jackson-Tal. 2003. „A Glass Pendant in the Shape of Harpokrates from Yavneh-Yam, Israel." *Journal of Glass Studies* 45:35–40.

Foerster, Werner. 1933. „βδελύσσομαι, βδέλυγμα, βδελυκτός." *TWNT* 1:598–600.

Garr, W. Randall. 2003. *In His Own Image and Likeness. Humanity, Divinity, and Monotheism.* CHANE 15. Leiden: Brill.

Griffith, Terry. 2002. „ΕΙΔΩΛΟΝ as ‚Idol' in Non-Jewish and Non-Christian Greek." *JTS* 53:95–101.

Hayward, Charles T. R. 2007. „Observations on Idols in Septuagint Pentateuch." Seiten 40–57 in *Idolatry. False Worship in the Bible, Early Judaism and Christianity.* Hrsg. von Stephen C. Barton. London: T&T Clark.

Heine, Heinrich. 1987. „Geständnisse." Seiten 9–57 in *Historisch-Kritische Gesamtausgabe der Werke.* Hrsg. von Manfred Windfuhr. Bd. 15. Hamburg: Hoffmann & Campe.

Hieke, Thomas. 2014. *Levitikus. Zweiter Teilband 16–27.* HThKAT. Freiburg im Breisgau: Herder.

Hossfeld, Frank Lothar, und Erich Zenger. 2008. *Die Psalmen 101–150.* HThKAT. Freiburg im Breisgau: Herder.

Jacob, Benno. 1997. *Das Buch Exodus.* Stuttgart: Calwer.

Joosten, Jan. 2016. „Septuagint Greek and the Jewish Sociolect in Egypt." Seiten 246–56 in *Die Sprache der Septuaginta / The Language of The Septuagint.* Hrsg. von Eberhard Bons und Jan Joosten. LXX.H 3. Gütersloh: Gütersloher Verlagshaus.

Lust, Johan. 2008. „Idols? גלולים and εἴδωλα in Ezekiel." Seiten 317–33 in *Florilegium Lovaniense. Studies in Septuagint and Textual Criticism in Honor of F. G. Martínez.* Hrsg. von Hans Ausloos, Bénédicte Lemmelijn, und Marc Vervenne. BETL 224. Leuven: Peeters.

Meadors, Edward P. 2006. *Idolatry and the Hardening of the Heart. A Study in Biblical Theology.* New York: T&T Clark.

Olofsson, Staffan. 1990. *God Is My Rock. A Study of Translation Technique and Theological Exegesis in the Septuagint.* ConBOT 31. Stockholm: Almqvist & Wiksell.

Peters, Melvin K. H. 2012. „Revisiting the Rock: Tsur as a Translation of Elohim in Deuteronomy and Beyond." Seiten 37–51 in *Text-Critical and Hermeneutical Studies in the Septuagint*. Hrsg. von Johann Cook und Hermann-Josef Stipp. VTSup 157. Leiden: Brill.

Pietersma, Albert. 1994. *The Apocryphon of Jannes and Jambres the Magicians. P. Chester Beatty XVI (with New Editions of Papyrus Vindobonensis Greek Inv. 29356 + 29828 Verso and British Library Cotton Tiberius B. v f. 87)*. Religions in the Graeco-Roman World 119. Leiden: Brill.

Plangger, Stefanie. 2018. „Gott im Bild, Eidôlon – Studien zur Herkunft und Verwendung des Septuagintabegriffes für das Götterbild." Diss. theol. Universität Straßburg.

Rad, Gerhard von. 1935. „εἰκών. A. Das Bilderverbot im AT" *TWNT* 2:378–80.

Rösel, Martin 1994. *Übersetzung als Vollendung der Auslegung. Studien zur Genesis-Septuaginta*. BZAW 223. Berlin: De Gruyter.

———. 2015. „»Du sollst die Götter nicht schmähen!« (LXX Ex 22,28[27]). Die Übersetzung Gottes und der Götter in der Septuaginta." Seiten 54–68 in *Der übersetzte Gott*. Hrsg. von Melanie Lange und Martin Rösel. Leipzig: Evangelische Verlagsanstalt.

———. 2018. „Eine Theologie der Septuaginta? Präzisierungen und Pointierungen." Seiten 25–43 in *Theologie und Textgeschichte. Septuaginta und Masoretischer Text als Äußerungen theologischer Reflexion*. Hrsg. von Frank Ueberschaer, Thomas Wagner, und Jonathan Miles Robker. WUNT 407. Tübingen: Mohr Siebeck.

———. 2019. „Vorlage oder Interpretation? Zur Übersetzung von Gottesaussagen in der Septuaginta des Deuteronomiums." Seiten 250–62 in *Ein Freund des Wortes*. Festschrift Udo Rüterswörden. Hrsg. von Sebastian Grätz, Axel Graupner, und Jörg Lanckau. Göttingen: Vandenhoeck & Ruprecht.

Saïd, Suzanne. 1987. „Deux noms de l'image en grec ancien: idole et icône." *Comptes rendus des séances de l'Académie des Inscriptions et Belles-Lettres*. 131:309–30.

Scheer, Tanja S. 2000. *Die Gottheit und ihr Bild. Untersuchungen zur Funktion griechischer Kultbilder in Religion und Politik*. Zetemata 105. München: Beck.

Schroer, Silvia, 1987. *In Israel gab es Bilder. Nachrichten von darstellender Kunst im Alten Testament*. OBO 74. Freiburg: Universitätsverlag; Göttingen: Vandenhoeck & Ruprecht.

Seebass, Horst. 2003. „The Case of Phinehas at Baal Peor in Num 25." *BN* 117:40–46.

Seeligmann, Isac L. 2004. *The Septuagint Version of Isaiah and Cognate*

Studies. Hrsg. von Robert Hanhart und Hermann Spieckermann. FAT 40. Tübingen: Mohr Siebeck.

Seybold, Klaus, 1977. „הבל." *TWAT* 2: 334–43.

Spaer, Maud, et al. 2001. *Ancient Glass in the Israel Museum. Beads and Other Small Finds*. Jerusalem: The Israel Museum.

Stählin, Gustav. 1964. „σκάνδαλον κτλ." *TWNT* 7:339–58.

Stendebach, Franz J. 1989. „צלם." *TWAT* 6:1046–55.

Ulrich, Eugene, und Peter W. Flint. 2010. *Qumran Cave 1 II: The Isaiah Scrolls*. DJD 32. Oxford: Clarendon.

Vernant, Jean-Pierre. 1990. „Figuration et image." *Métis* 5:225–38.

Wenham, Gordon J. 1994. *Genesis 16–50*. WBC 2. Dallas: Word.

Wevers, John W. 1978. *Text History of the Greek Deuteronomy*. MSU 13. Göttingen: Vandenhoeck & Ruprecht.

"You Saw No Form When YHWH Spoke to You at Horeb" (Deut 4:15): Antianthropomorphisms in the Greek Deuteronomy

Hans Ausloos

ABSTRACT: As literature making use of human language, it is unavoidable that the Hebrew Bible presents God in a so-called anthropomorphic way. Even within Deuteronomy, a book that clearly reacts against making carved images of God (Deut 4:16), God seems to have human characteristics: reference is made to God's mouth (8:3), it is often mentioned how God leads Israel through the desert with a mighty hand and an outstretched arm (e.g., 4:34), and how God has written the stone tablets with his finger (9:10). Besides these physical human characteristics, God also is referred to as having feelings or emotions similar to human ones. Whereas Fritsch was of the opinion that the Septuagint translation of Deuteronomy is characterized by an antianthropomorphic bias, Wittstruck considered this so-called antianthropomorphic tendency within the Septuagint as a mere stylistic issue, not influenced by any theological motivation. This chapter reevaluates this topic and investigates if and to what extent the anthropomorphic presentation of God in the Hebrew text of Deuteronomy troubled the Septuagint translator of this book.

1. Introduction

Talking about God requires the use of human language. Notwithstanding the acceptance of God being the completely different one, the only way to speak of him or to reflect on him is by doing this through human words, language and its metaphors. This is the reason why Old Testament authors have presented God as a judge, a shepherd, a father, or a mother. These characterizations of God evidently do not imply that God *is* a judge, *is* a shepherd, *is* a father, or *is* a mother. These are metaphors. God is *like* them:

righteous as a judge, caring as a shepherd, and comforting and providing as parents do for their children.

Besides making use of metaphors, but equally due to the fact that human language necessarily has to be used to talk about God as the one who transcends the world, biblical authors equally attribute human physical characteristics to God, which, in turn, can give the impression that God is as "bodily" as human people. Genesis 1:26, stating that God "made humankind in his image," could even strengthen this impression.

Also and even within the book of Deuteronomy, one of the biblical books that explicitly states that Israel has been forbidden to make graven idols "in the form of any figure—the likeness of male or female" (Deut 4:16), several physical human characteristics, in other words, anthropomorphisms, can be found.[1] It is often stated that God is "speaking" (making use of the verbs אמר and דבר, verbs that are also used with humans as subject). Moreover, within Deuteronomy explicit reference is made to God's mouth (פי יהוה, 8:3). In several instances (4:34; 5:15; 7:19; 11:2; 26:8) one reads that God delivered the Israelites out of Egypt with "a mighty hand and outstretched arm" (ביד חזקה ובזרוע נטויה). Further, Deut 9:10 narrates that Moses received the tables of stone that were written with "the finger of God" (באצבע אלהים). Moreover, God seems to have a nose, eyes, and even feet, as Deut 33:10, 11:12, and 33:3, respectively, suggest.

The anthropomorphic presentation of God is not limited to his external appearance. Quite often God is also internally depicted as having feelings, passions, and emotions.[2] God can be angry (אנף, Deut 1:37; 4:21; 9:8, 20), as he can be jealous (קנא, 4:24; 5:9; 6:15) or merciful (רחום, 4:31).

Even if an anthropomorphic and anthropopathic presentation of God is inevitable, a (too-)human presentation seems to have encountered resistance among some ancient readers of the Bible. Already within the Hebrew Bible itself, some seemingly antianthropomorphic tendencies can be detected.[3] Besides these reactions within the Hebrew Bible, some

---

1. See also the quotation in the title of this paper. In Deut 4:12, contrary to Exod 13:21, there is nothing to see. God reveals himself by words only. This presentation apparently has been the basis of the prohibition of a physical representation of God.

2. Here one often uses the term *anthropopathic*. Within the present essay, the term *anthropomorphism* also includes anthropopathisms.

3. Thus, for example, the intermediary role of the angels within some theophanies, as it is the case in Gen 16:7 or Num 22:24.

scholars posit that the oldest traces of this so-called antianthropomorphic tendency can be found within the Greek translation of the Bible, the Septuagint (LXX).

In his *Vorstudien zu der Septuaginta* (1841), Zacharias Frankel concisely dealt with an antianthropomorphic tendency of the LXX.[4] Frankel also mentioned this topic in his 1851 work *Über den Einfluss der palästinische Exegese auf die alexandrinische Hermeneutik*, albeit only sporadically.[5]

The first more or less encompassing analysis of the way in which the LXX translators dealt with the topic of anthropomorphisms was offered by Charles Fritsch in his PhD thesis at Princeton University, which was published, in a revised form, in 1943 as *The Anti-anthropomorphisms of the Greek Pentateuch*. As the title makes clear, Fritsch was only focusing on the anthropomorphisms in the Pentateuch. His conclusion was rather nuanced:

> Actual anthropomorphisms and anthropopathies are taken over into the Greek with comparatively few cases of alteration; on the other hand, there are some anthropomorphic expressions and metaphors which are quite consistently avoided in the Greek. … For the most part, the LXX reveals no consistent method of avoiding the anthropomorphisms of the Hebrew. Genesis and Leviticus, for instance, are singularly free from anti-anthropomorphisms in the Greek, whereas Exodus has the most examples of any book in the Pentateuch.… The tendency to spiritualize the conception of God in the LXX by avoiding anthropomorphic expressions was active; it was not strong enough, however, to make itself felt consistently, except in a comparatively few instances. In this connection it must be borne in mind that the Seventy did not undertake to rewrite the Pentateuch. They were translators, but in various passages their theology is brought out in this version.[6]

Despite these nuanced conclusions, Fritsch's analysis has been strongly criticized, first by Harry Orlinsky[7] and later by Thorne Wittstruck in "The So-Called Anti-anthropomorphisms in the Greek Text of Deuteronomy":

---

4. Frankel 1841, 174–79.
5. Frankel 1851, 30. On 216, Frankel very generally states, "Der Vert. des Deuteron. vermeidet … Anthropomorphismen."
6. Fritsch 1943, 62.
7. Orlinsky 1944, 156–60. See also Orlinsky's introductory essay on anthropomorphisms and anthropopathisms in the LXX and the Targum in Zlotowitz 1981, xi–xxiv.

There is no support for Fritsch's opinion that the LXX text of Deuteronomy exhibits an anti-anthropomorphic bias in its translation. The alleged examples of anti-anthropomorphisms are merely the result of a style which is not limited to theological matters, but rather is found throughout the entire book of Deuteronomy.[8]

In what follows, Fritsch's and Wittstruck's considerations with regard to the question whether or not the LXX translation of Deuteronomy should be characterized as more antianthropomorphic than the Hebrew form, the Masoretic Text (MT), of the book, will be reevaluated.[9] Within the scope of this essay, however, we will look only at some typical human physical characteristics that the MT attributes to God and the way they are dealt with in the LXX translation. As such, so-called anthropopathies (God who fears, is jealous, or is angry) as well as typical human activities that are attributed to God (God who carries, dwells, walks, and swears) will not be dealt with here. Also, instances of metaphoric conceptualization of God (God as a rock, shield, or sword) are not part of the present comparative analysis between the MT and the LXX.

2. The Mouth of God

In Deut 1:26, Moses reproaches the Israelites, according to the MT, for having "rebelled (against) the mouth of YHWH" (ותמרו את פי יהוה). The same Hebrew formula can be found in Deut 1:43 and 9:23. Finally, in Deut 34:5 it is said that Moses died in the land of Moab, "according to the mouth of YHWH" (על פי יהוה). In all four instances, the MT uses the noun פה in the sense of "word." As such, the LXX's equivalent τὸ ῥῆμα κυρίου is not at all strange and certainly cannot be labeled as antianthropomorphic. On the contrary, the LXX translator seems to give a very "faithful" rendering of his presumed Hebrew *Vorlage*.[10]

The fact that this rendering is hardly the result of an antianthropomorphic tendency becomes equally clear from Deut 8:3, where we read that one does not live by bread alone but "by everything that comes from the mouth of YHWH" (על כל מוצא פי יהוה). Here, due to the context,

---

8. Wittstruck 1976, 29–34, esp. 34.

9. For the MT of Deuteronomy, the edition of McCarthy 2007 has been used. For the LXX, I rely on the eclectic edition by Wevers and Quast 2006.

10. On this terminology, see, *inter alia*, Ausloos and Lemmelijn 2014, 53–69.

the Hebrew פה cannot be rendered as "words," even if the author wants to accentuate that one does not live by material food only but thanks to God's words. In this verse, no other rendering than a literal one—"mouth"—is possible.

In the LXX version of Deut 8:3, one reads: παντὶ ῥήματι τῷ ἐκπορευομένῳ διὰ στόματος θεοῦ (NETS: "by every word that goes through the mouth of God man shall live").[11] Even if ῥήματι is a *plus*, which does not have an equivalent in Hebrew, the expression על פי יהוה has διὰ στόματος θεοῦ as its "literal" translation equivalent.[12] This rendering can be compared to Deut 32:1, where Moses opens his song with the words "Let the earth hear the words of my mouth" (ותשמע הארץ אמרי פי), rendered adequately as καὶ ἀκουέτω γῆ ῥήματα ἐκ στόματός μου (NETS: "Let the earth hear words from my mouth").

These findings with regard to mentioning God's mouth and the equivalent readings in the LXX are relevant only for the book of Deuteronomy. With regard to the book of Numbers, for example, Martin Rösel has clearly indicated that the LXX's rendering of על פי יהוה by διὰ φωνῆς κυρίου in Num 3:16, 39 "is the result of a theological consideration" and that "the translator did not avoid the idea of a voice of God only that God had a mouth."[13]

3. The Ears of God

In Deut 1:45, it is told how the Israelites, returning from their unsuccessful expedition against the Amorites, cried out to YHWH. However, YHWH did not listen to their voice and did not "give ear," as the American Standard Version "literally" translates the Hebrew denominative verb אזן, to them.

In the LXX, there is no reference to the "ear" of God that is present in the MT. The LXX reads: οὐδὲ προσέσχεν ὑμῖν (NETS: "nor paid you any attention"). According to Fritsch, the use of the verb אזן was "objectionable," the reason why reference to God's ear, albeit implicitly, was avoided by the LXX translator.[14]

---

11. Peters 2007, 153.

12. On the distinction between "literal" and "free," and the role of quantitative representation as a criterion herein, see, *inter alia*, Ausloos forthcoming.

13. Rösel 2006, 247. Rösel indicates that, for example, in Num 4:27 the expression על פי אהרן has κατὰ στόμα Ααρων as equivalent.

14. Fritsch 1943, 3. Compare, however, to Num 11:1, where the "ears of YHWH" are explicitly mentioned (אזני יהוה). Instead of using a substantive as equivalent, the

The verb אזן occurs a second time in Deuteronomy; the noun אזן is never used in Deuteronomy with reference to God. In Deut 32:1, Moses asks the heavens to "give ear" (האזינו השמים) so that he can speak, as he asks the earth to listen to his words. Similar to Deut 1:45, the LXX reads a form of the verb προσέχω. Contrary to Deut 1:45, however, the translator's word choice in Deut 32:1 can hardly have been influenced by antianthropomorphic concerns, since it is Moses, not YHWH, who functions as the verb's subject.

Although he does not refer to the use of the verb אזן/προσέχω in Deut 32:1, Wittstruck does not agree with Fritsch's antianthropomorphic characterization of the LXX in Deut 1:45. In his view, Fritsch's argument is based on the premise that, "since the verb is translated idiomatically, it is an anti-anthropomorphism," and that, also in Fritsch's view, "only in translating it literally … [would] the translator be free of this charge."[15]

Wittstruck's observation makes sense. Nevertheless, a rash interpretation should be avoided. One should notice that, in the case of the Hebrew verb אזן, the Greek translator could have chosen another Greek term in which, nonetheless, the element of the "ear" also was present: ἐνωτίζομαι. In choosing this verb, a denominative from the noun οὖς ("ear"), the translator could have translated both idiomatically and "faithfully" to the Hebrew.[16] Although this verb, which is not found outside the LXX and therefore maybe can be characterized as LXX-Greek, does not occur in Deuteronomy, it can be found in Gen 4:23, Exod 15:26, and Num 23:18 as the equivalent of אזן.

The fact that the translator of Deut 32:1 equally prefers προσέχω as equivalent of אזן, although it is not used with God as subject, can be due to the fact that the translator aimed to be consistent in his use of translation equivalents, thus rendering consistently a given Hebrew term by one and the same Greek equivalent.[17] Consequently, one should be careful in using

---

LXX has opted to render the expression as ἔναντι κυρίου, thus avoiding an anthropomorphic presentation of God.

15. Wittstruck 1976, 30. See also Harl 1994, 214: "Les anthropomorphismes qui sont supprimés le sont le plus souvent au nom de la bonne grécité désirée pour la traduction. Il en reste cependant encore un bon nombre, surtout dans les livres traduits de façon littérale ou dans les livres révisés et rehébraisés."

16. See Helbing 1928, 157–58.

17. On consistency (often the term *stereotyping* is used in this regard) as a criterion for the characterization of the LXX translation technique, see Ausloos forthcoming.

this verse as an argument in the denial of a possible antianthropomorphical tendency of the LXX translator.

4. The Eyes of God

The expression בעיני יהוה is common within the book of Deuteronomy, occurring in Deut 4:25; 6:18; 9:18; 12:25, 28; 13:19; 17:2; 21:9; 31:29. Literally, it can be translated by "in the eyes of YHWH," as, for example, the NIV translates Deut 4:25: "doing evil in the *eyes* of the Lord." Other translations look for an alternative rendering of the noun עין—the NRSV, for example, renders as "in the *sight* of the LORD"—thus apparently avoiding an overly anthropomorphic presentation of God as having eyes.

In the LXX of Deuteronomy, the Hebrew formula בעיני יהוה is consistently rendered *ad sensum*, making use of the preposition ἐναντίον + genitive. The question could be asked whether this should be interpreted as indicative of an antianthropomorphic tendency of the LXX translator. Fritsch is of the opinion that "the original underlying anthropomorphic conception has been permanently eradicated in the LXX."[18]

Nevertheless, Fritsch's qualification of the LXX's rendering seems to be premature. First, the Greek rendering occurs not only in passages that refer to God but equally in cases where the formula is used in relation to human subjects. For example, in Deut 15:18, where the expression לא יקשה בעינך בשלחך אתו ("it shall not be hard to your eyes when you send him") refers to Israel, the construction equally has been rendered *ad sensum*: οὐ σκληρὸν ἔσται ἐναντίον σου.[19] Also in Deut 1:23, applying the formula to Moses (וייטב בעיני הדבר; "this case was good in my eyes"), the LXX renders the Hebrew בעיני equally as ἐναντίον μου. Thus choosing ἐναντίον + genitive as the translation equivalent to בעיני does not seem to be an indication as such of an antianthropomorphic tendency in the LXX but rather the result of the translator's attempt to provide an idiomatic translation.

Nevertheless, when the MT uses the noun עין to refer explicitly to the physical organ of the human eye, the LXX translates consequently by ὀφθαλμός, as in Deut 3:21, 27; 4:3, 9; 6:5; 7:16, 19; 10:21; 11:7, 12, 18; 13:9; 14:1; 15:9; 16:19; 19:13, 21; 21:7; 25:12; 28:32, 34, 54, 56, 65; 29:3; 34:4, 7. However, used as such in relation to God, the term occurs only in Deut

---

18. Fritsch 1943, 12–13.
19. See also, e.g., Deut 25:3; 28:31, 34.

32:10. Here, in his song, Moses describes God's care for Israel with the words: "He kept him as the pupil of his eye" (יִצְּרֶנְהוּ כְּאִישׁוֹן עֵינוֹ).

In the LXX, there is no equivalent for the suffix ‫ו‬-. Here, one reads: καὶ διεφύλαξεν αὐτὸν ὡς κόρην ὀφθαλμοῦ.[20] According to Fritsch, this should be seen as a deliberate omission by the LXX translator, witnessing "the tendency to separate God from that which is physical as well as from that which is unbecoming to his majesty."[21] According to Wittstruck, however, the "omission of the possessive pronoun is not restricted to the so-called anti-anthropomorphic passages." Therefore, he considers this *minus* to be "just a feature of the translator's style in general."[22] In this context, one can refer to Deut 3:27, a verse referring to the human eye as physical organ. Here, too, there is a minus in the LXX with regard to the suffix (עֵינֶיךָ – τοῖς ὀφθαλμοῖς).

However, one should be careful in generalizing. In Deut 3:21, for example, the LXX is completely in line with the MT: on the one hand, segmenting each part of the term, although, on the other, harmonizing with the second-person plural forms of the rest of the verse (עֵינֶיךָ – οἱ ὀφθαλμοὶ ὑμῶν).

Notwithstanding these observations, in Deut 3:21 (without possessive pronoun) and in 3:27 (with possessive pronoun), reference is made to the human eye, not to God's eye. The only text in Deuteronomy where the noun refers to God's "eye" is 32:10. Therefore, it is not impossible that the *minus* of the suffix in this verse indeed goes back to a deliberate decision of the translator.

5. The Nose of God?

As in many other books of the Old Testament, the author of Deuteronomy also refers to the "nose of YHWH" (אַף יהוה). This expression is used four times within Deuteronomy (6:15; 7:4; 11:17; 29:19).[23] As it is commonly accepted, in this formula the noun אַף ("nose") is used as a metonymy for

---

20. Compare, however, the translation by NETS: "He guarded him as the apple of his eye."
21. Fritsch 1943, 11.
22. Wittstruck 1976, 30.
23. See also Deut 13:18, which literally speaks about the "burning of his [YHWH's] nose" (מֵחֲרוֹן אַפּוֹ).

"anger," "by the natural association of heavy breathing or snorting in connection with this emotion."²⁴

The LXX interprets the noun אף in this metonymical sense, both in the context of humans and referring to God, rendering it by either θυμός (Deut 6:15; 7:4; 13:17; 29:22, 26, 28; 31:17; 32:22) or ὀργή (9:19; 29:19, 24).²⁵

Nevertheless, one particular case merits attention. In Deut 33:10, the term אף seems to refer literally to God's nose: "they shall put incense before your nose" (ישימו קטורה באפך).²⁶ In the LXX version of this verse, the term אף also has been rendered by ὀργή: ἐπιθήσουσιν θυμίαμα ἐν ὀργῇ σου (NETS: "They shall place incense in your wrath"). Because this translation does not make much sense, NETS indicates that "in your wrath" can possibly mean "on your wrath," or "when you are angry."

As to this translation equivalent of Deut 33:10, two possible explanations, both inspired by a deliberate choice of the translator, can be suggested: (1) the LXX translator aimed at a consistent rendering of the noun אף throughout the entire book of Deuteronomy;²⁷ (2) the translator rendered אף by ὀργή in order to avoid an anthropomorphic presentation of God.²⁸ One explanation does not necessarily exclude the other one. In any case, because Deut 33:10 is the only instance within the book of Deuteronomy in which the Hebrew term irrefutably refers to YHWH's nose as an olfactory organ, a sound decision is difficult to make.

6. The Face of God

Comparably to the construction בעיני יהוה, the Hebrew formulae לפני יהוה and מפני יהוה should be mentioned. Morphologically, this common expression—Waltke and O'Connor call it a "frozen prepositional expression"²⁹—consists of the combination of a prefix ל- or -מ followed

---

24. Fritsch 1943, 13. See, e.g., Deut 13:18,

25. In Deut 11:17, LXX reads θυμωθεὶς ὀργισθῇ κύριος ἐφ᾽ ὑμῖν, thus rendering the noun אף by a finite verb (וחרה אף יהוה בכם).

26. Some actual translations render this formula literally, whereas other prefer a less anthropomorphic rendering. See Otto 2017, 2212–13: "Sie legen Räucherwerk vor deine Nase." Also the Dutch *Statenvertaling* translates as such: "zij zullen reukwerk voor Uw neus leggen." Compare, however, with NRSV or ASV: "they place incense before you/thee."

27. So Wittstruck 1976, 31.

28. So Fritsch 1943, 14.

29. *IBHS*, §11.3.1.

by the lexeme פנה ("face"). Sometimes a pronominal suffix is added (such as לפניך); sometimes it is followed by a noun or a proper name (as in לפני יהוה).

In some contexts in the Greek Deuteronomy, the translator segmented this formula into its constitutive parts.[30] Being one of the classical criteria to measure the literalness of a translation, this segmentation can be seen, for example, in Deut 9:3, where לפניך occurs twice. Segmented into its constitutive parts, the formula is rendered as ἀπὸ/πρὸ προσώπου σου. The same procedure is followed in Deut 1:30, where לפניכם has been rendered by πρὸ προσώπου ὑμῶν, or in Deut 2:25, where מפניך has ἀπὸ προσώπου σου as a translation equivalent.

Much more in line with Koine Greek, however, is the rendering by the Greek preposition ἐνώπιον + genitive, as in Deut 1:8 (לפניכם – ἐνώπιον ὑμῶν), or by the Greek preposition ἐναντίον + genitive (22:17: לפני זקני העיר – ἐναντίον τῆς γερουσίας τῆς πόλεως) or ἔναντι + genitive (19:17: לפני הכהנים – ἔναντι τῶν ἱερέων).[31] Also the combination πρότερος (adjective) + genitive is used as an equivalent for the Hebrew לפני (1:22: לפנינו – προτέρους ἡμῶν).

There is no reason to argue that these Greek idiomatic equivalents would have been used out of an antianthropomorphic concern. Indeed, it is true that the prepositions ἐνώπιον, ἐναντίον, and ἔναντι are often used in combination with the name of God, as, for example, in Deut 16:16; 31:11 (ἐνώπιον κυρίου), in 4:10, 25; 6:18 (ἐναντίον κυρίου), and in 10:8; 15:20 (ἔναντι κυρίου). However, within the book of Deuteronomy, the "literal" translation by πρόσωπον is also used. In 5:4 the LXX renders the Hebrew פנים בפנים דבר יהוה עמכם "literally" (πρόσωπον κατὰ πρόσωπον ἐλάλησεν κύριος πρὸς ὑμᾶς). Also in 5:7 the Greek does not seem to react against a possible anthropomorphic reading of the MT, thus translating לא יהיה לך אלהים אחרים על פני ("You shall have no other gods before my face") by οὐκ ἔσονταί σοι θεοὶ ἕτεροι πρὸ προσώπου μου.

Nevertheless, according to Fritsch, in one passage in Greek Deuteronomy the translator clearly reacts against an overly anthropomorphic—a "surrogate for God"[32]—presentation. In Deut 4:37, the term בפניו is used to refer to the "own independent status as an *Erscheinungsform Gottes*"

---

30. On segmentation as a criterion for the analysis of the "translation technique," see Ausloos forthcoming.

31. On the Greek rendering, see in particular Sollamo 1979; 1975, 773–82.

32. Fritsch 1943, 47 n. 17.

(ויוצאך בפניו בכחו הגדל ממצרים).³³ In this passage, פנים "can mean ... only the person himself insofar as he is present." Therefore, in rendering בפניו as αὐτός (NETS: "and himself brought you out of Egypt"), the LXX both "has admirably reproduced its true meaning" and avoided a possible anthropomorphic presentation of God.³⁴ According to Wittstruck, however, the LXX rendering is the result of an incomprehensible Hebrew source text. When a source text does not make sense, as it is the case in the MT of Deut 4:37 ("he brought you forth with his face"), the translator has the duty to make an intelligible translation, trying to stay as close as possible to his source.³⁵

7. God's Arms, Hand and Fingers

Moreover, one can read about God's hand (יד), and this especially in Deut 3:24; 7:19; 11:2; 32:39; 33:3. In all these instances the LXX has the noun χείρ as its equivalent. In Deut 3:24 (ידך החזקה - τὴν χεῖρα τὴν κραταιάν) as well as in 11:2 (ידו החזקה - τὴν χεῖρα τὴν κραταιάν), the LXX has no equivalent for the pronominal suffix, contrary to 32:39 (מידי - τὴν χεῖρά μου) and 33:3 (בידך - τὰς χεῖράς σου).

God's finger is mentioned only once in the Hebrew text of Deuteronomy. In 9:33, one reads that YHWH gave to Moses the two tablets of stone, "written with the finger of God" (כתבים באצבע אלהים). The LXX's translation is close to the Hebrew: γεγραμμένας ἐν τῷ δακτύλῳ τοῦ θεοῦ.

Reference to God's arm (זרוע) is made only within the so-called Deuteronomic formula "with outstretched arm" (זרע הנטויה) in Deut 7:19; 9:29; 11:2. The Hebrew term is rendered by the usual Greek equivalent βραχίων, a noun that is also used to denote human arms.

Nevertheless, as Fritsch notes, in Deut 33:27 the expression זרעת עולם ("everlasting arms") has a *plus* in the LXX: ἰσχὺν βραχιόνων ἀενάων (NETS: "under the strength of the everlasting arms"). In Fritsch's view, "by introducing this abstract idea of power into the phrase the Greek has definitely weakened the anthropomorphism of the Hebrew."³⁶ Whether this can be

---

33. Fritsch 1943, 10.
34. Fritsch 1943, 12.
35. Wittstruck 1976, 30. See also Tov 1998, 203–18.
36. Fritsch 1943, 15.

considered as a case of an antianthropomorphic tendency in the LXX is questionable, since God's arm is still present in the verse.³⁷

8. The Feet of God

Finally, we arrive at the bottom of God's "body." Within Deuteronomy there is a single reference to God's feet.³⁸ In Deut 33:3, in his blessing, Moses proclaims that "all his saints are in your [God's] hand, and they sat down at your [God's] feet" (כל קדשיו בידך והם תכו לרגלך). Even if this verse is not easy to interpret,³⁹ it is interesting to note that, in the LXX, there is no "literal" equivalent for the Hebrew term רגל. The LXX reads: πάντες οἱ ἡγιασμένοι ὑπὸ τὰς χεῖράς σου καὶ οὗτοι ὑπὸ σέ εἰσιν (NETS: "all of the sanctified ones were under your hands—even these are under you"). Wevers suggests that the translator seems to have taken the enigmatic Hebrew והם תכו לרגלך as והם תחת רגלך, even if, as he admits, תכו ל- could hardly have been misread in this way.⁴⁰

Whether this rendering testifies to an antianthropomorphic tendency of the Greek translator is not at all certain. In the same verse, the translator apparently did not have a problem referring to God's hand. Similarly, the *minus* with regard to רגל in the LXX cannot be due to ignorance of a good equivalent, as becomes evident, for example, from Deut 8:4, in which the translator indeed renders רגל by πούς.

Nevertheless, it is not impossible that the translator was trying to avoid a possible allusion to Gods genitalia, due to the common euphemistic usage of the term. This puritan attitude would be confirmed by Deut 28:57 ("the afterbirth that comes out from between her feet"), where רגל has been rendered by μηρός ("thigh").

9. Conclusion

Coming at the end of this "body-scan" of God—sincere apologies for this anthropomorphism—it can be concluded that a simplistic treatment of

---

37. See also Wittstruck 1976, 31, who argues that the LXX translator often adds words that are not present within the Hebrew form of the text, as in Deut 2:5, 6; 8:20; 9:10, 18; 11:9; 15:9; 19:10; 21:6; 29:19(20).

38. Neither Fritsch 1943 nor Wittstruck 1976 mentions this case.

39. Cf. Otto 2017, 2212.

40. Wevers 1995, 540.

the question whether the LXX of Deuteronomy is more antianthropomorphic than the MT should be avoided.⁴¹

As the analysis of the Greek rendering of the terminology of the human body used to speak about God in the book of Deuteronomy has made clear, a univocal presentation is not possible.⁴² Only a nuanced answer to the question is valid, taking into account several elements.

First of all, an apparent antianthropomorphic tendency with respect to one or another particular case could have been caused by the translator's wish to translate in an idiomatic way. Second, the translator is often trying to find an appropriate *ad sensum* translation of a formula, which is also used *ad sensum* in the Hebrew text. Third, the search for antianthropomorphic tendencies within the Greek Deuteronomy should be part of a more encompassing analysis of the translation technique of the book. Finally, when a general presentation of a theme or a theological accent, such as an antianthropological bias, already seems to be difficult for a single book that has been translated by a single translator, it will be all the more difficult to draw general conclusions as to the LXX as a whole.

Bibliography

Ausloos, Hans. Forthcoming. "Translation Technique." In *Oxford Handbook of the Septuagint*. Edited by Alison Salvesen and Michael Law: Oxford: Oxford University Press.

Ausloos, Hans, and Bénédicte Lemmelijn. 2014. "Faithful Creativity Torn between Freedom and Literalness in the Septuagint's Translations." *JNSL* 40.2:53–69.

Frankel, Zacharias. 1841. *Vorstudien zu der Septuaginta*. Leipzig: Vogel.

———. 1851. *Über den Einfluss der palästinischen Exegese auf die alexandrinische Hermeneutik*. Leipzig: Barth.

Fritsch, Charles T. 1943. *The Anti-anthropomorphisms of the Greek Pentateuch*. Princeton: Princeton University Press.

Harl, Marguerite. 1994. "Les divergences entre la Septante et le texte massorétique." Pages 201–22 in *La Bible grecque des Septante: Du judaïsme*

---

41. Contrary to, for example, Lundbom 2013, 3: "The LXX appears not to manifest any anti-anthropomorphic bias in its translation, as might be expected."

42. Cf. Jobes and Silva 2015, 100: "As scholars continue to explore this issue in the biblical corpus as a whole, most of them conclude that no consistent anti-anthropomorphic pattern is found throughout the Greek Bible."

hellénistique au christianisme ancien. Edited by Marguerite Harl, Gilles Dorival, and Olivier Munnich. Initiations au christianisme ancien. Paris: Cerf.

Helbing, Robert. 1928. *Die Kasussyntax der Verba bei den Septuaginta: Ein Beitrag zur Hebraismenfrage und zur Syntax der Κοινή*. Göttingen: Vandenhoeck & Ruprecht.

Jobes, Karen H., and Moisés Silva. 2015. *Invitation to the Septuagint*. 2nd ed. Grand Rapids: Baker Academic.

Lundbom, Jack R. 2013. *Deuteronomy: A Commentary*. Grand Rapids: Eerdmans.

McCarthy, Carmel. 2007. *Deuteronomy*. BHQ 5. Stuttgart: Deutsche Bibelgesellschaft.

Orlinsky, Harry. 1944. "Review of Charles T. Fritsch, *The Anti-anthropomorphisms of the Greek Pentateuch*." *The Crozer Quarterly* 21:156–60.

Otto, Eckart. 2017. *Deuteronomium 12–34*. Vol. 2: *23,16–34,12*. Herders Theologischer Kommentar zum Alten Testament. Freiburg: Herder.

Peters, Melvin K. H. 2007. "Deuteronomion." Pages 141–73 in *A New English Translation of the Septuagint and the Other Greek Translations Traditionally Included under That Title*. Edited by Albert Pietersma and Benjamin G. Wright. New York: Oxford University Press.

Rösel, Martin. 2006. "Towards a 'Theology of the Septuagint.'" Pages 239–52 in *Septuagint Research: Issues and Challenges in the Study of the Greek Scriptures*. Edited by Wolfgang Kraus and R. Glenn Wooden. SCS 53. Atlanta: Society of Biblical Literature.

Sollamo, Raija. 1975. "Some 'Improper' Prepositions Such as ἐνώπιον, ἐναντίον, ἔναντι, Etc. in the Septuagint and Early Koine Greek." *VT* 25:773–82.

———. 1979. *Renderings of Hebrew Semiprepositions in the Septuagint*. AASF 19. Helsinki: Suomalain Tiedeakatemia.

Tov, Emanuel. 1998. "Did the Septuagint Translators Always Understand Their Hebrew Text?" Pages 203–18 in *The Greek and Hebrew Bible: Collected Essays on the Septuagint*. Edited by Emanuel Tov. VTSup 72. Leiden: Brill.

Wevers, John W. 1995. *Notes on the Greek Text of Deuteronomy*. SCS 39. Atlanta: Scholars Press.

Wevers, John W., and Udo Quast. 2006. *Deuteronomium*. 2nd ed. Septuaginta Vetus Testamentum Graecum Auctoritate Academiae Scientiarum Gottingensis editum 3/2. Göttingen: Vandenhoeck & Ruprecht.

Wittstruck, Thorne. 1976. "The So-Called Anti-anthropomorphisms in the Greek Text of Deuteronomy." *CBQ* 38:29–34.

Zlotowitz, Bernard M. 1981. *The Septuagint Translation of the Hebrew Terms in Relation to God in the Book of Jeremiah*. New York: Ktav.

Holiness and the Levites in MT and LXX Chronicles: An Avenue for Exploring the Theology of LXX Chronicles?

Louis C. Jonker

ABSTRACT: In a recent paper I argued that the relationship between holiness and the Levites in Chronicles provides us with valuable insight into the Chronicler's engagement in the discourses of his own time. It seems that the Chronicler, in contrast to those responsible for the Priestly literature, had no problem indicating that "the Levites were more holy than the priests." I argued that Chronicles latches onto a late stage in the development of the Pentateuch, namely, the Holiness Legislation (H), in order to develop a profile of the Levites that stands on a par with that of the Aaronide priesthood. This is particularly done through the development of the relationship between the Levites and holiness throughout Chronicles. In the Hezekiah narrative and in the Josiah Passover account, this development reaches its climax. The question that will be examined in this contribution is whether this same development is reflected in LXX Chronicles. Terminological patterns will be studied, particularly on the concept holiness, and it will be investigated how the LXX translators engaged with the profile of the Levites. The outcome of this investigation will be used as basis to ask whether the concept "holiness" may be used as possible avenue to explore the theology of LXX Chronicles.

1. Introduction

In recent years, the study of Chronicles has moved from historiographical interests to rhetorical interests.[1] This means that researchers are no longer primarily asking what historiographical value the book holds, in comparison to other historiographies such as the Primary History and the Deuteronomistic History (or, more pointedly, the books of Samuel–

---

1. See the description in chapter 1 of Jonker 2016.

Kings). One of the main foci in Chronicles research now is determining how the book communicated rhetorically by latching onto older traditions, while simultaneously contributing to the discourses of the late Persian or early Hellenistic periods.[2] A synoptic comparison with the (mainly biblical) sources used by the Chronicler assists scholars to determine the *Sondergut* of the writer and thereby the unique rhetorical contribution the Chronicler made to the discourse of his time. These discourses were strongly influenced by the cultic and religious but also political power dynamics of the late Persian and early Hellenistic phase in Jerusalem in the province Yehud.[3]

Whereas the focus in earlier studies was mainly on a comparison with the Deuteronomistic History, the most recent development in the field is to investigate how the book Chronicles, as one of the earliest readers (or even interpreters) of the Pentateuch (in whatever form), sheds light on the theological dynamics that contributed to the the formation of the Pentateuch.[4] Studies on the relationship between Chronicles and some pentateuchal materials increasingly emerge in our field.

One theme that is useful for determining the Chronicler's relationship to pentateuchal traditions is the portrayal of the Levites. Chronicles scholars are fairly convinced that the Chronicler—as an individual author or, more likely, a collective—had affiliations with the Levite priesthood in Jerusalem and that these literati wanted to profile the Levites in comparison with the Aaronide priesthood. In my investigations into the notion of holiness in the Pentateuch and Chronicles, I have come to the conclusion that the Chronicler uses the development of the Levites' profile in terms of holiness as a literary device to give legitimacy to his high view of the Levites in light of earlier pentateuchal traditions.[5]

In the present chapter, I will use the same heuristic strategy to investigate how the LXX translation of Chronicles engaged terminologically and thematically with the same issue. Can one observe any trends in LXX Chronicles that are unique to LXX, or does one see the same rhetorical strategy as in the Hebrew Bible? Answering this question will lead me to suggest some avenues for exploring the theology of LXX Chronicles.

---

2. Cf., e.g., Nihan 2013b, 2014, 2016; Becker and Bezzel 2014.

3. See chapter 3 of Jonker 2016.

4. See Jonker 2014a and 2014b, where I argue that Chronicles and pentateuchal studies should be brought into conversation with one another.

5. See Jonker 2020.

However, first I will provide a more elaborate explanation of my argument about Chronicles, the Levites, and holiness in MT.

2. The Chronicler's Discourse on the Status of the Levites

In contrast to the fairly negative portrayal of the Levites in some pentateuchal traditions, in parts of the book Judges, and in Ezekiel, Chronicles provides a more prominent and positive view of them. This already starts in the so-called genealogical preamble to the book, in which the Levite genealogy features right at the center of the concentric construction of the family lists.[6] First, in 1 Chr 5:27–41, the line of Levi to Jehozadaq is provided in order to elaborate on the priestly heritage of this family. Thereafter, in 1 Chr 6:1–38, the Levitical genealogies are provided, while 1 Chr 6:39–66 contains a description of the Levitical settlements. From the genealogical construction, it already becomes clear that the Levites take center stage in the Chronicler's mindscape.

A further major section is part of the Chronicler's *Sondergut* in 1 Chr 23–27, where the division of the Levites for various kinds of service is described and the organization of the cultic service in Jerusalem is explained. The narrative setting is the time of King David, who is portrayed as the originator of the cultic service. The term *Levite* is used generically (referring to the tribe) in this elaborate section of Chronicles but also technically (referring to specific parts of the cultic community). The Aaronides are thereby identified as Levites (generically), but they also share the cultic service with the Levites (in a cultic sense).[7] However, here it is still clear that the cultic Levites are portrayed as assistants to the Aaronide priests. Programmatic in this regard is 1 Chr 23:13: "The sons of Amram: Aaron and Moses. Moses was set apart to dedicate [*hiphil* of קדש] the most holy things [קדש קדשים], that he and his sons forever should make offerings before the LORD and minister to him and pronounce blessings in his name forever" (ESV).

The same portrayal continues into the Chronicler's Solomon narrative in 2 Chr 1–9 (e.g., 2 Chr 5:11–14) and in the narratives of the earlier kings of the kingdom of Judah. However, from 2 Chr 23 onward, it seems that a more positive portrayal of the Levites emerges. In 2 Chr 23:6 we

---

6. See, e.g., Kartveit 1989; Oeming 1990; Knoppers 1999, 2004; Klein 2006; Sparks 2008; Willi 2009; Jonker 2012, 2015.
7. Cf. Jonker 2010.

encounter the first indication in the book that the Levites, together with the (Aaronide) priests, could enter the temple for duty, because they (including the Levites) were holy (כי קדש המה). This stands in contrast to King Uzziah, who is reprimanded because he wanted to perform some priestly functions.

In the narratives of Kings Hezekiah (2 Chr 29–32) and Josiah (2 Chr 34–35), the positive development of the Levite profile reaches its climax. A contrast increasingly emerges between the (Aaronide) priests and the Levites. This becomes clear not only from the fact that the Levites increasingly take over some of the traditionally priestly functions but also from the fact that the Levites are deliberately contrasted to the priests in terms of holiness. The Chronicler seems to claim at least an equal position for the Levites together with the (Aaronide) priesthood.

This development has brought Chronicles scholars to the insight that, differently from some other pentateuchal traditions, Chronicles cannot be described as either exclusively pro-Priestly or pro-Levite. Gary Knoppers states:

> To be sure, the Chronicler does not jettison all distinctions between the two. The Aaronic priests have a distinct status within the tribe of Levi (secured by birth) and a different function—to officiate within the Temple and to make offerings (1 Chr 23:30–32). The sons of Aaron are "officers of the sanctuary and officers of God" (1 Chr 24:5). There is no firm evidence to suggest that the Chronicler holds to an absolute equality between priests and Levites. Nevertheless, the author does not emphasize hierarchy. Both the priests and the Levites are essential to the success of the Temple cultus. Rather than constituting evidence for a pro-Priestly author or redactor of Chronicles, the summary of levitical duties is evidence for the Chronicler's own distinctive stance, a *via media* between the positions of Deuteronomy, the Priestly source, and Ezekiel.[8]

At this point, it will be helpful for the present argument to provide brief remarks on key sections on holiness in other biblical traditions, because the Chronicler's use of this concept in connection with the Levites illustrates the above point well.

---

8. Knoppers 1999, 70–71.

3. Key Sections on Holiness

The concept "holy, holiness, holy person/thing/place" is well distributed over the Hebrew Bible, although some concentrations occur in the various strands of the Pentateuch, in the Deuteronomistic History, in the Major Prophets, in Psalms, and in Chronicles.[9] As expected, verbs with the root קדש occur twenty-eight times in Exodus, thirty-one times in Leviticus, eleven times in Numbers, and fifteen times in Ezekiel. However, it is surprising that the book with the highest frequency is Chronicles, with thirty-two occurrences (four times in *piel*, twice in *pual*, thirteen times in *hiphil*, and thirteen times in *hithpael*). A similar pattern emerges with reference to the noun: seventy occurrences in Exodus, ninety-two in Leviticus, fifty-seven each in Numbers and Ezekiel, and forty-seven in Chronicles.[10]

Although this is a frequently used concept, different parts of the Hebrew Bible provide different understandings of it. The following short subsections summarize the unique employment of the concept in the different strands:

3.1. Non-Priestly and Deuteronomic-Deuteronomistic Traditions (and Associated Literature)

Although the concept of holiness dominates in Priestly literature of the Pentateuch, there are also some instances in non-Priestly literature where it occurs. One such instance is the in the Covenant Code, in Exod 22:30, which indicates that the people of Israel (who are addressed by Yahweh through Moses) will/should be "people of holiness" to Yahweh. Likewise in Deuteronomy (e.g., 7:6, 14:1–2, 21), holiness is related to the community of Israel. It therefore shows that the envisioned relationship between holiness and the community of Israel was not a new invention of later traditions but was already present in some of the earliest pentateuchal material.

---

9. For statistics on the distribution of the concept, see Müller 2004, 594.

10. The adjective occurs once in Chronicles (2 Chr 35:3), while the noun derivative מקדש occurs five times in the book, all referring to the temple in Jerusalem.

3.2. Priestly Tradition (and Associated Literature)

The Priestly literature and Ezekiel differ remarkably from the above. Nowhere in this literature is holiness related to all people or the broader community. It is exclusively used in relation to cultic objects, places, rituals, and persons. This trend continues up to Lev 16, which is considered by many Pentateuch scholars as the end of the Priestly strand.[11] The frequent occurrence of the various forms of קדש in this literature proves that the cult was closely connected to the priests' understanding of "holiness."

3.3. The Holiness Legislation

However, in Lev 17–26 the situation is different. Traditionally, these chapters were seen as part of the Priestly strand in the Pentateuch. However, already in earlier scholarship some scholars started postulating the independent origin of these chapters, in contrast to the Priestly strand. On account of the fact that the so-called Holiness Legislation (H) contained in these chapters reflects ideas from both the Priestly tradition and the non-Priestly/Deuteronomic-Deuteronomistic traditions, scholars hypothesized that H is actually post-Priestly and reflects an attempt to merge the different traditions contained in the other pentateuchal strands.[12] Earlier scholars such as Milgrom and Knohl held to a dating in the monarchic period of H, but more recent studies, such as those of Otto and Nihan,[13] argue that H should rather be dated toward the end of the fifth century BCE.

However, it is not only the issue of dating H in relation to P that is important for our discussion, but also the fact that scholars observe in the Holiness Legislation some sort of an "ethical turn," that is, that holiness is extrapolated from the cultic sphere to include everyday life. Paradigmatic in this legislation is Lev 19, which states that "You should be holy, because the LORD your God is holy." Holiness, which should extend not only into the cultic sphere but also into everyday life, is motivated from the holiness of God.[14]

---

11. Cf., e.g., Nihan 2007; Meyer 2013.
12. Cf., e.g., Nihan 2004, 2013a; Meyer 2012, 2015.
13. Milgrom 2000, 2001; Knohl 1987, 1995; Otto 1999, 2000; Nihan 2004, 2007, 2013a.
14. Cf., e.g., Bibb 2009; Meyer 2013.

3.4. Other Post-Priestly Traditions

Research on H has sparked further theories on the late phases of composition of the Pentateuch. In a seminal study on the book of Numbers, Reinhard Achenbach argued, for example, that the development of the Holiness Legislation that had the intention of merging non-Priestly, Deuteronomic-Deuteronomistic, and Priestly traditions into a proto-Pentateuch gave rise to another attempt to bridge the gap between the Priestly/non-Priestly literature, on the one side, and the Deuteronomic-Deuteronomistic literature, on the other side.[15] This bridge was the book of Numbers, which grew through different phases. It is characteristic of the later compositional layers in this book that D and P ideas were both incorporated in another attempt toward merging the earlier traditions.

One section in Numbers stands out, however. The so-called Korah legend in Num 16–18 is considered to be a very late addition to the book. I have argued elsewhere that this could even be post-Chronistic and a response to some views on the Levites expressed in Chronicles.[16] The issue at stake in that legend is whether the sons of Korah (who constitute one of the foundational Levite families) could also claim that they are holy or whether this quality only belongs to Moses and Aaron and their priestly descendants. The narrative clearly sides with the Aaronide priesthood and against the Levite claims. The reason I see this as a very late, post-Chronistic addition to the book of Numbers, and therefore to the Pentateuch, will become clear from the following discussion on holiness in Chronicles.

3.5. Chronicles

We have already seen above that the Levite profile is developed throughout Chronicles and that it is explicitly done in terms of holiness. We have also seen that the Chronicler wanted to merge different Priestly and Levite traditions, as well as Priestly and Deuteronomic-Deuteronomistic ideas in his literary work. I have argued elsewhere that the Chronicler latched onto not only the Deuteronomistic History as main source, and to the D and P traditions, but also onto the Holiness Legislation.[17] Like the development of the book of Numbers, the book of Chronicles was probably a response

---

15. Achenbach 2003.
16. See Jonker 2019.
17. See again Jonker 2020.

to the new views expressed in H, namely, that holiness should not only be seen as an exclusive quality of the cultic sphere but should also be extrapolated into everyday life. This certainly had an influential impact on the understanding of the different factions in the priesthood in Jerusalem.

The first indication that the Levites had been consecrated comes in 2 Chr 23:6. This notion does not occur anywhere in the Priestly literature or Ezekiel or in the earlier parts of Chronicles. However, 2 Chr 23:6 indicates that the Levites—together with the priests—could enter the temple because they (including the Levites) were holy/consecrated. This development continues and is strengthened beginning in 2 Chr 29. The concept holiness is used twenty-six times in the Hezekiah narrative and four times in the Josiah narrative. In 2 Chr 29:5–11 Hezekiah orders the Levites to consecrate themselves to perform the temple purification. In 2 Chr 35:6 they are commanded to consecrate themselves to slaughter the Passover lambs. The indication in 2 Chr 29:34 is central in the Chronicler's development of the Levite profile because it constructs a contrast between the (Aaronide) priests and the Levites. It is indicated that the Levites were "more upright of heart" than the priests because they had consecrated themselves in time for the Passover, while the priests did not do so. This is also the reason given for the postponement of the Passover to the second month (2 Chr 30:3). The Levites even slaughtered the Passover lambs for the people (2 Chr 30:17) because there were not enough consecrated priests for the job.

The description is closed by a telling statement: "They [male Levites and priests] were enrolled with all their little children, their wives, their sons, and their daughters, the whole assembly, for they were faithful in keeping themselves holy" (2 Chr 31:18 ESV). It is thus clear that the Chronicler propagated the same idea as the Holiness Legislation, namely, that holiness is not a quality that belongs exclusively to the (Aaronide) priests and the cultic sphere but also to the Levites and even to the whole assembly. The same so-called ethical turn of the Holiness Legislation can be observed here.

Within this context, my earlier remark about the Korah legend in Num 16–18 being a late, post-Chronistic development makes sense. It seems that those theocrats (according to Achenbach's description) who concluded the book of Numbers, and thereby the Pentateuch, wanted to push back against the Chronicler's potent appropriation of the Holiness Legislation with reference to the Levites. The final phase of reworking of the book of Numbers probably sought to put the Levites back in their subservient place.

3.6. A Reflection of the Chronicler's Theology?

The developments described above might be a valuable window into the Chronicler's theological thinking during the late Persian and early Hellenistic period. Normally, when scholars discuss the rhetorical strategies of Chronicles, it is emphasized that obedience to Yahweh and his torah is central to the Chronicler's understanding of holiness, wellness, and peace. With reference to the priesthood, the Chronicler emphasizes that holiness is not a quality that belongs irrevocably and exclusively to some priestly groups or families on account of their descent but that holiness is something in reach of the Levites and the community as well, provided that they obey the torah of Yahweh. The Chronicler therefore does away with an essentialistic understanding of holiness and develops instead a relational understanding that stands much nearer to the Holiness Legislation.

Could we perhaps use this same window to get a glimpse of the Septuagint's theology as given expression in Chronicles? With a focus on LXX Chronicles, we take one further step to a later phase of transmission of this book, but perhaps even a phase of further interpretation. However, for that purpose, we will now focus on LXX Chronicles.

4. LXX Chronicles, the Levites and Holiness

4.1. The Greek Witnesses to Chronicles

Before embarking on an investigation into the holiness terminology in LXX Chronicles, it is prudent to look first at the Greek versions of Chronicles.[18] However, one should take note of the fact that comprehensive critical editions of Paraleipomena (the Greek Chronicles) have either not been created or are not yet completed. Some progress, however, has been made in studying the date and nature of the two LXX translations of Chronicles, that is, Paraleipomena, but also the sections of Chronicles included in 1 Esdras. The last-mentioned contains, among other materials from Ezra and Nehemiah, the final two chapters: 2 Chr 35:1–36:23. The Paraleipomena version follows the Hebrew Bible but lacks some small sections of 1 Chr 1 (vv. 11–16, 17b–24a, 27b) in the most reliable manuscript,

---

18. This section is based on the excellent discussion of the versions of Chronicles in Knoppers 2004, 55–65.

Codex Vaticanus. This manuscript also contains some minor additions to MT in 2 Paraleipomena 35:19a–d and 36:2a–c, 5a–d. Scholars are fairly convinced that these lines were not part of the Hebrew *Vorlage* of LXX Chronicles but were rather later developments in light of some Lucianic witnesses to the Greek book of Kings.

The two Greek translations of Chronicles differ in style of translation. While 1 Esdras offers an elegant and idiomatic Greek translation, LXX Chronicles is written in fairly literal and nonidiomatic Greek. When this literal translation is back-translated to Hebrew, it resembles the text of MT closely. This is not the place to discuss the elaborate debate on the relationship between 1 Esdras and the LXX versions of Chronicles, Ezra, and Nehemiah. Suffice it to quote Knoppers on the value of Paraleipomena as textual witness at this point:

> *Paraleipomena* belongs to the same textual tradition as the MT. This means that the value of *Paraleipomena* for reconstructing the earliest text does not approximate the textual value of the LXX for certain other books, such as Joshua, Samuel, and Jeremiah. As to the relationship between *Paraleipomena* and the Old Greek, *Paraleipomena* is generally thought to be a mixed text, a witness of uneven value. The recensional history of the Greek Chronicles is … a matter of continuing debate.[19]

With reference to the date of LXX Chronicles, Knoppers indicates that this should be established in connection with the date of 1 Esdras. He says:

> Although extreme positions have been taken on the relationship of LXX Chronicles to 1 Esdras, approaching either the Greek Chronicles or 1 Esdras as primary and dismissing the other as late, such views promote a false dichotomy. The relationship between the two is more complex. Neither the Greek Chronicles nor 1 Esdras need be viewed as late in its basic form. There is good reason to believe, in fact, that both stem from the second century B.C.E.[20]

Earlier studies, such as those of Gerleman and Allen, saw the provenance of LXX Chronicles in Egypt. However, more recent studies (particularly

---

19. Knoppers 2004, 59–60.
20. Knoppers 2004, 61.

Ralph Klein, also followed by Knoppers in his commentary) see its origin in Palestine.[21]

4.2. Holiness Terminology in the LXX

Before we come to how holiness terminology is used specifically in LXX Chronicles, it would be enlightening to first take note of its distribution in the LXX as a whole. Kornfeld provides an overview of how the different Hebrew terms are translated in the Septuagint. The table below is an adapted form of his discussion:[22]

Hebrew Term	Greek Equivalents
קדש noun (469x)	ἅγιος: 425x (adjective) ἁγίασμα: 13x (noun) ἁγιάζω: 6x (verb) ἁγιωσύνη: 2x (noun) other terms: 19x not translated: 4x
קדוש adjective (116x)	ἅγιος: 107x (adjective) ἁγιάζω: 4x (verb) other terms: 3x not translated: 2x
קדשה/קדש noun (11x)	πόρνη: 6x (noun) τελετή: 1x (noun) transliterated: 1x other terms: 2x not translated: 1x
מקדש noun (74x)	ἅγιος: 43x (adjective) ἁγίασμα: 22x (noun) other terms: 8x not translated: 1x
קדש verb (172x)	ἁγιάζω: 140x ἁγνίζω: 19x (15x in Chronicles) other terms: 13x

---

21. This view is expressed in Klein 1966, although he follows Leslie Allen's position in his commentary: Klein 2006, 26–28.

22. Kornfeld 2003, 543.

What interests us most in this overview is the use of the related verbs ἁγιάζω and ἁγνίζω as translations for the Hebrew verbs with the root קדש. Lust, Eynikel, and Hauspie provide the following renderings of ἁγιάζω: in the active form, the verb means "to hallow, to make sacred, to sanctify," while in the passive it can be rendered as "to be sanctified, to be holy." With reference to the term ἁγνίζω, Lust, Eynikel, and Hauspie translate the active form as "to cleanse, to purify, to sanctify," while the medio-passive form is rendered in the reflexive, "to purify oneself."[23] It thus seems that the latter, ἁγνίζω, is associated more with cultic contexts and cultic purity.

Louw and Nida place the term ἁγιάζω under the domain "Religious Activity," in the subcategory "Dedicate, Consecrate" (53.44), and explain it as "to dedicate to the service of and to loyalty to deity—'to consecrate, consecration, to dedicate to God, dedication.'" They add the following: "Though in certain contexts ἁγιάζω and ἁγιασμός suggest resulting moral behavior, the emphasis is not upon a manner of life but upon religious activity and observances which reflect one's dedication or consecration to God."[24] Louw and Nida also discuss ἁγιάζω in the domain "Moral and Ethical Qualities and Related Behavior," in the subcategory "Holy, Pure." It then means "to cause someone to have the quality of holiness—'to make holy'" (88.26) or "to feel reverence for or to honor as holy—'to hallow, to regard as holy, to honor as holy'" (88.27). These remarks are, of course, based on the use of the terms in the New Testament.

Louw and Nida also place ἁγνίζω in two domains: in the subcategory "Purify, Cleanse" of the main category "Religious Activity," and in the subcategory "Holy, Pure" of "Moral and Ethical Qualities and Related Behavior."[25] They render it as "to purify and cleanse ritually and thus acquire a state of ritual acceptability—'to purify, purification'" (53.30) and "to feel reverence for or to honor as holy—'to hallow, to regard as holy, to honor as holy'" (88.30). Thus in both cases the cultic connotation is predominant.

Kornfeld provides an interesting diachronic description of the development of these terms' meaning that may be significant for our own purposes. I quote him at length:

---

23. Lust, Eynikel, and Hauspie 2003, 4, 5.
24. Louw and Nida 1989, 537.
25. Louw and Nida 1989, 536, 746.

> The adj. *hágios* appears first in Herodotus (5.119; 2.41,44) and is probably related to the archaic verb *házomai*, "stand in awe of, dread." ... During the Hellenistic period, *hágios* was used as an epithet especially for gods whose cults had been imported from the east; but that it was never applied to a living human being means that expressions such as *éthnos hágion* (Ex. 19:6) or *laós hágios* (Dt. 7:6) were coined for the LXX. During the Homeric period, the adj. *hagnós*, which is related to *hágios*, also had a sacral meaning, though this meaning changed during the Ptolemaic period, when it came to mean "pure" (*hagneía*, "purity," *hagnízein*, "purify, cleanse"); so semantically *qādôš* is related to *tāhôr* the way *hágios* is related to *hagnós*, though the rendering of *qādaš* as *hagnízein* (19 times, 15 in Chronicles) shows that, as before, authors were aware of the kinship between *hágios* and *hagnós* and thus also closely associated "(ritual) purity" ... with "holiness." In the LXX the adj. *hierós*, which during the classical and Hellenistic periods was the regnant one, now refers only to the temple.... The reason for the different usage may well have been an altered understanding of holiness itself. The OT understanding of holiness was based on the historical proximity of the holy God who made Israel into a "holy people" in fellowship with him. Hence for semantic reasons the LXX preferred to render *qdš* as *hágios* rather than as *hierós*. Similarly it changed *hagi-* (*hagízein, hagismós*, etc.) into *hagia-* (*hagiázein, hagiasmós*, etc.) in search of a more appropriate expression of the biblical understanding of holiness.[26]

During the time when Kornfeld wrote this entry for *TDOT*, the latest research on the development of the concept of holiness in the Old Testament was not yet available. One thus understands why he departed from a view that the Old Testament had a more or less homogeneous understanding of the concept. However, his diachronic description of the development of the term has value in the sense that one may assume that the usage of the term ἁγνίζω, in contrast to ἁγιάζω, may be significant. Kornfeld's statement that fifteen of the nineteen occurrences of ἁγνίζω in the LXX are in Chronicles seems quite significant for our purposes.[27] Our

---

26. Kornfeld 2003, 543–44.

27. His count is not correct. According to a search with Logos software in the SESB LXX version, the verb ἁγνίζω appears thirty-four times in twenty-nine verses in the LXX, of which five are in Esdras A and 2 Maccabees, which were probably not counted by Kornfeld. The concentration in Chronicles is, however, still very clear. The majority, eighteen out of thirty-four, occur in Chronicles in fourteen verses.

192   Louis C. Jonker

next step will therefore be to look more closely at this conspicuous distribution in Chronicles.

4.3. Holiness and the Levites in LXX Chronicles

The following observations on the texts in Chronicles are important for our argument.

(1) The verb ἁγιάζω occurs fifteen times in LXX Chronicles, but in only one instance (2 Chr 35:3) is it related to the Levites. In the narrative, King Josiah speaks to the Levites, who are described as τοῖς δυνατοῖς ἐν παντὶ Ισραηλ τοῦ ἁγιασθῆναι αὐτοὺς τῷ κυρίῳ, that is, as those who taught the whole of Israel and who were consecrated to the Lord.[28] As indicated above, the Josiah narrative plays an important role in the development of the Levite profile in MT Chronicles.

(2) Except in two instances, the use of the verb ἁγνίζω is always related to the Levites in LXX Chronicles. In sixteen of the eighteen occurrences the verb it is used to describe the Levites positively as being, or having been, consecrated to perform certain duties. In the two instances where the verb does not refer to the Levites, it stands in negations. For example, 2 Chr 30:3 states that the priests and the people have not consecrated themselves for the celebration of the Passover; in 2 Chr 30:18, the verb is used to indicate that the majority of the people, including people from Ephraim, Manasseh, Issachar, and Zebulun, have not consecrated themselves for the Passover.

(3) The use of ἁγνίζω in LXX Chronicles is concentrated in specific sections. Two occur in 1 Chr 15, where the bringing of the ark to Jerusalem is the theme of the narrative. The Levites play a central role in that action. All other occurrences of the verb are in the narrative about King Hezekiah (which, we have seen above, plays a pivotal role in the development of the Levite profile in MT Chronicles).

(4) In all but three occurrences of ἁγνίζω in LXX Chronicles, the word translates some or other form of the verbal root קדש. In the other three (2 Chr 29:16, 18; 30:18), it translates the Hebrew root טהר (in the *piel* in the first two instances and in the *hithpael* in the last), which has the connotation of cleansing or purifying something or oneself (presumably for

---

28. The use of τοῖς δυνατοῖς in this verse, as a translation of the *hiphil* participle of בין, is also conspicuous as a description of the Levitical activity, but this is not the focus in this chapter.

cultic purposes).²⁹ Given the development of the terms ἁγιάζω and ἁγνίζω as described by Kornfeld, the translation of this specific Hebrew verb with ἁγνίζω is actually quite appropriate. However, its use in LXX Chronicles is somewhat puzzling. In 2 Chr 29:15, the Hebrew verb טהר (which refers to the cleansing of the temple in that context) is translated with καθαρίζω,³⁰ while it is translated with ἁγνίζω in the very next verse (29:16) and in 29:18, where the term is applied to the Levites. The same applies in 2 Chr 30:18, where the verb is negated to refer to the fact that many of the tribes did not clean themselves for the Passover.

These observations can lead us now to our synthesis in which we will ask whether the conspicuous use and distribution of the terms ἁγιάζω and ἁγνίζω reflect anything of LXX Chronicles' theology, in distinction from that of the MT version of the book.

5. Synthesis: A Reflection of LXX Theology?

From the descriptions above, it seems that the LXX translator(s) of Chronicles at least sensed something of the theological development that the Chronicler—in my opinion, deliberately—built into his literary work. We have seen that the climax of the development of the Levite profile in terms of holiness in 2 Chr 29–32 is also reflected in some terminological patterns in LXX Chronicles, where the concept holiness is suddenly expressed clearly with another Greek verb than the usual translation with ἁγιάζω. The massive concentration of ἁγνίζω in the Hezekiah narrative in Chronicles (in fact, in the whole Hebrew Bible) is indicative of some theological accent that the LXX translator(s) wanted to express.³¹ The question is, of course, which theological accent do we see here?

---

29. See *HALOT* and BDB.

30. The same in 2 Chr 34:3, 5, 8, where the verb refers to the purging of the temple and the land.

31. It is, indeed, as has been pointed out by Emanuel Tov during our symposium, conspicuous that ἁγιάζω mostly translates the *hiphil* form of קדש in Chronicles, while ἁγνίζω mostly translates the *hithpael* form. Could one therefore assume that the difference in translation is merely a linguistic matter? I am of a different opinion and think that the different translations have some ideological background. I argue on account of the fact that ἁγιάζω is also used in Chronicles (in 2 Chr 5:11) to translate the *hithpael* form, while ἁγνίζω occasionally translates the *piel* (2 Chr 29:16, 17, 18) and *hiphil* (2 Chr 29:19) forms. There is thus no clear-cut pattern. Furthermore, in all cases where it translates the *hithpael* form, the verb קדש is used reflexively, which is

It seems to me that LXX Chronicles is pushing back against the "liberal" understanding of the Levites as being holy, probably in line with some late developments in the Pentateuch (with reference to the Korah legend in Num 16–18, of course). The diachronic development of the word ἁγνίζω, in contrast to ἁγιάζω, has been described above. Kornfeld has indicated that from the Ptolemaic period onward the adjective ἁγνός and the related verb ἁγνίζω started having the semantic potential of "pure, purify, cleanse," which clearly have cultic overtones. As Kornfeld explained, the reason why a different form of the word started becoming dominant "may well have been an altered understanding of holiness itself." This is exactly the point that I argued in my description of how the Levite profile is developed in terms of holiness toward the end of MT Chronicles.

However, it seems the LXX translation tried to turn back the wheel by translating קדש in the Hezekiah and Josiah narratives with ἁγνίζω, a word with clear cultic overtones. It appears that the LXX translator(s) engaged in the same discourse about the status of the Levites that was given expression in the developments from the Holiness Legislation through Chronicles. But, an opposite position was taken in LXX Chronicles. My contention is that the use of ἁγνίζω was deliberate to cut down the Levites to their cultic size again. I also maintain that the translator(s) noticed that the Chronicler was leading his readers into a direction to believe that Levites, on account of their greater dedication to the torah of Yahweh, were actually more holy than the Aaronide priests. The LXX translator(s) wanted to return to a more essentialistic understanding of the Levites' position, in opposition to the MT Chronicler's more relational understanding.

In which context would such a backlash be understandable? We have seen that Knoppers dates LXX Chronicles more or less in the second century BCE, and we have seen that more recent views on the provenance of LXX Chronicles go in the direction of an origin in Palestine. From the beginning of the second century BCE, Seleucid domination became a prominent reality in Palestine, and it eventually led to the Maccabean revolt. This was a tumultuous era in terms of cultic and political leadership. The usurpation of the high priesthood during this period certainly

---

typically expressed with the *hithpael*. There is no indication that ἁγνίζω is preferred for the reflexive use in Greek. It thus seems safe to argue that the change in Greek wording particularly in the Chronicler's Hezekiah narrative is ideologically significant.

caused weighty debates again about the status of the different factions in the priestly guilds in Jerusalem.

Could we confirm that the conspicuous use of holiness terminology in relation to the Levites in LXX Chronicles gives a reflection on some theological discourses during the time of this translation? I would hypothesize at the end of this contribution that this is indeed the case. However, a few concluding remarks should now be made on the methodological aspects of this investigation.

6. Conclusion

In order to make a small and modest contribution to the theme of the symposium on a theology of the LXX, I will conclude with some methodological considerations. These considerations, which emerged from the case study that I have done on the use of holiness terminology in relation to the Levites in LXX Chronicles, summarize the approach that was followed in this contribution.

(1) It is necessary to take into account the semantic development of Greek vocabulary. Kornfeld's diachronic description of the development of terms related to holiness in the Hellenistic and Ptolemaic periods enlighten our understanding of the conspicuous differentiation in terminology that the LXX Chronicles translator(s) made in the book. It seems to me that any formulation of a theology of the Septuagint should take these diachronic semantic developments in terminology into account.

(2) It furthermore seems a responsible approach to develop a theology of the Septuagint in a comparative mode with the theological discourses reflected in Hebrew Bible corpora. It is of utmost importance to become aware of the theological discourses that are reflected in a specific book of the LXX, but also over coherent textual corpora, such as the Priestly material, the Holiness Legislation, Chronicles, and post-Chronistic literary developments. I hereby emphasize that any attempt to formulate a theology of the Septuagint should not only incorporate the theological developments in the *Vorlagen* into such an endeavor but should also concentrate on textual corpora instead of isolated textual examples. The theology of the Septuagint is one step removed from the theology of Hebrew Bible corpora. By engaging in comparative studies that involve larger textual corpora, one can determine which theological positions informed the *Vorlagen* of the Septuagint translations and, accordingly, which theological direction changes (or similarities) one can observe in the Septuagint. In a

certain sense, the treatment of the Septuagint in isolation for the purpose of formulating a theology of the LXX is reductionistic. The LXX, through its translation techniques and theological interpretations, constitutes an important further stage in the reception history of the Hebrew Bible. If the status of the LXX is elevated to an independent endeavor that does not stand in continuity and discontinuity with theological traditions reflected in the *Vorlagen*, a project to formulate a theology of the Septuagint is bound to produce superficial results.

(3) In my opinion, no theology originates or exists in a sociohistorical vacuum. This implies that, if the Septuagint does indeed reflect theological thinking, it must have been in response to some sociopolitical and particularly socioreligious realities of the time of translation. It thus follows that no formulation of a theology of the Septuagint can ignore the historical embeddedness of the different translations. The worldviews of the translators that are determinative in the formulation of certain theological ideas, in response to earlier theological discourses, were formed within concrete historical circumstances. The formulation of a theology of the Septuagint therefore cannot merely be a textual endeavor but should necessarily be a historical investigation.

Bibliography

Achenbach, Reinhard. 2003. *Die Vollendung der Tora: Studien zur Redaktionsgeschichte des Numeribuches im Kontext von Hexateuch und Pentateuch*. BZABR 3. Wiesbaden: Harrassowitz.

Becker, Uwe, and Hannes Bezzel, eds. 2014. *Rereading the Relecture? The Question of (Post)chronistic Influence in the Latest Redactions of the Books of Samuel*. FAT 2/66. Tübingen: Mohr Siebeck.

Bibb, Bryan D. 2009. *Ritual Words and Narrative Worlds in the Book of Leviticus*. LHBOTS 480. New York: T&T Clark.

Jonker, Louis C. 2010. "David's Officials according to the Chronicler (1 Chronicles 23–27): A Reflection of Second Temple Self-Categorization?" Pages 65–91 in *Historiography and Identity (Re)formulation in Second Temple Historiographical Literature*. Edited by Louis C. Jonker. LHBOTS 534. New York: T&T Clark.

———. 2012. "Reading the Pentateuch's Genealogies after the Exile: The Chronicler's Usage of Genesis 1–11 in Negotiating an All-Israelite Identity." *OTE* 25:316–33.

———. 2014a. "From Paraleipomenon to Early Reader: The Implications of Recent Chronicles Studies for Pentateuchal Criticism." Pages 217–54 in *Congress Volume: Munich, 2013*. Edited by Christl M. Maier. VTSup 163. Leiden: Brill.

———. 2014b. "Within Hearing Distance? Recent Developments in Pentateuch and Chronicles Research." *OTE* 27:123–46.

———. 2015. "Agrarian Economy through City Elite Eyes: Reflections of Late Persian Period Yehud Economy in the Genealogies of Chronicles." Pages 77–101 in *The Economy of Ancient Judah in Its Historical Context*. Edited by Marvin L. Miller, Ehud Ben Zvi, and Gary N. Knoppers. Winona Lake, IN: Eisenbrauns.

———. 2016. *Defining All-Israel in Chronicles: Multi-levelled Identity Negotiation in Late Persian Period Yehud*. FAT 106. Tübingen: Mohr Siebeck.

———. 2019. "Numbers and Chronicles: False Friends or Close Relatives?" *HeBAI* 8:332–77.

———. 2020. "Holiness and the Levites: Some Reflections on the Relationship between Chronicles and Pentateuchal Traditions." Pages 457–74 in *Eigensinn und Entstehung der Hebräischen Bibel: Erhard Blum zum siebzigsten Geburtstag*. Edited by Joachim J. Krause, Wolfgang Oswald, and Kristin Weingart. Tübingen: Mohr Siebeck.

Kartveit, Magnar. 1989. *Motive und Schichten der Landtheologie in I Chronik 1–9*. ConBOT 28. Stockholm: Almquist & Wiksell.

Klein, Ralph W. 1966. "Studies in the Greek Text of the Chronicler." Unpublished PhD dissertation, Harvard University.

———. 2006. *1 Chronicles: A Commentary*. Hermeneia. Minneapolis: Fortress.

Knohl, Israel. 1987. "The Priestly Torah versus the Holiness School: Sabbath and the Festivals." *HUCA* 58:65–117.

———. 1995. *The Sanctuary of Silence: The Priestly Torah and the Holiness School*. Minneapolis: Fortress.

Knoppers, Gary N. 1999. "Hierodules, Priests, or Janitors? The Levites in Chronicles and the History of the Israelite Priesthood." *JBL* 118:49–72.

———. 2004. *I Chronicles 1–9: A New Translation with Introduction and Commentary*. AB 12. New York: Doubleday.

Kornfeld, Walter. 2003. "קדש *qdš*. IV. LXX." *TDOT* 12:543–44.

Louw, Johannes P., and Eugene A. Nida. 1989. *Greek-English Lexicon of the New Testament: Based on Semantic Domains*. 2nd ed. New York: United Bible Societies.

Lust, J., E. Eynikel, and K. Hauspie. 2003. *Greek-English Lexicon of the Septuagint*. Rev. ed. Stuttgart: Deutsche Bibelgesellschaft.

Meyer, Esias E. 2012. "Leviticus 17 as a Bridge between P and H, with a Twist of D?" *JSem* 21:106–24.

———. 2013. "From Cult to Community: The Two Halves of Leviticus." *VetE* 34.2:1–7.

———. 2015. "Leviticus 17, Where P, H and D Meet: Priorities and Presuppositions of Jacob Milgrom and Eckart Otto." Pages 349–68 in *Current Issues in Priestly and Related Literature: The Legacy of Jacob Milgrom and Beyond*. Edited by Roy E. Gane and Ada Taggar-Cohen. RBS 82. Atlanta: SBL Press.

Milgrom, Jacob. 2000. *Leviticus 17–22: A New Translation with Introduction and Commentary*. AB 3A. New York: Doubleday.

———. 2001. *Leviticus 23–27: A New Translation with Introduction and Commentary*. AB 3B. New York: Doubleday.

Müller, Hans-Peter. 2004. "קדש *qdš* heilig." *THAT* 2:590–610.

Nihan, Christophe. 2004. "The Holiness Code between D and P: Some Comments on the Function and Significance of Leviticus 17–26 in the Composition of the Torah." Pages 81–122 in *Das Deuteronomium zwischen Pentateuch und Deuteronomistischem Geschichtswerk*. Edited by Eckart Otto and Reinhard Achenbach. FRLANT 206. Göttingen: Vandenhoeck & Ruprecht.

———. 2007. *From Priestly Torah to Pentateuch: A Study in the Composition of the Book of Leviticus*. FAT 2/25. Tübingen: Mohr Siebeck.

———. 2013a. "The Priestly Laws of Numbers, the Holiness Legislation, and the Pentateuch." Pages 109–37 in *Torah and the Book of Numbers*. Edited by Christian Frevel, Thomas Pola, and Aaron Schart. FAT 2/62. Tübingen: Mohr Siebeck.

———. 2013b. "Textual Fluidity and Rewriting in Parallel Traditions: The Case in Samuel and Chronicles." *JAJ* 4:186–209.

———. 2014. "Samuel, Chronicles, and 'Postchronistic' Revisions: Some Remarks of Method." Pages 57–78 in *Rereading the Relecture? The Question of (Post)chronistic Influence in the Latest Redactions of the Books of Samuel*. Edited by Uwe Becker and Hannes Bezzel. FAT 2/66. Tübingen: Mohr Siebeck.

———. 2016. "Cult Centralization and the Torah Traditions in Chronicles." Pages 253–88 in *The Fall of Jerusalem and the Rise of the Torah*. Edited by Peter Dubovský, Jean-Pierre Sonnet, and Dominik Markl. FAT 107. Tübingen: Mohr Siebeck.

Oeming, Manfred. 1990. *Das Wahre Israel: Die "genealogische Vorhalle" 1 Chronik 1–9*. Stuttgart: Kohlhammer.
Otto, Eckart. 1999. "Innerbiblische Exegese Im Heiligkeitsgesetz Levitikus 17–26." Pages 125–96 in *Levitikus als Buch*. Edited by Heinz-Josef Fabry and Hans-Winfried Jüngling. BBB 119. Berlin: Philo.
———. 2000. "Heiligkeitsgesetz." *RGG*[4] 3:1570–71.
Sparks, James T. 2008. *The Chronicler's Genealogies: Towards an Understanding of 1 Chronicles 1–9*. AcBib 28. Atlanta: Society of Biblical Literature.
Willi, Thomas. 2009. *Chronik (1 Chr 1,1–10, 14)*. BKAT 24.1. Neukirchen-Vluyn: Neukirchener Verlag.

Theology and Translation Technique in the Old Greek Version of Job 28

Jessie Rogers

ABSTRACT: Working within the broad consensus that Septuagint Job is a relatively free translation of a Hebrew *Vorlage* similar to MT, I conduct a reading of the unasterisked text of LXX Job 28, which is taken reliably to reflect OG Job. The study proceeds as a comparison of the Hebrew and the Old Greek, minimizing the theological import of those changes that are more easily explained as misreadings, driven by literary considerations, or examples of translation technique. I approach OG Job 28 not as a discrete wisdom poem but as the second part of Job's speech that begins in Job 27:1. The focus is on the one major plus in LXX Job 28:4, with the minuses largely attributed to an abbreviating tendency evident in the translator's rendering of the majority of the speeches in the book and driven by stylistic more than theological concerns. The change from third- to first-person pronominal suffix ("my eye") in 28:10 alters the theology of the passage but is nevertheless not indicative of theological *tendenz*, since it is more likely a misreading of the *Vorlage*. I suggest that, for OG Job, emulation is a more helpful model than interlinear translation for interpreting the changes made by the translator. Emulation allows for an integrated reading that respects the text of OG Job as an adaptation of Hebrew Job, an adaptation that is both a translation and a work of literature in its own right.

---

1. Introduction

The early Greek translations of the Hebrew Bible are an intriguing window into the thought world of early Hellenistic Judaism, since they are, in effect, the earliest commentaries on the Hebrew Bible.[1] Translation

---

[1]. This is not to deny the intratextual commentary that is found within the Hebrew canon itself.

is always interpretation, but translation is also technique. How were the translations from Hebrew into Greek made, and how much of that process reflects the theological convictions of the translators? Furthermore, what were those convictions, and how did they change over the centuries in which the Septuagint took shape? That is one series of questions that can be asked about the theology of the Septuagint. Another set of questions regarding theology and the Septuagint can be directed not at the production but at the product itself, paying attention to the theological dimensions of the meaning-world generated by the texts. It is the first, historical, set of questions that is the focus of Martin Rösel's project and thus the focus of this chapter's investigation of the Old Greek translation of Job 28. I will investigate the differences between the Hebrew and the Greek texts and what that might suggest about the translator's theological commitments. As Karl Kutz noted in regard to OG Job:

> the paraphrastic nature of the translator's rendering of the Hebrew often disclosed what he, and his religious community, considered implicit in the text—insights that would not be revealed in a more literal translation. The OG of Job is thus important because it reflects perhaps the earliest written interpretation of the book and because it illuminates, on a broader scale, the process of exegesis and translation within Hellenistic Judaism.[2]

The task is not as simple as mapping the differences between the Hebrew and the Greek texts and suggesting theological reasons for them. Differences between the MT and OG Job could be the result of a different *Vorlage*, of misreading by the translator, or indeed due to the employment of translation techniques that have no theological motivation. If the translator freely introduces changes in the rendering of the parent text for stylistic reasons, for instance, then one cannot simplistically attribute theological motives for those differences. Nor is theology reflected only in the differences between *Vorlage* and translation. The theology of the translators is also reflected in what they choose to keep unchanged. Not all theology is innovation. Still, it is in what appear to be deliberate alterations of the Hebrew that we have the clearest glimpses into the theological developments that may have been occurring at the time of translation. This study will therefore proceed as a comparison of the Hebrew and the Old Greek,

---

2. Kutz 2005, 345.

minimizing the theological import of those changes that are more easily explained as either misreadings or examples of translation technique.

As regards the theology of OG Job, Katherine Dell's remarks are typical of an older consensus:

> There is strong evidence ... that changes were made to the plot and theology of Job in the Septuagint version which toned down and sometimes eliminated Job's most impatient, presumptuous and impious remarks and exerted a great influence on later traditions of Job. These changes are more than literary; they are theological in motivation.[3]

This opinion was first argued for by Gilles Gerleman, Harry Gehman, and Donald Gard in the 1940s and 1950s.[4] In their treatments of LXX Job, they compared parts of the Hebrew and Greek line by line to demonstrate that changes were introduced to avoid anthropomorphisms and anthropopathisms and to ameliorate anything that might be offensive concerning God. Their approach was quite simplistic, however, in that they worked with isolated units. Writing a decade later in "Studies in the Septuagint of the Book of Job," a series of articles in the *Hebrew Union College Annual* between 1957 and 1965, Harry Orlinsky offered a robust critique of the earlier work. He examined the entire text of Septuagint Job for translation technique, use of anthropomorphisms, anthropopathism, and euphemisms, and indications of the underlying text and script.[5] Orlinsky convincingly demonstrated that the points that were made from one pericope could be contradicted by what the translator leaves unchanged in another place, often in close proximity. His other insights into translation technique will be summarized below.

2. The Text of OG Job

The Old Greek translation of the Hebrew book of Job was made in Egypt some time between the second and first centuries BCE.[6] It is striking for its literary quality and for the lack of interference from the Hebrew parent text. It reads well as a freestanding text without recourse to its *Vorlage*.

---

3. Dell 1991, 16.
4. Gerleman 1946; Gehman 1949; Gard 1952.
5. Orlinsky 1957, 1958, 1959, 1961, 1962, 1964, 1965.
6. Cox 2006, 106–8.

Practically all extant manuscripts reflect Origen's harmonized text. The Hexapla brought the Greek qualitatively in line with the Hebrew by adding to the shorter OG material drawn from a later more literal translation of the Hebrew attributed to Theodotion. This Hexaplaric version has strongly influenced subsequent copies of LXX Job so that only the fragmentarily attested Old Latin and the Coptic for the most part preserve the prerecensional text without the Theodotian additions.[7] This hybrid text is represented in both Rahlfs's and Ziegler's critical editions.[8] Fortunately, the material added to the OG by Origen is marked with an asterisk, and this asterisked material is noted in the critical editions. There are only four discrepancies between these editions with respect to the asterisked cola. One can therefore retrieve OG Job with a fair degree of confidence.

3. Translation Technique in OG Job

Natalio Fernández Marcos describes OG Job as "a new book, if not re-written, at least re-created in Greek."[9] It is generally accepted that OG Job is a work of good literary quality. It is more likely to reflect standard Greek usage than it is to use constructions that are indebted to underlying Hebrew phrasing.[10] A recent demonstration of this is provided by Douglas Mangum's study of how the Hebrew idiom נשא פנים is rendered in LXX Job. Mangum shows how the translator, despite being aware of the stereotypical rendering of the idiom by other LXX translators, typically chooses context-appropriate idiomatic Greek renderings.[11]

OG Job keeps the plot structure of the Hebrew texts.[12] It has a number of major additions in the narrative frame of the book: Job's wife is given a speech that makes her characterization more sympathetic; the friends are designated as kings or tyrants; there is a note about the certainty of Job's resurrection (though it is disputed whether this is OG); and there is an epilogue linking Job with the Jobab in Esau's genealogy. OG mirrors the pattern of the introductions to the speeches in the dialogue in MT exactly,

---

7. Cox 1986, 2; Pietersma 1985, 306.
8. Ziegler 1982; Rahlfs and Hanhart 2006.
9. Fernández Marcos 1994, 265.
10. Cox 2007, 667.
11. Mangum 2018.
12. Beck 2000, 125.

using set formulae to introduce each of Job's and the friends' speeches. OG Job, like MT, lacks a speech for Sophar in the third cycle.

OG Job does not exhibit consistency in rendering words from Hebrew to Greek and departs from stereotypical LXX translation equivalents.[13] There are two significant exceptions to this. All thirteen instances where the satan is named in the Hebrew are rendered by the term ὁ διάβολος and not transliterated as ὁ Σατανάς, a term that appears in the Testaments of the Twelve Patriarchs.[14] The divine name שדי is consistently rendered παντοκράτορος, an equivalence unique to Job in the LXX corpus.

For the most part, OG Job is considerably shorter than MT Job. Kutz has calculated that there are approximately 397 lines lacking in OG Job, of which only four appear in the prologue-epilogue narrative frame.[15] This is due in large part to the collapsing of parallelism and the shortening of speeches toward the end of each. Scholarly consensus is that the translator, not an alternative *Vorlage*, is responsible for the majority of these changes.[16] Fernández Marcos argues that the Greek translator tended toward paraphrase in order to create a meaningful text out of an often-obscure *Vorlage*, whereas Johann Cook suggests a combination of free translation and a slightly different source text to account for differences.[17]

Orlinsky, Heater, Kutz, and Dhont have conducted extensive studies of aspects of the translation techniques evident in OG Job.[18] What becomes clear is that the translator takes an essentially paraphrastic approach. He is more concerned with meaning than with grammatical structures and frequently transforms sentence types and even grammatical number, often for no discernible reason.[19] Condensed translations may be used to summarize a word pair, a phrase, a line, or even a whole verse.[20] He condenses two stichs into one while preserving information from each of the original Hebrew components.[21] We find inter/intra-textual readings with

---

13. Kutz 1997, 37.
14. Rogers 2013, 399–400.
15. Kutz 1997, 71.
16. Driver and Gray 1964, lxxiv–lxxvi; Dhorme 1926, clvii–clxii; Konkel 2010, 135–58, esp. 156; Cox 2014, 461–62; See most recently Eckstein 2018, 197–219, who uses the idiolect test developed by Hermann-Josef Stipp to reach the same conclusion.
17. Fernández Marcos 1994; Cook 1992.
18. Heater 1982; Dhont 2018.
19. Orlinsky 1958, 231–56.
20. Kutz 1997, 30.
21. Heater 1982, 2–3.

the interpolation of material from elsewhere in Job or from other biblical books, a technique Heater calls anaphoric translation.[22]

The pluses can be for clarification, harmonization, descriptive detail, midrashic expansion, and the preservation of alternative exegetical traditions.[23] There are small minuses where words are not considered essential for capturing the meaning of the verse, and metaphors and illustrations are often omitted. The translator frequently resolves a metaphor into a more literal statement.[24] Sometimes alternative lines are introduced as summarizing statements for passages that were omitted.[25] There are several examples of lines being omitted to bring connecting ideas or images closer together.[26] On the level of literary composition, it is clear that the translator does not recognize leitmotifs or copy word patterns closely but generates new ones.[27] Another point of note is that, where shortening of speeches occurs, it is less at the beginning and increases toward the end of a speech.

4. Reading Job 28

These side-by-side translations of MT Job and OG Job give a clear overview of what has been omitted (underlined in the first column), added (underlined in second column) or significantly changed (italicized in both).

MT Job 28 (NRSV)	OG Job 28 (NETS)
"Surely there is a mine for silver, and a place for gold to be refined.	"For silver has a place from which it comes, and gold a place from where it is sifted.
² Iron is taken out of the earth, and copper is smelted from ore.	² For whereas iron comes out of the earth, copper is quarried like stone.
³ *Miners* put an end to darkness, and search out to the farthest bound the ore in gloom and deep darkness.	³ *He* imposed order on darkness,
⁴ *They open shafts in a valley away from human habitation;* they are forgotten by travelers, they sway suspended, remote from people.	⁴ *and those of mortals who kept forgetting the righteous way became weak.*

---

22. Heater 1982, 6.
23. Kutz 1997, 60–61.
24. Kutz 1997, 76.
25. Kutz 1997, 78–79.
26. Kutz 1997, 81.
27. Beck 2000, 126.

⁵ As for the earth, out of it comes bread;
   but underneath it is turned up as by fire.
⁶ Its stones are the place of sapphires,
   and its dust contains gold.
⁷ "That path no bird of prey knows,
   and the falcon's eye has not seen it.
⁸ The proud wild animals have not trodden it;
   the lion has not passed over it.
⁹ "They put their hand to the flinty rock,
   and overturn mountains by the roots.   ⁹ And he overturned mountains from their
                                              roots
¹⁰ They cut out channels in the rocks,   ¹⁰ and broke whirlpools of rivers –
   and *their eyes* [lit: "his eye"] see every pre-   and *my eye* saw every precious thing.
   cious thing.
¹¹ The sources of the rivers they probe;   ¹¹ And he uncovered rivers' depths
   hidden things they bring to light.   and showed *his own power* to the light.
¹² "But where shall wisdom be found?   ¹² "But wisdom—where was it found?
   And where is the place of understanding?   And of what sort is the place of knowledge?
¹³ Mortals do not know the way to it,   ¹³ No mortal knows its way,
   and it is not found in the land of the living.   nor will it ever be discovered among
                                              human beings.
¹⁴ The deep says, 'It is not in me,'
   and the sea says, 'It is not with me.'
¹⁵ It cannot be gotten for gold,
   and silver cannot be weighed out as its
   price.
¹⁶ It cannot be valued in the gold of Ophir,
   in precious onyx or sapphire,
¹⁷ Gold and glass cannot equal it,
   nor can it be exchanged for jewels of fine
   gold.
¹⁸ No mention shall be made of coral or of
   crystal;
   the price of wisdom is above pearls.
¹⁹ The chrysolite of Ethiopia cannot compare
   with it,
   nor can it be valued in pure gold.
²⁰ "Where then does wisdom come from?   ²⁰ "But wisdom—where was it found?
   And where is the place of understanding?   And of what sort is the place of knowledge?
²¹ It is *hidden from the eyes of all living*,   ²¹ It has *escaped notice by any human*,
   and concealed from the birds of the air.
²² Abaddon and Death say,   ²² but we have heard of its renown.
   'We have heard a rumor of it with our
   ears.'

²³ "God understands the way to it, and he knows its place.	²³ God has established well its way, and he himself knows its place,
²⁴ For he looks to the ends of the earth, and sees everything under the heavens.	²⁴ for he observes all that is under heaven, since he knows all the earth contains, <u>that which he made</u>—
²⁵ When he gave to the wind its weight, and apportioned out the waters by measure;	²⁵the weight of winds and the measures of water!
²⁶ when he made a decree for the rain, <u>and a way for the thunderbolt;</u>	²⁶When he had done so, he looked and made a count²⁸
²⁷ <u>then he saw it and declared it;</u> he established it, and searched it out.	²⁷ since he prepared them, he kept track of them.
²⁸ And he said to humankind, 'Truly, the fear of the Lord, that is wisdom; and to depart from evil is understanding.'"	²⁸ And he said to humankind, 'Look, the worship of God is wisdom, and to stay away from evil is knowledge.'"

Although OG Job 28 follows the parts of the text it translates relatively closely, the multiple omissions mean that the literary structure changes completely. It is no longer three stanzas with a twice-repeated refrain. The introduction and conclusion are preserved intact, but the middle stanza has almost completely dropped out, transforming the refrain, "but where is wisdom to be found…" into an emphatically repetitive statement at the center. The opening metallurgical imagery that in the MT introduces a description of human ingenuity is both shortened and transferred onto God and God's powerful actions in creation.

We have only half the picture about the poetic structure if we read this chapter in isolation, which scholars are wont to do. That reading choice is driven by the MT. Most modern commentators, recognizing a difference in style, tone, and content from the surrounding speech of Job, treat Job 28 as an interlude, a self-contained speculative wisdom poem and not the words of Job. The opinion of Norman Habel is typical:

> The form of ch 28 differs radically from its surroundings.… It is not addressed to any of the participants of the dialogues in Job. There are no indictments, complaints, interactive comments, or direct responses to previous assertions of other speakers. The poem is a self-contained and measured reflection on access to wisdom.[29]

---

28. Or, following Ziegler 1982, "he counted rain."
29. Habel 1985, 392. See also Westermann 1981, 137; Gutiérrez 1987, 38.

This decision is based on the structure and contents of the poem and not on any explicit introductory formula; it is recognized as a specific genre. Carol Newsom uses the term "speculative wisdom poem" for Prov 8, Job 28, Sir 1 and 24, Bar 3:9–4:4, and perhaps 1 En. 42 and considers Prov 3:13–20 and Wisd 7–9 to exhibit many elements of the genre. The generic markers include: the topic of the place of wisdom in the cosmos and its relation to God and humanity/Israel; Wisdom as a feminine personification of a transcendent concept; the trope of seeking and finding; creation imagery and the syntactical style of creation accounts; economic imagery of buying and selling and comparison of value; a didactic quality; and the rhetorical aim of persuading the reader of the value of wisdom.[30] It is clear why these poems are often chosen as loci for reflection on the theological perspective of the books in which they appear.

But, as has been noted, the poem in Job 28 does not have any introductory formula to mark it off from what precedes it. In both MT and OG, Job's words are introduced in Job 27:1 and again in 29:1 without any introductory formula at the start of Job 28. There is no indication that the OG translator treats Job 28 as an interlude. Quite the opposite: the phrase εἶδέν μου ὁ ὀφθαλμός with its first-person pronoun in OG Job 28:10 is a clear indication that the translator read it as a continuation of Job's speech.

When OG Job 28 is read as the latter part of Job's speech begun in chapter 27, it follows a pattern of abbreviation often repeated in OG Job, where the first part of the speech is adhered to closely, with more and more omitted as the poem progresses. By Kutz's calculation the translator omits 1.7 percent of the first cycle, 13.5 percent of the second cycle, 27.7 percent of the third cycle, 34.6 percent of Elihu's speeches, and 16.3 percent of the Lord's speeches from the whirlwind.[31] Within these speeches, the omissions increase toward the end of the speeches. I illustrate this roughly by noting the verses omitted in the third cycle where OG Job follows the structure of MT in having no speech for Sophar: Eliphaz's speech in OG Job 22:1–30 lacks verses 3b, 13–16, 20, 24, and 29–30; Job's reply in OG Job 24:1–25:23 is missing 23:9, 15 and 24:4b, 5b, 8, 14–18a, and 25; Bildad's speech in OG Job 25:1–6 lacks verse 6b. Job's speech in OG Job 26:1–14 omits verses 5–11 and 14a. This pattern of increasing abbreviation continues in Job's speech in OG Job 27:1–28:28. The minuses are: 27:18b, 19b,

---

30. Newsom 2003, 172–73.
31. Kutz 1997, 71–72.

21–23, and 28:3bc, 4a, 5–8, 9a, 14–19, 21b, 22a, 26b, and 27a. In OG Job 27 the first part of the speech is followed closely, with some abbreviation of the section on the fate of the wicked where the parallelism is collapsed in verses 18–19 so that each verse loses a stich; then the passage where the derisive, punishing east wind is personified is omitted entirely. We have already noted the (much more frequent) abbreviating that occurs in OG Job 28.

4.1. Job 28:3–4

Although both the Hebrew and the Greek here have no named subject for the action in verse 3, it is clear from the context that MT is referring to humans who are mining. The OG reads most naturally as referring to God, particularly in light of what follows. The translator has therefore elided the references to mining activity and instead introduced the action of God, who imposes order on darkness in a moral way in verse 4. OG Job 28:4 reads quite differently from the MT. Nevertheless, it can largely be derived from the parent Hebrew text, as I indicate below. The Hebrew is difficult, and multiple emendations have been suggested.[32] It is thus unsurprising that the translator may have found it a challenge. I have supplied my own very literal translation of MT.

פָּרַץ נַחַל ׀ מֵעִם־גָּר הַנִּשְׁכָּחִים מִנִּי־רָגֶל דַּלּוּ מֵאֱנוֹשׁ נָעוּ׃
He breaks open a shaft from with [away from?] sojourning; the forgotten [pl] from foot, they languish from humankind they sway/totter.

οἱ δὲ ἐπιλανθανόμενοι ὁδὸν δικαίαν ἠσθένησαν ἐκ βροτῶν.
And those of mortals who kept forgetting the righteous way became weak. (NETS)

הַנִּשְׁכָּחִים	οἱ <u>δὲ</u> ἐπιλανθανόμενοι
מִנִּי־רָגֶל	ὁδὸν <u>δικαίαν</u>
דַּלּוּ	ἠσθένησαν
מֵאֱנוֹשׁ	ἐκ βροτῶν[33]
נָעוּ	–

---

32. Various interpretations are discussed by Yem Hing Hom 2017, 2–4.

33. Dafni (2007, 53) has noted that this Homeric Greek word for "mortal" is only

The translator appears to have taken discrete elements of the Hebrew and interpreted them in a way that is still within the semantic range of the words, though without much concern for the grammatical relationships within the Hebrew. The addition of the particle δέ is standard technique for the translator and need not concern us. The introduction of the modifier δικαίαν with ὁδὸν is significant. When Job 28 is read in isolation, it appears to be quite a radical shift on the part of the translator. However, when Job 28 is read as the continuation of Job's speech begun in Job 27:1, the shift is less dramatic. If the translator either did not recognize or chose to erase the miners' activity in Job 28, then this addition is importing the idea of judgement on the wicked from earlier in the same speech.

Perhaps verse 4 could be read as a more literal statement for the personification of the east wind that brings judgement and derision on the wicked that the translator omitted from the end of chapter 27:

> The east wind lifts him up and he is gone; It sweeps him out of his place.
> It hurls at him without pity; he flees from its power in headlong flight.
> It claps its hands at him, and hisses at him from its place. (Job 27:21–23 NRSV)

4.2. The Minus of Job 28:5–9a

It is hard to find any theological motivation for removing these verses. There is also no pressing literary reason beyond abbreviating the speech. In passing over verses 7–9a, the narrator has removed occurrences of the three motifs of "place," "way," and "discovery." But these are still found at the beginning, in the middle, and at the end of the chapter. What has been removed is the human quest to discover the place of these precious things. Habel, commenting on MT Job 28, notes that the underlying metaphor of the poem is the search for what is rare and precious.[34] This metaphor has not been consistently taken over by the translator, who appears to want to keep the focus on God's power and wisdom.

---

found in the LXX in OG Job, where it occurs as a translation of a number of different Hebrew terms.

34. Habel 1985, 19.

4.3. Job 28:9b

God is the subject in κατέστρεψεν δὲ ἐκ ῥιζῶν ὄρη, unlike in MT, where it is human beings mining the earth. God has been described as overturning mountains in an earlier speech of Job (OG Job 9:5): παλαιῶν ὄρη καὶ οὐκ οἴδασιν, ὁ καταστρέφων αὐτὰ ὀργῇ. The translator is thus internally consistent. Here, however, the purpose is not a display of wrath but a revelation of God's power.

4.4. Job 28:10

There is a change from "his eyes" (עֵינוֹ) in the MT to "my eye" (μου ὁ ὀφθαλμός) in OG, which substantially affects the meaning of the text. In the Hebrew, the miners in their subterranean explorations see every precious thing. But OG Job, having transposed the searching and uncovering of the hidden depths from humans onto God, has God uncovering the roots of the mountains and breaking whirlpools and Job as the observer of every precious thing. The text as it stands has Job at this stage in the narrative already the recipient of revelation of the hidden mysteries of the cosmos, in a manner that prefigures the voice from the whirlwind. That would be a significant theological shift. It is likely, however, that this is not a theological choice by the translator but simply a misreading of a *yod* for a *waw*: עיני instead of עינו. Kutz identifies twenty times where this confusion has occurred in relation to suffixes in OG Job.[35]

4.5. The Minus in Job 28:14–19

Habel describes the dynamics of the center of the poem in the MT:

> The poet employs a listing technique to underscore the unsurpassable value of Wisdom when weighed against all the gems of the earth (vs 15–19). He personifies Death, Sea, and Deep as the figures who are ignorant of Wisdom's whereabouts (vs 14, 22) and portrays Wisdom as the elusive and alluring woman behind the scenes whom God alone has found.[36]

---

35. Kutz 1997, 91 n 64.
36. Habel 1985, 394.

All of this has been removed by the translator of OG. The omission of Sea and Deep and their words in Job 28:14 and of Death and Abaddon in 28:22a may point to a demythologising tendency on the part of the translator. I note, however, that the translator does not avoid mythological references as a matter of course. In OG Job 7:12 Job asks if he is Sea or Dragon that God feels the need to put a guard on him, and God refers to monsters and the Dragon in the speech from the whirlwind (40:15, 25). Perhaps it is their agency as speakers that the translator objects to here.

Then again, there is nothing theologically objectionable about the comparison between wisdom and precious objects in verses 15–19, and these are also left out. Kutz noted that one of the techniques employed by the translator is to bring similar ideas closer together, and this is what happens here with the omission of these verses. The minus "allows for related ideas or identical words at distant points to be brought together by the removal of intervening material."[37] This tighter connection between verses originally functioning as refrains creates a very emphatic repetitive statement at the center of this chapter. I arrange it in two columns to make the parallelism explicit:

| But wisdom – where was it found? And of what sort is the place of knowledge? No mortal knows its way, nor will it ever be discovered among human beings. | But wisdom –where was it found? And of what sort is the place of knowledge? It has escaped notice by any human, but we have heard of its renown. |

Could it be that we are overinterpreting by seeking a motivation for the removal of these particular verses beyond the literary one of recrafting the central part of the poem as described here?

4.6. Job 28:21

In verse 21 we find an example of the translator altering the grammatical shape without altering the meaning of the parent text. Instead of wisdom being hidden from "the eyes of all the living", it "escapes notice". This does lose the contrast with Job 28:10, but the polarity within the original source text—that which the humans are able to see in precious stones compared to what they cannot see, wisdom—has been completely altered in the

---

37. Kutz 1997, 81. He gives as examples Job 29:24–30:1 and 33:31–34:2.

translator's poem anyway. The references to creation have been omitted earlier, so it becomes the human eye instead of "all the living". The Greek gives an elegant composition which fits in the new context without reflecting the literary workings of the MT.

The Hebrew has been shortened here by omitting the reference to Death and Abaddon speaking, with the action of hearing of wisdom's renown transposed onto the humans. This may be an instance of demythologising, with any reference to Abaddon and Death, potential rivals to God, effectively removed. As noted above, this echoes the omission of the east wind in Job 27:21–23 and the omission of Sea and Deep in Job 28:14. But it can also be explained at a literary level: the parallelism of the central assertion described above is enhanced by making it the humans who do not know and cannot discover the way to wisdom (OG Job 28:13), because they have not noticed and have only heard of her renown (OG Job 28:22)

4.7. Job 28:23

אֱלֹהִים הֵבִין דַּרְכָּהּ וְהוּא יָדַע אֶת־מְקוֹמָהּ
כִּי־הוּא לִקְצוֹת־הָאָרֶץ יַבִּיט תַּחַת כָּל־הַשָּׁמַיִם יִרְאֶה

God has understood its way, and he knows its place.
Because he, to the ends of the earth he looks and under all the heavens he sees.

ὁ θεὸς εὖ συνέστησεν αὐτῆς τὴν ὁδόν, αὐτὸς δὲ οἶδεν τὸν τόπον αὐτῆς·
αὐτὸς γὰρ τὴν ὑπ' οὐρανὸν πᾶσαν ἐφορᾷ εἰδὼς τὰ ἐν τῇ γῇ πάντα, ἃ ἐποίησεν
God established well its way, for he knows its place;
for all that is under heaven he observes, he knows all that is in the earth, that which he made.

There is a shift here from God understanding to God establishing, which appears to give God a more active role vis-à-vis wisdom. Cook has suggested that this is a deliberate alteration to reflect a stronger subordination of wisdom to God. In the first place, God has ordered/determined/established wisdom's path as opposed to "understanding" it. The addition of the adverb εὖ may also "underline the fact that God is solely responsible for the creation."[38] That is certainly possible, and the inclusion of εὖ is interest-

---

38. Cook 1997, 325.

ing. However, it is more likely to be a misreading of הכין for הבין, since *beth* and *kaph* are easily confused. Nevertheless, there is an addition at the end of the verse that reads more naturally as referring to God than to wisdom: ἃ ἐποίησεν, which would make God the creator. Thus Cook's observation about the explicitly subordinate role of wisdom still stands.

4.8. Job 28:26–27

The translator has abbreviated again here by taking the first stich of one verse and the second of the following one. There is no explicit direct object of God's preparing and keeping track (ἑτοιμάσας ἐξιχνίασεν), but the creation and not wisdom is in view. Consistent with the rest of OG Job 28, God is the one who knows creation, being its originator, and who thus can reveal its secrets.

We return to considering Job's speech as a whole. Read as a unit, OG Job 27–28 begins with Job taking an oath of integrity (27:1–6), followed by an imprecation against his adversary (27:7). Job then moves on to consider the position of the wicked before the Lord, their vulnerability and eventual destiny: the destruction of their family by sword and famine and the fragility of their abode and of their lives. The excision of the miners at the beginning of OG Job 28 streamlines this single speech of Job, which begins with the wicked and their punishment, then moves on to God and wisdom without the complicating factor of the play on human skill in relation to the rest of creation versus human inability to find wisdom. God is the subject of the verbs in OG Job 28:2–11. The imagery of the miners' skill has been converted into the power of God to attenuate the wicked and to reveal the hidden parts of the creation. The action of imposing order has been transposed onto God, and OG Job 28:4 then reads as the consequences of God imposing order. The order has also been transposed into a moral key, since what is forgotten is the "righteous way." The addition of δίκαιος in verse 4 is therefore less of a surprising addition because it is in line with the topic of the wicked and their punishment, which it brings to a conclusion. The transition from one focus (fate of the wicked) to the other (God's power to reveal creation's secrets) does not come at OG Job 28:1 but several verses later, at OG Job 28:9. The prior mention of silver and gold in OG Job 27:16 may also suggest that OG Job 28:1–2 links with what has gone before rather than with what comes after. As I have indicated, the actions of the miners in MT have become actions of God's power: overturning mountains, breaking whirlpools, and uncovering rivers' depths. This revelation of the hidden secrets of the cosmos to Job is the revelation of God's power (28:11). Then comes the question of where wisdom is to be found. Instead of reflecting on the value of wisdom, OG Job 28 asks the question twice and twice gives the answer: humans do not know. That leads into the assertion of God's wisdom. As creator, God knows everything God has made, and God then gives to humans their own wisdom, which is to worship God and shun evil. Thus the poem ends on the same point as the Hebrew but following a more direct route to get there.

5. Interlinear Translation or Emulation?

The NETS and the SBL exegetical commentary series on the Septuagint[39] are both indebted to Albert Pietersma's interlinear hypothesis, which has exerted a strong influence on studies of translation technique. In the opening words to the reader of NETS, Wright and Pietersma note that "for the vast majority of books the linguistic relationship of the Greek to its Semitic parent can best be conceptualized as a Greek interlinear translation of a Hebrew original within a Hebrew-Greek diglot."[40] They stress that this is a heuristic model and not a claim that such an interlinear or diglot translation ever actually existed. This model, whatever its merits for the other parts of the LXX,[41] is difficult to apply to OG Job. Here we have an earlier freer translation of a text that was not read in the synagogue and that self-evidently could be read as a literarily coherent self-contained text. The more literal translations (e.g., Theodotion), which are more conducive to being explained by the interlinear model, came later.

This is not to say that a comparison with the MT is not helpful. We have the preceding inspiration for this Greek text, and that gives us access to some of the choices made by the translator. It is a translation, so comparison with the Hebrew is an additional window onto the theology. But if the interlinear paradigm leads to reading OG Job verse by verse instead of according to larger pericopes, it distorts our understanding of the theology of Job. According to the interlinear model, one has to explain each of the subtractions, alterations, and additions piece by piece. Cook's treatment of Job 28 is a good example of this approach. He notes that some strophes

---

39. As this project is described in Büchner 2017.
40. Pietersma and Wright 2007, 18–19.
41. But see the critique of Joosten 2008; Schaper 2014, 34–39.

have been reinterpreted (vv. 4, 23, 24, 27) and comments that "it is also rather difficult to find a logical reason for these omissions/abridgements."[42] One suggestion that Cook makes is that there is a spiritualizing tendency, with "earthy things" omitted, "such as the earth, stones, birds of prey, the lion, the deep, gold and other precious stones," though he does concede that there are still a good number of earthly things that remain.[43] He sees in the addition of "righteous way" that has no justification in the Hebrew of Job 28 a moralizing tendency and the idea of the two ways that finds its way also into LXX Job. He notes in 28:23–24 that God's role is heightened vis-à-vis Wisdom. The notion of God understanding wisdom's way has been replaced with God establishing wisdom well, so God's primacy is being stressed.

This application on the interlinear model works with the assumption that a line-by-line comparison is the path to understanding the theology of the translator. But is this the best approach to a text such as OG Job? A more productive model when working with OG Job, in my opinion, is that of emulation, where the translator is attempting an improved rendition of his original text. Here I am indebted to Theo van der Louw, who has suggested that "LXX Job and Proverbs are translations that come close to the Roman practice of *aemulatio*."[44] To work within an emulation paradigm is to suggest that the translator is respectful of the source text but has the freedom to make changes to improve its literary quality in Greek. This freedom to adapt could include deleting or shortening passages, adding material for literary rather than theological reasons, and using the "textual elements as the building blocks of a new text."[45] The translator works not simply at the level of the line but within broader literary units. A change made in a particular verse may be influenced by the structure of the pericope as a whole.

In his study of storytelling in the Septuagint, John Beck has recognized that translation technique covers more than lexical choices. He argues for the importance of literary analysis of translated texts. He is concerned with the attributes of a text that can be uncovered by narrative criticism, in particular how the translator handles characterization, the use of time, and the patterning play of words in the parent text in

---

42. Cook 1997, 322.
43. Cook 1997, 323.
44. Van der Louw 2016, 461–62.
45. Van der Louw 2016, 461–62.

narrative texts. His method is applied, *inter alia*, to the prologue of Job, and he concludes that the Greek text presents "an enhanced version of the Job we meet in the Hebrew."[46] Of particular interest for this chapter is his observations about the translator's attention to the structure of the text. Beck notes that "the translator seemed less concerned about the symmetry of repeated formula" but that the Greek text "generates new patterns all its own."[47] Wordplay and patterning such as *Leitwort* repetitions in the Hebrew are not uniformly carried over into the Greek, but the plot sequence is followed closely. He concludes that "while the use of time is nearly identical the characterisation and patterning play of words create a very unique reading experience."[48] If the translation technique observed by Beck in the prose prologue carries over into the poetic sections of Job, then one would expect that, while the overall structure in terms of plot remains similar, changes will be introduced in literary structure, particularly as that is carried in the patterning play of words. The changes would not simply reflect a loss of the literary merits of the Hebrew but be a transformation of literary effect to create a distinctive literary product. The theology of the translated text would therefore be adducible not merely from alterations made in translation but also from the literary structure of the translation itself.

Drawing upon the emulation model, all of the omissions in OG Job 28 can be explained in terms of the translator's literary translation technique. We expect him to shorten the latter part of a speech, and he does not disappoint. He brings remote repetitions closer together by omitting most of the middle stanza of MT Job 28:13–19; metaphors and personifications have been resolved or removed (East Wind, Sea and Deep, Death and Abaddon); and a refocusing has occurred so that the second part of the speech becomes predominantly about God and God's relationship to the cosmos. The dynamics of OG Job 28 have been simplified. God is the powerful, knowing one; humans are not. It is humans, not mythical Death and Abyss, who have heard of wisdom's renown. Job is given a revelation of God's power. Only God, who knows and can turn the cosmos upside down, has established wisdom and therefore is able to say what wisdom is for humans.

---

46. Beck 2000, 123–25.
47. Beck 2000, 125.
48. Beck 2000, 126.

These omissions and refocusing do not appear to be as theologically significant when OG Job 28 is read as the second part of Job's speech begun at Job 27:1 and when OG Job 28:9, not OG Job 28:1, is seen as the turning point from the focus on the fate of the wicked (Job 27) to God's revelatory acts in the cosmos. Certainly there has been an elevation of God's role vis-à-vis wisdom and a simplifying of the dynamics of the poem to highlight God's activity. The technical explanations for why East Wind, Sea and Deep, Abaddon and Death have been removed do not alter the fact that it is precisely these mythological personifications that have been omitted. Their speaking role in MT Job 28 may have been an added impetus to silence them. In any case, the effect is to remove any potential rivals to God and thus to further elevate God in this speech of Job. The addition of "righteous way" in OG Job 28:4, however, has been shown not to be a moralizing tendency that was introduced *de novo* by the translator but a carryover from Job 27.

I return briefly to OG Job 28:10 with its reading "my eye" as a way of illustrating different approaches to the theology of OG Job. If OG Job is seen as a translation in the first place, then the fact that this reflects a misreading of the Hebrew and does not say anything about the translator's theological *Tendenz* would mean that it is not theologically significant. We could even point out that there is a break in logic here. Why suddenly bring in a revelation to Job? But if the theology is carried in the shape of the final form as a work in itself, then that *is* significant, and the revelation of the secrets of the cosmos to Job would need to be worked into an exposition of the theology of the passage.

6. Some Observations for Writing a Theology of the Septuagint

Emanuel Tov has argued that theological exegesis occurs primarily in the more freely rendered translations of books such as Isaiah, Daniel, Job, and Proverbs.[49] These books cannot be treated in precisely the same way as more literal translations within the Septuagint. The nature of OG Job is even more distinctive, given that it was not read in the synagogue. Cox has concluded that "it is very likely that the book's status at the edge [of the canon] permitted the translator to alter the text that was translated,

---

49. Tov 1999, 258.

to the extent that the translator almost becomes an author."⁵⁰ This makes OG Job a rich source for a theology of the Septuagint. It also highlights the importance of recognizing the specific profile of each translation and dealing with it on its own terms before bringing it into conversation with the wider corpus. OG Job's distinctive characteristics support Rösel's firm conviction that "a theology of the Septuagint cannot be based on the leveling of differences among the individual books or the specific profiles of the translators for the sake of a common edifice of ideas."⁵¹

The theology of the Septuagint is the theology of a translation of which we, broadly speaking and with allowances made for variations of *Vorlage*, have the parent text. This allows us to discern the theological lens in the translation process itself. As Cook observes: "What is clear to me is that 'theology' is to be located in the way any given translator in fact renders his parent text. It is in the differences between the source text and the target text that interpretation becomes evident."⁵² There is value in asking the question about the operative theology at play in the act of translation itself. Nevertheless, for a free-standing text with its own literary merits, it is also the shape and content of the text itself, including any intertextual dynamics that it sets up, that gives us the theology of that text and, by implication, of its translator.

My chosen text has not allowed for the exploration of theological themes in which OG Job may have been innovative, such as resurrection, angelology and demonology, or names for God. My contribution is on the level of method. What I have attempted to demonstrate is that, in working with OG Job, an interlinear comparison needs to be supplemented by attention to how larger literary units have been treated by the translator. I will give the last word to Harry Orlinsky, who noted that "in letting the data speak for themselves, it seems best in many instances to reproduce several verses together, or even an entire speech. In that way the crucial passages may be comprehended in the proper setting."⁵³

---

50. Cox 2006, 115. But Kutz (1997, 27) points to LXX Isaiah and LXX Psalms as counterexamples to prove that "a dynamic translation style does not … imply a diminished canonical status."
51. Rösel 2006, 240.
52. Cook 2017, 277.
53. Orlinsky 1961, 250.

Bibliography

Beck, John A. 2000. *Translators as Storytellers: A Study in Septuagint Translation Technique*. New York: Lang.
Büchner, Dirk, ed. 2017. *The SBL Commentary on the Septuagint: An Introduction*. SCS 67. Atlanta: SBL Press.
Cook, Johann 1992. "Aspects of Wisdom in the Texts of Job (Chapter 28): *Vorlage(n)* and/or Translator(s)?" *OTE* 5:26–34.
———. 1997. "Aspects of the Relationship between the Septuagint Versions of Proverbs and Job." Pages 309–28 in *IX Congress of the International Organization for Septuagint and Cognate Studies: Cambridge, 1995*. Edited by Bernard A. Taylor. SCS 45. Atlanta: Scholars Press.
———. 2017. "A Theology of the Septuagint?" *OTE* 30:265–82.
Cox, Claude E. 1986. *Hexaplaric Materials Preserved in the Armenian Version*. SCS 21. Atlanta: Scholars Press.
———. 2006. "The Historical, Social and Literary Context of Old Greek Job." Pages 105–16 in *XII Congress of the International Organization for Septuagint and Cognate Studies: Leiden, 2004*. Edited by Melvin K. H. Peters. Atlanta: Society of Biblical Literature.
———. 2007. "Iob." Pages 667–96 in *A New English Translation of the Septuagint and the Other Greek translations Traditionally Included under That Title*. Edited by Albert Pietersma and Benjamin G. Wright. Oxford: Oxford University Press.
———. 2014. "Does a Shorter Hebrew Parent Text Underlie Old Greek Job?" Pages 451–62 in *In the Footsteps of Sherlock Holmes: Studies in the Biblical Text in Honour of Anneli Aejmelaeus*. Edited by Kristin De Troyer, T. Michael Law, and Marketta Liljeström. CBET 72. Leuven: Peeters.
Dafni, Evangelia G. 2007. "*Brotos*: A Favourite Word of Homer in the Septuagint Version of Job." *VetE* 28:35–65.
Dell, Katherine. 1991. *The Book of Job as Sceptical Literature*. Berlin: de Gruyter.
Dhont, Marieke. 2018. *Style and Context of Old Greek Job*. JSJSup 183. Leiden: Brill.
Dhorme, Édouard P. 1926. *Le livre de Job*. Étude bibliques. Paris: Gabalda.
Driver, Samuel R., and George B. Gray. 1964. *A Critical and Exegetical Commentary on the Book of Job: Together with a New Translation*. ICC 14. Edinburgh: T&T Clark.

Eckstein, Juliane. 2018. "The Idiolect Test and the *Vorlage* of Old Greek Job: A New Argument for an Old Debate." *VT* 68:197–219.

Fernández Marcos, Natalio. 1994. "The Septuagint Reading of the Book of Job." Pages 251–66 in *The Book of Job*. Edited by Willem A. M. Beuken. BETL 114. Leuven: Leuven University Press.

Gard, Donald H. 1952. *The Exegetical Method of the Greek Translator of the Book of Job*. JBLMS 8. Philadelphia: Society of Biblical Literature.

Gehman, Harry S. 1949. "The Theological Approach to the Greek Translator of Job 1–15." *JBL* 68:231–40.

Gerleman, Gilles. 1946. *Studies in the Septuagint I: Book of Job*. Lund: Lunds Universitets Årsakrift.

Gutiérrez, Gustavo. 1987. *On Job: God-Talk and the Suffering of the Innocent*. Maryknoll, NY: Orbis Books.

Habel, Norman C. 1985. *The Book of Job: A Commentary*. OTL. Philadelphia: Westminster.

Heater, Homer 1982. *Septuagint Translation Technique in the Book of Job*. CBQMS 11. Washington, DC: Catholic Biblical Association.

Joosten, Jan 2008. "Reflections on the 'Interlinear Paradigm' in Septuagintal Studies." Pages 163–78 in *Scripture in Transition: Essays on Septuagint, Hebrew Bible, and the Dead Sea Scrolls in Honour of Raija Sollamo*. Edited by Anssi Voitila and Jutta Jokiranta. JSJSup 126. Leiden: Brill.

Konkel, August H. 2010. "The Elihu Speeches in the Greek Translation of Job." Pages 135–58 in *Translation Is Required: The Septuagint in Retrospect and Prospect*. Edited by Robert J. V. Hiebert. SCS 56. Atlanta: Society of Biblical Literature.

Kutz, Karl V. 1997. "The Old Greek of Job: A Study in Early Biblical Exegesis." Unpublished PhD dissertation, University of Wisconsin-Madison.

———. 2005. "Characterization in the Old Greek of Job." Pages 345–55 in *Seeking Out the Wisdom of the Ancients: Essays Offered to Honor Michael V Fox on the Occasion of His Sixty-Fifth Birthday*. Edited by Ronald L. Troxel, Kelvin G. Friebel, and Dennis R. Magary. Winona Lake, IN: Eisenbrauns.

Louw, Theo A. W. van der. 2016. "Did the Septuagint Translators Really Intend the Greek Text as It Is?" Pages 449–66 in *Die Septuaginta – Orte und Intentionen*. Edited by Siegfried Kreuzer, Martin Meiser, and Marcus Sigismund. WUNT 361. Tübingen: Mohr Siebeck.

Mangum, Douglas, 2018. "The Biblical Hebrew Idiom 'Lift the Face' in the Septuagint of Job." *HTS Teologiese Studies/Theological Studies* 74/3. doi: 10.4102/hts.v74i3.5025.

Newsom, Carol A. 2003. *The Book of Job: A Contest of Moral Imaginations.* Oxford: Oxford University Press.

Orlinsky, Harry M. 1957. "Studies in the Septuagint of the Book of Job I." *HUCA* 28:53–74.

———. 1958. "Studies in the Septuagint of the Book of Job II." *HUCA* 29:229–71.

———. 1959. "Studies in the Septuagint of the Book of Job III." *HUCA* 30:153–67.

———. 1961. "Studies in the Septuagint of the Book of Job III (Continued)." *HUCA* 32:239–68.

———. 1962. "Studies in the Septuagint of the Book of Job IV." *HUCA* 33:119–51.

———. 1964. "Studies in the Septuagint of the Book of Job V." *HUCA* 35:57–78.

———. 1965. "Studies in the Septuagint of the Book of Job V." *HUCA* 36:37–47.

Pietersma, Albert. 1985. "Review of Joseph Ziegler, ed., *Iob. Septuaginta: Vetus Testamentum Graecum*, 11/4." *JBL* 104:305–11.

Pietersma, Albert, and Benjamin G. Wright, 2007. "To the Reader of NETS." Pages 16–28 in *A New English Translation of the Septuagint and the Other Greek translations Traditionally Included under That Title.* Edited by Albert Pietersma and Benjamin G. Wright. Oxford: Oxford University Press.

Rahlfs, Alfred, and Robert Hanhart. 2006. *Septuaginta: Vetus Testamentum Graecum Auctoritate Scientiarum Gottingensis Editum.* Stuttgart: Deutsche Bibelgesellschaft.

Rogers, Jessie, R. 2013. "Testament of Job as an Adaptation of LXX Job." Pages 395–408 in *Text-Critical and Hermeneutical Studies in the Septuagint.* Edited by Johann Cook and Hermann-Josef Stipp. VTSup 157. Leiden: Brill.

Rösel, Martin. 2006. "Towards a 'Theology of the Septuagint.'" Pages 239–52 in *Septuagint Research: Issues and Challenges in the Study of the Greek Jewish Scriptures.* Edited by Wolfgang Kraus and R. Glenn Wooden. SCS 53. Atlanta: Society of Biblical Literature.

Schaper, Joachim. 2014. "The Concept of the Translator(s) in the Contemporary Study of the Septuagint." Pages 31–46 in *In the Footsteps of Sherlock Holmes: Studies in the Biblical Text in Honour of Anneli Aejmelaeus.* Edited by Kristin De Troyer, T. Michael Law, and Marketta Liljeström. CBET 72. Leuven: Peeters.

Tov, Emanuel 1999. "Theologically Motivated Exegesis Embedded in the Septuagint." Pages 257–69 in *The Greek and Hebrew Bible: Collected Essays on the Septuagint*. Edited by Emanuel Tov. VTSup 72. Leiden: Brill.

Westermann, Claus. 1981. *The Structure of the Book of Job: A Form-Critical Analysis*. Philadelphia: Fortress.

Yem Hing Hom, Mary Katherine. 2017. "Water, Wisdom, and Life: Literary Insights on the Use of נַחַל in Job 28:4 with Reference to 28:1–28 and 38:22–30." *VT* 67:1–8.

Ziegler, Joseph. 1982. *Job*. Septuaginta. Vetus Testamentum Graecum Auctoritate Scientiarum Gottingensis 11.4. Göttingen: Vandenhoeck & Ruprecht.

The Septuagint of Proverbs as a Jewish Document
Johann Cook

ABSTRACT: This paper argues that the time has arrived for other studies than text-critical ones, such as the question whether it is viable to formulate a theology of the Septuagint. During the current congress it has become clear that most scholars are, in fact, convinced that it is possible to apply hermeneutical principles to the Septuagint in order, among other things, to formulate a theology of the LXX. However, there are clear differences of opinion. This paper also demonstrates that LXX Proverbs is a Jewish document, which in the final instance will have an effect upon the "theology" that is formulated. Passages from this unit that are analyzed are Prov 2, 8, and 28. Examples of prerabbinic exegetical traditions, such as the so-called יצר הרע and יצר הטוב (the good and bad inclinations) are unearthed. Another example concerns the law of Moses that encircles the righteous. These are examples of Jewish traditions. I found no evidence of Greek philosophical, Platonic influence in this book, as is argued, inter alia, by Gerleman and D'Hamonville.

1. Introduction

I have made a number of pilot studies about the question whether it is viable to formulate a theology of the Septuagint.[1] During the current congress it has become clear that most scholars are in fact convinced that it is possible to apply hermeneutical principles to the Septuagint in order, among other things, to formulate a theology of the LXX.[2] However, there are clear differences of opinion. I, for one, have argued that a prerequisite

---

The financial and other assistance of the South African National Research Foundation (SANRF) and Stellenbosch University (SU) is acknowledged. The views expressed in this chapter are solely those of the author.

1. See Cook 2010a.
2. See Rösel 2018c.

for a hermeneutical approach should be an exegetical commentary, if at all possible.³ Martin Rösel does not agree with this point of view.

There is another issue at stake. In all my research into LXX Proverbs, I have become more convinced of the Jewish nature of this document, which in the final instance will have an effect upon the "theology" that is formulated. Two passages stand out in this regard, LXX Prov 2 and 28, which contain evidence of Jewish exegetical traditions.⁴ The first example contains prerabbinical exegetical traditions about the essence of humanity, the so-called יצר הרע and יצר הטוב (the good and bad inclinations). The second example concerns the law of Moses that encircles the righteous. These two passages are examples of direct Jewish exegetical influence in LXX Proverbs. There are also indirect examples. Because of the overwhelming influence of Jewish exegetical material in LXX Proverbs, I find no evidence of Greek philosophical, Platonic influence in this book, as is argued, inter alia, by Gerleman and D'Hamonville.⁵

This essay reflects work on Prov 2 previously published in the Festschrift for Professor Pieter de Villiers,⁶ on Prov 28, and in a book that Arie van der Kooij and I recently completed.⁷ As far as the question of Greek philosophical influence in the Septuagint is concerned, I focus on Stoicism. A contextual approach is adopted, leading to conclusions that have implications for the formulation of a theology of LXX Proverbs.

2. Textual and Thematic Issues

The book of Proverbs has been allocated to Peter Gentry in the Göttingen series, but it will be many years before this publication is completed. In the meantime, the pocket edition of Rahlfs and Hanhart must suffice.⁸

One of the advantages of an exegetical commentary is that one can analyze passages contextually.⁹ This ensures that researchers do not fall into the trap of ad hoc interpretations. In this regard, I will deal with two central issues in wisdom literature, the topos of wisdom, specifically the

---

3. See Cook 2016.
4. See Tov 2010, 22.
5. Gerleman 1950, 1956; D'Hamonville 2000, 194.
6. Cook 2015.
7. Cook and Van der Kooij 2012.
8. Rahlfs and Hanhart 2006.
9. *Text* and *context* should be accounted for in the exegesis of texts. Moreover, this translator had a contextual approach toward the parent text.

role of wisdom. I focus on Prov 2 and the role of the law of Moses in Prov 28, chapters that must act as pilot studies.

3. Wisdom in Proverbs 2

I have demonstrated in various contexts that the person(s) responsible for the book of Proverbs in its Greek guise adopted a fairly systematic approach toward the parent text.[10] As far as the figure of the strange woman (אשה זרה) is concerned, five chapters from the first nine chapters are relevant: Prov 2, 5, 6, 7, and 9.[11] This prominent figure plays a decisive role in the first part of the book. Scholars have divergent perspectives on the strange woman. Some see her as a foreigner, others as a literary figure. Fox interprets her in a literal sense, yet to others she is a personification of foreign wisdom.[12]

In the Hebrew, Prov 2 can be divided into two main parts: the protasis is found in 2:1–4; the rest of the chapter makes up the apodosis. Verses 11 and 16–19 are directly relevant to the issue at stake.

11 βουλὴ καλὴ φυλάξει σε,
ἔννοια δὲ ὁσία τηρήσει σε
11 *good* counsel will guard you,
and holy intent will protect you,

16 τοῦ μακράν σε ποιῆσαι ἀπὸ ὁδοῦ εὐθείας
καὶ ἀλλότριον τῆς δικαίας γνώμης.
16 in order to remove you far from *the straight way*
and to make you a stranger to a righteous opinion.

17 υἱέ, μή σε καταλάβῃ κακὴ βουλὴ
ἡ ἀπολείπουσα διδασκαλίαν νεότητος
καὶ διαθήκην θείαν ἐπιλελησμένη
17 *My son, do not let bad counsel overtake you,*
that which forsakes the teaching of youth
and has forgotten the divine covenant.

Chapter 2 can be divided into two parts that at the same time are contrasting. Verses 1–12 refer to the good realm, and verses 13–22 describe

---

10. Cook and Van der Kooij 2012, 117.
11. Cook 1994, 465.
12. Fox 2000, 361; see also Hengel 1973, 281.

the bad realm. Verses 11 and 17 are significant and contain related but contrasting concepts. Verses 16 and 17 are especially crucial and contain an addition compared to MT and the other witnesses. Verse 16 in MT and LXX read as follows:

להצילך מאשה זרה מנכריה אמריה החליקה
τοῦ μακράν σε ποιῆσαι ἀπὸ ὁδοῦ εὐθείας καὶ ἀλλότριον τῆς δικαίας γνώμης

It is clear that the translator does not deliberately avoid the אשה זרה but reinterprets it in order to make a theological point that is expressed even more clearly by the translation of verse 17. Whereas MT has two strophes, העזבת אלוף נעוריה ואת־ברית אלהיה שכחה, the LXX has three: υἱέ, μή σε καταλάβῃ κακὴ βουλή ἡ ἀπολείπουσα διδασκαλίαν νεότητος καὶ διαθήκην θείαν ἐπιλελησμένη. The first strophe has no equivalent in the other textual witnesses and is, in my view, a deliberate addition by the translator with reference to bad counsel (κακὴ βουλή). The antithesis of this concept, good counsel (βουλὴ καλή), is found in verse 11 and is, as stated above, part of the good realm.[13] I argued elsewhere that these two Greek concepts are not typical Greek but have as their cultural background the Jewish concepts יצר הרע and יצר הטוב.[14] Fox differs from this interpretation, since according to him "the counsels" described here are not internal impulses.[15] I think he does not take seriously enough the fact that the two concepts are part of the two realms, as I demonstrated above. I also think that our interpretations do not differ that much. After all, he concedes that good counsel is wisdom and bad counsel is folly. The difference lies in the fact that he does not accept a further level of abstraction, whereas I argue that bad counsel is indeed a metaphor for foreign wisdom, namely, Hellenism. He also seems to accept that the strange woman is a symbol, what he calls a stable metaphor.[16]

The term βουλή is a significant concept. It occurs frequently in the LXX and eighteen times in Proverbs. In most of the instances in Proverbs it is related to יעץ. Διάνοια also is used frequently in the LXX but only in Proverbs at 2:10, 4:4, 9:10, 13:15, and 27:19. In three cases, it is related to לב. Whereas διάνοια is situated, so to speak, inside the person, in the pas-

---

13. See Odeberg 1943, 78.
14. Cook 1997, 134–39.
15. Fox 2000, 361.
16. Fox 2000, 34 n. 7.

sage under discussion, βουλή is directly related to wisdom. Wisdom enters the διάνοια, and this leads to good counsel that saves one from the bad way. Wisdom in turn comes from the outside and is obtained by studying the law and teaching (see v. 6).

The other side of the coin, the lexeme יצר, is also significant, albeit problematic.[17] It appears forty-four times in the Hebrew Bible as a verb (most often by far in the book of Isaiah) and nine times as a noun. Neither the verb nor the noun appears in Proverbs, and I do not think that it should be retroverted into 2:17. In Gen 6:5 and 8:21 in the Hebrew the term concerns the ideas and plans of humans, and it stated that the יצר of humans is evil. The LXX translated these passages relatively freely; in Gen 6:5 יצר מחשבת is rendered by means of the verb διανοέομαι, and in 8:21 יצר לב האדם רע מנעריו is translated ἔγκειται ἡ διάνοια τοῦ ἀνθρώπου ἐπιμελῶς ἐπὶ τὰ πονηρά. The combination יצר מחשבת also occurs in 1 Chr 29:18, where the Greek equivalent is ἐν διανοίᾳ καρδίας λαοῦ. The noun ἡ διάνοια in turn is also a laden term. It occurs in Prov 2:10 (לב), 4:4 (לב), 9:10 (בינה), 13:15 (–), and 27:19 (לב). It seems to be the place where thinking and ideas take place.

To return to the addition under discussion, I have argued that bad counsel in this context is indeed a metaphor for foreign wisdom, namely, Hellenism. In this regard, I follow Hengel.[18]

In my view, we have a conservative Jewish translator at work[19] who has reused typical Jewish exegetical traditions regarding the good and evil inclinations that, according to Judaism, are found in each person. It is clear that the translator did not intend to avoid the sexual issues inherent in the Hebrew, since in Prov 7 a corresponding phrase is translated literally. I take this interpretation of אשה זרה to be a reference to foreign wisdom in the sense of un-Jewish/non-Israelite wisdom.[20]

Prov 7:5

לשמרך מאשה זרה מנכריה אמריה החליקה

To preserve you from the loose woman,
from the adventuress with her smooth words.

---

17. This paragraph is based upon dialogue between Arie van der Kooij and me.
18. Hengel 1973, 281.
19. See Rösel 2008.
20. Cook 1994, 465. For a different view, see Bledsoe 2016. It must be remembered that the intention of these two articles is different. Bledsoe hardly deals with the Jewishness of this translated unit. His focus is on the "strange" interpretations.

ἵνα σε τηρήσῃ ἀπὸ γυναικὸς ἀλλοτρίας καὶ πονηρᾶς,
ἐάν σε λόγοις τοῖς πρὸς χάριν ἐμβάληται
that she may keep you from a strange and sinful woman,
if she would assail you with words of charm.

In this regard, I find that the view of Yee, who has argued for a literary interpretation of the various speeches—the seductive words of the strange woman, on the one hand, and the words of the father, on the other hand—open interesting perspectives on the understanding of this figure.[21] According to Yee, it is not literal things such as the physical body of the woman that are dangerous but rather her words, her speeches. Hence I argue that also in the LXX it is not the אשה זרה herself who is dangerous but her words, or rather her bad words, her bad counsel.

I have, moreover, argued that bad counsel in this context is indeed a metaphor for foreign wisdom, or Hellenism. I follow Hengel, who states:

> Darauf könnt die Tatsache hinweisen, dass das in Prv. 1–9 häufig auftauchende fremde Weib (2, 16ff; c. 5; 6, 24ff; c. 7) und wohl auch die »Frau Torheit« schon in der Septuaginta von Prv. 2, 16–18 (διδασκαλίαν νεότητος V. 17) sinnbildlich auf die »fremde Weisheit« gedeutet wurden.[22]

However, he is not clear about what this strange wisdom is. To me, it is clear that it refers to the strange wisdom that is the Hellenism of the day.

4. The Law in Proverbs 28

Of special significance is the way the law of Moses is depicted in Prov 28. This chapter contains the highest number of occurrences of the lexeme תורה in Proverbs.

The LXX text of the first nine verses reads as follows:

1 φεύγει ἀσεβὴς μηδενὸς διώκοντος
δίκαιος δὲ ὥσπερ λέων πέποιθεν
2 δι' ἁμαρτίας ἀσεβῶν κρίσεις ἐγείρονται
ἀνὴρ δὲ πανοῦργος κατασβέσει αὐτάς
3 ἀνδρεῖος ἐν ἀσεβείαις συκοφαντεῖ πτωχούς
ὥσπερ ὑετὸς λάβρος καὶ ἀνωφελής

---

21. Yee 1980.
22. Hengel 1973, 281.

4 οὕτως οἱ ἐγκαταλείποντες τὸν νόμον ἐγκωμιάζουσιν ἀσέβειαν
οἱ δὲ ἀγαπῶντες τὸν νόμον περιβάλλουσιν ἑαυτοῖς τεῖχος
5 ἄνδρες κακοὶ οὐ νοήσουσιν κρίμα
οἱ δὲ ζητοῦντες τὸν κύριον συνήσουσιν ἐν παντί
6 κρείσσων πτωχὸς πορευόμενος ἐν ἀληθείᾳ πλουσίου ψευδοῦς
7 φυλάσσει νόμον υἱὸς συνετός
ὃς δὲ ποιμαίνει ἀσωτίαν ἀτιμάζει πατέρα
8 ὁ πληθύνων τὸν πλοῦτον αὐτοῦ μετὰ τόκων καὶ πλεονασμῶν
τῷ ἐλεῶντι πτωχοὺς συνάγει αὐτόν
9 ὁ ἐκκλίνων τὸ οὖς αὐτοῦ τοῦ μὴ εἰσακοῦσαι νόμου
καὶ αὐτὸς τὴν προσευχὴν αὐτοῦ ἐβδέλυκται

1 The impious flees when no one is pursuing,
but the righteous is confident like a lion.
2 By the sin of the impious disputes arise,
but a clever man will quell them.
3 A bold man blackmails the poor with impious acts.
Like a violent and useless rain,
4 so those who forsake the law praise impiety,
but those who love the law *build a wall around themselves*.
5 Evil men will not consider judgment,
but those who seek the Lord will have understanding in everything.
6 Better is a poor person who walks in truth than a rich liar.
7 An intelligent son keeps the law,
but he who feeds debauchery disgraces his father.
8 He who increases his wealth with interest and excess
gathers it for him who has empathy for the poor.
9 He who turns away his ear not to listen to the law—
he, too, has made his prayer abominable.

Again, the examples of contrasts are conspicuous. However, it is especially verse 4 that is crucial for the issue under discussion, as can be observed in the following translation of Prov 28:4:

עזבי תורה יהללו רשע ושמרי תורה יתגרו בם
Those who forsake the law praise the wicked, but those who keep the law struggle against them.

οὕτως οἱ ἐγκαταλείποντες τὸν νόμον ἐγκωμιάζουσιν
ἀσέβειαν οἱ δὲ ἀγαπῶντες τὸν νόμον περιβάλλουσιν ἑαυτοῖς τεῖχος
so those who forsake the law and praise impiety,
but those who love the law *build a wall around themselves*.

There seems to be no logical relationship between the LXX and the Hebrew.[23] It is nevertheless possible that the Hebrew reading (גרה) was understood as גדר ("wall"). Be that as it may, here the law has a protective function toward the righteous. One notes similar traditions in the Letter of Aristeas, which states the following:[24]

> When therefore our lawgiver, equipped by God for insight into all things, has surveyed each particular, he fenced us about with impregnable palisades and with walls of iron [περίφραξεν ἡμας ἀδιακόποις χάραξι καὶ σιδηροῖς τείχεσιν], to the end that we should mingle in no way with any other nations but remain pure in body and soul, free from all vain imaginations, worshiping the one Almighty God above the whole creation. (Let. Aris. 139)

That this is indeed a reference to the cultic laws is clearly observed in Let. Aris. 143: "Therefore lest we should be corrupted by any abomination, or our lives be perverted by evil communications, *he hedged us round on all sides by rules of purity*, affecting alike what we eat, or drink, or touch, or hear or see." Here we thus have an ancient exegetical tradition of the people of God being surrounded by the law in order to preserve them.[25]

These traditions are markedly different from the view found in some later rabbinical writings, for example, the Mishnah, and in even later rabbinical writings such as m. Avot 1:1, according to which the torah must be protected! (The latter used to say three things: Be patient in justice, rear many disciples, and make a fence around the torah).

In addition to these lexemes, the Greek noun νόμος appears as a plus in comparison to the Hebrew in two passages, Prov 9:10 and 13:15, which are highly significant.

Prov 9:10

תחלת חכמה יראת יהוה ודעת קדשים בינה
The fear of the LORD is the beginning of wisdom, and the knowledge of the holy one is insight.

ἀρχὴ σοφίας φόβος κυρίου

---

23. See Cook 1999, 458.
24. See also Cook 1999, 459.
25. The reference to "body and soul" in this passage naturally is an indication that ethical issues are also at stake.

καὶ βουλὴ ἁγίων σύνεσις
τὸ γὰρ γνῶναι νόμον διανοίας ἐστὶν ἀγαθῆς
The beginning of wisdom is the fear of the Lord,
and the counsels of saints is understanding,
for to know the law is the sign of a sound mind.

Prov 13:15

שכל־טוב יתן־חן ודרך בגדים איתן
Good sense wins favor, but the way of the faithless is their ruin.

σύνεσις ἀγαθὴ δίδωσιν χάριν
τὸ δὲ γνῶναι νόμον διανοίας ἐστὶν ἀγαθῆς
ὁδοὶ δὲ καταφρονούντων ἐν ἀπωλείᾳ
Sound discretion gives favor,
and to know the law is the sign of a sound mind,
but the ways of scorners end in destruction.

These passages have an identical addition ("to know the law is the sign of a sound mind") that is part of the translator's systematic application of exegetical perspectives. The only difference between these phrases is that the particle δέ is used in 13:15, whereas 9:10 uses γάρ. This is an indication of the literary approach of the translator, who preferred variation in literary style. Scholars have different views on these additions. In connection with 9:10, de Lagarde thinks that the addition is to be deemed the original.[26] Seeligmann, on the contrary, takes the added stich in 9:10 as a later, secondary addition; he calls it "eine Dublette": "Man hat auf Grund des Kontextes der Übersetzung den Eindruk, dass die zuletzt erwähnte Wiedergabe die ältere ist."[27] I think de Lagarde is correct to take this addition as coming from the hand of the translator. I also do not think it was drawn in secondarily from 13:15, as surmised by Seeligmann.

Be that as it may, double translations are difficult phenomena,[28] and the term *double translation* is used interchangeably with doublet. It is, first, not clear what is meant by such textual phenomena. Talmon presented an exhaustive approach on this matter.[29] His approach was not restricted to the MT but included the versional material, such as the LXX.

---

26. De Lagarde 1863, 30.
27. Seeligmann 1953, 179.
28. Cook 1997, 13.
29. Talmon 1984.

However, he does approach the double translations from the perspective of the Hebrew. He asks pertinent questions in this regard. Is a particular double translation peculiar to the translator, and is it ultimately derived from a Greek or a non-Hebrew tradition? It could have been taken over from an ancient Hebrew tradition. He also distinguishes various categories of double translations: (1) double translations that are the work of copyists who combined alternative renderings of a single Hebrew word or a different expression found in different manuscripts of the version in question; (2) conflate translations of different synonymous readings; (3) translations of double readings that had been incorporated as such in the Hebrew manuscripts used by the translator and whose conflated character escaped his notice or he did not presume to correct them. In these cases double translations derive from the Hebrew. Talshir, again, defines double translations as cases of one item in the MT being matched by two items in the LXX.[30] According to Tov, doublets pertain to single words and pairs of words; as a rule, the two elements of a double translation are juxtaposed in the same verse, although they are occasionally found in adjacent verses.[31]

There are thus various theoretical possibilities as to the origin of double translations. On the one hand, they could have arisen as a result of the transmission history of the text; on the other hand, they could be a device utilized by the original translator.

I think the second option is applicable in the case under discussion. I have demonstrated that this translator indeed makes use of intra-/intertextual readings and hence does consult previous passages, sometimes with a deliberate contention.[32] A crucial example is the quotation from Ps 111 (110):10 in Prov 1:7.[33] The first stich in 9:10 indeed corresponds largely with 1:7, which has the literary and ideological function of indicating where the wise should find wisdom in order to solve interpretational questions.[34] To be sure, the first six verses are closely knit together, inter alia, by the application of the particle τε. This particle has been used sparsely, in verses 2, 3 (2x), 4, and 6 (2x).

---

30. Talshir 1987, 21.
31. Tov 1990.
32. Cook 2006.
33. See my discussion in the Festschrift for Albert Pietersma: Cook 2001.
34. See Cook 1997, 262.

I have argued that it became necessary in the wake of a specific historical situation to stress the importance of the law of Moses. The translator, in other words, warns readers of the inherent "dangers" of foreign wisdom (the Hellenism of the day). One of these prominent dangers was the devaluation of the law of Moses.[35] Proverbs 28:7 is instructive in this regard. It reads: "An intelligent son keeps the law" (φυλάσσει νόμον υἱὸς συνετός).

The relationship between law and wisdom is seemingly at the background of these passages. On account of the added reference to the law, especially 13:15, Seeligmann suggested that there is a metaphorical relationship between law and wisdom. He offers a creative rabbinically based (Sifre Num. 14) interpretation of the first stich in 13:15 (שֵׂכֶל טוֹב יִתֶּן חֵן): "Wenn die Schrift von חֵן redet, so meint sie immer Thorah."[36] Thus, according to him, the translator deliberately added this reference to the law in the present context to identify חן and תורה.

Finally, Weingreen is of the opinion that Ps 111 (110) is deliberately quoted in order to underline the view that knowledge and wisdom are effectively the same attribute of religious fear. Weingreen defines this as rabbinic-type commentary.[37]

5. Greek Philosophical, Platonic Influence

Some scholars have argued that the translator of Proverbs was, in fact, influenced by Greek, philosophical, Platonic ideas. He seemingly had access to Plato and Aristotle. This first-hand knowledge has been interpreted by some scholars that the translator indeed applied aspects of the idea world of the Greeks in the translation. One example is the Stoic ideas that Gerleman located in LXX Proverbs. Gerleman argued that the addition of the adjectives καλή and κακή in conjunction with the noun βουλή in Prov 2:11 and 17 is evidence of Stoic influence: "The Greek translator thinks it necessary to emphasise their religious contents by making small alterations in wording."[38] These alterations are, according to him, based upon Stoic religious perspectives. However, I have demonstrated that they are actually based on Jewish, prerabbinic perspectives, since the Greek concepts represent the well-known Jewish tradition of the good and evil

---

35. See Cook 1994, 457.
36. Seeligmann 1953, 179.
37. See Weingreen 1973, 407–15.
38. Gerleman 1950, 19.

inclinations (יצר הרע and יצר הטוב) inherent in humans.[39] My argument is that the translator was influenced by Greek culture as far as the external form is concerned but not concerning the idea world.[40]

More recent views include those of Evangelia Dafni and Russel Gmirkin. Dafni is probably the most outspoken proponent of correspondences between the Semitic world of Gen 1–11, the Hellenistic world, and the classical world of Plato. In an article on Plato's *Symposium* and the LXX, her point of departure is that

> Plato's teachings have never lost their dominance in the intellectual scene or the general education system of the Hellenistic world. Therefore one cannot seriously dispute the encounter of the Old Testamental thoughts with Plato's thoughts. The crucial question is: Did the Septuagint (LXX) manage to absorb linguistic forms from Plato's work without at the same time absorbing basic Platonic, philosophical concepts? The LXX translators wanted to proclaim the Old Testament belief to the Hellenistic world via the Greek language. At the same time they wanted to prevent that polytheistic concepts were introduced into the world of the Old Testament via the language. The LXX has thus adopted the refined forms of expression of Plato's work, which represents the first and only completely handed-down philosophic work of the antique Greeks, and changed them as necessary. The Platonic linguistic forms in the LXX can be seen as a type of Old Testamental meta-language of great theological importance. This meta-language was created due to philosophic reflection about linguistic and mental constructs of the Old Testament.[41]

These statements are, to say the least, speculative. The same critique can be expressed against the recent work by Gmirkin.[42]

---

39. See Cook 2007; and Rosen-Zvi 2008, 527, who missed the point of the article, namely, the dating of the concepts under discussion.

40. On the external form, see Cook 1997, 201–46. Here I discuss Prov 8 and find no evidence of Greek philosophical ideas, such as Platonic and/or Stoic views, in this classic creational passage. On the idea world, see Skehan and Di Lella, 1987, 48 "Sanders offers a satisfying explanation of Ben Sira's manner of borrowing from Greek sources. Ben Sira used Hellenic material only when it suited his Jewish purpose...."

41. Dafni 2006, 584.

42. Gmirkin 2016.

6. Proverbs 8

This chapter contains one of the classic passages on creation in the Hebrew Bible. The other one is Job 28,[43] where the author tries his best to understand the creation. Proverbs 8 has been composed beautifully and has a structure of four sections in the Hebrew: 8:1–11, 12–21, 22–31, and a peroration in 32–36.[44] The first and third sections are made up of twenty-two lines, but the middle section has only twenty-one lines. However, this is the result of the transmission history of this chapter.[45] This chapter also contains crucial exegetical renderings, many of which seek to emphasize God's omnipotence. Here I will deal only with verse 30 against the larger background of verses 22–31.

Prov 8:30[46]

ואהיה אצלו אמון
ואהיה שעשעים יום יום
משחקת לפניו בכל־עת

Then I was beside him, like a master workman,
and I was daily his delight,
rejoicing before him always....

ἤμην παρ' αὐτῷ ἁρμόζουσα,
ἐγὼ ἤμην ᾗ προσέχαιρεν.
καθ' ἡμέραν δὲ εὐφραινόμην ἐν προσώπῳ αὐτοῦ ἐν παντὶ καιρῷ

I was beside him, fitting together;
it is I who was the one in whom he took delight.
And each day I was glad in his presence at every moment....

This verse is the *locus classicus* as far as arguments concerning the so-called Stoic coloring of the LXX. The verbal form ἁρμόζουσα has been taken as "to join, to accommodate, bring into harmony," which is then seen as an idea "indigenous to the Stoic view of nature."[47] The Greek lexeme ἁρμόζουσα occurs in only ten LXX passages: 2 Kgdms 6:5 (*) and 14 (עץ); Ps 151:2 (–); Prov 8:30 (אמון); 17:7 (נאוה); 19:14 (שכל); 25:11 (אפן); only in the corrected

---

43. See Cook 2010b.
44. See Cook 1997, 201.
45. See Cook 1997, 208f.
46. See Cook 1997, 33–50.
47. Gerleman 1950, 26.

wording of Codex Sinaiticus); Nah 3:8 (אמון); 2 Macc 14:22; and 3 Macc 1:19. It is thus used to render different lexemes in Proverbs. In Prov 17:7, the Hebrew contains a contrast between the speech of a fool and of a king:

לא־נאוה לנבל שפת־יתר אף כי־לנדיב שפת־שקר
οὐχ ἁρμόσει ἄφρονι χείλη πιστά οὐδὲ δικαίῳ χείλη ψευδῆ
Faithful lips will not suit a fool, nor false lips the righteous.

The idea of "fitting" clearly prevails. In Prov 19:14, the Hebrew and Greek read:

בית והון נחלת אבות ומיהוה אשה משכלת
House and wealth are inherited from parents, but a prudent wife is from the Lord
οἶκον καὶ ὕπαρξιν μερίζουσιν πατέρες παισίν, παρὰ δὲ θεοῦ ἁρμόζεται γυνὴ ἀνδρί
Fathers distribute house and substance to their children, but a woman is joined to a man by God.

Nahum 3:8 is the closest parallel to the passage under discussion.

התיטבי מנא אמון הישבה ביארים מים סביב לה אשר־חיל ים מים חומתה
Are you better than Thebes that sat by the Nile, with water around her, her rampart a sea and water her wall?

ἑτοίμασαι μερίδα, ἅρμοσαι χορδήν, ἑτοίμασαι μερίδα, Αμων ἡ κατοικοῦσα ἐν ποταμοῖς, ὕδωρ κύκλῳ αὐτῆς, ἧς ἡ ἀρχὴ θάλασσα καὶ ὕδωρ τὰ τείχη αὐτῆς
Prepare a portion, tune the cord, prepare a portion for Ammon; she that dwells among the rivers, water is around her, whose dominion is the sea, and whose walls are water.[48]

The Greek seems to be an interpretation of the Hebrew, and the verb ἁρμόσει could therefore be related to אָמוֹן, as suggested by Hatch-Redpath. The problem is that the Hebrew lexeme is also rendered literally as Αμων. In extrabiblical writings, this lexeme is used with other connotations. In Solon 36.17 it appears in the sense of "adapt, accommodate," and in Hegesippus Comicus 1.19 the nuance of "to prepare" applies. Also the sense of "joining, fitting together" occurs in classical Greek sources. It is used,

---

48. See Cook 1997, 230.

inter alia, to describe the work of a joiner in Homer, *Od.* 5.247, and Pindar, *Nem.* 8.11, applies it in the meaning of "to regulate, set in order, govern." It also appears in the meaning of "fitting," as in clothes or armor that fit well (Pindar, *Pyth.* 4.80).

It is therefore not easy to determine what the translator actually had in mind in Prov 8:30. The Hebrew lexeme אָמוֹן is already a problematic one, for it appears only twice in the Hebrew Bible (Jer 52:15; Prov 8:30). אָמוֹן as a proper noun is used for the Egyptian god Amun, and it can also be related to the root אמן ("support, assist, bind together"). A number of scholars have connected it to אָמָן ("master workman, craftsman"),[49] which is also how the author of the Wisdom of Solomon understood it. In Wis 7:21 and 8:6, wisdom is described as τεχνῖτις. It is not immediately evident how the author arrived at this interpretation. Taking into account the Hellenistic milieu in which he lived, it is equally possible that he could have interpreted it in a Platonic manner according to the idea of the Demiurge or that he simply understood the Hebrew אָמוֹן in that sense.[50] Because of the limited application of the Greek verb, it remains difficult to decide what nuance the translator of Proverbs actually had in mind. Consequently, the context must provide the decisive evidence.

First because of the limited evidence, I find it unacceptable to formulate a theory of possible external influence, as was done by Gerleman regarding Stoic perspectives allegedly adopted by the translator. Hengel followed Gerleman in this regard and on the basis of the passage under discussion referred to "popularphilosophischen Züge."[51] Indications of such signs are, according to him, the preexistence of wisdom (Prov 8:22), the fact that she was created for the sake of God's works (8:22), and the question of wisdom experiencing joy (8:30b and 31). Hengel poses the question whether the description of wisdom is not to be seen "als eine Art von Weltseele," which is the way it functions in Plato's *Timeaus*.[52] He opts for this explanation because the typical Stoic notion of the identification of God and matter would certainly have been a problem for a Jewish translator. According to Hengel, the Platonic version with its reference to Demiurges as personal creation gods would have been more acceptable to Jews. In the final analysis, I do not regard the small number of references

---

49. See Scott 1965, 72.
50. See Hengel 1973, 292.
51. See Gerleman 1950, 26; Hengel 1973, 285; Keel 1974, 17.
52. Hengel 1973, 293.

to typical Stoic or popular philosophical traits mentioned by these scholars as convincing evidence. The connotations of "to join, prepare, harmonize" for ἁρμόζουσα, which are certainly found in extrabiblical writings, need not be reconstructed in this context. In my view, the verb ἁρμόζουσα actually describes wisdom's relationship with the creator. It is not used to depict wisdom's relation to creation. This relationship is described in the rest of verse 30 as well. The Greek ἐγὼ ἤμην ᾗ προσέχαιρεν ("I was the one in whom he took delight") is less ambiguous than the MT. Conspicuous is the addition of the personal pronoun ἐγώ. It could be a case of stressing the subject, underlining the privileged role wisdom actually had beside God. The final hemistich is a literal rendering of the Hebrew.

The emphasis of the whole pericope in its Greek version is on God's activity in the creation process. Wisdom has no other role than that of being happy and joyful, which also need not be seen as an exclusive characteristic of Stoicism. Therefore, I translate ἁρμόζουσα with "fitting together," a nuance that appears in specific contexts. In my view, the translator underscores the creative role of God in the creation.

7. Application

From the preceding discussion it should be clear that the Septuagint of Proverbs is first and foremost a Jewish document. Hence, when it comes to the application, that is, the formulation of a theology of LXX Proverbs, there is first a question of discontinuity. The law of Moses is primarily to be approached from a Judaic perspective. The depiction of the law as a wall surrounding the righteous is a typical Jewish image. The righteous can therefore be no one else than Jewish righteous individuals.

The addition of the lexeme *torah* in this book is also to be interpreted as a Jewish motivated addition. To be sure, my interpretation of the provenance of this book,[53] if correct, can be deemed as Jewish motivated. Thus part of the discontinuity. This has implications for the seventh conclusion by Rösel.[54]

Having said that, I have to agree with Rösel's statement, after accepting the reality that the LXX is fundamentally a Jewish document: "Das schließt aber nicht aus, dass man sich der LXX nicht mit spezifisch christ-

---

53. Cook and Van der Kooij 2012, 117.
54. Rösel 2018a, 16.

lichen Fragestellungen nähern kann."⁵⁵ I would, nevertheless, add that this should be done with care. I remain skeptical of all theological interpretations involving the understanding of the OG based on the reception of this text.

8. Conclusion

The Septuagint of Proverbs is fundamentally a Jewish document. Its theology can therefore not be exclusively Christian. The view of Siegert is worth noting in this regard, however, with a provisio, as can be gleaned from the following statement by Rösel: "In eine ähnliche Richtung geht die Definition von Folker Siegert in Bezug auf das hellenistische Judentum, die explizit die Septuaginta mit einbezieht: 'hellenistisch-jüdische Theologie … ist … denkerisches Bemühen um Gottes Wort.'"⁵⁶ As far as LXX Proverbs is concerned, in the light of the above, I would rather say not Hellenistic-Jewish but *Jewish*-Hellenistic theology.

Bibliography

Bledsoe, Seth A. 2016. "'Strange' Interpretations in LXX Proverbs," Pages 671–93 in *XV Congress of the International Organization for Septuagint and Cognate Studies: Munich, 2013*. Edited by Wolfgang Kraus, Michaël N. van der Meer, and Martin Meiser. SCS 64. Atlanta: SBL Press.

Cook, Johann. 1994. "אִשָּׁה זָרָה (Prov 1–9 in the Septuagint): A Metaphor for Foreign Wisdom?" *ZAW* 106:458–76.

———. 1997. *The Septuagint of Proverbs: Jewish and/or Hellenistic Proverbs? Concerning the Hellenistic Colouring of LXX Proverbs*. VTSup 69. Leiden: Brill.

———. 1999. "The Law of Moses in Septuagint Proverbs." *VT* 49:448–61.

———. 2001. "Inter-textual Relations between the Septuagint Versions of the Psalms and Proverbs." Pages 218–28 in *The Old Greek Psalter: Studies in honour of Albert Pietersma*. Edited by Robert J. V Hiebert, Claude E. Cox, and Peter J. Gentry. JSOTSup 332. Sheffield: Sheffield Press.

---

55. Rösel 2018a, 16.
56. Rösel 2018b, 5; see also Siegert 1998, 11.

———. 2006. "Intertextual Readings in the Septuagint." Pages 117–34 in *The New Testament Interpreted: Essays in Honour of Bernard C. Lategan*. Edited by Johan C. Thom, Jeremy Punt, and Cilliers Breytenbach. NovTSup 124. Leiden: Brill.

———. 2007. "The Origin of the Tradition of the היצר הטב and היצר הרע." *JSJ* 38:80–91.

———. 2010a. "Towards the Formulation of a Theology of the Septuagint." Pages 621–40 in *Congress Volume: Ljubljana, 2007*. Edited by André Lemaire. VTSup 133. Leiden: Brill.

———. 2010b. "Were the Septuagint Versions of Job and Proverbs Translated by the Same Person?" *HS* 51:129–56.

———. 2015. "A Theology of the Greek Version of Proverbs." *HTS Teologiese Studies/Theological Studies* 71.1. doi: 10.4102/hts.v71i1.2971.

———. 2016. "Between Text and Interpretation: An Exegetical Commentary on LXX Proverbs." Pages 653–70 in *XV Congress of the International Organization for Septuagint and Cognate Studies: Munich, 2013*. Edited by Wolfgang Kraus, Michaël N. van der Meer, and Martin Meiser. SCS 64. Atlanta: SBL Press.

Cook, Johann, and Arie van der Kooij. 2012. *Law, Prophets, and Wisdom: On the Provenance of Translators and Their Books in the Septuagint Version*. CBET 68. Peeters: Leuven.

D'Hamonville, David-Marc. 2000. *Les Proverbes*. BdA 17. Paris: Cerf.

Dafni, Evangelia. 2006. "Genesis 1–11 und Platos Symposion: Überlegungen zum Austausch von hebräischem und griechischem Sprach- und Gedankengut in der Klassik und im Hellenismus." *OTE* 19:584–632.

Fox, Michael V. 2000. *Proverbs 1–9: A New Translation with Introduction and Commentary*. AB 18A. New York: Doubleday.

Gerleman, Gilles, 1950. "The Septuagint Proverbs as a Hellenistic Document." *OTS* 8:15–27.

———. 1956. *Studies in the Septuagint III: Proverbs*. Lund: Gleerup.

Gmirkin, Russell E. 2016. *Plato and the Creation of the Hebrew Bible*. Copenhagen International Seminar. New York: Routledge.

Hengel, Martin, 1973. *Judentum und Hellenismus: Studien zu ihrer Begegnung unter besonderer Berücksichtigung Palästinas bis zur Mitte des 2. Jh. V. Chr*. WUNT 10. Tübingen: Mohr Siebeck.

Keel, Othmar, 1974. *Die Weisheit spielt vor Gott: Ein ikonographischer Beitrag zur Deutung des mᵉsaḥäqät in Sprüche 8,30f*. Freiburg: Universitätsverlag; Göttingen: Vandenhoeck & Ruprecht.

Lagarde, Paul A. de. 1863. *Anmerkungen zur griechischen Übersetzung der Proverbien*. Leipzig: Brockhaus.

Odeberg, Hugo. 1943. *Pharisaism and Christianity*. St Louis: Concordia.

Rahlfs, Alfred, and Robert Hanhart. 2006. *Septuaginta: Vetus Testamentum Graecum Auctoritate Scientiarum Gottingensis Editum*. Stuttgart: Deutsche Bibelgesellschaft.

Rösel, Martin, 2008. "Schreiber, Übersetzer, Theologen: Die Septuaginta als Dokument der Schrift-, Lese- und Übersetzungskulturen des Judentum. Pages 83–102 in *Die Septuaginta – Texte, Kontexte, Lebenswelten*. Edited by Martin Karrer, Wolfgang Kraus, and Martin Meiser. WUNT 219. Tübingen: Mohr Siebeck.

———. 2018a. "Projekt: Theologie der Septuaginta: Forschungsgeschichte." Unpublished document.

———. 2018b. "Projekt: Theologie der Septuaginta: Methodische Grundlegung." Unpublished document.

———. 2018c. "Eine Theologie der Septuaginta? Präzisierungen und Pointierungen." Pages 25–44 in *Theologie und Textgeschichte: Septuaginta und Massoretischer Text als Äusserungen theologischer Reflexion*. Edited by Frank Ueberschaer, Thomas Wagner, and Jonathan Miles Robker. WUNT 407. Tübingen: Mohr Siebeck.

Rosen-Zvi, Ishay. 2008. "Two Rabbinic Inclinations? Rethinking a Scholarly Dogma." *JSJ* 39:513–39.

Scott, R. B. Y. 1965. *Proverbs*. AB 18. New York: Doubleday.

Seeligmann, Isac L. 1953. "Vorauszetzungen der Midraschexegese." Pages 150–81 in *Congress Volume: Copenhagen, 1953*. Edited by G. W. Anderson et al. VTSup 1. Leiden: Brill.

Siegert, Folker. 1998. "Die hellenistisch-jüdische Theologie als Forschungsaufgabe." Pages 9–30 in *Internationales Josephus-Kolloquium: Münster, 1997*. Edited by Folgert Siegert and Jürgen U. Kalms. Münsteraner judaistische Studien 2. Münster: Lit.

Talmon, Shemaryahu, 1984. "Double Readings in the Massoretic Text." *Textus* 1:144–84.

Talshir, Zipora, 1987. "Double Translations in the Septuagint." Pages 21–63 in *VI Congress of the International Organization for Septuagint and Cognate Studies*. SCS 23. Atlanta: Scholars Press.

Tov, Emanuel. 1990. "Recensional Differences between the Masoretic Text and the Septuagint of Proverbs." Pages 43–56 in *Of Scribes and Scrolls: Studies on the Hebrew Bible, Intertestamental Judaism, and Christian Origins Presented to John Strugnell*. Edited by Harold W. Attridge, John

J. Collins, and Thomas H. Tobin. Lanham, MD: University Press of America.

———. 2010. "Reflections on the Septuagint with Special Attention Paid to the Post-pentateuchal Translations." Pages 1–22 in *Die Septuaginta – Texte, Theologien, Einflüsse*. Edited by Wolfgang Kraus, Martin Karrer, and Martin Meiser. WUNT 252. Tübingen: Mohr Siebeck.

Weingreen, Jacob. 1973. "Rabbinic Type Commentary in the LXX Version of Proverbs." Pages 407–15 in vol. 1 of *Proceedings of the Sixth World Congress of Jewish Studies*. Edited by Avigdor Shinan. Jerusalem: World Union of Jewish Studies.

Yee, Gale A. 1980. "An Analysis of Prov 8:21–22 according to Style and Structure." *ZAW* 94:58–66.

"To Shine" or "To Show"?
A Conceptual and Theological Exploration of Light in the LXX

Joel D. Ruark

ABSTRACT: This essay examines the metaphorical use of the physical concept of light in the Greek Septuagint in comparison with the Hebrew Masoretic Text, with specific focus on the conceptualization of the light of God's face. The LXX is more diverse than the MT in its lexical symbols for the concept of light but utilizes the same foundational conceptual metaphors: WISDOM IS LIGHT and LIFE IS LIGHT. The chapter explores some comparative trends regarding how the LXX translates the concept of light from its Hebrew *Vorlage* in comparison with the MT and draws some methodological and theological conclusions of a comparative linguistic approach toward a sound methodology for a theology of the LXX.

Introduction

As a Hebraist, I approach the topic of a methodology for a theology of the Septuagint (LXX) via comparative semantics, working from a cognitive linguistic paradigm and using the topic of light as a case study. In this chapter, I will examine the use of light as a theological metaphor in the Old Testament through the lens of cognitive semantics: first comparing the linguistic construal of the concept of light in the Hebrew Masoretic Text (MT) with the linguistic construal in the Greek LXX, then identifying some implications of the conceptual similarities/differences toward a specific theological question in the LXX. To do this, I will start with a brief lexical survey and then move "upward" through concentric circles of conceptual meaning from the less abstract to the more abstract in accordance with conceptual metaphor theory (see below). I will then explore some of the similarities and differences between the apparent conceptualizations of light in the Greek LXX versus the Hebrew MT. Finally, I will draw out some methodological and theological implications concerning the understanding and translation of the specific concept "the light of God's face" in the Old Testament.

The principles of cognitive semantics affirm that semantic meaning in language is organized according to prototype structures with "fuzzy" and overlapping boundaries.[1] Zoltán Kövecses, a prominent linguist who specializes in the phenomena of metonymy and metaphor in human cognition and language, has defined conceptual metaphor theory as "a view of metaphor in which metaphorical meaning construction is simply a matter of how our metaphors arise from correlations in experience … or from similarities between experiential domains."[2] In other words, the conceptual theory of metaphor posits that humans "typically conceptualize the nonphysical in terms of the physical—that is, we conceptualize the less clearly delineated in terms of the more clearly delineated."[3] Thus, when the Old Testament uses light as a metaphor for wisdom, for example, the conceptualization of wisdom is cognitively dependent in some way on the conceptualization of light as light actually operates in the physical world. One can say that light is a *vehicle* concept used to conceptualize the *target* concept of wisdom; the vehicle concept is less abstract, and the target concept is more abstract. I have argued elsewhere that two of the foundational metaphors operative in the Old Testament (both the MT and LXX) that use the concept of light are WISDOM IS LIGHT and LIFE IS LIGHT.[4] In both cases, light is the vehicle concept: wisdom is the target concept for the first metaphor; life is the target concept for the second.

The specific theological problem targeted by this chapter concerns the meaning of the verb ἐπιφαίνω ("to appear, shine") in reference to the concept of the light of God's face in numerous Old Testament passages. In this specific context, does the verb express the concept of illumination ("to shine") or the concept of visibility ("to show")? The standard lexica list both meanings, although Montanari allows only variations of the concept of visibility for this particular verb.[5] NETS alternately trans-

---

1. Rosch 1973, 1975; Rosch and Mervis 1975; Lakoff 1987, 1–76; Taylor 1989, 51–69; Dirven and Verspoor 2004, 25–48; Kövecses 2005; Lewandowska-Tomaszczyk 2007; Riemer 2010, 46–81, 136–71, 224–59.

2. Kövecses 2015, 1.

3. Lakoff and Johnson 1980, 59. See also Grady 2007; Fauconnier and Turner 2008; Ritchie 2013, 68–87; Kövecses 2015, 73–96.

4. Ruark 2017, 89–95.

5. See LSJ, s.v. "ἐπιφαίνω," 669; BDAG, s.v. "ἐπιφαίνω," 385; Montanari 2015, 801.

lates both meanings in the LXX: Num 6:25, "*make* your face *shine*"; Pss 31 (30):17, "*Shine* your face"; 67 (66):2, "*display* your face"; 80 (79):4, 8, 20, "*show* your face"; 119 (118):135, "*make* your face *shine*" (emphasis added). I will argue that the verb ἐπιφαίνω in these instances most likely means *to shine*, as per the Hebrew MT, but that further investigation is warranted concerning the semantic value of the verb and its cognates in reference to specific situational contexts in ancient Greek literature.

Lexical Survey

The LXX is more diverse than the MT in the lexical symbols it uses for the concept of light. As might be expected, the Hebrew lexeme אוֹר (consisting of a primitive noun, denominative verb, and a derivative noun) in the MT loosely correlates to the Greek lexical root ΦΩ- in the LXX, which includes the following terms: φῶς ("light"); φωτίζω ("to shine, appear"); φωστήρ ("luminary"); φωτισμός ("illumination"); διαφωτίζω ("to enlighten"); also φωτεινός ("shining, bright") twice in Sir 17:31; 23:19.[6] The primitive noun אוֹר ("light") in the MT most often reads as the noun φῶς in the LXX (102/122 attestations),[7] five times as the noun φωτισμός,[8] and once each as the verbs

---

6. I have used the Hebrew lexeme for light as the point of departure for this study because of the extremely primitive nature of the concept of light. The noun אוֹר in Biblical Hebrew is biconsonantal, lacking a triconsonantal counterpart, following a general but not universal trend in languages where semantically primitive concepts (e.g., body parts) are symbolized by shorter lexical words and characterized by certain other cognitive and linguistic features. See Rosch, Mervis, Gray, Johnson, and Boyes-Braem 1976; see also Dirven and Verspoor 2004, 127–34; Rohrer 2007. This accords with one of the axioms of the cognitive approach to language, that "simplicity of cognition is reflected in simplicity of form" (Lakoff 1987, 60). This suggests that the relationship between the lexical symbol אוֹר and the concept of light in the conceptual world of a Hebrew speaker is quite close and that cognitive shifts would be more readily reflected by lexical shifts, both in the Hebrew *Vorlage* and (perhaps) in the Greek translated text. Thus if one wants to know what an ancient Israelite thought about light, it is only natural to start by examining the lexeme אוֹר in Biblical Hebrew.

7. Gen 1:3 (2x), 4 (2x), 5, 18; Exod 10:23; Judg 16:2; 1 Kgdms 25:34, 36; 2 Kgdms 17:22; 23:4; 4 Kgdms 7:9; Esth 8:16; Pss 4:7; 36 (35):10 (2x); 37 (36):6; 38 (37):11; 43 (42):3; 49 (48):20; 56 (55):14; 89 (88):16; 97 (96):11; 104 (103):2; 112 (111):4; 119 (118):105; 136 (135):7; 139 (138):12; 148:3; Job 3:16, 20; 12:22, 25; 17:12; 18:5, 6, 18; 24:16; 26:10; 28:11; 29:3, 24; 33:28, 30; 36:32; 37:3, 11, 15, 21; 38:15, 19; Prov 4:18; 6:23; 13:9; 16:15; Eccl 2:13; 11:7; 12:2; Hos 6:5; Amos 5:18, 20; 8:9; Mic 7:9; Hab 3:4, 11; Zeph 3:5; Zech 14:6, 7; Isa 2:5; 5:20 (2x); 9:1 (2x); 10:17; 13:10 (2x); 18:4; 30:26 (3x);

φωτίζω (Mic 7:8) and διαφωτίζω (2 Esd 18:3, but ὄρθρου ["dawn"] in 1 Esd 9:41). The denominative verb אוֹר ("to shine, brighten") in the MT less often reads as the verb φωτίζω in the LXX (16/43 attestations).[9] Of the nineteen attestations of the derivative noun מָאוֹר ("luminary") in the MT, five read as the noun φῶς;[10] four as the noun φωστήρ (Gen 1:14, 16 [3x]); once as the noun φωτισμός (Ps 90 [89]:8); and once as a participle of the verb φωτίζω (Num 4:9). In total, the family of words from the lexical root ΦΩ- account for 136 of the 186 attestations of the lexeme אור in the MT (73.1 percent).[11]

The lexical data show a few general trends regarding the use of specific terms to describe certain referential contexts. There appear to be two primary pairs of synonymous terms: the verbal pair φωτίζω and φαίνω (both meaning "to shine"); and the nominal pair φωτισμός and φαῦσις (both meaning "illumination"). The primary difference between the individual items in these pairs is the specific form of the lexical root, that is, the apparently more primitive root ΦΑ- versus the derivative root ΦΩ-.[12] Excluding the noun φῶς, which in the LXX is disproportionately attested much more frequently than other terms from the same lexical root, the number of attestations of the lexical roots ΦΩ- and ΦΑ- as apparent translations from the Hebrew lexeme אור are roughly similar.[13] The Hebrew noun אוֹר appears five times as the noun φωτισμός and once as the verb φωτίζω; and twice as the verb διαφαύσκω and once as the verb φαίνω; the *hiphil* stem of the Hebrew verb אור appears twelve times as the verb φωτίζω; and six

---

42:6, 16; 45:7; 49:6; 51:4; 58:8, 10; 59:9; 60:1, 3, 19 (2x), 20; Jer 4:23; 13:16; 25:10; 31:35 (38:36) (2x); Lam 3:2; Ezek 32:7, 8.

8. Pss 27 (26):1; 44 (43):4; 78 (77):14; 139 (138):11; Job 3:9.

9. Num 8:2; 1 Kgdms 29:10; 1 Esd 8:76; 2 Esd 19:12, 19; Pss 13 (12):4; 18 (17):29; 19 (18):9; 76 (75):5; 105 (104):39; 119 (118):130; 139 (138):12; Prov 4:18; Eccl 8:1; Isa 60:1, 19.

10. Exod 27:20; 35:14; 39:16; Lev 24:2; Num 4:16.

11. This includes the Masoretic *qere* reading of 1 Sam 14:27.

12. According to Metzger (1998, 70), φῶς is a contracted form of the word φάος. The remainder of words in the LXX within the family of the lexical root ΦΩ- are then derivatives from the primitive noun φῶς.

13. That is, twenty-nine attestations of the lexical root ΦΩ- versus twenty-one attestations of the lexical root ΦΑ-. These twenty-one occurrences include the verb φαίνω (Gen 1:15, 17; Exod 25:37; Pss 77 [76]:19; 97 [96]:4; Ezek 32:7, 8), the verb ἐπιφαίνω (Num 6:25; Pss 31 [30]:17; 67 [66]:2; 80 [79]:4, 8, 20; 118 [117]:27; 119 [118]:135), the verb διαφαύσκω (Gen 44:3; Judg 19:26; 1 Kgdms 14:36; 2 Kgdms 2:32), and the noun φαῦσις (Gen 1:15; Ps 74 [73]:16).

times as the verb φαίνω and eight times as the verb ἐπιφαίνω; the *qal* stem appears three times as the verb φωτίζω; and twice as the verb διαφαύσκω. The derivative Hebrew noun מָאוֹר appears once as the noun φωτισμός and once as the verb φωτίζω; and twice as the noun φαῦσις. As a general principle, when expressing the Hebrew construal of the concept of light, the Greek lexical roots ΦΩ- and ΦΑ- appear to be used synonymously.

There seems to be no definitive organizing principle concerning the selection of specific Greek terms to render the presumed Hebrew *Vorlage* other than a general trend to use certain words to describe the concept of light (and its lexical corollaries) in certain situational contexts. The verb διαφαύσκω ("to dawn") always describes the dawning of the day, although not to the exclusion of other Greek verbs. The lexical root ΦΩ- is utilized when referring to the "light of the eyes" and never any form of the lexical root ΦΑ-, but again, not to the exclusion of other verbs. Most important for this study, the LXX nearly always uses the verb ἐπιφαίνω to describe the "shining of God's face," the only exception being Dan 9:17, although Theodotion's version also reads ἐπιφαίνω. Furthermore, this also suggests that the LXX translators did not use formal one-to-one equivalence when translating terms related to light, even though they plausibly could have. The primitive noun אוֹר in Hebrew corresponds quite well to the noun φῶς in Greek, likewise for the verbs אוֹר and φωτίζω as well as the derivative nouns מָאוֹר and φωστήρ. However, the LXX exhibits significant "cross-pollination" between these terms as well as between the broader word families from the lexical roots ΦΩ- and ΦΑ-, as described above.

Conceptual Analysis

The lexical data examined in the previous section show two different thresholds in the degree of correspondence between the prototypical construals of the concept of light in the Hebrew MT and the Greek LXX. First, the correspondence between the Hebrew noun אוֹר and the Greek noun φῶς forms a dense *prototypical core*, accounting for a total 102/186 attestations (54.8 percent). In this core group of attestations, the specific referential concepts include: celestial light (i.e., the sun, moon, stars, and the light which comes from them), with a staggering sixty-six attestations;[14]

---

14. Gen 1:18; Exod 10:23; Judg 16:2; 1 Kgdms 25:34, 36; 2 Kgdms 17:22; 23:4; 4 Kgdms 7:9; Pss 36 (35):10; 37 (36):6; 38 (37):11; 49 (48):20; 56 (55):14; 97 (96):11; 112 (111):4; 136 (135):7; 139 (138):12; 148:3; Job 3:16, 20; 12:22; 17:12; 18:18; 24:16; 26:10;

lightning, with four attestations;[15] firelight, with seven attestations;[16] divine light, with three attestations;[17] "the light of the eyes," with one attestation (Ps 38 [37]:11); "the light of the face," with four attestations;[18] light as a generic substance, with four attestations;[19] and, finally, references to light where the specific physical referent cannot be conclusively determined, with thirteen attestations.[20] For many of these attestations, the concept of light (especially sunlight and/or firelight) also serves as a vehicle concept for some metaphorical target concept such as wisdom or life (both of which entail the concepts of emotional pleasantness and moral righteousness), sometimes both simultaneously.[21] This high degree of congruity between the most cognitively primitive words for light in Hebrew and Greek is strong anecdotal evidence that the Greek translators understood the Hebrew concept of light; that is, they correctly interpreted the lexical symbol אור. At the very least, this congruity demonstrates that the LXX translators were not generally confused by the Hebrew word, although this does not necessarily preclude the possibility of misunderstanding in some cases. In other words, perhaps the LXX translators did not understand correctly every attestation of אור in their Hebrew *Vorlage*, but they were certainly not "shooting in the dark," so to speak.

Second, the correspondence between the broader Hebrew lexeme אור and the pair of Greek lexical roots ΦΩ- and ΦΑ- forms a *prototypical cloud*, accounting for a total 157/186 attestations (84.4 percent). The referential concepts in this prototypical cloud are exactly the same as in the prototypical core, but there are markedly fewer attestations outside the

---

28:11; 33:28, 30; 37:21; 38:19; Prov 4:18; Hos 6:5; Amos 5:18, 20; 8:9; Mic 7:9; Hab 3:4, 11; Zeph 3:5; Isa 2:5; 9:1 (2x); 13:10 (2x); 18:4; 30:26 (3x); 42:6; 45:7; 49:6; 51:4; 58:8, 10; 59:9; 60:1, 3, 19 (2x), 20; Jer 4:23; 31:35 (38:36) (2x); Lam 3:2; Ezek 32:7, 8.

15. Job 36:32; 37:3, 11, 15.
16. Ps 119 (118):105; Job 18:5, 6; 29:3; Prov 6:23; 13:9; Jer 25:10.
17. Pss 43 (42):3; 104 (103):2; Isa 10:17.
18. Pss 4:7, 89 (88):16; Job 29:24; Prov 16:15.
19. Eccl 2:13; 11:7; 12:2; Isa 42:16.9
20. Gen 1:3 (2x), 4 (2x), 5; Esth 8:16; Ps 36 (35):10; Job 12:25; 38:15; Isa 5:20 (2x); Zech 14:6, 7.
21. Esth 8:16; Pss 4:7; 36 (35):10; 38 (37):11; 43 (42):3; 89 (88):16; 97 (96):11; 104 (103):2; 112 (111):4; 119 (118):105; Job 12:22, 25; 17:12; 18:5, 6; 29:3; 38:15; Prov 6:23; 13:9; Hos 6:5; Amos 5:18, 20; Mic 7:9; Isa 2:5; 5:20 (2x); 9:1 (2x); 49:6; 51:4; 58:8, 10; 59:9; 60:1; Jer 13:16; Lam 3:2.

core (55) than inside it (102).²² Celestial light remains the most commonly attested referential concept in the prototypical cloud (89x) in comparison with lightning (6x), firelight (21x), divine light (6x), "the light of the eyes" (4x), and "the light of the face" (14x), which further strengthens the conclusions from the data evinced in the prototypical core (see paragraph above). Again, this expanded congruity of prototypicality does not prove conclusively that the LXX translators always understood correctly the Hebrew lexeme אור, but it reasonably demonstrates that they were not confused by the lexeme in their Hebrew *Vorlage*. However, the fact that the prototypical cloud makes up such a high percentage of the total semantic cloud (nearly 85 percent) strongly suggests that the LXX translators correctly understood the overall Hebrew conceptualization of light, that is, how the Israelites thought about light generally. The linguistic evidence seen in the two texts is exactly what one would expect to find in a reasonably accurate translation. Short of the modern exegete being able to ask the actual Hebrew writer and Greek translator for confirmation, this represents nearly the strongest possible anecdotal evidence to demonstrate that the Greek LXX correctly construes the Hebrew conceptualization(s) of light within the MT.

To summarize: in those places where the MT appears more prototypical in its lexical and conceptual use of light, the LXX also appears more prototypical, and in places where the Hebrew construal appears less prototypical, the Greek construal also appears less prototypical. This general trend applies to all the linguistic data throughout the Old Testament, both lexically and conceptually, and it holds true across all conceptual domains and degrees of abstractness. These data reasonably demonstrate that the prototypical structure of the *conceptualization* of light matches the prototypical structure of the *lexicalization* of light for both the Hebrew and Greek construals of the concept. In practical terms, this comparative study

---

22. References within the prototypical cloud but outside the prototypical core include the following: celestial light: Gen 1:14, 15 (2x), 16 (3x), 17; 44:3; Judg 19:26; 1 Kgdms 14:36; 29:10; 2 Kgdms 2:32; 2 Esd 18:3; Pss 74 (73):16; 139 (138):11, 12; Prov 4:18; Job 3:9; Mic 7:8; Isa 60:1, 19; Ezek 32:7, 8; lightning: Pss 77 (76):19, 97 (96):4; firelight: Exod 25:37; 27:20; 35:14; 39:37 (16); Lev 24:2; Num 4:9, 16; 8:2; 2 Esd 19:12, 19; Pss 18 (17):28; 78 (77):14; 105 (104):39; 119 (118):130; divine light: Pss 27 (26):1; 76 (75):5, 118 (117):27; "the light of the eyes": 1 Esd 8:76; Pss 13 (12):4; 19 (18):9; "the light of the face": Num 6:25; Pss 31 (30):17; 44 (43):4; 67 (66):2; 80 (79):4, 8, 20; 90 (89):8; 119 (118):135; Eccl 8:1.

of the lexical data shows no sign that the LXX translators either misunderstood or were confused by the Hebrew lexeme אור, at least to the degree that the MT and the Hebrew *Vorlage* for the LXX actually match. The reader of the LXX has good evidence to suppose that the Greek translators understood and translated the Hebrew conceptualization of light with reasonable accuracy.

Moving outside the prototypical cloud (i.e., where the LXX translation uses terms other than the ΦΑ- and ΦΩ- lexical roots), nearly all the translated occurrences of the term light in the LXX either appear to have little to no theological significance whatsoever or require deeper investigation than can be done in this essay in order to draw a conclusion. Six attestations of the lexeme אור in the MT are altogether missing from the LXX for some unknown reason.[23] There are eight additional attestations where the LXX selects other lexical terms but conveys the same conceptual meaning as the MT.[24] Only a handful of attestations appear to introduce genuine conceptual changes from the MT; nearly all of them are in the book of Job, which is known to be a more free translation of the Hebrew in the first place.[25] Some of these changes can be accounted for via a metaphorical use of light in the MT (Job 24:13, 14; 25:3; 33:30); I argue that in these cases the LXX simply explicates the target concept of the metaphor, whereas the MT retains the vehicle concept of light. The other five attestations (Exod 14:20; Job 36:30; 38:24; 41:24; Isa 27:11) would need to be studied much more thoroughly than can be done here in order to ascertain if the apparent conceptual differences between the MT and LXX amount to genuine theological changes or can be accounted for in some other way. Finally, it should also be noted that there are some instances where the LXX uses light terminology but the MT does not.[26] The resulting corollary of these attestations outside the prototypical cloud is that the LXX appears to be slightly more interpretive than the MT in regard to its use of the concept of light, but only very slightly.

Two specific Hebrew concepts merit closer examination in regard to their translation in the LXX: "the light of the eyes" and "the light of the

---

23. Exod 13:21; 25:6; 35:8, 14, 28; Isa 5:30.

24. Job 22:28; 30:26; 31:26; 41:10; Mic 2:1; Mal 1:10; Isa 30:26; Ezek 43:2.

25. Exod 14:20; Job 24:13, 14; 25:3; 33:30; 36:30; 38:24; 41:24; Isa 27:11. See Cox's discussion of the characterization of the translation of Hebrew into Greek in LXX Job in his introduction to the book in NETS: Cox 2007, 667–69.

26. See Gen 1:14; Hos 10:12 (cf. Jer 4:3); Isa 60:1.

face." Neither concept is attested often in the Old Testament, although I have argued elsewhere that they are important clues for understanding the conceptual metaphors regarding light in the Old Testament.[27] In regard to both of these concepts in the LXX, one observes the same general trends that have been characteristic of the data all the way through: (1) the selection of Greek terms to translate Hebrew terms for light appears to be based more on situational context than any strict one-to-one correspondence of lexical terms; (2) the more prototypical construals of the concept in the MT align with more prototypical construals in the LXX, and less prototypical Greek construals align with less prototypical construals in Hebrew; and (3) the LXX appears to be slightly more interpretive than the MT in regard to its use of light.

In regard to the concept "the light of the eyes," the LXX exhibits a standard linguistic construction when rendering a more prototypical Hebrew linguistic construction; that is, the *hiphil* of the verb אור with the noun עַיִן ("eye") as object in the MT is prototypically seen in the LXX as the Greek verb φωτίζω with the accusative of the noun ὀφθαλμός ("eye").[28] Four attestations of the concept lie on the edge of the prototypical cloud: 1 Kgdms 14:27, 29, where there is a *qere/ketiv* variant in the MT indicative of both textual and conceptual problems to be addressed; and Prov 15:30, 29:13, where the conceptual differences between the LXX and MT are too complex to be covered here. Much more can and should be said regarding the concept "the light of the eyes" in the Hebrew MT, but the issue is too deep to adequately discuss within this essay.

In regard to the concept "the light of the face," I will not treat here the attestations of the concept in Pss 4:7, 90:8, or Prov 16:15, for similar reasons.[29] As with the others before, these attestations require more detailed study in order to comment on their specific theological significance for the LXX. In Eccl 8:1, however, a similar Hebrew expression is used in reference to a human face as is used for human eyes; that is, a *hiphil* form of the verb אור with the noun פָּנִים ("face") as object in the MT appears in the LXX as

---

27. Ruark 2017, 91–95.

28. In various phrasing, the concept "the light of the eyes" is found in the MT in 1 Sam 14:27 [*qere*], 29 (cf. 1 Kgdms 14:27, 29); Pss 13 (12):4; 19 (18):9; 38 (37):11; Prov 15:30; 29:13; Ezra 9:8 (cf. 1 Esd 8:76).

29. In various phrasing, the concept "the light of the face" is found in the MT in Num 6:25; Pss 4:7; 31 (30):17 (16); 44 (43):4; 67 (66):2; 80 (79):4, 8, 20; 89 (88):15; 90 (89):8; 119 (118):135; Job 29:24; Prov 15:30; 16:15; Eccl 8:1; Dan 9:17.

the verb φωτίζω with the accusative of the noun πρόσωπον ("face"). This fact is unsurprising. But when referring to "the light of the face" of God, the LXX consistently uses the verb ἐπιφαίνω, not φωτίζω. This is not totally unexpected, given the linguistic patterns already observed, but the question remains open regarding the semantic meaning of the verb ἐπιφαίνω in these cases: Does it mean "to shine" or "to show"? Does the Greek intend to communicate a conceptualization of *illumination* or *visibility*?

I contend that this concept of "the light of the face" in the Hebrew MT is synonymous with the concept of "the lifting of the face" and describes the favorable quality of an interpersonal relationship, referring to smiling and/or looking on another person with grace or favor.[30] Based on the patterns of collocation of cognate terms in the MT, I argue that the Hebrew metaphor here accesses a conceptualization of illumination and not visibility.[31] The same is also true when the concept is used of the face of YHWH (Num 6:25; Ps 67:2), but it is applied more broadly in collocation with concepts of YHWH's salvation (Pss 31:17; 80:4, 8, 20), blessing (67:2), and instruction (119:135). The consistent selection of a *prototypical* verb ἐπιφαίνω to describe a *prototypical* verbal action of the "shining" of God's face would appear to indicate that this was a specific

---

30. See BDB, s.v. "נָשָׂא," 670; *HALOT*, s.v. "נשׂא," 725; *DCH* s.v. "נשׂא," 5:760. The argument for the semantic concordance between the concepts "the shining of the face" and "the lifting of the face" begins with the parallel collocation of the two concepts in the priestly blessing (Num 6:25; cf. also Ps 4:7). The concept "the lifting of the face" is a complex metaphor that functions more generally than the concept "the shining of the face" but is fundamentally a relational concept and collocates with the Hebrew verb חָנַן ("to show grace, favor") (Num 6:25–26; Deut 28:50; Mal 1:8–9; Lam 4:16). The concept sometimes describes the literal inclination of a person's head (2 Kgs 9:32; perhaps also 2 Sam 2:22; 2 Kgs 3:14), and a "lifted face" can indicate a person's status as wealthy or honored within the community (2 Kgs 5:1; Isa 3:3; 9:14; Job 22:28; also perhaps Job 11:15). To "lift the face" *of another person* unquestionably refers to a good or favorable relationship between the two persons, usually described in terms of a person of higher social status lifting the face of a person of lower social status (Gen 19:21; 32:21; 1 Sam 25:35; Mal 1:8–9; Ps 82:2; Job 13:8; 32:21; 42:8–9; Prov 6:35; 18:5; Lam 4:16). Finally, the concept can also describe the lifting *of one's own face* toward another person, often in a judicial context to describe a favorable relationship in a negative way, i.e., "favoritism" (Lev 19:15; Deut 10:17; 28:50; Mal 2:9; Job 13:10; 34:19; Prov 18:5). It is this latter sense that is most closely related to the concept "the shining of the face," referring to the "lifting" of the facial features, i.e., smiling. Job describes that the light of his own face "was not caused to fall" (*hiphil* of נפל ["to fall"], Job 29:24).

31. Ruark 2017, 25–42, 55–57, 93–95.

and deliberate choice on the part of the LXX translators. One can reasonably argue that they understood the Hebrew *hiphil* form as a verb of illumination and selected the Greek verb ἐπιφαίνω to refer to the concept of illumination based on the specific situational context. Thus one could consistently understand the Greek verb ἐπιφαίνω in these instances as meaning "to shine."

However, the verb ἐπιφαίνω in the LXX as a whole most often appears to access a conceptualization of visibility, not illumination. Surveying the Old Testament passages: "God *appeared* to Jacob," as from the Hebrew גלה ("to reveal") (Gen 35:7); "God *will reveal* himself to Israel," as from the Hebrew מצא ("to find") (Jer 29 [36]:14) and גלה (Ezek 39:28); "YHWH *will be revealed* to Israel," as from the Hebrew נורא ("to fear") or perhaps נראה ("to appear") (Zeph 2:11). In Ezek 17:6, the verb ἐπιφαίνω appears as the Hebrew פנה ("to turn") in the MT, which would seem to indicate visibility over above illumination in that context, but not necessarily so. The apparent rendering of the Hebrew אור in Ps 118 (117):27 could reflect either meaning, "God *has appeared* to us" or "God *has shined* for us." Surveying the deuterocanonical texts, the verb ἐπιφαίνω describes the *appearing* of Judas Maccabeus and his men (2 Macc 12:22); the *appearance* of a wonderfully arrayed gray-haired man (15:13); the *displaying* of God's mercy (3 Macc 2:19); *showing forth* the light of God's mercy (6:4); God *manifesting* himself to Israel (6:9); the *shining/showing* of God's holy face as angels descend (6:18); God gloriously *manifesting* his mercy (6:39); God *shining* on the one sitting in darkness and the shadow of death (Ode 9:79); and the *flashing* of lightning (Ep Jer 60). The LXX uses both the active and passive voice of ἐπιφαίνω to access both concepts of visibility and illumination in various contexts, so the specific verbal form is not a selector for the semantic meaning of this verb.

Thus one might also plausibly argue that, either when in doubt or when the verb is used metaphorically, the use of the Greek ἐπιφαίνω simply follows the pattern of frequency and expresses the concept of visibility when referring to the light of God's face. But this is unnecessary, in my view; there is sufficient semantic evidence to allow the verb ἐπιφαίνω to select alternate meanings based on specific contextual use in consideration of the available Hebrew MT. However, this is an issue that would need to be decided by a semantic study of the verb ἐπιφαίνω and its cognates in ancient Greek, especially Koine, both in terms of the specific conceptualization underlying the Greek construal of light as well as which specific contexts of Greek construal access the concept of illumination versus the concept of visibility. This remains fertile ground for further linguistic and semantic study in ancient Greek.

But even if the Greek construal of the "shining of God's face" selects a conceptualization of visibility in contrast to a Hebrew conceptualization of illumination, this could very well be an example of two different languages simply using different conceptualizations to express the same abstract metaphorical concept. The Greek work *Physiognomics*, commonly attributed to Aristotle, repeatedly uses cognates of the verb φαίνω to refer to *facial expressions*, twice including the verb ἐπιφαίνω.[32] Simply put, it makes intuitive sense to think that one culture might conceptualize a smiling face using the concept of illumination whereas a different culture might conceptualize a smiling face using the concept of visibility. Humans are *embodied* beings, which means that, for us, in the physical world illumination and visibility are highly congruent phenomena. For human persons, the action of sight requires light, and the perception of light requires sight.

To recap the options: (1) in both the MT and the LXX, the metaphorical concept "the light of the face" utilizes the concept of illumination, which I consider the most likely (see Ps 118 [117]:27). One could also make the argument that (2) the Hebrew construal utilizes the concept of illumination, while the Greek construal utilizes the concept of visibility. In my view, this is the second most likely possibility, but even this change in conceptualization would not necessarily indicate a change in textual meaning. It is also possible that I have misunderstood the Hebrew concept "the light of the face" in the MT and that (3) the construals in both Hebrew and Greek utilize the concept of visibility. There is not much linguistic evidence to support this view, but it is possible. Perhaps (4) the Hebrew construal utilizes the concept of visibility, while the Greek construal utilizes the concept of illumination, but this would be extremely strange in terms of the construal of the concept of light in *both* the Hebrew MT and the Greek LXX. Finally, it could also be argued that (5) the construals in both Hebrew and Greek select alternate concepts in various contexts, but, intuitively, I do not consider it very plausible. The congruity of prototypicality between the Hebrew MT and the Greek LXX suggests a standard conceptualization for all occurrences of the verb ἐπιφαίνω in specific reference to the light of God's face.

---

32. Hett 1936, 95, 101, 103, 123. These also include the verbs φαίνω (4x) and ἐμφαίνω (1x), although the reason(s) for the variance in verbal selection is not readily ascertainable.

Theological Implications

In regard to the linguistic construal of "the shining of God's face" in the Old Testament, the conceptualization in the Greek LXX might be different from the conceptualization in the Hebrew MT, or it might not be. But even if the conceptualization is different, the intended conceptual referent (both physical and metaphorical) might still be the same in the LXX and the MT. In terms of the physical referent, it is perfectly plausible that a Hebrew speaker might conceptualize a smiling face using the concept of illumination, while a Greek speaker might utilize the concept of visibility. In terms of the metaphorical referent, it is also perfectly plausible that a Hebrew speaker might conceptualize a favorable interpersonal relationship using the concept of illumination, while a Greek speaker might conceptualize a favorable interpersonal relationship using the concept of visibility. To borrow a colloquial expression, it could very well be that the LXX and the MT are simply "saying the same thing in different words," using different conceptualizations to express the same conceptual meaning.

Drawing a conclusion most relevant for the current topic, I think the greater danger lies in making too much of this distinction rather than too little, given the fact that the LXX is a *translated* text. This short study aptly illustrates just how fine the line can be between a *reception* of a source text and a *theology* of a target text. If the LXX simply translates a Hebrew idiom using a Greek idiom, even for so abstract and complex a metaphor as the "light" of God's face, then this difference in conceptualization is rightly considered as a reception of the Hebrew *Vorlage* and not a theology of the Greek translation. Furthermore, this remains true even if one supposes that the LXX translators misunderstood their Hebrew *Vorlage* when translating the concept. In order for a difference in conceptualization to be considered genuine theology, one should be able to demonstrate that the LXX translators understood the Hebrew conceptualization and then deliberately changed or adapted it for theological purposes as opposed to mere linguistic expression or conceptual idiom. That is, one could argue for a genuine theological innovation in the LXX if the Greek translators *intentionally* chose the verb ἐπιφαίνω to express the concept of visibility over against the concept of illumination for a theological reason, for example, to refer to the actual visibility of the divine face rather than merely the expression on the face. This could be true for the present case, but it is certainly not assured based on the current study.

Finally, one additional corollary bears consideration in light of the fact that both language and theology, as phenomena of abstract cognition, share a common human (i.e., personal) ontology. If one strives to articulate a theology of the LXX, and if theology is provisionally defined as "thinking/speaking/living about God," then theology is something that only a person can do, not a collection of linguistic symbols. Not only this, but I also argue that the very use of linguistic symbols to express theological ideas necessarily presupposes the person(s) who did the symbolizing. No linguistic text can be existentially separated from its writer. In actual practice, then, one speaks of a theology of the LXX only as a theology of the persons who wrote it down, and that holds true even when the LXX is treated as an entire wholistic work of religious literature. In other words, both the LXX and the MT are theological phenomena on the basis of *personal cognitive ontology* prior even to *religious literary ontology*. This further strengthens the position that a specific theology of the LXX (as distinct from a theology of either the MT or the Old Testament) must be considered a function of the LXX translators and not something purely latent in the text itself.

Therefore, based on all these implications, the following protocol can be derived. If one attempts to construct a theology of the LXX based on its differences from the Hebrew MT, then ideally, variations in the text would need to be sifted according the general method that I have followed here: first lexically, then conceptually, and then—and only then—theologically. This level of comprehensive thoroughness cannot be fully achieved, of course; the task is simply too great for this kind of analysis in each and every case in the whole Old Testament. So, to say the least, strict and careful judgment must be exercised.

Conclusion

In this essay I have examined the use of the concept of light in the Greek LXX compared with the Hebrew MT from a cognitive semantic perspective, using what linguists commonly call conceptual metaphor theory. This study has identified three general trends applicable for all the lexical data. First, the selection of specific Greek terms to refer to the concept of light appears to be based on situational context more than strict linguistic equivalence with Hebrew counterparts. Second, the spectrum of more prototypical to less prototypical linguistic construals of the concept of light in the LXX aligns with that in the MT to a very high degree. Third, the LXX leans a little more than the MT toward interpreting light metaphors, but this slant is slight indeed. There are several specific texts on the edges of the semantic prototypical cloud for which further study is required to determine their exact theological significance, although the impact of these passages would, at the most, be quite minimal when considering a theology of the LXX as a whole.

However, the nearly universal use of the verb ἐπιφαίνω in the LXX when describing "the light of the face" of God could be an example of a theological innovation from the MT, partially depending on which semantic meaning of ἐπιφαίνω is being selected in this specific situational context. In my view, the term most likely means exactly the same as its MT counterpart, only using a Greek idiom as opposed to a Hebrew idiom. But if it could be demonstrated that the LXX conceptualization of the "shining of God's face" was different from the MT conceptualization in ways that could not be accounted for either lexically or conceptually, then this shift might raise some interesting diachronic questions concerning the development of (1) the pre-Christian messianic expectation and eschatological vision in the Old Testament literature, and (2) an incarnational theology in the Scriptures as a whole, in both the Christian and pre-Christian eras. After all, it is quite a different thing to see the physical face of God—vis-á-vis Jesus of Nazareth—as opposed to merely in the mind's eye. But for this specific concept, it would have to be determined by methods other than cognitive semantics based on comparison with the MT.

Bibliography

Cox, Claude E. 2007. "Iob." Pages 667–96 in *A New Translation of the Septuagint and the Other Greek Translations Traditionally Included under That Title*. Edited by Albert Pietersma and Benjamin G. Wright. New York: Oxford University Press.

Dirven, René, and Marjolijn Verspoor. 2004. *Cognitive Exploration of Language and Linguistics*. 2nd ed. Amsterdam: Benjamins.

Fauconnier, Gilles, and Mark Turner. 2008. "Rethinking Metaphor." Pages 53–66 in *The Cambridge Handbook of Metaphor and Thought*. Edited by Raymond W. Gibbs. Cambridge: Cambridge University Press.

Grady, Joseph E. 2007. "Metaphor." Pages 188–213 in *The Oxford Handbook of Cognitive Linguistics*. Edited by Dirk Geeraerts and Hubert Cuyckens. New York: Oxford University Press.

Hett, W. S. trans. 1936. *Aristotle XIV: Minor Works*. LCL. Cambridge: Harvard University Press.
Kövecses, Zoltán. 2005. "A Broad View of Cognitive Linguistics." *Acta Linguistica Hungarica* 52:135–72.
———. 2015. *Where Metaphors Come From: Reconsidering Context in Metaphor*. Oxford: Oxford University Press.
Lakoff, George. 1987. *Women, Fire, and Dangerous Things: What Categories Reveal about the Mind*. Chicago: University of Chicago Press.
Lakoff, George, and Mark Johnson. 1980. *Metaphors We Live By*. Chicago: University of Chicago Press.
Lewandowska-Tomaszczyk, Barbara. 2007. "Polysemy, Prototypes, and Radial Categories." Pages 139–69 in *The Oxford Handbook of Cognitive Linguistics*. Edited by Dirk Geeraerts and Hubert Cuyckens. New York: Oxford University Press.
Metzger, Bruce M. 1998. *Lexical Aids for Students of New Testament Greek*. 3rd ed. Grand Rapids: Baker Academic.
Montanari, Franco. 2015. *The Brill Dictionary of Ancient Greek*. Edited by Madeleine Goh and Chad Schroeder. Leiden: Brill.
Riemer, Nick. 2010. *Introducing Semantics*. Cambridge: Cambridge University Press.
Ritchie, L. David. 2013. *Metaphor*. Cambridge: Cambridge University Press.
Rohrer, T. 2007. "Embodiment and Experientialism." Pages 25–47 in *The Oxford Handbook of Cognitive Linguistics*. Edited by Dirk Geeraerts and Hubert Cuyckens. New York: Oxford University Press.
Rosch, Eleanor H. 1973. "Natural Categories." *Cognitive Psychology* 4:328–50.
———. 1975. "Cognitive Reference Points." *Cognitive Psychology* 7:532–47.
Rosch, Eleanor H., and Carolyn B. Mervis. 1975. "Family Resemblances: Studies in the Internal Structure of Categories." *Cognitive Psychology* 7:573–605.
Rosch, Eleanor H., Carolyn B. Mervis, Wayne D. Gray, David M. Johnson and Penny Boyes-Braem. 1976. "Basic Objects in Natural Categories." *Cognitive Psychology* 8:382–439.
Ruark, Joel D. 2017. "The Theological Significance of Light (אוֹר) in the OT: An Applied Cognitive Linguistic Study." Unpublished MTh thesis, Stellenbosch University.
Taylor, John R. 1989. *Linguistic Categorization: Prototypes in Linguistic Theory*. New York: Oxford University Press.

Part 4
Theological Perspectives of the Greek Bible 2:
Greek Literature

Sophia as Second Principle in Wisdom of Solomon
Johan C. Thom

ABSTRACT: Much has been written on the role and function of Sophia in the theology of Wisdom of Solomon. A broad consensus is that Sophia functions as more than just a poetic personification but less than a full-blown hypostasis. In a recent study Gregory Sterling contends that Sophia should indeed be understood as a second divine principle similar to what we encounter in Middle Platonism. I examine this proposal in the light of other contemporary philosophical texts, in particular the Pseudo-Aristotelian *De mundo*.

1. Introduction

The Wisdom of Solomon was composed in Greek and therefore presents us with a different set of questions than septuagintal texts that were translated from a Hebrew or Aramaic original. It also originated in the Hellenistic Diaspora and contains several important theological topics influenced by this context. These topics include the relation between human and divine justice, the immortality of the soul and eschatology, natural theology and providence, universalism and particularism, freedom and determinism, monotheism versus polytheism, sapiential theology and creation, and the relation between wisdom and torah. In this paper I will not attempt to provide a survey of these topics, but I will rather focus on a particular issue: the nature and function of the figure of Wisdom, that is, Sophia.

When we compare the figure of Sophia in Wisdom of Solomon with Sophia in other wisdom texts such as Proverbs or Sirach, there is a noticeable difference: in the latter texts, the personification of Sophia functions as a poetic metaphor, but in Wisdom, Sophia appears to be more than that. The basic question is thus whether Sophia functions as a poetic personification in Wisdom or as a hypostasis, an expression of the deity, that is, an intermediate divine being similar to the Logos in Philo of Alexandria. Extensive research has been done on this question over the past fifty years, which I will not rehearse here. Although there is difference of opinion about details and about influences on Wisdom, a general scholarly consensus seems to be emerging that Sophia in Wisdom lies somewhere on the trajectory between a mere poetic personification and a full-blown hypostasis.[1]

In a recent essay contributed to the volume *From Stoicism to Platonism*, Gregory Sterling, however, contends that Sophia in Wisdom of Solomon functions as a second divine principle like that found in contemporary Middle Platonism.[2] I will explore this suggestion further here by looking at other texts beyond Platonism.

2. Passages in Wisdom of Solomon

Let us begin by looking at some crucial passages in Wisdom of Solomon.[3]

2.1. Sophia as a Divine Spirit

There are scattered references in Wisdom to Sophia as a spirit closely associated with or emanating from God. Sophia is called a "holy spirit" (1:5; also 9:17) and a "kindly spirit" (1:6), abhorring and rebuking unrighteousness, but also the "spirit of the Lord" that "fills the world" and "that which holds all things together" (1:7). God's "incorruptible spirit is in all things" (12:1). Elsewhere the "spirit of Sophia" is said to be coming from God (7:7), "having a shared life with God" (8:3). Sophia shares God's throne (9:4) and was present when he made the world (9:9). She is indeed "the fashioner of all things" (7:22; 8:6).

In these verses Sophia represents God on the microcosmic, anthropological level, as the one who upholds and reinforces righteousness and

---

1. See, e.g., Neher 2004, 240, who concludes: "Für das Vermittlungsproblem kann am Ende der Untersuchung festgehalten werden, dass sich an keiner Stelle der biblischen Belege ein eindeutiger Hinweis feststellen ließ, dass die Weisheit als Hypostase zu verstehen ist. Erst bei Philo von Alexandrien lassen sich konkrete Zwischenwesen in Gestalt des λόγος, und der δυνάμεις nachweisen. Die σοφία [sc. in Wisdom of Solomon] befindet sich noch auf dem Weg zur Hypostasierung." Similarly already Zeller 1919–1923, 3.2:292, cited by Neher 2004, 240 n. 1.

2. Sterling 2017, 198–213, esp. 207–10. He uses "'Second Principle' to signal the state of Wisdom as an intermediary Principle between God and humanity in Wisdom" (208 n. 57). See also 207: "Our author has taken the traditional personification of wisdom in the Jewish tradition and recast her into a hypostasis by using Greek philosophical categories."

3. I am using the Göttingen edition of Ziegler 1980 and the translation of NETS.

grants understanding, but also on the macrocosmic, cosmological level, as the one sustaining the world order.

2.2. The Hymn to Sophia

The important passage for our present purposes is, however, Wis 7:22–8:1.

> 7:22 For there is in her a spirit that is intelligent, holy,
> unique, of many parts, subtle,
> free-moving, lucid, unpolluted,
> distinct, invulnerable, loving the good, sharp,
> 23 unhindered, beneficent, loving towards humanity,
> firm, unfailing, free from care,
> all-powerful, all-surveying
> and penetrating all spirits
> that are intelligent, pure, most subtle.
> 24 For wisdom moves more freely than any movement;
> she pervades and penetrates all things because of her pureness.
> 25 For she is a breath of the power of God
> and an emanation of the pure glory of the Almighty;
> therefore nothing defiled gains entrance into her.
> 26 For she is a reflection of eternal light
> and a spotless mirror of the activity of God
> and an image of his goodness.
> 27 Although she is one, she can do all things,
> and while remaining in herself, she renews all things,
> and in every generation she passes into holy souls
> and makes them friends of God and prophets;
> 28 for God loves nothing except the person who lives with wisdom,
> 29 for she is more beautiful than the sun
> and above every constellation of stars.
> Compared with the light, she is found to be more radiant;
> 30 for this is succeeded by the night,
> but against wisdom wickedness does not prevail.
> 8:1 She reaches with might from one end of the world to the other
> and orders all things well.

I cannot here do justice to the rich detail of this beautiful hymn,[4] but I wish to underline the following characteristics of Sophia found here.

---

4. See the discussion by Hübner 1993, 58–74; Cox 2007, 64–70; Engberg-Pedersen 2010, 22–24; Sterling 2017, 207–10.

Sophia is intelligent (7:22), all-powerful and all-surveying (7:23). She pervades and penetrates all things (7:24), including intelligent human minds (7:23). She can do all things and renew all things (7:27); she strongly reaches from one end to the other and orders all things well (8:1). These verses depict Sophia's creative and administering activity throughout the world. At the same time, she is called a breath of the power of God and an emanation of the pure glory of the Almighty (7:25), a reflection of eternal light and a spotless mirror of the activity of God, and an image of his goodness (7:26), all of which are images to express Sophia's relationship to God.[5] Sophia is not identical to God but represents him and makes him visible.[6]

3. Stoic and Platonic Ideas in Wisdom of Solomon

It has often been suggested that Wisdom of Solomon makes use of both Stoic and Middle Platonic ideas.[7]

In the passages we looked at, Sophia as a pure, subtle, and all-powerful spirit (πνεῦμα), pervading, sustaining and administering everything in the world, closely echoes the Stoic doctrine of the active principle pervading and structuring everything. This principle is called πνεῦμα, λόγος, designing fire, God, and so on. It is a very fine material force that penetrates everything and gives everything its form and internal cohesion. It orders the world in a rational manner so that it is also identified with providence and fate. The divine principle in Stoicism is immanent in this world; there is no transcendent God in Stoicism. This raises the question how a Hellenistic-Jewish author could accommodate such ideas derived from Stoic immanentism and pantheism.

Some of the other ideas found in the hymn to Sophia reflect the tension between divine immanence and transcendence.[8] The phrases used to describe Sophia in 7:25–26 all serve to make a distinction between the transcendent God and Sophia who is active within the cosmos. Some of the terms and ideas are also found in Stoic texts,[9] but the idea of Sophia

---

5. See Engberg-Pedersen 2010, 23.

6. See also Lorenzen 2008, 47.

7. See Hübner 1993; Collins 1997, 196–202; Engberg-Pedersen 2010, 22–23; Cox 2007, 64–67; Sterling 2017, 207–10.

8. The question of immanence versus transcendence in Wis 7 is treated at length by Hübner 1993, 62–81.

9. The usage of ἀπόρροια for an emanation of God is elsewhere first found in Marcus Aurelius 2.4. Sterling (2017, 209) cites Dodds 1963, 214, who suggests that this

as an image and emanation of God is more typical of Middle Platonism. In order to separate the transcendent God from involvement in the world, that is, to keep God completely transcendent, Middle Platonists devolved the demiurgic function of God to a second divine principle, variously identified as the world soul, the cosmic intellect, the second demiurge, and the like.[10] As I noted earlier, Gregory Sterling suggests that Sophia fulfils this role in Wisdom of Solomon.[11]

Much of the scholarly discussion of these ideas in Wisdom focuses on their philosophical or theological origin.[12] In a recent dissertation, Martin Neher, for example, considers the possible Platonic or Stoic sources for Wisdom at great length and comes to the conclusion that Wisdom may have used a philosophical *koine* but that there is no evidence of direct influence from first-century BCE philosophical contemporaries such as Posidonius, Antiochus of Ascalon, or Eudorus.[13] In this essay I adopt a slightly different approach: instead of attempting to trace the sources of philosophical ideas and motifs in Wisdom, I seek to contribute to an understanding of the intellectual environment in which the text originated.[14] In order to do so, I will briefly discuss a contemporary text in which we find a similar tension between immanence and transcendence, namely, *On the Cosmos* attributed to Aristotle.

4. Pseudo-Aristotle, *On the Cosmos*

Like Wisdom of Solomon, the Pseudo-Aristotelian treatise *On the Cosmos* (= *De mundo*) cannot be dated with any certainty, but again, like Wisdom, a date around the turn of the era seems probable.[15] One of the main

---

idea developed within the Middle Stoa in an attempt to distinguish between God and the cosmos. One may also point to the distinction made between Zeus and the λόγος in Cleanthes's *Hymn to Zeus*; see, e.g., vv. 12, 21; also Thom 2009, 202.

10. See Opsomer 2005, 51–99.

11. Sterling 2017, 209.

12. Apart from Platonism and Stoicism, Isis theology has also been suggested as a source; see Reese 1970, 40–52; Mack 1973, passim; Kloppenborg 1982, 57–84; Collins 1997, 203–4.

13. See Neher 2004, 164–208.

14. For the importance of focusing on the intellectual environment of a text instead of on influences or sources, see Malherbe 2014. On Malherbe's approach, see also Thom 2014b, 2018.

15. See the discussion in Thom 2014c, 3–8. I use the text and translation of *On the Cosmos* in Thom 2014d. Recent scholars accept the suggestion of Collins (1997,

purposes of this treatise appears to be to provide an alternative to Stoic immanence to explain divine involvement in the world.[16] Within an Aristotelian context, God is completely transcendent, the Unmoved Mover with no direct involvement with the cosmos. The question the author tries to address is how it is possible for God to be responsible for the order and preservation of the world without giving up his self-sufficiency and independence, that is, his transcendence.[17]

After an elaborate description of the diverse geographical features and meteorological phenomena of the world with their potential for conflict and mutual destruction, the author states in chapter 6 that "the cause holding the universe together" is indeed God:

> It now remains to speak in summary fashion about the cause holding the universe together, as has also been done about the rest; for it would be wrong when speaking about the cosmos—even if not in detail, then at least for a knowledge in outline—to pass over that which is most important in the cosmos. There is indeed an ancient account, native to all people, that all things have come into existence from God and because of God, and that no thing by itself is self-sufficient, if deprived of the preservation deriving from him. Therefore some of the ancients were also led to say that all these things that appear to us through the eyes and hearing and every sensation are full of gods, presenting an idea appropriate to the divine power, not however to the divine essence. For God is really the preserver of all things and the begetter [creator] of everything however it is brought about in this cosmos, without indeed enduring the hardship of a creature hard at work for itself, but by making use of an untiring power, by means of which he prevails even over things that seem to be far away. He has been allotted the highest and first place, and is therefore called Supreme, established according to the poet "on the highest peak" of the whole heaven. The body closest to him has most benefit of his power, and then the body next to it, and so on in sequence until the regions where we are. So the earth and the things on the earth, being at the greatest distance from the assistance of God, seem to be weak and incongruous and full of much confusion; but nevertheless, in as far as the divine naturally penetrates to everything, it happens to the

---

178–79) that Wisdom could have been written at any time from 30 BCE to 70 CE; see, e.g., Winston 2005, 14; Sterling 2017, 199.

16. For a fuller discussion, see Thom 2014a and 2020.

17. For the problem of the concept "transcendence" in *On the Cosmos*, see Thom 2020, 135.

things in our region in the same way as to the things above us: they share to a greater or lesser extent in God's assistance according to whether they are closer or further from him. (398a) It is therefore better to suppose—which is also fitting and most appropriate to God—that the power based in heaven is the cause of preservation for all things, even those furthest separated, one may say, rather than that it pervades and goes to where it is not honourable or dignified that it should, and of itself performs the things on earth. (397b9–398a6)

It is more dignified and becoming for him to be based in the highest region and for his power, penetrating through the whole cosmos, to move the sun and moon and to cause the whole heaven to revolve and to be the cause of preservation for the things on earth. (398b6–10)

The notion that there is a divine force holding the world together and thus preserving it from chaos was already present in the time of Plato and Aristotle,[18] but the phrase συνεκτική αἰτία seems to be a direct reaction to Stoic doctrine because it is a variant of the formula συνεκτικὸν αἴτιον coined by the Stoics.[19] The transcendent Aristotelian god is thus put in place of the immanent Stoic πνεῦμα as cohesive cause of the cosmos.

The author refers to "an ancient account" (397b13–20) with which he apparently agrees, according to which everything owes its existence and continued preservation to God; all things have come to be "from God and because of God" (ἐκ θεοῦ πάντα καὶ διὰ θεόν).[20] Nothing is self-sufficient (αὐτάρκης), that is, can exist in and of itself, if deprived of God's preservation. The author immediately corrects the wrong inference by "some of the ancients" that this means that everything is full of God,[21] that God himself is immanently present in the world. The author again takes up a position against Stoic immanentism and pantheism.[22]

According to the author, one should instead distinguish between God's essence (οὐσία) and his power (δύναμις): "God is really the preserver

---

18. Cf. Aristotle, *Pol.* 7.4.1326a32–33; Xenophon, *Mem.* 4.3.13; see also Reale and Bos 1995, 313 n. 233; Duhot 1990, 195; Opsomer 2006, 7.

19. See Duhot 1990, 197–98; Mansfeld 1992, 401; Opsomer 2006, 7–8.

20. Cf. *Mund.* 2, 391b12: ὑπὸ θεοῦ τε καὶ διὰ θεόν.

21. This view may refer to Thales; cf. Thales 11 A 22 (Diels-Kranz, *Fragmente der Vorsokratiker*) = Aristotle, *De an.* 411a7.

22. Pohlenz (1965, 377–78) even speaks of a "Kampfansage" against Stoicism. See also Moraux 1984, 39.

[σωτήρ] of all things and the begetter [γενέτωρ] of everything however it is brought about in this cosmos, without indeed enduring the hardship of a creature hard at work for itself, but by making use of an untiring power, by means of which he prevails even over things that seem to be far away." God himself is established in the highest region and does not do any work himself, because it would not be "appropriate" (πρέποντα) (397b19–27).

The statement that all things have come to be "from God and because of God" (ἐκ θεοῦ πάντα καὶ διὰ θεόν) furthermore identifies God as efficient cause of the cosmos.[23] God effects all of this without having to act directly himself, however; active involvement in the world is relegated to the power (δύναμις) of God instead.[24] The author describes the way God's power is transmitted through the cosmos by saying that the power is physically transmitted from one body to the next, gradually weakening in proportion to the distance from its origin until it reaches earth. God's preservative and beneficial influence (ὠφέλεια) nevertheless penetrates down to the lowest level (397b27–35). A formulation such as "in as far as the divine naturally penetrates to everything" (καθ' ὅσον ἐπὶ πᾶν διικνεῖσθαι πέφυκε τὸ θεῖον) again sounds Stoic, but the gradual, physical transmission of power envisaged here is quite different from the Stoic πνεῦμα that permeates everything equally.

In the rest of chapter 6, the author uses various metaphors and comparisons to describe how it is possible for God to act on the world through his power, but we need not concern ourselves with them here.[25]

For our present purposes, the most important feature of *On the Cosmos* is the distinction made between God and his power (δύναμις). By means of this differentiation, the author tries to uphold the transcendence of God, while at the same time allowing for divine action in the world: God himself is not in direct contact with the world, and therefore his dignity is maintained, but he is still able to administer and sustain the world by means of his power. As we have seen, a similar concern to keep the supreme god separate from the world motivated the devolving of the

---

23. Cf. Opsomer 2006, 8.

24. There is some confusion between god and his power in 398a1–6, but it is clear from texts such as 398b6–10 that god's power penetrates through the whole cosmos. On the confusion between these passages, see also Duhot 1990, 203–4.

25. A good discussion of the comparisons is found in Betegh and Gregoric 2014, 574–91.

demiurgic functions to a second divine principle in Middle Platonism.²⁶ An important difference between *On the Cosmos* and the various Middle Platonic texts, however, is that the δύναμις of God is not personified nor developed into a fully formed hypostasis; in *On the Cosmos*, God is still the ultimate cause of what happens in the cosmos.²⁷ This may be because *On the Cosmos* was written at the beginning of this process of distinguishing different divine principles²⁸ or because the Peripatetic author of the work had a stricter monotheistic worldview than his Platonic contemporaries.

5. Wisdom of Solomon in Its Intellectual Environment

Compared to the δύναμις in *On the Cosmos*, the figure of Sophia in Wisdom of Solomon is evidently closer to the kind of second principle that we find in Middle Platonic authors. Sophia is also closer in the way she is described to the Logos in John 1:2–3, who was in the beginning with God and through whom all things came into being; to Christ as the "image of God" (εἰκὼν τοῦ θεοῦ) in 2 Cor 4:4 and Col 1:15;²⁹ and to the Son in Heb 1:3, who "is the reflection of God's glory and the exact imprint of God's very being" (ἀπαύγασμα τῆς δόξης καὶ χαρακτὴρ τῆς ὑποστάσεως αὐτοῦ) and who "sustains all things by his powerful word" (φέρων τε τὰ πάντα τῷ ῥήματι τῆς δυνάμεως αὐτοῦ).³⁰

We may perhaps postulate a trajectory in terms of historical development or a spectrum of possibilities from an ontological perspective for where a particular divine figure or principle may be located; that is, the divine figure or principle could be more or less independent of the transcendent God. This could vary from being a mere extension of God, as in the case of the δύναμις in *On the Cosmos*, to an independent hypostasis, as in Platonic authors.

This move, to distinguish between the transcendent God and his activity in the world, is, however, not limited to Platonic authors. The Aristotelian author of *On the Cosmos*, as we have seen, also makes such a distinction, and as I have argued elsewhere even Stoic authors such as Cleanthes and Epictetus sometimes differentiate between God and the

---

26. See also Opsomer, 2005, 61–62.
27. Festugière 1983, 515–16; Gottschalk 1987, 1136, 1138; Opsomer 2006, 16–17.
28. Thus Opsomer 2006, 10.
29. For a discussion of "the image of God" in Wisdom and Paul, see Lorenzen 2008.
30. See also Thom 2012a.

λόγος or God and a personal *daimon*.³¹ Instead of trying to identify the source of this idea with a specific philosophical tradition, it would be better to view the idea itself as part of the shared intellectual environment within which Wisdom of Solomon also originated. I have elsewhere argued that this environment was influenced by popular philosophy.³²

This does not mean that the separation between God and his activity in the world had the same nature or function in all texts within this shared environment. How this idea manifests itself in each text is determined, at least in part, by the ideological orientation and purpose of the text. Each text therefore has to be investigated on its own to see how this idea is implemented or appropriated.

In *On the Cosmos*, the δύναμις itself has no characteristics or independent existence; it is depicted as an impulse setting things in motion in a mechanical manner. Its function is merely to explain how God can cause events at a distance without being in the world itself.

Sophia in Wisdom of Solomon, on the other hand, has clearly defined material and personal characteristics. On the material side, she is a quick-moving, very fine spirit (πνεῦμα) that is able to penetrate and pervade all things; as a person, she is described as intelligent, discerning, kind, loving humans, and so on. She shares a life with God and is responsible for the creation of all things; therefore she can also give humans understanding and wisdom. Compared to the δύναμις of *On the Cosmos*, she is depicted as an independent entity with a very different role than the δύναμις.

How do we explain the role of Sophia in Wisdom within the context of Judaism? Martin Neher's conclusion that Sophia should not be understood as an intermediate being ("Zwischenwesen") and that she is still "on the way to hypostasisation" seems to underplay the characteristics I have just noted.³³ Gregory Sterling's identification of Sophia as a second divine principle, "an intermediary … between God and humanity," is closer to the text.³⁴ He notes that the author of Wisdom appropriated contemporary philosophical concepts that were then subordinated to Judaism but that

---

31. Cleanthes, *Hymn to Zeus*, 12, 21; see Thom 2009, 202–3; Epictetus, *Diatr.* 1.14.

32. See Thom 2012b, 2015. Sterling (2005, 217) is correct in noting that the term *popular philosophy* is often limited to moral philosophy and to simplistic concepts, but I have argued that the concept can be used in a broader sense, covering different areas of philosophy and different levels of technical sophistication.

33. See Neher 2004, 240.

34. See Sterling 2017, 208 n. 57. Cf. Lorenzen 2008, 47: "Die Weisheit in der

in the process also transformed Judaism, although Sterling does not spell out what this transformation entails.[35] It includes, however, the fact that the transcendent God works through an intermediary, Sophia, to become present and immanent in the world.[36] Such a transformation was taken a step further in the New Testament, when the Logos became flesh.

Bibliography

Betegh, Gábor, and Pavel Gregoric. 2014. "Multiple Analogy in Ps.-Aristotle, *De mundo* 6." *ClQ* 64:574–91.
Collins, John J. 1997. *Jewish Wisdom in the Hellenistic Age*. OTL. Louisville: Westminster John Knox.
Cox, Ronald. 2007. *By the Same Word: Creation and Salvation in Hellenistic Judaism and Early Christianity*. BZNW 145. Berlin: de Gruyter.
Dodds, Eric R. 1963. *The Elements of Theology*. 2nd ed. Oxford: Oxford University Press.
Duhot, Jean-Joël. 1990. "Aristotélisme et Stoïcisme dans le *peri kosmou* pseudo-aristotélicien." *Revue de philosophie ancienne* 8:191–228.
Engberg-Pedersen, Troels. 2010. *Cosmology and Self in the Apostle Paul: The Material Spirit*. Oxford: Oxford University Press.
Festugière, André-Jean. 1983. *Le dieu cosmique*. Vol. 2 of *La révélation d'Hermès Trismégiste*. Paris: Gabalda, 1949. Repr., Paris: Belles Lettres.
Gottschalk, Hans B. 1987. "Aristotelian Philosophy in the Roman World from the Time of Cicero to the End of the Second Century AD." *ANRW* 36.2:1079–174.
Hübner, Hans. 1993. "Die Sapientia Salomonis und die antike Philosophie." Pages 55–81 in *Die Weisheit Salomos im Horizont Biblischer Theologie*. Edited by Hans Hübner. Biblisch-Theologische Studien 22. Neukirchen-Vluyn: Neukirchener Verlag.

SapSal [wird] stark personalisiert, so dass sie beinahe als eigenständige Person neben Gott erscheint."

35. Sterling 2017, 211–13.

36. Cf. also Hübner 1993, 79: "Gottes Wirken durch die Weisheit bzw. den der Weisheit innewohnenden Geist geschieht als Wirken des transzendenten Gottes inmitten der in seiner Raumhaftigkeit reflektierten Welt, die als Immanenz begriffen ist. Kurz: Der transzendente Gott wirkt kraft seines Geistes, seiner Weisheit in der immanenten Welt." According to Lorenzen (2008, 47), Sophia makes the divine order visible in the world.

Kloppenborg, John S. 1982. "Isis and Sophia in the Book of Wisdom." *HTR* 75:57–84.

Lorenzen, Stefanie. 2008. *Das paulinische Eikon-Konzept: Semantische Analysen zur Sapientia Salomonis, zu Philo und den Paulusbriefen.* WUNT 2/250. Tübingen: Mohr Siebeck.

Mack, Burton L. 1973. *Logos und Sophia: Untersuchungen zur Weisheitstheologie im hellenistischen Judentum.* Göttingen: Vandenhoeck & Ruprecht.

Malherbe, Abraham J. 2014. "Introduction." Pages 1–8 in *Light from the Gentiles: Hellenistic Philosophy and Early Christianity; Collected Essays, 1959–2012.* Edited by Carl R. Holladay, John T. Fitzgerald, Gregory E. Sterling, and James W. Thompson. NovTSup 150. Leiden: Brill.

Mansfeld, Jaap. 1992. "ΠΕΡΙ ΚΟΣΜΟΥ: A Note on the History of a Title." *VC* 46:391–411.

Moraux, Paul. 1984. *Der Aristotelismus im I. und II. Jh. n. Chr.* Vol. 2 of *Der Aristotelismus bei den Griechen von Andronikos bis Alexander von Aphrodisias.* Peripatoi 6. Berlin: de Gruyter.

Neher, Martin. 2004. *Wesen und Wirken in der Sapientia Solomonis.* BZAW 333. Berlin: de Gruyter.

Opsomer, Jan. 2005. "Demiurges in Early Imperial Platonism." Pages 51–99 in *Gott und Götter bei Plutarch: Götterbilder – Gottesbilder – Weltbilder.* Edited by Rainer Hirsch-Luipold. RVV 54. Berlin: de Gruyter.

———. 2006. "Over de wereld en haar bestuur." Unpublished paper delivered in honor of Prof. Dr. A. P. Bos at the Free University, Amsterdam, 28 April.

Pohlenz, Max. 1965. "Philon von Alexandreia." Pages 305–83 in vol. 1 of *Kleine Schriften.* Edited by Heinrich Dörrie. Hildesheim: Olms.

Reale, Giovanni, and Abraham P. Bos. 1995. *Il trattato Sul cosmo per Alessandro attribuito ad Aristotele: Monografia introduttiva, testo greco contraduzione a fronte commentario, bibliografia ragionata e indici.* 2nd ed. Studi e testi 42. Milan: Vita e Pensiero.

Reese, James M. 1970. *Hellenistic Influence on the Book of Wisdom and Its Consequences.* AnBib 41. Rome: Biblical Institute Press.

Sterling, Gregory E. 2017. "The Love of Wisdom: Middle Platonism and Stoicism in the Wisdom of Solomon." Pages 198–213 in *From Stoicism to Platonism: The Development of Philosophy, 100 BCE–100 CE.* Edited by Troels Engberg-Pedersen. Cambridge: Cambridge University Press.

Thom, Johan C. 2009. "Wisdom in the Wisdom of Solomon and Cleanthes' Hymn to Zeus." Pages 195–207 in *Septuagint and Reception*. Edited by Johann Cook. VTSup 127. Leiden: Brill.

———. 2012a. "Kosmiese Mag in Pseudo-Aristoteles, *De mundo*, en die Nuwe Testament." *HTS Teologiese Studies/Theological Studies* 68/1. doi: 10.4102/hts.v68i1.

———. 2012b. "Popular Philosophy in the Hellenistic-Roman World." *Early Christianity* 3:279–95.

———. 2014a. "The Cosmotheology of *De mundo*." Pages 107–20 in *Cosmic Order and Divine Power: Pseudo-Aristotle, "On the Cosmos."* Edited by Johan C. Thom. SAPERE 23. Tübingen: Mohr Siebeck.

———. 2014b. "Greeks Seeking Wisdom: Abraham Malherbe's Contribution to Hellenistic Philosophy and Early Christianity." *BR* 59:35–44.

———. 2014c. "Introduction." Pages 3–17 in *Cosmic Order and Divine Power: Pseudo-Aristotle, "On the Cosmos."* Edited by Johan C. Thom. SAPERE 23. Tübingen: Mohr Siebeck.

———. 2014d. "Text, Translation and Notes." Pages 20–66 in *Cosmic Order and Divine Power: Pseudo-Aristotle, "On the Cosmos."* Edited by Johan C. Thom. SAPERE 23. Tübingen: Mohr Siebeck.

———. 2015. "Paul and Popular Philosophy." Pages 47–74 in *Paul's Graeco-Roman Context*. Edited by Cilliers Breytenbach. BETL 277. Leuven: Peeters.

———. 2018. "Review of Abraham J. Malherbe, *Light from the Gentiles*." *Early Christianity* 9:369–72.

———. 2020. "The Power of God in Pseudo-Aristotle's *De mundo*: An Alternative Approach." Pages 135–52 in *World Soul – Anima Mundo: On the Origins and Fortunes of a Fundamental Idea*. Edited by Christoph Helmig. Topics in Ancient Philosophy 8. Berlin: de Gruyter.

Winston, David. 2005. "A Century of Research on the Book of Wisdom." Pages 1–18 in *The Book of Wisdom in Modern Research: Studies on Tradition, Redaction, and Theology*. Edited by Aangelo Passaro and Giuseppe Bellia. Berlin: de Gruyter.

Zeller, Eduard. 1919–1923. *Die Philosophie der Griechen in ihrer geschichtlichen Entwicklung*. 3 vols. Leipzig: Reisland.

Ziegler, Joseph. 1980. *Sapientia Salomonis*. Septuaginta. Vetus Testamentum Graecum 12.1. 2nd ed. Göttingen: Vandenhoeck & Ruprecht.

The Joseph Narratives in the LXX, Philo, and Josephus
Philip R. Bosman

ABSTRACT: This essay analyzes two Hellenistic reworkings of the biblical Joseph narratives in relation to the Septuagint version and to the authors' stated view of the authority of the Hebrew Bible's translation into Greek. The LXX version of the Joseph narratives remains closely faithful to the Hebrew wording, by which method the narrative openness of the original telling is retained. The technique gives scope for retellings to be elaborated in various directions by authors writing for Hellenistic audiences. While Philo and Josephus sometimes suppress and depersonalize reference to God, they also occasionally add a divine perspective in their embellishments, which occur mostly in the form of added speeches in the mode of Greek historiography. Philo retains Joseph's moral ambiguity to a certain degree, while Josephus renders the protagonist more consistently in a positive light, seemingly in service of a self-apology.

1. Introduction

In this essay I compare the text of the LXX with two early Hellenizing interpreters of biblical material: Philo of Alexandria and Flavius Josephus. I will conclude with brief remarks on what such a comparison may suggest about the theology of the LXX, albeit with a number of provisos and restrictions. A theology of the LXX can entail a range of issues, among others, whether or not the kind of thinking about God reflected in a text should be considered in contradistinction to its Hebrew *Vorlage*. My focus here will rather be on how the text was viewed by its interpreters and how such views influenced their interpretations. In other words, what did Philo and Josephus allow themselves, and what were they inclined to do with an authoritative text such as the LXX? Both authors are for considerable parts of their oeuvres engaging with the Hebrew scriptures, so that an exhaustive study is not feasible. Consequently, I will provide mere glimpses on the issue by means of their use of small sections from the Joseph story at the end of the book of Genesis. More specifically, I will look at what these authors make of the moral ambiguity of the protagonist and how they embellish the compact biblical original with rhetorical extensions. The narrative culminates in Joseph revealing his identity to his brothers, so a few notes on the episode of Joseph's self-revelation to his brothers are included. Hovering in the background will be the question whether the authors in fact thought of the narrative as a theological text.

2. The LXX as Viewed by Philo and Josephus

I start with brief notes on how Philo and Josephus saw the status of the Greek translation of the Hebrew scriptures in order to gauge what they allowed themselves to do with it. This consideration needs to be preceded by yet another issue, namely, these two authors' use of the Greek text as opposed to its Hebrew/Aramaic *Vorlage*. Philo's command of Hebrew is contentious, but we may safely claim that he resorted in his exegetical commentaries to a translation of the Hebrew Bible.[1] The situation is more complex for Josephus. First, it remains uncertain whether Josephus's "native tongue" (*B.J.* 1.3; 5.361) was Hebrew or Aramaic.[2] Second, while he does not seem to quote from a Greek translation in his *Jewish Antiquities*, Feldman argues that he had a multilingual approach to his treatment of the Hebrew scriptures, probably using Aramaic, Hebrew, and Greek versions. The circumstances under which he decided to consult the Greek text remain unclear.[3]

More clearly evident is both authors' exceptionally high regard for the Greek translation of the Hebrew Bible, with both devoting extensive passages to its legendary origins, which are otherwise best known from the Letter of Aristeas: Philo in *Vit. Mos.* 2.25–45 and Josephus in *A.J.* 12.2. In his account, Philo evidently endeavors to promote the status of the "laws in the Chaldaean tongue" (2.6) even further. While Aristeas's translators compared their work as they went along and produced an agreed-upon text, Philo stresses divine intervention in the process, which culminated in

---

1. Cf. Feldman 1997, 80 n. 13.

2. For a summary of the issue, see Rajak 1983, 230–32.

3. Feldman (1997, 45) claims "good reason to believe that he had access to three textual traditions, one in Hebrew, two in Greek (the Septuagint and a proto-Lucianic text), and one in Aramaic"; see also nn. 21 and 22 below and Rajak 1983, 46–64, 230–36.

an inspired text. The ὑποβολεῖς ("interpreters") were explicitly ἐνθυσιῶντες, with the miraculous result that their separate translations on comparison after the event corresponded perfectly with each other. Furthermore, the words in the translation corresponded perfectly to the objects they referenced, just like the Chaldean words of the original text managed to do.[4] The translators, characterized as notable Hebrews with a Greek and a Hebrew education, were not simply ἑρμηνεῖς but ἱεροφάντες ("initiates") and προφῆται ("prophets"), perfectly attuned to the spirit of Moses himself. Josephus's paraphrase of Aristeas (his account reduces the original letter by two-thirds) is less miraculous and more practical. In *A.J.* 12.2, Josephus mentions how the interpreters were carefully scrutinized and how, after completion, the translated text was kept stable, with the possibility of correction if an addition or omission could be proved. Josephus uses a number of terms for the act of putting text into another language, including (μεθ-)ερμηνεύω, μεταγράφω, μεταφράζω, and μεταβάλλω, and does not seem to distinguish sharply between the acts of "translating" and "interpreting." In fact, he sees his own rewriting of the history of the Jews as a continuation of the work done by the translators of the LXX.[5] While the authors share a high regard for the translation as the result of God's πρόνοια, the existence of an authoritative text did not exclude the possibility of elaboration and manipulation, as is evident from their respective treatments of the Joseph narratives. Both stress that it stood in need of further interpretation, and both were quite liberal in their retelling. Refashioning the original was not meant to undermine its authority nor to displace it, and both authors claim at least some authority for their own interpreted versions.

3. The Joseph Narratives in Greek

3.1. The LXX Version: Respect for the Original

The Joseph narratives are among the best known and the most entertaining to be found in the Hebrew Bible and, consequently, among the best scrutinized. With sixteen chapters in the Hebrew text, they are also quite extensive, so that the current format will allow only a mere dipping into

---

4. Presumably Philo's language theory comes into play here and in extension his view that the texts are primarily allegories referring to (Platonic) reality.

5. Cf. Feldman 2000, 3–5 n. 4: "he did not conceive himself as adding or subtracting anything if he continued the LXX's tradition of liberal clarification."

the narrative and its accompanied scholarship. On LXX Genesis, Scarlata's valuable survey of scholarship and Hiebert's translation notes for the NETS edition are especially valuable.[6] The literature on what Philo and Josephus wrote about Ἰωσήφ (Philo) and Ἰώσηπος (Josephus) is equally extensive, with more recent in-depth treatments by Niehoff and Feldman's commentary of the *Jewish Antiquities*.[7] The contradicting evaluations of the biblical Joseph in Philo have been extensively discussed in scholarship but are only of peripheral interest to the current investigation, which will focus on the *De Iosepho*.[8]

While Feldman notes that LXX Genesis text does include some veering away from the *Vorlage*,[9] Scarlata stresses the "close lexical and syntactical relationship to the Hebrew parent text," even though the "translator was not slavishly dependent on the Hebrew, but did, at times, depart from the original to produce renderings for stylistic and, perhaps, theological reasons."[10] Hiebert seems circumspect in noting the heterogeneity of the translation technique in Genesis as in the LXX as a whole, "the marked swings from idiomatic to painfully literal renderings, sometimes within the same verse."[11] Hiebert proposes a particular understanding of the "interlinear model" as a way of dealing responsibly with the unevenness in translation mode, that is, the varying degrees of dependence on the (Hebrew/Aramaic) *Vorlage*. He prefers to use the model as "a metaphor to conceptualize the linguistic relationship between the Semitic and Greek texts rather than as a hypothesis that the LXX translators actually produced a diglot."[12] Such a conceptualization stresses the translation's educational aims over against cultic use. For this study, I assume that the relevant chapters, Gen 37–50, share the assumptions regarding the early layers of the translation, namely, that the Greek narratives of the Pentateuch go back even to the third century, regardless of how much of a historical kernel Aristeas's legend is seen to retain, and that it is first and foremost a translation. This may, of course, mean a range of things, but we may assume that the translators attempted

---

6. Scarlata 2015; Hiebert 2006.

7. Niehoff 1992; Feldman 2000.

8. Feldman remarks in an aside that he views the LXX as an interpretation, betraying perhaps a particular view of what a real translation should look like.

9. Feldman 2000, 3.

10. Scarlata 2015, 13.

11. Hiebert 2006, 85.

12. Hiebert 2006, 102.

to remain truthful to the conceptuality of their original text, with the safest way to accomplish this aim being to remain as literally close as possible. The sections I examined confirm this assumption, with correspondence to the original text often overriding clarity of meaning in the target community. Some sentences certainly fit Hiebert's verdict of "painfully literal," for instance, the following from Gen 37:13:

> καὶ εἶπεν Ἰσραὴλ πρὸς Ἰωσήφ Οὐχ οἱ ἀδελφοί σου ποιμαίνουσιν ἐν Συχέμ; δεῦρο ἀποστείλω σε πρὸς αὐτούς. εἶπε δὲ αὐτῷ Ἰδοὺ ἐγώ.[13]
> And Israel said to Joseph, "Are not your brothers herding in Sychem? Come, let me send you to them." And he said to him: "Look, I."

Here a meticulous rendition of the Hebrew text overrides intelligibility, or, as Wright notes, the Greek text "does not stand on its own feet."[14] It is possible but not likely that the response ἰδοὺ ἐγώ (cf. Hebrew הִנֵּנִי) could have been intelligible to a nonnative Greek speaker. Rather, two other possibilities are more plausible: either the translation was meant to be used in conjunction with the original, or the (divine) authority of the original determined the translation method. I suggest that the latter played an important part in how the Greek text was formulated.

3.2. Joseph's Moral Ambiguity

Turning to the Joseph narratives themselves, the fact that the LXX stays so close to the Hebrew text means that it also retains the compact style of the biblical narrative. Robert Alter in particular made us attentive to how the marvelously terse prose can contain huge narrative potential. At the start of the Joseph narratives, the LXX version of Gen 37:2 still packs a whole story into a single verse, the details of which are left to the imagination of the reader:

> LXX Gen 37:1–4: Κατῴκει δὲ Ἰακὼβ ἐν τῇ γῇ, οὗ παρῴκησεν ὁ πατὴρ αὐτοῦ, ἐν γῇ Χανάαν. αὗται δὲ αἱ γενέσεις Ἰακώβ· Ἰωσὴφ δέκα καὶ ἑπτὰ ἐτῶν ἦν ποιμαίνων μετὰ τῶν ἀδελφῶν αὐτοῦ τὰ πρόβατα ὢν νέος, μετὰ τῶν υἱῶν Βάλλας καὶ μετὰ τῶν υἱῶν Ζέλφας τῶν γυναικῶν τοῦ πατρὸς

---

13. The LXX Genesis text used is that of Wevers 1974.
14. Wright 2006, 49, quoting Pietersma 2002 in connection with the interlinear model.

αὐτοῦ· κατήνεγκεν δὲ Ἰωσὴφ ψόγον πονηρὸν πρὸς Ἰσραὴλ τὸν πατέρα αὐτῶν. Ἰακὼβ δὲ ἠγάπα τὸν Ἰωσὴφ παρὰ πάντας τοὺς υἱοὺς αὐτοῦ, ὅτι υἱὸς γήρους ἦν αὐτῷ· ἐποίησεν δὲ αὐτῷ χιτῶνα ποικίλον. ἰδόντες δὲ οἱ ἀδελφοὶ αὐτοῦ ὅτι αὐτὸν ὁ πατὴρ φιλεῖ ἐκ πάντων τῶν υἱῶν αὐτοῦ, ἐμίσησαν αὐτόν, καὶ οὐκ ἐδύναντο λαλεῖν αὐτῷ οὐδὲν εἰρηνικόν.

Jacob settled in the land where his father sojourned, in the land Canaan. These are the generations of Jacob: Joseph was seventeen years old, herding sheep with his brothers, being young, with the sons of Balla and with the sons of Zelpha, the women of his father; Joseph brought a malicious censure to Israel their father. But Jacob loved Joseph beyond all his sons, because he was a son of old age to him; he made him a colorful chiton. When his brothers saw that their father loves him [more than] all his sons, they hated him, and they could not speak to him anything peaceful.

The verse relates how Joseph at the age of seventeen was herding the sheep of his father with his brothers. Some suggestive detail follows: he was still a νέος,[15] while the brothers referred to are not the whole group but more specifically the boys of Jacob's two slave concubines. Something happened in the pastures of which we are not informed, but Joseph eventually returns home with a ψόγος πονηρός, an evil/bad "censure," presumably a report meant to put his half-brothers in a bad light.[16] Everything remains half-said and uncommented-upon, so that the reader is not sure but suspects that the information is intended to reflect on Joseph's character as much as it does on that of his half-brothers. Joseph's apparent lapse in judgment is mitigated by his age, but the reader is already aware of a fissure among the siblings—potentially worsened by Jacob's greater love for Joseph. Potential for filial conflict increases when Joseph receives from Jacob a χιτὼν ποικίλον, the LXX rendition of the Hebrew כתנת פסים, which scholars prefer to translate as "long-sleeved garment." In response, the brothers—apparently all of them—now positively hated him, and they were henceforth incapable of conversing with him peaceably.

Philo's references to Joseph are spread through his oeuvre but concentrated in the jarring depictions of the *De somniis* and the *De Iosepho*. His interpretation of Joseph in the *De somniis* is remarkably negative and differs quite drastically from the *De Iosepho*, a full treatise devoted to Joseph

---

15. Westermann 1986 speculates that the Hebrew term נער might be technical, but it attains a different nuance in the LXX; cf. also Niehoff 1992, 27 n. 29.

16. On the verse in the Hebrew narrative, see Niehoff 1992, 28 n. 32.

and situated among his exegetical commentaries on the patriarchs.[17] I will restrict my current remarks to the latter, which is certainly more positive but retains, albeit to a lesser extent, the ambiguity of the biblical version. The *De Iosepho*, partly narration and partly allegory, interprets the figure of Joseph as representing the statesman.[18] While Philo makes use of the generic features of a βίος (the ancient term for the genre of biography), his interest in the patriarchs in the *Exposition of the Law* lies primarily with what he perceives to be their allegorical meaning. The first three patriarchs—Abraham, Isaac, and Jacob—represent the triad of μάθησις ("learning," a life resulting from teaching), φύσις ("nature," a self-taught life), and ἄσκησις ("training," a life formed by practice). To these three modes of life Philo adds a fourth as presented by Joseph, that of the πολιτικός. To Philo, the stories about the patriarchs were included in the Torah because they signify humankind before the law was available for regulating human life. This scheme does not work consistently, and even the ingenious Philo, though ploughing on relentlessly, labors to sustain his line of thinking.[19] Ambiguity is inevitably attached to Joseph because the life he represents, that of the politician, is of necessity accompanied by dubious aspects and moral snares. A threefold division between modes of living was already attributed to Pythagoras: the life of pleasure (characterized by the pursuit of things, especially money, and the default mode of the masses), the life of politics, and the life of contemplation, the mode of the wise. The βίος πολιτικός is suspended between the two extremes, not as an Aristotelean mean but rather as a mode of compromise: its objectives are not altogether base, but it comes with that dubious attachment to ambition, the craving for acknowledgment and success, and the surrender of personal autonomy to those being governed. Although Philo's Joseph is mainly an idealized portrayal, he cannot escape the fate of the mode he represents.

The marvel of compact Hebrew narrative is not completely lost on Philo and Josephus, even if neither of them elaborates on the ψόγος πονηρός that introduces the shadow of ambiguity in the protagonist. Philo, intent on presenting Joseph as a natural politician, rather elaborates on the

---

17. Cf. *Somn.* 2.43, 116 versus the authorial summaries of *Ios.* 157, 268. Different solutions to the discrepancy have been offered by, among others, Bassler 1985.

18. See a detailed treatment of the treatise in relation to the biblical Joseph, with rich footnoting, in Niehoff 1992, 54–83.

19. Cf. Niehoff 1992, 57 and n. 15

reason why Jacob sent him to shepherd: his father saw in him a φρόνημα εὐγενές ("noble mind") and dispatched him to tend the sheep as the best preparation for managing a state. Philo also identifies the brothers' hatred as φθόνος, adding (on the line οὐκ ἠδύναντο λαλεῖν αὐτῷ οὐδὲν εἰρηνικόν) the fine psychological insight of how destructive pent-up hatred inevitably turns into even greater bitterness: "For emotions that are cooped up," says Philo, "and find no vent become more violent because expression is stifled." But their silence also meant, ominously, that Joseph remained unaware of their envy, which is why he innocently went on to tell them the explosive content of his two dreams. In his allegorical interpretation of this first part of the narrative, Philo interprets Joseph's coat (in his view "multicolored") as signifying political life, for "the politician needs be a man of many sides and many forms," different in war from when there is peace, vigorously opposing the few but skilled in persuading the many. The politician can rightly be considered as "sold" just as Joseph was sold: he seems to be receiving honors, but only in exchange for his captivity by the fickle and insatiable masses.

The ascetic, other-worldly philosopher Philo retains a critical distance from the type represented by Joseph and, consequently, also the ambiguity of Joseph's character cryptically embedded in the LXX narrative. The Judean nobleman Josephus is less critical of his inherited character and shows less interest in moral subtleties. Working in the tradition of "rhetorical historiography" probably best known to him through Dionysius of Halicarnassus and his *Roman Antiquities*, he devotes a considerable part of book 2 of his *Antiquities* to his famous namesake.[20] Josephus saw many similarities between himself and his forebear: he, too, had problems with envious family; he, too, was exiled from his homeland; and he, too, "became a prominent member of a foreign court."[21] But Joseph also played an important part in Josephus's project. From Niehoff's analysis emerges a very personal motive for his Joseph depiction, evident especially from the protagonist's relationship with his father, his brothers, the women in the story, and the Egyptians: Josephus's Joseph becomes in many ways an autobiographical apology. But apart from the personal interest, Feldman stresses the nationalistic motive running through the *Antiquities* as a whole that is also present in his treatment of the Joseph

---

20. On Josephus's Greek education and familiarity with Greek literature, see Feldman 1997, 64–73.

21. Feldman 2000, 134.

narrative: he wished to answer critics of the Jews that they were not capable of producing illustrious men despite their long history, and an idealized Joseph could fit this purpose very well.

In Josephus's opening sequence of the narrative, therefore, we do not find the moral ambiguity of the LXX. Josephus, for instance, suppresses the implied story of what happened in the pastures and the ugly gossip that Joseph brought back. Instead, he dwells on the reasons why Jacob loved Joseph more than his other children, namely, for his physical beauty (a result of his noble birth) and for his virtuous soul, as was evident from his practical wisdom (διά τε τὴν τοῦ σώματος εὐγένειαν καὶ διὰ ψυχῆς ἀρετήν, φρονήσει γὰρ διέφερε, A.J. 2.9). From the outset, therefore, we see Josephus portraying his protagonist as a καλὸς κἀγαθός, a Jewish nobleman.[22]

When Joseph then tells his dreams to his family, there is no indication that they should reflect negatively on the dreamer: the brothers immediately realize that Joseph was predetermined for power, greatness, and authority, which together with their father's preference for the son of Rachel a invoked envy and hatred (φθόνον ἐκίνησε καὶ μῖσος, A.J. 2.10). Josephus prided himself in the ability to interpret dreams and records some forty-four dreams in the *Antiquities*, all of which turn out to be true. But Joseph's dream interpretation is not used to promote dream interpretation as such. Focusing rather on how Joseph's dreams affected his relationships with his brothers, Josephus reads the story in the light of his own experiences during the Jewish Revolt, that is, how he would have wished events of his own life to have played out.[23] There is no indication in Josephus that Joseph deserved at least some of his family's scorn.

Philo, with his more ambiguous attitude toward Joseph, differs in this regard.[24] Philo depicts the father, Jacob, as being afraid that Joseph might have made an error—not by telling everyone the dream but by dreaming such preposterous dreams. Philo can be quite acute in his psychological observations, and his Jacob thinks the dreams might just be expressions of wish fulfillment instead of sent by God: τὸ γὰρ τὴν ἐπὶ τοῖς οἰκείοις ἐλπίζειν καὶ καραδοκεῖν ἡγεμονίαν ἀπευκτὸν ἄγαν παρ' ἐμοὶ κριτῇ ("To hope and eagerly expect to lord it over your family I would regard repulsive," *Ios.* 9). Jacob consequently warns Joseph to let the memory of what he saw in his dreams quietly fade away. But there is more to the original narra-

---

22. Cf. Feldman 2000, 131–33.
23. See Niehoff 1992, 89–90.
24. On Joseph's dreams in Philo, see Reddoch 2011.

tive's depiction of Joseph revealing his dreams to his family than youthful naïveté. For a character who later in the story becomes famous for his skills in dream interpretation, it would be difficult to imagine that the meaning of sun, moon, and eleven stars could have passed him by, nor to try and imagine what προσκυνήσις could have looked like for heavenly bodies, even in a dream! It is up to the reader to decide whether Joseph was naïve, perplexed, or arrogant and taunting. The fact that the dreams turned out only relatively accurate—Jacob never προσκυνεῖ before Joseph—does not excuse the boast.[25]

3.3. Rhetorical Elaboration

In the next scene (Gen 37:12–35), the brothers plot against Joseph, and Rouben manages to save his life but not his sale into slavery. Where Rouben pleads with his brothers, the LXX text affords him two sentences: οὐ πατάξομεν αὐτὸν εἰς ψυχήν ("We shall not strike him to the soul") and μὴ ἐκχέητε αἷμα· ἐμβάλετε αὐτὸν εἰς τὸν λάκκον τοῦτον τὸν ἐν τῇ ἐρήμῳ, χεῖρα δὲ μὴ ἐπενέγκητε αὐτῷ ("Do not shed blood; throw him into this pit in the wilderness, but do not lay a hand on him"). Philo reports the eldest brother's words in a brief indirect speech (*Ios.* 13) as that they should keep their souls clear from ἀδελφοκτονία ("fratricide"); the emphasis on the effect of their actions on themselves should count as typical to a late Hellenistic philosopher. The politically minded Josephus, on the other hand, cannot resist exploiting the situation for a proper deliberation by Roubelos that would attempt to set before them "the magnitude of the shameless deed and the resulting defilement" (ἐπειρᾶτο κατέχειν ὑποδεικνὺς τὸ μέγεθος τοῦ τολμήματος καὶ τὸ ἐπ'αὐτῷ μύσος).[26] Also in indirect speech, Josephus's rhetoric goes on for a good number of lines (*A.J.* 2.21–31), mostly appealing to reason and the consideration of consequences: any murder is considered wicked (πονηρόν), by God as much as by unholy people, but

---

25. Alter 1980 is worth quoting: "Joseph is, of course, the magisterial knower in this story, but at the outset even he has a lot to learn—painfully, as moral learning often occurs. In his early dreams, he as yet knows not what he knows about his own destiny, and those dreams which will prove prophetic might well seem at first the reflex of a spoiled adolescent's grandiosity, quite of a piece with his nasty habit of tale-bearing against his brothers and with his insensitivity to their feelings, obviously encouraged by his father's flagrant indulgence."

26. The translation is quoted from Feldman 2000, 138.

to slaughter a brother is repulsive (μιαρώτερον); they should think of and have compassion for their father and mother; God is a witness to their plot but would welcome that if they would even now yield to μετάνοια and τὸ σοφρωνεῖν; however, if they decide to continue with profaning God's πρόνοια, he will punish them severely. What is more, they will be confronted by their συνειδός—that inner enemy none can escape. The term for conscience in Philo and Joseph, συνειδός is an inescapable inner accuser set next to God and exacting God's retribution. As conscience as a component of the human soul is absent from the Hebrew Bible, its introduction here may be regarded as a form of Hellenizing the biblical content. Roubelos continues by mentioning Joseph's youth, which should elicit sympathy instead of envy and murder. What is more, by killing Joseph, the brothers will not be able to share in the blessings God intended for Joseph. In the end, Roubelos settles for convincing them to commit a lesser crime.

Josephus's deliberative speech should be seen at least partly as an opportunity to display his rhetorical training as a member of the Hellenistic elite.[27] Philo would have had similar training, but being a philosopher he would have been aware of the continued enmity between philosophers and rhetoricians: the former searching for truth, the latter for persuasion. Thus he lets this scene pass but grabs onto the next, where Reuben finds out that Joseph is no longer in the well (*Ios.* 16–21). The eldest brother's grief is typically exaggerated, crying and shouting, ripping his clothes, rushing up and down, wringing his hands, and pulling at his hair (ἐβόα καὶ κάτω καθάπερ ἐμμανὴς ἐφέρετο τὰς χεῖρας κροτῶν καὶ τὰς τρίχας τίλλων, *Ios.* 16). This is followed by a lament, then by an extended, sarcastic, and, given the dramatic circumstances, an improbably detailed series of accusations against his brothers—even eventually turning to the Socratic dictum that it is worse to do wrong than to be wronged (τοῦ ἀδικεῖσθαι τὸ ἀδικεῖν χαλεπώτερον, *Ios.* 21).[28]

Philo must have had a penchant for depicting grief, since a few lines further he is at it again, this time with an even longer elaboration on Jacob's grief when confronted by Joseph's blood-stained χιτών (*Ios.* 22–27). As in the case of Reuben, Philo starts by describing the physical gesturing associated with intense grief: overwhelmed by the intensity of his emo-

---

27. While Josephus in his writings only mentions one rhetorician, he would have gained the skills for writing embedded speeches from the numerous historiographers he seems to have encountered in his studies of Greek culture; see Feldman 1997, 65–66.
28. See Plato *Gorg.* 469c, 508b, 509c; see Colson 1935, 600.

tions, Jacob simply faints, but after a while he starts wailing bitterly, his tears pouring as from a fountain and wetting his face, his beard, and his garment. The again dramatically improbable direct speech that follows is substantially longer than that of Reuben. In the historical treatise *In Flaccum*, Philo also pulls out all stops and, as here, depicts the lamenter in a state of temporary derangement, not so much of mind—the speeches are completely rational—as of control over bodily movements.[29] While some scholars see parallels to Flaccus's laments in the slightly later genre of the novel, the literary lament was part of Greek literature since Homer and, of course, well developed in tragedy, so someone eager to display skill in describing the soul overwrought with grief had a considerable literary tradition to tap into. All of this, of course, in contrast to the beautifully evocative two simple sentences of LXX Gen 37:30 as Rouben's reply: τὸ παιδάριον οὐκ ἔστιν· ἐγὼ δὲ ποῦ πορεύσομαι ἔτι; ("The little boy is not [here]; and I, where shall I go now?").

The episode in the Joseph narrative in which both authors obviously took great pleasure reimagining is that of Joseph and the wife of Potiphar, or Petephres, as in the LXX, or Josephus's Pentephres. The LXX also mentions that he was the eunuch of Pharaoh (Gen 39:1), a fact kept by Philo (*Ios.* 27, 37) but omitted by Josephus, who probably understood the Hebrew סריס as more generally an officer.[30] Whether the term εὐνοῦχος in the LXX was a mere mistranslation or served as an explanation for the lasciviousness of Potiphar's wife, Philo does not give it much thought: he simply goes on to elaborate on how Joseph's training in οἰκονομία ("household management") prepared him for a successful political career (*Ios.* 37–39). Josephus, interestingly, is interested not only in practical training; his Joseph gets a παιδεία ἐλευθέριον, the liberal education that the nobleman Josephus himself probably received—another way in which the biblical Joseph was his very own precursor.[31] Even more interesting for the current investigation is that neither Philo nor Josephus grabs the opportunity to elaborate on the repeated remark in the LXX that ὁ κύριος ἦν μετ' αὐτοῦ ("the Lord was with him").[32] Josephus completely omits any

---

29. For a discussion, see Bosman 2020.
30. Feldman 2000, 142 n. 131
31. Feldman 2000, 142–43 n. 135.
32. The notion is strengthened by the observations that his master knew that it was the Lord who caused everything he did to prosper (Gen 39:3) and that God blessed Potiphar's house and possessions for the sake of Joseph (Gen 39:5).

reference to God's supervision or blessing, while Philo retains it as from the perspective of his Egyptian master, who noticed rather neutrally that everything Joseph did was οὐκ ἄνευ θειας ἐπιφροσύνης ("not without divine wisdom," *Ios.* 37).

According to Feldman,[33] Josephus tends to deemphasize the role of God when he wishes to highlight the accomplishments of his human heroes. This episode is used primarily to illustrate Joseph's virtue and how his φρόνημα ("mind") could overcome any challenge. This comes in the form of Pentephres's wife, who fell not only for his εὐμορφία ("attractiveness") but also for the δεξιότητα, his dexterity in managing the household. In the LXX, she is not the most discreet of lovers: κοιμήθητι μετ' ἐμοῦ, she says after looking the young man up and down, "come sleep with me." Both our Hellenistic authors, however, dwell quite a bit longer on the ensuing drama, with Josephus extending the fourteen verses of the original text to a mini-novella, complete with the woman feigning illness during a festival to seek out Joseph and the narrator reporting the persuasive displays of both parties before the denouement. Philo makes up for what he may lack in narrative with a huge speech in the first-person inserted where the wife of Potiphar had been worked up into a mad frenzy (τῇ γὰρ εὐμορφίᾳ ἐπιμανεῖσα τοῦ νεανίσκου καὶ ἀκαθέκτως περὶ τὸ πάθος λυττῶσα), and the lad "stoutly resisted" her indecent proposals by virtue of the decency and temperance (κοσμιότητα καὶ σωφροσύνη) derived from his nature and nurture (ἐκ φυσέως καὶ μελέτης). But, quoting further from Colson's rendering of Philo's melodramatic text,

> as she fed the fire of lawless lust till it burst into a blaze, her constant efforts to gain him as constantly failed, at last in an accession of passion she was fain to employ violence. She caught hold of his outer garment and powerfully drew him to her bed with superior force, since passion which often braces even the weakest gave her new vigour (*Ios.* 41–42).[34]

Joseph, however, matched her power and burst himself—not of passion but into a long and overdrawn speech that surely ought to have been, under the circumstances, a passion-killer (*Ios.* 42–48). But she clung to the garment as he fled, and Philo comes as close to a tongue-in-cheek observation as we could imagine, noting that the ἐσθης ("garment") that

---

33. Feldman 2000, 143.
34. Colson 1935, 163.

she showed to her husband as proof should rather have been evidence of violence against Joseph. Philo blames Potiphar for poor lack of judgment in not seeing through the ruse (*Ios.* 52–53).

Scholars have in the past noted the similarities between the narratives of the wife of Potiphar and the Phaedra-Hippolytus myth dramatized by both Sophocles and Euripides. The story was popular in Roman times,[35] which may be the reason why Josephus presents the biblical narrative with some parallels to renditions of the Phaedra myth.[36] Unlike Euripides's version, however, Josephus found the moral of the story in the κοσμιότητα and σωφροσύνη of Joseph, with which he with considerable irony ends the section as the virtues that Pentephres claims to have recognized in his wife. Philo, on the other hand, finds the virtue epitomising the narrative to be ἐγκράτεια (or καρτερία), which together with ποιμενικός and οἰκονομικός are the distinguishing virtues of the politician that Moses wished to set before his readers.

4. A Theological Text?

The analysis above has shown that Philo and Josephus shared a high regard for the Hebrew scriptures and that Philo at least transferred this high regard to the Greek Bible as well. It is not equally evident what Josephus thought of the LXX specifically, since he seems to have made only occasional use of it and viewed his own rendition of the Jewish history as continuing in similar vein as the LXX translators. We may assume, however, that he regarded it as authoritative inasmuch as it rendered the Hebrew scriptures into the lingua franca of his times. We also saw that both Philo and Josephus did not subscribe to the scriptures in whatever format as self-sufficient, since they were in need of proper interpretation. They considered their own work as the consequence of this fact. The originals' authority did not deter them from expanding and elaborating nor of suppressing parts of the texts they found less useful or even inappropriate to their own textual goals.

The question may be asked whether they regarded texts such as the Joseph narratives as conveying a particular theology and that their task as μεθερμηνεῖς included a responsible rendition of and elaboration on such

---

35. Cf. Pausanias, *Descr.* 1.22.1.
36. Cf. Feldman 2000, 146–49 nn. 158, 167, 177.

theological views. This does not seem to be the case. A striking feature, in my view, of both the authors is that the texts are not amplified on aspects that might be considered as in the ambit of theology but that they are rather pulled into more Hellenistic *cum* secular contexts, for purposes other than theology: philosophical allegory, moral exempla, historiography. Philo is explicit throughout that Joseph's history should be interpreted allegorically to elucidate the topic of the political, and God features only at the margins of his interpretation. Josephus is again more complex. There are quite a number of instances where Josephus gives God a role or heightens God's role in comparison to the original narrative,[37] but he also occasionally omits the original's reference to God or refers to the more impersonal τὸ θεῖόν.[38] Feldman notes that Josephus introduces God into the narrative for the first time after the episode with Pentephres's wife in *A.J.* 2.60, where, interestingly, Philo mentions only Joseph's virtue, and that the narrator mainly downplays the role of God when he wishes to give his human protagonist full focus. There is no clear pattern to be observed, however, and Josephus does hold to his initial theological purpose with the work, to show that God is steering events behind the scenes and that he makes use of human "assistants" (συναίτιοι) to accomplish his πρόνοια.

The Joseph narrative culminates in the episode where the protagonist finally makes his true identity known to his brothers. In the LXX, Joseph relieves his siblings from their guilt toward him by stating that it was in fact God who steered the course of his fate (Gen 45:5, repeated in v. 7) and made him into a powerful figure in Egypt (Gen 45:8)—the message they had to convey to Jacob as well (Gen 45:9). Considering that Josephus at the start of the *Antiquities* gives his work an explicitly theological aim (*A.J.* 14–25), it may be expected that he would use the opportunity to elaborate on one of his favorite themes: God's πρόνοια. The speech he sets in Joseph's mouth is, however, little more than a paraphrase of the biblical text, expressing his gratitude toward his brothers for acting as allies in executing God's plans. Philo similarly does not elaborate on the beautifully crafted plan of God but merely states God to be the real agent behind what happened to Joseph for the benefit of the whole family. A hesitant conclusion would be that neither Philo nor Josephus wishes to excise God from the Joseph narratives, but they did not feel obliged to elaborate on God's

---

37. *A.J.* 2.25, 60, 63, 74, 86, 117, 129, 136, 137.
38. *A.J.* 2.39, 42, 80, 84, 89, 118, 121. For τὸ θεῖόν, see, among others, *A.J.* 13.

role. Rather, we find their emphases wandering to issues their contemporary readerships would have regarded as more appropriate and interesting in their respective genres. This may be considered a consequence of the LXX translation itself. Exactly because the translator/translators aimed to render the Hebrew text as faithfully as they could, they managed to translate the suggestive potentiality of the Hebrew narratives into a different world of significations and interlocking conceptuality. In this way, their evocative power could be channeled into and utilized in hitherto unforeseen literary and cultural settings.

Bibliography

Alter, Robert 1980. "Joseph and His Brothers." *Commentary* 7:59–68.

Bassler, Jouette M. 1985. "Philo on Joseph: The Basic Coherence of *De Iosepho* and *De somniis ii*." *JSJ* 16:240–55.

Bosman, Philip R. 2020. "Philo's Flaccus: Trauma, Justice, and Revenge." In *Emotional Trauma in Greco-Roman Literature*. Edited by Andromache Karanika and Vassiliki Panoussi. Oxford: Routledge.

Colson, F. H. 1935. *Philo: On Abraham. On Joseph. On Moses*. LCL. Cambridge: Harvard University Press.

Feldman, Louis H. 1997. "Torah and Greek Culture in Josephus." *The Torah U-Madda Journal* 7:41–87.

———. 2000. *Judean Antiquities 1–4*. Vol. 3 of *Flavius Josephus Translation and Commentary*. Leiden: Brill.

Hiebert, Robert J. V. 2006. "The Hermeneutics of Translation in the Septuagint of Genesis." Pages 85–103 in *Septuagint Research: Issues and Challenges in the Study of the Greek Jewish Scriptures*. Edited by Wolfgang Kraus and R. Glenn Wooden. SCS 53. Atlanta: Society of Biblical Literature.

Niehoff, Maren 1992. *The Figure of Joseph in Post-biblical Jewish Literature*. AGJU 16. Leiden: Brill.

Pietersma, Albert. 2002. "A New Paradigm for Addressing Old Questions: The Relevance of the Interlinear Model for the Study of the Septuagint." Pages 337–64 in *Bible and Computer—The Stellenbosch AIBI-6 Conference: Proceedings of the Association Internationale Bible et Informatique 'From Alpha to Byte,' University of Stellenbosch 17–21 July, 2000*. Edited by Johann Cook. Leiden: Brill.

Rajak, Tessa. 1983. *Josephus: The Historian and His Society*. London: Duckworth.
Reddoch, M. Jason. 2011. "Philo of Alexandria's Use of Sleep and Dreaming as Epistemological Metaphors in Relation to Joseph." *International Journal of the Platonic Tradition* 5:283–302.
Scarlata, Mark W. 2015. "Genesis." Pages 13–28 in *The T&T Clark Companion to the Septuagint*. Edited by James K. Aitken. London: Bloomsbury.
Westermann, Claus 1986. *Genesis 37–50: A Continental Commentary*. Minneapolis: Fortress.
Wevers, John W., ed. 1974. *Genesis*. Vol. 1 of *Septuaginta: Vetus Testamentum Graecum*. Göttingen: Vandenhoeck & Ruprecht.
Wright, Benjamin G., III. 2006. "Translation as Scripture: The Septuagint in Aristeas and Philo." Pages 47–61 in *Septuagint Research: Issues and Challenges in the Study of the Greek Jewish Scriptures*. Edited by Wolfgang Kraus and R. Glenn Wooden. SCS 53. Atlanta: Society of Biblical Literature.

Toward Defining the Fourth Quest in 2 Maccabees Theological Research

Pierre J. Jordaan

ABSTRACT: The aim of this essay is to demonstrate the main features of theologically based research on 2 Maccabees over the past century. This will be done by dividing this period into four quests. These quests represent chronological periods wherein certain theological leitmotifs surfaced. The fourth quest research represents current theological endeavors in 2 Maccabees. This quest, dating from after the 2012 publications until the present day, has yielded some unique approaches to the study of 2 Maccabees.

1. Introduction

The book 2 Maccabees may be considered atypical in various ways. First, it was written in Greek and has no Semitic *Vorlage* for the purposes of comparison. Thus, 2 Maccabees is not merely a translation wherein subtle theological nuances might surface. Second, its theological content deviates considerably from other Septuagint books. In this regard, Otto Kaiser mentions certain aspects (although there are many) found solely in 2 Maccabees.[1] For example, in 2 Macc 7 there is a reference to the future resurrection of the dead as well as a statement that strongly implies that God made heaven and earth and everything that fills it from nothing. Therefore it involves both an early witness to the concept of the bodily resurrection of the pious and serves as a precursor to the doctrine of *creatio ex nihilo*. Another unique feature, according to Kaiser, is found in 2 Macc 12:40–45: the oldest attestation of faith apropos the efficacy of intercession and atonement for the dead.[2] The third peculiarity is the

---

1. Kaiser 2004, 22.
2. Kaiser 2004, 19.

fact that 2 Maccabees has a large number of neologisms. Daniel Schwartz mentions 2,200 words that are found only in 2 Maccabees.[3] Later studies, such as the one of Nikolaos Domazakis, limits the actual (*hapax legomena*) neologisms to fifty-nine.[4] Nevertheless, considering the abovementioned claim that 2 Maccabees is somewhat idiosyncratic, it is safe to assume that new words were employed to denote new ideas or even possibly a new theology. Accordingly, 2 Maccabees creates the expectation of something different. Research on 2 Maccabees, especially from a theological perspective, has shown a remarkable development over the past century.

The aim of this essay is to demonstrate the main features of theologically based research on 2 Maccabees over the past century. This will be done by dividing this period into four quests. These quests represent chronological periods wherein certain theological leitmotifs surfaced. The fourth quest in 2 Maccabees research represents current theological endeavors in 2 Maccabees. This quest dates from after the 2012 publications until the present day. This quest is different from the others in that it does not center on a book but focuses rather on articles published since 2013, as no new commentary has been published since that date. The fourth quest also has different approaches that incorporate all sorts of methods that have been used to scrutinize the text of 2 Maccabees.

2. The First Quest (1891–1937)

The first commentator here is Otto Böckler. In his *Die Apokryphen des Alten Testaments* (1891), Böckler discusses extensively why 2 Maccabees was not taken up in the Protestant canon.[5] His main contribution, theologically, was twofold. First, he acknowledged the importance of the Jerusalem temple,[6] which he saw as the center of the author's theocratic/pragmatic historical approach. Second, he saw 2 Maccabees as an orthodox Pharisaic book over against the theological beliefs of the Sadducee party.[7]

---

3. Schwartz 2008, 71–72.
4. Domazakis 2018, 352.
5. Böckler 1891.
6. Böckler 1891, 93.
7. Böckler 1891, 93.

In 1913, James Moffatt wrote the introduction to and translation of 2 Maccabees in *The Apocrypha and Pseudepigrapha of the Old Testament*, edited by Robert H. Charles.[8] Moffatt, like Böckler, regarded 2 Maccabees as Pharisaic. He also noted a few theological ideas.

He sees the theology of punishment and reward as especially important. This system, according to Moffatt, is worked out with special care in 2 Maccabees. Unfortunately, he does not refer to any other texts where this scheme is mentioned.[9] Furthermore, Moffatt saw the suffering of the martyrs as an expiation for the sins of the nation. Thus, as the righteous, they placate God's anger toward their fellow Jews.[10] Moffatt also noted that the righteous who suffer and die will be raised up in the afterlife.[11]

The third person from the first quest who needs to be mentioned is Elias Bickerman, with his 1937 book *Der Gott der Makkabäer: Untersuchungen über Sinn und Ursprung der makkabäischen Erhebung* (ET 1979). Bickerman claims that the religious conflict in 2 Maccabees was not only between Jews and Seleucids but also among the Jews themselves.[12] The clash was between an orthodox group and a reformist group of Jews. The orthodox group was conservative and monotheistic, while the reformed group was pro-Hellenistic and possibly even polytheistic in nature. In this book Bickerman states that, theologically, 2 Maccabees belongs to the genre of "pathetic historiography" of the Hellenistic age. He also states that this genre is highly rhetorical and attempted to awake fear and sympathy in the heart of the reader.[13] In 1937 Bickerman already went so far as to say that modern scholars completely underestimate 2 Maccabees as being purely "rhetorical" in character.[14] Bickerman, in effect, pleads for future scholars to take seriously the rhetorical value of 2 Maccabees as a unique Hellenistic writing. A graphic depiction of the first quest is presented below:

---

8. Moffatt 1913, 125–54.
9. Moffatt 1913, 131.
10. Moffatt 1913, 131.
11. Moffatt 1913, 131.
12. Bickerman 1979, 90.
13. Bickerman 1979, 96.
14. Bickerman 1979, 95–96.

Table 1: A Summary of the First Quest (1891–1937)

Böckler	Moffatt	Bickerman
Prominent Theological Issue		
Jerusalem temple	reward and punishment; God's anger taken away by martyrs; the pious will rise bodily after death.	monotheism versus polytheism in Jerusalem
Conflict		
Pharisees versus Sadducees	Pharisees versus Sadducees	orthodox versus reformist Jews
Type of Literature		
temple history	no mention	pathetic historiography; highly rhetorical

Indeed, the following quests built upon certain key themes. Some commentators would refine these themes, and others would add new themes. This brings me to the second quest in 2 Maccabees research, which did not commence until 1959 as a result of the Second World War.

3. The Second Quest (1959–1985)

The second quest began with the publication of Victor Tcherikover's *Hellenistic Civilization and the Jews* (1959). Tcherikover adopts and extends the German word "Erhebung," meaning revolt or revolution, used by Bickerman in the title of his 1937 publication. Tcherikover saw the uprising in Jerusalem as coming from the populace and spreading to the countryside against the aristocracy and the temple elite.[15] The temple in Jerusalem was ruled by a pro-Hellenistic high priest. The temple, of course, was the hub of economic activity. The faithful came from all around to Jerusalem to sacrifice and make their offerings. The pro-Hellenistic temple elite disenfranchized the general population and deprived them of doing business. This resulted in dissatisfaction, which quickly spread from Jerusalem to the surrounding areas. This disenfranchisement was eventually developed

---

15. Tcherikover 1982, 192–93.

into a theological issue. The temple of the Lord had been polluted by gentiles and pagan rites. Tcherikover further states that the Hasidim were the driving force behind this popular revolt. The Hasidim's interpretation of the ancestral laws was made redundant by Jason the high priest. When the populace took up arms to oppose the Hellenizing government and pollution of their temple, the Hasidim were the unsurprising popular directors and leaders of the revolution. The pro-Hellenistic movement saw the Hasidim as a threat to the welfare and, in effect, undermining the state's political and social equilibrium. This hostility between these opposing parties became more and more evident, such that civil war became inevitable. The value of Tcherikover's contribution lies in the fact that he more accurately describes the parties in the revolution and their theological tendencies. The Seleucid colonists, with their temple-polluting polytheistic religion, wanted to turn Jerusalem into a Greek polis. According to Tcherikover, the Jewish masses would not accept what was happening to their temple.[16] The defilement to the temple and not being able to sell and buy in its vicinity became offensive to the Jewish populace. Tcherikover also states that 2 Maccabees looked upon Judas the Maccabee as the leader of the Hasidim.[17]

The second person who merits discussion with regard to the second quest is Robert Doran, with his *Temple Propaganda: The Purpose and Character of 2 Maccabees* (1981). Incidentally, this book was published one hundred years after the time of Böckler. Doran maintains the supremacy of the Jerusalem temple and its role in 2 Maccabees.[18] Naturally, a temple was protected by its patron deity and the deity's accomplices against other deities.[19] Doran thus propagates a distinct temple theology. Furthermore, his literary approach toward 2 Maccabees is important. He describes it as a highly emotional and dramatic rhetoric. Doran is thus advancing what Böckler (first quest) said about the temple. He also concurs with Bickerman on the rhetorical value of the text. Doran will be discussed in more detail in the third quest, where he further refined his ideas.

The third member of the third quest Elias Bickerman's doctoral student, Jonathan A. Goldstein, who first published his commentary on 2 Maccabees in 1983. He differed from his *Doktorvater* on various aspects

---

16. Tcherikover 1982, 195.
17. Tcherikover 1982, 198.
18. Doran 1981, 110, 114.
19. Doran 1981, 104.

of 2 Maccabees. He did not see 2 Maccabees, as Bickerman did, as a Hellenistic pathetic history but rather as ordinary history recorded by a more than capable historian, Jason of Cyrene.[20] Goldstein further openly refuted Bickerman on the source of the conflict in Judea. The conflict, according to Goldstein, was not among the Jews but rather came from outside, namely, from Antiochus IV Epiphanes, the Seleucid king.[21] Goldstein also does not see the temple in 2 Maccabees as being so important. He states that "the holiness of the temple is no guarantee that God will protect it. If the Jews sin the anger of the Lord will strike it too."[22] In summary, Goldstein takes a more conservative approach toward 2 Maccabees. He leaves the impression that the Jews are quite unique in the book of 2 Maccabees. They hardly borrowed anything from Hellenism and were victimized by the Seleucids. A graphic depiction of the second quest is presented below:

Table 2: A Summary of the Second Quest (1959–1985)

Tcherikover	Doran	Goldstein
Prominent Theological Issue		
the interpretation of ancestral law by Hasidim on temple defilement	the Jerusalem temple	typical Jewish focus, i.e., not Hellenistic.
Conflict		
temple elites versus Hasidim/population	the defenders and attackers of the temple	Antiochus IV and Jewish population
Type of Literature		
the dynamic history (clashes of classes)	highly dramatic and emotional rhetoric	highly structured history

In the second quest, Tcherikover refined the identity of the conflicting religious parties in Jerusalem in terms of a Greek polis. His notion that the populace around the temple were being deprived of business opportunities, as well the theological sidelining of the Hasidim, was valuable. Doran

---

20. Goldstein 1983, 21.
21. Goldstein 1983, 112.
22. Goldstein 1983, 17.

also acknowledged the importance of the temple but for another reason. Doran saw the Jerusalem temple as a space in which a clash of deities took place. Goldstein did not add much but rather reacted upon certain arguments of Bickerman. Nevertheless, the second quest was a step forward in 2 Maccabees research, but much still needed to be done.

4. The Third Quest (1986–2012)

In the third quest, it was perceived that the second quest had not really addressed the Hellenistic underpinning of 2 Maccabees. In the same vein, much more still needed to be said about 2 Maccabees from a theological perspective. The third quest may be seen as beginning in 1986 when Jan-Willem van Henten brought the Hellenistic background into 2 Maccabees again. The third quest (1986–2012) was also limited by the fact that the main contributors, Van Henten, Schwartz, and Doran, all employed a largely narrative critique when looking at 2 Maccabees.

The year 1986 brought a new approach to 2 Maccabees research with the Dutch dissertation of Jan-Willem van Henten, "De Joodse Martelaren als grondleggers van een nieuwe orde: Een studie uitgaande van 2 en 4 Makkabeën." Van Henten claimed that, in 2 Maccabees, Jerusalem is depicted as a typical Greek polis with a patron deity based on the Greco-Roman model. The patron deity of the city needs to be honored by the city. Whenever the patron deity is shamed by the conduct of the city, he or she is unable to defend the city. Consequently, atonement has to be undertaken by the city in order to repair the damaged relationship with the city's patron deity. The patron deity will again look favorably at the city when atonement has been completed.[23] Van Henten had now in effect made a theological transfer from the deities of the Greco-Roman world to the God of the Jews. Van Henten encountered serious criticism for this from his fellow European scholars. They claimed that the texts of 2 Maccabees should be scrutinized not just from a Greco-Roman point of view but also in comparison with other Jewish texts, as Jewish texts also have martyrs. Van Henten later admitted to the value of Jewish texts in his reworked book, the 1997 English version titled *The Maccabean Martyrs as Saviours of the Jewish People: A Study of 2 and 4 Maccabees*. In this work he typifies his approach to 2 Maccabees as "apologetic historiography."

---

23. Van Henten 1997, 243–67.

He defines this as a method that is usually employed by a member of a subgroup within a community. This person follows the traditions of the subgroup but Hellenizes the traditions in an effort to establish the identity within the setting of a larger world.[24] Van Henten makes the important statement that the author of 2 Maccabees used all means, from both Jewish and Greco-Roman sources, to reinvent the identity of the Jewish people.[25] Therefore, Greco-Roman and Jewish texts should not be seen as opposites but rather as complementing each other in order to establish a new identity. This is an important admission by Van Henten, and it means that theologically progress is facilitated and a new identity created. Van Henten, however, made another significant contribution to 2 Maccabees research, namely, his recognition of the importance of narrative critique. He distinguished six successive elements when looking at the martyr narratives of 2 and 4 Maccabees.[26] The importance of narrative on this literature is likewise recognized by George Nickelsburg when he states:

> I am interested not simply or primarily in ideas or motifs or in contents in some amorphous sense, but in literature that has form and direction: in narrative that has plot with beginning, middle and end (or situation complication and resolution); in other types of literature that use particular forms and rhetorical devices with consistency and purpose. The critic's task is to find these forms and directions and to interpret the text with reference to them.[27]

The timely contribution of Van Henten to a theological understanding of 2 Maccabees cannot be underestimated. He broke the stereotypical "either or" approach to 2 Maccabees, seeing it as either Jewish or Greco-Roman. He opened the door to the possibility that it might be both. He also stressed the importance of looking at the narrative.

David DeSilva (2004) and Nickelsburg (2005) picked up on certain themes of Moffatt (first quest) and elaborated on them. Both authors reiterated the importance of the punishment and reward system, which they called the Deuteronomistic philosophy of history. This system carried the promise of reward for obedience and punishment for disobedience. Both

---

24. Van Henten 1997, 20.
25. Van Henten 1997, 295–304.
26. Van Henten 1997, 26.
27. Nickelsburg 2005, 3.

authors saw the martyrs' obedience as a turning point in the narrative. DeSilva posited that the martyrs displayed covenant loyalty and that God's wrath was turned to mercy.[28]

The next important commentator of the third quest was Schwartz with his 2008 commentary, *2 Maccabees*. Schwartz recognized the value of Van Henten's contribution on various levels: on the use of narratives[29] and with regard to the use of Greek topoi. However, like Van Henten, he did not see the necessity of choosing between a uniquely Jewish or Greco-Roman background for interpreting 2 Maccabees. Like DeSilva and Nickelsburg, he also recognized the importance of the Deuteronomistic philosophy to interpret 2 Maccabees. Schwartz did not prefer a specific approach for history but merely called his focus the history of Jerusalem.[30] Schwartz did not add much new to the interpretation of 2 Maccabees

This brings me to the last and most recent contribution to the third quest: Doran with his *2 Maccabees: A Critical Commentary* (2012). On the very first page of his commentary Doran states: "It is a highly rhetorical narrative that sets out not to give a blow-by-blow description of events but to move the audience to commit to faithfully following the ancestral traditions of Judaism."[31] Doran hereby recognizes important aspects of 2 Maccabees: the rhetoric and the narrative that has a purpose to lead the audience toward Judaism. The mere characterization of 2 Maccabees as Hellenistic history is not enough for Doran to describe its complicated narrative. In order to arrive at a better understanding, Doran employs the subgenre of theomachy (the clash of deities) to describe the narrative.[32] However, there is still more to it. The deity is also, as Frank Moore Cross describes him, the "divine warrior in Israel's early cult"[33] who clashes with other divinities. For example, King Antiochus IV Epiphanes thought himself to be a god.[34] Doran also refers to the "divine warrior" on several occasions.[35] Thus God as the divine warrior has all the traits of a deity, such as a temple, certain accomplices, and an

---

28. DeSilva 2004, 275.
29. Schwartz 2008, 55–66.
30. Schwartz 2008, 6.
31. Doran 2012, 1.
32. Doran 2012, 6.
33. Cross 1966.
34. Doran 2012, 6.
35. Doran 2012, 44, 198, 202.

obvious need to be worshiped. Doran states: "The success of Judas comes because he fights for God, who is defending his temple."[36] Judas in this sense is secondary to the main protagonist, God.

Doran therefore argues that the purpose of 2 Maccabees is to show how God defended his temple from attackers.[37] In addition, 2 Maccabees promotes the inauguration of new festivals, whereby the author seeks to impress his audience about the high honor in which the God of the Jews is to be held.[38] In addition, the text demonstrates the need to participate in the festivals inaugurated to commemorate these events. In order to convince the reader, the author has arranged his text in such a way as to exhort the reader (rhetoric). The first method is by means of figures of style—different literary devices.[39] The second is by means of words and narrative structure.[40] A graphic depiction of the third quest is presented below:

Table 3: A Summary of the Third Quest (1986–2012)

Van Henten	DeSilva, Nickelsburg	Schwartz	Doran
Prominent Theological Issue			
the establishing of Jewish identity	the Jerusalem temple		the defense of Jerusalem temple
Conflict			
the patron deity versus own subjects	the defenders and attackers of the temple	Jews versus Hellenizers	divine warrior versus other deities
Type of Literature			
apologetic historiography	Deuteronomistic scheme	history in general	rhetorical narrative on theomachy

The third quest looked afresh at the theology of 2 Maccabees. The much-neglected Greco-Roman background was finally put on the same level

---

36. Doran 2012, 9.
37. Doran 2012, 2.
38. Doran 2012, 3–4.
39. Doran 2012, 4–5.
40. Doran 2012, 5.

as Jewish texts by Van Henten. Naturally, this had a huge impact when scrutinizing 2 Maccabees theologically. This leveling of the fields between Greco-Roman and Jewish antecedents opened the door for demonstrating new (progressive) theological ideas. Furthermore, Van Henten and Doran valued rhetoric as highly as Bickerman pleaded for it in the first quest. However, each followed his own specific rhetorical method that would most certainly render specific results. Nevertheless, this means that Bickerman's plea in the first quest to see 2 Maccabees as rhetorical begun to gain traction.[41] Most scholars, for various reasons, have seen the temple as important, as Böckler already stated in the first quest. However, Van Henten only sees the temple as pertaining to the city's patron deity, whereas Doran sees the temple distinctively as the space of the divine warrior. Schwartz, again, seems to view the temple as a mere symbol of God.[42] From the second quest to the third quest the source of the conflict shifted dramatically from "strife between people" to "strife between a deity and his people" (Van Henten) and "hypothetical strife between deities" (Doran).[43] Furthermore, DeSilva, Nickelsburg, and Schwartz saw the Deuteronomistic theological scheme as significant for 2 Maccabees. This means that, since Moffatt's observation in the first quest that postulated a theology based on punishment and reward, research has come a long way. Van Henten, Schwartz, and Doran all emphasized the importance of the narrative critique. However, each stressed different aspects of this. This is why Jordaan commented that narrative critique is a "free for all" when it comes to interpreting 2 Maccabees narratively.[44]

Research on 2 Maccabees has now come full circle. Most themes from the first quest have been addressed. However, there still does not seem to be consensus about the theological issues of 2 Maccabees. Rather, there seems to be both a majority and minority standpoint. The question can now be asked: What is the way forward for theological research on 2 Maccabees? This brings me to the fourth quest. That is the time frame from 2013 to the present. As already noted, no commentaries (as yet) have been published in this time. This research pertains to certain areas relevant to the theology of 2 Maccabees, whether the temple, rhetoric, theology, or

---

41. Doran 2012, passim.
42. Cf. Schwartz 2008, 164.
43. Van Henten 1997, 297–99; Avemarie and Van Henten 2002, 44; Doran 2012, 44, 198, 202.
44. Jordaan 2016, 91.

narrative critique. However, what really stands out in the fourth quest is the different methods that are used to arrive at some meaning for 2 Maccabees, methods such as narratology, cognitive linguistics, and semiotic theory etc.

5. The Fourth Quest (2013 to the Present)

Nicholas Allen read a paper titled "The Epitome of 2 Maccabees: The Rhetoric of Selling a New Theology of Salvation" at the Rhetoric in 2 Maccabees: Deities at War conference held in Potchefstroom on 2 and 3 December 2018.[45] His latest research shows that 2 Maccabees has the following narratological structure:

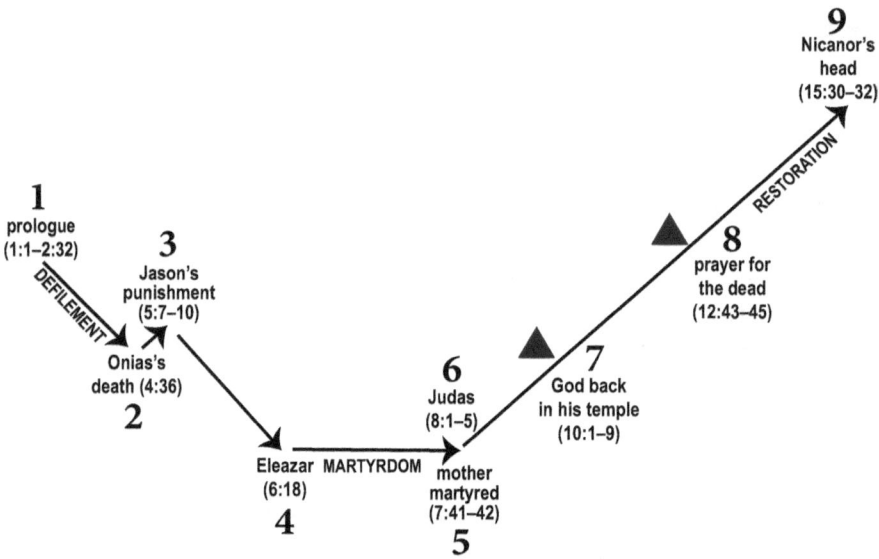

Fig. 1: The narratological structure of 2 Maccabees (Allen 2018)

According to Allen, the author of 2 Maccabees seems to have a deliberate narratological structure that seeks to entice and engage the reader for as long as possible (1–9). It starts out with the *status quo ante* (1) (prologue) when, everything is, according to Schwartz, in equilibrium.[46] God

---

45. Allen 2018.
46. Schwartz 2008, 184.

is in his temple, where the high priest, Onias III, is presiding with good results. However, when the temple is polluted during Jason's reign, the problems escalate (3–6). These problems prevail for a long time to keep the reader in suspense, awaiting a possible outcome. The restoration does not come before 2 Macc 8 (7), and still there are minor relapses along the way. However, this does not detract from the overall positive momentum of the narrative immediately after the martyrdom accounts (5). From (6) the introduction of Judas Maccabeus, the narrative literally takes off and climaxes with the removal of Nicanor's head (9). Regardless, everything does not always go according to plan, as when idols are found under the tunics of the dead (8) (2 Macc 12:40–45). However, in the end (2 Macc 15) everything works out fine. Allen argued that the temple serves as an indicator in the text for when God is acting on behalf of the Jewish nation. The narratological structure seems to indicate that God leaves the temple after Jason the high priest sent 300 drachms of silver for the sacrifice to Herakles (2 Macc 4:19–20). This was an extremely disrespectful act that prioritized a heathen demigod over the Jewish deity by the high priest, who was supposed to preserve and maintain God's divine will. This event also marks the beginning of the more dramatic decline in the narrative (3–5). Finally, Allen supports the more recent notion that the epitome of 2 Maccabees was most likely written and composed by a single authority. In short, he doubts that this text contains interpolations as suggested by, inter alia, Daniel McClellan.[47]

Another scholar who has shown that the epitome of 2 Maccabees is more likely a unified composition created by a single author is Domazakis. In his recent doctoral dissertation, he investigated previously underresearched Septuagint neologisms, specifically in 2 Maccabees. Here Domazakis examined how the neologisms have thus far been treated in Septuagint studies and lexicography and proposes a method for their identification based on a thorough search of the electronic databases of ancient Greek literary and nonliterary texts rather than of the existing Greek lexica. The main part of his thesis consists of a detailed commentary on some sixty neologisms of various types that occur in 2 Maccabees—neologisms first attested in this book that do not occur anywhere else in the Septuagint or other Greek works (absolute *hapax legomena*). This examination sought to trace the intertextual connections that link 2 Maccabees with

---

47. McClellan 2009.

such texts as the Greek Pentateuch, the Greek Psalter, Old Greek Daniel, 1 Esdras, 3 and 4 Maccabees, Addition E to Esther, and the Alpha Text of Esther; the study explores the possible influence on the deuterocanonical book's diction of secular Greek literary and nonliterary texts such as Polybius's *Histories* and the Hellenistic honorific decrees. Domazakis's findings provide chronological clues that suggest a date of composition or final redaction of 2 Maccabees in the first century BCE, or around the turn of the Common Era, rather than in the last third of the second century BCE, as is more commonly believed. Importantly, Domazakis provided good linguistic evidence (e.g., diction) to show that 2 Macc 7 was *not* an interpolation and that the entire book was written by one and the same author.[48]

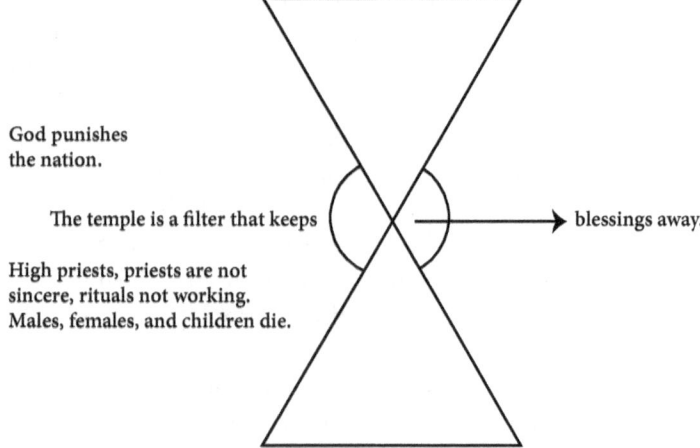

Fig. 2: Depiction of dynamic between God, temple, and nation (Jordaan 2015, 357)

The research of Jordaan in "The Temple in 2 Maccabees: Dynamics and Episodes" made use of another narratological approach.[49] Here Jordaan divides 2 Maccabees into three temple episodes; 2 Macc 3, 2 Macc 4–7, and 2 Macc 8–15. He shows that, if God is pleased with his people, the temple acts as a funnel that lets blessings through to his people. On the other hand, if God is displeased with his people, the temple acts as a filter that keeps blessings away.[50] The temple is thus a barometer that

---

48. Domazakis 2018, 354; on 2 Macc 7 as an interpolation, see McClellan 2009.
49. Jordaan 2015.
50. Jordaan 2015, 357.

measures the quality of the relationship between God and his people.⁵¹ These contributions by Allen and Jordaan indicate the importance of narrative criticism for 2 Maccabees and reaffirm the importance of the Jerusalem temple. The diagram below illustrates Jordaan's observations. However, this idea is taken even further in a paper by Jordaan titled "Body, Space and Narrative in 2 Macc 1:1–10a,"⁵² where the role of the mediator in the temple is discussed. In this regard, the diagram below illustrates Jordaan's observations.

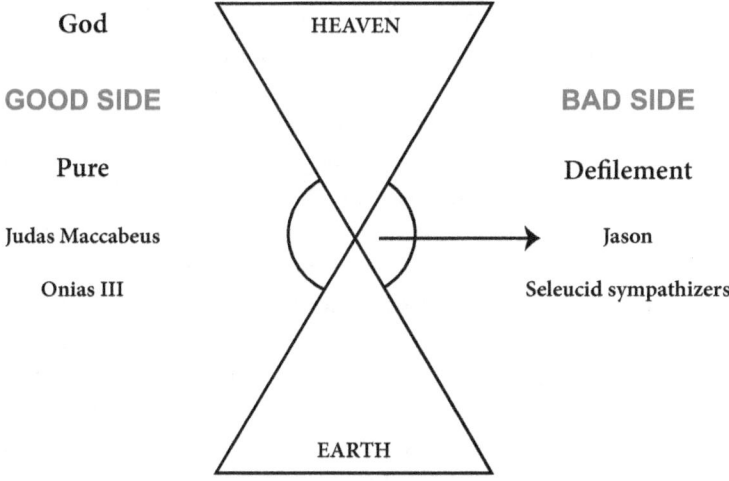

Fig. 3: Depiction of dynamic between priests and Seleucid sympathizers (Jordaan 2016, 99)

The diagram depicts the mediation of priests at the temple in Jerusalem. The lefthand side represents the pure mediation by a priest such as Onias III. The link between heaven and earth is sanctified. The righthand side represents the opposite. It is mediation gone wrong because of the actions of the corrupt Jason. The temple is defiled, and the channel between heaven and earth blocked.⁵³ Thus 2 Maccabees does not just have temple theology but also mediation theology. A pious priest such as Onias III qualifies as a mediator between God and his people. Jason does not qualify, as he defiled the temple by mingling with the Seleucids. This mediation is taken to a

---

51. Allen 2018 came to the same conclusion.
52. Jordaan 2016.
53. Cf. Ego 2017, 177.

next level in 2 Macc 15:12–16, where the now-deceased priest Onias III is praying in a vision on behalf of the Jews. The prophet Jeremiah is also present in this vision and hands a sword to Judas the Maccabee. In this vision, even after their deaths Onias and Jeremiah mediate between God and his people. This makes 2 Maccabees an example of mediation theology. These pious mediators operate during their lives and even after their deaths.[54] These three papers as part of quest four show the significance of the temple and mediation.

However, other contributions using other methods were also made, such as on the level of semiotics. In a paper presented by Jordaan at the IOSCS conference in Stellenbosch in 2016, semiotics was used to determine the appeal of the phrase "widows and orphans" in 2 Macc 3. Jordaan argued that "widows and orphans" were used as an index.[55] This means that this term denoted "the lowest of low" in Jewish society. On the other hand, the phrase "widows and orphans" included the acknowledgment that God would surely intervene on their behalf.[56] "Widows and orphans" is therefore a loaded concept. Theologically speaking, when one sees the "widows and orphans," one can expect action from God. This is the case in 2 Maccabees. In this sense, 2 Maccabees displays a theology of the underdog. The pious underdogs such as "widows and orphans" will prevail. This also seems to be the case with Judas Maccabeus, who fights the massive Seleucid armies and wins. The same can be said about Onias III, the pious priest who stood up with the population of Jerusalem against the mighty Heliodorus (2 Macc 4).

The fourth quest also makes primary use of cognitive linguistics as popularized by George Lakoff and Mark Johnson in *Philosophy in the Flesh*.[57] In this respect, Jordaan produced a range of articles that emphasized that bodily parts have distinctive meaning in 2 Maccabees. In this context, interesting findings resulted. (1) *Head* in 2 Macc 1:16 was shown as an organ housing the higher faculties such as worship and intelligence. However, if a head did not display these higher functions and, for instance, blasphemed, as Antiochus IV Epiphanes did, then a person would be decapitated. This is what happened to blasphemous heads of

---

54. Coetzer 2019 focuses on the excellent example set by the three elders: Onias III, Eleazar, and Razis.
55. Jordaan 2019.
56. Jordaan 2019.
57. Lakoff and Johnson 1999.

Goliath of Gad, Nicanor in 2 Macc 14:33, and Antiochus IV Epiphanes.[58] (2) *Heart* in 2 Macc 1:3–4 was shown not to be a human organ that pumps blood but, used with the adjectives *big* and *small*, denoting commitment to God. Thus, *heart* denotes commitment.[59] (3) Nicanor's arm was held out against the temple in 2 Macc 14:33, and he spoke blasphemous words against the temple. His arm, as well as his tongue, thus became degrading symbols against the temple. Consequently, both were cut off in 2 Macc 15:30–33.[60] An approach that makes use of cognitive linguistics reveals that the above-mentioned human organs are hardly neutral; quite to the contrary, they contribute substantially to the theological interpretation of 2 Maccabees.

In his paper "2 Maccabees 9, the Demise and Death of Antiochus IV Epiphanes as Dramatic Irony" (2017), Jordaan illustrates that Antiochus IV Epiphanes is unknowingly, like Sophocles's *Oedipus Tyrannus*, a victim of his own stupidity. Jordaan shows how the typical characteristics of a Greek tragedy, such as blasphemy and irony, are revealed here. Also, as the narrative progresses, Antiochus IV Epiphanes paints himself more and more into a corner. This illustrates the point that the author of 2 Macc 9 borrowed from Greek literature to convey his message and his efficiency in handling Greek.

Allen and Jordaan recently commented on the more traditional appraisal of the notion of atonement as contained in 2 Maccabees.[61] As is well-known, the novel idea portrayed in 2 Maccabees, that it is now possible to pray for the dead, was subsequently employed by the Catholic Church to justify, inter alia, the concept of purgatory. Here these scholars point out that, normally, traditional Judaism emphasizes personal, individual responsibility and accountability for transgressions against the deity. However, in 2 Maccabees the Jewish deity is suddenly portrayed as requiring financial payment as compensation for wrongdoing and not individual *teshuvah*. Indeed, even dead, unrepentant, Jewish soldiers are forgiven their transgressions, even something as abominable as idolatry. In short, Jewish transgression has now metamorphosed into something resembling Christian sin. Furthermore, the "sinner" does not need personally to atone for the misdeed. Money may now be paid to the deity

---

58. Jordaan 2013a, 724–25.
59. Jordaan 2016, 97–98.
60. Jordaan 2013b, 69.
61. Allen and Jordaan 2018.

on behalf of the transgressor and his or her "debt" repaid. In addition, this new theology is "sold" to the reader by misleadingly presenting it as though it was somehow in total accord with the more traditional "atonement for your lives" concept as proclaimed in, inter alia, Exod 30:11–16. In one sense, this finding mirrors that of Coetzer and Jordaan when they argue that 2 Macc 7 seems to be attempting to make sense of God through a modified doctrine in terms of suffering and sells it through emotional appeal.[62]

In a similar way, Coetzer realizes that 2 Maccabees is attempting to realign the thinking of the typical reader.[63] The text is trying to make the reader accept a new Jewish theology. In his study "A Rhetorical Analysis of 2 Maccabees," Coetzer presents an investigation into the various strategies applied in 2 Maccabees in order to move the reader to adopt certain ideas. The chief objective is to provide a layout of the communicative strategies applied throughout the text. In order to reach a satisfactory conclusion to this objective, his study set as goals a structural and pragmatic analysis. The structural analysis consists of the delimitation of the various pericopes in 2 Maccabees, a syntactical and semantic analysis, and a formulation of the proposition and argumentation of the author in each pericope. The pragmatic analysis consists of an explication of the communicative strategy, real- and alternative text-world, and transuniversal relations. The core findings of the study may be divided into four categories: (1) the main ideas communicated, (2) the strategies applied in order to encourage the reader to adopt these ideas, (3) the elements that make up these strategies, and (4) the possible impact of each of these elements on the reader. Interestingly, the author uses a technique of creating a contract of trust between the reader and a specific group within the text. A graphic depiction of the fourth quest is presented below:

---

62. Coetzer and Jordaan 2009.
63. Coetzer 2015.

Table 4: A Summary of the Fourth Quest (2012–Present)

Allen	Allen, Jordaan	Jordaan	Coetzer	Domazakis
Prominent Theological Issue				
the establishing of a new Jewish theology	the establishing of a new Jewish theology of atonement	the establishing of a new Jewish theology	the establishing of a new Jewish theology	number of neologisms
Importance of Temple				
important	important	important	N/A	N/A
Conflict				
the patron deity versus own subjects and outsiders	the patron deity versus own subjects and outsiders	the patron deity versus outsiders	the patron deity versus outsiders	N/A
Type of Literature				
narrative history	socially constructed/ tiered	cognitive constructed/ intertextual	rhetorically loaded	comparative literacy analysis

6. Conclusions

The fourth quest is identifiable by the advent of newer methods of interpretation to 2 Maccabees. Since quests one, two, and three, some refinement has taken place. For example, narratological analyses have shown that the temple may now be considered as a barometer indicating the status of the relationship between God and the Jewish nation. The importance of requiring an unblemished mediator to serve as intercessor between the nation and God has also been shown.

Research on 2 Maccabees has surely entered an exciting phase. The new theology portrayed in 2 Maccabees by, among others, Allen, Coetzer, Domazakis, and Jordaan, has begun to gain traction. This theology, however, is not named but seems to be a form of proto-Christianity. Here we take note that the Jewish deity seems to have evolved from one who constantly and willingly forgives those who demonstrate genuine repentance to suddenly requiring the torturous sacrifice of the only most righteous members of Jewish society. In addition, the Jewish deity is strangely portrayed as also forgiving dead and quite unrepentant idolaters in exchange for hard currency.

In conclusion, it can be said that the time for a new commentary on 2 Maccabees has come. The more stereotypical approaches have been surpassed.

Bibliography

Allen, Nicholas P. L. 2018. "The Epitome of 2 Maccabees: The Rhetoric of Selling a New Theology of Salvation." Paper presented at the Rhetoric in 2 Maccabees: Deities at War conference, North-West University, Potchefstroom, 3–4 December.

Allen, Nicholas P. L., and Pierre J. Jordaan. 2018. "Counting Half-Shekels—Redeeming Souls? in 2 Maccabees 12:38–45." *HTS Teologiese Studies/Theological Studies* 74/3. doi: https://doi.org/10.4102/hts.v74i3.5011

Avemarie, Friedrich, and Jan Willem van Henten. 2002. *Martyrdom and Noble Death: Selected Texts from Graeco-Roman, Jewish and Christian Antiquity.* New York: Routledge.

Bickerman, Elias. 1979. *The God of the Maccabees: Studies on the Meaning and Origin of the Maccabean Revolt.* Leiden: Brill.

Böckler, Otto. 1891. *Die Apokryphen des Alten Testaments nebst einem Anhang über die Pseudepigraphenliteratur.* Munich: Beck.

Coetzer, Eugene. 2015. "A Rhetorical Analysis of 2 Maccabees." Unpublished PhD dissertation, North-West University.

———. 2019. "Three Elders: Onias III, Eleazar, and Razis as the Embodiment of Judaism in 2 Maccabees." Pages 53–65 in *XVI Congress of the International Organization for Septuagint and Cognate Studies: Stellenbosch, 2016.* Edited by Gideon R. Kotzé, Wolfgang Kraus, and Michaël N. van der Meer. SCS 71. Atlanta: SBL Press.

Coetzer, Eugene, and Pierre J. Jordaan. 2009. "Selling Religious Progress to a Nostalgic Nation: Jewish Doctrinal Revolution in 2 Maccabees 7." *Ekklesiastikos Pharos* 91:179–88.

Cross, Frank Moore. 1966. "Divine Warrior in Israel's Early Cult." Pages 11–30 in *Biblical Motifs: Origins and Transformations.* Edited by Alexander Altman. Cambridge: Harvard University Press.

DeSilva, David A. 2004. *Introducing the Apocrypha: Message, Context and Significance.* Grand Rapids: Baker Academic.

Domazakis, Nikolaos. 2018. "The Neologisms in 2 Maccabees." Unpublished PhD dissertation, Lund University.
Doran. Robert. 1981. *Temple Propaganda: The Purpose and Character of 2 Maccabees.* CBQMS 12. Washington, DC: Catholic Biblical Association of America.
———. 2012. *2 Maccabees: A Critical Commentary.* Hermeneia. Minneapolis: Fortress.
Ego, Beate. 2017. "The Temple as a Place of Worship and the God of Heaven in 2 Maccabees." Pages 167–79 in *Various Aspects of Worship in Deuterocanonical and Cognate Literature.* Edited by Géza G. Xeravits, József Zengellér, and Ibolya Balla. Berlin: de Gruyter.
Goldstein, Jonathan A. 1983. *II Maccabees: A New Translation with Introduction and Commentary.* AB 41A. Garden City, NY: Doubleday.
Henten, Jan-Willem van. 1997. *The Maccabean Martyrs as Saviours of the Jewish People: A Study of 2 and 4 Maccabees.* JSJSup 57. Leiden: Brill.
Jordaan, Pierre J. 2013a. "A Clash of Deities in 2 Maccabees 1:10b–17 in Terms of Space, Body and Narrative." *OTE* 26:718–29.
———. 2013b. "A Clash of Hands and Tongues—2 Maccabees 14 and 15 in the Framework of Cognitive Linguistics." *JECH* 3.2:62–72.
———. 2015. "The Temple in 2 Maccabees: Dynamics and Episodes." *JSem* 24:352–65.
———. 2016. "Body, Space and Narrative in 2 Macc 1:1–10a." *BN* 168:89–103.
———. 2017. "2 Maccabees 9, the Demise and Death of Antiochus IV Epiphanes as Dramatic Irony." Paper presented at the Passion, Persecution, and Epiphany in Early Jewish Literature conference, Károli Gáspár University, Budapest, 20–23 September.
———. 2019. "A Semiotic Approach to Analyzing the Widows and Orphans as an *Index* in 2 Maccabees 3:10." Pages 95–102 in *XVI Congress of the International Organization for Septuagint and Cognate Studies: Stellenbosch, 2016.* Edited by Gideon R. Kotzé, Wolfgang Kraus, and Michaël N. van der Meer. SCS 71. Atlanta: SBL Press.
Kaiser, Otto. 2004. *The Old Testament Apocrypha: An Introduction.* Peabody, MA: Hendrickson.
Lakoff, George, and Mark Johnson. *Philosophy in the Flesh: The Embodied Mind and Its Challenge to Western Thoughts.* New York: Basic Books.
McClellan, Daniel O. 2009. "A Reevaluation of the Structure and Function of 2 Maccabees 7 and Its Text-Critical Implications." *Studia Antiqua* 7:81–95.

Moffatt, James. 1913. "The Second Book of Maccabees." Pages 125–54 in vol. 1 of *The Apocrypha and Pseudepigrapha of the Old Testament*. Edited by R. H. Charles. Oxford: Clarendon.

Nickelsburg, George W. E. 2005. *Jewish Literature between the Bible and the Mishnah*. Minneapolis: Fortress.

Schwartz, Daniel R. 2008. *2 Maccabees*. CEJL. Berlin: de Gruyter.

Tcherikover, Victor. 1982. *Hellenistic Civilization and the Jews*. Repr., New York: Atheneum.

Contributing toward Theologies of the LXX: The Use of the Terms θεός and κύριος in 1 and 2 Maccabees

Peter Nagel

ABSTRACT: There is an ongoing debate among scholars on whether and to what extent a theology, or theologies, of the LXX is in fact possible. Is it reasonable and fair to speak of an *implicit* LXX theology? Does the LXX merely reproduce theological content within a Greek frame of reference? Is *theologizing* not a natural consequence when reproducing texts? These and other questions encouraged me to contribute to the debate by investigating the use of theologically significant terms such as θεός and κύριος in 1 and 2 Maccabees. This investigation will first look at how these terms were used in 1 and 2 Maccabees, respectively. Second, these uses will be compared with one another to determine unique characteristics as well as overlaps.

1. Introduction

An investigation into a theology (or theologies) of the Septuagint (LXX) is as exciting as it is complex. The default position when constructing any theology is to define, describe, and explain the characteristics, epithets, and nature of a particular deity in predominately positive terms.[1] It is an attempt to construct what a God is, what a God does, how a God relates, and so on, as inferred from the literature. It is to track and trace the interaction of a deity with human reality through the history of relevant literature.[2] This is also my approach; however, my theological endeavors

---

1. I agree with Foshay 1992, who remarks that it is inevitable that modernity's concern with differences, discontinuity, and the novelty of an evolving, unfolding, unfinished (and unfinishable) experience should issue in a progressive sensitivity to and wariness of all positive terms, predications, equations, adequations.

2. As Kreuzer aptly puts it, "Zum einen geht es mir um den genauen Wortlaut und die genaue Gestalt des Textes, und diese kann man nicht haben ohne

are skeptical, pessimistic, and critical in nature. I would want to ask what a deity is not, what a deity simply cannot be, an so on. I am interested in determining whether a "traditional" theology has failed and what the potential impact of such a failure might be. My contention is that a reconstruction, or rather a "construction," of a LXX theology (or theologies) cannot escape accounting for, reflecting on, and rebutting the failures of a theology.³ Responding to a so-called failed theology can produce the following results. On the one hand, it can lead to a *silencing* theology, which is characterized by a failure to explicitly acknowledge a deity. It is a theology that is vague, it generalizes, causing the deity to appear inactive, uninvolved, and of little value or relevance. On the other hand, the supposed failures are countered by explicitness, being elaborative, extravagant, using absolutisms, and being descriptive. Hence my contribution to the "theology(ies) of the LXX venture" is undertaken from the vantage point of a potentially failed theology.

The starting point is the terms θεός and κύριος in 1 and 2 Maccabees; these terms are theologically significant in that they are Greek terms used to refer specifically to a Hebrew deity. The premise here is that the use of the terms θεός and κύριος has the potential to reveal a response to a failed theology. These terms, by definition, do not signify a response to a failed theology, but they do signal theological intent. The book of Esther serves as a good example; the explicit references to the Hebrew deity by using the terms θεός and κύριος are deliberate and theologically intentional; they reveal a theology of explicitness. In the Hebrew version, the deity is implicitly acting, so one assumes, but the Greek scribes changed that by

---

die Geschichte des Textes. Zum anderen geht es mir um die Inhalte der Texte, die nicht nur theologische, sondern auch kulturgeschichtliche, historische und andere Themen umfassen, die aber doch wegen ihrer theologischen Inhalte und deren bleidender Bedeutung überliefert wurden" (2018, 1). Bloesch rightly remarks that "theology must do more than simply repeat the mainly figurative language of the biblical narrative" (1995, 31). He says that it should also draw upon the conceptual language of philosophy to illuminate the mystery of the God who revealed himself in biblical history. According to Goldstein 2002, there is a logical connection between the beliefs of the Israelites as a people of an almighty god and the peculiar phenomena of the Jews' history and literature.

3. It would be a fair inference to connect what I term a failed theology with the notion of negation or negative theology. Negative theology is also known as apophatic theology, a form of theological thinking that attempts to approach God, the Divine, by negation of concepts that might be applied to him.

explicitly making known who is at work (see Esth 2:20; 4:8, 14, 6:1, 13).[4] These explicit references to the Hebrew deity were made at crucial points in the narrative and are theologically motivated and deliberate. The additions to the narrative are so theologically unequivocal that they overshadow the core of the narrative in part. This is, in my view, not simply a matter of interpretive intent, but these insertions and additions are driven by much larger theological challenges, namely, accounting for and responding to the traditional theologies and their failures in particular.[5] The zeitgeist of the third century BCE onward created an ideal opportunity to reflect on and respond to the traditional theologies that undergirded Israelite theology. A noteworthy case in point is the theologically critical response by Job and Ecclesiastes to the predictability theology of *Proverbia* (Proverbs). Job to a lesser and Ecclesiastes to a larger degree question, critique, and respond to the failures of the predictability theology (cause and effect) as aptly represented in *Proverbia*. It is therefore not such an outlandish idea that one of the motivations for translating the Hebrew Scriptures into a Greek idiom was to engage the theologies of the Hebrew Scriptures critically and to scrutinize their so-called successes. Whether this notion is accepted or not does not change the fact that the Hebrew Scriptures were translated and that theological reflection was inevitable.

The theory offered here is that the theological reflection—a theology of *silencing* and *explicitness* in 1 and 2 Maccabees, respectively—suggests that they both reflect in broad terms on the failure of, among other things, a theology of omnipotence. The failure of a Hebrew deity to prove that he is all-powerful, possessing the ability to be more powerful than any other deity, is theologically defined and explained by the notion of a victorious warrior deity.[6] The theology of the *almighty* is a theology informed by peoples waging war against their enemies and the ability of their deity to defeat the enemy and to be hailed a victorious warrior.

---

4. For a detailed reflection on these explicit references, see Nagel 2008.

5. One such failure was the "omnipotence" of a Hebrew deity, the "ability" of the Hebrew deity, YHWH, who was responsible for the flourishing and thriving of the Hebrew people, the Israelites. Flourishing and thriving included, but were not limited to, having land, producing offspring, having access to goods, and, of course, winning wars. On all these fronts, the Hebrew people were consistently challenged.

6. Signori (2012, 1) suggests that defending faith through violence gradually took shape following the decision of Antiochus Epiphanes (174–164 BCE) to suppress Judaism, by profaning the temple and forcing the Jews not to follow the torah.

An almighty deity is a deity who protects his people against the enemy. A deity who fails at war, who is defeated by the enemy, cannot by definition be an almighty deity.[7] The persistent persecution of the Hebrew people and the repeated destruction of the temple and everything they held dear "theologically" had to have an impact on how scribes understood their deity's role in the life of his people. The text of 1 Maccabees is a product of such a response, a negation by way of a theology of silencing, an implicit theology that is anthropologically centered. It produced a theology of *disappointment, resentment,* and *pessimism.* The text of 2 Maccabees offers a noticeably different approach; here an explicit, elaborative, descriptive, and explanatory theology is revealed, a theology that is characterized by extravagant claims as a countermeasure for the failed theology of almightiness.

Goldstein summarizes the tension between the two books as follows:

> These two books present sharply different accounts; indeed, we shall find that their authors were bitter opponents. The webs of doctrinal subtleties, of charge and counter charge, which characterize the polemics of monotheistic sects against the rivals they call "heretics"—these webs give rise to some of the most complicated puzzles in the history of literature. So, it is with our two books. First Maccabees and the original of which [2 Maccabees] is an abridgment were written in close succession as propaganda after decades of controversy.

I interpret the propaganda Goldstein refers to as opposing attempts to come to grips with the failure of the Hebrew deity's ability to defeat the enemy. This study is an attempt to test whether the theory that 1 and 2 Maccabees were responses to the failed theology of an almighty deity holds any water.[8] The theory will be tested by focusing on the theological character of both 1 and 2 Maccabees in general and how the use, and absence, of the terms θεός and κύριος influenced the theological character of these two books.

---

7. Goldstein (2002, 3) defines a people of an almighty god as "one which believes that a god stronger than all other powers combined is ultimately committed to be their protector, though temporarily the people may suffer adversity."

8. It must be noted that most scholars and specialists on 1 and 2 Maccabees will not agree with this theory.

2. 1 Maccabees: A Theology of Silencing

There seems to be consensus among scholars that 1 Maccabees is a Greek translation of a Hebrew *Vorlage*.[9] The book accounts for the history of the rise of the Hasmonean dynasty from the zealous priest Mattathias to the reign of John Hyrcanus, high priest and prince of the Jews.[10] The contents of 1 and 2 Maccabees account for the revolt against Antiochus Epiphanes IV, the Seleucid king of Syria, who profaned the temple and persecuted Judaism in 175–164 BCE.[11] The profanity included the erection of an altar to Zeus in the temple and compelling the Jews to violate the laws of the torah.[12] What is strikingly obvious is the *silence* and inactivity of a Hebrew deity in 1 Maccabees. The absence of the terms θεός and κύριος perpetuates the silencing of a Hebrew deity and subverts his active role in protecting his people.

2.1. General Theological Character

The book 1 Maccabees offer a dually motivated response to the prevailing sociocultural circumstances. It is directed first against the atrocities committed by Antiochus Epiphanes, but also against those who turned their backs on the covenant, the law, Jewish practices in general, and joined the impious, immoral nation.[13] Second, it is inspired by the failure of the *almighty* theology as defined during the Late Bronze Age and

---

9. See Zervos 2007, 478. Goldstein (1976, 37), in turn, states that all the documents in 1 Maccabees are authentic and that no document were forged. See also Van der Woude and Vriezen 2005, 555.

10. Goldstein 1976, 4; cf. Schwartz 2008, 3. Berthelot (2007, 45) argues that the wars led by the Hasmoneans were in fact inspired by the biblical model of the conquest of the promised land at the time of Joshua. The aim was to reconquer the land that "God" gave to his people.

11. Rocca (2008, 4) considers this a golden age when the Jews achieved complete political independence.

12. Cohen 2006, 3.

13. For Kampen (2007, 13), the ideological conflict within the Maccabean compositions demonstrates the central issue they want to address. This issue, according to him, is found in 1 Macc 1:10–15, where the scribe talks about "sinful root" (Antiochus Ephiphanes), "lawless," "made a covenant with the nations around us," "turned aside from the holy covenant." The central issue is not limited to threats from the "outside," but also because of traitors from the "inside" (see also Goldstein 1976, 199–200).

refined during the Early Iron Age, a theology inspired by the notion of a victorious warrior deity.[14] It is therefore not surprising to read of victorious human warriors sanctifying and purifying the "holy places" in 1 Maccabees.[15] There is a shift away from a transcendent-centered theology to an anthropologically oriented theology. The savior(s) of the Judeans and their heritage are Mattathias and his sons, Judas called Makkabaios and Simon, among others. It is Mattathias who is the ruler, great and glorious (1 Macc 2:17); he and his sons walk in the commandments of their fathers (2:19–20). They were the ones purifying the "holy places"; they were zealous about keeping the commandments and walking in the covenant of their fathers (2:19–22). The extent of their zeal[16] was so extreme that Mattathias killed a Jew when he made an offering on the altar in accordance with the ordinance of the king (2:23–25).[17] The notion that "Judas caused the prosperity of salvation" is introduced in 1 Macc 3:6. All the nations will know that there is only one who redeems and saves Israel (4:11); Judas's victory over Gorgias is known as the great salvation of Israel (4:25). When Judas lost his life in battle, all of Israel mourned while they cried out: Πῶς ἔπεσε δυνατὸς σώζων τὸν Ισραηλ, "How did the mighty savior of Israel fall?" They sang hymns and directed blessings toward the heavens while saying: καλόν, ὅτι εἰς τὸν αἰῶνα τὸ ἔλεος αὐτοῦ, "for he is good, and his mercy is forever" (4:23). The sentence is ambiguous; on the one hand, it could mean the "silent" Hebrew deity is acknowledged here, but, on the other hand, it could also mean that gratitude is directed to the heavens for the blessing of having someone like Judas. Referring to Judas as the mighty savior of

---

14. I agree with Goldstein 2002, 4 who asserts that people who defined their deity as being almighty must resolve the problem of "revelation by authoritative means" and "suffering continuous adversity." The issue here is the duration of expiation of sin. However, I want to argue that the notion of "expiating sin" is an easy way out of the dilemma caused by an almightiness theology. Cf. Goldstein 1976, 3 on how the Jews interpreted their circumstances: "God's favour had departed from Israel in the dark days of the destruction of the two kingdoms. If now God's favour had fully returned after the harshest time of troubles, it was necessary for the people to know how and why: otherwise, the might again lose His favour."

15. Cohen, 2006, 2 states that in 164 BCE the Maccabees reconquered and purified the Temple.

16. 1 Macc 2:50: ζηλώσατε τῷ νόμῳ.

17. According to Trampedach 2012, 61 the act of Mattathias (1 Macc 2:24–26) was the catalyst for the Maccabean Revolt. For Trampedach the revolt contains all the elements of a holy war.

Israel, and his existential prominence in deliverance, certainly allows for such an interpretation. This idea, however, is countered with the words in 1 Macc 4:30, when Judas, after seeing the mighty army of Lysias, started praying and said:

> Εὐλογητὸς εἶ ὁ σωτὴρ Ισραηλ ὁ συντρίψας τὸ ὅρμημα τοῦ δυνατοῦ ἐν χειρὶ τοῦ δούλου σου Δαυιδ καὶ παρέδωκας τὴν παρεμβολὴν τῶν ἀλλοφύλων εἰς χεῖρας Ιωνάθου υἱοῦ Σαουλ καὶ τοῦ αἴροντος τὰ σκεύη αὐτοῦ.
> Blessed are you, the savior of Israel, who smashed the attack of the powerful one by the hand of your slave Dauid and delivered the camp of the allophyles into the hands of Ionathes son of Saoul and of the bearer of his armor. (NETS)

The uncertainty of the verse is palpable: Did the scribe intend to convince the reader that Judas genuinely evoked a Hebrew deity when he referred to the savior of Israel? Alternatively, could it be a lame attempt to soften the impact that their deity had failed to protect them and they themselves had to step up to the plate and fend for themselves? The references to other prayers and supplications such as Σὺ ἐξελέξω τὸν οἶκον τοῦτον ἐπικληθῆναι τὸ ὄνομά σου ἐπ' αὐτοῦ εἶναι οἶκον προσευχῆς καὶ δεήσεως τῷ λαῷ σου ("You selected this house to evoke your name, a house for prayer and supplication by your people," 1 Macc 7:37) legitimizes Judas's prayer. That said, the scattered and brief prayer accounts do make it difficult to make any final assertions.[18] The scribe is not yet ready to subscribe to the idea that the Hebrew deity as failed to protect his people effectively and can therefore no longer be considered almighty. The scribe opted for a theology of silence and generalization of the Hebrew deity as highlighted by phrases such as:

> Οἱ παρὰ τοῦ βασιλέως ὅτε ἐδυσφήμησαν, ἐξῆλθεν ἄγγελός σου καὶ ἐπάταξεν ἐν αὐτοῖς ἑκατὸν ὀγδοήκοντα πέντε χιλιάδας, "When the men from the king blasphemed, your Angel came out and killed one hundred eighty-give thousand of them" (1 Macc 7:41).

> ἔχομεν γὰρ τὴν ἐξ οὐρανοῦ βοήθειαν βοηθοῦσαν ἡμῖν, "for we have the help from heaven helping us" (1 Macc 12:15).

The indirect nature of a Hebrew deity's response is clear in the statement made in 1 Macc 7:41, while the generalization is striking in 12:15. In

---

18. Cf. 1 Macc 11:71; 12:11.

addition to this, a Hebrew deity is not involved with the purification and sanctification of the temple and the most holy of places, neither is he active in battle.[19] The zealous leaders of the Judeans take center stage; they are the high priests (1 Macc 13:41; cf. 16:24), the righteous or self-righteous judges, the implementers of the law.[20] They are the ones who purify the sanctuaries while waging war against the enemies of the Judeans and their heritage. The prayers and supplications point to the reservations of the scribe about expressing disappointment at the Hebrew deity's inability to defeat the enemy and subsequently save his people.

2.2. κύριος and θεός Terms in 1 Maccabees

Zervos, the NETS translator for 1 Maccabees, translated the phrase ἵλεως ἡμῖν καταλιπεῖν νόμον καὶ δικαιώματα as "God help us if we abandon the law and the statutes" (1 Macc 2:21). The reasoning behind this is that the use of ἵλεως in the Greek Old Testament (LXX) is always "of God,"[21] or so the interpretation goes. This might be true, but it is rather the absence of θεός and κύριος that forces one to translate this term with "God." The addition of "God" in the NETS translation creates an expectation of an active, explicitly engaged deity, an expectation that 1 Maccabees fails to meet. The terms θεός or κύριος, however, are used to call other entities and ideas to mind. The first such use is found in 1 Macc 2:53, Ιωσηφ ἐν καιρῷ στενοχωρίας αὐτοῦ ἐφύλαξεν ἐντολὴν καὶ ἐγένετο κύριος Αἰγύπτου ("Joseph, during the time of personal distress, kept the command and became lord of Egypt"). The idea of Joseph becoming a lord forms part of a rhetorical question: "Was not Abraam found faithful in temptation, and it was accounted to him as righteousness?" (1 Macc 2:52: Αβρααμ

---

19. Berthelot (2007, 51) states that the reasoning about the wrath of God (1 Macc 1:64), and the turning away from this wrath (3:8) is in accordance with Deut 13:18, which states that the eradication of the idolaters will cause the Lord to "turn from the fierceness of his anger and show you mercy." Trampedach's (2012, 65) view that the Hasmoneans demanded respect for the Torah's rule of warfare, which entails the blowing of trumpets, among other actions, "assuring steady communication with God and both the visibility and audibility of his assistance," is contrary to mine, in that he is of the opinion that for them God would have been visibly assisting.

20. Cf. Van der Woude and Vriezen 2005, 556. Berthelot (2007, 49–50) notes that deliverance came from God for the sake of Israel but that the military and political achievements of the leaders "elected" by God were also prominent.

21. See BDAG, s.v. "ἵλεως," 376.

οὐχὶ ἐν πειρασμῷ εὑρέθη πιστός, καὶ ἐλογίσθη αὐτῷ εἰς δικαιοσύνην;). In addition, it is said that "Phinees, our father, by becoming zealous with zeal, received a covenant of everlasting priesthood" (2:54: Φινεες ὁ πατὴρ ἡμῶν ἐν τῷ ζηλῶσαι ζῆλον ἔλαβε διαθήκην ἱερωσύνης αἰωνίας), followed by "Iesous, by fulfilling the command, became a judge in Israel" (2:55: Ιησοῦς ἐν τῷ πληρῶσαι λόγον ἐγένετο κριτὴς ἐν Ισραηλ); Caleb received an inheritance of Land after bearing witness in the assembly (2:56); David inherited the throne of a kingdom forever (2:57), and so on and so forth.[22] The underlying logic is one of cause and effect: the one who causes something to happen is awarded a position of power and status. In the case of Joseph, he kept a command and became a lord of Egypt. If this is the logic applied to the narrative, it seems appropriately important to ask: What position, status, and title should be ascribed to a Hebrew deity? The most logical answer seems to be none, and the reason for this is that the deity does not feature in the narrative. The reasoning is that there is obviously no inclination to reference or call to mind a deity who failed to protect his people from their adversaries. The theological relevance of explicitly evoking or even referencing a Hebrew deity would therefore be superfluous. A theology of *subversion* seems appropriate for a deity who, for all practical purposes, failed to act as an almighty deity. While the term κύριος is used to designate authority and rule in 1 Macc 2:53, the term θεός is used as reference to deities' carvings (of the allophyles) in 1 Macc 5:68. The use of the term κύριος in 1 Macc 8:30 also designates authority,[23] and the same applies for its use in 1 Macc 9:25, when Bacchides elected impious husbands and made them rulers of the region.[24] A fair inference to draw from the literary evidence is that the term θεός is used as reference to a deity, and the term κύριος designates a ruler who possesses authority. There is no indication that either term was used to refer to a Hebrew deity or that there was a desire to call upon and acknowledge a Hebrew deity by using these terms.[25] The use of the terms κύριος and θεός—the former for a ruler in Egypt and the latter for deities worshiped by the enemy—is

---

22. This, according to Trampedach 2012, 64.

23. 1 Macc 8:30: ἐὰν δὲ μετὰ τοὺς λόγους τούτους βουλεύσωνται οὗτοι καὶ οὗτοι προσθεῖναι ἢ ἀφελεῖν, ποιήσονται ἐξ αἱρέσεως αὐτῶν, καὶ ὃ ἐὰν προσθῶσιν ἢ ἀφέλωσιν, ἔσται κύρια.

24. 1 Macc 9:25: καὶ ἐξέλεξε Βακχίδης τοὺς ἀσεβεῖς ἄνδρας καὶ κατέστησεν αὐτοὺς κυρίους τῆς χώρας. See also Kampen 2007, 14.

25. Cf. Van der Woude and Vriezen 2005, 556–57.

simultaneously theologically insignificant and significant: insignificant because the terms do not reproduce or reference a Hebrew deity but significant enough because they are used to refer to Joseph as a mortal ruler and to call to mind "pagan" deities. The absence of θεός and κύριος speaks to a theology of silencing and subversion, traces of which presumably would have been evident in the Hebrew version of the narrative. It is plausible to argue that the Hebrew *Vorlage* did not attest to any explicit references to the Hebrew deity, and the Greek scribe simply repeated the absence of any explicit references. It is highly unlikely that a scribe would omit an explicit reference to a Hebrew deity. Does this imply that the scribe simply "copied" the theological intent of the Hebrew scribe? The answer remains uncertain, since the relationship between Greek 1 Maccabees and its Hebrew *Vorlage* are speculative. Irrespective, 1 Maccabees in its Greek form reveals a theology of *silencing*.

3. 2 Maccabees: A Theology of Explicitness

The narratives compiled in 2 Maccabees attest to a supposed "original" Greek version of the events that took place in and around Jerusalem during the first quarter of the second century BCE.[26] The body of the text (2 Macc 3:1–15:36) is a literary creation without a Hebrew parent text.[27] The sections 2 Macc 1:1–10a and 1:10b–2:18 present two letters referring to the feast of Sukkoth in the month of Kislev, most likely a translation of Hebrew and Aramaic originals.[28] Notwithstanding this, there is no confusion about the subject being addressed in 2 Maccabees: it is the history of the city of Jerusalem from around 175 BCE until 161 BCE.[29] This Greek

---

26. Cf. Zervos 2007, 478.
27. Schaper 2007, 503.
28. Schaper 2007, 503. A prooemium is found in 2 Macc 2:19–32 and epilogue in 15:37–39; both are the work of the epitomizer. Schwartz 2008 convincingly argues that the first two chapters of 2 Maccabees are two separate letters prefixed to the book, with the story of Heliodorus serving as prologue, followed by the real story, which starts at 2 Macc 4:4–6, 7. In terms of the compilation of 2 Maccabees, Goldstein (1976, 28) mentions that Dan 7–12 was used by the scribes of both 1 and 2 Maccabees, whom he considers exceptional historians.
29. The date 175 BCE is generally accepted as the beginning of institutionalized Hellenization under the high priest Jason. See Schwartz 2008, 3. The date 161 BCE is when Judas Maccabeus defeated the Seleucid general Nicanor. See Schwartz 2008, 3. According to Goldstein (1976, 3), no harsher trial ever tested the monotheistic faith of

version differs from 1 Maccabees in that it frequently uses the terms κύριος and θεός, compared to the absence of these terms in 1 Maccabees. Furthermore, 1 Maccabees has no reference to a deity being almighty, but the Hebrew deity in 2 Maccabees is all-powerful.[30] This is due either to a different theological predisposition or to the scribe simply having more scribal freedom because there was no Hebrew *Vorlage*.

3.1. General Theological Ideas

A Hebrew deity as depicted in 2 Maccabees and referenced using the terms θεός and κύριος is a deity who is *all-powerful*. The battlefield, as one would expect, is the backdrop against which this deity is considered almighty. The warrior deity as nonentity in 1 Maccabees has morphed into a victorious all-powerful deity in 2 Maccabees, as aptly expressed by the words Θεοῦ νίκην (2 Macc 13:15: "divine victory"). A Hebrew deity is called upon as κύριος, the almighty, "while they were calling upon the almighty Lord" (2 Macc 3:22: οἱ μὲν οὖν ἐπεκαλοῦντο τὸν παγκρατῆ κύριον). Although κύριος is called upon as the almighty, it is θεός who manifests himself, resulting in many being astonished by his power, greatness (2 Macc 3:24; cf. 3:34, 36, 38), and dominance (3:28).[31] During the battle with Nicanor, Judas and his men approach the enemy with invocations and prayers, and θεός again manifests himself on the battlefield (2 Macc 15:27). The concept of the almighty is further developed in 2 Macc 8:18, when it is said: "but we trust in the almighty God" (ἡμεῖς δὲ ἐπὶ τῷ παντοκράτορι θεῷ δυναμένῳ ... πεποίθαμεν). One can only "trust" in the ability of a deity if such a deity is trustworthy, and trustworthiness is determined on the battlefield, more

---

the Jews than that under the rule of the Seleucid king, Antiochus IV (167–164 BCE), when obedience to the commandments of the Hebrew deity became a crime punished with extreme severity.

30. Schwartz (2008, 38) makes an interesting remark that the field was dominated by the axiom that 1 Maccabees is the more accurate of the two books (this presumption still prevails, according to him). He makes a compelling argument that 2 Maccabees stands alongside 1 Maccabees as a firm foundation for the construction of the history of the period with which it deals. He makes a valuable point that "2 Maccabees is the main source not only for the Hellenistic world in which the story played itself out, but also for the Jewish world within which that happened—the world which the author of 1 Maccabees, for readily understandable reasons, had to portray in a way that was monochromic and only background for his own heroes" (2008, 44).

31. The Hebrew deity also appeared in the temple as κύριος (2 Macc 3:30).

specifically when battles are won by a more powerful deity. According to the scribe of 2 Maccabees, a Hebrew deity is such a deity. The introductory verses of 2 Maccabees introduce a Hebrew deity in an extravagant manner, with phrases such as Κύριε κύριε ὁ θεός ("Lord, Lord, the God"), who is ὁ μόνος χορηγός ("the sole provider"), ὁ μόνος δίκαιος ("the only righteous one"), and καὶ παντοκράτωρ καὶ αἰώνιος ("almighty and eternal," 1:25). Using extreme terminology is one way to construct a Hebrew deity in a positive light amid challenging socioreligious circumstances. Antiochus Epiphanes IV is a major cause of these circumstances, which severely challenges the supremacy of a Hebrew deity; the scribe of 2 Maccabees is countering by way of making it explicit that the Hebrew deity is all-powerful. An all-powerful deity had to have the ability to create (see 2 Macc 7:22–23; 13:14); furthermore, an all-powerful deity is by default an all-seeing deity: ὁ δὲ παντεπόπτης κύριος ὁ θεὸς τοῦ Ἰσραηλ (2 Macc 9:5: "The all-seeing Lord, the God of Israel"). It is pointless if one is an all-powerful deity but this ability remains an abstract, hypothetical idea; it must manifest itself in real terms. The scribe presumably knows this and thus makes it a point to mention that the power of θεός is in fact displayed (2 Macc 9:8, 17; 11:4).

The reference to a Hebrew deity as almighty in 2 Macc 5:20 demands a closer examination of the verse, which reads:

ὁ καταλειφθεὶς ἐν τῇ τοῦ παντοκράτορος ὀργῇ πάλιν ἐν τῇ τοῦ μεγάλου δεσπότου καταλλαγῇ μετὰ πάσης δόξης ἐπανωρθώθη
What was forsaken in the wrath of the Almighty was restored again in all its glory when the great Lord became reconciled.

The phrase is significant in two ways: the first is due to the use of the term δεσπότης; the second is the issue of the reconciliation of the great Lord as the almighty one. The term δεσπότης is used in 2 Macc 5:17 in an explanation as to why the δεσπότης ("Lord") was disregarded in the most holy part of the temple by Antiochus. I believe that using the term θεός or κύριος with reference to the disregarding of the Hebrew deity in the context of the most holy of holy places in the temple could have resulted in theological suicide, an implicit way of committing blasphemy. The use of the term κύριος in 5:19, given the context, is not problematic, because it speaks of the Lord's decision not to elect the nation for the sake of the place but to choose the place for the sake of the nation. The term δεσπότης is repeated in 5:20 with reference to the restoration of the Almighty's wrath, when the great δεσπότης became reconciled. The latter use supports the theory that, when speaking of the misfortunes of the most holy of holy places, the restoration of the Almighty, and the reconciliation of the "Lord," the theologically sensitive term to use is δεσπότης. The use of the term in 2 Macc 6:14, however, cannot be explained by the same arguments as in 5:17 and 20. The use of δεσπότης here relates to the patience of δεσπότης in punishing the other nations. One can argue that the failure of a Hebrew deity to act justly and decisively is why the term δεσπότης is used in this instance. This explanation, however, will not work for δεσπότης in 2 Macc 9:13, neither for its use in 15:22. The use of δεσπότης in 9:13 should be understood as the most appropriate term to use when a vow is made to a Hebrew deity, especially by Antiochus, who is busy rotting from the inside. As for the use of δεσπότης in 15:22, the interpretation is less certain; it can be argued that its use is to evoke the epithet "master" used for a Hebrew deity and not the "lordship" in terms of the Tetragrammaton. This argument finds support in similar uses of the term in Gen 15:2, 8; Jdt 5:20; 11:10; Jonah 4:3; Isa 1:24; 3:1; 10:33; Jer 1:6; 4:10; and Dan 9:15. In sum, none of these explanations is certain, but they are all reasonably plausible. What is important for this study is that the use of δεσπότης reveals a reservation about representing a Hebrew deity using the rule of thumb terms θεός and κύριος when the failure of such a deity is on the cards.

3.2. κύριος and θεός in 2 Maccabees

In 2 Maccabees, the terms θεός and κύριος are used primarily as references for a Hebrew deity. The explicit use of these terms are introduced in 2 Macc 1 with the phrase ἀγαθοποιήσαι ὑμῖν ὁ θεὸς καὶ μνησθείη τῆς διαθήκης αὐτοῦ τῆς πρὸς Αβρααμ καὶ Ισαακ καὶ Ιακωβ τῶν δούλων αὐτοῦ τῶν πιστῶν (1:2: "May *theos* do good to you, and may he remember his covenant with Abraam and Isaac and Jacob, his faithful servants"). When things turned out for the worse, like the gatehouse burning down and innocent blood being shed, the Judeans commit themselves to κύριος (1:8).[32] There is no vagueness about who is responsible for saving the Judeans: it is θεός who saved them from great danger (1:11; cf. 2:16).[33] It is because of this

---

32. 2 Macc 1:8: καὶ ἐνεπύρισαν τὸν πυλῶνα καὶ ἐξέχεαν αἷμα ἀθῷον, καὶ ἐδεήθημεν τοῦ κυρίου.

33. 2 Macc 1:11: ἐκ μεγάλων κινδύνων ὑπὸ τοῦ θεοῦ σεσῳσμένοι μεγάλως εὐχαριστοῦμεν αὐτῷ.

act of salvation that he should be blessed in many ways, according to 2 Macc 1:17. But the phrase in 1:24, Κύριε κύριε ὁ θεός, ὁ πάντων κτίστης, ὁ φοβερὸς καὶ ἰσχυρὸς καὶ δίκαιος καὶ ἐλεήμων, ὁ μόνος βασιλεὺς καὶ χρηστός, ("*Kyrios, kyrios,* the *theos,* the Creator of all, the awesome, mighty, and just one; the one who is merciful, the only good and kind king") emphasizes the explicit, extravagant, and elaborative nature of the theology found in 2 Maccabees. It is not surprising that all the nations knew that this θεός was the θεός of the Judeans (1:27). In 2 Macc 2:2, the notion of commandments is connected with the term κύριος; it is the prophets who gave the law so that the commandments of κύριος are not forgotten (see 2:22). In 2 Macc 2:4, inheritance is discussed in connection with the term θεός; it is the inheritance envisaged by Moses when he went up the mountain. This θεός will also gather all his people (2:7). It is presumably during this gathering that κύριος will disclose things and his glory will be revealed (2:7–8). The same Moses who went up the mountain to see the inheritance of θεός is the one praying to κύριος (2:10). Supplication and directing prayer to a Hebrew deity are not uncommon in 2 Maccabees. In 2 Macc 10:25 it is Makkabaios and his men who sprinkle dust on their heads and gird their loins with sackcloth in supplication to θεός. It is again Makkabaios and his men praying to κύριος when they approach a stronghold.[34] The "calling upon" by the women in sackcloth and by the virgins in 2 Macc 3:22 is connected to κύριος, as the "expected" one to be called upon, when the concept of the almighty is at the forefront. The term κύριος is always used in praying to or calling upon a Hebrew deity. This might also explain why the scribe differentiates between calling upon this deity using the terms δεσπότης and κύριος. The exception, though, is when a Hebrew deity is called upon during battle; then one would expect θεός to manifest his powers.

According to the scribe, it is κύριος who is worthy of praises (2 Macc 3:30), whose grace is revealed, and who gives life (3:33), who is also deserving of sacrifices (3:35), and who repays through punishment (4:38). It is to be expected that κύριος is the one who also elects (5:19). It is, however, ὁ κύριος ὁ θεός who watches over his people with truth and compassion (7:6) but θεός who can raise one if and when one is put to death by the hands of a human (7:13–14). On the flipside, one can also be forsaken by θεός (7:16–19). Any text with explicit references to a Hebrew deity that does not at the same time account for judgment and mercy would be odd;

---

34. A similar use is found in 2 Macc 12:36; 13:10; 14:35–36, 46.

2 Maccabees does not disappoint in this regard. There are only two references made to justice: one in relation to παντοκράτωρ (8:11), and the other in relation to θεός (8:13), but references to the Hebrew deity as being just or righteous are found in a few instances (see 1:24, 25). The book also attests to the righteous judgment of θεός in 2 Macc 7:36 and 9:18. It is θεός who is none other than the righteous judge (12:6). The act of judging, to be just and righteous, seems to be reserved for θεός,[35] while mercy can be shown by either θεός (11:9) or κύριος (8:27; 11:10; 13:12). As expected, a Hebrew deity is also a warrior deity whose intervention (3:29) and help (8:23; 13:13) are characterized as divine. Such interventions are always associated with a battle or war scenario. It is θεός who explicitly fights in battles (10:16; 12:11). "Divine intervention," "divine help," and actively engaging in warfare or battle are reserved for θεός. Moreover, the τοῦ θεοῦ θελήσει (12:16: "the will of *theos*") speaks to the idea of doing battle, presumably to be victorious. A deity who wills is a deity who is almighty, and a deity who is considered almighty must wage war to prove his all-powerfulness. It is, however, κύριος who led them (Makkabaios and his men) to recover the temple and city (10:1). Moreover, the praise in reference to a Hebrew deity is confined to κύριος in 3:30, 8:27, 10:38, and 12:41. The final reference I want to deal with is by Nicanor in 2 Macc 14:33. The use of the terms κύριος is not limited to the Judeans only; even Nicanor, when he demands that Judas be handed over to him, states:

> προτείνας τὴν δεξιὰν ἐπὶ τὸν νεώ ὤμοσε ταῦτα·Ἐὰν μὴ δέσμιόν μοι τὸν Ἰούδαν παραδῶτε, τόνδε τὸν τοῦ θεοῦ σηκὸν εἰς πεδίον ποιήσω καὶ τὸ θυσιαστήριον κατασκάψω καὶ ἱερὸν ἐνταῦθα τῷ Διονύσῳ ἐπιφανὲς ἀναστήσω
> He stretched out his right hand toward the shrine and swore this oath: if you do not hand Ioudas over to me as prisoner, I will level this precinct of *theos* to the ground and tear down the altar and build here a notable temple to Dionysus.

This direct reference and subsequent acknowledgement of a Hebrew deity in explicit terms is unusual and risky. The scribe would not have entertained such an utterance if the outcome had been negative, that is, if Nicanor had been victorious. The priests responded to this challenge by stretching out their hands and calling upon κύριος the holy one (2 Macc

---

35. There is one exception found in 2 Macc 12:41, where the righteousness judge κύριος is praised.

14:35–36). Explicitly referencing a Hebrew deity as the victorious one is a highly effective way to counter any critique against him as all-powerful. The explicit and extensive use of both the term θεός and κύριος throughout the narrative made a Hebrew deity explicit. It allowed for a Hebrew deity to be interpretative as an active, relevant, significant, accomplished, and all-powerful deity. The use of these terms introduces a theology of explicitness, elaboration, and adoration of a Hebrew deity actively, wilfully, and competently acting on behalf of his people.

4. Concluding Remarks

A Hebrew deity as an active theologically significant agent is evoked in 2 Maccabees with the use of terms θεός and κύριος. The scribe of 1 Maccabees conveyed the opposite by simply following his *Vorlage*; in fact, these terms are used for human agents and when reference is made to the deities of the enemy. The absence of these terms in 1 Maccabees, particularly in relation to a Hebrew deity, is a sign of a theology of *silencing*, almost to the extent of a theology characterized as being subversive. It enforces an anthropologically centered theology with political and nationalistic tendencies. The active role played by the zealous leaders to save their people and their heritage, while purifying the holy places in combination with a silent and inactive Hebrew deity, opens the possibility of a self-righteously oriented theology, a theology of taking the law into one's own hands, so to speak. It is a theology that opens the possibility to consider a deity that is distant and irrelevant, as opposed to a tangible human being with "pure" intentions who accomplishes things in real terms. The nature of the narrative in combination with the lack of acknowledgment of a Hebrew deity is enough evidence to infer, within reason, that a Hebrew deity as an all-powerful deity has failed his people, at least for the scribe of 1 Maccabees. The most appropriate response is to silence such a deity, while raising the voices of those fighting for the law, for justice, for purity. In all cases, the zealous religious leaders are active agents, while a Hebrew deity is unsettlingly silent. The explicit and extensive use of terms θεός and κύριος in evoking and acknowledging a Hebrew deity in 2 Maccabees stands in direct opposition to 1 Maccabees. The traditional notions about the Hebrew deity are kept intact. It is a recognizable theology; it is a theology of playing it safe. The Hebrew deity is active in all cases, both in purifying the most holy of holy places and actively involved in waging war on the battlefield. The notion of a Hebrew deity as an absolute all-powerful merciful righteous judge and victorious warrior as the only deity is reinforced. Second Maccabees is an ideal case of a lost opportunity to creatively address failed and questionable theologies. The scribe opted for the traditional and did so excessively. The response of 1 and 2 Maccabees, whether it was deliberate to respond to what I call failed theologies or not, contribute toward theologies of the LXX. A theology of the LXX should acknowledge and account for failed theologies and the various responses to such theologies. It should allow for negative theology (what the Hebrew deity is not) and an optimistic theology (what believers hope and believe the Hebrew deity ought to be).

Bibliography

Berthelot, Katell. 2007. "The Biblical Conquest of the Promised Land and the Hasmonaean Wars According to 1 and 2 Maccabees." Pages 45–60 in *The Books of the Maccabees: History, Theology, Ideology*. Edited by Géza G. Xeravits and József Zsengellér. JSJSup 118. Leiden: Brill.

Bloesch, Donald G. 1995. *God the Almighty: Power, Wisdom, Holiness, Love*. Downers Grove, IL: Intervarsity Press.

Cohen, Shaye J. D. 2006. *From the Maccabees to the Mishnah*. 2nd ed. Louisville: Westminster John Knox.

Foshay, Toby. 1992. "Introduction: Denegation and Resentment." Pages 1–24 in *Derrida and Negative Theology*. Edited by Harrold Coward and Toby Foshay. New York: SUNY Press.

Goldstein, Jonathan A. 1976. *1 Maccabees: A New Translation with Introduction and Commentary*. AB 41. New York: Doubleday.

———. 2002. *Peoples of an Almighty God: Competing Religions in the Ancient World*. New York: Doubleday.

Kampen, John. 2007. "The Books of the Maccabees and Sectarianism in Second Temple Judaism." Pages 11–30 in *The Books of the Maccabees: History, Theology, Ideology*. Edited by Géza G. Xeravits and József Zsengellér. JSJSup 118. Leiden: Brill.

Kreuzer, Siegfried. 2018. "Textgeschichte und Theologie." Pages 1–24 in *Textgeschichte und Theologie: Septuaginta und Masoretischer Text als Äußerungen theologischer Reflexion*. Edited by Frank Ueberschaer, Thomas Wagner, and Jonathan Miles Robker. WUNT 407. Tübingen: Mohr Siebeck.

Nagel, Peter. 2008. "LXX Esther: More God Less Theology." *JSem* 17:129–55.

Rocca, Samuel. 2008. *The Forts of Judaea 168 BC–AD 73: From the Maccabees to the Fall of Masada.* Oxford: Osprey.

Schaper, Joachim. 2007. "2 Makkabees." Pages 503–20 in *A New Translation of the Septuagint and the Other Greek Translations Traditionally Included under That Title.* Edited by Albert Pietersma and Benjamin G. Wright. New York: Oxford University Press.

Schwartz, Daniel R. 2008. *2 Maccabees.* CEJL. Berlin: de Gruyter.

Signori, Gabriela. 2012. "Introduction." Pages 1–38 in *Dying for the Faith, Killing for the Faith: Old-Testament Faith-Warriors (1 and 2 Maccabees) in Historical Perspective.* Edited by Gabriela Signori. Brill's Studies in Intellectual History 206. Leiden: Brill.

Trampedach, Kai. 2012. "The War of the Hasmoneans." Pages 61–78 in *Dying for the Faith, Killing for the Faith: Old-Testament Faith-Warriors (1 and 2 Maccabees) in Historical Perspective.* Edited by Gabriela Signori. Brill's Studies in Intellectual History 206. Leiden: Brill.

Woude, Adam S. van der, and Theodorus Christian Vriezen. 2005. *Ancient Israelite and Early Jewish Literature.* Leiden: Brill.

Zervos, George T. 2007. "1 Makkabees." Pages 478–502 in *A New Translation of the Septuagint and the Other Greek Translations Traditionally Included under That Title.* Edited by Albert Pietersma and Benjamin G. Wright. New York: Oxford University Press.

Israel und die Völker in Texten der Septuaginta

Wolfgang Kraus

ABSTRACT: The relationship between Israel being God's people and the other peoples is a central theme within the Bible. There are texts expressing both a positive view on this relationship but also very negative statements. An important question in this respect is whether a legitimate worship of the God of Israel is possible for non-Israelites and, if so, under what conditions, and whether such worship affects the position of the peoples: Are they equated with the people of Israel as God's people? Are they included into the people of God? Are there then several "peoples of God"? Within the Tanak the problem is not finally solved. There are different statements that may be assigned to different theological tendencies. A detailed discussion of selected texts (Ps 47:10; Zech 2:14-15; Isa 19:16-25; 56:3-18; 66:18-24; Gen 12:1-3) will show how the translators of the Septuagint dealt with this problem.

1. Problemanzeige

Gedaliah Alon, der bedeutende Historiker und erste Träger des Israel-Preises schreibt in seinem postum erschienenen Buch *The Jews and Their Land in the Talmudic Age*: „One of the more difficult problems in the study of Jewish history is the question of the relationship between Jews and gentiles".[1]

Genau diesem Problem wollen wir uns im Folgenden zuwenden und dabei fragen, wie bestimmte Überlieferungen des TaNaKh in der LXX übersetzt und verstanden wurden.[2]

---

1. Alon 1984, 548. Zitat bei Haarmann 2008, 54 Anm. 161.

2. Ich knüpfe mit dem Folgenden an Überlegungen an und führe sie fort, die ich in meiner Habilitationsschrift unterbreitet habe: Kraus 2004. (Selbst-)Zitate aus diesem Buch sind im vorliegenden Beitrag nicht eigens gekennzeichnet. Die Arbeit

Mein Ausgangspunkt für die Fragestellung liegt im Neuen Testament bei Gal 3,26–29:

> [26] Denn ihr alle seid durch den Glauben Gottes Kinder [υἱοὶ θεοῦ] in Christus Jesus. [27] Denn ihr alle, die ihr auf Christus getauft seid, habt Christus angezogen. [28] Hier ist weder Jude noch Grieche, hier ist weder Sklave noch Freier, hier ist weder männlich noch weiblich; denn ihr seid allesamt eins in Christus Jesus. [29] Gehört ihr aber Christus an, so seid ihr ja Abrahams Nachkommenschaft und Erben gemäß der Verheißung.

Wie kommt Paulus dazu, so etwas zu formulieren: „Hier ist weder Jude noch Grieche", d.h. die heilsgeschichtliche Differenzierung soll „in Christus" aufgehoben sein? Die Glaubenden sollen „Abrahams Nachkommenschaft" und damit „Erben gemäß der Verheißung" sein, d.h. die Glaubenden würden in die von Abraham herkommende erwählungsgeschichtliche Linie integriert? Basiert seine Ansicht, wie Josef Klausner es formulierte, auf einer hellenistischen Fehlinterpretation der Überlieferung oder gibt es Anlass für seine Position bereits in der biblischen bzw. nachbiblischen Tradition? Nach Klausner erbaute Paulus sein Christentum „auf den Trümmern des entwurzelten Diaspora-Judentums".[3] Doch lässt ein Blick in antike jüdische Texte auch den gegenteiligen Schluss zu (vgl. etwa *1.Hen* 10,21–22; 90,37–38).[4]

In seinem Artikel „Septuaginta-Forschung" in der *RGG*[4] schreibt Johann Cook bezüglich der künftigen Forschungsperspektiven: „Schließlich sind hermeneutische Untersuchungen des gesamten LXX-Korpus erforderlich. Ihre Ergebnisse werden für den Forschungsbereich LXX und NT von großer Tragweite sein. Dadurch wird es sich vermeiden lassen, an das NT lediglich als hell[enistisches] Schriftstück heranzugehen und seinen jüdischen Hintergrund zu unterschätzen, wie es in der Vergangenheit geschah".[5]

Nach Röm 3,29 gibt es nur einen einzigen Gott. Der Gott der Ἰουδαῖοι ist auch der Gott der ἔθνη. Insofern muss die Frage *theologisch* beantwortet

---

von Carolin Ziethe 2018, bietet keine grundsätzlich neuen Aspekte, sondern bestätigt die Diversität.

3. Siehe Klausner 1980, 62; nach Klausner war Jesus „ein durchaus palästinischer Jude", Paulus hingegen als Diasporajude, „losgerissen vom Mutterboden" (538).

4. Siehe Kraus 2004, 53–57.347–50.

5. Cook 2004, 1219.

werden, wie das Verhältnis JHWHs zu den Völkern zu bestimmen ist – und damit auch das Verhältnis Israels zu den Völkern.

Dabei erscheint es mir wichtig zu beachten, dass die Definitionen, wie sie uns später in der rabbinischen Literatur begegnen, in der biblischen Tradition erst angebahnt werden. Es gibt in der biblischen Tradition – im TaNaKh – noch im Widerstreit miteinander liegende Aussagen. Dies wird fortgeführt in den Schriften des antiken Judentums, in Qumran, in der apokalyptischen Literatur usw.

Wie die Überlieferungen des TaNaKh in der LXX aufgenommen und verarbeitet werden, ist die Frage, die uns beschäftigen soll. Auf den ersten Blick scheint es sich – nach meiner gegenwärtigen Erkenntnis – so zu verhalten, dass bestimmte Aussagen des TaNaKh sinnentsprechend wiedergegeben werden, wohingegen an anderen Stellen deutliche Modifikationen festzustellen sind. Alle Belege sind daher gesondert wahrzunehmen.[6] Ein System oder eine einheitliche Linie scheint mir nicht erkennbar zu sein. Was ich hier allerdings nur leisten kann, sind einige „Probebohrungen". Ein umfassendes Bild ist nicht zu erwarten – es würde mindestens ein Buch erfordern.[7]

Bevor wir auf die Texte eingehen, sind noch zwei Vorbemerkungen notwendig: 1. eine terminologische Klärung und 2. ein Blick auf Kategorien:

2. Zur Terminologie

Die rabbinische Auffassung unterscheidet zwischen „Proselyt" (גר צדק) und „Sympathisant" (גר תושב). Der eine wird ins Volk Israel integriert. Der andere verehrt JHWH an seinem Ort, ohne ins Gottesvolk aufgenommen zu werden.[8] Eine Auflösung oder Veränderung des Gottesvolk-Konzeptes ist

---

6. Zur Art und Weise, wie die LXX-Übersetzer ihre hebräischen Vorlagen gelesen und verstanden haben, siehe van der Kooij 2008.

7. Eine eingehende Behandlung des Themas ist innerhalb der alttestamentlichen Wissenschaft nach wie vor ein Desiderat, und zwar sowohl was den TaNaKh angeht (v.a. eine Untersuchung des Verhältnisses von Zions-Motivik und JHWH-Volk-Konzeption; so Groß 1989b, 38 A.9) als auch eine Untersuchung der Zusammenhänge in der LXX (und zwar bezogen auf verschiedene Schriften/Schriftengruppen).

8. Naaman in 2.Kön 5,17 gehört in letztere Kategorie. Die Besonderheit bei ihm besteht allerdings darin, dass er Erde aus dem Heiligen Land nach Damaskus mitnimmt. D.h. JHWH kann nur auf israelitischem Boden verehrt werden, weil er nur dort anzutreffen ist; vgl. 5,15b (siehe dazu Haarmann 2008, 132–69). Das ist anders in Jes 19,19: Dort wird das Land durch neue Grenzsteine erweitert (es gibt auch nach

mit beiden Optionen nicht verbunden. Die Bezeichnung „Gottesvolk" bleibt für Israel reserviert. Eine Auflösung bzw. Erweiterung desselben ist nach rabbinischer Auffassung auch für die Endzeit nicht im Blick. Dass die *Gerim* das eschatologische Heil erreichen können, steht gleichwohl außer Frage.[9]

Im TaNaKh und in der LXX (und von dort ausgehend auch im Neuen Testament) werden hingegen auch andere Völker mit der Bezeichnung „Gottesvolk" belegt: In Jes 19,24 MT werden Ägypten und Assyrien mit dieser Begrifflichkeit bezeichnet, in Sach 2,14f MT und LXX andere Völker. Im Neuen Testament wendet Paulus in Röm 9,25-26 und 2.Kor 6,16 Zitate aus Hos 2,1 bzw. Ez 37,27 auf die *Ekklesia* an. Andererseits spricht Paulus in Röm 15,10 unter Zitat von Dtn 32,43 LXX davon, dass sich die *Ethne* mit (μετά) dem Volk Gottes freuen sollen.[10] In der Apk lesen wir in 21,3 von der σκηνὴ τοῦ θεοῦ, die bei den Menschen sein wird. Diese werden dann seine λαοί sein – Plural.

3. Zu den Kategorien

Im Folgenden werde ich Texte, die eine Vernichtung der Völker zum Inhalt haben, nicht besprechen, z.B. Joel 4 (3 LXX); Sach 14,1-5; Obadja. Es soll vielmehr um positive Verhältnisbestimmungen gehen. Ein alle Aspekte umfassendes Bild müsste allerdings auch jene Texte in den Blick nehmen.

Für positive Verhältnisbestimmungen, die im TaNaKh vorkommen, hat Walter Groß drei Modelle unterschieden: (1) Verehrung JHWHs durch Völker in den jeweiligen Ländern, (2) Eingliederung eines Fremdvolkes in das Gottesvolk, (3) eine – wie er es nennt – „vermittelnde" Lösung: Völkerwallfahrt zum Zion und JHWH-Verehrung dort (ohne Eingliederung). Das entscheidende Problem benennt Groß folgendermaßen: Wie kann das Hinzukommen der Nichtjuden gedacht werden, ohne den Gottesvolk-Gedanken zu sprengen?[11]

---

der LXX eine „Säule an der Grenze für den Herrn"). Neben 2.Kön 5 fallen Jon 1,14.16; Zef 2,11 und Mal 1,11 ins Auge. Hier werden dem Gott Israels Gebete und Opfer wie selbstverständlich von Heiden dargebracht (vgl. 1.Kön 8,41-43; Jes 45,22.23; Ps 22,28; 72,11.17; 86,9; 102,23; 145,10.21; vgl. auch 4QOrNab). Zur Fragestellung vgl. grundsätzlich Haarmann 2008.

9. Zur Sache siehe Novak 1983; Porton 1988,1994.

10. Die Diskussion über die Relevanz dieser Fragestellung bei Paulus ist im Gange. Zu Dtn 32,43 vgl. Kraus 2007. Ein besonderes Problem stellt Gal 6,16 dar. Vgl. dazu Kraus 2004, 247-52.

11. Groß 1989b, 38-40.

M.E. ist zu den Modellen bei Groß noch eine 4. Möglichkeit hinzuzufügen: (4) Israel bleibt das Gottesvolk, aber andere Völker werden ebenso Gottesvolk genannt. D.h., es gibt nicht nur ein Gottesvolk, sondern mehrere – so wie dies in Apk 21,3 explizit zum Ausdruck kommt.[12]

Ich gehe so vor, dass ich zwei Texte kurz anspreche (Sach 2,14f; Ps 47 [46],10), um danach Texte aus dem Jesajabuch und der Genesis zu diskutieren. Voraussetzung dabei ist, dass (a) das Verständnis der LXX-Texte nicht vom MT her präjudiziert sein darf und (b) sie aus dem Kontext des jeweiligen Buches und nicht nur für sich allein gelesen werden müssen.[13]

4. Beispiel 1: Sach 2,14–15[14]

Gott verheißt gemäß Sach 2,14, nach erfolgtem Gericht an den Völkern, die Israel bedrängt haben, in Zion Wohnung zu nehmen.[15] V. 15 gehört in den Traditionskreis der Völkerwallfahrt zum Zion. Viele Völker werden sich „an jenem Tage" JHWH zuwenden. Dabei werden diese selbst zum עַם יהוה.[16] Dies führt „über bloße Wallfahrten hinaus, hier klingt ja direkt die Erwählungsformel Israels an: ‚Ihr sollt mein Volk sein'."[17]

---

12. Ziethe 2018, 44–74, unterscheidet unter der Überschrift „Heil für die Völker" zwölf „Topoi": (1) Bundesschluss mit der ganzen Schöpfung, (2) Die Menschheitsfamilie, (3) Segen für alle Völker, (4) Der Lebensraum für alle Völker – der Weltenbaum, (5) Israel als Lebensraum des Fremden, (6) Tora für die Völker, (7) Gottesfürchtige und einzelne JHWH-Verehrer unter den Völkern, (8) Fremde Völker als Gottesvolk, (9) Die Völkerwallfahrt, (10) Das Völkermahl, (11) Gottes explizites Rettungsangebot für die ganze Welt, (12) Die Antwort der Schöpfung – das Lob Gottes durch Rühmen, Anbetung und Opfer (2018, 75). Dabei ist zu bedenken, dass auch Überschneidungen vorliegen.

13. Zur methodischen Vorgehensweise siehe auch Kraus 2009, 152–55; Van der Kooij 1997a, 384.

14. Zu Sach 2,15 vgl. Hanhart 1998, 114–60, bes. 132–33.152–56.

15. Aus dem Zusammenhang ergibt sich m.E. unzweifelhaft, dass es sich um das von JHWH in Zion in Aussicht genommene Wohnen handelt.

16. Sach 2,15 gehört nicht in einen Kontext mit Jes 14,2 (bzw. Sach 8,20–23), denn es heißt hier ausdrücklich גוים und nicht גרים (gegen Wildberger 1978, 526). TgSach 2,15 fügt (diff. MT) ausdrücklich hinzu, dass sich viele Völker an das „Volk" JHWHs anschließen werden. Zur zeitlichen Einordnung des Tg s. Cathcart und Gordon 1989, 16–18, die die Endredaktion v.a. aufgrund von TgNah 1,9 in die Zeit nach 70 n.Chr. datieren.

17. Rudolph 1976, 91.

Die LXX hat die Aussage aufgenommen und dahingehend modifiziert, dass sie (diff. zum hebräischen Text, wo dies von Gott ausgesagt wird) das „Wohnen" (V. 15b) auf die Völker bezieht. Sie sollen innerhalb Israels leben: καὶ ἔσονται αὐτῷ εἰς λαὸν καὶ κατασκηνώσουσιν ἐν μέσῳ σοῦ.[18] An der Aussage, dass diese Völker als „Gottesvolk" gelten, wird nichts zurückgenommen.

In V. 16 rückt dann Juda/Jerusalem wieder ins Zentrum[19]: Mit adversativem Anschluss heißt es, dass der Herr Juda in Besitz nehmen und sein Erbteil im Heiligen Land sein werde, und dass er Jerusalem wiederum erwählen werde. Der Möglichkeit, dass die Völker auch als „Gottesvolk" gelten, entspricht auf der anderen Seite die Zentrierung auf Juda – und Jerusalem.[20]

5. Beispiel 2: Ps 47 (46),10

Ein Text, der eine der Bezeichnung „Gottesvolk" analoge Begrifflichkeit auf Heiden anwendet, findet sich in Ps 47,10: „Die Fürsten/Edlen der Völker (עמים) sind versammelt (נאספו) als Volk des Gottes Abrahams (עם אלוהי אברהם). Denn Gott gehören die Mächte; er ist hoch erhaben".

Erich Zenger interpretiert den Vers so: „Insofern die ‚Edlen der Völker' sich von ihren Göttern abkehren und JHWH den einzig wahren Gott als ihren Gott-König anerkennen, werden bzw. sind sie ‚Volk des Gottes *Abrahams*'."[21] Es geht dabei nicht um das Thema der Aufnahme von Heiden ins Gottesvolk, sondern darum, dass die Völker dem Gottesvolk gleichgestellt werden. Über das Verhältnis zu Israel ist dabei explizit nichts ausgesagt.[22]

---

18. Erich Zenger (1994, 127) setzt den Text in Beziehung zu Ps 87,4–6, wo von Zion als der Mutter aller gesprochen wird. Vgl. auch Kraus 2004, 27–28. Der Übersetzer hat in Ps 86 LXX diese Aussage völlig umgebogen.

19. Vgl. Preuß 1992, 313.

20. Vgl. Hanhart 1998, 153. Nach Rudolph (1976, 91), fällt sich damit „der Prophet selbst ins Wort". Eine Einschränkung der universalistischen Weite von V. 15 sieht auch Beuken 2018, 325.

21. Zenger 1989, 429; vgl. so schon Schreiner 1962, 13. Schreiner konzediert jedoch, dass der Heilsempfang für die Völker nicht direkt ausgesprochen sei.

22. So mit Recht Zenger 1989, 429. Nach Jeremias (1987, 67–68), schließen V. 10b wie auch der Kontext die Annahme aus, dass es sich um eine Aufhebung der Grenze zwischen Israel und den Völkern handeln könne. Möglicherweise verbanden

Die Septuaginta übersetzt עם אלוהי אברהם durch μετὰ τοῦ θεοῦ Αβρααμ („mit dem Gott Abrahams"). Hans-Joachim Kraus nimmt für den hebräischen Text Haplographie an und liest: „versammelt mit dem Volk des Gottes Abrahams" (עם עם אלוהי אברהם).[23] Eine andere Vokalisation als Voraussetzung für die Übersetzung der LXX ist durchaus möglich. Allerdings wird das Verbum אסף im AT stets mit על, אל oder ל konstruiert, nicht aber mit עם.[24] Daher ist die Wahrscheinlichkeit einer Haplographie gering. Näher liegt die Möglichkeit, dass dem Übersetzer des Psalms die Aussage zu weit ging, weshalb er עם anders vokalisiert und durch μετά übersetzt hat.

Mit diesen beiden Beispielen haben wir zwei gegenläufige Tendenzen festgestellt. Es waren Einzelbelege. Machen wir jetzt einen Versuch an mehreren Texten aus einem Buch.

6. Texte aus dem Jesajabuch

6.1. Jes 25,6–8

Die Verse gehören in den Zusammenhang der Jesaja-Apokalypse und stellen vermutlich einen der jüngsten Texte des Jesajabuches dar.[25] Die universale Perspektive ist kaum mehr zu überbieten: Das Freudenmahl soll für alle (!) Völker stattfinden. Es wird eine „Überhöhung wie Ausweitung des Bundesmahles Israels auf dem Sinai" geben (Ex 24,10–1).[26] Alle Völker sollen Anteil bekommen an einem opulenten Mahl, das JHWH bei seiner Thronbesteigung und der endgültigen Aufrichtung der Gottesherrschaft ausrichten wird. An eine Aufnahme der Völker ins Gottesvolk ist nicht gedacht, jedoch werden die Völker, indem sie am Mahl teilnehmen, kultisch dem Gottesvolk gleichgestellt. Otto Kaiser stellt fest: „Mit dieser Mahlgemeinschaft sind die Völker in die Gottesgemeinschaft aufgenommen".[27]

---

sich jedoch mit dem Abschluss des Psalms spätere Hoffnungen auf universale Anerkenntnis des Gottes Israels.
23. Kraus 1972, 348.
24. Jeremias 1987, 54 Anm. 4.
25. Steck (1991a, 30) setzt den Text gleichzeitig mit Jes 19,18–25, d.h. zu Beginn des 3. Jhs. v.Chr. an; vgl. Steck 1985, 40 Anm. 5, 64, 75 Anm. 81, 90. Zum redaktionellen Ort des Textes, siehe auch Preuß 1992, 300–301 (Lit.).
26. Preuß 1992, 322, im Anschluss an Wildberger 1977.
27. Kaiser 1983, 161.

Die Jesaja LXX ist vermutlich um 140 v.Chr. entstanden. Gewichtige textliche Gründe (siehe z.B. Jes 3,18–24; 10,24; 11,16; 19,18–9. 24–5 LXX) sprechen dafür, dass dies im ptolemäischen Ägypten,[28] näherhin in Leontopolis geschah.[29]

Der Abschnitt Jes 25,6–8 LXX darf nicht isoliert verstanden, sondern muss im Kontext der vorausgehenden und nachfolgenden Verse interpretiert werden. Die LXX hat V. 5b ausgelassen.[30] V. 5 LXX spricht jetzt von kleinmütigen Menschen auf dem Zion, die Gott den Feinden (gottlosen Menschen) ausgeliefert hat. V. 6–8 knüpft daran an. Es scheint, dass Zion den Völkern durch Gottes Ratschluss zeitweilig preisgegeben wurde. Doch dies ist nicht das Ende. Gott wird Rettung schenken. Die überaus positive Aussage über eine Teilhabe der Völker an einem endzeitlichen Freudenmahl ist reduziert. Ebenso fehlt, dass es „auf diesem Berg" eine Offenbarung für die Völker geben wird, bei der die Hülle von den Völkern (עמים) genommen und die Decke, die auf dem Angesicht der *Gojim* liegt, beseitigt wird.

Dagegen wird jetzt von einer zeitweiligen „Plünderung der Reichtümer Sions durch Feindvölker" gesprochen.[31] Doch am Ende steht die Vernichtung der Widersacher. Das wird durch die Verse 9–12 zum Ausdruck gebracht.

Der/die Übersetzer des Jesaja-Buches hat/haben den Text somit erheblich modifiziert. Es fehlt auch, dass der Tod auf immer vernichtet wird (V. 8 MT). Dies stimmt damit überein, dass auch in Jes 26,19 LXX gegenüber dem MT eine Änderung festzustellen ist: Zwar spricht V. 19a LXX von einer Auferstehung Toter. Dabei handelt es sich jedoch um eine

---

28. Ziegler 1934, 175–212; Seeligmann 1948, 42, 87; van der Kooij 1981, 60–65; vgl. das Referat bei Troxel 2008, 20–25. Ob es sich um einen einzelnen Übersetzer oder eine Gruppe gehandelt hat, muss hier nicht entschieden werden. Nach Hurvitz 1957 ist davon auszugehen, dass Kap. 36–39 von einem anderen Übersetzer stammen; vgl. Troxel 2008, 1 Anm. 3.

29. Van der Kooij und Wilk 2011a, 2493. Michael Tilly (2010, 214–15) geht davon aus, dass aufgrund von Jes 23,1 LXX die Übersetzung *vor* der Zerstörung Karthagos durch die Römer im Jahr 146 V.Chr. entstanden sein muss. Doch das scheint mir nicht zwingend, im Gegenteil: Karthago ist nach Jes 23,1 LXX bereits zerstört. Zu den Fragen der Interpretation von Jes 23 LXX siehe die Diskussion bei Troxel 2008, 194–99.

30. Es ist unklar, ob wegen Hom.tel. (so van der Kooij und Wilk 2011b, 2567) oder mit Absicht.

31. Van der Kooij und Wilk 2011b, 2568.

metaphorische Aussage analog zu Ez 37,9.12. Und die Herausgabe der Schatten aus der Erde wurde zu einem Gegensatz ausgebaut, wonach das Land der Gottlosen fallen wird. Es scheint v.a. darum zu gehen, dass in einem Bildwort von den Personen, die aus der Diaspora zurückkehren werden, gesprochen wird, nicht von eigentlich Toten.[32]

6.2. Jes 19,16–25[33]

Hier wird keine Völkerwallfahrt zum Zion erwartet, sondern die Offenbarung Gottes vor den Ägyptern (V. 21). Daraufhin werden diese sich zu JHWH bekehren. Für die Darbringung der Opfer wird es in Ägypten selbst einen legitimen Altar geben (V. 19).[34] Und auch das Heilige Land wird erweitert, denn an der Grenze Ägyptens wird ein Steinmal für JHWH stehen (V. 19b).[35] Auch Assur wird zusammen mit Ägypten Gott dienen.[36] Es fällt auf, dass Ägypten und Assur nicht auf die Einhaltung der Tora verpflichtet werden.

Die Erwartung der Anerkennung JHWHs durch die Völker findet sich auch sonst im AT (z.B. Ez 29,6.9.16; 30,8.19.25–6; 32,15.19). In der vorliegenden Spruchfolge jedoch sehen wir eine sonst in dieser Eindeutigkeit kaum belegbare konsequente Übertragung des Gottesvolkkonzepts auf Assur und Ägypten.[37] Dabei stehen „mein Volk" – „Werk meiner Hände" – „mein Erbbesitz" in Parallele zu einander. Nach Jes 19,16–25 MT wird es mehrere Gottesvölker geben: Ägypten, Assur und Israel. Jes 19,24–5 stellen m.E. jene Verse im TaNaKh dar, die sich am weitesten vorwagen hinsichtlich eines heilvollen Verhältnisses JHWH – Israel – Völker.

---

32. Van der Kooij und Wilk 2011b, 2571; dazu vgl. van der Kooij 1997b, 23–24.

33. Zu den Details im Vergleich zwischen MT und LXX siehe van der Kooij 1987; Baer 2001, bes. 214–17.

34. Westermann 1987, 73, sieht Jes 45,20–25 im Hintergrund des Textes stehen (wie auch bei Jes 66,18–24), wobei jedoch das „Motiv der Darbringung von Geschenken (an Könige) und von Opfergaben (an Heiligtümer) von Gästen oder Pilgern" dahingehend abgewandelt sei, dass die Völker ein grundlegend gewandeltes Verhältnis zu Israel haben würden und in eine „gemeinsame Gottesbeziehung" einträten.

35. Zur Deutung der מצבה (die LXX hat στήλη) als Grenzstein siehe Gen 31,44–54; dazu Gamberoni 1984, 1071; gegen Wildberger 1978, 740, zu V. 19. Aus V. 20 geht m.E. eindeutig hervor, dass es sich nicht um ein Kultobjekt handeln kann; vgl. Wildberger 1978, 740, zu V. 20.

36. עבד ist hier im Sinn des Opferdienstes zu verstehen; Wildberger 1978, 740.

37. Vgl. Wildberger 1978, 745–46; Zenger 1991, 107.

Ist damit die Fragestellung „Israel und die Völker" gelöst? Einerseits wird Ägypten ein JHWH-Volk, andererseits bleibt Israel Erbteil JHWHs. Ein Oberbegriff, der beide zusammenfassen könnte, wird nicht gebildet.[38] Nach Groß führt dies „zur Konzeption mehrerer YHWH-Völker, einem Unding, das freilich im Alten Testament nicht ausformuliert wurde".[39] Aber warum sollte das ein „Unding" sein? In Sach 2,14–15 MT wird die Bundesformel auch auf andere Völker angewendet. Nach Ps 47,10 MT werden die „Edlen der Völker" zum „Volk des Gottes Abrahams". Blicken wir auf die LXX in Jes 19:

Auch die LXX bietet mehrere Einheiten, die jeweils mit „an jenem Tag" beginnen: V. 16.18.19.21b.23.24. Dabei werden verschiedene Bereiche angesprochen:

V. 18: Man schwört beim Namen des Herrn.

V. 19: Es gibt einen legitimen Altar in Ägypten und eine „Säule für den Herrn". Dass hinter dem „Altar" der JHWH-Tempel in Leontopolis stehen kann, ist denkbar.[40]

V. 20: Beides sei für immer ein Zeichen für den Herrn im Gebiet Ägyptens.

V. 21: Der Herr sendet ihnen einen Retter. Darin ist vom Kontext her wohl impliziert, dass dieser aus dem Gottesvolk kommt.[41] Die Ägypter erkennen den Herrn an und bringen ihm Opfer dar. Sie legen ihm Gelübde ab und erfüllen diese.

V. 22: Die Ägypter werden vom Herrn geschlagen und geheilt.

---

38. Anders z.B. Schreiner 1968, 110; 1962, 22. Zu diesem Problem und seiner Ausprägung in Jes 56 und 66 vgl. im Detail weiter unten. Nach Judith Gärtner (2006, 66, vgl. 99.128.314) ist in Jes 66,23 unter dem Stichwort כל בשר ein „Gottesvolk zu verstehen", welches neben den Israeliten auch „die Frommen aus den Völkern umfasst, sofern sie sich wie die frommen Fremden aus Jes 56,6–7. verhalten und Sabbat und Bund wahren".

39. Groß 1989a, 21; 1993, 157.

40. Vgl. Clements 1980, 171.

41. Van der Kooij 1987, 142: „the saviour-judge is a Jew", vgl. 143.157.

V. 23: Es wird einen Weg von Ägypten zu den Assyrern geben, allerdings so, dass die Ägypter den Assyrern dienen. „LXX Isa 19:23 refers to a military campaign by the Assyrians against Egypt, and to subjection of the Egyptians to the Assyrians. Having conquered Palestine, they shall go to Egypt by 'the way to Egypt.'"[42]

V. 24: Israel wird Dritter sein bei den Ägyptern und Assyrern, gesegnet auf der Erde, die der Herr segnete. „[T]his points to an important role of Israel."[43]

V. 25: Die LXX unterscheidet sich in V. 25 deutlich vom MT. „Gesegnet ist mein Volk, das in Ägypten und das bei (unter) den Assyrern, und mein Volk Israel." Wer ist gemeint mit der Ausdrucksweise „mein Volk, das in Ägypten und das bei (unter) den Assyrern"? Ist es die jüdische Diaspora? Es fällt auf, dass „Ägypter" und „Ägypten" in V. 24 und 25 wechseln. Anders als im MT spricht die LXX stets von „Assyrern", nicht von „Assyrien" (als Werk der Hände Gottes).[44] Das stimmt mit V. 23 zusammen, wonach die Assyrer Ägypten erobert haben. „Mein Volk in Ägypten" meint in Jes 11,16 LXX die Israeliten beim Auszug. In 10,24 LXX werden Israeliten durch den Schlag, der von Gott ausgeht, den Weg nach Ägypten gewiesen. Diese Stellen gelten als Indizien dafür, dass in der LXX-Jesaja die jüdische Diaspora in Ägypten im Blick ist.[45]

Nach Georg Bertram handelt es sich bei dieser Ausdrucksweise um eine „judaistische Verengung".[46] Dem widersprechen Arie van der Kooij und Florian Wilk: Der Segen für „mein Volk" betreffe die ganze Erde.[47] Ist es denkbar, hinter der Formulierung „mein Volk, das in Ägypten und das bei (unter) den Assyrern" eine andere Größe als die jüdische Diaspora zu

---

42. Van der Kooij 1987, 147.155.
43. Van der Kooij 1987, 150.
44. Vgl. auch Baer 2001, 215 Anm. 44.
45. Van der Kooij 1987, 146. Zur Sache vgl. auch de Vos, 2011, 96–100.
46. Bertram 1957, 227. In diese Richtung geht auch die Interpretation bei Baer 2001, 214–17.
47. Van der Kooij und Wilk 2011b, 2555; sie sehen den Vers auf einer Ebene mit Gen 12,3. Den Bezug auf Ägypten als Gottesvolk in Jes 19,25 LXX findet Monsengwo-Pasinya (1985, 204), doch das scheint so nicht ausreichend begründet, denn Subjekt in V. 25 ist Israel; vgl. van der Kooij 1987, 152–55 (unter Verweis auf die gleiche grammatische Konstruktion in Jes 48,1 LXX und 2.Makk 1,1).

verstehen? Von V. 21 her könnten auch die Ägypter ein Volk des Herrn bilden. Aber das wird so in V. 25 nicht wieder aufgenommen.[48] Gleichwohl bleibt es dabei, dass die Ägypter legitime Opfer darbringen und dem Herrn Gelübde ablegen.

6.3. Jes 56,3–8 (gegen Ez 44,6–11.15)

Mit Jes 56,1–8 wird der dritte Teil des Jesajabuches eröffnet. Die neuere Forschung betont die Beziehung dieses Textes zu Jes 66,18–24 und sieht einen gemeinsamen Redaktor am Werk.[49] Ein Vergleich von Jes 56,3ff. und 66,18ff. ergibt jedoch hinsichtlich des Verhältnisses von Nichtjuden zum Gottesvolk mindestens unterschiedliche Akzente,[50] was der Annahme einer einheitlichen Redaktionsschicht entgegenstehen und auf unterschiedliche Redaktoren schließen lassen könnte,[51] es sei denn, man löst das Problem wie Judith Gärtner, die erklärt, es werde in Jes 66 auch inhaltlich eine weitere Stufe der Fortschreibung erreicht.[52] Dabei versteht sie Jes 66,23 als „Quintessenz" aus Jes 66 und 56,1–7.8.[53]

Der Text bezieht sich in V. 3 auf die Klagen des Fremden (בן הנכר) und des Verschnittenen (הסריס), nicht als Mitglieder des Gottesvolkes anerkannt zu sein. Resigniert stellen sie fest, vom Volk Gottes getrennt gehalten zu werden. In V. 4–7 findet sich in Form eines Gottesspruches die

---

48. Siehe auch Harl, Dorival, und Munnich 1994, 217.

49. Zur Auslegung und Datierung siehe Gärtner 2006, bes. 54–66.93–101.103–34.213–20.311–20 (Lit.!); 2013 (Lit.!); Haarmann 2008, 206–46 (Lit.!); daneben aus der älteren Literatur v.a. Donner 1985; außerdem Hanson 1975, 388–89 (Hanson rechnet 56,1–8 wie 66,17–24 zum „redactional framework" und ordnet die Texte zeitlich etwa wie Sach 14 ein); Koenen 1990, 27–32.223–24; Bultmann 1992, 207–12 (Bultmann setzt den Text zeitlich in der 2. Hälfte des 5. Jhs. an). Nach Steck (1991a 94–95.98; vgl. Groß 1989a, 27) gehört Jes 56,1–8 zusammen mit 63,7–66,24 zu einer dritten Redaktionsschicht des Jesajabuches. Auch Kellermann (1991, 46–47.64–65.72) und Koenen (1990, 28–32.212–14) ordnen Jes 56,3ff. und 66,18–24 derselben Schicht zu (Koenen datiert jedoch anders).

50. Vgl. Groß 1989a, 30, Haarmann 2008, 216.

51. Die zeitliche Ansetzung dieser Fortschreibung des Jesajabuches dürfte nach Steck 1991a, 197, an der Wende vom 4. zum 3. Jh. v.Chr. anzusetzen sein.

52. Gärtner 2013, 12–13.27–28. Gärtner (2013, 2–3) schließt sich grundsätzlich den literarkritischen Ergebnissen von Steck an; vgl. Gärtner 2006, 60–62 mit Anm. 214.

53. Gärtner 2006, 59–62 (Zitat 59).

Begründung für die Abweisung dieser Klage und in V. 8 der Abschluss in Gestalt eines prophetischen Botenspruches.[54]

Die Zugehörigkeit zum Gottesvolk wird für diese Personengruppe künftig entschieden durch die Einhaltung des Sabbat, das Erwählen dessen, was JHWH gefällt, und das Festhalten an der ברית.[55] Worin diese ברית besteht, wird nicht näher definiert.[56] Fremdlinge und Verschnittene dürfen am Tempelgottesdienst teilnehmen.[57] Der Tempel soll „Haus des Gebets für alle Völker" heißen.[58] Dadurch ist für diese Personen die Unterscheidung Israels und der Völker, die sich u.a. im Verbot des Zutritts zum inneren, eigentlichen Tempelbezirk niederschlägt, nicht mehr relevant.[59]

Dass damit das Gottesvolk-Konzept insgesamt in Frage gestellt werde, wird von Volker Haarmann bestritten.[60] Nach ihm handelt es sich um

---

54. Zur formgeschichtlichen Bestimmung siehe Haarmann 2008, 208–10. Kraus (1990, 177) möchte V. 8 von V. 3–7 absetzen, dies ändert jedoch nichts an der Bedeutung von V. 4–7.

55. Der MT spricht in 56,3a.6a von einem Anschluss an JHWH, wohingegen der Targum dies als Anschluss an das „Volk" JHWHs interpretiert (vgl. TgSach 2,15). Darüber hinaus geht es hier ausdrücklich um „Heiden", die Anschluss an das Gottesvolk suchen.

56. Nach Kutsch (2004, 350) der *Berit* dezidiert als „Verpflichtung" interpretiert, besteht die Verpflichtung in Jes 56,4 in der Einhaltung des Sabbat; daneben Westermann 1976, 250: „Bundessatzung", „Gesetz"; Fohrer 1964, 189: „Religion," „Gesetzesfrömmigkeit"; Kraus 1990, 178: „Gottesgebote"; vgl. sachlich gleich: Ex 31,16 (Priesterschrift); Kutsch 2004, 350. Bultmann (1992, 210) sieht darin im Anschluss an Duhm die Beschneidung angesprochen; vgl. Rendtorff 2001, 73. Dagegen argumentiert Haarmann 2008, 219–20.

57. Die Aussage könnte sich nach Steck (1991b, 246–47 Anm. 111) direkt antithetisch auf die Separationsaussagen in Esr 9–10; Neh 9–10; 13 beziehen. Eine Antithetik zu Esr/Neh und deren Ausgrenzungspolitik wird auch von Koenen 1990, 223–24, gesehen, wenngleich er sich in seiner Datierung des Redaktors von Steck unterscheidet.

58. Dabei ist (entgegen der Benutzung des Verses in Mk 11) keine opferlose Gottesverehrung anvisiert, sondern die Teilnahme der Verschnittenen und Fremden am Opferkult.

59. Koenen 1990, 29, sieht in 56,6 die priesterliche Tätigkeit der Fremden angezeigt.

Einzelne, die als JHWH-Verehrer aus den Völkern zu bezeichnen seien.⁶¹ Haarmann betont hingegen die Opposition, in der Jes 56,3–8 zu Ez 44,6–11.15 steht. Dort wird explizit die Position vertreten, dass es ein Gräuel sei, Unbeschnittene ins Heiligtum vorzulassen (s.u.). Nur die Leviten seien dafür vorgesehen.

Haarmann⁶² wendet sich auch dagegen, mit Herbert Donner u.a. in Jes 56,3–8 eine sakralrechtliche Außerkraftsetzung von Dtn 23,2–9⁶³ und damit verbunden eine grundlegende Wandlung der Gestalt des Gottesvolkes zu erkennen, deren Voraussetzungen in der „Trennung der Jahwe-Gemeinde vom Staatswesen" und in dem „Heilsangebot Jahwes an die Völker" (vgl. Jes 45,20–25) zu suchen seien.⁶⁴ Nach Haarmann geht es nur um Einzelpersonen, die das Gottesvolkkonzept nicht tangieren. Sie schließen sich der JHWH-Verehrung, nicht dem Volk Israel an.⁶⁵

Immerhin wird man sagen dürfen, dass der Verschnittene *Yad waShem* erhält und der Fremdling nicht vom Volk Gottes getrennt gehalten wird. Dass es sich um Einzelpersonen handeln mag, spricht nicht gegen eine grundsätzliche Fragestellung. Die Frage, ob diese Fremden analog den Priestern Israels auch Opfer darbringen, entscheidet sich an der Interpretation von V. 6, insbesondere der des Infinitivs לשרתו im Verbund mit den Aussagen in V. 7. Nach der ausführlichen Diskussion bei Haarmann ist wohl davon auszugehen, dass – im Unterschied zu anderen alttestamentlichen Belegen – in Jes 56 „ausdrücklich" davon gesprochen wird, dass „von den Fremden, die JHWH zu seinem Tempel führt ... deren Opfer auf dem Altar wohlgefällig" angenommen werden.⁶⁶

Die LXX bietet gegenüber dem hebräischen Text einige gewichtige Veränderungen. Der Eunuch bekommt einen „namhaften Platz". Betont

---

61. Haarmann 2008, 206–46. So bereits Zenger 1991, 106: Das in Jes 56 vorgestellte Modell eigne sich nur „für die Integration von Individuen, aber nicht von Ethnien in das Gottesvolk". Ähnlich auch Welten 1986, 134. Nach Welten geht es nicht generell um Integration der Fremden, sondern lediglich um eine Ausnahme. Es soll ihnen der Weg zur gottesdienstlichen Gemeinde geöffnet werden.

62. Siehe dazu Haarmann 2008, 220–26, bes. 223–24.

63. Donner 1985, 87–88; so schon Westermann 1976, 249–50.252.

64. Westermann 1976, 249–50.

65. Haarmann 2008, 243.244. Den gleichen Sachverhalt sieht Haarmann in Jes 2,1–5 vorliegen: „Die Völker werden dabei nicht zu Israel, sondern pilgern als JHWH-Verehrer der Völker zum Zion" (253–54 mit Anm. 1097, im Anschluss an Levenson 1996, 164).

66. Haarmann 2008, 237 (innerhalb von 232–42), vgl. allerdings 232 mit Anm.

wird, dass davon „alle" Eunuchen betroffen sein werden. Die Opfer der Fremdstämmigen werden Gott willkommen sein. Sie werden auf „seinem Altar" dargebracht – der Begriff θυσιαστήριον signalisiert einen legitimen Altar.[67] Ob er in Jerusalem steht, ist damit nicht gesagt. Es ist möglich, dass die LXX 56,6 im Sinn von Proselyten verstanden hat.[68] Diese Fremdstämmigen werden in der LXX ausdrücklich als „Diener und Dienerinnen" Gottes bezeichnet. Das bedeutet zum einen, dass Frauen einbezogen werden.[69] Zum anderen ist der hebräische Infinitiv לשרתו in V. 6 mit dem Begriff δουλεύειν unspezifisch wiedergegeben, was (analog zum Text von Jes 56,6 in 1QJes^a) eine Abschwächung bedeuten könnte. „Möglich wäre auch eine Übersetzung mit λειτουργέω gewesen."[70] Durch die Erwähnung von Frauen könnte der Übersetzer den Ausschluss der Fremden vom Priesterdienst intendiert haben.[71] Es bleibt im Gegenüber zum MT in der LXX unklar, ob die Fremdstämmigen aktiv gottesdienstliche Handlungen übernehmen dürfen.[72] In V. 7 wird allerdings explizit davon gesprochen, dass die Opfer der Fremden von Gott akzeptiert werden. Die Opfer heißen ausdrücklich ὁλοκαυτώματα und θυσίαι. Das scheint dafür zu sprechen, dass auch in der LXX die Fremden am Heiligtum aktiv Dienst tun. Der Tempel soll ein „Haus der Anbetung für alle *Ethne*" heißen. Auch wenn es *nur* um Einzelpersonen gehen sollte, so werden deren Opfer jedenfalls anerkannt.

Jes 56,3–8 steht in explizitem Widerspruch zu Ez 44,6–11.15.[73] In V. 7.9 wird dort ausdrücklich kritisiert, dass unbeschnittene Fremde (בני נכר) ins Heiligtum zugelassen wurden.[74] „Jes 56,1–8 und Ez 44,6ff. stellen demnach zwei konträre Positionen in einem Diskurs über die Frage der

---

67. Zur Bedeutung von θυσιαστήριον als „legitimer Altar" (im Unterschied zu βωμός) siehe van der Kooij und Wilk 2011b, 2554; vgl. van der Kooij 1987, 162 Anm. 38 mit Hinweis auf Daniel 1966, 18–19; Troxel 2008, 153.

68. Burchard 1983, 676 Anm. 7 und 8.

69. Koenen 2011, 2678, weist auf Joel 2,29 (3,2) und 2.Esdr 20,28–29 (Neh 10,29–30) als Parallelen hin.

70. Haarmann 2008, 206.

71. So Haarmann 2008, 206–7 im Anschluss an Van Winkle 1997.

72. Haarmann 2008, 207 (Z. 11) ist allerdings zu korrigieren: Auch Jes 56,6 LXX spricht davon, dass die Fremden den Namen Gottes „lieben", 1QJes^a hingegen hat an dieser Stelle „segnen".

73. Vgl. hierzu Haarmann 2008, 229–32.

74. Nach Lev 22,25 ist es verboten, Opfermaterie aus der Hand eines בן נכר entgegenzunehmen.

Beteiligung von Fremden am Tempelkult dar".[75] Dahinter scheint somit ein tatsächliches Problem aus nachexilischer Zeit zu stehen, das zu unterschiedlichen Positionen führte.

Die LXX hat die Aussage insofern verschärft, als es nun die Fremden selbst sind, die durch ihre Anwesenheit das Heiligtum „entweiht" haben (V. 7, verbum finitum). Im MT geschieht dies durch die Israeliten, die durch das Hineinlassen der Fremden die Entweihung provoziert haben. In Ez 44 scheint es aber eigentlich um die Reduktion des Anspruchs der Leviten zu gehen. Sie sollen künftig nur noch als Wächter dienen. Als Begründung wird ihr Fehlverhalten gegenüber den Fremden angegeben.

Bezieht man noch Ez 47,22–3 in die Überlegungen mit ein, so bestätigt sich, dass es in Ez 44,6–11.15 um das Problem der Zulassung von unbeschnittenen Fremden (בני נכר) ins Heiligtum ging. Nach Ez 47,22–23 MT sollen die Schutzbürger (גרים) bei der neuen Landverteilung mitberücksichtigt werden, und zwar so, dass sie in dem Stamm, in dem sie wohnen, Landanteil bekommen. Die LXX hat die „Schutzbürger" als „Proselyten" interpretiert. Und sie hat in V. 23 sogar einen eigenen „Stamm der Proselyten" eingeführt. Für sie sind die Proselyten beschnittene Nicht-Israeliten.[76]

6.4. Jes 66,18–24[77]

Jes 66,18–24 gehört wie Jes 2,1–5; Sach 2,15 in den Traditionskreis der Völkerwallfahrt zum Zion.[78] Auf den ersten Blick könnte es scheinen, als lägen in unserem Text zwei Tendenzen, die sich nicht im Sinn eines zeitlichen Nacheinander auflösen lassen, miteinander im Streit: auf der einen Seite das Herzukommen der Völker, die Mission an anderen Völkern durch Abgesandte aus den Herzugekommenen und die Einsetzung von Priestern und Leviten aus ihren Reihen,[79] auf der andern Seite eine

---

75. Haarmann 2008, 230–31.
76. Zur Sache siehe Konkel 2011, 2991.
77. Zu diesem Text siehe insbesondere die Arbeiten von Gärtner 2006; 2013; daneben 2018, bes. 140–45. Für die Akzente der Jes 66,18–24 LXX siehe Tilly 2010; Baer 2001, 231–76.
78. Allerdings gibt es keine literarischen, sondern nur traditionsgeschichtliche Beziehungen zwischen diesen Texten. Für das Jesaja-Buch betont Gärtner 2018, 140–41, die unterschiedlichen Konzeptionen. Den Kompositionsbogen zwischen dem Buchanfang und -schluss in Jesaja sieht Gärtner in der Sabbatthematik vorliegen (2018, 142–43).
79. Zu den Ländernamen in V. 19 vgl. *Jub* 9,1.14.

Tendenz, dann doch Israel in den Mittelpunkt zu rücken. Ging es in V. 18.19.21 um eine zentrifugale Bewegung hin zur Völkerwelt, so findet sich in V. 20.22-24 deren zentripetale Umkehrung hin zum Zion und zu Juda.[80] Der Text hat zu literar- bzw. redaktionskritischen Überlegungen Anlass gegeben.[81] Nach Durchmusterung vieler Vorschläge empfiehlt es sich, den Abschnitt doch als literarische Einheit aufzufassen.[82]

V. 18 überträgt die häufig belegte Erwartung, wonach Gott die Zerstreuten Israels sammelt, auf die Heiden.[83] Es liegt eine steigernde Anknüpfung an Jes 45,20-25 vor.[84] Eine direkte Aufnahme von Jes 56,8 (vgl. 60,3.4a) ist evident.

V. 19 wird den Völkern eine Funktion zugewiesen, die Jes 42,1.4; 49,6 dem Gottesknecht zukommt: Sie werden zu „Missionaren der Weltvölker".[85]

In V. 20 scheint sich zunächst die gegenläufige Tendenz Gehör zu verschaffen.[86] Das Gegenteil trifft jedoch zu: Dass sie „eure Brüder aus den Völkern als Opfergabe für JHWH herbeibringen", bedeutet eine weitere Steigerung, nämlich die kultische Gleichsetzung mit Israel. Die Völker werden kultfähig.

---

80. Vgl. Westermann 1976, 336. Westermann (1976, 336-38.338-40) legt die V. 18.19.21 und 20.22-24 strikt getrennt aus.

81. Kraus 1990, 253, rechnet mit Einschüben in einen ursprünglich tritojesajanischen Text; Koenen 1990, 208.257, hält den Text insgesamt für redaktionell, V. 23.24 für Zusätze, ebenso die Namenslisten in V. 19.20. Die Überlegung von Westermann 1976, 336, wonach sich V. 20.22-24 wie eine „bewußte Korrektur" des „Unerhörten" in V. 18.19.21 ausnehmen, hat sich in der Forschung nicht durchsetzen können. Schreiner 1968, 111-12; Groß 1989b, 38 Anm. 10; 1989a, 27-28; Sehmsdorf 1972, 573; Steck 1985, 72.74-75; 1991b, 262-65, gehen von einer literarischen Einheit aus, ebenso Kellermann 1991, 64-66, bes. Anm. 80. Die zahlreichen Versuche zeigen zumindest, dass im Text unterschiedliche Tendenzen vorliegen. Auch Gärtner 2006, 34-62, geht von literarischer Einheit aus.

82. Siehe insbesondere die Argumentation bei Gärtner 2006, 61-62. mit Anm. 214.

83. Vgl. Dtn 30,4; Jes 11,12; Jer 23,3; 29,14; 31,10-11; 32,37; Ez 11,17; 20,34.41; 34,13; 36,24; Zef 3,19; Jes 40,11; 43,5; 54,7; Kellermann 1991, 68-69.

84. Vgl. Westermann 1976, 337.

85. Kellermann 1991, 71. Dies ist ein gravierender Unterschied zu Sach 14,16: gegen Kellermann 1991, 70.

86. So Westermann 1976, 339; Vermeylen 1978, 501.514.

V. 21: Aus welcher Gruppe sollen Priester und Leviten zusätzlich genommen werden, aus den heimkehrenden Exulanten oder aus den Völkern? Es liegt nahe, den Abgesandten aus den Völkern diese Funktion zuzuschreiben, denn sie sind in V. 19.20 auch grammatikalisch jeweils handelnde Subjekte. Der hebräische Text erschwert aufgrund der Syntax eine eindeutige Entscheidung.[87] Die Vokalisation der Masoreten von ללוים und לכהנים jeweils mit Artikel bedeutet, dass die Ankommenden nur zu Dienern der Priester und Leviten gemacht werden.[88] Dies könnte schon den Versuch einer Abmilderung darstellen. Setzte man eine Nachinterpretation voraus, so wäre eventuell mit einer bewussten Sinnverschiebung zu rechnen: Die Priester und Leviten sollen jetzt aus den zurückkommenden Israeliten stammen. Stellt jedoch V. 20 keine spätere Korrektur, sondern eine Steigerung von V. 19 dar, dann bedeutete V. 21 nur die konsequente Fortsetzung der Gleichstellung der Heidenvölker mit dem Gottesvolk. V. 21 beinhaltete dann, dass Gott selbst aus den Heidenvölkern Priester und Leviten erwählen werde, die am Heiligtum Dienst tun sollten.[89] Dies würde eine Änderung der gängigen Gliederung des Gottesvolkes in Priester, Leviten und Israeliten und den Eintritt von Heiden in dessen innersten Kreis bedeuten.[90] Im Vergleich zu Jes 56,7 beinhaltet Jes 66,21 mindestens eine Akzentverschiebung.

---

87. So auch Kellermann 1991, 73. Auch die Übersetzung in TgJes 66,20ff. lässt keine eindeutige Entscheidung zu (engl. Übersetzung bei Chilton 1987). Bei literarkritisch einheitlicher Beurteilung geht Groß 1989a, 29, im Anschluss an Feldmann von den Völkern aus; ebenso Steck 1991a, 95, im Anschluss an Beuken 1989, 142–43; anders Kraus 1990, 254, der an die heimkehrenden Exulanten denkt und 66,21 im Kontext von 61,6 sieht. Haarmann (2008, 216.232 mit Anm. 1017) bezieht die Aussage auf die mitgebrachten „Brüder"; Gärtner (2006, 37 mit Anm. 133) bezieht das מהם auf die ankommenden Völker (siehe dazu weiterhin unten).

88. Vgl. Koenen 1990, 211 Anm. 15. Zur Übersetzung der Asyndese und dem Verständnis von ללוים als Apposition siehe Koenen 1990, 211. V. 21 stellt m.E. jedoch keine Parallele zu Jes 60,9 dar, sondern geht weit darüber hinaus (gegen Koenen 1990, 213).

89. Vgl. Westermann 1976, 338. Weitere Argumente bei Kellermann 1991, 73–74; Groß 1993, 163; Lohfink 1994, 57 (unter Bezug auf Franz Delitzsch). Hanson (1975, 388) sieht in 66,21 „close resemblance to the tolerant spirit of Zech 14,20–21" und eine Attacke gegen die zadokitische Priesterschaft (1975, 389).

90. Vgl. Westermann 1976, 338; Zenger 1991, 106; vgl. Koenen 1990, 211; Sehmsdorf 1972, 573; Kellermann 1991, 75.

V. 23 heißt es, „alles Fleisch" werde *wöchentlich* kommen, „um sich anbetend niederzuwerfen". Dies geht über die Pilgerfahrten in Sach 8,20-22; 14,16-17 hinaus[91] und setzt eine andauernde Teilnahme am Tempelgottesdienst voraus.

Geht es zu weit, wenn man sagt: Jes 66,18-24 geht von einer (endzeitlichen) Aufhebung des Unterschiedes zwischen Israel und den Völkern aus – und geht damit auch über Jes 56,3-8 hinaus?

Blicken wir auf die LXX:

V. 18: Die LXX geht weitgehend parallel mit dem hebräischen Text: Gott wird kommen, um alle Völkerschaften und Sprachen zu versammeln, damit diese seine Herrlichkeit zu sehen.[92]

V. 19: Gerettete aus dem Kreis derer werden zu Missionaren ausgesandt in die ganze Welt. Sie verkünden den *Ethne* von der Herrlichkeit des Gottes Israels.

V. 20: Sie bringen die Brüder als Gabe (δῶρον) aus den *Ethne* nach Jerusalem und zwar so, wie die Söhne Israels ihre Opfer (θυσίας) unter Psalmengesang zum Haus des Herrn brachten (ἄν + Optativ Aorist: es handelt sich um eine vorsichtige Behauptung über die Vergangenheit).[93] Allerdings hat sich die Zuordnung und Bezeichnung der Opfer gegenüber dem hebräischen Text verschoben: Nach dem MT bringen die Ausgesandten die Israeliten als מנחה für Gott mit sich zurück so wie die Söhne Israels dem Herrn eine „Opfergabe" (מנחה) darbringen. Die LXX spricht nur von einer Gabe (δῶρον) der Völker. Das führt Michael Tilly zu folgender Einschätzung: „Während die Gabe Israels somit explizit als eine

---

91. Vgl. Groß 1989a, 30 Anm. 54. Zu Pilgerfahrten von Heiden nach Jerusalem und der Frage der Teilnahme am Tempelkult siehe Kraus 2004, 16 Anm. 3; Haarmann (2008, 232-42) geht auch bei Jes 56,7 von einer Teilnahme von Nicht-Israeliten am Tempelkult aus (s.o.). Damit argumentiert er mit Recht gegen Daniel Schwartz (2008, 237).

92. Im MT steht nicht „ich komme", sondern die 3. Sg. fem. באה. BHS schlägt vor, בא zu lesen.

93. Koenen (2011, 2690, mit Bezug auf Helbing) fragt, ob damit evtl. die vorexilische Zeit gemeint sein könnte. Anders Baer 2001, 259-61: er denkt an „some undefined point in the future" (2001, 261).

kultische ‚*Opfergabe*' im Kontext des Tempelkultes erscheint (vgl. Lev 2,1 sowie Jes 1,11; 19,21; 34,6; 43,23f.; 56,7; 57,6f.) wird die – als Opfer völlig ungeeignete – Gabe der Heiden in unspezifischer Weise als bloßes ‚*Geschenk*' ausgewiesen (vgl. 1Chr 16,28f.; 2Chr 32,23)".[94]

Damit werde die Völkerwelt ein „untergeordneter Überbringer von Tributen".[95] Doch so sehr diese Überlegung auf den ersten Blick besticht, ist sie auf den zweiten nicht zwingend: Zum einen ist der Begriff δῶρον in der LXX die gängige Übersetzung des „priesterlichen Obergriff[es]" für Opfer: קרבן.[96] Zum andern werden auch in der LXX-Jesaja θυσίαι von Nichtisraeliten dargebracht: Jes 19,21; 56,7. Daher kann es sein, dass die Geretteten aus den Völkern im Blick auf ihre Darbringung den Israeliten doch gleichgestellt werden. Auffällig ist, dass die Gabe, die für den Herrn dargebracht wird, nach V. 20 LXX nicht wie im MT zu „meinem heiligen Berg Jerusalem" kommt, sondern „in meine heilige Stadt Jerusalem". Ob man daraus folgern soll, dass damit ein „down-grading of access for the Gentiles"[97] erfolgt, erscheint mir nicht zwingend, denn die LXX schließt die Transportmittel unter die nach Jerusalem gebrachten Güter mit ein.

V. 21: „Von ihnen" werden Priester und Leviten genommen. Wer ist mit „von ihnen" gemeint? Gerettete aus den Völkern? Zurückgekehrte Israeliten? Das „auch" im hebräischen Text ist ausgelassen. Die Beziehung des ἀπ' αὐτῶν ist wie das מהם im MT nicht vollkommen eindeutig zu bestimmen. Trotzdem bezieht sich „sie" wohl auf die Völker. Denn bei den Exilierten waren bereits Priester und Leviten dabei. Daher würde ein Bezug auf sie nichts Erwähnenswertes bedeuten.[98]

V. 23: Wie im MT wird auch in der LXX davon gesprochen, dass „alles Fleisch" an jedem Neumond und Sabbat kommen wird, um anbetend niederzufallen. Das Ganze, so ergänzt die LXX, wird in Jerusalem stattfinden. Kann man das anders verstehen, denn als Huldigung der ganzen Welt vor dem Gott Israels? Mir scheint daher die von Baer postulierte Tendenz, wonach LXX-Jesaja einen „nationalistic" Akzent habe, nicht völlig

---

94. Tilly 2010, 218 (kursiv im Original) im Anschluss an Baer 2001, 265.274; und im Anschluss an Tilly: Gärtner 2013, 10–11 mit Anm. 27; ähnlich Koenen 2011, 2690.
95. Tilly 2010, 218.
96. Siehe dazu Eberhart 2014, 314 (vgl. Mk 7,11).
97. Baer 2001, 266.276; im Anschluss an ihn Tilly 2010, 219.
98. Koenen 1990, 209 Anm. 7 (im Anschluss an Westermann).

schlüssig. Die Völker sollen nach Baer „participate in that city's final glories, but only as tribute-bearers who remain in the moral shadow of those returned Jews who offer eschatological sacrifice to the Lord himself in his own house."[99] Die Wortwahl „nationalistic" evoziert Assoziationen, die den Texten m.E. nicht gerecht werden. Eher scheint es mir angebracht danach zu fragen, ob sich nicht die Diaspora-Situation im 2.Jh. v.Chr. in den Texten niederschlägt. Doch vorher soll noch einmal die Bedeutung von Jesaja 66 MT angesprochen werden, um den Hintergrund der LXX-Aussagen präziser profilieren zu können.

6.5. Die Bedeutung von Jesaja 66 MT für das Jesaja-Buch

Judith Gärtner hat die These vertreten, dass das Thema des Schicksals der Völker eine Deutungsperspektive für das Groß-Jesaja-Buch darstellt. Damit bekommt Jesaja 66 eine zentrale Funktion für die Gesamtbedeutung des Prophetenbuches. Zu Jes 66,18-21.22-23 stellt sie fest: „Die über den Begriff כל־בשׂר bereits [in V. 16] angeklungene universale Ausdehnung des endzeitlichen Gerichts- und Heilshandelns Jhwhs wird im folgenden Abschnitt zum zentralen Thema, in dem das Schicksal der Völkerwelt in den Blick genommen wird".[100] Gärtner sieht dabei Beziehungen zu weiteren Texten in Trito-Jesaja:

> Wenn nun in Jes 66,23 כל־בשׂר kommt, um Jhwh zu huldigen, sind jetzt all die Übriggebliebenen aus dem Gericht Jhwhs an allem Fleisch gemeint (V. 15–17). Dies bedeutet im literarischen Zusammenhang von Jes 66,23: die Knechte Jhwhs (65,8ff.), die neuen Zionskinder (66,7–14), die dem Wort Jhwhs Entgegenzitternden (66,2.5), die Entronnenen aus den Völkern (66,19–21) und die nach 56,6–7 als fromme Fremde und „Verschnittene" den Sabbat wahren und zu Knechten Jhwhs geworden sind. Von Jes 66,23 her ist es nun eindeutig, dass sich כל־בשׂר auch in Jes 66,15–17 nicht auf das Gottesvolk beschränken lässt, sondern die in Jes 66,18ff. entfaltete universale Dimension impliziert und sein positives Pendant im Völkerzug in Jes 66,23 hat. Diejenigen aus allem Fleisch, die sich Jhwh gemäß verhalten, wie es in Jes 56,2ff. ausgeführt wird, bilden nun das neue Gottesvolk und kommen Sabbat um Sabbat, Neumond um Neumond, um Jhwh zu huldigen.[101]

---

99. Baer 2001, 276.
100. Gärtner 2006, 34.
101. Gärtner 2006, 54.

Jes 66,23 bekommt damit die Funktion einer „Quintessenz" aus 56,1–7.8 und Jes 65f.[102]

> Die endzeitliche Herrschaft Jhwhs wie sie Jes 66 entfaltet, bildet die Voraussetzung des endzeitlichen Gottesvolkes, wie es in Jes 56,1–7.8 beschrieben wird. Denn die universale Herrschaft Jhwhs, deren Dimension die Neuschöpfung von Himmel und Erde umfasst, impliziert auch ein Gottesvolk, zu dem Fremde und „Verschnittene" gehören, sofern sie Sabbat und Bund wahren. Dies halten Jes 66,22 und 66,23, die eine Brücke zwischen Tempel, Schöpfung und Sabbatobservanz schlagen, abschließend fest und resümieren, dass die universale Herrschaft Jhwhs über Himmel und Erde, die Neuschöpfung von Himmel und Erde ebenso umfasst wie das endzeitliche Gottesvolk aus allem Fleisch ... Konzeptionell gesehen bildet damit Jes 66 das zentrale Kapitel der redaktionellen Bearbeitung am Buchschluss.[103]

Den Völkern kommt in diesem Kontext eine „besondere Funktion" zu.[104] Gärtner verfolgt diese Linie, die die Bedeutung der Völker hervorhebt, durch das gesamte Jesajabuch.[105] Sie resümiert:

> Die Komplexität der mit Zion und Völkern verbundenen Thematik in Jes 66, wie sie sich in der Analyse als eine Summe jesajanischer Theologie erwiesen hat, macht Jes 66 zu einem einzigartigen Textstück schriftgelehrter Prophetie. Über Jes 60* und 30,27–33 hinausgehend werden jetzt nicht nur Völkergericht und Völkerzug in schriftgelehrter Manier für das Jesajabuch entfaltet, sondern beide Vorstellungen abschließend miteinander verbunden.[106]

6.6. Israel und die Völker in der LXX-Jesaja

Diese positive Sicht auf die Völker, wie sie nach Gärtner MT-Jesaja betrifft, lässt sich für die LXX-Jesaja so nicht nachweisen. Wo liegen hier im Blick

---

102. Gärtner 2006, 61, vgl. 59.
103. Gärtner 2006, 65.
104. Gärtner 2006, 65.
105. Gärtner 2006, 103–34.
106. Gärtner 2006, 129–30, vgl. nahezu wortgleich 315. Diese positive Beurteilung des Völkerthemas im Jesaja-Buch erkennt Gärtner im XII-Propheten-Buch hingegen nicht (2006, 209–13.219–20).

auf die Völker die wichtigen Akzentsetzungen? Ein gerraffter Durchgang durch das Jesajabuch wird Hinweise geben.[107]

Nach Jes 2,6 und 3,8 LXX hat Gott sein Volk, das Haus Israels/Jerusalem aus seiner Obhut „entlassen". Nach Jes 5,6 LXX wird der Weinberg, der Gottes Volk symbolisiert, „aufgelassen". Wird deshalb jetzt „mein Volk, das in Ägypten und das unter den Assyrern" gesegnet? In Jes 19,19.20.21 LXX wurde gesagt, es werde einen legitimen Altar in Ägypten geben, die Ägypter würden sich dem Herrn zuwenden, ihm Gelübde halten und dem Herrn Opfer darbringen. Sie werden damit nicht zum „Volk Gottes". „Mein Volk" bleibt für die (Diaspora der) Israeliten in Ägypten reserviert.

In Jes 3,10 LXX heißt es (diff. MT) lasst uns den Gerechten fesseln, denn er ist uns lästig. Dabei handelt es sich um einen Vorblick auf den Gottesknecht. Dieser ist ein Gerechter.[108] Versteht man ihn als Chiffre für den Kreis um Onias III, dann könnte das eine Bestätigung für die Interpretation von Jesaja 19 LXX als Diaspora darstellen.

Jes 6,10 LXX gehört ebenfalls in diesen Kontext. Die LXX macht aus dem sogenannten Verstockungsauftrag des hebräischen Textes eine Aussage über das Verstockt-Sein des Volkes: Sie können nicht hören, *denn* sie sind verhärtet.

Jes 10,5–34 LXX enthält Weherufe gegen Assur.[109] Auch hier taucht schon Ägypten auf: Ägypten–Israel–Assur. Assur hat sich als „Stock des Herrn" überheblich gezeigt und wird deshalb geschlagen, so V. 15–16. In 10,24 stellt der durch Assur ausgeführte Schlag in Wahrheit einen Schlag Gottes dar, der das Volk, das in Zion wohnt, auf den Weg nach Ägypten weist.[110]

Nach Jes 11,12 LXX richtet Gott ein Zeichen auf für die *Ethne*, um die Verstreuten Israels zu sammeln. Das klingt wie ein Vorblick auf Jes 56,3–8; 66,18–24.

Jes 11,15–16 LXX beinhaltet gravierende Unterschiede zum MT: „Und der Herr wird ⁺ das Meer Ägyptens *zur Einöde machen* und seine Hand an

---

107. Es kann auch hier nur um Hinweise gehen, nicht um eine vollständige Analyse der LXX-Jesaja.
108. Zum Verständnis des Gottesknechtes in der LXX-Jesaja siehe Kraus 2009, 155–67; und ders., Zur Rezeption von Jes 53 LXX, im Druck.
109. Zu diesem Text siehe Wilk 2010, bes. 193–95, der im Anschluss an Robert Hanhart den Bezug auf Antiochus Epiphanes betont (dort auch die Ablehnung der Position von Troxel).
110. Van der Kooij und Wilk 2011b, 2533.

den Fluss legen mit gewaltigem Wind ⁺ und wird ⁺ sieben Täler schlagen, sodass *es* auf Sandalen hindurchgeht; und es wird einen Durchgang geben für *mein* übrig gebliebenes Volk ⁺ *in Ägypten, und es wird* für Israel *sein wie* der Tag, als es aus dem Land Ägyptens auszog".[111] Die Art der Erwähnung des Windes erinnert an den Exodus aus Ägypten, Ex 14,21. Der in V. 15 genannte Fluss meint einen Fluss in Ägypten.[112] Bedeutsam ist insbesondere in V. 16 die Veränderung von „der übrig gebliebene Rest seines Volkes in Assur" zu „mein übrig gebliebenes Volk in Ägypten". Dieser Rest wird von Gott gerettet (vgl. V. 11: „seine Hand zeigen", „eifern"). Der Bezug auf die Diasporasituation ist eindeutig.[113]

Nach Jes 14,1–2 LXX kommt es zu einer Neuerwählung Israels. Der Fremde (γιωράς) wird sich Israel und dem Haus Jakob anschließen. Nach dem MT werden die Völker zu Knechten und Mägden Israels, Israel wird sie „besitzen". Nach der LXX werden auch die Völkerschaften im Land Gottes Besitz erhalten. Sie werden sich auf dem Land Gottes mehren.[114]

Jes 19,16–25 wurde oben ausführlich diskutiert. Die Diaspora-Perspektive ist eindeutig.

Jes 27,13 LXX: Die Verlorenen im Gebiet der Assyrer und die Verlorenen in Ägypten werden kommen und den Herrn anbeten auf dem Heiligen Berg in Jerusalem. Hier sind in der Tat die Exilierten gemeint.

Jes 29,22 bietet der MT: „der Abraham erlöst hat." „Anders als der MT bezieht die LXX den Relativsatz (…) auf das ‚Haus Jakob' als eine bestimmte Gruppe aus Abrahams Nachkommenschaft".[115]

Jes 42,1 LXX: Der Knecht (Jakob) bringt den Völkerschaften Recht. Der Knecht ist Licht der *Ethne*. Die Völkerschaften hoffen auf sein Gesetz (V. 4).

Jes 49,6 LXX: Der Knecht ist eingesetzt zum Licht für die *Ethne*, zur Rettung bis an die Enden der Erde. Aber es wird nicht näher spezifiziert,

---

111. Übersetzung nach LXX.D. *Kursive Auszeichnung* bedeutet eine Differenz zum MT, das ⁺ bedeutet, dass der MT hier erkennbar mehr Text bietet.

112. Van der Kooij und Wilk 2011b, 2536.

113. Van der Kooij und Wilk 2011b, 2536; vgl. van der Kooij 1997a, 388–96; Troxel 2008, 157–58; Baer, 2001, 199–200, mit Anm. 1.230 (Troxel und Baer mit Bezug auf Seeligmann 1948, 110–11.117).

114. Van der Kooij und Wilk 2011b, 2540.

115. Van der Kooij und Wilk 2011b, 2581–82; vgl. Harl, Dorival, und Munnich 1994, 217.

wie diese Rettung aussehen soll. In V. 8 heißt es, er sei eingesetzt zur *Diatheke* für die *Ethne*.

Jes 49,22 LXX: Die *Ethne* bringen die Söhne Israels im Gewandbausch mit. Gott gibt den *Ethne* dazu das Signal. Sie werden Pfleger und Ammen Israels.

Jes 51,4 LXX: Das Gesetz geht von Gott aus und sein Recht wird zum Licht der *Ethne*. Die Inseln hoffen auf ihn.

Jes 55,4 LXX: Einer aus dem Haus Davids wird zum Zeugnis unter den Völkerschaften. Er herrscht über sie und befehligt sie.

Jes 60 LXX: Nach V. 3.5 kommen die *Ethne* nach Jerusalem, um den Glanz zu sehen. Der Reichtum der Völkerschaften und der Völker (ἐθνῶν καὶ λαῶν) kommt in die Stadt. Nach V. 8f. haben die Inseln auf den Herrn geharrt. Die Tarsisschiffe bringen die Söhne und Töchter Israels, weil der Herr hoch im Ansehen steht. Nach V. 10 helfen Fremdstämmige beim Aufbau der Mauern. In V. 12 heißt es, dass Völkerschaften, die nicht dienen wollen, zugrunde gehen werden. Nach V. 16 wird Israel die Milch der *Ethne* saugen.

Jes 61,5–6 LXX: Fremdstämmige weiden Israels Vieh. Israel wird die Kraft der *Ethne* verzehren.

Jes 63,1–6 LXX: Die *Ethne* werden in der Kelter von Gott, dem Keltertreter, zertreten.

Jes 65,1 LXX: Gott wurde denen offenbar, die ihn nicht suchten, ließ sich finden von denen, die nicht nach ihm fragten, sprach zu den *Ethne*, die seinen Namen nicht angerufen hatten: Siehe ich bin es. Der Vers wird in Röm 10,20 als Begründung für das Hinzukommen der Völker zur Endzeitgemeinde zitiert.

Jes 66,18 LXX: Von Gott heißt es: Ich komme, um alle *Ethne* und alle Sprachen zusammenzuführen und sie werden kommen und meine Herrlichkeit schauen.

Lässt sich aus den genannten Texten eine Gesamtperspektive für das Thema „Israel und die Völker in der LXX-Jesaja" entwickeln? Nach meinem gegenwärtigen Eindruck ist das nicht der Fall. Dennoch bedeutet eine Fehlanzeige auch eine Antwort. Es gibt in der LXX-Jesaja Texte, die von Unterwerfung der Völker und Dienstbarkeit an Israel reden, aber auch von Integration einzelner in das Gottesvolk und von endzeitlicher Gleichstellung der *Ethne* mit demselben. Eine konsistente Lösung der Frage bedeutet das nicht.

Eindeutiger scheint jedoch die Diaspora-Perspektive in LXX-Jesaja durchzuschlagen. Geht man mit Arie van der Kooij u.a. davon aus, dass die LXX-Jesaja in Alexandrien um 140 v.Chr. entstanden ist, so könnte darin das Selbstverständnis der Onias-Gruppe zum Ausdruck kommen. Sie dienen jetzt an einem legitimen Altar in Ägypten, hoffen aber darauf, dass es schlussendlich wieder nach Jerusalem gehen wird (66,23). Wenn es sich in der LXX-Jesaja um eine aktualisierende Interpretation des Textes hin auf die Situation der Onias-Gruppe in Ägypten handelt, dann ist das „nationalistische" Verständnis, das David Baer in der LXX-Jesaja zu finden meint, nicht überzeugend. Es handelt sich dann nicht um eine nationalistische Verengung, sondern um eine Zuspitzung auf eine konkrete Situation. Im Vergleich zu MT-Jesaja werden dabei „Engführungen" sichtbar, die aber mit dem Stichwort „Nationalismus" nicht angemessen bezeichnet werden.

7. Die Verheissung an Abraham

7.1. Gen 12,3 und Parallelen (18,18; 22,18; 26,4; 28,14)

Die Verheißung an Abraham nimmt eine besondere Stellung ein, denn sie begegnet in Variationen mehrfach im AT (und später auch in den Apokryphen) und hat schon innerhalb des AT eine Wirkungsgeschichte (vgl. Jes 19,24; Sach 8,13; Jer 4,2; Ps 72,17).[116]

Die traditionelle Auslegung deutete die Verse im Sinn einer universalistischen Segenszusage, die die Segens*mittlerschaft* Abrahams/Israels für alle Völker beinhaltet.[117] Doch handelt es sich in V. 3b, „in dir sollen sich Segen wünschen alle Sippen[118] des Erdbodens", wirklich um eine alle Völker einschließende Aussage?

Der Sinn wird deutlicher, wenn V. 3 im Zusammenhang mit V. 2b gelesen wird: „du sollst ein Segen sein" bzw. „sei ein Segen".[119] Die Diskussion drehte sich lange um die Übersetzung von ונברכו. Doch die Entscheidung, das verwendete Nif'al in V. 3b reflexiv oder passiv (bzw. rezeptiv)

---

[116]. Dazu Schreiner 1962, 12–31; nach Schmitt 1980, 170, ist die Vorstellung, dass ein Mensch zum „Segen" werde, aus der Königsideologie herzuleiten, wie sie sich in dem vorexilischen Text Ps 21,7 niedergeschlagen hat.

[117]. Vgl. v.a. Wolff 1973.

[118]. Zum Begriff משפחת siehe Zobel 1986, bes. 92–93.

[119]. Die LXX hat ברכה abgeändert in εὐλογητός, die Vulgata in *benedictus*, Targum und die syrische Übersetzung lesen מברך.

zu verstehen, bedeutet keinen prinzipiellen Unterschied.[120] Die reflexive Übersetzung ist die philologisch wahrscheinlichere, doch sagt sie – wie Claus Westermann feststellt –

> in Wirklichkeit nicht weniger als die passive oder rezeptive. Wenn „die Geschlechter der Erde" sich „in Abraham segnen", d.h. sich unter Nennung seines Namens Segen wünschen […], so ist dabei natürlich vorausgesetzt, daß sie dann auch Segen empfangen. Wo man sich mit dem Namen Abrahams segnet, da wird tatsächlich Segen verliehen und Segen empfangen.[121]

Die Übersetzung ändert somit am Sinn so gut wie nichts. Jedoch ist zu fragen, worin die eigentliche Spitze der Segenszusage des Erzählers zu suchen ist. Ist es wirklich der Segen für die Völker, also die Segens*mittlerschaft* Abrahams/Israels?

Sieht man die Segenszusage an Abraham im engen Zusammenhang der Verheißung, ihn zu einem großen Volk zu machen, dann wird klar, wie V. 3b gemeint ist: „Die Völker werden zueinander sagen: Sei gesegnet wie Abraham"[122] (vgl. Gen 48,20; Jer 29,22). D.h. Gott möge es dir (hinsichtlich deiner Nachkommen und auch sonst) ergehen lassen, wie er es dem Abraham ergehen ließ.[123] Von einer Segens*mittlerschaft* ist dabei nichts zu spüren.[124]

Es geht um die hervorgehobene Stellung, die JHWH Abraham/Israel verleihen wird. Und genau dies sagt auch V. 3b: „und so können in dir (= unter Berufung auf dich) alle Sippen der Erde für sich Segen erwerben".[125] Abraham wird zu einer ברכה, einer „Verkörperung des Segens",[126] und dadurch bekommt er Bedeutung für die Menschheit.

---

120. Vgl. dazu im einzelnen Westermann 1981, 175–76; Schmitt 1980, 103 Anm. 45; Köckert 1988, 298 Anm. 657.

121. Westermann 1981, 176.

122. So nach Neue Jerusalemer Bibel, Anm. zu Gen 12,3.

123. So auch Ehrlich 1908, 47: „Die Völker der Erde, einander segnend, sollen Abraham in ihren Segnungen als Muster eines gesegneten und glücklichen Mannes nennen".

124. Vgl. Schmidt 1975, *passim*; Schmitt 1980, 108–12; Köckert 1988, 267 Anm. 506.

125. Zur Übersetzung siehe Schmidt 1975, 138; Scharbert 1973, 829; Westermann 1981, 176.

126. Schmidt 1975, 139. Abraham soll ein „Gestalt gewordener Segen sein"; Schreiner 1962, 5.

Nun hat Gen 12,3 mehrere Parallelen in der Genesis und darüber hinaus. Adressaten sind Abraham, Isaak und Jakob. Teilweise wird von den *Mischpachot ha-Adamah*, teilweise von den *Goje ha-Aretz* gesprochen. In Gen 22,18 und 26,4 wird formuliert: sie sollen „in deinem Samen" Segen gewinnen. Bei den angeführten Parallelen fällt auf, dass ברך Nif'al neben Gen 12,3 noch in 18,18 (Abraham) und 28,14 (Jakob) gebraucht wird. Gen 22,18 (Abraham); 26,4 (Isaak) gebrauchen die Hitpa'el-Form. Die Hitpa'el-Form begegnet also dann, wenn das Segen-Gewinnen auf den Samen Abrahams bezogen ist. Am nächsten kommt Gen 12,3 die Formulierung in 28,14.

Gen 18,18 (an Abraham) bietet die Segensaussage im Nif'al. Auch hier ist von einer Segens*mittlerschaft* Abrahams an die Völker nichts zu spüren.

Gen 22,18 (an Abraham): „Segnen" steht hier in der Hitpael-Form. Es heißt „mit/in deinem Samen (sollen sich segnen)".

Gen 26,4 (an Isaak): Die Erfüllung der Mehrungsverheißung führt dazu, dass die Völker sich im Namen Abrahams Segen wünschen.

Gen 28,14 (an Jakob): Unter Berufung auf den Samen Jakobs sollen sich die Geschlechter der Erde Segen wünschen.

Es ist somit festzuhalten: Gen 12,3 und seine Parallelen haben nicht in erster Linie eine Segensverheißung an die Völker im Blick und verstehen Abraham/Israel in keinem Fall als Segens*mittler*.

Blicken wir auf die LXX:

Das auffälligste Kennzeichen nenne ich gleich zu Beginn. Die LXX übersetzt an allen Stellen, ganz gleich ob im Hebräischen Nif'al oder Hitpa'el verwendet wird, passiv mit ἐνευλογέομαι ἐν: „durch dich/ihn/seine Nachkommen sollen gesegnet werden alle Völker/Stämme der Erde". Das ἐν hat dabei instrumentalen Sinn, und die Aussage wird verstärkt durch das Kompositum ἐνευλογέω. Das Verbum ἐνευλογέομαι im Passiv stellt einen Neologismus dar und ist außerhalb der LXX und von ihr unabhängiger Literatur nicht belegt.[127] Auch die Pseudepigraphen bieten keine Belege. Im AT begegnet es an den genannten Genesis-Stellen (Gen 12,3; 18,18; 22,18; 26,4; 28,14), sodann in Ps 10 (9),3 (24); 72 (71),17 (als v. l. in Cod. Sinaiticus) und in Sir 44,21. 1.Sam 2,29 ist die Verwendung unsicher.[128]

---

127. So die Auskunft des Thesaurus Linguae Graecae der University of California.
128. Vgl. MT; LSJ vermuten hier medialen Gebrauch.

Die sechs Belege bei Philon (*Migr.* 1.118.122; *Her.* 8; *Somn.* 1,3.176) sind LXX-Zitate aus der Genesis (Gen 12,3; 26,4; 28,14). Das bedeutet, dass alle passivischen Belege bis auf Ps 10 (9),3 (24) zu Gen 12,3 in Beziehung stehen.

Hier ist nun in der Tat von einer universalistischen Segens*mittlerschaft* Abrahams/Israels in der Formulierung von Gen 12,3 parr zu sprechen. *Mischpachot* in Gen 12,3 und 28,14 wird mit φυλαί, *gojim* jeweils mit ἔθνη übersetzt. Durch Abraham soll der Segen Gottes an alle Völker und Sippen weitergegeben werden. Hier liegt dann auch der Punkt, an den Paulus in Galater 3 anknüpfen wird.

7.2. Zusammenschau der Genesis-Texte

Zu Gen 12,3 und seinen Parallelen ist somit festzuhalten, dass die Segenszusage eine Bedeutung Abrahams als Segens*mittler* für „alle Sippen des Erdbodens" zunächst nicht im Blick hat, sondern es darin um die Bewahrheitung der Verheißung an Abraham geht. Um eine Gleichstellung der Völker mit Israel geht es dabei nirgends, vielmehr hat der Erzähler von Genesis 12 die Bedeutung des Segens Abrahams unterstreichen wollen.

Die LXX hat jedoch aus Abraham einen Segens*mittler* für alle Völker/ Sippen gemacht und ist damit für den universalen Charakter der Aussage, woran Gal 3,8 und Apg 3,25 anknüpfen, verantwortlich.

Fragt man, wie der/die Übersetzer der LXX-Genesis dazu kommt/ kommen, Abraham, Isaak und Jakob als Segens*mittler* für alle Völker/ Stämme der Erde zu interpretieren, so könnte ein Blick auf die Umstände helfen, in der die LXX-Genesis entstanden ist. Nach Überzeugung der Mehrzahl der Forscher ist sie im 3. Jh. v.Chr. in Alexandrien entstanden. Und zwar in einer Zeit, in der Juden in Ägypten in einem gesellschaftlichen Milieu lebten, das geeignet war, positive Beziehungen zum Diaspoara-Umfeld zu fördern. Dass es in einer solchen Situation nötig wurde, sein Selbstverständnis zum Ausdruck zu bringen und zugleich positive Signale an die Umwelt auszusenden, liegt auf der Hand.[129] Darin zeigt sich jedoch keine generelle Tendenz *der* LXX, wie dies in anderen Bereichen der LXX deutlich wird (s.o. zu Ps 47 [46],10). Um dieser Fragestellung gerecht zu werden, müssen alle Teilbereiche der LXX je für sich untersucht werden.[130]

---

129. Zur Situation der Entstehung und Publikation der ursprünglichen Septuaginta siehe Kreuzer 2004 2016.

130. Dieses Thema wird in einem weiteren Band des LXX.H zur Sprache kommen.

8. Perspektiven für eine „Theologie der Septuaginta"

In der vorliegenden Darstellung war es nur möglich, einen kleinen Teilbereich abzuschreiten. In einer „Theologie der Septuaginta" müssten weitere Bereiche zur Sprache kommen:
- Texte, die von der Vernichtung der Völker sprechen.
- Texte, in denen es um die Völkerwallfahrt zum Zion in ihren vielen Schattierungen geht: Aspekte der Unterwerfung, der Gottesverehrung sowie der Eingliederung.
- Texte, in denen es um Verehrer des Kyrios aus den Völkern geht, ohne dass diese ins Gottesvolk eingegliedert werden (Jona, Zefanja, Maleachi).
- Texte, in denen die Frage der Übernahme der Tora durch die Völker zur Sprache kommt: Jesaja 2; 11; Micha 4 sowie die Rezeption dieser Vorstellung z.B. in *Sib. Or.* 3 und bei Philon.[131]

Was kann die vorliegende Fragestellung theologisch leisten?
- Sie kann Strömungen im TaNaKh und im Antiken Judentum erkennen lassen – an die dann z.B. die Autoren des NT anknüpfen konnten.
- Sie kann Einsicht bringen in das Selbstverständnis von Übersetzern/Übersetzerkreisen, die ihre eigene Lage in die Übersetzung der Texte eingeschrieben haben.

Literatur

Alon, Gedaliah. 1984. *The Jews and Their Land in the Talmudic Age (70–640 C.E.)*. Bd. 2. Jerusalem: Magnes.

Baer, David A. 2001. *When We All Go Home: Translation and Theology in LXX Isaiah 56–66*. JSOTSup 318. Sheffield: Sheffield Academic.

Bertram, Georg. 1957. „Praeparatio Evangelica in der Septuaginta." *VT* 7:225–49.

Beuken, Willem A. M. 1989. *Jesaja deel IIIA*. POT. Nijkerk: Callenbach.

———. 2018. *Haggai – Sacharja 1–8. Studien zur Überlieferungsgeschichte der frühnachexilischen Prophetie*. SSN 10. Leiden: Brill.

Bultmann, Christoph. 1992. *Der Fremde im antiken Juda. Eine Untersuchung zum sozialen Typenbegriff ,ger' und seinem Bedeutungswandel*

---

[131]. Siehe dazu Kraus 2004, 84–90.

in der alttestamentlichen Gesetzgebung. FRLANT 153. Göttingen: Vandenhoeck & Ruprecht.

Burchard, Christoph. 1983. *Joseph und Aseneth*. JSHRZ 2.4. Gütersloh: Gütersloher Verlagshaus.

Cathcart, Kevin J., und Robert P. Gordon 1989. *The Targum of the Minor Prophets*. ArBib 14. Wilmington, DE: Glazier.

Chilton, Bruce D. 1987. *The Isaiah Targum*. ArBib 11. Wilmington, DE: Glazier.

Clements, Ronald E. 1980. *Isaiah 1–39*. NCB 12.1. Grand Rapids: Eerdmans.

Cook, Johann. 2004. „Septuaginta-Forschung." *RGG*⁴ 7:1217–20.

Daniel, Suzanne. 1966. *Recherches sur le vocabulaire du culte dans la Septante*. Études et commentaires 61. Paris: Klincksieck.

Donner, Herbert. 1985. „Jesaja LVI.1–7: Ein Abrogationsfall innerhalb des Kanons – Implikationen und Konsequenzen." Seiten 81–95 in *Congress Volume: Salamanca, 1983*. Hrsg. von James A. Emerton. VTSup 36. Leiden: Brill.

Eberhart, Christian. 2014. „Beobachtungen zu Opfer, Kult und Sühne in der Septuaginta." Seiten 297–314 in *Die Septuaginta – Text, Wirkung, Rezeption*. Hrsg. von Wolfgang Kraus und Siegfried Kreuzer. WUNT 325. Tübingen: Mohr Siebeck.

Ehrlich, Arnold B. 1908. *Randglossen zur hebräischen Bibel*. Leipzig: Hinrichs.

Fohrer, Georg. 1964. *Das Buch Jesaja III*. Zürich: TVZ.

Gamberoni, Johann. 1984. „מצבה." *TWAT* 4:1064–74.

Gärtner, Judith. 2006. *Jesaja 66 und Sacharja 14 als Summe der Prophetie. Eine traditions- und redaktionskritische Untersuchung zum Abschluss des Jesaja- und des Zwölfprophetenbuches*. WMANT 114. Neukirchen-Vluyn: Neukirchener Verlag.

———. 2013. „Das eine Gottesvolk aus Israel und den Völkern in Jes 66 – Zur Bedeutung der Völkerwelt in der späten jesajanischen Tradition." Seiten 1–29 in *Der eine Gott und die Völker in eschatologischer Perspektive. Studien zur Inklusion und Exklusion im biblischen Monotheismus*. Hrsg. von. Luke Neubert und Michael Tilly. BThS 137. Neukirchen-Vluyn: Neukirchener Verlag.

———. 2018. „Die Völker und der Tag-JHWHs im Horizont des Jesaja- und des Zwölfprophetenbuches." Seiten 131–56 in *The Books of the Twelve Prophets: Minor Prophets—Major Theologies*. Hrsg. von Heinz-Josef Fabry. BETL 295. Leuven: Peeters.

Groß, Walter. 1989a. „Wer soll YHWH verehren? Der Streit um die Aufgabe und die Identität Israels in der Spannung zwischen Abgrenzung und Öffnung." Seiten 11–32 in *Kirche in der Zeit*. FS Walter Kasper. Hrsg. von Hermann J. Vogt. München: Wewel.

———. 1989b. „YHWH und die Religionen der Nicht-Israeliten." *ThQ* 169:34–44.

———. 1993. „Israel und die Völker. Die Krise des YHWH-Volk-Konzepts im Jesajabuch." Seiten 149–67 in *Der Neue Bund im Alten*. Hrsg. von Erich Zenger. QD 146. Freiburg: Herder.

Haarmann, Volker. 2008. *JHWH-Verehrer der Völker. Die Hinwendung von Nichtisraeliten zum Gott Israels in alttestamentlichen Überlieferungen*. AThANT 91. Zürich: TVZ.

Hanhart, Robert. 1998. *Dodekapropheton 7.1. Sacharja 1–8*. BKAT 14.7.1. Neukirchen-Vluyn: Neukirchener Verlag.

Hanson, Paul D. 1975. *The Dawn of Apocalyptic*. Philadelphia: Fortress.

Harl, Marguerite, Gilles Dorival, und Olivier Munnich. 1994. *La Bible grecque des Septante. Du Judaïsme hellénistique au Christianisme ancien*. 2. Aufl. Paris: Cerf.

Hurvitz, Marshall S. 1957. „The Septuagint of Isaiah 36–39 in Relation to That of 1–35.40–66." *HUCA* 28:75–83.

Jeremias, Jörg. 1987. *Das Königtum Gottes in den Psalmen*. FRLANT 141. Göttingen: Vandenhoeck & Ruprecht.

Kaiser, Otto. 1983. *Der Prophet Jesaja Kapitel 13–39*. 3. Aufl. ATD 18. Göttingen: Vandenhoeck & Ruprecht.

Kellermann, Ulrich. 1991. „Tritojesaja und das Geheimnis des Gottesknechts. Erwägungen zu Jes 59,21; 61,1–3; 66,18–24." *BZ* 58:46–82.

Klausner, Josef. 1980. *Von Jesus zu Paulus*. Königstein: Jüdischer Verlag.

Köckert, Matthias. 1988. *Vätergott und Väterverheißung*. FRLANT 142. Göttingen: Vandenhoeck & Ruprecht.

Koenen, Klaus. 1990. *Ethik und Eschatologie im Tritojesajabuch*. WMANT 62. Neukirchen-Vluyn: Neukirchner Verlag.

———. 2011. „Erläuterungen zu Jes 56–66." Seiten 2673–90 in Bd. 2. von *Septuaginta Deutsch. Erläuterungen und Kommentare*. Hrsg. von Martin Karrer und Wolfgang Kraus. Stuttgart: Deutsche Bibelgesellschaft.

Konkel, Michael. 2011. „Erläuterungen zu Ez 40–48." Seiten 2968–92 in Bd. 2. von *Septuaginta Deutsch. Erläuterungen und Kommentare*. Hrsg. von Martin Karrer und Wolfgang Kraus. Stuttgart: Deutsche Bibelgesellschaft.

Kooij, Arie van der. 1981. *Die alten Textzeugen des Jesajabuches.* OBO 35. Fribourg: Universitätsverlag.

———. 1987. „The Old Greek of Isaiah 19:16–25: Translation and Interpretation." Seiten 127–66 in *VI Congress of the International Organization for Septuagint and Cognate Studies: Jerusalem, 1986.* Hrsg. von Claude E. Cox. SCS 23. Atlanta: Scholars Press.

———. 1997a. „'The Servant of the Lord': A Particular Group of Jews in Egypt according to the Old Greek of Isaiah. Some Comments on LXX Isa 49,1–6 and Related Passages." Seiten 383–97 in *Studies in the Book of Isaiah.* FS Willem A. M. Beuken. Hrsg. von Jaques van Ruiten und Marc Vervenne. BETL 122. Leuven: Peeters.

———. 1997b. „Zur Theologie des Jesajabuches in der Septuaginta." Seiten 9–25 in *Theologische Probleme der Septuaginta und der hellenistischen Hermeneutik.* Hrsg. von Henning Graf Reventlow. VWGTh 11. Gütersloh: Gütersloher Verlagshaus.

———. 2008. „The Septuagint of Isaiah and the Mode of Reading Prophecies in Early Judaism." Seiten 596–611 in *Die Septuaginta – Texte, Kontexte, Lebenswelten.* Hrsg. von Martin Karrer, Wolfgang Kraus, und Martin Meiser. WUNT 219. Tübingen: Mohr Siebeck.

Kooij, Arie van der, und Florian Wilk. 2011a. „Einleitung." Seiten 2484–504 in Bd. 2. von *Septuaginta Deutsch. Erläuterungen und Kommentare.* Hrsg. von Martin Karrer und Wolfgang Kraus. Stuttgart: Deutsche Bibelgesellschaft.

———. „Erläuterungen zu Jes 1–39." Seiten 2505–607 in Bd. 2. von *Septuaginta Deutsch. Erläuterungen und Kommentare.* Hrsg. von Martin Karrer und Wolfgang Kraus. Stuttgart: Deutsche Bibelgesellschaft.

Kraus, Hans-Joachim. 1972. *Psalmen 1–63.* 4. Aufl. BKAT 15.1. Neukirchen-Vluyn: Neukirchener Verlag.

———. 1990. *Das Evangelium des unbekannten Propheten. Jes 40–66.* Neukirchen-Vluyn: Neukirchener Verlag.

Kraus, Wolfgang. 2004. *Das Volk Gottes. Zur Grundlegung der Ekklesiologie bei Paulus.* 2. Aufl. WUNT 85. Tübingen: Mohr Siebeck.

———. 2007. „Die Septuaginta als Brückenschlag zwischen Altem und Neuem Testament? Dtn 32 als Fallbeispiel." Seiten 266–90 in *Im Brennpunkt: Die Septuaginta. Studien zur Theologie, Anthropologie, Ekklesiologie, Eschatologie und Liturgie der Griechischen Bibel.* Hrsg. von Heinz-Josef Fabry und Dieter Böhler. BWANT 174. Stuttgart: Kohlhammer.

———. 2009. „Jes 53 im frühen Christentum – eine Überprüfung." Seiten 148–79 in *Beiträge zur urchristlichen Theologiegeschichte*. Hrsg. von Wolfgang Kraus. BZNW 163. Berlin: de Gruyter.

———. Im Druck. „Zur Rezeption von Jes 53 LXX." In *Die Septuaginta – Themen, Manuskripte, Wirkungen*. Hrsg. von Eberhard Bons et al. WUNT. Tübingen: Mohr Siebeck.

Kreuzer, Siegfried. 2004. „Entstehung und Publikation der Septuaginta im Horizont frühptolemäischer Bildungs- und Kulturpolitik." Seiten 61–75 in *Im Brennpunkt: Die Septuaginta. Studien zur Entstehung und Bedeutung der griechischen Bibel*. Hrsg. von Siegfried Kreuzer und Jürgen Peter Lesch. BWANT 161. Stuttgart: Kohlhammer.

———. 2016. „Entstehung und Überlieferung der Septuaginta." Seiten 30–88 in *Einleitung in die Septuaginta*. Hrsg. von Siegfried Kreuzer. LXX.H 1. Gütersloh: Gütersloher Verlagshaus.

Kutsch, Ernst. 2004. „בְּרִית‎ b^{e}rīt Verpflichtung." *THAT* 1:339–52.

Levenson, Jon D. 1996. „The Universal Horizon of Biblical Particularism." Seiten 143–69 in *Ethnicity and the Bible*. Hrsg. von Mark G. Brett. BibInt 19. Leiden: Brill.

Lohfink, Norbert. 1994. „Bund und Tora bei der Völkerwallfahrt." Seiten 37–83 in *Der Gott Israels und die Völker. Untersuchungen zum Jesajabuch und zu den Psalmen*. Hrsg. von Norbert Lohfink und Erich Zenger. SBS 154. Stuttgart: Katholisches Bibelwerk.

Monsengwo-Pasinya, Laurent. 1985. „Isaïe XIX 16–25 et universalisme dans la LXX." Seiten 192–207 in *Congress Volume: Salamanca, 1983*. Hrsg. von James A. Emerton. VTSup 36. Leiden: Brill.

Novak, David. 1983. *The Image of the Non-Jew in Judaism: An Historical and Constructive Study of the Noachide Laws*. Toronto: Mellen.

Orlinsky, Harry M. 1970. „Nationalism-Universalism and Internationalism in Ancient Israel." Seiten 206–36 in *Translating and Understanding the Old Testament*. FS Herbert G. May. Hrsg. von Harry T. Frank und William L. Reed. Nashville: Abingdon.

Porton, Gary G. 1988. *Goyim: Gentiles and Israelites in Mishnah-Tosefta*. BJS 155. Atlanta: Scholars Press.

———. 1994. *The Stranger within Your Gates: Converts and Conversion in Rabbinic Literature*. Chicago: University of Chicago Press.

Preuß, Horst Dietrich. 1992. *Theologie des Alten Testaments II*. Stuttgart: Kohlhammer.

Rendtorff, Rolf. 2001. *Theologie des Alten Testaments. Ein kanonischer Entwurf*. Bd. 2. Neukirchen-Vluyn: Neukirchener Verlag.

Rudolph, Wilhelm. 1976. *Haggai – Sacharja 1–8 – Sacharja 9–14 – Maleachi*. KAT 13.4. Gütersloh: Gütersloher Verlagshaus.
Scharbert, Josef. 1973. „ברך." *TWAT* 1:808–41.
Schmidt, Ludwig. 1975. „Israel ein Segen für die Völker?" *ThViat* 12:135–51.
Schmitt, Hans-Christoph. 1980. *Die nichtpriesterliche Josephsgeschichte*. BZAW 154. Berlin: de Gruyter.
Schreiner, Josef. 1962. „Segen für die Völker in der Verheißung an die Väter." *BZ* 6:1–31.
———. 1968. „Berufung und Erwählung Israels zum Heil der Völker." *BibLeb* 9:94–114.
Seeligmann, Isac L. 1948. *The Septuagint Version of Isaiah: A Discussion of Its Problems*. MVEOL 9. Leiden: Brill (= ders., *The Septuagint Version of Isaiah and Cognate Studies*. Hrsg. von Robert Hanhart und Hermann Spieckermann. FAT 40. Tübingen: Mohr Siebeck 2004, 119–294).
Sehmsdorf, Eberhard. 1972. „Studien zur Redaktionsgeschichte von Jesaja 56–66 I.II." *ZAW* 84:517–76.
Steck, Odil Hannes. 1985. *Bereitete Heimkehr*. SBS 121. Stuttgart: Katholisches Bibelwerk.
———. 1991a. *Der Abschluß der Prophetie im Alten Testament*. BThS 17. Neukirchen-Vlyun: Neukirchener Verlag.
———. 1991b. *Studien zu Tritojesaja*. BZAW 203. Berlin: de Gruyter.
Tilly, Michael. 2010. „Das Heil der Anderen im hellenistischen Diasporajudentum. Anmerkungen zur griechischen Übersetzung von Jesaja 66,14b–24." Seiten 209–21 in *Das Heil der Anderen. Problemfeld: ,Judenmission'*. Hrsg. von Hubert Frankemölle und Josef Wohlmut. QD 238. Freiburg: Herder.
Troxel, Ronald L. 2008. *LXX-Isaiah as Translation and Interpretation*. JSJSup 124. Leiden: Brill.
Van Winkle, Dwight W. 1997. „An Inclusive Authoritative Text in Exclusive Communities." Seiten 423–40 in Bd. 1. von *Writing and Reading the Scroll of Isaiah: Studies of an Interpretative Tradition*. Hrsg. von Craig A. Evans und Peter W. Flint. VTSup 70.1. Leiden: Brill.
Vermeylen, Jaques. 1978. *Du prophète Isaïe à l'Apocalyptique II*. Paris: Cerf.
Vos, Cornelius de. 2011. „Das Land Israel in der Sicht der Septuaginta: Beispiele aus Exodus, Josua und Jesaja." Seiten 87–105 in *Die Septuaginta und das frühe Christentum / The Septuagint and Early Christianity*. Hrsg. von Hermann Lichtenberger und Thomas Scott Caulley. WUNT 277. Tübingen: Mohr Siebeck.

Welten, Peter. 1986. „Zur Frage nach dem Fremden im Alten Testament." Seiten 130–38 in *Wie gut sind deine Zelte, Jaakov... FS Rudolf Mayer*. Hrsg. von Ernst Ludwig Ehrlich und Bertolt Klappert. Gerlingen: Bleicher Verlag.

Westermann, Claus. 1976. *Das Buch Jesaja Kapitel 40–66*. 3. Auflage. ATD 19. Göttingen: Vandenhoeck & Ruprecht.

———. 1981. *Genesis 12–36*. BKAT 1.2. Neukirchen-Vluyn: Neukirchener Verlag.

———. 1987. *Prophetische Heilsworte*. FRLANT 145. Göttingen: Vandenhoeck & Ruprecht.

Wildberger, Hans. 1977. „Das Freudenmahl auf dem Zion." *TZ* 33:373–83.

———. 1978. *Jesaja 13–27*. BKAT 10.2. Neukirchen-Vluyn: Neukirchener Verlag.

Wilk, Florian. 2010. „Between Scripture and History: Technique and Hermeneutics of Interpreting Biblical Prophets in the Septuagint of Isaiah and the Letters of Paul." Seiten 189–209 in *The Old Greek of Isaiah: Issues and Perspectives*. Hrsg. von Arie van der Kooij und Michael N. van der Meer. CBET 55. Leuven: Peeters.

Wolff, Hans Walter. 1973. „Das Kerygma des Jahwisten." Seiten 345–73 in *Gesammelte Studien zum Alten Testament*. Hrsg. von Hans Walter Wolff. 2. Aufl. ThB 22. München: Kaiser.

Zenger, Erich. 1989. „Der Gott Abrahams und die Völker. Beobachtungen zu Psalm 47." Seiten 413–30 in *Die Väter Israels*. FS Josef Schabert. Hrsg. von Manfred Görg. Stuttgart: Katholisches Bibelwerk.

———. 1991. „Israel und Kirche im einen Gottesbund? Auf der Suche nach einer für beide akzeptablen Verhältnisbestimmung." *Kirche und Israel* 6:99–114.

———. 1994. „Zion als Mutter der Völker." Seiten 117–50 in *Der Gott Israels und die Völker. Untersuchungen zum Jesajabuch und zu den Psalmen*. Hrsg. von Norbert Lohfink und Erich Zenger. SBS 154. Stuttgart: Katholisches Bibelwerk.

Ziegler, Joseph. 1934. *Untersuchungen zur Septuaginta des Buches Isaias*. ATA 12.3. Münster: Aschendorff.

Ziethe, Carolin. 2018. *Auf seinen Namen werden die Völker hoffen. Die matthäische Rezeption der Schriften Israels zur Begründung des universalen Heils*. BZNW 233. Berlin: de Gruyter.

Zobel, Hans-Jürgen. 1986. „משפחה." *TWAT* 5:86–93.

Septuagint Influence on the Formation of Early Christian Theology: ἐπαγγελία in the Book of Hebrews and Its Substantiation from the LXX Pentateuch

Gert J. Steyn

ABSTRACT: The theology of the Jewish Scriptures shaped the theology of the New Testament authors. The author of the book of Hebrews, for example, regularly connects ἐπαγγελία at strategic points in his theological exposition with passages from Scripture that he understood, by means of *retrodiction*, to be affirmations, predictions, and promises of God. Given the leitmotif of ἐπαγγελία in Hebrews and its deliberate connections with the Jewish Scriptures, this paper serves as an experiment for how available terminology from these Scriptures in their Septuagint versions contributed to the formation of early Christian theology in a particular New Testament book. Seven identified promise trajectories in Hebrews with their connections to the LXX Pentateuch are studied in order to establish their theological impact on this early Christian author.

1. Introduction

It might be stated that the New Testament developed at the nexus where two tradition trajectories intersected with each other: the Christ-event and the long-established hermeneutical tradition that interpreted the Jewish Scriptures within ever-changing contexts. Developing as a particular hermeneutical branch of the Jewish religion, early Christianity naturally faced the challenge from its earliest beginnings to prove from the same Jewish Scriptures that Jesus of Nazareth was the long-expected Jewish messiah. Furthermore, it needed to prove convincingly to its converts why particularly this messiah had to suffer and why he had to die. Even beyond this, they had to prove from their Scriptures that this messiah who died would be raised from death, depart to the heavens, and, even more, still return to earth. The interpretation of the Jewish Scriptures would be key for this new movement. Particularly the gospel writers report in their versions that this perspective on the interpretation of the Scriptures can be traced back to the sayings of Jesus himself, to his engagement with and explanation of these Scriptures.

The New Testament writers utilized the Scriptures in different ways. Most common and most clear are their *explicit quotations*, that is, those quotations that are introduced with clear introductory formulae. But beyond this obvious use of the Scriptures, there are also clear traces of *references* to the Scriptures and their contents. There are also numerous *allusions and echoes* to the Scriptures, often probably not used in a conscious manner but rather subconsciously. Aside from these modes of scriptural use, one can also trace particular *motifs* or broader *themes* across the New Testament documents and their writers. Some New Testament documents, such as Hebrews, Romans, Luke-Acts, and Matthew, quote extensively from the Jewish Scriptures, while others, such as Revelation, hardly contain a single explicit quotation but have a high density of allusions. Needless to say, the New Testament documents display a high frequency of scriptural material and engage strongly with the Jewish scriptural traditions. Such existing traditions are often referred to and most often newly reinterpreted by the New Testament writers from a christological perspective. Differently formulated: *scriptural traditions that were driven by messianic expectations were understood and applied by the New Testament writers in connection with Jesus as messiah*. Given this continuation of interpretation of the Jewish Scriptures in early Christianity, it is logical to assume that this interaction with the theology of these Jewish Scriptures would greatly impact on this new Jewish, that is, early Christian, movement. Differently formulated: *the theology of the Jewish Scriptures shaped the theology of the New Testament authors*. Important in this regard to note, is the fact, now well-proven and well-accepted, that it was almost exclusively the Greek versions of these Jewish Scriptures that were used by the New Testament writers, who wrote in Greek themselves, for their exegetical and hermeneutical engagement with these Scriptures. This phenomenon, where mainly the LXX was used, can be traced not only but particularly in Paul's letters, Luke-Acts, Hebrews, and 1 Peter.

This intertextual junction poses several methodological challenges. How does one approach this nexus between the Jewish Scriptures and the earliest Christian writings in order to determine the theological impact of the former on the latter? How can one clearly trace and prove that it was definitely the Greek versions of the Jewish Scriptures that contributed to a *praeparatio evangelica*? How does one responsibly differentiate between the different versions of "the" Septuagint? Furthermore, what would be the best modus operandi for such an experiment: to investigate the phenomenon from the perspective of the influence of a particular LXX book on the New Testament writers or, rather, to trace LXX theological influence receptionally back via a particular New Testament book? Either way, the researcher might continually be confronted by the danger of insufficient literary context to responsibly justify such identified theological positions by the ancient authors.

While being fully aware of at least some of these dangers and methodological pitfalls, this essay will trace and follow experimentally one such theological motif in one of the New Testament books. The New Testament writers read their Scriptures with a view to understand and substantiate the Christ-events. I have argued elsewhere that this was done by means of retrodiction.[1] One of the hermeneutical filters that they deployed in their quest for information about the events that happened was their theological assumption that the Scriptures somehow predicted those events. They were aware of the promises of a coming messiah, someone like Moses and the prophet Elijah, someone like King David. They studied the Scriptures in their quest to make sense of the person and life of Jesus of Nazareth as the long-awaited messiah. In this quest, they took special note of references in their Scriptures that they understood to be predictions and promises of God. They were actually quite familiar with these promises of God—to Abraham, for instance—so that these became a natural point of entry for their hermeneutical engagement with these Scriptures. They could easily associate the Christ-events with many of these promises, but they could also expand on them and add to them. This phenomenon becomes vividly clear from the number of occurrences where ἐπαγγελία occurs in the New Testament. In the much smaller (than LXX) New Testament corpus, ἐπαγγελία occurs much more frequently and surfaces fifty times,[2] which is a clear indication of its prominence here in comparison to the LXX. The noun ἐπαγγελία is rarely used in the much larger LXX corpus[3] and occurs

---

1. See Steyn 2015.

2. See, for instance, Acts 1:4; 2:33, 39; 7:17; 13:23, 32; 23:21; 26:6; Gal 3:14, 16, 17, 18, 21, 22, 29; 4:23, 28; Rom 4:13, 14, 16, 20; 9:4, 8, 9; 15:8; 2 Cor 1:20; 7:1; Eph 1:13; 2:12; 3:6; 6:2; 1 Tim 2:10; 4:8; 6:21; 2 Tim 2:1.

3. Schniedewind is even of the opinion that ἐπαγγελία is never used in the Old Testament in a theological sense (Schniedewind and Friedrich 1964, 579).

elsewhere in Amos 9:6; Ps 55:9; Ode 12:6; Pss. Sol. 12:6; 1 Esd 1:7; Esth 4:7; 1 Macc 10:15; and 4 Macc 12:9. The theological inclination of two of these cases is particularly aligned with that of the New Testament authors: Ode 12:6–7 and Pss. Sol. 12:6.

… <u>ἀμέτρητόν τε καὶ ἀνεξιχνίαστον τὸ ἔλεος τῆς ἐπαγγελίας σου,</u> ⁷ ὅτι σὺ εἶ κύριος ὕψιστος, εὔσπλαγχνος, μακρόθυμος καὶ πολυέλεος καὶ μετανοῶν ἐπὶ κακίαις ἀνθρώπων

… <u>both immeasurable and inscrutable is the mercy of your promise</u>, because you are Lord Most High, compassionate, slow to anger and abounding in mercy and repenting at ills of human beings. (Ode 12:6–7 NETS)

τοῦ κυρίου ἡ σωτηρία ἐπὶ Ισραηλ παῖδα αὐτοῦ εἰς τὸν αἰῶνα, καὶ ἀπόλοιντο οἱ ἁμαρτωλοὶ ἀπὸ προσώπου κυρίου ἅπαξ, <u>καὶ ὅσιοι κυρίου κληρονομήσαισαν ἐπαγγελίας κυρίου.</u>

The salvation of the Lord is upon Israel his servant forever, and may the sinners perish altogether from the presence of the Lord, <u>and may the devout of the Lord inherit the promises of the Lord</u>. (Pss. Sol. 12:6 NETS)

The verb ἐπαγγέλλω is even more rare and occurs only in Prov 13:12, Wis 2:13, Sir 20:23, and 3 Macc 1:4. Philo uses the noun ἐπαγγελία only once (*Mut.* 201) but the noun ἐπάγγελμα much more regularly (*Post.* 139; 146; *Flacc.* 54; *Plant.* 81; *Congr.* 133; 148; *Mut.* 128; *Leg.* 2.99; *Virt.* 64). The latter, plus the verb ἐπαγγέλλω (fifteen times), are usually deployed by Philo in the sense of "command."

The New Testament book where this term ἐπαγγελία occurs not only regularly but also at strategic points in the exposition of the author's theological expositio is (the so-called Letter to the) Hebrews, which contains more than a fifth of all the cases in the New Testament. In this sense, one might call Hebrews a "book of promises."[4] These references to God's promises are distributed throughout the book. The theme starts at the beginning of Hebrews and runs through until the end of the book. The author's opening lines about "God who spoke to the fathers and prophets in the past but in these last days through the Son" (Heb 1:1), as well as all the introductory formulae to the quotations in Hebrews, which almost exclusively utilize a verb of "saying," all point in the same direction of God's authoratative

---

4. See Steyn 2011, 212.

announcements. A striking phenomenon of the author's use of ἐπαγγελία is that he connects this leitmotif regularly with some passages from Scripture. The following table provides an overview of the distribution of the seven ἐπαγγελία texts in Hebrews and the LXX passages connected with them by the unknown author of Hebrews:

Hebrews	Reference	LXX Texts
theme: promise of rest		
3:7–4:13	ἐπαγγελίας εἰσελθεῖν εἰς τὴν κατάπαυσιν (4:1)	Ps 95:7–11; Gen 2:2
theme: inheritors of God's promise to Abraham		
4:14–7:28	κληρονομούντων τὰς ἐπαγγελίας (6:12) -A. οὕτως μακροθυμήσας ἐπέτυχεν τῆς ἐπαγγελίας (6:15) -ὁ θεὸς ἐπιδεῖξαι τοῖς κληρονόμοις τῆς ἐπαγγελίας (6:17) -A. τὸν ἔχοντα τὰς ἐπαγγελίας εὐλόγηκεν (7:6)	Ps 2:7; Ps 110 (109):4; Gen 22:17; Gen 14:17–20; Ps 110 (109):4
theme: better promise: covenant renewal		
8:1–10:18	J. κρείττοσιν ἐπαγγελίαις νενομοθέτηται (8:6)	Exod 25:40; Jer 31 (38):31–34
theme: promise of eternal inheritance		
8:1–10:18	τὴν ἐπαγγελίαν λάβωσιν οἱ κεκλημένοι τῆς αἰωνίου κληρονομίας (9:15)	Exod 24:8; Ps 40 (39):7–9
theme: endurance to receive the promise		
10:19–39	ἵνα τὸ θέλημα τοῦ θεοῦ ποιήσαντες κομίσησθε τὴν ἐπαγγελίαν (10:36)	Deut 32:35, 36; Hab 2:3, 4
theme: faith and God's promises		
11:1–12:11	Πίστει παρῴκησεν εἰς γῆν τῆς ἐπαγγελίας (11:9) -Κατὰ πίστιν ἀπέθανον οὗτοι πάντες, μὴ λαβόντες τὰς ἐπαγγελίας (11:13) -ὁ τὰς ἐπαγγελίας ἀναδεξάμενος, (11:17) -οὗτοι πάντες μαρτυρηθέντες διὰ τῆς πίστεως οὐκ ἐκομίσαντο τὴν ἐπαγγελίαν (11:39)	Gen 21:12; Prov 3:11
theme: apocalyptic promise		
12:12–29	νῦν δὲ ἐπήγγελται (12:26)	Deut 9:19 Hag 2:6, 21

Given then the leitmotif of ἐπαγγελία in the book of Hebrews and its deliberate connections with the Jewish Scriptures, this essay serves as an experiment for how available terminology from these Scriptures in their LXX versions contributed to the formation of early Christian theology in a particular New Testament book. The seven promise trajectories identified above, with their connections to the LXX Pentateuch as presented by the unknown author of Hebrews, will be surveyed in order to establish the theological impact of these LXX Pentateuch quotations on the theology of this early Christian author. This experiment is limited to the LXX Pentateuch, largely based on selected data and some slight reworking of the relevant passages taken from my 2011 study, *A Quest for the Assumed LXX Vorlage of the Explicit Quotations in Hebrews*, where more detailed information on the LXX text forms of all the quotations in Hebrews can be found.

2. Seven "Promise" Trajectories in Hebrews Based on LXX Pentateuch Theology

2.1. Hebrews' Promise of "Rest" (Heb 4:1) and LXX Gen 2:2 in the Light of LXX Ps 95 (94):7–11

The unknown author of Hebrews deals with the exodus theme in Heb 3:7–4:13. He starts with a long quotation from LXX Ps 95 (94):7–11, which refers to the rebellious reaction of the forefathers during their journey through the desert. Directly after presenting this quotation, the author proceeds to an exposition and contemporary application of the psalm for his readers, which highlights his actual purpose with the quotation. The readers ("brothers") are exhorted to ensure that an attitude of unbelief does not germinate in their midst and that they do not "turn away from the living God" (Heb 3:12). What is at stake is their faith in Christ (see 3:14), but the author of Hebrews argues that they would actually become unfaithful to the living God himself. This unfaithfulness to the living God strongly recalls the covenant that God entered into with his people when he led them out of Egypt. He would give them the promised land, and they had to worship, obey, and never forget him. The exodus motif is thus interwoven into the author's argument.

The author then starts the section of Heb 4:1–11 with the remark that the promise (ἐπαγγελίας, 4:1) about entering into God's κατάπαυσιν still stands (4:1). He picks this issue up from 3:6, where he stated that they are holding on to courage and hope. The term κατάπαυσιν becomes a new *Leitthema* that is to be found eleven times exclusively here between 3:11 and 4:11. The author now places himself alongside his readers when he refers to "we" (4:2, 3) and calling them οἱ πιστεύσαντες (4:3). He continues thus with his comparison of the two groups: "we/you" and "they" (κἀκεῖνοι, 4:2). That generation's exposure to the message and their reaction to it is compared with this generation: "we also have had the gospel preached to us, just as they did; but the message they heard [ὁ λόγος τῆς ἀκοῆς ἐκείνους] was of no value to them, because those who heard did not combine it with faith [μὴ συγκεκερασμένους τῇ πίστει τοῖς ἀκούσασιν]" (4:2). There is a connection between ἀκοῆς and ἀκούσασιν here in 4:2 and ἀκούσητε in the quoted psalm (Heb 3:7b). God's promise and the people's response to it by faith here go hand in hand. The difference with that generation was that they merely heard the message but did not combine it with faith. They are contrasted with the group to whom the author of Hebrews belongs: "Now, we who have believed enter that rest" (4:3). The bridge has been built for a new group who can claim the very same promise. The promise (ἐπαγγελία) thus remains the same, but the previous group did not succeed in entering God's rest. The current group has access to it because they believe, combining the hearing of the promise with faith. The element of faith thus becomes a prerequisite for entering into the rest, and the author of Hebrews contrasts warning and promise with each other. The author now requotes part of the initial quotation a second (4:3) and third time (4:5). Both these are taken from Ps 95 (94):11. Between these two recurrences of Ps 95 (94):11 stands the quotation from Gen 2:2. The author uses Scripture here to explain Scripture by means of employing the rabbinical *gezerah shawah* technique.[5] It is on the basis of the combined strength of the two Scripture passages (Ps 95[94]:11 and Gen 2:2) that the author draws the conclusion that those who believe shall enter God's rest.[6] This exegesis and its theological interpretation is deeply rooted in the LXX translation and the author of Hebrews' careful selection of Greek *Stichwörter* to substantiate his "promise theology."

The reference to Gen 2:2 is dealt with again later, in Heb 4:9. It is at this point, at the core of that ring compositional argument, in quoting Gen 2:2,

---

5. So also Attridge 1989, 128–29; Weiss 1996, 681; Koester 2001, 278; Karrer 2002, 216; Lincoln 2006, 71.

6. See Kistemaker 1961, 110. He states that Hebrews employs the word "rest" *sensu pleniore* by combining the two passages (1961, 113).

where the transition from κατάπαυσιν as the promised land (location, i.e., a spatial dimension) of that generation to κατάπαυσιν as a sabbatical period (state or condition, i.e., a temporal dimension) for this generation takes place.[7] By using Gen 2:2, the author reinterprets the key term κατάπαυσιν in Ps 95 (94) in terms of the Sabbath,[8] which is now different from the promised land of the exodus as a place and from the place in heaven (as described, e.g., in Joseph and Aseneth). Acknowledging some kind of a threefold rest, one could actually connect God's creation rest (a condition) with the quotation from Gen 2:2, Israel's Canaan rest (a place) with the quotation of Ps 95 (94):11 just prior to Gen 2:2, and the true rest of God's people (a condition) with the second quotation from Ps 95 (94):11.[9] The motif of rest is firmly rooted in the importance of the Sabbath as such and substantiated on the basis of God who rested on the seventh day after he had created everything.[10] This same motivation, that God rested on the seventh day, is to be found in the quotation from Gen 2:2,[11] presented by the author as the center of his commentary on Ps 95 (94):7–11. The quotation from Gen 2:2 has been embedded within the midrash on Ps 95 (94), and it is clear that there is a wordplay on the substantive κατάπαυσιν (Ps 95[94]:11) and the verb κατέπαυσεν (Gen 2:2), which in turn confirms that Greek versions were used for these quotations. One could say that the

---

7. Kistemaker (1961, 110) already pointed out that in Heb 4:4 the concept of rest is placed in the realm of spiritual things. So also Attridge 1989, 116, who states that in the author's suggestion in 4:4–5 "the term 'rest' has a different sense from that accorded in the psalm, where it refers primarily to the resting place of Canaan." Similarly Enns 1997, 359: "By citing Gen. 2.2, our author is arguing that the rest that is the reward to the faithful new exodus community is to be understood not as physical land, but as an eschatological rest; specifically the rest God has enjoyed since the completion of his creative work."

8. Karrer 2002, 216: "Die Ruhe, die Gott den Vätern ihrer Anmaßung wegen versagte, ist deshalb weit mehr als die Ruhe eines verheißenen irdischen Landes um den irdischen Ruheort Gottes (den Tempel in Jerusalem)."

9. Kistemaker identified a "threefold rest" of which Ps 95 speaks: "God's rest after creation, Israel's rest in Canaan, and the true rest for the people of God" (1961, 132).

10. Attridge reminds that "in some apocalyptic texts, and particularly in Philo, it is ultimately the primordial sabbath of God's own rest that is in view" (1989, 129).

11. See Steyn 2002. In addition, Bauernfeind highlights the role of Gen 2:2 in this regard, saying, "As the promise of Scripture undoubtedly points beyond the servant Moses to fulfilment by the Son (3:1–6), so the rest mentioned on the very first page (Gn. 2:2) points beyond Joshua (4:8) and David (4:7) to the last things" (1963, 628).

Sabbath becomes the symbol of eschatological salvation.[12] From the preceding exposition (Heb 3:16–18), κατάπαυσιν would seem to refer then to the promised land[13] during the times of the exodus generation, although it might have been used by the worshiper in Ps 95 (94) in terms of the temple as the resting place[14] (closer to the idea of Joseph and Aseneth?). The author is at least fully aware of the original context of the promised land, as his exposition shows here in Heb 3:16–18. However, as his exposition develops, the term is reinterpreted in terms of a sabbatical period that does not need to be detached necessarily from a temple context.[15]

The noun κατάπαυσιν is used in the LXX for the promised land (Deut 12:9), when the ark of the covenant came to rest (Num 10:35, 36; 1 Chr 6:31; 2 Chr 6:41), for the Sabbath (Exod 34:21; 35:2), or for the Jubilee (Lev 25:28). Another interesting passage that refers to κατάπαυσιν is 3 Kgdms 8:56: Εὐλογητὸς κύριος σήμερον, ὃς ἔδωκεν κατάπαυσιν τῷ λαῷ αὐτοῦ Ισραηλ κατὰ πάντα, ὅσα ἐλάλησεν.[16] Both the motifs of "rest" and of "today" are combined here with "his people Israel" (see Heb 4:9: τῷ λαῷ τοῦ θεοῦ) and with his promise. It is clear that God's people already received the κατάπαυσιν in 3 Kingdoms.[17] So why would the author of Hebrews state that they had not received it? In Heb 4:8 the author refers to the fact that, "if Joshua [Ἰησοῦς] had given them rest, God would not have spoken later about another day [οὐκ ἂν περὶ ἄλλης ... ἡμέρας]" (4:8). Is he now referring to another κατάπαυσιν, perhaps a sabbatical period, instead of the land itself? Does he imply then that this other Joshua (Jesus) would be able to lead them to this rest (a Sabbath period)? Scholars have offered several solutions to this issue. Attridge finds the "key to understanding how it is that the promise remains open to see that God's promised 'rest' is not the earthly land of Canaan but a heavenly reality, which God entered upon the completion of creation (vss 3b-5), ... and it remains open for those who currently hear the psalm to join in the festive sabbath rest that God

---

12. Attridge 1989, 129.
13. Karrer 2002, 205, writes: "Er 'geht ein' in die 'Ruhe' wie ein gelobtes Land."
14. See Braulik 1986, 43; also Karrer 2002, 210: "Sie werden anders als die jetzigen Beter des Psalms nicht zu seiner Ruhestätte, dem Tempel kommen."
15. Karrer 2002, 218: "Die Verheißung ist ... verblieben. Sie bestimmt für das Volk Gottes die Ruhe des siebten Schöpfungstages, die Sabbatruhe und Sabbatfeier Gottes."
16. An "association of the temple with the divinely provided κατάπαυσιν" (Attridge 1989, 126) is probably to be found here in 3 Kgdms 8:54–56.
17. See also Josh 1:13, 15; 21:44; 22:4; 23:1.

enjoys (vss 9–10)."[18] Slightly different is the theory of Käsemann, who emphasizes a "wandering motif"[19] of God's people ("das wandernde Gottesvolk") from the earthly world to the heavenly as the underlying motif of Hebrews. He bases his argument on Heb 3:7–4:13, as well as on 10:19–20, and understands the rest as the "Gott verheißenen himmlische Heimat. … Das Gottesvolk verlasse die irdische Welt und wandere der himmlischen Heimat zu."[20] Gäbel rightly points out that there is no reference to a "wandering people of God" in Hebrews but rather to an "addressed people."[21] It is the faithful listening to the divine speech that becomes the prerequisite for the entry into the heavenly rest at the end of time.[22] It is therefore, in this sense, a "gegenwärtige Teilnahme am himmlischen Kult." He makes it clear that one ought to distinguish here between the following: "Eines ist die Rede von dem von Gott angeredeten Israel der Wüstenzeit, ein anderes die Rede vom himmlischen Vaterland, ein anderes das gegenwärtige Hinzugetreten-Sein der Adressaten zum himmlischen Kult."[23] The suggestion of Hofius about entry into the eschatological temple (i.e., that God's κατάπαυσιν is identical with the heavenly sanctuary) would perhaps make sense within the broader context and theology of Hebrews, a viewpoint similar to that of Gäbel: "Eintritt in die κατάπαυσιν (4,1.11) bzw. in das himmlische Allerheiligste in der Folge des Eintretens Christi (6,19 f)."[24] Do we have here a connection between the rich cultic imagery of the temple, sacrifices, and the high priest that will still be discussed later in Hebrews, on the one hand, and the author's understanding of a Sabbath period with its liturgical setting, on the other hand? It is stated in Heb 2:17 that Jesus became "a merciful and faithful high priest in service to God" and that he makes atonement for the sins of the people. The Sabbath was a time of festive praise and celebration, not a time of quiet and inactivity in

---

18. See Attridge 1989, 123.

19. Enns holds a similar view: "In the same way that the original exodus community, which rebelled at Meribah and Massah, was a community wandering through the wilderness, so too is the church a community of wilderness wanderers living between Egypt and Canaan with the ever present possibility of rebellion" (1997, 352).

20. The position of Käsemann as summarized by Gäbel 2006, 427.

21. Gäbel 2006, 427: "es müsste nach Maßgabe der Einleitung dieses Abschnitts (Hebr 3,7–11) mit dem Zitat aus Ψ 94 (Ps 95),7 nicht vom 'wandernde[n]', sondern vom angeredeten Gottesvolk gesprochen werden."

22. Gäbel 2006, 427.

23. Gäbel 2006, 428.

24. Gäbel 2006, 428.

the Jewish tradition. The link with praise and thanksgiving to God during an eschatological Sabbath rest (condition) in a heavenly sanctuary (place) seems thus to be a logical one.[25] There are indeed some indicators that confirm this change from κατάπαυσιν as the promised land (location) to a Sabbath period (state or condition): (1) the application of Gen 2:2, which clearly refers to the Sabbath day (ἐν τῇ ἡμέρᾳ τῇ ἑβδόμῃ) in Heb 4:4; (2) it is clear that this rest is a "rest from work" (τῶν ἔργων) in 4:3, 4; (3) God's setting of a "certain day" (τινὰ ... ἡμέραν) in 4:7; (4) the reference to "another day" (ἄλλης ... ἡμέρας) in 4:8 and then (5) the sudden use of σαββατισμός in 4:9. The occurrence of this word here in Heb 4:9 is the oldest evidence of the noun, although it occurs several times in later early Christian writings, independently from Hebrews.[26] The word σαββατισμός should not be seen to be identical in meaning or being interchangeable with κατάπαυσιν (cf. Heb 3:11, 18; 4:1, 3, 5, 10) but rather designates what God's people should expect when they enter God's κατάπαυσιν (compare 4:9 with 4:6a). The author thus understands σαββατισμός probably as an "eternal Sabbath celebration of salvation, i.e., the perfected community's worship before God's throne."[27]

When surveying Heb 3:7–4:11 and the prominence of the motif of rest or resting place (εἰς τὴν κατάπαυσιν, 3:18; σαββατισμός, 4:8), one becomes aware of the possibility that the author and his readers might have been converts from a group who held the Sabbath in high regard. The two keywords used by the author of Hebrews within this motif of rest are σήμερον and κατάπαυσιν. It is thus noteworthy that the author's delimitation of the quoted section (i.e., the beginning and end of the section that he quotes) is probably chosen because it starts with σήμερον (Ps 95[94]:7) and ends with κατάπαυσιν (Ps 95[94]:11). Both terms also play a prominent role in Deuteronomy. For σήμερον, compare, for instance, Deut 11:2, 8; 29:9, 14; for κατάπαυσιν, compare Deut 12:8–9. It is clear that one cannot argue in favor of the author's reliance on Deuteronomy here for these motifs in the light of his use and application of Ps (95)94. What is clear, however,

---

25. See Attridge 1989, 131.
26. Cf. Justin *Dial.* 23.3; *Orat.* 27.16; Epiphanius *Haer.* 30.2.2; 66.85.9; Acts Pet. Paul 1; Apos. Con. 2.36.2; Pseudo-Macarius (Symeon) Homily 12.2.4. The only non-Christian occurrence is in Plutarch (ca. 46–120 CE), *Superst.* 3 (166A). See Hofius 1993, 219.
27. Hofius 1993, 219. Attridge refers to the term as "sabbath observance" (1989, 130).

is that Deuteronomy equates the promise of rest with the "inheritance of the promised land."²⁸ By using and applying Ps 95 (94), Moses and the people of God (that generation) are compared with the new dispensation in Christ (this generation), who share in the promise of God's rest—today. So, when should this rest be pursued? The time that the promise is due for the new group is identified as today, σήμερον.

2.2. Hebrews' "Inheritors of God's Promise to Abraham" (Heb 6:12, 17) in the Light of LXX Gen 22:17 and LXX Gen 14:17–20

One encounters in Heb 5–7 an important promise, namely, that made to Abraham (Τῷ γὰρ Ἀβραὰμ ἐπαγγειλάμενος, 6:13), which the author of Hebrews connects closely with the inheritors of this promise in Heb 6:12 (κληρονομούντων τὰς ἐπαγγελίας) and 6:17 (τοῖς κληρονόμοις τῆς ἐπαγγελίας). The argument regarding Abraham, Melchizedek, and the high priesthood of Christ in Heb 5–7 seemed to be composed on the basis of several LXX passages and composed in the following manner.

(1) A combination of quotations from LXX Ps 2:7 (with which Hebrews opened in 1:5) and LXX Ps 110 (109):4 is presented in Heb 5:5–6, dealing with the appointment of the Son as HIGH PRIEST according to the order of Melchizedek (κατὰ τὴν τάξιν Μελχισέδεκ).²⁹

(2) Then a quotation from LXX Gen 22:17 is presented in Heb 6:14, dealing with God's promise to Abraham (Τῷ γὰρ Ἀβραὰμ ἐπαγγειλάμενος), when God swore by himself (ὁ θεός ... ὤμοσεν καθ' ἑαυτοῦ, Heb 6:13). The emphasis lies here on God's oath, which qualifies the authority and importance of the promise. Hebrews 6:13–15 is a closed unit and a commentary on LXX Gen 22:16–20. It should be noted that Gen 22:16 (the verse prior to that quoted in Heb 6:14) is alluded to in Heb 6:13, after which the explicit quotation from Gen 22:17 follows in Heb 6:14. This implies broader contextual knowledge of the passage from which the author of Hebrews quoted here. Alluding thus to the words of the angel to Abraham (λέγων Κατ' ἐμαυτοῦ ὤμοσα, λέγει κύριος, Gen 22:16), the author of Hebrews introduces in Heb 6:13–14 the explicit quotation in the next verse with the words: Τῷ γὰρ Ἀβραὰμ ἐπαγγειλάμενος ὁ θεός, ἐπεὶ

---

28. Kistemaker 1961, 115; see also Allen 2008.
29. See also Ellingworth 2000, 281: "The purpose of vv. 5 f. is to bind together the titles of Son and (high) priest as being equally conferred on Christ by God, as scripture attests."

κατ' οὐδενὸς εἶχεν μείζονος ὀμόσαι, ὤμοσεν καθ' ἑαυτοῦ λέγων. This results again in the introductory formula λέγων, with a verb of saying, as direct speech from God.³⁰ "In as much as the Greek translators have correctly rendered the Hebrew יְהוָה by κύριος, the author introduces the quotation with ὁ θεός, thereby indicating that it was God who swore and gave his promise to Abraham."³¹ The author thus distinguishes explicitly between the κύριος (Jesus) and ὁ θεός (God) in his theology. After Abraham was willing to sacrifice his son, God promised to him: "By myself have I sworn ... [that] in blessing I will bless you, and in multiplying I will multiply your seed" (Κατ' ἐμαυτοῦ ὤμοσα, λέγει κύριος, ἦ μὴν εὐλογῶν εὐλογήσω σε καὶ πληθύνων πληθυνῶ τὸ σπέρμα σου, Gen 22:16-17).

(3) Furthermore, the priesthood according to Melchizedek, its superiority to Abraham, and its connections with Christ's appointment are discussed on the basis of a paraphrase from LXX Gen 14:17-20 and several references to (e.g., κατὰ τὴν τάξιν Μελχισέδεκ, Heb 7:17) and a quotation from LXX Ps 110 (109):4 (ὤμοσεν κύριος, Heb 7:21) in Heb 7. The γάρ in Heb 7:1 with its commentary function makes Heb 7 in effect an exposition of LXX Ps 110 (109):4, which is interpreted with the aid of LXX Gen 14. Reference to Melchizedek in the Old Testament is only made in these two passages,: Gen 14:1-20 and Ps 110 (109):4.

With the little information from Gen 14 the author of Hebrews constructs his theological argument and reasons from the silence of Scripture in order to interpret the status of Jesus's high priesthood along the lines of that of Melchizedek.³² *Stichwörter* from LXX Ps 110 (109) and LXX Gen 14 are employed by means of a *gezerah shawah* argument and interpreted on the basis of the midrash-pesher method. The link with the paraphrase from LXX Gen 14:17-20 is established first through the name Melchizedek when Ps 110 (109):4 is quoted in Heb 7:17, then through the term ἱερεύς when Ps 110 (109):4 is quoted in Heb 7:17 and again in 7:21—now with the added element of the duration of this term of appointment: εἰς τὸν αἰῶνα. By applying Ps 110 (109):4 at different points in his argument and by linking it with analogous passages, the author succeeds in providing

---

30. Weiss 1991, 359.
31. Kistemaker 1961, 38.
32. On the silence of Scripture, see Kistemaker 1961, 133. Braun 1962, 29: "Man erkannt aber ... kaum noch den Jesus, der – sehr wenig priesterlich – Sabbat, levitische Reinheit und Tempelopfer angreift und all sein Wirken in das Wort und die helfende Tat verlegt."

scriptural confirmation from the LXX for the following aspects relating to the status of Christ: he was appointed by God, not by himself; he was appointed as high priest; his priestly order resembles that of Melchizedek; his term of office is eternal.

2.3. Hebrews on "Better Promises" (Heb 8:6) in the Light of LXX Exod 25:40

The term ἐπαγγελία is used again in Heb 8:6 in connection with the promise of a better covenant (κρείττοσιν ἐπαγγελίαις). This follows immediately after the author's quotation of LXX Exod 25:40 in Heb 8:5. The point of departure for the author of Hebrews is that God spoke in the past to their ancestors but in these last days through the Son (1:1). For the author of Hebrews, the vision of Moses in Exod 24–25 during which he received the pattern, or design, (τὸν τύπον,[33] Heb 8:5) for the tabernacle belongs to those voices from the past. The author of Hebrews continues this line of thought by means of the way in which he uses and presents the LXX quotation from Exod 25:40 in Heb 8:5: (1) He clearly indicates that it is God who spoke these words by means of his insertion of γάρ φησιν, as an introductory formula at the beginning of the quotation. (2) He is also probably responsible for the temporal change from δεδειγμένον (LXX Exod 25:40) to δειχθέντα as an indication that the earthly tabernacle belongs to the past and is thus temporary. (3) The presence of the term τύπον might have played a role in the author's selection of this passage,[34] in the sense that it "attests the 'shadowy' character of the earthly sanctuary and its liturgy."[35]

---

33. Contrary to Bruce 1985, 165, n. 27, Ellingworth states that it is an unnecessary complication to read into Hebrews "the idea that God showed to Moses a τύπος (in the sense of 'model') which was itself only a copy of a heavenly reality. This misunderstanding arises from an attempt to treat τύπος as a technical term which must have the same meaning in all contexts. On the contrary, what Moses is shown is constituted a τύπον simply by the fact that he is told to copy it" (2000, 408). Schröger 1968, 159, argued similarly. Klijn suggests in this regard that "Het woord 'voorbeeld' (typos) kan men vergelijken met het woord antitypa, dat in 9:24 voorkomt" (1975, 96).

34. See Strobel 1975, 164: "Hat in der LXX der Begriff 'Urbild' (griech. typos) wohl stärker die Bedeutung 'Vorlage, Muster', so wird nun mit Hilfe der alexandrinischen Hermeneutik der Ton auf die minderwertige Abbildlichkeit des irdischen Heiligtums und seiner Einrichtungen gelegt."

35. So, correctly, Lane 1998, 207.

The word occurs fourteen times in the New Testament,[36] but only here and in Stephen's Speech (Acts 7:43) within quotations.

The gist of the author's use of this quotation from Exod 25:40 "is to show from scripture itself that the Mosaic tabernacle, and by implication the whole OT cultus, was only a copy of the heavenly reality."[37] It can be assumed that the author of Hebrews must have known ("read") the broader context, "as the addition of πάντα would already suggest. Ex. 25:10–40 is drastically summarized in Heb. 9:1–5, and Ex. 24:8 is quoted in Heb. 9:20."[38] This is a piece of the puzzle by the author as part of his bigger argument that the earthly cultic worship belongs to a previous era.[39] The earthly priests were only serving in a shadowy copy of the heavenly sanctuary. Our observations regarding the quotation from Exod 25:40 in Heb 8:5 might be concluded with the statement that the author of Hebrews portrays the superior offering of the heavenly high priest in Heb 8:3–10:18 in a typological manner and in the light of salvation history.[40] The fairly close proximity of the only two passages that are quoted from Exodus by the author of Hebrews (i.e., Exod 24:8 and 25:40) confirms the prominence of the cultic theme for the author of Hebrews.

2.4. Hebrews on "the Promise of Eternal Inheritance" (Heb 9:15) in the Light of LXX Exod 24:8

Hebrews 9 continues with "the promise of eternal inheritance" (τὴν ἐπαγγελίαν ... τῆς αἰωνίου κληρονομίας (9:15). The tradition of the first covenant was transferred to early Christianity. The institutional formula of the covenant, which refers to the role of the blood, forms a key element in establishing the covenant. It is this formula (LXX Exod 24:8)

---

36. Cf. John 20:25; Acts 7:43, 44; Rom 5:14; 6:17; 1 Cor 10:6; 16:17; Phil 3:17; 1 Thess 1:7; 2 Thess 3:9; 1 Tim 4:12; Tit 2:7; Heb 8:5; and 1 Pet 5:3.

37. Ellingworth 2000, 408; also Schröger 1968, 160. Theißen (1969, 91) sees Exod 25:40 as a kind of "hermeneutisches Prinzip," with possible influence from the Alexandrian hermeneutics.

38. Ellingworth 2000, 408.

39. The quotation is found "in the introduction to Hebrews' extensive treatment of Christ's superior high-priestly offering (8:3–10:18)" (Guthrie 2007, 968).

40. So similarly Strobel with regard to the closure of the Jeremiah quotation: "Indem der Verfasser das Zitat mit der Zusage der Sündenvergebung abschließt, steht er wiederum beim größeren Thema, das vom hohenpriesterlichen Dienst des Christus handelt, der eine Reinigung von den Sünden bewirkt hat (1,2)" (1975, 166).

that is quoted in Heb 9:20. The similarity between this formula and that of the institution of the Eucharist, as the new covenant, is obvious. The author of Hebrews interprets the covenantal events in the light of Christ, who is now the mediator of a new covenant (διὰ τοῦτο διαθήκης καινῆς μεσίτης ἐστίν), by means of his death in order to save people from their disobedience regarding the requirements of the first covenant (9:15).[41] The author draws attention to the link with, and the importance of, the blood (9:18).[42] In referring to the events of the first covenant, the author included more elements—that are absent in the narrative of Exod 24: (1) Moses took the "water and the blood" (λαβὼν τὸ αἷμα ... μετὰ ὕδατος); (2) the blood belonged to "calves and goats" (τῶν μόσχων καὶ τῶν τράγων);[43] (3) he sprinkled it with "red wool and hyssop" (καὶ ἐρίου κοκκίνου καὶ ὑσσώπου); and (4) Moses sprinkled the blood not only on the people but also on "the book" (τε τὸ βιβλίον καὶ πάντα τὸν λαὸν ἐρράντισεν, 9:19). This might have been a development by the author himself or traces of an expansion or mutation of the existing tradition during the course of time. It might even have been ritual elements during a feast,[44] such as for a covenantal renewal, if such a feast existed. More possible is a probable merging between the traditions of the first covenantal events and the celebration of the Day of the Atonement, referred to in the preceding context of Heb 9:12.[45] Rather than speculating here about how the additional elements found their way into the author of Hebrews' narrative, what should

---

41. The account is mostly a summary of these events with some modifications. See Bruce 1985, 214; Wilson 1987, 160.

42. See Van Oyen 1962, 149: "Het oude verbond is derhalve met bloed ingewijd, zo redeneert de schrijver, eveneens het nieuwe met het bloed van Christus, en het oude is op deze wijze schaduwbeeld van het nieuwe en volmaakte." Karrer makes it explicit: "Das ist das Blut (nämlich der zum Inkrafttreten notwendige Tod und der aus dem Tod resultierende Blutritus) des Testaments, das Gott zu euren Gunsten verfügt hat" (2008, 163). Note that the word "blood" appears six times in Heb 9:18–22 alone (Kistemaker 1984, 257).

43. Some manuscripts omit "and goats" [καὶ τῶν τράγων]: P[46] ℵ[2] K L Ψ 0150. 0278. 1241. 1319. 1505. 1739. 1852. 1881 al sy[(p)] h pal Chrysostom. The inclusion of goats is found in the broader context where reference was already made to it in Heb 9:12, probably influencing the reading here in Heb 9:19. Bruce (1985, 214), too, is of the opinion that it was probably a later addition to the text of Hebrews in 9:19.

44. See Strobel 1975, 183: "daß ein festlicher Gottesdienst, der als 'Sitz-im-Leben' der Homilie angenommen werden darf, die Assoziation mit den Einsetzungsworten jederzeit begünstigen konnte."

45. Bruce signals a similar possible link between Exod 24 and Num 19 regard-

be noted is the "blood formula" and its connection to the covenant. It is within this context that the author argues about a new covenant and in which he interprets the role of Jesus's death.⁴⁶ This is enhanced with the blood-formula quotation from the first covenant (LXX Exod 24:8) and its allusion to the institution of the Eucharist.

2.5. Hebrews on "Endurance to Receive the Promise" (Heb 10:36) in the Light of LXX Deut 32:35, 36

The tone of Heb 10:19–12:29 changes to an exhortation to proceed in full assurance of faith (ἐν πληροφορίᾳ πίστεως, 10:22), with the confession of their hope (τὴν ὁμολογίαν τῆς ἐλπίδος, 10:23), provoking each other with love and good deeds (ἀγάπης καὶ καλῶν ἔργων, 10:24), not to abandon their confidence (Μὴ ἀποβάλητε τὴν παρρησίαν, 10:35) and to pursue endurance (ὑπομονῆς γὰρ ἔχετε χρείαν, 10:36). The theme of judgment is being picked up (κρίσεως, 10:27; ἀποθνῄσκει, 10:28; ἀξιωθήσεται, 10:29) and leads to the quotation from the Canticum Mosis in which the keywords ἐκδικήσεως and κρινεῖ appear. Judgment becomes a major topic in Heb 10:19–39, within which the quotations from LXX Deut 32:35–36 and Hab 2:3–4 are embedded. The author first presents a quoted text from the Torah—actually a hymnic text that he splits up into two quotations—then proceeds a few verses further with another quotation, consisting of a possible conflation of texts from the Prophets (Isa 26:20 and Hab 2:3–4). These last two texts combine the theme of judgment with the promise (τὴν ἐπαγγελίαν, Heb 10:36) of the one who will come soon (ὁ ἐρχόμενος, Hab 2:3b in Heb 10:37).

For the first text, the text from the Torah, the author of Hebrews quotes here for a second time from the Song of Moses. In Heb 1:6, he quoted LXX Deut 32:43 (Ode 2:43), and he quotes in Heb 10:30 a few lines earlier from the same Song. A longer quotation from the Song of Moses is thus found here in Heb 10:30, corresponding with Deut 32:35, 36.

---

ing the triennial synagogue lectionary that "would have been read around the same season of the year in the second and third years respectively" (1985, 216).

46. See also Schröger 1968, 172: "Durch den Vergleich mit dem Sinai-Bundesschluß, der mit Blut geschlossen wurde, wird u. a. klargestellt, daß der Neue Bund, verheißen vom Propheten Jeremias, bereits besteht, beschlossen im Blute Jesu Christi." Similarly Guthrie 2007, 973.

The quotation is introduced with the words οἴδαμεν γὰρ τὸν εἰπόντα (10:30).[47] Although the quotation is part of Moses's speech in Deuteronomy, the author of Hebrews gives it authority with the formula τὸν εἰπόντα as the direct words of God.[48] Hebrews does not quote the entire section from Deut 32:35–36 but selects only two lines and omits the rest. These two lines—one quoted text but actually two quotations—"establish two facts with regard to the divine judgment."[49] These lines confirm that it is in God's nature to be just and to judge.[50] The first line points to the vindication of the righteous and innocent and to the condemnation of the wicked.[51] The author starts his double quotation with "mine is" (ἐμοί) in an emphatic position similar to that of Rom 12:19. The second part of the double quotation points to the fact that God's people will be judged—now not referring to Israel but applied to the recipient congregation[52] as "eschatological judgment."[53] What the judgment will be, lies within themselves.[54] The saying that "God will judge his people" became a "geflügelten Wort" in Israel—identical to the wording of Ps 135 (134):14—that was understood in a positive sense.[55]

2.6. Hebrews on "Faith and God's Promises" (Hebrews 11) in the Light of LXX Gen 21:12

The recipients have heard God speaking in the past. Here he spoke again through the words of his promise to Abraham. It stands within the list of passages previously quoted in Hebrews where God communicated his

---

47. The meaning is ambiguous: "we know God, who said in scripture," and "we know that it was God who said in scripture." Ellingworth (2000, 541) reckons that the latter is perhaps more prominent in this context.

48. See Grässer 1997, 48: "Der εἰπόν ist der κύριος von V 30c." Paul, on the other hand, states explicitly λέγει κύριος with his introductory formula to this quotation in Rom 12:19.

49. Westcott 1974, 332. Similarly Guthrie 2007, 981.

50. Similarly Van Oyen 1962, 178.

51. See Wilson 1987, 195.

52. Weiss 1991, 542; Grässer 1997, 49.

53. See Guthrie 2007, 981.

54. Westcott 1974, 332. Wilson points out that the "actual form of words is the same, but the emphasis suggested by the context is different" (1987, 195). So, similarly, Bruce 1985, 262; Karrer 2008, 214.

55. Karrer 2008, 228.

relationship by means of visions or oracles. Philo interprets the situation similarly with regard to Abraham (*Mut.* 39; *Somn.* 1.64). The history of Abraham and Sarah is encountered in Heb 11:8–13 with the author's own theological interpretation of the events in Heb 11:13–16. Hereafter follow the other patriarchs, Isaac and Jacob, with Abraham in Heb 11:17–21. In his list of faith heroes (Heb 11), the author's focus on God's promise (11:17) is again here connected with a LXX Pentateuch quotation that follows. The immediate context of LXX Gen 21, from which Hebrews quotes the phrase, is interesting. The Abrahamic promise is made within the context of God referring to Abraham's two children. The text refers to Isaac as "the child" (περὶ τοῦ παιδίου, Gen 21:12) and Ishmael as "the son" (καὶ τὸν υἱόν, 21:13) of the slave woman. The terminology is striking and reminds of terms used, not only in Heb 2 when Jesus expressed his relation with the believers (πολλοὺς υἱούς, 2:10), but also in Heb 12 when the believers are referred to within a similar relationship (ὡς υἱοῖς, 12:5, 7; υἱέ μου, 12:5). The concept of God as the Father and believers as his children is firmly rooted within the theology of early Christianity.

Two clear theological motifs, further, surface in Heb 11:17 within the immediate context of the quotation: (1) the story of Abraham (and Isaac) is connected with the motif of God's testing (πειραζόμενος); and (2) the quoted passage is intended as a reminder of the very words of God's promise (ὁ τὰς ἐπαγγελίας), the latter of which is confirmed by the divine passives ἐλαλήθη and κληθήσεταί, as well as by the direct speech of the quotation itself.

The citation of LXX Gen 21:12 in Heb 11:17–19 cannot be understood without the context of the author's own interpretation. It is embedded within the history of God's test to Abraham to be willing to sacrifice Isaac,[56] despite the promise that God had made about the descendants through Isaac.[57] Abraham's perseverance in his faith goes beyond the questioning of God's promise and beyond the test itself. According to Hebrews, he

---

56. Abraham's test is described particularly in Gen 22. Bruce makes the point that "the 'Binding of Isaac', as the story of Gen. 22 has traditionally been called among the Jews, is treated in Jewish interpretation as the classic example of the redemptive efficacy of martyrdom" (1985, 309). Abraham's willingness to obey and the focus of this obedience as an act of Abraham (not on Isaac here) should be noted. See also Van Oyen 1962, 203; Strobel 1975, 218; Wilson 1987, 209; Schunack 2002, 178.

57. "Gottes Weisung an Abraham, Isaak als Opfer darzubringen, steht im Widerspruch zu seiner eigenen Verheißung bzw. stellt sie radikal in Frage" (Weiss 1991, 597).

believed that God would be able even to resurrect Isaac from death. The list of faith heroes continues to the beginning of Heb 12, where the example of Jesus himself is presented. All of these were believers who suffered in the past but who did not abandon their faith. The Abrahamic promise was already encountered in Heb 6:14 when Gen 22:17 was quoted in connection with the near sacrifice of Isaac (Akedah). Abraham's test stands thus in stark contrast with God's promise, which in turn puts the recipients' suffering in perspective.

The author of Hebrews presents an important theological perspective in his interpretation of God's promise to faith heroes such as Abraham. He points to the fact that they died without always having the opportunity to see these promises fulfilled: ἀπέθανον οὗτοι πάντες, μὴ λαβόντες τὰς ἐπαγγελίας (11:13; also 11:9, 17, 33, 39). This implies for him that these believers continued to believe God's promises even when they died without seeing the promises fulfilled and that the fulfillment of God's promises continues to take place even after the recipients have died.

2.7. Hebrews on God's "Current Promise" (12:26) in the Light of LXX Deut 9:19 (+ LXX Pss 17/76)

In Heb 12:26, the author refers to God's current promise (νῦν δὲ ἐπήγγελται),[58] which is an apocalyptic promise that God will once more shake not only the earth but also the heaven.

The author proceeds in Heb 12:12–17 with a list of instructions, the first three of which are imperatives: ἀνορθώσατε in 12:12, ποιεῖτε in 12:13, and διώκετε in 12:14. The last instruction is a participle (ἐπισκοποῦντες, v. 15) that leads into three μή τις constructions. Then follows the motif of receiving the law on Sinai (12:18–24). This forms the immediate context of the pair of quotations within which the first quotation, probably taken from Deut 9:19, is embedded. Although it is introduced with a clearly formulated introductory formula, the text of the quotation as presented in Heb 12:21 is nowhere to be found in the Old Testament in this particular format and sequence. Some phrases, however, show agreement with a number of texts. The closest is probably that of LXX Deut 9:19, which is in agreement with the first part of this brief quotation.[59] It is only one of two

---

58. Ἐπήγγελται surfaces in Paul's letters in Gal 3:19 and Rom 4:21.
59. Bruce 1985, 372. So also Guthrie 2007, 988: "Rather than drawing … from the passages to which he has been alluding thus far, the author seems to allude here to

places where the word ἔκφοβος is found in the LXX; the other is 1 Macc 13:2, which provides a close parallel with regard to the wording (but not the context) of the Hebrews quotation: καὶ εἶδεν τὸν λαόν, ὅτι ἔντρομός ἐστιν καὶ ἔκφοβος (1 Macc 13:2). However, interesting parallels are also to be found in LXX Ps 17:8 and LXX Ps 76:19, two of three places where the term ἔντρομος occurs. (The third place is LXX Dan 10:11, which describes Daniel's state during the epiphany and speech of the angel.) The context in which the term is used in both LXX Pss 17 and 76 is similar to that as described in Hebrews. The quotation of what Moses would have said contains only part of the actual words of LXX Deut 9:19. The rest is nowhere to be found from the same passage among the textual witnesses of the LXX or the MT and were probably added by the author of Hebrews. As mentioned, these might have arrived via LXX Ps 17:8 and/or LXX Ps 76:19 (both which read καὶ ἔντρομος), thus presenting us with a possible conflated quotation from the LXX. The other element encountered in LXX Pss 17 and 76, that of the earth's shaking (ἐσαλεύθη), will be picked up in the introductory formula of the second quotation from Hag 2: οὗ ἡ φωνὴ τὴν γῆν ἐσάλευσεν τότε (Heb 12:26). It seems quite possible that the author of Hebrews might have included different elements from LXX Deut 4 and 9, together with the quotation from LXX Deut 9:19, into the broader context of his argument. The quotation thus seems like a conflation between LXX Deut 9:19 (ἔκφοβος) and the concept of the earth trembling (ἔντρομος) from LXX Pss 17/76, when God spoke at that time.

3. Conclusion

The theology of the LXX played an important role in the formation of New Testament theology. This study traced the leitmotif of ἐπαγγελία in the book of Hebrews in order to identify its connection with LXX Pentateuch quotations and its theological impact on the theology of this New Testament document. Seven such trajectories were identified.

(1) The promise (ἐπαγγελία) about entering into God's κατάπαυσιν still stands (Heb 4:1). The term κατάπαυσιν became a theological leitmotif for the eschatology of the author. He found the term in his LXX from pas-

---

Deut. 9:19a." Similarly Wilson 1987, 229: "There is nothing to correspond to this in the Exodus theophany at Sinai, and the closest parallel is in Dt. 9:19." So also Kistemaker 1984, 390: "The accounts recorded in Exodus 19–20 and Deuteronomy 4–5 are silent about the fear of Moses."

sages in Gen 2:2 and LXX Ps 95 (94):7–11 and constructed an eschatology based on God's κατάπαυσιν as a sabbatical period after the creation and the κατάπαυσιν of the promised land as destination for the exodus people. It is clear that the quotation from LXX Gen 2:2 has been embedded within the midrash on LXX Ps 95 (94) with a wordplay on the substantive κατάπαυσιν (LXX Ps 95[94]:11) and the verb κατέπαυσεν (LXX Gen 2:2).

(2) The promise made to Abraham (Τῷ γὰρ Ἀβραὰμ ἐπαγγειλάμενος, 6:13) when God swore by himself (ὁ θεός … ὤμοσεν καθ' ἑαυτοῦ, 6:13) is closely connected to the inheritors of this promise in Heb 6:12 (κληρονομούντων τὰς ἐπαγγελίας) and 6:17 (τοῖς κληρονόμοις τῆς ἐπαγγελίας). Hebrews 6:13–15 is a closed unit and a commentary on LXX Gen 22:16–20, with an explicit quotation from LXX Gen 22:17 in Heb 6:14. The term ὤμοσεν became another theological leitmotif for the eschatology of the author. He found the term in his LXX from the text in Gen 22:17. The author of Hebrews introduced the quotation with ὁ θεός, thereby indicating that it was God who swore and gave his promise to Abraham—despite the correct rendering of the Hebrew Tetragrammaton with κύριος by the LXX translators—and in this manner distinguished explicitly between the κύριος (Jesus) and ὁ θεός (God) in his theology. The leitmotif of God's oath to Abraham continues in Heb 7 with the superiority of the priesthood according to Melchizedek and its connections with Christ's appointment, based on a paraphrase from LXX Gen 14:17–20, several references (e.g., κατὰ τὴν τάξιν Μελχισέδεκ, Heb 7:17), and a quotation from LXX Ps 110 (109):4 (ὤμοσεν κύριος, Heb 7:21). The latter psalm is interpreted with the aid of LXX Gen 14.

(3) In Heb 8:6, the promise of a better covenant (κρείττοσιν ἐπαγγελίαις, 8:6) is introduced. This follows directly after reference was made in Heb 8:5 of Moses's vision by means of the LXX quotation from Exod 25:40, where he received the design (τὸν τύπον, Heb 8:5) for the tabernacle. The LXX term τύπον probably played a key role in the author's selection of this passage, due to his understanding of the "shadowy" character of the earthly sanctuary.

(4) Hebrews 9:15 refers to the promise of eternal inheritance (τὴν ἐπαγγελίαν … τῆς αἰωνίου κληρονομίας). The institutional formula of the covenant, the "blood formula" as it occurs in LXX Exod 24:8, is shortly thereafter quoted in Heb 9:20. The author draws attention to the link with, and the importance of, the blood (9:18), which forms a key element in establishing the covenant. This context of the first covenant (LXX Exod 24:8) provides the backdrop for the author to refer to a new covenant,

which he interprets in connection with Jesus's death and alludes to the institution of the Eucharist.

(5) In Heb 10, the theme of judgment is combined with the promise (τὴν ἐπαγγελίαν, 10:36). The author selects two lines from LXX Deut 32:35–36 for his quotation in order to establish two facts with regard to the divine judgment. The first points to both the vindication of the righteous and the condemnation of the wicked. The second points to the fact that God's people will be judged—now not referring to Israel but applied to the recipient congregation as "eschatological judgment."

(6) In his catalog of *exempla fidei* in Heb 11, the author's focus on God's promise (11:17) is again here connected with a LXX Pentateuch quotation. The context of the citation from LXX Gen 21:12 refers to Abraham's two children. Isaac is "the *child*" (περὶ τοῦ παιδίου, Gen 21:12) and Ishmael "the *son*" (καὶ τὸν υἱόν, Gen 21:13) of the slave woman. In the theological interpretation of this LXX quotation in Heb 11:17–19, Abraham's story is closely connected with the motif of God's testing (πειραζόμενος), as well as with the reminder of God's promise (ὁ τὰς ἐπαγγελίας), the latter of which is confirmed by the divine passives ἐλαλήθη and κληθήσεταί, as well as by the direct speech of the quotation itself. The author of Hebrews finds important theological roots for perserverance in faith in Greek Scriptures. Abraham, for example, died without seeing these promises fulfilled: ἀπέθανον οὗτοι πάντες, μὴ λαβόντες τὰς ἐπαγγελίας (11:13; also 11:9, 17, 33, 39). Based on his theological interpretation, God's oath stands, and his promises will always be fulfilled. Hence these are still valid and open and are now relevant for the current audience. It reinforces the theological leitmotif as expressed in Heb 10:36: "For you need endurance, so that when you have done the will of God, you may receive what was promised."

(7) God's current promise (νῦν δὲ ἐπήγγελται) in Heb 12:26 is understood by Hebrews as an apocalyptic promise about the shaking of earth and heaven. A theological link is created between the term ἔκφοβός in Heb 12:21 (embedded in 12:18–24 with the motif of receiving the law on Sinai) and the LXX. The term ἔκφοβός surfaces in Deut 9:19 and in 1 Macc 13:2, which provides a close parallel with regard to the wording (but not the context) of the Hebrews quotation: καὶ εἶδεν τὸν λαόν, ὅτι ἔντρομός ἐστιν καὶ ἔκφοβος (1 Macc 13:2).

Septuagint terminology from the Pentateuch became theological levers by which the early Christian author of Hebrews shunted his case of God's promises in a particular theological direction. The rhetorical power of the LXX terms and phrases he uses goes beyond the mere identification of these terms: it finds its persuasive power as *Gottessprache* fundamentally in the New Testament author's Jewish exegetical techniques. Two of these are most appropriate in Hebrews.

(1) Especially based on "the exposition of proof," the principle of midrash haggadah provided an apt theological exposition method where passion for God and his embracement of humanity were important. The most fundamental presupposition of midrash haggadah was that a particular text does not mean per se what it says and that it can have different meanings. These are often introduced not by the text itself but rather by other Scripture passages, which the interpreter then connects with the original passage. The most prosaic or blunt verse is then elevated with the theological insights of the prophets by means of the combination of the original passage.

(2) Another kind of midrash as expressed in the seven rules of Rabbi Hillel (ca. 110 BCE–10 CE) is the principle of *gezerah shewah*. An argument gains persuasive power by means of the analogy of identical or similar words. These synonymns or homonyms are then subjected to identical definitions and applications.

Our experiment with ἐπαγγελία in the book of Hebrews and its connection with the Jewish Scriptures in their Greek versions—in this essay illustrated only by *Stichwörter* from the LXX Pentateuch—undergirds the theology of Hebrews, which is on a par with that of Pss. Sol. 12:6, where "the devout of the Lord inherit the promises of the Lord."

Bibliography

Allen, Dave M. 2008. *Deuteronomy and Exhortation in Hebrews*. WUNT 238. Tübingen: Mohr Siebeck.
Attridge, Harold W. 1989. *The Epistle to the Hebrews*. Hermeneia. Philadelphia: Fortress.
Bauernfeind, Otto. 1964. "κατάπαυσις." *TDNT* 3:628.
Braulik, Georg. 1986. "Gottes Ruhe – Das Land oder der Tempel?" Pages 33–44 in *Freude an der Weisung des Herrn: Beiträge zur Theologie der Psalmen; Festgabe zum 70. Geburtstag von Heinrich Groß*. Edited by Ernst Haag and Frank-Lothar Hossfeld. SBB 13. Stuttgart: Verlag Katholisches Bibelwerk.
Braun, Herbert. 1962. "Das Alte Testament im Neuen Testament." *ZThK* 59:16–31.

Bruce, Frederick F. 1985. *The Epistle to the Hebrews*. NICNT. Grand Rapids: Eerdmans.
Ellingworth, Paul. 2000. *The Epistle to the Hebrews*. NIGTC. Grand Rapids: Eerdmans.
Enns, Peter. 1997. "The Interpretation of Psalm 95 in Hebrews 3.1–4.13." Pages 352–63 in *Early Christian Interpretation of the Scriptures of Israel: Investigations and Proposals*. Edited by Craig A. Evans and James A. Sanders. JSNTSup 148. Sheffield: Sheffield Academic.
Gäbel, Georg. 2006. *Die Kulttheologie des Hebräerbriefes*. WUNT 2/212. Tübingen: Mohr Siebeck.
Grässer, Erich. 1997. *Hebr 10,19–13,25*. Vol. 3 of *An die Hebräer*. EKK 17.3. Zürich: Benziger Verlag.
Guthrie, George H. 2007. "Hebrews." Pages 919–95 in *Commentary on the New Testament Use of the Old Testament*. Edited by Greg K. Beale and Donald A. Carson. Grand Rapids: Baker Academic.
Hofius, Otto. 1993. "Σαββατισμός." *EDNT* 3:219.
Karrer, Martin. 2002. *Der Brief an die Hebräer: Kapitel 1,1–5,10*. ÖTK 20.1. Gütersloh: Gütersloher Verlagshaus.
———. 2008. *Der Brief an die Hebräer: Kapitel 5,11–13,25*. ÖTK 20.2. Gütersloh: Gütersloher Verlagshaus.
Kistemaker, Simon J. 1961. *The Psalm Citations in the Epistle to the Hebrews*. Amsterdam: Van Soest.
———. 1984. *Exposition of the Epistle to the Hebrews*. Grand Rapids: Baker Academic.
Klijn, Albertus F. J. 1975. *De Brief aan de Hebreeën*. PNT. Nijkerk: Callenbach.
Koester, Craig. 2001. *Hebrews*. AB 36. New York: Doubleday.
Lane, William L. 1998. *Hebrews 1–8*. WBC 47A. Dallas: Word.
Lincoln, Andrew T. 2006. *Hebrews: A Guide*. London: Continuum.
Oyen, Hendrik van. 1962. *De Brief aan de Hebreeën*. Nijkerk: Callenbach.
Schniewind, Julius, and Gerhard Friedrich. 1964. "ἐπαγγελία." *TDNT* 2:576–86.
Schröger, Friedrich. 1968. *Der Verfasser des Hebräerbriefes als Schriftausleger*. BU 4. Regensburg: Pustet.
Schunack, Gerd. 2002. *Der Hebräerbrief*. ZBK. Zürich: Theologischer Verlag.
Steyn, Gert J. 2002. "A Note on the Vorlage of the Citation from Gen 2,2 in Heb 4,4." *Ekklesiastikos Pharos* 84:43–50.

———. 2011. *A Quest for the Assumed LXX Vorlage of the Explicit Quotations in Hebrews*. FRLANT 235. Göttingen: Vandenhoeck & Ruprecht.

———. 2015. "Retrodiction of the Old Testament in the New: The Case of Deut 21:23 in Paul's Letter to the Galatians and the Crucifixion of Yehoshua ben Yoseph." *HTS Teologiese Studies/Theological Studies* 71.3. doi: 10.4102/hts.v71i3.3091.

Strobel, August. 1975. *Der Brief an die Hebräer*. NTD 9. Göttingen: Vandenhoeck & Ruprecht.

Theißen, Gerd. 1969. *Untersuchungen zum Hebräerbrief*. SNT 2. Gütersloh: Gütersloher Verlagshaus.

Weiss, Hans-Friedrich. 1991. *Der Brief an die Hebräer*. KEK 13. Göttingen: Vandenhoeck & Ruprecht.

———. 1996. "Sabbatismos in the Epistle to the Hebrews." *CBQ* 58:674–89.

Westcott, Brooke F. 1974. *The Epistle to the Hebrews*. Grand Rapids: Eerdmans.

Wilson, Robert M. 1987. *Hebrews*. NCB. Grand Rapids: Eerdmans.

„Binde die Gebote auf Deine Seele".[1] Zum Einfluss anthropologischer Begrifflichkeiten der Septuaginta auf die patristische Ethik

Ulrich Volp

ABSTRACT: "It was through the church fathers that anthropological terminologies of the Septuagint influenced the Christian tradition" (Martin Rösel). Fundamental differences in the conceptions of humanity in the MT and the Septuagint have been discussed since the days of Zacharias Frankel (1851). The fact that the translation of נֶפֶשׁ with ψυχή gave dichotomic patristic anthropologies a certain biblical authority is immediately obvious. This essay, however, will sketch the consequences for the development of Christian ethics. The fathers developed their ethical concepts as a result of a complex struggle with philosophical teachings and competing Christian thoughts. A basic consensus was reached in the late fourth century. It is a development whose dynamics and autonomy have come to the fore again only recently. The Septuagint was often the most important reference text of the church fathers, who formulated their ethical ideas in a complex philosophical, theological, social, and ritual context. Neither the model of a simple "derivation" of ethical concepts from philosophical schools or "biblical ethics" nor an understanding on the basis of perpetual Christian values (justice, discipleship, faith, love) can therefore do justice to this development, especially since the question of God's revelation before the incarnation was intimately linked to the fathers' view of human beings and what they should do. An exemplary look at some of the Septuagint terminology relevant to the fathers, such as ὁμοίωσις τοῦ θεοῦ, ψυχή, and προαίρεσις, may indeed shed some light on these issues.

---

[1]. Spr 6,20–21 LXX: υἱέ φύλασσε νόμους πατρός σου καὶ μὴ ἀπώσῃ θεσμοὺς μητρός σου ἄφαψαι δὲ αὐτοὺς ἐπὶ σῇ ψυχῇ διὰ παντὸς καὶ ἐγκλοίωσαι ἐπὶ σῷ τραχήλῳ („Sohn, bewahre die Gebote deines Vaters und lass nicht fahren die Anordnungen deiner Mutter. Binde sie dir auf deine Seele allezeit und hänge sie um deinen Hals").

1. Einleitung

> Der Lektor lese von einem erhöhten Ort in der Mitte die Bücher des Moses und Josua, die der Richter und Könige, die Paraleipomena[2] und was über die Rückkehr des Volkes in der Schrift enthalten ist, dazu die Bücher Jobs und Salomons, auch die sechzehn Propheten.... Bei Lesung des Evangeliums sollen es alle Priester und Diakonen und das ganze Volk in tiefem Stillschweigen stehend anhören, denn es steht geschrieben: „Schweige und höre, Israel" [vgl. Dtn 4,1 LXX] und außerdem: „Du bleib hier und höre" [Vgl. Dtn 5,3 LXX].[3]

Diese Anweisung für einen christlichen Gottesdienst in der Antike belegt die Präsenz der Septuaginta im christlichen Leben. Sie gibt einen Eindruck vom Kontext, in dem die Kirchenväter ihre theologischen Schriften verfassten. Das hier vorgeschriebene Programm deckt sich mit dem Anspruch an biblische Lesungen im antiken Gottesdienst, wie er auch in tausenden erhaltenen patristischen Predigten eingefordert wird. In diesen Predigten geht es oft um ethische Fragen, um ethische Ermahnung und die Definition ethischer Standards für die christliche Gemeinde.[4] Das ist insofern vielleicht überraschend, weil die christliche Identität seit den Kontroversen mit der Gnosis und Markion im zweiten Jahrhundert ganz wesentlich an der Frage der Integration der Inkarnation in die Gotteslehre hing – und nicht an der Ethik, die in den Glaubensbekenntnissen deshalb auch nicht explizit vorkommt.[5] Anders als im spätantiken Judentum, in dem Spekulationen über die Gotteslehre doch eher einen akademischen Charakter

---

2. Gemeint ist in der Begrifflichkeit der Septuaginta 1.Chronik und 2.Chronik.

3. Apos. Con. 2,57: Μέσος δὲ ὁ ἀναγνώστης ἐφ' ὑψηλοῦ τινος ἑστὼς ἀναγινωσκέτω τὰ Μωϋσέως καὶ Ἰησοῦ τοῦ Ναυῆ, τὰ τῶν Κριτῶν καὶ τῶν Βασιλειῶν, τὰ τῶν Παραλειπομένων καὶ τὰ τῆς Ἐπανόδου, πρὸς τούτοις τὰ τοῦ Ἰὼβ καὶ τὰ Σολομῶντος καὶ τὰ τῶν Ἑξκαίδεκα προφητῶν.... Καὶ ὅταν ἀναγινωσκόμενον ᾖ τὸ Εὐαγγέλιον, πάντες οἱ πρεσβύτεροι καὶ οἱ διάκονοι καὶ πᾶς ὁ λαὸς στηκέτωσαν μετὰ πολλῆς ἡσυχίας· γέγραπται γάρ· Σιώπα καὶ ἄκουε Ἰσραήλ, καὶ πάλιν· Σὺ δὲ αὐτοῦ στῆθι καὶ ἀκούσῃ (SC 320, 312,19–314,36). Vgl. zu der Stelle Volp 2011, 50–51.

4. Bereits das umfangreiche Corpus an Kommentierungen alttestamentlicher Texte durch den Alexandriner Origenes († um 254 n. Chr.) ist ohne diese Lese- und Predigtpraxis nicht zu verstehen. Einen Höhepunkt der ethisch-homiletischen Zuspitzung stellt das homiletische Werk des Johannes Chrysostomus († 407 n. Chr.) dar, von dem Auslegungsreihen u.a. zu Genesis LXX, zu den Septuagintatexten des Hiob- und des Psalmenbuchs sowie zu Jes 1–8.10 LXX erhalten geblieben sind.

5. Vgl. in diesem Sinne zuletzt Kinzig 2019.

hatten und in dem die Einhaltung ethischer und ritueller Normen viel stärker die Zugehörigkeit zum Judentum und seiner Identität bestimmte,[6] wurde im Christentum das Bekenntnis des inkarnierten Gottes zu einer unabdingbaren Voraussetzung für das Christsein und für die richtige Lebensführung.[7] Im antiken Christentum folgte deshalb die Aufforderung zu einer bestimmten Lebensweise, also dem, was man „präskriptive Ethik" nennen kann, schon in frühen Texten der Bekenntnisformulierung. So heißt es etwa im Polykarpbrief:

> Darum ... glaubt an den, der unseren κύριος Jesus Christus von den Toten auferweckt und ihm Herrlichkeit und den Thron zu seiner Rechten verliehen hat. Ihm ist alles untertan im Himmel und auf Erden, ihm dient jegliches Leben,[8] ... Blut wird Gott fordern von denen, die nicht an ihn glauben.[9] Der aber ihn von den Toten auferweckt hat, wird auch uns auferwecken, wenn wir seinen Willen tun und in seinen Geboten wandeln und lieben, was er geliebt hat, und uns frei halten von jeder Ungerechtigkeit, Habsucht, Geldgier, übler Rede, falschem Zeugnis; wenn wir Böses nicht mit Bösem vergelten oder Schmähung nicht mit Schmähung, noch Faustschlag mit Faustschlag; noch Fluch mit Fluch.[10]

---

6. Vgl. dazu nur etwa die Studien Jacob Neusners über die Bildung von Verständniskategorien im antiken Judentum (z.B. Neusner 1994). Auch wenn etwa Neusners vielleicht zu starke Betonung des rituellen Fokus des antiken pharisäischen Judentums umfassender Kritik unterzogen worden ist (vgl. etwa die Position E. P. Sanders zu den Speiseregeln), so steht doch außer Zweifel, dass in den in Frage stehenden antiken Richtungen des Judentums Fragen der Lebensführung wesentliche Identitätsfragen gewesen sind.

7. So bezeichnet etwa Tertullian, *Virg.* 1,4–5, die *lex fidei*, also die Zustimmung zum einen Schöpfergott, zur Gottheit, Auferstehung und Richteramt Christi als primär und unveränderlich, während Fragen der *disciplina*, also der Ethik und Lebensführung sekundär und Gegenstand laufender Verbesserung seien.

8. Vgl. Ps 150,6 LXX (πᾶσα πνοὴ αἰνεσάτω τὸν κύριον); vgl. Jes 57,16 LXX und 3.Kgt 15,29.

9. Vgl. Gen 42,22 LXX; Ez 3,18.20 LXX; 33,6.8 LXX.

10. Polykarp, *Phil.* 2,1: Διὸ ... πιστεύσαντες εἰς τὸν ἐγείραντα τὸν κύριον ἡμῶν Ἰησοῦν Χριστὸν ἐκ νεκρῶν καὶ δόντα αὐτῷ δόξαν καὶ θρόνον ἐκ δεξιῶν αὐτοῦ· ᾧ ὑπετάγη τὰ πάντα ἐπουράνια καὶ ἐπίγεια, ᾧ πᾶσα πνοὴ λατρεύει ... οὗ τὸ αἷμα ἐκζητήσει ὁ θεὸς ἀπὸ τῶν ἀπειθούντων αὐτῷ. ὁ δὲ ἐγείρας αὐτὸν ἐκ νεκρῶν καὶ ἡμᾶς ἐγερεῖ, ἐὰν ποιῶμεν αὐτοῦ τὸ θέλημα καὶ πορευώμεθα ἐν ταῖς ἐντολαῖς αὐτοῦ καὶ ἀγαπῶμεν, ἃ ἠγάπησεν, ἀπεχόμενοι πάσης ἀδικίας, πλεονεξίας, φιλαργυρίας, καταλαλιᾶς, ψευδομαρτυρίας· μὴ ἀποδιδόντες κακὸν ἀντὶ κακοῦ ἢ λοιδορίαν ἀντὶ λοιδορίας ἢ γρόνθον ἀντὶ γρόνθου ἢ κατάραν ἀντὶ κατάρας (vgl. BKV[2] 35, 164).

Dieser Text macht die Bedeutung der Septuaginta für die Entwicklung der altkirchlichen Christologie gut deutlich. Jesus ist hier für den Christen κύριος, genauso wie JHWH für die in christlicher Zeit gebräuchlichen Septuagintahandschriften[11] κύριος ist. Die auf den κύριος-JHWH bezogenen Septuagintaaussagen konnten also auf den κύριος-Christus übertragen werden. Bereits neutestamentliche Bestimmungen von Jesus Christus nehmen nicht selten einen wörtlichen Bezug auf Septuagintaformulierungen zu Gott.[12] So findet sich Jes 8,13 LXX („heiligt ihn, den κύριος und er sei eure Furcht")[13] fast wörtlich im Petrusbrief – aber nun auf den zu heiligenden κύριος Christus bezogen.[14] Ähnliche Parallelisierungen finden sich im Römerbrief (zur Joel LXX)[15] oder im Brief an die Philipper (zur Jesaja LXX).[16] Für Athanasius[17] oder Ambrosius[18] belegte vor diesem

---

11. Tatsächlich weisen ältere Handschriftenfragmente zum Beispiel „ΙΑΩ" und andere Umschriften oder Ersatzzeichen (z.B. vier Punkte, vgl. Rösel 1998, 54) für JHWH-Namen auf. Schon Josephus bezeugt aber die Schreibweise κύριος an den Stellen, an denen JHWH gemeint ist. Josephus, *Ant.* 13,68 und 20,90.

12. Es versteht sich von selbst, dass das nicht durchgängig geschah – die neutestamentliche Verwendung des Kyrios-Titels ist nicht einheitlich und Gegenstand umfangreicher und auch kontroverser Untersuchungen geworden. Vgl. nur etwa die klassische Studie von Hahn 1995, zu κύριος 67–132.

13. Jes 8,13 LXX: κύριον αὐτὸν ἁγιάσατε καὶ αὐτὸς ἔσται σου φόβος.

14. 1.Petr 3,15: κύριον δὲ τὸν Χριστὸν ἁγιάσατε ἐν ταῖς καρδίαις ὑμῶν, ἕτοιμοι ἀεὶ πρὸς ἀπολογίαν παντὶ τῷ αἰτοῦντι ὑμᾶς λόγον περὶ τῆς ἐν ὑμῖν ἐλπίδος („Heiligt aber den κύριος Christus in euren Herzen. Seid allezeit bereit zur Verantwortung vor jedermann, der von euch Rechenschaft fordert über die Hoffnung, die in euch ist"). Vgl. zum Begriff der „Heiligung" den Beitrag von Louis Jonker in diesem Band.

15. Vgl. Joel 3,5 LXX: πᾶς, ὃς ἂν ἐπικαλέσηται τὸ ὄνομα κυρίου, σωθήσεται („jeder, der den Namen des Kyrios anrufen wird, der soll errettet werden") und Röm 10,12–13: ὁ γὰρ αὐτὸς κύριος πάντων, πλουτῶν εἰς πάντας τοὺς ἐπικαλουμένους αὐτόν· πᾶς γὰρ ὃς ἂν ἐπικαλέσηται τὸ ὄνομα κυρίου σωθήσετα („es ist über alle derselbe Kyrios, reich für alle, die ihn anrufen. Denn jeder, der den Namen des Kyrios anrufen wird, wird gerettet werden").

16. Vgl. Jes 45,23–24 LXX: κατ' ἐμαυτοῦ ὀμνύω ῏Η μὴν ἐξελεύσεται ἐκ τοῦ στόματός μου δικαιοσύνη, οἱ λόγοι μου οὐκ ἀποστραφήσονται ὅτι ἐμοὶ κάμψει πᾶν γόνυ καὶ ἐξομολογήσεται πᾶσα γλῶσσα τῷ θεῷ λέγων Δικαιοσύνη καὶ δόξα πρὸς αὐτὸν ἥξουσιν („bei mir selbst schwöre ich: Wahrlich, Gerechtigkeit wird aus meinem Munde kommen, meine Worte werden nicht rückgängig gemacht werden, denn vor mir wird sich jedes Knie beugen, und jede Zunge wird sich bekennen vor Gott und sagen: ‚Gerechtigkeit und Herrlichkeit werden zu ihm kommen'"), und Phil 2,9–11: διὸ καὶ ὁ θεὸς αὐτὸν ὑπερύψωσεν καὶ ἐχαρίσατο αὐτῷ τὸ ὄνομα τὸ ὑπὲρ πᾶν ὄνομα, ἵνα ἐν τῷ ὀνόματι ᾿Ιησοῦ πᾶν γόνυ κάμψῃ ἐπουρανίων καὶ ἐπιγείων καὶ καταχθονίων καὶ πᾶσα γλῶσσα ἐξομολογήσηται

Hintergrund der heilige Septuagintatext geradezu die Gleichrangigkeit von Vater und Sohn. An dessen durch den Heiligen Geist verbürgten Autorität gab es kaum Zweifel, selbst wenn hebräische Textfassungen einen anderen Sinn als die Formulierungen in der Septuaginta nahelegten. Berühmt ist die Kontroverse zwischen Augustinus und Hieronymus über die Heiligkeit des Septuagintatextes: Für Augustinus war es angesichts von dessen Würde geradezu unerheblich, was der hebräische Text des Hieronymus oder dessen Übersetzung auf hebräischer Grundlage sagten, erst recht im Hinblick auf den kirchlichen Gebrauch.[19]

Ich möchte im Folgenden die These vertreten, dass sich ein ähnliches Vorgehen und eine ähnliche Umgangsweise der Kirchenväter mit der Septuaginta auch auf einem anderen Feld abzeichnet, und zwar im Bereich der reflektierenden Aussagen über den Menschen und seine ethisch relevanten Entscheidungen.[20] Die im antiken christlichen Gottesdienst regelmäßig und ausführlich vorgelesenen Septuagintatexte boten zahlreiche Anknüpfungspunkte für die ethische Weisung. Jesu Predigt selbst formulierte den Anspruch, „das Gesetz und die Propheten nicht aufzulösen, sondern zu erfüllen" (Mt 5,17). Die Septuaginta, etwa mit ihrer Formulierung des Dekalogs (Ex 20,2–17 LXX; Dtn 5,6–21 LXX) oder der Nächstenliebe (Lev 19,18 LXX; vgl. Mk 12,28–34), stellte der altkirchlichen Predigt Grundtexte präskriptiver Ethik zur Verfügung. Damit ist die

---

ὅτι κύριος Ἰησοῦς Χριστὸς εἰς δόξαν θεοῦ πατρός („darum hat ihn auch Gott erhöht und hat ihm den Namen gegeben, der über alle Namen ist, dass in dem Namen Jesu sich beugen sollen aller derer Knie, die im Himmel und auf Erden und unter der Erde sind und jede Zungen bekennen soll, dass Jesus Christus der Herr ist, zur Herrlichkeit Gottes, des Vaters").

17. So z.B. in seiner Parallelisierung von Jes 44,24 („ich bin der κύριος, der den Himmel ausbreitet allein") mit Joh 1,3 („ohne den Logos ist nichts gemacht, was gemacht ist"). Vgl. Athanasius, *Decr.* 9 u.ö. Zur Verwendung des Septuagintatextes durch Athanasius vgl. die detailreiche Studie von Metzler 1997.

18. Vgl. nur z.B. das Psalmenverständnis des Ambrosius, der die Kyrios-Anrede in Psalm 36 (35) (Christus als Kyrios/*dominus* und Gottesknecht: Ambrosius, *Exp. Ps.* 35), Psalm 38 (37) (Christus als *dominus* und *deus*: Ambrosius, *Exp. Ps.* 37) und Psalm 41 (40) (Leiden Christi: Ambrosius, *Exp. Ps.* 40) direkt auf Christus als Adressaten des Psalms bezieht. Vgl. dazu: auf der Maur 1977, 46–47.88.107–9 u.ö.

19. Vgl. etwa Augustinus, *Ep.* 71,4–6 und 82,34. Vgl. zum Briefwechsel Hennings 1994. Zum Septuagintagebrauch bei Augustinus, siehe Schirner 2015. Zur Autorität der Septuaginta, insbes. 260–87; zu konkreten textkritischen Entscheidungen zugunsten der LXX, vgl. 525–44 u.ö.

20. Vgl. zu diesem Thema allgemein etwa Volp 2018.

Rolle der Septuaginta für die Genese und Entwicklung der antiken christlichen Ethik aber nicht ansatzweise vollständig erfasst, denn eine noch fundamentalere Rolle spielte die anthropologische Begrifflichkeit der Septuaginta für die reflexive Durchdringung ethischer Entscheidungen hinsichtlich ihrer leitenden Normen mit dem Ziel einer Bewertung[21] – also dem, was im Gegensatz zur präskriptiven und deskriptiven Ethik gelegentlich mit dem anachronistischen Begriff der „Metaethik" bezeichnet wird. Im Gegensatz zur Metaethik der Philosophie des 20. Jahrhunderts ging es freilich den antiken christlichen Autoren nicht um eine neutrale Reflexion, sondern um eine wertende und dennoch fundamental reflektierende Verständigung über Natur und Zielrichtung ethischer Entscheidungen. Eine solche fundamentale Rolle lässt sich meines Erachtens jedenfalls dann nicht verneinen, wenn man sich der These anschließt, die patristische Anthropologie sei eine wichtige Voraussetzung für das ethische Denken der Kirchenväter gewesen und der Grundkonsens über den Menschen, wie er in der langwierigen und konfliktuösen Auseinandersetzung mit der Gnosis, mit Markion und mit enkratistischen und rigoristischen Strömungen, aber auch mit der antiken Philosophie im zweiten und dritten Jahrhundert erreicht wurde, habe erst die intellektuelle und dann auch institutionelle Zuwendung zur Ethik ermöglicht, die sich in der antiken Kirche des vierten und fünften Jahrhunderts beobachten lässt.[22] Dabei war der Rückgriff auf die Begrifflichkeiten der Septuaginta meiner Ansicht nach nicht nur im Sinne eines „Einflusses" auf die patristische Theologie bedeutsam. Die Würde des Septuagintatextes war vielmehr eine entscheidende Voraussetzung dafür, dass sich die darauf berufenen Positionen in der christlichen Theologie durchsetzen konnten. Die Plausibilität dieser These soll im Folgenden mit einem notwendigerweise kurzen und exemplarischen Blick auf einige für die Kirchenväter wichtige Begrifflichkeiten der Septuaginta deutlich gemacht werden.

---

21. Diese Definition verdankt sich den Mainzer Forschungen zur antiken, neutestamentlichen und patristischen Ethik („Ethik in Antike und Christentum", www.ethikmainz.de). Vgl. dazu nur etwa die Paradigmen und Überlegungen bei Horn, Volp, und Zimmermann 2013; Volp, Horn, und Zimmermann 2016.

22. Siehe in diesem Sinne Volp 2006.

2. Anthropologische Begrifflichkeiten der Septuaginta: drei Beispiele

Die für diesen Zweck ausgewählten drei Beispiele haben für die patristische Anthropologie und Ethik eine herausragende Rolle gespielt und sind in mancherlei Hinsicht mit dem erwähnten κύριος-Titel vergleichbar, der über die Septuagintatexte von JHWH auf Christus übertragen wurde: Es handelt sich um die Septuagintabegrifflichkeit der Ebenbildlichkeit des Menschen (2.1), um den Terminus ψυχή („Seele"), der häufig, aber nicht immer von der Septuaginta als Übersetzung für נפש im hebräischen Text gewählt wurde (2.2), und schließlich um den für die antike philosophische Ethik wichtigen Begriff der προαίρεσις, der ebenfalls in der Septuaginta auftaucht und von den Kirchenvätern außerordentlich oft verwendet wird (2.3).

2.1. Die Rede von der Ebenbildlichkeit des Menschen

Die Doppelbestimmung der Gottebenbildlichkeit des Menschen mit der εἰκών und der ὁμοίωσις in Gen 1,26 LXX zählt zu den für die christliche Theologie folgenschwersten Übersetzungsentscheidungen der Septuaginta (εἰκών für צלם אלהים und ὁμοίωσις für דמות). Schon früh wurde diese doppelte Bestimmung des frisch geschaffenen Menschen christlich rezipiert, etwa im ersten Clemensbrief (1.Clem 33,4–5; um 100 n. Chr.), bei Justin (*Dial.* 62,1–3; ca. 155–160) oder Athenagoras (um 180).[23] Den Kontext der Rezeption der Schöpfungsgeschichte im späten zweiten Jahrhundert bildete die Auseinandersetzung um die leibliche Auferstehung. Der Glauben an die leibliche Auferstehung, wie er zum Beispiel in den Paulusbriefen vertreten wurde, musste vor allem gegen die leibfeindlichen Gnostiker, aber auch gegen philosophische Einwände verteidigt werden. Wenn Gott den Menschen nach Genesis 1 *ex nihilo* hat erschaffen können (die Erde war nach Gen 1,2 LXX ἀόρατος καὶ ἀκατασκεύαστος),[24] so ein wichtiger

---

23. Hier beziehe ich mich auf den „pseudo-justinischen", von Heimgartner Athenagoras zugeschriebenen Traktat *De resurrectione* (*CPG* 1081; vgl. Heimgartner 2001), der um das Jahr 180 entstanden sein dürfte und der nicht zu verwechseln ist mit dem traditionell unter dem Namen des Athenagoras überlieferten Traktat mit dem gleichen Thema (*CPG* 1071). Dieser nimmt nur implizit Bezug auf die Schöpfungsgeschichte, vor allem unter Hinweis auf die *creatio ex nihilo* des Menschen, die auch eine analoge Neuschöpfung am Ende der Zeiten *ex nihilo*, jedenfalls unabhängig von einem bestimmten Zustand menschlicher Überreste möglich erscheinen lässt. Siehe Ps.-Athenagoras, *Res.* 3 u.ö.

24. Vielleicht am ehesten zu übersetzen mit: „unsichtbar und unausgestattet".

Gedankengang, so wird Gott auch eine Neuschöpfung am Ende der Zeiten mit seiner Allmacht vornehmen können – und zwar ohne Rücksicht auf naturwissenschaftliche Zusammenhänge oder die angebliche Unwürdigkeit von körperlichen Bestandteilen. Folgenschwer war die systematische Einbettung von Gen 1,26 LXX in diesen heilsgeschichtlichen Zusammenhang von Schöpfung und Auferstehung. Ein gutes Beispiel dafür ist der theologische Ansatz des Irenäus von Lyon († um 200 n. Chr.). Irenäus wollte bewusst eine „biblische Theologie" gegen die Gnosis entwerfen und unternahm dies unter Rückgriff auf die Septuaginta und auf Paulus. In der Anthropologie ist seine wichtigste argumentative Grundlage die Septuagintafassung von Gen 1,26 LXX (mit Gen 2,7 LXX), die zum Ausgangspunkt einer heilsgeschichtlichen Rekapitulationslehre wird. Diese *recapitulatio* oder ἀνακεφαλαίωσις soll den theologischen Bezug zwischen Schöpfung und Erlösung herstellen:

> Und Gott sprach: Lasst uns einen Menschen machen nach unserem Bild und nach Ähnlichkeit[25] ... Und Gott formte den Menschen als Auswurf von der Erde und blies in sein Angesicht Lebensatem, und der Mensch wurde zur lebendigen Seele.[26]

Durch die Sünde Adams ging die ὁμοίωσις, die Ähnlichkeit des Menschen mit Gott, verloren. Bei Paulus hieß dieses Verlorengegangene δόξα τοῦ θεοῦ (Röm 3,23) aber bei Irenäus wird daraus in Aufnahme der Septuagintabegrifflichkeit die ὁμοίωσις τοῦ θεοῦ. Auch die platonischen Philosophumena von Bild/Abbild/Ähnlichkeit/Verähnlichung stehen bei dieser Wahl zweifellos im Hintergrund.[27] Der Mensch ist nach dem Fall unfähig zur Vergöttlichung, zur Annäherung an das Göttliche, und damit unfähig zur Erkenntnis und zu einem ethisch perfekten Leben. Auch bei Justin findet sich schon ein ähnlicher Gedanke.[28] Jesus Christus war der erste

---

25. Gen 1,26 LXX: καὶ εἶπεν ὁ θεός· Ποιήσωμεν ἄνθρωπον κατ' εἰκόνα ἡμετέραν καὶ καθ' ὁμοίωσιν.

26. Gen 2,7 LXX: καὶ ἔπλασεν ὁ θεὸς τὸν ἄνθρωπον χοῦν ἀπὸ τῆς γῆς καὶ ἐνεφύσησεν εἰς τὸ πρόσωπον αὐτοῦ πνοὴν ζωῆς καὶ ἐγένετο ὁ ἄνθρωπος εἰς ψυχὴν ζῶσαν.

27. Vgl. dazu Volp 2006, 121–24 u.ö. Diese Adaption hat natürlich eine ähnliche Vorgeschichte bei Philo von Alexandrien. So zitiert Philo, *Fug.* 63, im Zusammenhang mit der Schöpfung ὁμοίωσις τοῦ θεοῦ Platon, *Theaet.* 176ab.

28. Justin konnte mit seiner Theorie vom λόγος σπερματικός, der zwischen Weltentstehung und Inkarnation als „Keim" in der Welt war und demnach sogar im Hinblick auf das philosophische Denken der vorchristlichen Antike Wirksamkeit entfaltete,

Mensch, dem diese ὁμοίωσις wieder zu eigen war. Diese Fleischwerdung des „Wortes Gottes" war für Irenäus die endliche *recapitulatio* und Vollendung des ursprünglich von Gott nach seinem „Bilde" gestalteten und in reiner Idealität gewollten Menschen. Der Fleischgewordene wurde Anfang einer neuen Menschheit. Irenäus entwickelt vor diesem Hintergrund als wohl erster Theologe der Alten Kirche eine umfassende Gesamtschau von Geschichte in Form einer progressiv voranschreitenden Heilsgeschichte. Der Mensch und seine ethischen Möglichkeiten und Aufgaben werden nicht zeitlos gesehen (anders als in der Philosophie), sondern in den heilsgeschichtlichen Fortschritt eingebettet:[29]

Adam	Fall	Moses	Christus
gutes Urbild, aber mit *infirmitas*, *naturalia praecepta Dei*	durch Sünde verdorben	*legislatio*	*recapitulatio* gefallener Schöpfung: non *dissolvit legem, sed extendit et implevit*

Der Sündenfall wurde zum Grund für den Tod, aber nach der Inkarnation ist die Macht des Todes durch die Gerechtigkeit Christi aufgehoben.[30] Christus ist für Irenäus ein Mensch nach dem Willen Gottes. Er ist im Vollsinn εἰκὼν τοῦ θεοῦ, wie es schon im Kolosserhymnus heißt, und zwar wiederum im Anschluss an die Septuaginta (vgl. Gen 1,2.26 LXX u.ö.):

> [Christus] ist das Ebenbild des unsichtbaren Gottes, der Erstgeborene vor aller Schöpfung.[31]

---

nicht nur pagane Kosmogonie und alttestamentliche Schöpfungslehre positiv miteinander in Beziehung setzen, sondern versuchte auch die Vorstellung von der Ebenbildlichkeit des Menschen mit der paganen Philosophie zu vermitteln. Der Mensch ist danach im Urzustand Bild Gottes, diese Gottebenbildlichkeit ist jedoch größtenteils verloren gegangen. Nur die Restbestände des λόγος σπερματικός bewahren ein Stück dieser Ebenbildlichkeit, sie bleiben damit auf die Schöpfungsgeschichte rückbezogen. Justin fordert von allen Christen ein tugendhaftes Leben nach dem Logos, das er im sprachlichen Anschluss an die platonische Tradition als Angleichung an Gott versteht. Vgl. dazu Volp 2006, 130–34 (mit Lit.).

29. Zum Fortschrittsbegriff bei Irenäus vgl. grundlegend Kinzig 1994 (mit weiterer Lit.).

30. Vgl. Röm 3–6.

31. Kol 1,15: ὅς ἐστιν εἰκὼν τοῦ θεοῦ τοῦ ἀοράτου, πρωτότοκος πάσης κτίσεως.

Den Menschen wird dadurch eine teilweise ὁμοίωσις im Sinne einer Angleichung an Christus durch ein auf Christus ausgerichtetes Leben ermöglicht, mit dem man allmählich zur Nachahmerin und zum Nachahmer Christi und damit zur Nachahmerin und zum Nachahmer des Vaters wird – indem man Gott nahe (ἐγγὺς θεοῦ) wird, eine Formulierung, die Irenäus der Septuagintafassung von Weish 6,19 entnimmt.[32]

Diese Konstruktion wurde für die Ethik deshalb richtungsweisend, weil es damit gelang, eine auf der Septuaginta basierende Schöpfungsethik mit der jesuanischen Nachfolgeethik zusammenzubringen. In Christus ist für Irenäus die Natur erschienen, damit ist das richtige, christlich-ethische Handeln zugleich schöpfungsgemäßes, naturgemäßes Handeln. Man hat in Irenäus darum faktisch einen Begründer des christlichen Naturrechts gesehen.[33] Die Rekapitulation hat ja die Wiederherstellung eines natürlichen Urzustands zum Ziel, der auch der Maßstab für richtig und falsch ist. Im Gegensatz aber zu naturrechtlichen Vorstellungen etwa in der Stoa machte das durch den Septuagintatext der Schöpfungsgeschichte begründete heilsgeschichtliche Modell die Differenz zwischen defizitärer – christlich gesprochen: sündhafter – Welt und diesem guten Naturzustand verstehbar. Dies erklärt den außerordentlichen Erfolg, den diese heilsgeschichtliche Übertragung der Septuagintaunterscheidung von εἰκών und ὁμοίωσις in der patristischen Theologie erlebte. Die Kirchenväter unterschieden fortan zwischen dem wahren Menschen, dem *homo primigenius* (εἰκὼν καὶ ὁμοίωσις), und dem *homo lapsus* (mit verlorengegangener ὁμοίωσις), zwischen dem *status naturae integrae* und dem *status naturae lapsae*. Der wahre Mensch stand als Christus und damit als eschatologische Größe vor Augen, aber eben auch als ethisches Vorbild.

---

32. Irenäus, *Adv. haer.* 4,38,3: „Der Mensch musste zunächst einmal entstehen, dann wachsen, dann kräftig werden, dann sich vermehren, dann stark werden, dann verherrlicht werden und dann seinen Gott schauen. Denn Gott ist es, den wir schauen sollen; die Anschauung Gottes führt zur Unvergänglichkeit, ‚die Unvergänglichkeit aber macht uns Gott nah'". *Oportuerat autem hominem primo fieri, et factum augeri, et auctum corroborari, et corroboratum multiplicari, et multiplicatum convalescere, convalescentem vero glorificari, et glorificatum videre suum dominum: Deus enim est qui habet videri, visio autem Dei efficax est incorruptelae,* „*incorrupta vero proximum facit esse Deo*" (ἀφθαρσία δὲ ἐγγὺς εἶναι ποιεῖ θεοῦ Weish 6,19). (SC 100/2,956,19–25; vgl. FC 8/4,339–41).

33. Vgl. etwa Flückiger 1954.

2.2. ψυχή

Irenäus lokalisierte den Sitz der ὁμοίωσις eindeutig in der ψυχή, der Seele, die den Geist Gottes aufnehmen kann und soll.[34] Das ist nicht erstaunlich, denn die Kirchenväter gingen häufig von einer dreifachen Anthropologie aus, indem sie zum Beispiel zwischen Körper, Seele und Geist unterschieden.[35] Diese Dreiheit spielt auch als Hintergrund zu den christologischen Debatten eine wichtige Rolle.[36] Schon in Platons *Timaios* findet sich eine solche Dreiheit von ψυχή, νοῦς und σῶμα.[37] Dazu kommt Platons wohl an Sokrates anschließende Überzeugung, die Seele sei der Ort ethischer Entscheidungen.[38] Sie findet sich auch bei dem ebenfalls dem Platonismus zugeneigten Philo.[39] Es greift aber zu kurz, wenn man nur dem Platonismus die Schuld am Seelenbegriff der Kirchenväter geben wollte. Sie fanden ihn nämlich ihrer Ansicht nach in der Bibel, in der Septuaginta, die im Detail auch gegen Platon ins Feld geführt wurde.[40] Insgesamt findet sich hier der griechische Begriff ψυχή fast 1000 mal, häufig, aber nicht nur als Übersetzung von נפש.[41] Dabei sind es gerade die bei den Vätern immer wiederkehrenden Eigenschaften der ψυχή, die dem Körper das Leben gibt, die Sitz ethischer Entscheidung ist, damit das „Eigentliche" des Menschen ausmacht und von Gott zu einem bestimmten Zeitpunkt geschaffen wurde, aber als Ganzes unsterblich ist, so lange Gott das will.

---

34. Irenäus benutzt die ψυχή-Terminologie alleine in *Adv. haer.* fast 100 mal.
35. Vgl. Volp 2006, 104–232.
36. Vgl. dazu z.B. Thümmel 1998.
37. Plato, *Tim.* 28a-29a. Innerhalb der ψυχή unterscheidet Platon auch noch drei Seelenteile (λογιστικόν, θυμοειδές, ἐπιθυμητικόν. Platon, *Resp.* 4,439c-441b u.ö.), auch dies wird von den Kirchenvätern breit rezipiert, vgl. dazu Volp 2006, *passim*.
38. Vgl. dazu zuletzt Drews 2013, außerdem etwa die Beiträge von Christoph Horn und Christian Pietsch in dem genannten Band.
39. Philo bezieht diese den Menschen im Gegensatz zu Tieren auszeichnende Seelenauffassung auf die (biblische) Schöpfung durch Gott. Philo, *Deus* 46-48 (zu Gen 1 und Gen 6,5-12 LXX; Mosés 1963, 84,5–86,6); an der Stelle rechtfertigt Philo u.a. die Bestrafung allein für menschliche Seelen auf Grund ethisch falscher Entscheidungen. Vgl. dazu etwa Frick 1999, 153–67.
40. So kritisiert Irenäus etwa die Lehre von der Seelenwanderung. Vgl. seine harsche Kritik am Schlussmythos der Politeia (Platon, *Resp.* 10, 619b-621b) in *Adv. haer.* 2,33,2. Vgl. Justin, *Dial.* 5-7.
41. Vgl. dazu etwa Rösel 2009.

Es sind dies Bestimmungen, die sie in der Septuaginta fanden. In Gen 2,7 LXX heißt es zum Beispiel:

> [Gott] blies in sein Angesicht den Odem des Lebens, und der Mensch wurde zur lebendigen Seele.[42]

Irenäus zitierte (*Adv. haer.* 5,7,1) diese Stelle im Zusammenhang mit Ps 22 (21),30.[43] Beide Stellen im Zusammenhang definierten für ihn alle die genannten Eigenschaften: Die ψυχή ist belebend, entscheidend, eigentlich, geschaffen und unsterblich. Ganz unplatonisch ist dabei die bei Irenäus zum Ausdruck kommende völlige, auch erkenntnistheoretische Abhängigkeit vom Schöpfer:

> Der Herr lehrte uns, dass niemand Gott kennen kann, wenn nicht Gott ihn belehrt. Das heißt, dass ohne Gott Gott nicht zu erkennen ist. Und dass das ihn-Erkennen genau Wille des Vaters ist. Es erkennen ihn nämlich diejenigen, denen der Sohn es offenbart.[44]

Origenes band diese Auffassungen von der menschlichen Seele in seine großangelegte Kosmologie ein. Darin interpretierte er den Fall Adams als Fall der Gott überdrüssig gewordenen Vernunftwesen. Diese νόες verdichteten sich in ihrem Fall durch „Abkühlung" (ἀποψύχεσθαι) zu ψυχαί bzw. ψυχικαί, also „Seelen"-Wesen.[45] Eines dieser Wesen freilich fiel nicht, sondern nahm in der Inkarnation in der Gestalt Jesu Fleisch an, eine mit dem Logos vereinte Seele.[46] Clemens von Alexandrien hatte Gen 1,26 LXX dahingehend interpretiert, dass der Mensch nur Abbild des Logos, der Logos aber Abbild Gottes sei:

> Abbild Gottes ist sein Logos ... Abbild des Logos ist aber der wahrhaftige Mensch, der Geist im Menschen, von dem es deswegen heißt, dass

---

42. Gen 2,7 LXX: καὶ ἐνεφύσησεν εἰς τὸ πρόσωπον αὐτοῦ πνοὴν ζωῆς καὶ ἐγένετο ὁ ἄνθρωπος εἰς ψυχὴν ζῶσαν.
43. Ps 22 (21),30: καὶ ἡ ψυχή μου αὐτῷ ζῇ („Und meine Seele wird für ihn leben").
44. Irenäus, *Adv. haer.* 4,6,4: Ἐδίδαξεν ἡμᾶς ὁ Κύριος ὅτι Θεὸν εἰδέναι οὐδεὶς δύναται μὴ οὐχὶ Θεοῦ διδάξαντος, τουτέστιν ἄνευ Θεοῦ μὴ γινώσκεσθαι τὸν Θεόν· αὐτὸ δὲ τὸ γινώσκεσθαι αὐτὸν θέλημα εἶναι τοῦ Πατρός· γνώσονται γὰρ αὐτὸν οἷς ἂν ἀποκαλύψῃ ὁ Υἱός (frg. 5 Holl 61; SC 100/2, 446). Vgl. Mt 11,27.
45. Origenes, *Princ.* 2,8,3.
46. Origenes, *Comm. Jo.* 20,19,162, und *Princ.* 2,6,3

er nach dem Bild Gottes und seiner Ähnlichkeit[47] geschaffen worden sei. Der Mensch, der durch das Denken in seinem Herzen dem göttlichen Logos ähnlich und dadurch vernünftig geworden ist.[48]

Origenes bezog dieses Abbild, das ja platonisch gedacht immer auch Seinsmitteilung ist, auf die ψυχή:

> Es gibt nun aber einen, den Sohn Gottes, der Bild des unsichtbaren Gottes ist, und dessen Bild, das sogenannte Bild des Sohnes Gottes. Ich meine, dass dieses Bild die menschliche Seele (ψυχή) ist, die der Sohn Gottes angenommen hat, als solche, die durch die Tugend Bild des Bildes Gottes geworden ist.[49]

Nach Origenes ist also nichts anderes als die ψυχή Bild Gottes – und zwar die ψυχή, die der Sohn angenommen hat durch ihre ἀρετή. Eine – im Einzelnen dann zuweilen unterschiedlich bestimmte – Verbindung von ψυχή, Ebenbild und Tugend findet sich wieder und wieder bei den späteren Kirchenvätern.[50] Die Septuaginta schien dieser Verbindung auch nicht zu widersprechen, wenn es in den *Proverbia* zum Beispiel heißt (eine Stelle, auf die sich der große Prediger Johannes Chrysostomus[51] oder Ephraem der Syrer[52] beziehen): „Binde [die Gebote und Weisungen] auf deine Seele allezeit".[53]

---

47. Gen 1,26 LXX.
48. Clemens Alexandrinus, *Protr.* 10,98,3: Εἰκὼν μὲν γὰρ τοῦ θεοῦ ὁ λόγος αὐτοῦ ..., εἰκὼν δὲ τοῦ λόγου ὁ ἄνθρωπος ἀληθινός, ὁ νοῦς ὁ ἐν ἀνθρώπῳ, ὁ κατ' εἰκόνα τοῦ θεοῦ καὶ καθ' ὁμοίωσιν διὰ τοῦτο γεγενῆσθαι λεγόμενος, τῇ κατὰ καρδίαν φρονήσει τῷ θείῳ παρεικαζόμενος λόγῳ καὶ ταύτῃ λογικός (GCS 12, 71,26–29; vgl. BKV² 2.R. 7, 174).
49. Origenes, *Comm. Rom.* = *Philoc.* 25,2: Ἔστιν οὖν τις ὁ υἱὸς τοῦ θεοῦ, εἰκὼν τυγχάνων τοῦ θεοῦ τοῦ ἀοράτου, καὶ τούτου εἰκὼν ἡ λεγομένη εἰκὼν τοῦ υἱοῦ τοῦ θεοῦ· ἥντινα νομίζω εἶναι ἣν ἀνέλαβεν ψυχὴν ὁ υἱὸς τοῦ θεοῦ ἀνθρωπίνην, γενομένην διὰ τὴν ἀρετὴν τῆς εἰκόνος τοῦ θεοῦ εἰκόνα (SC 226,218).
50. Vgl. z.B. Lactantius, *Ir.* 19; Epiphanius Salaminis, *Ancoratus* 55f. (mit aufschlussreichen kritischen Überlegungen zu der Dreiheit von Seele, Ebenbild und Tugend); Augustinus, *Sermo de Symbolo* 11 u.ö.; Johannes Damascenus, *Expositio fidei* 3,18 u.a.
51. Johannes Chrysostomus, *Frag. Prov.* 676 (PG 64).
52. Ephraem Syrus (Ephraem Graecus), *De his, qui animas ad impudicitiam pelliciunt, cum dicant nihil mali esse* (Phrantzoles 1994, 207–23, 210,3).
53. Spr 6,20f. LXX: [νόμους καὶ θεσμοὺς] ἄφαψαι δὲ αὐτοὺς ἐπὶ σῇ ψυχῇ διὰ παντός. (siehe oben Anm. 1).

Immer wieder geht es dabei um die Frage, weshalb der Mensch oft nicht das Richtige – die Tugend – tut, und warum auch Christen oft nicht das tun, was ihnen die christliche Predigt als richtig aufgezeigt hat. Es gibt dafür im Wesentlichen zwei Antworten: Entweder haben sie ihre Seele noch nicht ausreichend an Gott angenähert oder es handelt sich schlicht um den in diesem Leben unausräumbaren Konflikt zwischen Seele und Körper. Letzteren beschrieb etwa Ambrosius von Mailand mit nachhaltiger Wirkung. Im Urzustand waren seiner Ansicht nach Körper und Seele eins und taten stets dasselbe. Seit dem Fall gibt es jedoch einen Zwiespalt im Menschen:

> Wie man sehen kann, drang der Zwiespalt zwischen Körper und Seele durch die Untreue des ersten Menschen in die Natur ein, so dass sie [sc. Körper und Seele] sich nicht mehr im gleichen Tugendstreben begegneten.[54]

Ambrosius unterschied den geistigen und „wahren" Menschen, das menschliche *nos*, vom *nostra* und vom *circa nos*, also vom äußeren Menschen, das heißt Körperteile, Sinne etc. und den Dingen, die den meisten Menschen besonders wichtig sind, aber mit dem Menschsein eigentlich nichts zu tun haben, also etwa Geld, Sklaven und Güter. Die Seele ist *imago* Gottes, der Körper verbindet die Menschen dagegen mit den Tieren.[55] Unsere Seele ist

> nach dem Bild Gottes. In ihm, Mensch, ruht dein ganzes Sein; denn ohne es bist du nichts, sondern du bist Erde und wirst in Erde aufgelöst.[56]

Auch das Paradies konnte Ambrosius insgesamt als „Seele" deuten.[57] Nach dem Septuagintatext wurde nämlich das Paradies von Gott geschaffen als

---

54. Ambrosius, *Exp. Luc.* 7,141: *Possunt etiam uideri caro atque anima ... dissensio per praeuaricationem primi hominis in naturam uerterit, ut nequaquam sibi paribus ad uirtutem studiis conuenirent* (CCSL 14, 263,1521–23).

55. Ambrosius, *Hex.* 6,42–46.

56. Ambrosius, *Hex.* 6,43: *...ad imaginem dei est. In hac totus es, homo, quia sine haec nihil es, sed es terra et in terram resolueris* (CSEL 32/1, 234,13–16). Vgl. auch noch Ambrosius, *Exp. Luc.* 2.

57. Ambrosius, *Parad.* 3,12: „Also ist das Paradies gewissermaßen eine fruchtbare Seele." *Est ergo paradisus terra quaedam fertilis hoc est anima fecunda.*

ein Gewimmel von ψυχαὶ ζωσαί.⁵⁸ Auch die Menschenschöpfung ist nichts anderes als eine Schaffung „zur lebenden Seele", εἰς ψυχὴν ζῶσαν (Gen 2,7 LXX). An anderer Stelle greift Ambrosius die Formulierung aus Gen 1,21 LXX auf, wonach Gott jede Seele der Kriechtiere geschaffen hat⁵⁹ – eine erhebliche Abweichung von der hebräischen Syntax, die eine dichotome Anthropologie gut anschlussfähig machte. Ambrosius verwies außerdem auf Ez 18,20 LXX, wonach die Seele, die sündigt, sterben wird.⁶⁰ Der Septuagintatext ergab für Ambrosius nur einen Sinn, wenn es um den Ausschluss derjenigen Seelen von der Auferstehung ging, die sich durch keinen tugendhaften Lebenswandel ausgezeichnet hatten. Auch hier bestimmte also die Septuagintabegrifflichkeit von ψυχή Anthropologie und Ethik.

2.3. προαίρεσις

Abschließend sei mit der προαίρεσις hier ein dritter Grundbegriff ins Gespräch gebracht, der für die ethischen Überlegungen mancher Kirchenväter wie Clemens von Alexandrien, Origenes oder Johannes Chrysostomus und Philosophen wie Aristoteles und Epiktet eine herausragende Rolle spielte,⁶¹ dessen Rolle in der Septuaginta aber meines Wissens nach bisher nicht umfänglich untersucht worden ist.⁶² Der Begriff der προαίρεσις ist deshalb besonders interessant, weil sein Gebrauch unweigerlich in den Bereich metaethischer Reflexion hineinreicht. Die προαίρεσις ist in der ethischen Theorie bei Aristoteles,⁶³ in

---

58. Gen 1,20 LXX: Καὶ εἶπεν ὁ θεός Ἐξαγαγέτω τὰ ὕδατα ἑρπετὰ ψυχῶν ζωσῶν καὶ πετεινὰ πετόμενα ἐπὶ τῆς γῆς κατὰ τὸ στερέωμα τοῦ οὐρανοῦ. καὶ ἐγένετο οὕτως. „Und Gott sprach: Die Wasser sollen Kriechtiere mit lebenden Seelen hervorbringen und Flugtiere, die auf der Erde am festen Himmelskörper entlangfliegen. Und so geschah es" (LXX.D).
59. Ambrosius, Hex. 5,1,1 und 5,2,5 u.ö.
60. Ez 18,20 LXX: ἡ δὲ ψυχὴ ἡ ἁρματάνουσα ἀποθανεῖται („Die Seele aber, die sündigt, wird sterben") (LXX.D).
61. Vgl. dazu etwa den Überblick bei Laks 1989. Zum Gebrauch bei Aristoteles vgl. außerdem z.B. Chamberlain 1984. Zu Epiktet vgl. z.B. Dobbin 1991; Long 2002. Ein ausführlicher Vergleich des Gebrauchs bei Aristoteles und Epiktet findet sich bei Dragona-Monachou 1978–1979.
62. Vgl. aber dazu z.B. Siegert 2001, 261–62.
63. Aristoteles, Eth. nic. 3,4,1112a; 4,2,1139ab u.ö.

der Stoa[64] oder auch im antiken forensischen Kontext[65] die bewusste Entscheidung für oder gegen eine bestimmte Handlungsalternative, eine Wahl im Sinne des Vorziehens einer von mehreren Möglichkeiten. Eine προαίρεσις-Entscheidung ist moralisch und intellektuell qualifiziert – anders als eine triebhafte Entscheidung (aus ὁρμή) oder ein Beschluss vor dem Hintergrund von Unwissenheit (ἀγνοία). Clemens von Alexandrien kann vor dem Hintergrund eines solchen Gebrauchs die Verdienstlichkeit guter Taten von einer vorausgegangenen Entscheidung auf Grund von προαίρεσις abhängig machen:

> Denn manchmal möchten wir durch eine Geldgabe oder durch eine persönliche Hilfeleistung Barmherzigkeit erweisen, zum Beispiel einem Bedürftigen helfen oder einen Kranken pflegen oder einem, der ins Unglück geraten ist, beistehen. Aber wir sind, entweder wegen Armut oder Krankheit oder hohen Alters (auch dieses ist ja eine natürliche Krankheit) nicht dazu imstande, unseren Vorsatz auszuführen, zu dem wir uns getrieben fühlen, so dass wir das, was wir wollten, nicht zu Ende führen können. Die gleiche Ehre also wie die, die etwas tun konnten, werden die erlangen, die den Willen dazu hatten, bei denen die Absicht (προαίρεσις) die gleiche war, wenn auch das Vermögen bei anderen größer war.[66]

Eine nur zufällig gute Entscheidung hat für Clemens keinerlei Verdienstlichkeit, ja, sie ist in eschatologischer Perspektive – *coram Deo* – gar keine Entscheidung, und sie ist auch nicht ethisch relevant.[67]

Auch die Septuaginta kennt diesen Begriff. Er kommt 15 mal vor, darunter zweimal bei Jeremia (8,5; 14,14 [2x]), im Richterbuch (5,2), in den Makkabäerbüchern,[68] bei Kohelet (1,14.17; 2,11.17.22.26; 4,4.6.16) und

---

64. Epictetus, *Diatr.* 1,17,21–4,29,39; 4,5,12 u.ö.
65. Vgl. etwa Polybius, *Hist.* 12,12,4f.
66. Clemens Alexandrinus, *Strom.* 4,38,3–4: ἐνίοτε γὰρ βουλόμεθα δι' ἀργυρίου δόσεως ἢ διὰ σωματικῆς σπουδῆς ἔλεον ποιῆσαι, ὡς δεομένῳ ἐπαρκέσαι ἢ νοσοῦντι ὑπουργῆσαι ἢ ἐν περιστάσει γενομένῳ παραστῆναι, καὶ οὐχ οἷοί τέ ἐσμεν ἤτοι διὰ πενίαν ἢ νόσον ἢ γῆρας (φυσικὴ γὰρ νόσος καὶ τοῦτο) ἐξυπηρετῆσαι τῇ προαιρέσει ἐφ' ἣν ὁρμώμεθα, μὴ δυνηθέντες ἐπὶ τέλος ἀγαγεῖν ὃ βεβουλήμεθα. τῆς αὐτῆς οὖν τιμῆς μεθέξουσι τοῖς δυνηθεῖσιν οἱ βεβουλημένοι, ὧν ἡ προαίρεσις ἴση, κἂν πλεονεκτῶσιν ἕτεροι τῇ περιουσίᾳ. (GCS 15⁴, 265,17–24; vgl. BKV² 2. R. 19,33).
67. Bei Serapion von Thmuis († um 370 n. Chr.) finden sich ähnliche Aussagen: Serapion von Thmuis, *Adv. Man.* 4 (PG 40, 904).
68. 2.Makk 2,6; 9,27; 11,26 sowie 3.Makk 6,10 und 7,2.

in den Sprüchen Salomos.⁶⁹ Meistens geht es dabei der Sache nach um eine bewusste und schwerwiegende Handlungsentscheidung – auch wenn der hebräische Text natürlich nicht die eben genannten metaethischen Konnotationen rechtfertigt, die jemand wie Clemens von Alexandrien oder andere philosophisch gebildete antike Zeitgenossen mit dem Wort προαίρεσις verbunden haben dürften.⁷⁰ Das „Siegeslied Deboras" im Richterbuch etwa verwendet προαίρεσις für die Entscheidung des Volkes, JHWH und ihr zu folgen und Sisera und die Kanaaniten zu besiegen:

> Weil Führer in Israel führten in der Entscheidung (προαίρεσις) des Volkes: Preist den Herrn.⁷¹

In Jer 8,5 und 14,14 geht es bei der προαίρεσις καρδίας um die Entscheidung gegen JHWH – ebenfalls eine Entscheidung aus freien Stücken, was Grundlage für die Verwerfung durch den Propheten ist:

> Warum wandte sich dieses mein Volk in schamloser Abwendung ab? Warum hielten sie an ihrer Entscheidung (προαίρεσις) fest und wollten nicht umkehren?⁷²

Die Kirchenväter haben diese Stellen rezipiert. Bei Origenes etwa wird deutlich, dass er den Begriff der προαίρεσις auch deshalb ausgiebig – an mindestens 164 Stellen des erhaltenen Werkes – verwendet, weil er ihn in der Septuagintaübersetzung von Jer 8,5 und 14,14 findet. An einer entscheidenden Stelle beschreibt Origenes in seinem Jeremiakommentar ausführlich, wie christliche Lebensführung idealerweise auszusehen hat, wie ethische Entscheidungen zu treffen sind, und an welchen Vorbildern sich die Christen orientieren sollten:

> Und wenn wir die Angelegenheiten wahrhaftig in Wahrheit und nicht mit dem Mob beurteilen, wenn wir die Angelegenheiten aus freien Stücken bewusst (προαίρεσις) beurteilen und nicht auf die Meinung der versammelten Vielen blicken, werden wir sehen, dass wir jetzt nicht gläubig

---

69. Spr 21,25, hier allerdings in der finiten Verbalform προαιροῦνται.
70. Vgl. auch die Lit. und Quellen oben in Anm. 61, 63, und 64.
71. Ri 5,2 LXX: Ἐν τῷ ἄρξασθαι ἀρχηγοὺς ἐν Ισραηλ ἐν προαιρέσει λαοῦ εὐλογεῖτε τὸν κύριον.
72. Jer 8,5 LXX: διὰ τί ἀπέστρεψεν ὁ λαός μου οὗτος ἀποστροφὴν ἀναιδῆ καὶ κατεκρατήθησαν ἐν τῇ προαιρέσει αὐτῶν καὶ οὐκ ἠθέλησαν τοῦ ἐπιστρέψαι;

sind. Damals aber gab es Gläubige, als die echten Martyrien geschahen, als wir, nachdem wir den Märtyrern das letzte Geleit gegeben hatten, von den Begräbnisstätten aus zu den Versammlungshäusern gingen und sich die ganze Gemeinde ohne irgendwelche Furcht einfand, als die Katechumenen bei den Bezeugungen derer belehrt wurden, welche, ‚nicht eingeschüchtert' (Phil 1,28) und nicht verwirrt, die Wahrheit ‚bis in den Tod' (Offb 2,10) ‚zum lebendigen Gott hin' (Apg 14,15) bekannten.[73]

Ein besonderer Fall ist der häufige Gebrauch von προαίρεσις bei Kohelet,[74] denn hier taucht immer wiederkehrend die Formel προαίρεσις πνεύματος auf: Der Septuagintaübersetzer verwendet προαίρεσις πνεύματος, um רְעוּת רוּחַ und רַעְיוֹן רוּחַ zu übersetzen, also das unnütze „Streben nach dem Wind" bzw. „Haschen nach dem Wind", wie wir es aus der Lutherbibel seit 1912 kennen.[75] Da προαίρεσις πνεύματος aber für griechische antike Ohren die freie Willenswahl des Geistes bezeichnet, entspricht dies kaum dem Sinn der Stelle, wie er von der antiken Leserschaft der Septuaginta aufgefasst wurde.[76]

---

73. Origenes, *Hom. Jer.* 4,3: Καὶ ἀληθῶς ἐὰν κρίνωμεν τὰ πράγματα ἀληθείᾳ καὶ μὴ ὄχλοις, καὶ κρίνωμεν τὰ πράγματα προαιρέσει καὶ μὴ τῷ βλέπειν πολλοὺς συναγομένους, ὀψόμεθα νῦν ὡς οὐκ ἐσμὲν πιστοί· ἀλλὰ τότε ἦσαν πιστοί, ὅτε τὰ μαρτύρια τὰ γενναῖα ἐγίνοντο, ὅτε ἀπὸ τῶν κοιμητηρίων προπέμψαντες τοὺς μάρτυρας ἠρχόμεθα ἐπὶ τὰς συναγωγάς, καὶ ὅλη ἡ ἐκκλησία μὴ θλιβομένη παρεγίνετο, καὶ οἱ κατηχούμενοι ἐπὶ τοῖς μαρτυρίοις κατηχοῦντο καὶ ἐπὶ τοῖς θανάτοις τῶν ὁμολογούντων τὴν ἀλήθειαν μέχρι θανάτου, μὴ πτυρόμενοι μηδὲ ταρασσόμενοι 'ἐπὶ τὸν ζῶντα θεόν' (SC 232, 264, 12–21; vgl. BGrL 10, 74).

74. Die reichliche und frühe Ecclesiasteskommentierung der Väter hat in der Forschung durchaus zu Verwunderung geführt: Hippolyt, Origenes, Gregorius Thaumaturgos, Dionysius von Alexandrien, Didymus der Blinde, Gregor von Nyssa – sie alle haben sich ausführlich mit Kohelet beschäftigt. Martin Hengel vermutete hierin schlicht den Zwang zur Allegorese, der die Kommentierung dieser seiner Ansicht nach theologisch wenig gehaltvollen Texte intellektuell reizvoll machte. Hengel 1994, 230.

75. Luther selbst übersetzte hier freier, z.B. „muehe und jamer" (1534) oder „eitel vnd jamer" (Biblia devtsch 1545). Die Formulierung „Haschen nach dem Wind" wird 1848 in der kommentierten Lutherausgabe von Bindseil/Niemeyer vorgeschlagen: Bindseil und Niemeyer 1848, 404, Anm. zu Koh 6,9.

76. Koh 1,17–18 nach Lutherbibel 2017: „Und ich richtete mein Herz darauf, dass ich lernte Weisheit und erkennte Tollheit und Torheit. Ich ward aber gewahr, dass auch dies ein Haschen nach Wind ist. Denn wo viel Weisheit ist, da ist viel Grämen, und wer viel lernt, der muss viel leiden".

So kommt es etwa Clemens von Alexandrien auf die προαίρεσις πνεύματος an, also auf die richtige Auswahl des Geistes, „ob mit einer Fülle von Weisheit auch eine Fülle von Erkenntnis verbunden ist", oder ob es eben nichtiges Wissen bleibt:

> Es steht ja im Prediger geschrieben: „Und ich gewann mehr Weisheit als alle, die vor mir in Jerusalem gewesen sind; und mein Herz sah vieles, Weisheit und Erkenntnis; Gleichnisse und Wissenschaft lernte ich kennen; denn auch dies ist die bewusste Entscheidung (προαίρεσις) des Geistes, dass mit einer Fülle an Weisheit auch eine Fülle an Erkenntnis verbunden ist"[77] … „Reichtum an Erkenntnis der Weisheit wird dem das Leben schenken, der von ihr abstammt"[78] … „Denn Weisheit ist mehr wert als kostbare Steine, alle Kleinodien wiegen sie nicht auf"[79].[80]

Statt des unnützen Anhäufens von Wissen erkennt Clemens angesichts der für ihn ganz positiv besetzten προαίρεσις πνεύματος hier geradezu ein pädagogisches Programm!

In einer zugespitzten Form begegnet das Konzept bei dem für seine moralischen Ermahnungen bekannten Kirchenvater Johannes Chrysostomos. Er verwendet den Begriff προαίρεσις mehr als alle anderen Kirchenväter. Fast 800 Erwähnungen finden sich alleine in den erhaltenen Schriften.[81] In seinen berühmten Taufkatechesen etwa läuft am Ende alles auf den Moment der προαίρεσις zu. Nachdem der Kirchenvater die ethischen Konsequenzen des neuen Lebens den Taufbewerbern eindringlich und in immer neuen Beispielen vor Augen gestellt hat,[82] kann er am

---

77. Vgl. Koh 1,16–18 LXX.
78. Vgl. Koh 7,13 LXX.
79. Vgl. Spr 8,9–11 LXX.
80. Clemens Alexandrinus, *Strom.* 1,13,58,1–4: γέγραπται γοῦν ἐν τῷ Ἐκκλησιαστῇ· καὶ προσέθηκα σοφίαν ἐπὶ πᾶσιν, οἳ δὴ ἐγένοντο ἔμπροσθέν μου ἐν Ἰερουσαλήμ· καὶ ἡ καρδία μου εἶδεν πολλά, σοφίαν καὶ γνῶσιν, παραβολὰς καὶ ἐπιστήμην ἔγνων. ὅτι καί γε τοῦτό ἐστι προαίρεσις πνεύματος, ὅτι ἐν πλήθει σοφίας πλῆθος γνώσεως … περισσεία γνώσεως τῆς σοφίας ζωοποιήσει τὸν παρ' αὐτῆς … κρείσσων γὰρ σοφία λίθων πολυτελῶν, πᾶν δὲ τίμιον οὐκ ἄξιον αὐτῆς (GCS 15⁴, 37,2–15; BKV² 2. R. 17, 57).
81. Anthropologisch reflektiert er die προαίρεσις z.B. in Chrysostomus, *Hom. Gen.* 19 (*CPG* 4409; PG 53, 158). Vgl. zur ethischen Konkretion seines προαίρεσις-Begriffs etwa Chrysostomus, *Stat.* 16,2 (*CPG* 4330).
82. Dazu gehört auch etwa das Almosengeben, das aber ohne προαίρεσις wertlos ist. Chrysostomus, *Catech. illum.* 1,14 (PG 49, 237; *CPG* 4330).

Schluss fordern: „Nötig ist alleine deine προαίρεσις", also deine freie Entscheidung für oder gegen Gott.[83]

An der προαίρεσις hängt für Chrysostomos letztlich alles. Sie steht für die Wahl zwischen einem Leben in Christus oder einem Tod in Gottesferne.[84] Es erscheint mir kaum denkbar, dass es zu einer solch radikalen Zuspitzung des προαίρεσις-Begriffes ohne die Verwendung in den prophetischen Texten der Septuaginta gekommen wäre. Die akademisch-elitären Ausführungen zu ethischen Handlungsalternativen in der nikomachischen Ethik des Aristoteles reichen als Hintergrund jedenfalls nicht aus.

3. Fazit

„Brich nicht die Ehe. Stiehl nicht. Morde nicht".[85] Der Wortlaut der Septuaginta prägt ganz wesentlich die christliche Ethik der Antike. Es sind diese prohibitiven Formen im griechischen Konjunktiv Aorist, die als Gottes Gebote aus der Septuaginta Eingang in die präskriptive christliche Ethik fanden, in ethische Ermahnungen und in auf die Lebensführung zielende Predigt. Einzelne Formulierungen der Septuaginta wurden aber auch zum Anknüpfungspunkt für mehr. Ich habe versucht, deutlich zu machen, inwiefern das für die Unterscheidung von εἰκών und ὁμοίωσις, und für die Begriffe ψυχή und προαίρεσις gelten kann. Man könnte Ähnliches für andere Begriffe aufzeigen. Die Vorstellung, dass der Mensch als εἰκών und in der ὁμοίωσις Gottes geschaffen wurde, dass die erfahrene, ethisch defizitäre Existenz des Menschen Zeichen des Verlustes der ὁμοίωσις ist, aber auch der durch den Fall verursachten Spannung zwischen menschlicher ψυχή und menschlicher Körperlichkeit; dass es seit der Inkarnation am einzelnen Christen selbst liegt, diese Diskrepanzen durch eine freie Entscheidung – προαίρεσις – aufzulösen: dieses Grundschema heilsgeschichtlichen Denkens bestimmt die Ethik der hier untersuchten Kirchenväter durchaus im Widerspruch zu den philosophischen Tugendlehren. Ohne Grundlage in ihrem biblischen Text – der Septuaginta – wäre dies meiner Ansicht nach kaum vorstellbar gewesen. Es lag mithin in

---

83. Chrysostomus, *Catech. ult.* 3,6: τῆς προαιρέσεώς σου γὰρ δεῖται μόνης (SC 366, 234, 12f.; *CPG* 4462). Vgl. Chrysostomus, *Catech. ult.* 3/1, 10 (*CPG* 4465).

84. Dass die προαίρεσις nie das Werk Gottes sein kann, sondern alleine eine menschliche Entscheidung *coram Deo*, sagt Chrysostomos verschiedentlich. Siehe z.B. Chrysostomus, *Diab.* 1,5 (*CPG* 4495/34; PG 49, 251).

85. Ex 20,13–15 LXX: οὐ μοιχεύσεις. οὐ κλέψεις. οὐ φονεύσεις.

der Terminologie der Septuaginta begründet, dass die Kirchenväter der Ansicht waren, in ihren Überlegungen zur Ethik und Anthropologie keine „Hellenisierung" der biblischen Überlieferung vorzunehmen, wie ihnen später vorgeworfen werden sollte,[86] sondern vielmehr gut biblisch zu argumentieren. Die Differenz der Septuagintaworte zum hebräischen Bibeltext ist auch deshalb relevant, weil wir uns damit auch einer Differenz bewusst werden zwischen der heutigen, durch die historisch-kritische Exegese geschulten Lektüre der Väter und der damaligen theologischen Welt, in der die Septuaginta „the first Bible of the church"[87] war.

Literatur

Bindseil, Heinrich Ernst, und Hermann Agathon Niemeyer. 1848. *Dr. Martin Luther's Bibelübersetzung nach der letzten Original-Ausgabe kritisch bearbeitet 3. Die poetischen Bücher des Alten Testaments, Hiob – Hoheslied*. Halle: Canstein.

Chamberlain, Charles. 1984. „The Meaning of Prohairesis in Aristotle's Ethics." *Transactions of the American Philological Association* 114:147–57.

Dobbin, Robert. 1991. „Prohairesis in Epictetus." *Ancient Philosophy* 11:111–35.

Dragona-Monachou, Myrto. 1978–1979. „Η προαίρεσις στον Αριστοτέλη και στον Επίκτητο. Μια συσχέτιση με την έννοια της πρόθεσης στη φιλοσοφία της πράξης (Prohairesis in Aristotle and Epictetus. A Comparison with the Concept of Intention in the Philosophy of Action)." *Φιλοσοφία* 8–9:265–310.

Drews, Friedemann. 2013. „Die Theorie der Seele als Voraussetzung der Ethik bei Platon, Apuleius, Augustinus, Proklos und Dionysius Areopagita." Seiten 49–90 in *Ethik des antiken Platonismus. Der platonische Weg zum Glück in Systematik, Entstehung und historischem Kontext.* Hrsg. von Christian Pietsch. Stuttgart: Steiner.

Flückiger, Felix. 1954. *Geschichte des Naturrechtes 1. Altertum und Frühmittelalter*. Zollikon-Zürich: Evangelischer Verlag.

Frick, Peter. 1999. *Divine Providence in Philo of Alexandria*. TSAJ 77. Tübingen: Mohr Siebeck.

---

86. Berühmt ist etwa die entsprechende Formulierung Harnacks in von Harnack 1931, 18 bzw. 20. Vgl. dazu etwa Meijering 1985; Nippel 2003.

87. Vgl. Müller 1996, insbes. 20–24.

Hahn, Ferdinand. 1995. *Christologische Hoheitstitel. Ihre Geschichte im frühen Christentum*. 5. Aufl. Göttingen: Vandenhoeck & Ruprecht.

Harnack, Adolf von. 1931. *Lehrbuch der Dogmengeschichte*. 5. Aufl. Tübingen: Mohr Siebeck.

Heimgartner, Martin. 2001. *Pseudojustin – Über die Auferstehung. Text und Studie*. PTS 54. Berlin: de Gruyter.

Hengel, Martin. 1994. „Die Septuaginta als ‚christliche Schriftensammlung', ihre Vorgeschichte und das Problem ihres Kanons." Seiten 182–284 in *Die Septuaginta zwischen Judentum und Christentum*. Hrsg. von Martin Hengel und Anna Maria Schwemer. WUNT 72. Tübingen: Mohr Siebeck.

Hennings, Ralph. 1994. *Der Briefwechsel zwischen Augustinus und Hieronymus und ihr Streit um den Kanon des Alten Testaments und die Auslegung von Gal. 2,11–14*. VCSup 21. Leiden: Brill.

Horn, Friedrich W., Ulrich Volp, und Ruben Zimmermann. 2013. *Ethische Normen des frühen Christentums: Gut – Leben – Leib – Tugend*. Kontexte und Normen der neutestamentlichen Ethik/Contexts and Norms of New Testament Ethics 4. WUNT 313. Tübingen: Mohr Siebeck.

Kinzig, Wolfram. 1994. *Novitas Christiana. Die Idee des Fortschritts in der Alten Kirche bis Eusebius*. FKDG 58. Göttingen: Vandenhoeck & Ruprecht.

———. 2019. „Warum es im Glaubensbekenntnis keine Ethik gibt. Überlegungen aus kirchenhistorischer Perspektive." *Journal of Ethics in Antiquity and Christianity* 1:39–53.

Laks, André. 1989. „Prohairesis." Seiten 1451–58 in Bd. 7 von *Historisches Wörterbuch der Philosophie*. Hrsg. von Joachim Ritter et al. Basel: Schwabe.

Long, Anthony Arthur. 2002. *Epictetus: A Stoic and Socratic Guide to Life*. Oxford: Clarendon.

Maur, Hansjörg auf der. 1977. *Das Psalmenverständnis des Ambrosius von Mailand. Ein Beitrag zum Deutungshintergrund der Psalmenverwendung im Gottesdienst der Alten Kirche*. Leiden: Brill.

Meijering, Eginhard J. 1985. *Die Hellenisierung des Christentums im Urteil Adolf von Harnacks*. Amsterdam: Kampen.

Metzler, Karin. 1997. *Welchen Bibeltext benutzte Athanasius im Exil? Zur Herkunft der Bibelzitate in den Arianerreden im Vergleich zur ep. ad epp. Aeg*. ANRhAW 96. Wiesbaden: Westdeutscher Verlag.

Mosés, André. 1963. *Les oeuvres de Philon d'Alexandrie 7/8*. Paris: Cerf.

Müller, Mogens. 1996. *The First Bible of the Church: A Plea for the Septuagint.* JSOTSup 206. Sheffield: Sheffield Academic.

Neusner, Jacob. 1994. *Die Gestaltwerdung des Judentums. Die jüdische Religion als Antwort auf die kritischen Herausforderungen der ersten sechs Jahrhunderte der christlichen Ära.* JudUm 51. Frankfurt: Lang.

Nippel, Wilfried. 2003. „,Hellenismus' – von Droysen bis Harnack – oder: Interdisziplinäre Mißverständnisse" Seiten 15–28 in *Adolf von Harnack: Christentum, Wissenschaft und Gesellschaft.* Hrsg. von Kurt Nowak et al. Göttingen: Vandenhoeck & Ruprecht.

Phrantzoles, Konstantinos G. 1994. Ὁσίου Ἐφραίμ τοῦ Σύρου ἔργα 5. Thessaloniki: To Perivoli tis Panagias.

Rösel, Martin. 1998. „Theo-Logie der griechischen Bibel. Zur Wiedergabe der Gottesaussagen im LXX-Pentateuch." *VT* 48: 49–62.

———. 2009. „Die Geburt der Seele in der Übersetzung. Von der hebräischen *näfäsch* über die *psyche* der LXX zur deutschen Seele." Seiten 151–70 in *Anthropologische Aufbrüche. Alttestamentliche und interdisziplinäre Zugänge zur historischen Anthropologie.* Hrsg. von Andreas Wagner. FRLANT 232. Göttingen: Vandenhoeck & Ruprecht.

Schirner, Rebecca. 2015. *Inspice diligenter codices. Philologische Studien zu Augustins Umgang mit Bibelhandschriften und -übersetzungen.* Millennium-Studien 49. Berlin: de Gruyter.

Siegert, Folker. 2001. *Zwischen Hebräischer Bibel und Altem Testament. Eine Einführung in die Septuaginta.* Münsteraner Judaistische Studien 9. Münster: LIT.

Thümmel, Hans Georg. 1998. „Die Seele im Platonismus und bei den Kirchenvätern." Seiten 243–54 in ΨΥΧΗ – *Seele – anima.* FS Karin Alt. Hrsg. von Jens Holzhausen. BzA 109. Stuttgart: Teubner.

Volp, Ulrich. 2006. *Die Würde des Menschen. Ein Beitrag zur Anthropologie in der Alten Kirche.* VCSup 81. Leiden: Brill.

———. 2011. „Ritus und Ethik. Die Konstituierung des Ethos nachkonstantinischer Gemeinden." Seiten 43–68 in *Liturgie und Ritual in der Alten Kirche.* Hrsg. von Wolfram Kinzig, Ulrich Volp, und Jochen Schmidt. Patristic Studies 10. Leuven: Peeters.

———. 2018. „Der Mensch. Kirchen- und theologiegeschichtliche Perspektive." Seiten 105–40 in *Mensch.* Hrsg. von Jürgen van Oorschot. Themen der Theologie 11. Tübingen: Mohr Siebeck.

Volp, Ulrich, Friedrich W. Horn, und Ruben Zimmermann. 2016. *Metapher – Narratio – Mimesis – Doxologie. Begründungsformen frühchristlicher und antiker Ethik. Kontexte und Normen der neutesta-*

mentlichen Ethik/Contexts and Norms of New Testament Ethics 7. WUNT 356. Tübingen: Mohr Siebeck.

Contributors

Hans Ausloos, Université catholique de Louvain (Belgium) / University of the Free State, Bloemfontein

Philip R. Bosman, Stellenbosch University (South Africa)

Dirk Büchner, Trinity Western University, Langley (Canada)

Johann Cook, Stellenbosch University (South Africa)

Evangelia G. Dafni, Aristotle University of Thessaloniki (Greece) / University of Pretoria

Louis C. Jonker, Stellenbosch University (South Africa)

Pierre J. Jordaan, North-West University, Potchefstroom (South Africa)

Gideon R. Kotzé, North-West University, Potchefstroom (South Africa)

Wolfgang Kraus, Universität des Saarlandes, Saarbrücken (Germany) / University of Pretoria

Peter Nagel, Stellenbosch University (South Africa)

Stefanie Peintner (born Plangger), Independent scholar, Vienna (Austria)

Jessie Rogers, St Patrick's College Pontifical University, Maynooth (Ireland)

Martin Rösel, Universität Rostock (Germany) / Stellenbosch University

Joel D. Ruark, Stellenbosch University (South Africa)

Gert J. Steyn, Theologische Hochschule Ewersbach (Germany) / University of Pretoria

Johan C. Thom, Stellenbosch University (South Africa)

Emanuel Tov, The Hebrew University of Jerusalem (Israel)

Ulrich Volp, Johannes Gutenberg Universität Mainz (Germany)

Kyle Young, Trinity Western University, Langley (Canada)

Ancient Sources Index

Old Testament/Septuagint

Genesis
1:2	85, 87, 403
1:20	411
1:26–27	157–58, 164, 403–4
2:2	375–78, 381, 392
2:7	404, 408
3	101–2
3:5	102
3:15	103
3:17	35–36
5:3	159
6:5	229
8:21	35–36, 229
12:3	360–62
14:1–20	383
14:17–20	375, 382–83, 392
16:7	164
17:1	12
18:18	362
21:12	375, 388–89, 393
21:13	389, 393
22:16	382
22:16–17	383
22:16–20	382, 392
22:17	375, 382, 390, 392
22:18	362
26:4	362
26:5	126
28:14	362
29:35	126
31	150
31:18	147
35:7	255
35:11	12
37:2	281–82
37:12–35	286
37:13	281
37:30	288
38	127
39:1	288
39:3	288
39:5	288
45:5	291
45:7	291
45:8	291
45:9	291

Exodus
12:43	124
15:3	26–27
19:3–4	39
19:6	191
19:10	38
20:4	151, 156
20:13–15	416
22:30	183
24–25	384
24:8	375, 385, 387, 392
24:10	39
25:10–40	385
25:40	375, 384–85, 392
30:11–16	312
33:7	38

Leviticus
3:4	128
3:9	121–22
3:10	128

Leviticus (cont.)		4:37	172
3:15	128	5:3	397
4:22	134	5:7	172
5:22	134	5:8	151, 156
6	124	7:6	183, 191
6:3	122	8:3	166
13	128	8:4	174
14:32	122	9:3	172
16	184	9:10	164
17–26	184	9:19	375, 390–91
18:4	131–33, 135	9:33	173
18:4–5	131, 135	11:17	171
18:5	132–35	13:18	324
18:11	136	15:18	169
18:14	128	23:2–9	348
19:4	152	29:16–17	147, 151
19:14	136	32	148, 154
20:20	128	32:1	166, 168
22:25	349	32:4	9, 33
23:39	122	32:10	170
23:40	122	32:35	375, 387
23:41	122	32:35–36	387–88, 393
25	127	32:36	375, 387
25:21	122	32:43	387
25:22	122	33:3	174
		33:10	171
Numbers		33:27	173
5:19	128		
6:25	247, 254	Joshua	
16–18	185–86, 194	1:8	40
22:18	116–17	2:9	38
25:1–3	147, 151, 153	6:8	41
33:52	147, 151, 158	6:9	40
36:13	125, 127	6:13	40
		6:20	40
Deuteronomy			
1:23	169	Judges	
1:26	166	5:2	413
1:45	167–68		
3:27	170	Ruth	
4:1	397	1:20	12
4:12	157, 164		
4:15	163	1 Samuel/1 Kingdoms	
4:16	151, 164	2:2	32
4:25	169	16–18	24

3:17–18	107	3:6	322
17:43	149	3:48	154–55
31:9	147	4:11–23	322
		4:30	323
1 Kings/3 Kingdoms		7:37	323
8:54–56	379	7:41	323
8:56	379	8:30	325
11	147	9:25	325
11:7	144	12:15	323
		13:2	391, 393
2 Kings/4 Kingdoms			
5:17	337	2 Maccabees	
23:24	150	1:3–4	311
		1:8	329
1 Chronicles		1:11	329
5:27–41	181	1:16	310
15	192	1:17	330
23–27	181	1:24	330
23:13	181	2:19–32	326
23:30–32	182	3	308, 310
24:5	182	3:22–28	327, 330
29:18	229	3:30	330
		4	310
2 Chronicles		4–7	308
1–9	181	4:19–20	307
17:3	149	5:17	328–29
23:6	181, 186	5:20	328–29
29–30	186, 193	6:14	329
29:15–16	193	7	295, 308, 312
30:3	192	7:22–23	328
30:18	192–93	8–15	308
31:18	186	8:11	331
35–36	187	8:18	327
35:3	183, 192	9	311
		9:5	328
1 Esdras	187–88	10:25	330
		12:40	149
1 Maccabees		12:40–45	295, 307
1:43	153	12:41	331
2:17	322	13:15	327
2:19–25	322	14:33	311, 331
2:21	324	14:35–36	332
2:50	322	15:12–16	310
2:52–53	324	15:22	329
2:54–57	325	15:30–33	311

Psalms

2:7	375, 382	27:1	209, 215, 219
3:4	9	27:21–23	214
7:12	13	28	201–20
8:7	75	29:1	208
10 (9):9	363	31:33	108
16 (15):10	102	38:2	104, 106, 109
17:8 (LXX)	391	42:3	105–6, 109
18 (17):3	9		
24 (23):10	12	Proverbs	
24 (23):5	13	1:7	234
31 (39):17	247	1:10	31
38 (37):11	250	2:1–4	227
40 (39):7–9	375	2:1–12	227
40 (39):11	109	2:6	229
47 (46):10	340–41, 344, 362	2:10	228–29
62 (61):13	75	2:11	227–28, 235
67 (66):2	247	2:13–22	227
68 (67):19	75	2:16	227–28, 230
76 (75):4	27	2:16–18	230
76:19 (LXX)	391	2:16–19	227
80 (79):2	247	2:17	227–30, 235
90 (89):2–3	13	3:11	375
95 (94):7	380–81	4:4	228–29
95 (94):7–11	375–76, 378, 392	6:20–21	397, 409
95 (94):11	377–78, 381, 392	7:5	229–30
110 (109):4	375, 382–83, 392	8:1–11	237
111 (110):10	234	8:12–21	237
117 (116):1	77	8:22	239
117 (116):2	77	8:22–31	237
118 (117):27	255–56	8:30	237, 239–40
119 (118):11	109	8:31	239
119 (118):135	247, 254	8:32–37	237
135 (134):14	388	9:10	228–29, 232–34
150:6	399	13:15	228–29, 232–33, 235
151:6	149	17:7	237–38
151:7	155	19:14	237–38
		27:19	228–29
		28:1–9	230–31
Odes		28:4	231
2:43	387	28:7	235
12:6–7	374		
		Ecclesiastes	
Job		1:17–18	414
7:12	213	8:1	253
9:5	212		

Song of Songs
1:1	37

Wisdom of Solomon
1:5	264
1:6	264
1:7	264
1:13–14	102
6:19	406
7:7	264
7:21	239
7:22	264, 266
7:22–8:1	265
7:23	266
7:24	266
7:25	266
7:25–26	266
7:26	266
7:27	266
8:1	266
8:3	264
8:6	239, 264
9:4	264
9:9	264
9:17	264
12:1	264
14:11	155, 158
14:23–26	156
14:29	155

Jesus Sirach
17:31	247
23:19	247

Psalms of Solomon
12:6	374, 394

Isaiah
1:29	153
2:1–5	348
2:6	357
3:8	357
6:1	31
6:9–10	76
7:14	76
8:13	399
8:23–9:1	76
10:5–34	357
11:12	357
11:15–16	357–58
14:1–2	358
19:16–25	343–46, 358
19:19	337, 357
19:24	338
22 (21):30	408
25:6–8	341–43, 349
26:19	342
26:20	387
27:13	358
29:13	76
29:22	358
30:29	37
37:19	148
40:3	76
41:28	150
42:1	358
42:1–4	76
44:24	401
45:23–24	400
49:6	358
49:22	359
51:4	359
53:4	76
55:4	359
56:3–8	346–49, 353
56:7	76, 352
57:5	153
60	359
61:5–6	359
65:1	359
66	355–56
66:18–24	350–55, 359

Jeremiah
8:5	413
9:14	149
14:4	36
14:14	413
29 (36):14	255
31:8	36

Jeremiah (cont.)
- 31 (38):31–34 — 375
- 38:8 — 37
- 38 (45):14 — 107
- 38 (45):25 — 107

Ezekiel
- 6:5 — 152
- 17:6 — 255
- 18 — 131, 134
- 18:20 — 411
- 18:22 — 135
- 20 — 131, 134
- 36 — 153
- 39:4–29 — 34
- 44:6–11 — 348–49
- 47:22–23 — 350

Daniel
- 3:12 — 145, 147
- 3:18 — 145
- 7–12 — 326
- 9:17 — 249
- 10:11 — 391

Hosea
- 2:20 — 27
- 4:13 — 153, 155
- 4:17 — 155
- 8:13 — 157
- 13:1–2 — 157
- 13:4 — 158
- 14:9 — 154

Joel
- 2:25 — 34
- 3:5 (LXX) — 400

Amos
- 3:13 — 12
- 7:1 — 34

Jonah
- 2:1 — 77
- 2:2 — 77
- 2:3 — 77
- 2:4 — 77
- 2:7 — 77

Micah
- 7:6 — 127

Nahum
- 3:8 — 238

Habakkuk
- 2:3 — 375, 387
- 2:3–4 — 387
- 2:4 — 375

Haggai
- 2:6 — 375
- 2:21 — 375

Zechariah
- 2:14–15 — 339–40, 344

Malachi
- 3:6–7 — 102
- 3:8 — 103, 110
- 3:11 — 102

New Testament

Matthew
- 1:23 — 76
- 3:3 — 76
- 4:15–16 — 76
- 5:17 — 401
- 8:17 — 76
- 12:18–21 — 76
- 12:40 — 77
- 13:13–15 — 76
- 15:8–9 — 76
- 21:13 — 76
- 27:51–53 — 77

John
- 1:2–3 — 271
- 1:3 — 401

Ancient Sources Index

Acts		2:17	380
3:25	362	3:1–6	378
		3:6	376
Romans		3:7	377
1	127	3:7–11	380
2	127	3:7–4:11	381
2:6	75	3:7–4:13	375–76, 380
3:29	336	3:11	381
5:16	127	3:11–4:11	377
5:18	127	3:12	376
10:12–13	400	3:14	376
12:19	388	3:16–18	379
15:7–14	76	3:18	381
15:8–9	77	4:1	375–76, 380–81, 391
15:11	77	4:1–11	376
		4:2	377
1 Corinthians		4:3	377, 381
15:27	75	4:3–5	379
		4:4	378, 381
2 Corinthians		4:4–5	378
4:4	271	4:5	377, 381
		4:6	381
Galatians		4:7	378, 381
3:8	362	4:8	378–79, 381
3:26–29	336	4:9	377, 379, 381
		4:9–10	380
Ephesians		4:10	381
4:8	75	4:11	380
		4:14–7:28	375
Philippians		5–7	382
2:9–11	400	5:5–6	382
		6:12	375, 382, 392
Colossians		6:13	382, 392
1:15	271, 405	6:13–14	382
		6:13–15	382, 392
1 Peter		6:14	382, 390, 392
3:15	400	6:15	375
		6:17	375, 382, 392
Hebrews		6:19	380
1:1	374, 384	7:1	382
1:2	385	7:6	375
1:3	271	7:17	383, 392
1:5	382	7:21	383, 392
1:6	387	8:1–10:18	375
2:10	389	8:3–10:18	385

Hebrews (cont.)		12:26	375, 390–91, 393
8:5	384–85, 392		
8:6	375, 384, 392	Revelation	
9	127	15:4	127
9:1–5	385	19:8	127
9:12	386	21:3	338–39
9:15	375, 385–86, 392		
9:18	386, 392	Second Temple Literature	
9:18–22	386		
9:19	386, 393	Josephus, *Antiquitates judaicae*	
9:20	385–86, 392	2.9	285
9:24	384	2.10	285
10:19–20	380	2.21–31	286
10:19–39	375, 387	2.25	291
10:19–12:29	387	2.39	291
10:22	387	2.42	291
10:23	387	2.60	291
10:24	387	2.63	291
10:27	387	2.74	291
10:28	387	2.80	291
10:29	387	2.84	291
10:30	387–88	2.86	291
10:35	387	2.89	291
10:36	375, 387, 393	2.117	291
10:37	387	2.118	291
11:1–12:11	375	2.121	291
11:8–13	389	2.129	291
11:9	375, 390, 393	2.136	291
11:13	375, 390, 393	2.137	291
11:13–16	389	12.2	278–79
11:17	375, 389, 390, 393	13	291
11:17–19	389, 393	14–25	291
11:17–21	389		
11:33	390, 393	Josephus, *Bellum judaicum*	
11:39	375, 390, 393	1.3	278
12:5	389	5.361	278
12:7	389		
12:12	390	Letter of Aristeas	
12:12–17	390	139	232
12:12–29	375	143	232
12:13	390		
12:14	390	Philo, *De Deo*	
12:15	390	46–48	407
12:18–24	390, 393		
12:21	390, 393		

Ancient Sources Index

Philo, *De fuga et inventione*
63   404

Philo, *De Iosepho*
9   285
13   286
16   287
16–21   287
21   287
22–27   287
27   288
37   288–89
37–39   288
41–42   289
42–48   289
52–53   290
157   283
268   283

Philo, *De somniis*
2.43   283
2.116   283

Philo, *De vita Mosis*
2.6   278
2.25–45   278

Philo, *Quaestiones et solutiones in Genesin*
4.184   126–27

Rabbinic Works

m. Avot
1:1   232

Sifre Numbers
14   235

Greek and Latin Authors

Aristophanes, *Vespae*
314   143

Aristotle, *De anima*
411a7   269

Aristotle, *Ethica nichomachea*
3.4.1112a   411

Aristotle, *Politica*
7.4.1326a32–33   269

Cleanthes, *Hymn to Zeus*
12   267, 272
21   267, 272

Epictetus, *Diatribai*
1.14   272
1.17.21   412

Hegesippus Comicus
1.19   238

Herodotus, *Historiae*
1.51   145

Homer, *Odyssea*
5.247   239

Pausanias, *Graeciae description*
1.22.1   290

Pindar, *Nemeonikai*
8.11   239

Pindar, *Pythionikai*
4.80   239

Plato, *Gorgias*
469c   287
508b   287
509c   287

Plato, *Leges*
715d   124
770e   135

Plato, *Phaedrus*
68d   135

Plato, *Politicus*
- 369 — 97
- 370 — 97
- 375–376 — 98
- 377 — 99
- 377–383 — 98
- 378 — 99
- 379 — 95, 100
- 380 — 100
- 382–383 — 100–101
- 427 — 99–100
- 589c — 108

Plato, *Symposium*
- 180b — 103

Plato, *Theaetetus*
- 176ab — 404

Plato, *Timaeus*
- 28a–29a — 407

Plutarch, *De Iside et Osiride*
- 359b — 145

Pseudo-Aristotle, *De mundo*
- 391b12 — 269
- 397b9–398a6 — 268–69
- 397b13–20 — 269
- 397b19–27 — 270
- 397b27–35 — 270
- 398a — 269
- 398a1–6 — 270
- 398b6–10 — 269–70

Solon
- 36.17 — 238

Thales
- 11 A 22 — 269

Xenophon, *Memorabilia*
- 4.3.13 — 269

Early Greek Papyri

CPJud
- 1.128 — 120

P. Oxy.
- 8.1119 — 125
- 46.3285 — 119

P. Petr.
- 3.29 — 119, 125

Ancient Christian Texts

1 Clement
- 33:4–5 — 403

Ambrose, *Expositio Evangelii secundum Lucam*
- 7.141 — 410

Ambrose, *Expositio Psalmi*
- 40.401

Ambrose, *Hexaemeron libri sex*
- 5.11 — 411
- 6.42–46 — 410

Ambrose, *De paradiso*
- 3.12 — 410

Apostolic Constitutions and Canons
- 2.57 — 398

Athanasius, *De decretis*
- 9 — 401

Athenagoras, *De resurrectione*
- 3 — 403

Augustine, *Epistulae*
- 71.4–6 — 401

Clement of Alexandria, *Protrepticus*
- 10.98.3 — 409

Ancient Sources Index

Clement of Alexandria, *Stromata*
1.12.58	415
4.38.3–4	412

Irenaeus, *Adversus haereses*
4.38.3	406
2.33.2	407
5.7.1	408

John Chrysostom, *Catecheses ad illuminandos*
1.14	415

John Chrysostom, *Catechesis ultima ad baptizandos*
3.6	416

John Chrysostom, *Fragmenta in Proverbia*
676	409

John Chrysostom, *Homiliae in Genesim*
19	415

Justin, *Dialogus cum Tryphone*
62.1–3	403

Origen, *Commentarii in evangelium Joannis*
20.19.162	408

Origen, *Commentarii in Romanos*
25.2	409

Origen, *De principiis*
2.8.3	408

Origen, *Homiliae in Jeremiam*
4.3	414

Polycarp, *To the Philippians*
2.1	399

Tertullian, *De virginibus velandis*
1.4–5	399

Modern Authors Index

Achenbach, Reinhard — 185
Aejmelaeus, Anneli — 9, 13–14, 50, 72, 82–84, 87, 130
Aitken, James K. — 4, 143
Albertz, Rainer — 50, 61
Allen, Dave M. — 382
Allen, Nicholas, P. L. — 306–7, 309, 311, 313
Alter, Robert — 281, 286
Amara, Dalia — 28
Apelt, Otto — 97
Attridge, Harold W. — 377–81
Ausloos, Hans — 6, 10, 25, 50, 72, 85, 166–68
Avemarie, Friedrich — 305
Baer, David A. — 343, 345, 350, 353–55, 358, 360
Barr, James — 53, 55–59, 61–63
Barthélemy, Dominique — 24
Bassler, Jouette M. — 283
Bauernfeind, Otto — 378
Beale, Greg K. — 74, 76
Beck, John A. — 204, 206, 217–18
Becker, Uwe — 180
Berthelot, Katell — 324
Bertram, Georg — 7–8, 11, 36, 345
Betegh, Gábor — 270
Bezzel, Hannes — 180
Bibb, Bryan D. — 184
Bickerman, Elias — 297–301, 305
Bledsoe, Seth A. — 229
Bloesch, Donald G. — 318
Böckler, Otto — 296, 298–99, 305
Bos, Abraham P. — 269
Bosman, Philip R. — 288
Boyd-Taylor, Cameron — 81, 83–84
Braulik, Georg — 379
Braun, Herbert — 383
Brockington, Leonard H. — 32
Brooke, George J. — 49
Brown, William P. — 30
Bruce, Frederick F. — 34, 384, 386, 388–90
Bruneau, Philippe — 150
Büchner, Dirk — 121, 216
Bultmann, Christoph — 346
Burchard, Christoph — 349
Bury, R. G. — 135
Cadell, Hélène — 119, 125, 126
Carson, D. A. — 76
Chamberlain, Charles — 411
Childs, Brevard S. — 53, 57–58
Clements, Ronald E. — 344
Coetzer, Eugene — 310, 312–13
Cohen, Shaye J.D. — 321–22
Collins, John J. — 61, 266–67
Colson, F. H. — 287, 289
Cook, Johann — 6, 10, 31, 49–50, 71–73, 75, 79–81, 83, 117, 214, 216–17, 220, 225–29, 232, 233–37, 240, 336
Cox, Claude — 74, 203–4, 219–20
Cox, Ronald — 265–66
Cross, Frank Moore — 303
Dafni, Evangelia G. — 15, 28, 50–51, 96, 108, 110, 210, 236
Dähne, August F. — 7
Daniel, Suzanne — 349
Deissmann, Adolf — 7–8
Dell, Katherine — 203
DeSilva, David A. — 302–5
De Troyer, Kristin — 33

D'Hamonville, David-Marc	226	Gooding, David	24
Dhont, Marieke	205	Goodwin, William	133–34
Di Lella, Alexander A.	236	Gottschalk, Hans B.	271
Dines, Jennifer	26	Grässer, Erich	388
Dodd, Charles H.	13	Gregoric, Pavel	270
Dodds, Eric R.	266	Griffith, Terry	144, 146
Dogniez, Cécile	125	Grossfeld, Bernard	33
Domazakis, Nikolaos	296, 307–8, 313	Groß, Walter	338, 346, 351, 353
Donner, Herbert	348	Guthrie, George H.	385, 387–88, 390
Doran, Robert	299–301, 303–5	Gutiérrez, Gustavo	208
Dorival, Gilles	151, 346	Haarmann, Volker	335, 337–78, 346–50, 352–53
Douglas, Alex	27, 50, 83		
Drews, Friedemann	407	Habel, Norman	208, 211–12
Duhot, Jean-Joël	269, 270	Hahn, Ferdinand	400
Eberhart, Christian	354	Hanhart, Robert	8, 204, 226, 334, 339
Ego, Beate	309	Hanson, Paul	346, 352
Ehrlich, Arnold B.	361	Harl, Marguerite	36, 125, 168, 346
Eichrodt, Walther	49–50, 54	Harlé, Paul	134–35
Ellingworth, Paul	382, 384–85, 388	Harrington, Daniel J.	54
Engberg-Pedersen, Troels	265–66	Hayes, John H.	51
Engel, Helmut	156	Heater, Homer	205–6
Enns, Peter	378, 380	Helbing, Robert	168
Fabry, Heinz-Josef	49, 150	Hendel, Ronald	30
Feldman, Louis H.	278–80, 284–291	Hengel, Martin	48, 53, 227, 229–30, 239, 414
Feldmeier, Reinhard	5		
Fernández Marcos, Natalio	204–5	Hennings, Ralph	401
Festugière, André-Jean	271	Henten, Jan-Willem van	301–5
Flashar, Martin	9	den Hertog, Cornelis	122, 129
Flückiger, Felix	406	Heschel, Susannah	8
Foshay, Toby	317	Hessen, Johannes	96
Fox, Michael V.	227–28	Hett, W. S.	256
Frankel, Zacharias	7–8, 11, 165, 397	Hiebert, Robert J. V.	280–81
Friedrich, Gerhard	373	Hieke, Thomas	152
Fritsch, Charles T.	29, 165–67, 169–74	Hofius, Otto	380–81
Gäbel, Georg	380	Honigman, Sylvie	123
Gamberoni, Johann	343	Horbury, William	26
Gärtner, Judith	344, 346, 350–52, 354–56	Horn, Friedrich-Wilhelm	402
Geiger, Abraham	7, 11, 28, 34	Hossfeld, Frank-Lothar	149
Gerleman, Gilles	226, 235, 237, 239	Huber, Karl	121–22
Gerstenberger, Erhard	51	Hübner, Hans	265–66, 273
Gese, Hartmut	53	Jaeger, Werner	95
Glenny, W. Edward	8, 57–58	Jeppesen, Knud	57
Gmirkin, Russel	236	Jeremias, Jörg	54–55, 340–41
Goldstein, Jonathan A.	299–301, 318, 320–22, 325	Jobes, Karen H.	74, 76, 175
		Johnson, Mark	310

Modern Authors Index

Jones, Spencer A. 117
Jonker, Louis C. 179–81, 185
Joosten, Jan 10, 13, 28, 50, 72, 142–43, 216
Jordaan, Pierre J. 305, 308–13
Kaiser, Otto 295, 341
Kaminka, Armand 11
Kampen, John 321, 325
Karrer, Martin 4, 49, 74, 377–79, 386, 388
Kartveit, Magnar 181
Keel, Othmar 52, 60–61, 239
Kellermann, Ulrich 346, 351–52
Kinzig, Wolfram 398, 405
Kistemaker, Simon J. 377–78, 382–83, 386, 391
Klausner, Josef 336
Klein, Ralph 181, 189
Klijn, Albertus F. J. 384
Kloppenborg, John S. 267
Knibb, Michael 120, 131
Knierim, Rolf 51
Knohl., Israel 184
Knoppers, Gary 181–82, 187–88, 194
Köckert, Matthias 361
Koenen, Klaus 346–47, 349, 351–54
Koester, Craig 377
Konkel, Michael 350
Kooij, Arie van der 76, 226–27, 229, 240, 337, 339, 342, 344–45, 349, 357–59
Kornfeld, Walter 189, 191, 193–95
Kövecses, Zoltan 246
Kraft, Robert A. 52
Kraus, Hans-Joachim 341, 347, 351
Kraus, Wolfgang 4, 14, 49, 79, 80, 225–26, 335, 338–39, 353, 357, 364
Kreuzer, Siegfried 4, 25–26, 74, 317, 363
Kutsch, Ernst 347
Kutz, Karl 202, 205–6, 208, 212–13, 220
Lagarde, Paul A. de 233
Lakoff, George 24–27, 310
Laks, André 411
Lange, Armin 49
Lane, William L. 384
Law, Timothy M. 74, 76

Le Boulluec, Alain 125
Lee, James A. 13
Lemmelijn, Bénédicte 166
Levenson, Jon D. 348
Lim, Timothy H. 49
Lincoln, Andrew T. 377
Lohfink, Norbert, 352
Lorenzen, Stefanie 266, 271–72
Louw, Theo van der 36, 217
Lundbom, Jack R. 175
Lust, Johan 10, 28, 152
Lustig, Christian 38–39
Mack, Burton L. 267
Malherbe, Abraham J. 267
Mangum, Douglas 204
Mansfeld, Jaap 269
Marcus, Ralph 127
Maur, Hansjörg auf der 401
Mazor, Leah 41
McClellan, Daniel O. 307–8
McDonald, Lee Martin 48, 57
McGrath, Alister E. 62
McLay, R. Timothy 14, 51, 54, 73–74, 77–78, 83
Meer, Michaël van der 15
Meiser, Martin 33
Meijering, Eginhard J. 417
Metzger, Bruce M. 248
Metzler, Karin 401
Meyer, Esias E. 184
Milgrom, Jacob 128, 133–35, 184
Modrzejewski, Joseph Mélèze 119–20, 123–24
Moffat, James 297–98, 302, 305
Moraux, Paul 269
Móses, André 407
Müller, Hans-Peter 183
Müller, Mogens 5, 16, 417
Nagel, Peter 319
Neher, Martin 264, 267, 272
Neusner, Jacob 399
Newsom, Carol 208
Nickelsburg, George W. E. 52, 302–5
Niehoff, Maren 280, 282–85
Niehr, Herbert 52

Nihan, Christophe	180, 184	Scharbert, Josef	361
Nippel, Wilfried	417	Scheer, Tanja	143–44
Novak, David	338	Schirner, Rebecca	401
Odeberg, Hugo	228	Schlund, Christine	117
Olofsson, Staffan	9, 12–13, 33, 84, 154	Schmid, Konrad	48–49, 52–53, 58, 61–62
Opsomer, Jan	267, 269–71		
Orlinsky, Harry M.	29, 165, 203, 205, 220, 347	Schmidt, Ludwig	361
		Schmidt, Werner H.	57, 61
Otto, Eckart	174, 184	Schmitt, Hans-Christoph	360–61
Pajunen, Mika	49	Schmitz, Barbara	26
Pape, Wilhelm	125	Schniewind, Julius	373
Passioni dell' Aqua, Anna	33	Schreiner, Josef	344, 360–61
Paul, Shalom M.	35	Schröger, Friedrich	384–85, 387
Peintner, Stefanie. See Plangger, Stefanie		Schunack, Gerd	389
		Schuster, Dirk	8
Perkins, Larry	14, 26	Schwartz, Daniel R.	296, 301, 303–6, 321, 325, 327, 353
Peters, Melvin K. H.	9, 154, 166		
Pietersma, Albert	28, 79, 81–82, 130–31, 204, 216, 281	Scott, Robert Y. B.	239
		Screnock John	14
Plangger, Stefanie	146, 152, 156–59	Seeligmann, Isac L.	8, 11, 25, 28, 37, 142, 233, 235, 342, 358
Pohlenz, Max	269		
Porton, Gary G.	338	Seebass, Horst	151
Pralon, Didier	134–35	Sehmsdorf, Eberhard	351–52
Preuß, Horst-Dietrich	340–41	Siegert, Folker	241, 411
Prijs, Leo	11	Signori, Gabriela	319
Prussner, Frederick	51	Silva, Moisés	74–76, 175
Rad, Gerhard von	50, 54	Skehan, Patrick W.	236
Rahlfs, Alfred	204, 226	Smyth, Herbert	133–34
Rajak, Tessa	278	Sollamo, Raija	172
Reale, Giovanni	269	Sommer, Benjamin D.	38
Reddoch, M. Jason	285	Sousa, Rodrigo de	10
Reese, James M.	267	Sparks, James T.	181
Rocca, Samuel	321	Spieckermann, Hermann	5
Rogers, Jessie	205	Stählin, Gustav	155
Rosch, Eleanor	24–27	Steck, Odil H.	341, 346–47, 351–52
Rösel, Martin	4, 6, 9, 25–28, 30, 31, 36, 42, 48–50, 52, 55, 64, 71–75, 79–81, 83–84, 86, 88, 117–18, 129, 142–43, 147, 154, 159, 166, 202, 220, 225–26, 229, 240–41, 397, 399, 407	Sterling, Gregory E.	264–68, 272–73
		Steyn, Gert J.	74, 76, 373–75, 378
		Stipp, Hermann-Josef	205
		Strobel, August	384–86, 389
Ruark, Joel	246, 254	Stuckenbruck, Loren	57–58
Rudolph, Wilhelm	339–40	Swete, Henry Barclay	48
Saïd, Suzanne	144–45	Talmon, Shemaryahu	233
Sandevoir, Pierre	125	Talshir, Zipora	234
Scarlata, Mark W.	280	Tcherikover, Victor	298–300
Schaper, Joachim	5, 28, 216, 325	Theißen, Gerd	385

Thom, Johan C.   60, 267–68, 271–72
Thümmel, Hans Georg   407
Tilly, Michael   342, 350, 354
Tov, Emanuel   10, 17, 24, 29–30, 32, 35–36, 41, 49, 74, 83–84, 86, 125, 154, 173, 219, 226, 234
Trampedach, Kai   322, 324–25
Troxel, Ronald L.   28, 342, 349, 357–58
Uehlinger, Christoph   52, 60
Ulrich, Eugene   49
Vahrenhorst, Martin   134
VanderKam, James C.   49
Van Oyen, Hendrik   386, 388–89
Van Winkle, Dwight   349
Vermeylen, Jaques   351
Vernant, Jean-Pierre   144–45
Volp, Ulrich   398, 401–2, 404, 407
Vos, Cornelius de   345
Vries, Johannes de   74
Wagner, J. Ross   58
Weingreen, Jacob   235
Weischedel, Wilhelm   95
Weiss, Hans-Friedrich   377, 383, 388–89
Wenham, Gordon   150
Westcott, Brooke F.   388
Westermann, Claus   50, 54, 57, 208, 282, 343, 347–48, 351–52, 361
Wevers, John W.   85, 122–23, 151, 174, 281
Wiegand, A.   33
Wildberger, Hans   339, 341, 343
Wilk, Florian   74, 76, 342, 345, 357–58
Willi, Thomas   181
Wilson, Robert M.   386, 388–89, 391
Winston, David   268
Wittstruck, Thorne   165–66, 168, 170–71, 173–74
Wolff, Hans-Walter   360
Wooden, R. Glenn   57–58
van der Woude, Adam   321, 324–25
Wright, Benjamin G.   216, 281
Yee, Gale A.   230
Yem Hing Hom, Mary K.   210
Zeller, Eduard   264
Zenger, Erich   149, 340, 343, 348, 352

Zervos, George T.   321, 325
Ziegler, Joseph   7–8, 77, 204, 208, 264, 342
Ziethe, Carolin   336, 339
Zimmermann, Ruben   401
Zipor, Moshe   33
Zobel, Hans-Jürgen   360
Zurawski, Jason M.   13

www.ingramcontent.com/pod-product-compliance
Lightning Source LLC
Chambersburg PA
CBHW021231300426
44111CB00007B/508